VOLUNTARY ACTION

VOLUNTARY ACTION

brains, minds, and sociality

Edited by

SABINE MAASEN

Science Studies
Universität Basel
Switzerland

WOLFGANG PRINZ

Max Planck Institute for Psychological Research
München
Germany

and

GERHARD ROTH

HWK – Hanse Institute for Advanced Study
Delmenhorst
Germany

OXFORD
UNIVERSITY PRESS

OXFORD
UNIVERSITY PRESS

Great Clarendon Street, Oxford OX2 6DP

Oxford University Press is a department of the University of Oxford.
It furthers the University's objective of excellence in research, scholarship,
and education by publishing worldwide in

Oxford New York

Auckland Bangkok Buenos Aires Cape Town Chennai Dar es Salaam Delhi
Hong Kong Istanbul Karachi Kolkata Kuala Lumpur Madrid Melbourne
Mexico City Mumbai Nairobi São Paulo Shanghai Taipei Tokyo Toronto

Oxford is a registered trade mark of Oxford University Press
in the UK and in certain other countries

Published in the United States
by Oxford University Press Inc., New York

A catalogue record for this title is available from the British Library

Library of Congress Cataloging in Publication Data
(Data available)

ISBN 0 19 857228 X (Hbk)

    0 19 852754 3 (Pbk)

10 9 8 7 6 5 4 3 2 1

Typeset by Cepha Imaging Pvt Ltd, India
Printed in Great Britain
on acid-free paper by Biddles Ltd, Guildford and King's Lynn

ACKNOWLEDGEMENTS

This book is based on a conference on 'Voluntary Action: Joint (Ad-)Ventures at the Interface of Nature and Culture', held at the Hanse Institute for Advanced Study in Delmenhorst, Germany, from March 16 to 18, 2000. We gratefully acknowledge the financial support received from the Hanse Institute for Advanced Study. Moreover, we owe special thanks to Heide John and Lilo Jegerlehner for diligently handling the manuscript, as well as to Martin Baum, Oxford University Press, for accompanying the process with utmost competence and care.

Sabine Maasen (Basel)   January 2003
Wolfgang Prinz (München)
Gerhard Roth (Bremen)

CONTENTS

Section III

Section IV

Section V

LIST OF CONTRIBUTORS

Ute C. Bayer	Universität Konstanz, Fachbereich Psychologie, Germany
Björn Burkhardt	Universität Mannheim, Fakultät für Rechtswissenschaft, Schloss, Germany
Naomi Eilan	University of Warwick, Project on Consciousness and Self-Consciousness, Department of Philosophy, UK
Melissa Ferguson	Cornell University, Department of Psychology, Ithaca, NY, USA
Peter M. Gollwitzer	Universität Konstanz, Fachbereich Psychologie, Germany
Thomas Goschke	Technische Universität Dresden, Institut für Allgemeine Psychologie, Germany
Klaus Günther	Fachbereich Rechtswissenschaften, Johann-Wolfgang-v.-Goethe Universität Frankfurt, Germany
Bernhard Hommel	Cognitive Psychology Unit, University of Leiden, The Netherlands
Marc Jeannerod	Institut des Sciences Cognitives, Lyon, France
Sabine Maasen	Wissenschaftsforschung/Science Studies, Universität Basel, Switzerland
Charles W. Nuckolls	Department of Anthropology, University of Alabama, USA
Wolfgang Prinz	Max-Planck-Institut für Psychologische Forschung, München, Germany
Joëlle Proust	CNRS/EHESS, Institut Jean-Nicod Paris, France
Gerhard Roth	HWK – Hanse Institute for Advanced Study, Delmenhorst, and Brain Research Institute, University of Bremen, Germany
Jürgen Schröder	Institut für Philosophie, Universität Karlsruhe (TH), Germany
Rüdiger J. Seitz	Neurologische Klinik, Heinrich-Heine-Universität Düsseldorf, Germany
Richard A. Shweder	Committee on Human Development, University of Chicago, USA
Tillmann Vierkant	Max-Planck-Institut für Psychologische Forschung, München, Germany
Wilhelm Vossenkuhl	Philosophie-Department, Ludwig-Maximilians-Universität München, Germany

GENERAL INTRODUCTION

VOLUNTARY ACTION: BRAINS, MINDS, AND SOCIALITY

SABINE MAASEN, WOLFGANG PRINZ,
AND GERHARD ROTH

1 Voluntary Action

In one sense, everybody knows what voluntary action is. We are all experts on this matter. Every day and every hour we perform a vast number of actions under the control of our will, and so we understand much of what other people do as well. By saying this, we do not mean to say that all actions people perform are voluntary. People act voluntarily in certain situations, but not (or less so) in certain others. This capacity to perform voluntary actions is tightly linked to our understanding of what it means to be an autonomous agent or person. By knowing what voluntary actions are, we also have a sense of what it means to be a person and vice versa.

Yet, in another sense, nobody knows what voluntary action is. We may be expert performers of such actions, but we are not expert 'knowers' of what this notion implies. In fact, like many other concepts adopted from folk psychology, the notion of voluntary action is as fuzzy as it can be. What counts as an action? When does it begin? When does it terminate? What makes an action voluntary, as opposed to non-voluntary? What kinds of non-voluntary actions should we distinguish? Is there a sharp demarcation between voluntary and non-voluntary actions? What exactly is it that volition adds to the action? Nobody has any ready-made answers to these and related questions—despite the fact that we are all expert performers. We may have some feeling of knowing, but we do not really know.

Still, despite its elusive character, it is generally believed that there is no way to avoid the notion of voluntary action and replace it by something less elusive. This is because this notion goes far beyond a psychological construct supposed to capture certain mental operations in individual minds. Our shared mutual belief that we can control our actions by will and are, hence, responsible for their outcomes, is a prerequisite not only for the theoretical purpose of understanding people's actions, but also for the practical purpose of exerting social control over those actions. Therefore, even if psychology were in a position to escape from the fuzzy notion of voluntary action, politics, law and ethics could not easily do without it.

Therefore, we need this book. The notion of voluntary action is as indispensable as it may be elusive. We need to take joint efforts to counteract its elusiveness. As we shall see, this task is pursued in two different ways. While in some cases authors are of the opinion that they can and, indeed, should do away with this fuzzy concept, others insist on its usefulness—if not necessity. In actual fact, this difference largely, if not exclusively, corresponds to the Nature/Culture-divide. Neurocognitive approaches try to recast the notion of voluntary action in cognitive functions and their underlying neural activity. Social scientists, in turn, not only insist on its indispensable social function, but also ask the sciences to explain this very fact, rather than to explain it away.

Philosophers, while responsive to the neurocognitive challenge, are strongly divided on this issue. The authors represented in this volume try to escape eliminativist stances by either arguing against the experience of volition as 'epiphenomenal' or by demonstrating how voluntariness relates to the (externally perceived) 'rationality' of an action. Hence, counteracting the elusiveness of voluntary action obviously means different things to different (sub-)disciplines. Before exploring the intricacies of these debates in further detail, let us briefly address three more basic issues, namely what actions, goals, and volitions actually are.

1.1   Actions

What counts as an action? What do we mean when we individuate certain actions within the stream of our own ongoing mental and physical activity, or in the stream of someone else's ongoing behaviour? How do we determine an action's beginning and end? What is confusing about actions is that they can be defined at various levels of granularity or time-scales. Pressing a key in a reaction-time experiment may be considered an action, but so may going on a 2-week vacation on the Bahamas. Somewhere in between the two extremes are everyday actions like brushing one's teeth, having a meal, watching a movie or going shopping. In all of these examples we have a clear sense of specifying when the action begins and when it ends.

With short-lived actions like pressing a key or closing a window, one possibility is that we detect both an action's onset and offset as salient perceptual events that attract our attention. For instance, if a person sits still for a while, then gets up to close the window, sits down again, and is quiet for a while, the action's onset and offset may be said to be two salient events. However, when it comes to more complex actions, which are embedded in all kinds of other activities and that extend over a longer period, the individuation of an action cannot rely on purely perceptual criteria. For instance, if brushing my teeth is preceded by drying my face with a towel and followed by combing my hair, transitions between those actions are much less salient in perceptual terms. Furthermore, when it comes to more extended actions, such as going shopping or even going on vacation, there is no longer perceptual coherence of the total action. Obviously, in such cases, the individuation of an action cannot exclusively rely on perception.

Instead, we need to refer to a conceptual basis for action individuation. The classical solution to the problem is to individuate actions in terms of their goals: Actions are segments of ongoing behaviour that are directed towards certain goals. This notion has two important implications. One is that goal achievement serves as the criterion that determines not only when the action comes to its end (i.e., after the goal has been achieved), but also when the action starts (i.e., when the first behavioural activity directed towards that goal occurs). The other implication is that actions are units of behaviour that can fail. For instance, one brushes one's teeth in order to clean them. Usually, this may work but there may be cases where the brushing, for one or the other reason, may not lead to the cleaning. Accordingly, talking about actions always entails talking about *ongoing events* (body movements) *with reference to intended events* (environmental effects).

1.2 Goals

How, then, do we know about goals? When it comes to goals, we need to draw a distinction between our own actions and other people's actions. This is because what we know about the goals underlying other people's actions appears to be different from what we know about the goals underlying our own actions. When we watch other people, young infants, animals, or animates, we can only infer goals from the behaviour we observe (as long as we have no way of talking to these agents). This is the third-person's perspective. Conversely, with respect to our own actions, we often have access to explicit mental representations of the goals our actions are directed at. This is the first-person's perspective. Accordingly, it has often been claimed that we have direct, privileged access to our own mental activity, whereas we have only indirect access to the mental state of others. Furthermore, it has often been claimed that the way we understand other people's actions is a secondary, indirect derivative of the way we understand ourselves. According to this claim, we project, as it were, our own mentality onto others.

This may be true or not true. More important is realizing that the term of goals refers to two entirely different things in the two cases. When we talk about goals inherent in other agents' actions (i.e. from a third-person's perspective), we talk about certain goal states their actions are presumably directed at (goals-in-the-world, such as having clean teeth or having a good time at the movies). However, when it comes to one's own goals (from a first-person's perspective), we often use the term of goals to refer to mental representations of those goal states (i.e. to goals-in-the-mind). It is often believed that one cannot talk about goals in the world without inferring goals in the mind. Yet, we need to be careful. Animals or animates may achieve certain goals in the world without being controlled by goals in the mind at all. Taking the argument one step further, it has even been claimed that the belief that goals-in-the-mind lead to the actions by which we eventually achieve corresponding goals-in-the-world may be illusory. In any case, we should not fail to see that the relationship between the two goal concepts is an empirical question. We must be careful not to be trapped by the fact that the same word is used for two different things. Goals-in-the-mind are often organized in hierarchies, and so are the actions directed at those goals. Accordingly, any given small-scale action (e.g. brushing one's teeth) forms part of a nested set of actions at larger scales (e.g. one's grooming in the morning or engaging in the prevention of tooth decay) and their respective goals. Obviously, small-scale actions pursue more concrete goals than large-scale actions. Still, it is an open empirical question whether or not goal hierarchies reflect certain features of the functional mechanisms involved in the control of complex action sequences or whether they just serve the function of a convenient tool for describing such sequences.

Sometimes, in order to avoid confusion, the term of intention is used to refer to the representational structures underlying goals-in-the-mind. One problem with all terms and terminologies in this field is that they carry the burden of being used for two purposes:

- to give a descriptive account of conscious experience from a first-person's perspective;
- to provide a theoretical account of representational mechanisms involved in the control of goal-directed action.

We believe that the term of intention is well suited for this latter purpose. Accordingly, intentions are representational structures that refer to action goals and link these goal representations to representations of actions suited to achieve those goals.

1.3 Volition

With that scheme in mind, we may now come back to the notion of voluntary action. What does the notion of volition add to the notion of goal-directedness inherent in action? There seems to be no sharp demarcation line between cases where volition is present versus absent in ongoing action. Rather, we speak of voluntary control or volition to the extent people have conscious access (or are believed to have conscious access) to the intentional antecedents underlying their actions. To the extent such conscious access exists, people can communicate about the goals they are striving for, and their motives and reasons for doing so. Likewise, they can be instructed to pursue certain goals and commit themselves to those goals.

Of course, there may be borderline cases. Consider once more brushing one's teeth in the morning. Should we consider it a voluntary action? It used to be a sequence of voluntary actions earlier in our life when we were trained to do so twice a day. Accordingly, we have built up long-term intentions to do so every day on certain occasions. However, under ordinary circumstances, these intentions do their work without conscious access. Therefore, when we brush our teeth in the morning, we do not do so for the sake of certain motives or reasons, but rather because it is just part of our habitual grooming procedure. However, when it comes to public discourse about those morning habits we tend to resort to reasons and motives implying that, though the individual instance of the action may be under the automatic control of certain habits, these habits themselves are under voluntary control.

To conclude, the notion of volition as we use it does not refer to specific mechanisms underlying action planning and control, but rather to specific conditions for conscious access to and, hence, communication about these underlying intentional processes. Accordingly, the will may be an emergent property of the workings of these mechanisms, rather than a causal agent working on them.

2 Folk psychology

How can we explain voluntary action? This question seems to address scholars from various branches of scientific study, such as psychology, philosophy, ethology, neurobiology, law, sociology, and anthropology. Yet, before we consider their contributions, we first turn to 'Everybody' again. In the same sense as Everybody knows what voluntary action is, Everybody also knows how to explain it. We know it by virtue of the logic of folk psychology, as we have imbibed it from earliest infancy. This logic is incorporated in the jargon of will and free will as we use it all the time every day. It provides an extremely powerful explanatory programme of voluntary action. Historically, since folk psychology is much older than science and even older than philosophy, it serves as the point of departure for scientific explanatory programmes as well. Much of our scientific theorizing about voluntary action is still very strongly dominated by folk psychology intuitions and has a hard time to liberate itself from these intuitions—much to the pleasure of some theorists and to the displeasure of some others, depending on their respective appreciation of folk psychology intuitions.

2.1   Psychological explanation

A major part of our everyday mental life is filled up with thoughts we have about actions—about our own actions or the actions of others. On the one hand, these ideas can be directed towards the future—for example, when they concern possible, intended, or expected actions that we are planning or anticipating. On the other hand, they can be directed toward the past—that is, to actions that have already occurred and that we subsequently think about. A major part of everyday conversation consists of communicative exchange over which persons have done what on which occasion, why they have done it, and what one thinks about what they have done. The action jargon in which we phrase our thoughts and conversations is always the same. It applies to past and to future actions as it occurs in our own, as well in other people's minds.

To explain actions a person carries out under specific circumstances, folk psychology's action jargon has a ready answer. We attribute most of the actions that people perform to mental states that precede the action. For instance, we think that someone attended a certain opera performance because they wanted to see or listen to a certain opera singer; or that my friend washes her car because she believes that she will create a better impression if she goes to the job interview in a clean car. Naturally, the mental states that are viewed as causes of subsequent actions do not explain the course of actions in detail. However, they do explain why the particular action came about. Common sense has no problem at all with the fact that this explanation views a mental event (the person believes, wants, fears something) as the cause of a subsequent physical event (the action itself).

The mental states that can be viewed as causes of actions can be of different types and can bring different variants of action explanations into play. The simplest case is when we explain an action by assuming that it is based on an intention that is directed toward the attaining of a specific goal. This is the ideal case of an act of will in which we assume that the person has planned and carried out the action in order to achieve specific goals through it. If we were to ask the persons why they had carried out the action, they would name reasons.

Other explanations of action, in contrast, operate with the logic of causes. For example, someone who hurls his alarm clock at the wall in anger at having overslept does not, according to the common sense interpretation, act according to the logic of reasons, but rather to the logic of causes. We understand the mental state of anger as the cause for the destructive act, but not as the reason for it. In this case, the action is not based on an intention directed towards attaining a particular goal. Accordingly, we do not understand it as a rational voluntary action.

This is, then, in a nutshell, the structure of psychological action explanations the jargon of everyday language provides us with. Voluntary actions come about because actors have a certain goal they want to attain and because they believe that this goal can be attained with the help of a certain action. When these preconditions are given, the thought becomes the deed—mental states evoke physical processes and reasons function as causes.

2.2   Moral judgment

The action jargon of everyday discourse is by no means confined to the causal explanation of the transition from thoughts to deeds. It likewise applies to the evaluation and, finally, the moral justification of actions. There are two aspects here: at one level we talk about actions and their consequences. At this level we evaluate actions and their (desired or unde-sired) effects, as well as their mental antecedents. At the second level we then judge actors, rather than actions. At this level actors are attributed with the evaluated actions and their effects. Thus, everyday discourse on the judgment of actions is not just directed toward actions, but also toward persons. We hold that persons are responsible for their actions and we justify this belief by assuming that they are basically free to choose their own actions.

These basic beliefs have long been reflected in the jargon of free will in everyday lan-guage. Their basic ingredients have become so much second nature to us that they hardly need any explanation. We assume that in nearly all situations we could always have acted otherwise—if only we had wanted to. This implies that we understand our factual action as the outcome of a free choice. Of course, we concede that the decisions we make are always co-determined by a series of circumstances of which we may be more or less aware. Nonetheless, we are responsible for the decision on what we do. It is our responsibility to decide which circumstances we take into account and which not. For this reason, we always have the possibility of deciding against options that are suggested by the circumstances, in which case we require a particularly high degree of willpower. It is in this sense of 'decid-ing otherwise' or even 'deciding against' that we experience freedom of choice, and we attribute this it to our fellow human beings as well.

The jargon of free will has two faces, however: on the one hand, it accounts for a funda-mental psychological fact—the experience of free will that each person considers self-evident and beyond any doubt (see, for example, Kuhl, 1996). On the other, it serves a fundamental moral function, namely, the attribution of the consequences of actions to the perpetrator. At this point, we have to leave open whether the psychological facts entail the moral function or whether the moral function creates the psychological fact.

2.3 Trouble with the action jargon

Could anything be wrong with the action jargon? Do we need anything beyond? In fact, it does satisfy all our practical needs in everyday discourse. It is not really satisfactory from a more theoretical point of view. In fact, if one takes a closer look at the logic inherent in it, one discovers some deep-lying problems and inconsistencies.

First, the notion of free will requires us to accept local pockets of indeterminism in an otherwise deterministically conceived world view. Though this view appears to be evident and obvious for the common sense mentality of folk psychology, it is certainly not com-patible with more rational and scientific mentalities. Importantly, the implied indetermin-ism does not just concern an absence of determination or determinableness, but something completely different and more radical: nothing less than the replacement of usual causal determination through another, causally inexplicable form of determination. This is based on the assumption of a subject who is conceived as autonomous, who is personally free, i.e. non-determined in him or herself. In a way, the idea of free will requires us to see each subject as an independent, autonomous source of action determination.

Secondly, folk psychological common sense believes in both psychophysical dualism and mental causation, which comes close to the squaring of the circle. On the one hand, com-mon sense takes it as a matter of course that there are mental and physical phenomena, that the one is completely alien and disparate from the other, and that they cannot be related or reduced to each other in an understandable way. Thoughts and feelings are things that are entirely different from, e.g. hands, tulips, or rocks. For our common sense, this dualism is entirely evident and undeniable, and it is usually taken as a dualism of essential substances and not only of mere superficial properties.

On the other hand, there is one peculiar exception. The action jargon implies that certain mental states can cause certain mental events. When a person decides to switch off the radio, he or she will finally get up and activate the corresponding switch. We understand the physical action as a direct causal consequence of the mental intention—just like we see the movement of a billiard ball as the direct causal consequence of its being struck by the cue. We do not even notice the categorical rift over which we spring with such an explanation, and we do not even realize that the explanatory pattern of mental causation, when looked at clearly, is not very compatible with the principal psychological dualism we otherwise cultivate.

Thirdly, and closely related to this, folk psychology does not distinguish between observations from conscious experiences and the functional mechanisms that may be involved in generating them. Instead, it takes observations for mechanisms and identifies data with theory. The fact of observation that we feel ourselves to be free in our choice of actions is understood as an indication of the theoretical fact that we actually are free. Likewise, the observation that we experience the mental causation of physical action all the time is interpreted as an expression of the theoretical fact that mental states do cause physical actions. More precisely, the one is not really taken as an indication of the other, but rather the two facts—observational and theoretical—coincide. Conscious experience is the sole fundament the action jargon rests on. There is not the slightest awareness of the possibility that what appears in personal conscious experience might not be the fundament for everything else, but rather the selective outcome of the workings of sub-personal non-conscious mechanisms.

In conclusion, on the one hand, for a number of strong reasons, science cannot do with folk psychology and it needs to go beyond it. On the other hand, folk psychology's action jargon seems to provide an essential, if not indispensable ingredient to the 'mental glue' that keeps social systems together. From this perspective, voluntary action serves the important function of assigning each other responsibility for actions and their consequences. It seems, therefore, that we cannot do with folk psychology any more and we cannot do without it. What, then, can we do?

3   Folk psychology revisited

The schism between scientific and socio-cultural perspectives on voluntary action has motivated this book and is one of the recurring themes in a number of chapters. The schism is alive in the way issues of voluntary action are taken up in scientific discourses. Basically, there are two diverging streams of thought: one tries to uncover the workings of the sub-personal machinery that goes along the personal experience of voluntary action and presumably underlies it. Researchers are concerned with how minds work, how brains work, and how the working of minds and brains is related. Conversely, the other stream of thought tries to uncover how people work in their social context: researchers study how what people do at the personal level is related to and depends on their respective socio-cultural contexts at the supra-personal level. In conclusion, besides going into the two major research traditions on minds, brains, and people, we will also adopt a meta-perspective on discourses about minds, brains, philosophies, and social discourses.

3.1 Minds and brains, philosophies and social discourses

As has been mentioned earlier in this introduction, the disciplines involved in re-assessing voluntary action differ considerably in their respective direction of reasoning. If anything, they are united by their general procedure of analysis. Fundamentally, all efforts at recasting voluntary action are characterized by de-constructing it. Namely, each single approach inquires into basic structures and/or functions that eventually result in our 'feeling of knowing', which cause us act on the basis of our will. Not surprisingly though, the approaches differ with respect to the specific targets of deconstruction: the contributions convened in this book look at targets as different as cognitive mechanisms or neural activities, philosophical considerations, and social discourses. They address the individual or the collective level, empirical research or philosophical reasoning. A brief *tour d'horizon* is meant to highlight their general outlook on voluntary action—later in the book, each part is preceded by a more detailed description of each contribution.

1. *Psychologists* deconstruct the functional mechanisms that give rise to actions that are represented as 'voluntary' or 'conscious'. Notably, they ask how intentional representations interact in order to generate voluntary action. While cognitive psychologists emphasize the performance of an action, social and volitional psychologists stress the role of conscious experience resulting from or leading to certain functionally defined states. Both types of scholars, however, follow the same basic pattern in their explanatory programme for voluntary action: Whether the prime explanation is physical performance or conscious experience, it is considered to reflect and arise from the operation of a sub-personal machinery that accounts for the subject's performance and/or experience—irrespective of the experiential phenomenon that the subject deems the action 'voluntary' or 'conscious'. In terms of cognitive psychology, voluntary action is but a manner of speech—convenient, yet utterly misleading, and thus should be abandoned. In terms of volitional psychology, voluntary action grants the possibility of balancing various, if not antagonistic constraints on action. In terms of social psychology, voluntary action emerges from action perception, rather than action control. Different kinds of intention, as well as ascriptions of intentionality lead to different kinds of effects on people's thoughts, feelings, and actions. Hence, social and volitional psychologists do not abandon the notion of voluntary action. Rather, they recast it in terms of balancing conflicting demands and modes of perceiving actions. Yet they, too, do away with basic folk psychological assumptions. Neither does volition necessarily have to be conscious (rather than unobserved and subtle) in order to generate action, nor is conscious will the first and only causal impetus behind an action.

2. *Neuroscientists*, in turn, deconstruct voluntary action by way of looking at neural activities in the brain. In their view, the experience of mental volition is generated through interactions of various cortical and sub-cortical regions in the brain. The latter differ with respect to their accessibility to consciousness. While the prefrontal cortex gives rise to conscious or voluntary actions, they have to pass the 'subcortical censorship' of the basal ganglia in order to check back with the limbic experiential memory, which stores the long-term evaluations of the systems (experience). Whether or not voluntary actions are actually

carried out, is thus subject to 'subcortical decisions', which are, in fact, inaccessible to consciousness. Hence, neuroscientists, too, target the sub-personal machinery when conceiving of voluntary action. Although action decisions are only partly amenable to consciousness, volition still plays an important role. Namely, volition is understood as a mechanism for monitoring actions, attributed *post hoc* to the acting self, thereby assigning him/her to be the author of that action. This becomes particularly noticeable whenever an action fails or remains incomplete. As result of a mismatch between the 'intended action' and the 'factual outcome', the subject will regularly (albeit unconsciously) respond with a corrective procedure. In summary, the brain processes observed differ between the neural correlates for initiating and evaluating (as well as correcting) behaviour for action. Those processes are more or less amenable to consciousness, yet—by way of highly interconnected circuits— eventually lead to highly flexible, situation-dependent behaviour, which folk psychology re-interprets in terms of actions having been caused by 'will'.

3. *Philosophers* reconsider the notion of voluntary action, too. Recent findings in the neurocognitive realm hold the prospect of finally coming to terms with the most prominent self-insistent paradox: while we believe ourselves to be physical beings, we also believe we are conscious beings whose awareness of physical beings cannot be physical. It thus seems that we are both physical and non-physical. The problem is: how do the physical and non-physical relate? More specifically, how does the physical lead to the non-physical or how does the non-physical lead to the physical? By definition, the physical and the non-physical have no means of 'communication'—hence, the problem. Eliminativists, such as the Churchlands, suggest to forget about issues such as voluntary action altogether. Yet, the philosophers convened in our book do not agree with a deconstructivist stance as radical as that, but rather argue two different, more moderate positions. On the one hand, they try to demonstrate that voluntary action is not just an epiphenomenon of something more fundamental and physical. Rather, they either deem representational contents of consciousness as causally relevant or they make an even stronger claim. There is no way to give a perspective-free information-processing explanation of what consciousness is. Namely, such attempts circumvent what is most acute for the acting subject: its particular perspective that deeply influences the ways in which she/he conceives of the relationship between conscious perception and action or judgment. On the other hand, philosophers investigate the role of 'rationality' by, first, discerning different senses in which one may speak of an action being voluntary (the feeling of actions being wilful, the conception of actions being reasoned, or embedded in long-term volitions). While the first sense acknowledges the scientific findings that basically abandon volition as causal for action, the latter two senses acknowledge the philosophical discourse on reasoned action and second-order volitions that do play a causal role in action planning. Moreover, the rationality branch argues that intentions—like all volitional attitudes—have external meanings; hence, they are individuated by the objects they are directed to and not by the mental acts themselves. In all cases, philosophers take up the challenge posed by the neurocognitive approaches, yet insist on philosophical insights from discourses on epiphenomenalism and rationality as well, which hint at subtle distinctions about the 'degree' of causality and the internal rational structure connected to various types, forms, and intensities of volition. Still, even philosophical proponents of a strong status for our folk psychological intuitions find it very difficult to say in exactly which way these intuitions could be justified.

4. *Social scientists* insist rather strongly on a folk psychological notion of voluntary action as being a *sine qua non* in the social sphere. We just cannot do without attributing authorship of action to ourselves or to others. Notably, if it comes to sanctioning irresponsible or criminal behaviour, we need the notion of selves who—in their own as well as in the observer's view—could have acted otherwise or even contrary to options suggested by the circumstances. The criminological approaches considered in this book pursue two lines of reasoning. In one instance, it is argued that the acting (criminal) subject must act *as though she/he were free.* Likewise, society must treat the (criminal) subject *as though she/he were free to choose between right and wrong.* In the social realm, we thus talk about accountability, a paramount imperative in (post-)modern society. Ultimately, the complementary notions just mentioned safeguard social order by way of making people obey to the law 'voluntarily', invest money according to 'their interests', and vote according to their 'own conviction'. Social accountability is thus the flip-side of individual responsibility— an organizing principle, based upon (self-)discipline and (self-)control. From this point of view, voluntary action could be defined in purely sociological and functional terms, albeit subject to socio-historical transformations. Still, as anthropological studies show, there are some universals guiding our notion of voluntary action that, fundamentally, is an ambiguous concept. Namely, both the concept and the perception of voluntary action develops through and is based upon multiple and conflicting childhood-derived concepts of agency and action, penetrated by the desires and frustrations of development. More specifically, it responds to the following question: just how dependent or independent do we really want to be from the sources of our deepest attachment, i.e. from our mothers? While this conflict is a universal one, the instantiations differ from culture to culture. In summary, criminological and anthropological accounts do not deny that human behaviour is shaped by brain processes, yet social scientists plead for identifying the social processes and functions that shape the concept of voluntary action (as the former are shaped by it).

All their deconstructions considered, the contributions in this book entail an important message: The folk psychological notion of voluntary actions that implies volition to be either the cause of or the reason for action needs to be revisited. Granting its significance in everyday communication and interaction, the cognitive and neurosciences, philosophy, and the social sciences all have important insights to add to the concept. Ultimately, they all reject to tackle voluntary issue at face value; most of all they reject its explanatory power for issues such as intentionality, consciousness, etc. Rather, they deconstruct it by taking recourse to cognitive, neural, and social functions and/or processes that account for goal-directed actions, as well as to philosophical considerations regarding the notion of causality and rationality. These perspectives shed a new light on folk psychological intuitions. Beyond the simple dualism of either embracing or excluding it from the scientific discourse altogether, a new relation emerges. Voluntary action in its folk psychological form can be said to be the selective result of all those mechanisms considered, interacting in ways yet to be explained. At the same time it remains valid that the folk psychological concept of voluntary action, in turn, does not explain the functional architecture of the neural, cognitive, motivational, and social processes involved in producing goal-directed actions, just because it is far too selective. In other words, while voluntary action is not scientific, but a psychic and social concept, it is both amenable to and in need of (social) scientific explanations; yet, not of just one explanation, so it seems.

3.2 A plea for multiple explanations and inter-disciplinarities

So far we have considered various deconstructions of voluntary action, in turn. It should have become evident that they—although enlightening in and of themselves—do not lend themselves to easy cross-talks, as much as this would be desirable. For one thing, they differ epistemologically along the dimension of individual versus collectivist approaches. For another, they differ along a continuum of reductionist appeal—they imply either more or less 'scientification' of voluntary action. This could prove to be a real obstacle to a multi- or even inter-disciplinary discourse on voluntary action. In this introduction, we choose to refrain from delving into the thorny issue of inter-disciplinarity as such. Suffice it to say that, since the inception of this very notion it has been accompanied by enthusiasm and rejection alike. While enthusiasts hope to counter over-specialization by way of a more encompassing understanding of any issue in question, opponents most of all fear all kinds of reductionism, as well as the impossibility of finding a 'common ground'. The latter phenomenon is well illustrated by innumerable accounts of the difficulty to find a 'joint language'—this problem is often recast metaphorically as the 'Tower of Babel'.

When it comes to voluntary action, there is perhaps some reason to be more optimistic. Being an issue at the interface of nature and culture, various (sub-)disciplines deal with aspects of voluntary action. Therefore, why not try and find some bridges? Indeed, there are some relationships that seem interesting to pursue. Consider just two examples that have been chosen arbitrarily. For instance, there is the idea that third-order conceptions of voluntary action (i.e. scientific ones) should count as abstractions of first-order accounts (folk psychological ones)—hence, their epistemic relationship would be not one of replacement, but of complementarity. On this view, both accounts, scientific and folk psychological, could mutually enrich, rather than oppose each other. Then there is another idea in the realm of the social sciences that, in a way, goes back to the neurocognitive challenge. As the social sciences can show the enormous importance of the social concept named voluntary action, they urge the neurocognitive sciences to take responsibility for the ways in which they specify responsibility. Put to the extreme, one-dimensional 'neural redefinitions' of volition could lead to social redefinitions of responsibility. Could society handle a purely neurocognitive understanding of voluntary actions in, say, the juridical sphere? These are but two examples or pleas for a more dialogical way to find and process bridges and interfaces. On a general note, this is to say that we should not attempt an all encompassing, possibly reductionist view of voluntary action. As may have become apparent throughout the last section, the concept does mean different things to different (sub-)disciplines. Inter-disciplinarity in terms of a 'fruitful dialogue' should aim at integration where possible, acknowledging the differences wherever they are necessary and maybe even beneficial for further exchange.

It is in this spirit that the book as a whole has been designed, knowing that the first step toward a more balanced view of voluntary action needs stocktaking first. Therefore, Sections I–IV deal with voluntary action in the various fields just mentioned. Most of them address possibilities of fruitful, if always very specific forms of inter-disciplinary dialogue.

While these suggestions largely remain tentative, we took pains to explicitly address the epistemological implications concerning the ways of integrating multiple notions of voluntary action or consciousness, respectively. In the last Section, two articles plead for inter-disciplinarity in the plural—inter-disciplinarities, that is. While one advances a decidedly 'polytheistic approach' toward voluntary action by way of accepting 'the reality of a loose assemblage of differently focused, rather self-involved, and variably overlapping research communities in both the human and natural sciences' (Geertz), the other studies the intricacies of multidisciplinary discourse as evidenced for consciousness research. Looking at all discourses engaged in this research topic over 30 years with bibliometric methods, it becomes evident that the concept of consciousness is best described as a hybrid (e.g. a loosely coupled ensemble of a neural activity, a cognitive function, a collective representation, a transpersonal event, . . .), engaging the disciplines involved in different ways. Due to epistemic tensions between matter and mattering, or physicalist and phenomenalist accounts, consciousness is likely to stay on the academic agenda for quite some time. It will also continue to mean many different things to many different discourses—and so does voluntary action.

This book is thus making a start with some stocktaking, and preliminary ideas as to where and how we might look for interfaces—in the plural, that is.

References

Kuhl, J. (1996) Wille und Freiheitserleben: Formen der Selbststeuerung. In Kuhl, J. and Heckhausen, H. (eds), *Motivation, Volition und Handlung (Enzyklopädie der Psychologie, Serie Motivation und Emotion, Band IV)*. Göttingen: Hogrefe. pp. 665–765.

SECTION I

SECTION I

BETWEEN MOTIVATION AND CONTROL: PSYCHOLOGICAL ACCOUNTS OF VOLUNTARY ACTION

WOLFGANG PRINZ

1   Stimuli, responses, and goals

Psychologists are experimentalists. They run experiments—mostly inspired by theoretical considerations. They ask theoretical questions and use experimental methods to answer them. In psychological experiments participants are exposed to well-controlled experimental environments. Experimental environments and experimental tasks need to be decontextualized—in the sense that one tries to exclude or neutralize all kinds of uncontrollable factors. In one sense, environments like this put severe constraints on the participant's room for manoeuvrings, since they require her to perform certain pre-specified responses to certain pre-specified stimuli. Hence, there seems to be no room for voluntary action. Still, even in a highly constrained situation like this, voluntary action comes into play at the time when the participant listens to the instruction and tries to prepare herself for performing the task accordingly (assuming she is co-operative and does not wish to thwart the experiment altogether). At this time participants need to create in their mental systems a representational configuration that captures the intention:

* to perform certain actions on certain conditions (e.g., press certain keys in response to certain stimuli);
* to do this as fast as they can.

In a way, then, each and every experiment has two stages: one at which an intentional representational set is established and one which is used for doing the task.

Remarkably, much of classical experimental research has focused on Stage Two and disregarded Stage One. Psychological theories consider what happens between stimuli and responses, but they do not often take into account that, whatever happens, there depends on the intentional structures that were created before the first stimulus arrived. Accordingly, the operations that translate stimuli into responses are treated as transformational operations that compute responses from stimuli—just as if the stimuli and the information inherent in them would be sufficient to specify the proper responses.

However, this is obviously not the case. Stimuli will only be capable of eliciting appropriate responses if and only if appropriate intentional sets have been formed and implemented in the first place. Therefore, the theoretical analysis of the task needs to start with the formation and implementation of intentional structures, rather than the presentation of the stimuli. Intentions need to be implemented first, and it is only then that the stimuli attain the capability of eliciting their appropriate responses.

This fact is too obvious to overlook and we may therefore wonder why it has been so much neglected in psychological theory. It seems that this neglect is deeply rooted in the way we conceive the relationship between perception and action. Over decades we have been educated to believe that stimuli come first and responses second. Likewise, over centuries, our philosophical forerunners have believed that knowing about the world comes first and acting upon it comes second. As a consequence, in both method and theory, psychological research has become used to starting with stimuli, ending up with responses, and ignoring what happened before.

When people perform voluntary actions, they want to attain particular goals. Goals have, in a way, two faces: On the one, the goal itself, i.e. the goal state in the world, can, by definition, be reached only after the action has been completed. However, on the other face, a representation of the goal may be involved in the actor's mind before the action commences, i.e. at early stages of action planning. There is a dual sense in which we say that actions are goal-directed. Goals-in-the-mind are already involved in their planning and control and, accordingly, goals-in-the-world are attained through their execution. According to the testimony of introspection we entertain anticipatory representations of the goals to be reached and it seems that these anticipatory representations somehow gain control over the execution of the actions themselves. At the end, then, we may compare the goal we have attained (in the world) with the goal we have been striving towards (in the mind) and, hence, evaluate our actions' success.

How can goals-in-the-mind come to play a causal role in action planning and control? In principle, the answer to this question is to invoke anticipatory goals representations that are somehow furnished with the power to elicit body movements suited to reach these goals. In the literature there have been various attempts to solve this seeming puzzle, like Ach's determining tendencies (Ach, 1905), Hull's fractional antedating goal response (Hull, 1931, 1952), Greenwald's ideomotor mechanism (Greenwald, 1970), or Schmidt's recall schema (1975, 1982). Though these mechanisms differ in detail, they share the common principle that anticipatory goal representations derive from previous learning of relationships between movements and their outcomes.

2 Persons, intentions, and mechanisms

Psychology has a long history of struggling with conscious experience. In the late nineteenth century when experimental work on cognition and action began, psychology was defined as the study of conscious experience. Later, the schools of thought like behaviourism brought conscious experience into discredit and emphasized the role of behaviour and performance as psychology's ultimate explanation. Today psychology deals with both conscious experience and performance, and many theorists are opportunistic in the sense that they wish to account for both sides of mental life. Still, as can be seen from the chapters in this section, some differences have survived in theoretical flavour and methodological focus. Scholars whose background is in social psychology and motivation, like Bayer, Ferguson, and Gollwitzer and, to some extent, Goschke, put much more weight on conscious experience than scholars whose background is in experimental cognitive psychology, like Prinz and Hommel. Social psychologists consider conscious experience in both of its potential roles, i.e. as resulting from and leading to certain functionally defined states. Experimental psychologists tend to adopt a somewhat different perspective, stressing the selective nature of conscious experience. They see their main job in accounting for performance and tend to assign to conscious experience a marginal, if not epiphenomenal role.

However, despite these differences, they all follow the same basic pattern in their explanatory programme for voluntary action: Whatever the prime explanation is—conscious experience or physical performance—it is considered to reflect and arise from the operation of a sub-personal machinery that accounts for participants' experience and/or performance. Over the past decades it has become customary to describe the working of this machinery in the metaphoric terminology of information processing, i.e. in close analogy to the way we describe what is going on in computers.

In a nutshell, present-day psychology's basic explanatory scheme is this: to construct a hypothetical functional system such that it accounts for the physical performance and—if possible—for conscious experience, as well. Moreover, the modern psychologists' dream is this: that this basic explanatory scheme provides us with a functional description of the same system that the neurosciences study in terms of its instantiation in the brain. Therefore, to the extent the scheme is valid and the dream is true, they study physical performance, conscious experience, and brain processes at the same time.

The four chapters in this section are arranged in an ascending order of complexity and contextualization with respect to both the experimental tasks under consideration and the theoretical issues addressed. Accordingly, and not surprisingly, as we proceed through the four chapters, we find increasing attention allotted to the role that conscious awareness (in terms of thoughts, deliberations, motives, beliefs, or intentions) play in the generation of voluntary action.

The general picture emerging at the end is two-fold. The four chapters do agree in the bad news they have for folk psychology. They all struggle against the folk psychology intuition that actions follow from intentions in a simple causal step. Instead, they argue for new views of the role of intentions and their underlying representations. On the other hand, the chapters differ in the major good news they have to offer about voluntary actions and their functional underpinnings.

The chapters by Prinz and by Hommel focus on short-lived actions on narrow timescales. Prinz discusses ways of knowing about one's own actions, contending that we know about our actions not by virtue of being their mental authors, but rather by being their mental observers. He suggests that two independent functional modules may be involved in voluntary action—a fast one for generating action, and a slower one for interpreting action in physical and mental terms. Accordingly, he sees no support for the folk psychology intuition that the mental causes the physical. Hommel's chapter deals with the mechanisms of action control and their acquisition in learning. He adopts the classical ideomotor view that actions are planned and controlled in terms of their represented effects. He discusses ways in which representations of these effects interact with representations of actual stimulus conditions in action execution. Moreover, he discusses the learning mechanisms involved in building associations between actions and their effects, which can be used in either direction.

With respect to the role of conscious experience, Hommel takes a functional stance claiming that the conscious experience of volitional involvement just does not make a difference in terms of the functional mechanisms that lead to the actions.

The chapters by Goschke and Bayer *et al.* consider actions on broader time-scales. Goschke considers both intentions and actions in the comprehensive framework of the requirements a large-scale theory of cognitive control and action control must meet. He views the cognitive system in a basic dilemma between conservative demands that require the system to maintain certain functional configurations over time and more progressive demands that require moment-to-moment flexibility. With this broad perspective voluntary actions are one of the outcomes of the operation of a number of context-sensitive control processes that operate to negotiate the basic stability/flexibility dilemma. The constraints arising from this dilemma act as long-term intentions that are satisfied by voluntary actions. Voluntary action emerges from a distributed system that has specialized modules for intentional representation, sensory information, and the interaction between the two.

Bayer *et al.* consider voluntary action from a more contextualized perspective as is usually adopted in social psychology and personality psychology. In the first part, they consider mechanisms underlying the long-term pursuit of goals. How are goals selected and set, and what mechanisms are involved in striving for goals? In the second part they consider how people perceive the intentionality of other people's actions and what role is played by conscious volition in the control of their own actions. The authors suggest three important conclusions:

- that goal-directed thoughts, feelings, and behaviour can emerge without a person's conscious intent;
- that we often perceive goal-directedness and intentionality in other's thoughts, feelings, and behaviour, regardless of whether or not their behaviour is guided by conscious intentions;
- that behaviour can often be explained without invoking intentional guidance as a causal factor in the game.

Taken together, these conclusions seem to suggest that, contrary to folk psychology intuitions, the experience of conscious volition may emerge from action perception rather than action control.

References

Ach, N. (1905) *Über die Willenstätigkeit und das Denken.* Göttingen: Vandenhoeck & Ruprecht.

Greenwald, A.G. (1970) Sensory feedback mechanisms in performance control: with special reference to the ideo-motor mechanism. *Psychol Rev* **77**, 73–99.

Hull, C.L. (1931) Goal attraction and directing ideas conceived as habit phenomena. *Psychol Rev* **38**, 487–506.

Hull, C.L. (1952) *A Behaviour System.* New Haven: Yale University Press.

Schmidt, R.A. (1975) A schema theory of discrete motor skill learning. *Psychol Rev* **82**, 225–60.

Schmidt, R.A. (1982) The schema concept. In Kelso, J.A.S. (ed.), *Human Motor Behaviour: An Introduction.* Hillsdale: Erlbaum, pp. 219–35.

CHAPTER 1

HOW DO WE KNOW ABOUT OUR OWN ACTIONS?

WOLFGANG PRINZ

1   The folk psychology of voluntary action

The history of psychology is, to some extent, the story of a never-ending struggle against folk psychology. In a way, folk psychology provides us with ready-made answers to many of the questions we ask in science. As a consequence, everybody who shares a particular system of folk psychology convictions and beliefs is an expert in psychological matters. People already know the answers to the questions we pose and, therefore, they find much of our scientific effort redundant and superfluous.

Consider, as an example, what folk psychology takes for granted about voluntary actions. When a person performs a voluntary action, e.g. brushing his/her shoes, we usually distinguish between the physical action itself and its mental antecedents that we believe causes the action. Typically, these mental causes take the form of beliefs, desires, or reasons. For instance, people polish their shoes on Saturday afternoon because they are attending an opera on Saturday night and want to look smart.

This is, in a nutshell, what folk psychology takes for granted. In the following I will examine two implications of the distinction between actions and their mental antecedents. One refers to the notion of mental causation. Folk psychology intuitions imply that reasons *cause* actions, i.e. that mental events cause physical events. As philosophers keep telling us, a view like this goes along with strong epistemological and ontological commitments. Interestingly, however, folk psychology does not have the slightest problem with this tricky relationship.

The second implication refers to the way we know about actions and their antecedents. We can *observe* people brushing their shoes, but we cannot observe in the same way their reasons for doing so. Depending on context, we may perhaps *infer* what their reasons are and/or ask them why they are doing what they are doing. However, there seems to be an interesting exception to the distinction between observation and inference. When it comes to understanding my own actions, I need not infer my reasons nor ask myself why I am doing what I am doing. Instead, I am *directly aware* of my actions' mental antecedents—much in the same way as I am aware of their physical realization. I'm quite at home with my mind, perhaps even more so than with my body.

Philosophical reflections on the wisdom of folk psychology have ever been concerned about the relationship between reasons and actions. These reflections have addressed both the doctrine of mental causation and the doctrine of direct access to mental events from a first-person's perspective. An influential example is Cartesian Dualism that, on the one hand, reflects basic notions of western-civilization folk psychology and, on the other, reflects *on* these notions in a particular way (see, e.g. Descartes, 1685). Of crucial importance has been Descartes' discussion of the way we access our own mental contents. According to Descartes, mental content has a privileged epistemological status. To *physical* events (in both the world and our body) our mind has access through the medium of perception. Of our own *mental* events, however, our mind simply becomes aware in a direct and unmediated fashion. As a consequence, we can be deceived about physical events, but not about mental events. Hence, our knowledge about what is going on in our own minds is privileged in two ways: it is immediate and infallible.

The scope of this doctrine goes far beyond the analysis of voluntary action. It has ever since played an important role in the history of philosophy and science (see, e.g. Brentano, 1874/1924; Mach, 1922). Not surprisingly, it has also inspired the major founding fathers of modern psychology in the nineteenth century (e.g. Lotze, 1852; Wundt, 1874; Helmholtz, 1879; James, 1890). More recently, it has attracted considerable interest in the rich literature on the development of agency in infancy (see, e.g. Russell, 1996, 1997, in defence of the Cartesian doctrine; and, e.g. Gopnik, 1993; Barresi & Moore, 1996, for a more critical position).

In this chapter I will discuss the Cartesian doctrine in the light of experimental evidence taken from research on voluntary actions in adult subjects. The questions I will raise are simple enough. How do we know about our own actions? How does the way our mind perceives our actions relate to the way our body performs them? Is it really true that we have privileged access to the mental causes of our actions? Of course, I realize that these questions continue to be discussed in philosophical discussions, too (see, e.g. the chapters by Eilan and Proust, this volume). However, unlike philosophers, I will not be concerned with the conceptual issues involved in them. Instead, I will take the naïve stance of a cognitive scientist who treats them as empirical questions.

2   Experimental observations

In this section I will discuss some experimental observations on the fine-grained time course of action. My basic message is that there is not much reason to believe that our folk psychology intuitions about voluntary action do, in fact, reflect or even come close to the way we actually perform and perceive our actions. At least for the simple tasks I will consider, there is no reason to believe in both mental causation and privileged access. Rather, it appears that we perceive our actions in exactly the same way as we perceive any other event.

In the tasks I shall consider people perform simple actions, like lifting their fingers or pressing response keys. These actions can be triggered in two different ways: self-triggered (i.e. by internal decisions) or stimulus-triggered (i.e. by external stimuli). For the self-triggered mode it is obvious that it reflects the basic constituents of voluntary action: a bodily movement (e.g. lifting a finger) and a mental antecedent (the decision to lift). For the stimulus-triggered mode that, for a number of methodological reasons, is more widespread in experimental research, it is less obvious how it fits into this scheme. On the one hand, one may argue that volition plays no role because the trigger is external and physical, rather than internal and mental. On the other hand, as I have argued elsewhere, volition is still involved because it is only by virtue of a voluntary act that the role of the trigger is delegated to the stimulus (Prinz, 1997, 1998). Correspondingly, our folk psychology intuitions make us believe that, in a situation like this, it is the percept of the stimulus that takes the role of the mental cause of the subsequent movement: the performance of the movement follows the perception of the stimulus in both temporal and causal terms.

2.1 On relationships between acting and knowing

2.1.1 Self-triggered movements

A famous series of experiments on spontaneous action has been performed by Libet and his colleagues (Libet *et al.*, 1983a,b; Libet, 1985, 1993, 1996). The basic task was to perform a quick, abrupt flexion of the fingers of the right hand whenever the participant felt like doing so. Participants were encouraged 'to let the urge to act appear on its own at any time without preplanning or concentrating on when to act'—an instruction meant to elicit spontaneous voluntary acts that are 'freely capricious in origin'. On each occurrence of a finger flexion the times of three events were recorded, two physical and one mental event. The first was the time of the onset of the movement, as defined by the onset of supra-threshold electromyographic activity in the muscles involved in the movement. The second was the onset of the readiness potential, as defined by the onset of supra-threshold EEG activity recorded at the vertex of the participant's scalp. The readiness potential (RP) is considered to reflect the brain's preparation of the motor act, i.e. to be a causal physiological antecedent of the overt movement itself. The third measure refers to the time of one of two mental events. In one condition participants were asked to judge the time of movement onset, i.e. the time at which they actually moved (condition M). In another condition, they were required to judge the time of the appearance of the conscious awareness of wanting to perform the movement, that is, the time-point at which they felt a decision or an urge to move (condition W). Unlike the times for the two physical events, which were recorded by straightforward electrophysiological measurement, the times of the mental events could only be recorded in an indirect fashion. Participants were required to watch a light spot revolving at constant velocity on a clockwise circle, and to indicate the spot's spatial position on the circle at the moment they felt W or M.

As a result, Libet and his colleagues then mapped the two physical events and the two mental events onto a common time scale whose zero-point was fixed at EMG onset. The basic observation was that the two mental events, W and M, preceded EMG onset by about 200 and 85 ms for W and M, respectively. In other words, the onset of a movement is perceived 85 ms before it is actually recorded in the muscles and the urge to move is perceived about 200 ms before its actual occurrence (and, hence, 115 ms before its perceived occurrence). More importantly, however, the onset of the readiness potential preceded the time of W by another 300–500 ms (depending on the exact technical definition of RP onset, i.e. the threshold applied to the raw data for determining RP onset).

Therefore, if one trusts the validity of the measurement procedures applied, one has to conclude that the physical preparation of the action commences much ahead of its mental initiation. There are, however, a number of reasons to distrust the validity of the measurements recorded. For instance, we do not know which constant and variable errors may be involved in the required mapping of the times of mental events onto spatial positions of the revolving spot. Furthermore, as has been argued by Dennett & Kinsbourne (1992), it is by no means clear to which extent it is legitimate to map mental times and physical times of events onto the same scale. Yet, even if one adopts a more cautious interpretation, one is still faced with the puzzling observation of a substantial lag of the person's mental initiative behind the brain's physical initiative to act.

As has recently been shown by Haggard & Eimer (1999) the times of W and M are not different for fixed movements (that are predetermined over a series of trials as was always the case in Libet's experiments) and free movements (that are selected and determined anew on each particular trial). In their free movement condition participants were instructed to 'decide of their own free will during each trial *which hand to use* for the impending movement'. Though it may not be too surprising that the time of M was identical for the two conditions, it is certainly not trivial that the same applied to the time of W. For instance, one might have expected that W occurs earlier for free than for fixed movements due to the difference in their cognitive requirements: fixed movements need to be initiated only, but free movements need first to be selected before they can then be initiated.

One of three possible conclusions can be drawn at this point. The first option is to believe that Libet's method to assess the time of W is valid. In this case, it is not obvious how W can play a causal role in physical action (whose preparation starts much earlier in the brain). This option saves privileged access at the expense of mental causation. The second option is to distrust Libet's method and maintain the notion of a causal role for W, assuming that its time is just misperceived or misjudged in the experimental set-up. This option saves mental causation at the expense of privileged access. The third and most radical option is to believe in the method, and conclude that there is no such thing as an action's mental cause. The elusive urge to move is just a phantom, re-constructed from the hindsight, rather than perceived in the process. This option gives up both mental causation and privileged access.

2.1.2 Stimulus-triggered movements

When actions are performed in response to stimuli our folk psychology intuitions make us believe that we first identify the stimulus and only then select the appropriate response. An intuition like this is contained in numerous processing models from the family of linear stage models of reaction processes (see, e.g. Sanders, 1980, 1998). These models believe that first comes stimulus identification and only then comes response selection. Of course, there is also an important difference between folk psychology notions and linear stage models. Stages in information-processing models are always defined in functional terms and not in terms of mental experiences related to them. Still, the basic logic is the same: there is an early stimulus-related operation whose results make the information available, which then determines the selection and initiation of the response to be performed.

Though these intuitions appear to be quite natural, there is now a substantial body of evidence questioning them, which is derived from observations about dissociations between acting and perceiving. In the following, I discuss two examples of such dissociations that speak to the details of the time-course of stimulus identification and response specification.

The first example refers to a reaching task studied by Castiello & Jeannerod (1991; Castiello *et al.*, 1991). In this task, participants had to reach for dowels, which were mounted on a table in front of them. Each dowel was equipped with a light, which was either off or on. On each trial, then, the light in one of the dowels was switched on, and participants were required to reach for this particular dowel as fast as possible, and to eventually grasp and lift it. Hence, right after the light in the dowel went on, the participant's hand would leave its resting position and move towards the dowel.

There were two types of trials: (frequent) control trials and (infrequent) perturbation trials. On control trials, participants grasped the dowel that was lit. On perturbation trials, the onset of the hand's movement triggered a shift of the illumination from one dowel to another one. If that occurred participants were required to do two things simultaneously:

- to emit a short vocal utterance ('tah') in response to the sudden change in the stimulus;
- to reorientate the already ongoing reach towards the newly lit dowel.

How did performance on perturbation trials differ from control trials? First, and not too surprisingly, movement times were longer on perturbation trials than on control trials. Secondly, the authors studied how long it takes for the reaching hand to show the earliest indication of a response to the perturbation applied. For this purpose they identified the point at which trajectories from perturbation trials started to depart from trajectories from control trials. Naturally, this departure point was strongly dependent on the nature of the perturbation applied. In one study in which the perturbation referred to *the location* of the dowel to be grasped, the departure point was observed as early as 100 ms after the location shift, indicating a very short correction delay. In another experiment, where the perturbation referred to *the size* of the dowel to be grasped (at constant location), the departure point was as late as 300 ms after the size shift, indicating a much longer correction delay. However, in both of these studies the vocal utterance occurred at exactly the same time— i.e. at 420 ms after perturbation onset—in any case much later than the departure points in the movement trajectories for the two conditions.

There are two points of interest here. One is that people appear to correct their movements much before they become consciously aware of the perturbation. This conclusion is based on the assumption that the time of the vocal utterance reflects the time of becoming aware of the perturbation. However, a conclusion like this is certainly questionable in view of the fact that the time of the utterance will, to an unknown amount of time, lag behind the time of awareness.

Less questionable and more important is the second implication of the results, which refers to the dissociation between perceiving and acting. The fact that identical vocal detection times go along with vastly different correction delays for the two perturbations appears to be incompatible with the folk psychology intuition that the physical event reflected in the correction is grounded in the mental event reflected in the vocal utterance. Rather, this finding seems to suggest the notion of two independent pathways, a fast one for physical action and a slow one for mental representation. First comes the action and only then comes the conscious awareness of its cause.

The second example comes from reaction-time tasks. In these tasks, participants are required to press certain response buttons when certain stimulus events appear and to do so as fast as they can. With a task like this, Neumann and colleagues have recently observed a similar dissociation between the conscious awareness of certain stimulus events, and their impact on the selection and initiation of motor responses (Neumann & Klotz, 1994; Neumann *et al.*, 1998).

This dissociation can be observed under so-called meta-contrast conditions. Meta-contrast is typically obtained in situations in which two adjacent stimuli are presented in immediate succession. For instance, in the classical version of the task, the first stimulus (the test stimulus) is a filled circle (disk) and the second stimulus (the mask) a ring that surrounds the disk. Under conditions where the test stimulus is first presented in a brief flash (say, for 20 ms presentation time) and is then followed by the mask (say, 40 ms after test stimulus offset), it is usually observed that the test stimulus can barely be seen. This is the meta-contrast phenomenon. It belongs to the class of backward masking phenomena that share 'the apparent paradox that a later presented stimulus (the mask) influences the perception of an earlier presented stimulus (the test stimulus), seemingly exerting its effect backward in time' (Neumann & Klotz, 1994, p. 125).

Interestingly, however, the invisible test stimulus appears to trigger motor responses just in the same way as it does in non-masked control conditions. For instance, Fehrer & Raab instructed participants to press a button as soon as a stimulus appeared. There were two stimulus conditions: disk/ring combinations and unmasked disks alone. Quite surprisingly, they observed that stimulus detection times were the same for the two conditions, suggesting that the masking of the test stimulus, though it does affect its availability to conscious awareness, does not affect its capacity to trigger a motor response. Once more, this observation questions the view that physical action goes back to mental causes.

Over the past decade, the meta-contrast dissociation has been extensively explored by Neumann and his colleagues. An important clarification arising from that work is that the test stimulus' power to elicit a motor response is even preserved under conditions under which the test stimulus is absolutely invisible and, hence, inaccessible to subjective report. This seems to lend strong support to the notion of two pathways that are strictly independent—one for conscious perception and one for action control. Another important clarification is that the dissociation between action control and awareness does not only pertain to simple reactions that depend on stimulus detection (as shown by Fehrer & Raab), but also to choice reactions that depend on stimulus identification. In other words, under conditions where the pathway for conscious perception is shut down, the pathway for action is still capable of identifying the stimulus and selecting the appropriate response. Apparently, action can be sighted when perception is blind.

2.1.3   Summary

We may summarize the evidence from these studies as follows: (1) There appears to be no support for the folk psychology notion that the act follows the will, in the sense that physical action is caused by mental events that precede them and to which we have privileged access. (2) It seems that the way we perceive our actions does not reflect the functional mechanisms that lead to them—at least not in a simple and straightforward way. (3) Experimental evidence suggests that two different pathways, or modules, may be involved in action—one for the generation of physical action and one for the mental awareness of its causal antecedents. If anything, the second follows the first, and not vice versa. The will follows the act: first comes the initiation of physical action and only later emerges the awareness of its mental cause.

2.2   On relationships between actions and events

Folk psychology makes us believe that we know of our actions by virtue of authorship: it is us who generate them and therefore we have privileged, first-hand knowledge about them. When we abandon this belief, we are faced with the question of how else we know about our actions and on what other evidence our knowing is possibly grounded.

One obvious possibility is that we perceive our own actions in exactly the same way as we perceive any other events in the world, that is, that there is nothing special about action at all. In this section I will discuss some evidence in support of the view that action perception and event perception are, in fact, made of the same stuff. The evidence is taken from experiments that study interactions between actions and external events with respect to the times at which their occurrence is perceived.

2.2.1   Sensorimotor synchronization

In sensorimotor synchronization tasks, participants are exposed to isochronous sequences of auditory stimuli (like short beeps or metronome clicks) and required to perform simple movements (like key-presses) in exact synchrony with the stimuli. The task is easy in the sense that everybody can do it. People first listen to three or four clicks, then start accompanying clicks with taps, and soon they feel to tap in perfect synchrony.

One of the interesting observations with this task is that the feeling of synchrony requires that taps lead over clicks by about 20–80 ms. This lead interval is called the negative asynchrony. Interestingly, its size does not decrease with practice. On the contrary— when one applies a feedback-based training procedure that urges people to perform taps in *physical* synchrony with clicks, they tend to lose the feeling of *mental* synchrony, believing that taps now lag behind clicks.

Most of the literature on this task is concerned with the mechanisms underlying negative asynchronies and the isochronous timing of actions. In the present context I would like to consider a somewhat different, although related aspect. What can we learn from the task about the way we perceive our actions?

The synchronization task allows us to study how self-generated actions (taps) get synchronized with external events (clicks). The fact that the task appears to be so simple conceals the fact that the functional problems involved in performing it are certainly not simple at all. Even if one considers clicks as (more or less) punctate events, self-generated actions are made up of a number of functional components that are extended over quite some time like, for example, the formation of the motor command in the brain, the execution of the physical movement, and the subsequent perception of re-afferent information arising from the movement. What, then, exactly is it in the tap that gets synchronized with the click?

There are two ways to approach this problem, direct and indirect. The direct way is to study which components of taps and clicks coincide in time. For instance, in one of the classical models of the negative asynchrony advanced by Fraisse (1956, 1980) and Paillard (1949), it has been argued that synchrony is achieved when the re-afferent information arising from the tap arrives in the brain at the same time at which the information from the click arrives (cf. Aschersleben & Prinz, 1995). According to this view, negative asynchronies arise, because the neural pathway from the fingertip to the brain is longer than from the ear to the brain, so that in order to achieve synchrony of arrival times in the brain, a certain amount of asynchrony needs to be maintained in their corresponding departure times in the world. However, the logic of the direct approach has been criticized because of its inherent assumption that the representation of time is based on the time of representation, i.e. that the mental synchrony of two events is based on the physical synchrony of the brain processes representing them (cf. Dennett & Kinsbourne, 1992).

Consider now the indirect approach. Its logic is to manipulate certain features of the actions to be performed and study how the size of the asynchrony is affected by this manipulation. For instance, in one of our experiments we studied the impact of the amplitude of the tapping movement (Aschersleben *et al.*, 2000). In two different conditions, we had participants practice *large* taps in one condition and *small* taps in another condition (defined in terms of two non-overlapping ranges of amplitudes of tapping movements). Much to our surprise this simple manipulation had a strong impact on asynchronies: negative asynchronies were smaller with large than with small amplitudes, indicating that taps resulting from large movements are perceived to occur earlier than taps resulting from small movements.

We then reasoned that this difference could arise from two aspects of the movements' sensory consequences: proprioceptive feedback arising from the fingers' downward strokes (which differed in both amplitude and peak velocity for the two conditions) or tactile feedback arising from the fingers' contact with the response pad (which differed in pressure for the two conditions). In order to pull these two factors apart we ran an isometric version of the task where the finger did not move at all. Participants kept their fingers on the response pad all the time and in two different conditions they were trained to exert strong versus weak key-presses in synchrony with clicks. Again, we observed smaller asynchronies for strong than for weak presses, supporting the view that it may be the intensity of the tactile feedback from the fingertip (rather than the movement-related proprioceptive feedback from the downward stroke) that determines the perceived time of the action.

In another set of studies we added an extrinsic auditory feedback signal (beep) to the intrinsic feedback signal provided by proprioceptive and tactile information (Aschersleben & Prinz, 1995). Consider first the situation where the delivery of that beep is triggered by the onset of the tap. In this situation the occurrence of the combined tap/beep event is signalled to the brain via two pathways—somatosensory and auditory. Since the auditory pathway is shorter than the somatosensory, the auditory information should arrive earlier than the tactile information. In fact, we did observe that the amount of negative asynchrony was reduced under this condition, that is, the combined tap/beep event was perceived earlier than the tap-alone event in the control condition (where extrinsic feedback was absent).

In two further experiments we studied what happens when the delivery of the beep is shifted forward or backward in time, relative to tap onset. In the first study the delivery of the auditory feedback signal was *delayed* up to 80 ms after tap onset—a range within which people still perceive the feedback signals in perfect synchrony with their taps (Aschersleben & Prinz, 1997). What we observed was that negative asynchronies increased within increasing delays in feedback delivery. More specifically, our results indicated that the two feedback signals—intrinsic and extrinsic—get integrated and that the time of the integrated signal is computed as a linear combination of the times of its two components.

A different picture emerged in the second study, where the beep *preceded* tap onset (to the effect that it coincided in time with the fingers' downward stroke; cf. Mates & Aschersleben, 2000). Under this condition we observed almost no effect of the beep on the size of the asynchrony. Hence, the integration of feedback information appears to be asymmetric. Feedback sources that precede the onset of the tap tend to be disregarded, whereas feedback sources that follow tap onset get integrated and determine the time at which the tap is perceived. In summary, these observations suggest that the perceived time of an action is much more determined by its consequences than by its antecedents.

An important implication of these findings seems to be that the perception of one's own action appears to follow the same principles as the perception of external events, at least as regards the time dimension. For instance, as has been shown in both reaction time studies and studies based on temporal order judgements, it also holds for the perceived times of physical events like flashes or light patches that high-intensity stimuli tend to be perceived earlier than low-intensity stimuli (see, e.g. Pieron, 1925; Roufs, 1963, 1974; Teichner & Krebs, 1972; Sanford, 1974). The same applies to the linear combination of information from different modalities. For instance, when one uses an auditory beep and a visual flash as a combined pacing signal in a synchronization task, the time at which the pacing signal is perceived seems to be computed from a linear combination of the times at which its two components are presented (Aschersleben & Bertelson submitted).

These may be surprising analogies as long as one believes that access to one's own actions is privileged over and different from access to other events. However, they turn into natural homologies under the assumption that the way we perceive our own actions does not differ at all from the way we perceive events in the world, and that they are both grounded on the same information.

2.2.2 Self-triggered movements

A similar conclusion has emerged from another recent study in which we explored how the perceived time of intrinsic actions and extrinsic events is modulated by actions and events preceding or succeeding them (Haggard *et al.*, 2002). The basic method of the study was modelled after the logic of Libet's experiments. In one set of conditions, participants were required to judge the time at which an extrinsic event occurred (an auditory beep). In another set of conditions they had to judge the time of their own action (key pressing). The beep was presented in three different ways:

- it could either happen alone;
- it could be an imperative signal to which the participant had to react;
- it could occur as an effect caused by a self-triggered response.

Likewise, the key press could either happen alone, it could cause a beep following it, or it could happen in response to a beep preceding it. In all cases, the temporal separation between the event whose time was to be judged, and the event that either preceded or followed it was about 200 ms.

Interestingly, we observed a complete analogy between the times of beeps and the times of actions. Beeps happening alone were slightly antedated (–30 ms relative to physical beep onset). When the beep called for a subsequent response its perceived time was slightly postponed (−19 ms). However, when the beep occurred in response to a preceding action its occurrence was perceived much earlier (−71 ms). The same pattern was observed for the time of the action. When the action happened alone it was slightly antedated, too (−9 ms). When the action caused a subsequent beep its time was slightly postponed (+1 ms). However, when the action occurred in response to a preceding beep its occurrence was perceived much earlier (−57 ms).

2.2.3   Summary

In summary, our studies suggest that there may be nothing special about action at all. On the one hand, we see strong interactions between intrinsic and extrinsic action effects with respect to action timing. On the other hand, we see strong analogies, if not homologies, between the way actions are affected by events preceding or succeeding them, and the way events are affected by actions preceding or succeeding them. Clearly, we see no indication of any form of privileged access to intrinsic, action-related knowledge.

3   Theoretical conclusions

In conclusion, let me come back to the question raised in the title and draw a more general picture of what can be learned from the experiments discussed on how we know about our own actions. In doing so, I would like to stress that my conclusions are exclusively based on observations from simple actions like finger lifts or key pressing, and that it is uncertain to what extent such observations can help to reveal mechanisms that also apply to more complex actions.

With this restriction in mind, I have two broader conclusions to offer in the end: deconstructionist disillusions and constructionist consolations.

3.1   Deconstructionist disillusions

The evidence seems to suggest that we perceive our own actions like any other events. Though we often perceive both mental antecedents and physical movements, there is no support for the folk psychology notion that the mental precedes or even causes the physical. Rather it seems that physical action and mental awareness of its causes arise in two independent modules that operate in parallel, and often it appears to be the case that action is fast and conscious awareness is slow. In any case, we see no indication of privileged access to first-person knowledge, that is, to knowledge referring to the mental preparation of the upcoming action and arising before the fact. Rather, like any other event, both the physical action itself and its mental antecedents appear to be perceived after the fact. The mental representation (= perception) seems to follow the physical event it represents (= action). A radical way to summarize this picture is to think of two separate modules involved in action, one for its physical generation and the other one for its mental interpretation.[1] This brings me to the constructionist part of my conclusions.

---

[1]   As noted, I have confined my discussion to very simple, short-lived actions, whose physical performance may be over before their mental representation commences. When one also wants to consider more complex actions,

3.2   Constructionist consolations

If it is true that we know about our actions only from the physical outside and not from the mental inside, the question arises how awareness of mental antecedents and causes can arise at all. Why do we perceive such mental things as reasons, intentions, or goals, rather than pure sequences of physical movements?

My answer to this question is bluntly this: that's the way perception is. Contrary to folk psychology intuitions, perception is never confined to simply reproduce the information inherent in the underlying stimulation. Instead, as we have been told by Bruner half a century ago, perception always goes beyond the information given (Bruner, 1957). For instance, we cannot see a person's face without recognizing the face as a face. Likewise, we cannot look at a written word without hearing, as it were, how it sounds and understanding what it means. In these cases, the stimulus information on which perception is grounded is purely visual, but the information that is perceived goes far beyond—capturing sound, meaning, and so on. The same applies to the perception of physical events. When we observe a billiard ball that hits another, the information our percept is grounded on is, again, purely visual, but the information contained in our percept also implies the causal relationship between the movements of the two balls. In the same vein, when we watch other people's actions, what we see goes far beyond what is contained in the underlying stimulus configurations. We see, for example, what objects people are reaching for, what goals they strive for, and whether they fail or succeed.

That's the way perception works. We may characterize it from two different perspectives. On the one hand, when one adopts a functional stance, one usually emphasizes the functional *difference* between two types of information made available by perception—information inherent in the stimulus itself, and information added to or associated with it. On the other hand, when one adopts a subjective or phenomenal stance, one usually emphasizes the phenomenal *equivalence* of these two kinds of information. Phenomenally speaking, there is no difference between primary information inherent in the stimulus and secondary information associated with it. Phenomenally speaking, perception is egalitarian: it makes information from different sources equal.

Given this general picture, it becomes apparent that there is nothing special about the way we perceive our own actions. Just in the same way as we perceive the goals and the motives underlying other people's actions (which clearly go beyond the visual and auditory information this perceiving is grounded on), we also perceive the mental background underlying our own bodily activity. Moreover, the functional fact that the information about the mental is derived from the information about the physical is not reflected in our phenomenal awareness at all. We perceive the mental as inherent in and intimately connected with the physical.

Thus, the answer I offer to the question raised in the title is simple and straightforward. We know about our actions in exactly the same way as we know about anything else in the world. We do it by way of ordinary perception—which, by definition, implies that we go beyond the information given.

---

whose execution is extended over time, the functional situation may be different. In this case, representation may act back on performance, and may thereby get a chance to intervene in the further course of action.

References

Aschersleben, G. & Bertelson, P. (subm.) Temporal ventriloquism: crossmodal interaction on the time dimension. 2. Evidence from sensory-motor synchronization. Manuscript submitted for publication.

Aschersleben, G. & Prinz, W. (1995) Synchronizing actions with events: the role of sensory information. *Percept Psychophys* **57**, 305–17.

Aschersleben, G. & Prinz, W. (1997) Delayed auditory feedback in synchronization. *J Motor Behav* **29**, 35–46.

Aschersleben, G., Gehrke, J. & Prinz, W. (in press). A psychophysical approach to action timing. In Kaernbach, C., Schröger, E. & Müller, H. (eds), *Psychophysics Beyond Sensation: laws and invariants in human cognition.* Mahwah: Erlbaum.

Barresi, J. & Moore, C. (1996) Intentional relations and social understanding. *Behav Brain Sci* **19**, 107–54.

Brentano, F. (1874/1924) *Psychologie vom empirischen Standpunkte, Bd. 1 [Psychology from an empirical perspective, Vol. 1].* Leipzig: Meiner.

Bruner, J.S. (1957) On perceptual readiness. *Psycholog Rev* **64**, 123–52.

Castiello, U. & Jeannerod, M. (1991) Measuring time to awareness. *NeuroReport,* **2**, 797–800.

Castiello, U., Paulignan, Y. & Jeannerod, M. (1991) Temporal dissociation of motor responses and subjective awareness. *Brain* **114**, 2639–55.

Dennett, D.C. & Kinsbourne, M. (1992) Time and the observer: the where and when of consciousness in the brain. *Behavior Brain Sci* **15**, 183–247.

Descartes, R. (1685) *Meditationes de Prima Philosophia.* Amsterdam: Blaviana.

Fraisse, P. (1956) *Les structures rythmiques.* Louvain: Editions Universitaires.

Fraisse, P. (1980) Les synchronisations sensori-motrices aux rythmes. In J. Requin (ed.), *Anticipation et comportement.* Paris: Centre National, pp. 233–57.

Gopnik, A. (1993) How we know our minds: the illusion of first-person knowledge of intentionality. *Behavior Brain Sci* **16**, 1–14.

Haggard, P. & Eimer, M. (1999) On the relation between brain potentials and the awareness of voluntary movements. *Exp Brain Res* **126**, 128–33.

Haggard, P., Aschersleben, G., Gehrke, J. & Prinz, W. (2002) Action-binding and awareness. In Prinz, W. & Hommel, B. (eds), *Common Mechanisms in Perception and Action: Attention and Performance,* Vol. XIX. Oxford: Oxford University Press, pp. 266–85.

Helmholtz, H. von (1879) *Die Thatsachen in der Wahrnehmung.* Berlin: Hirschwald.

James, W. (1890) *The Principles of Psychology.* New York: Holt.

Libet, B. (1985) Unconscious cerebral initiative and the role of conscious will in voluntary action. *Behavior Brain Sci* **8**, 529–66.

Libet, B. (1993) The neural time factor in conscious and unconscious events. In Ciba Foundation, Symposium 174, *Experimental and theoretical studies of consciousness.* Chichester: Wiley, pp. 123–46.

Libet, B. (1996) Neural processes in the production of conscious experience. In M. Velmans (ed.), *The Science of Consciousness: psychological, neuropsychological, and clinical reviews.* London: Routledge.

Libet, B., Gleason, C.A., Wright, E.W. & Pearl, D.K. (1983) Time of conscious intention to act in relation to onset of cerebral activity (readiness potential): the unconscious initiation of a freely voluntary act. *Brain* **106**, 623–42.

Libet, B., Wright, E.W. & Gleason, C.A. (1983) Preparation- or intention-to-act in relation to pre-event potentials recorded at the vertex. *Electroencephalogr Clin Neurophysiol* **56**, 367–72.

Lotze, R.H. (1852) *Medicinische Psychologie oder Physiologie der Seele.* Leipzig: Weidmann'sche Buchhandlung.

Mach, E. (1922) *Die Analyse der Empfindungen und das Verhältnis des Physischen zum Psychischen,* 9th edn. Jena: Gustav Fischer.

Mates, J. & Aschersleben, G. (2000) Sensorimotor synchronization: the impact of temporally displaced auditory feedback. *Acta Psychol* **109**, 29–44.

Neumann, O. & Klotz, W. (1994) Motor responses to nonreportable, masked stimuli: where is the limit of direct parameter specification? In Umiltà, C. & Moscovitch, M. (eds), *Attention and Performance, Vol. XV: Conscious and nonconscious information processing.* Cambridge: MIT Press, pp. 123–50.

Neumann, O., Ansorge, U. & Klotz, W. (1998) Funktionsdifferenzierung im visuellen Kortex: Grundlage für motorische Aktivierung durch nicht bewusst wahrgenommene Reize? *Psycholog Rundsch* **49**, 185–96.

Paillard, J. (1949) Quelques données psychophysiologiques relatives au déclenchement de la commande motrice. *L'Ann Psychol* **48**, 28–47.

Pieron, H. (1925) Des données que fournit sur le mechanisme de l'excitation lumineuse, l'étude du temps de latence sensorielle. *Ann Psychol* **26**, 92–106.

Prinz, W. (1997) Why Donders has led us astray. In Hommel, B. & Prinz, W. (eds), *Theoretical Issues in Stimulus-Response Compatibility.* Amsterdam: North-Holland, pp. 247–67.

Prinz, W. (1998) Die Reaktion als Willenshandlung. *Psycholog Rundsch* **49**, 29/30.

Roufs, J.A.J. (1963) Perception lag as a function of stimulus luminance. *Vision Res* **3**, 81–91.

Roufs, J.A.J. (1974) Dynamic properties of vision. V: Perception lag and reaction time in relation to flicker and flash thresholds. *Vision Res* **14**, 853–69.

Russell, J. (1996) *Agency: its role in mental development.* Hove: Psychology Press.

Russell, J. (1997) How executive disorders can bring about an inadequate 'theory of mind'. In Russell, J. (ed.), *Autism as an Executive Disorder.* Oxford: Oxford University Press, pp. 256–304.

Sanders, A.F. (1980) Stage analysis of reaction processes. In Stelmach, G.E. & Requin, J. (eds), *Tutorials in Motor Behaviour.* Amsterdam: North-Holland, pp. 331–54.

Sanders, A.F. (1998) *Elements of Human Performance: reaction processes and attention in human skill.* Mahwah: Erlbaum.

Sanford, A.J. (1974) Attention bias and the relation of perception lag to simple reaction time. *J Exp Psychol* **102**, 443–6.

Teichner, W.H. & Krebs, M.J. (1972) Laws of the simple visual reaction time. *Psycholog Rev* **79**, 344–58.

Wundt, W. (1874) *Physiologische Psychologie,* Vols I–III, 1st edn. Leipzig: Engelmann.

CHAPTER 2

ACQUISITION AND CONTROL OF VOLUNTARY ACTION

BERNHARD HOMMEL

Abstract

This chapter deals with the cognitive underpinnings of voluntary action, here defined as goal-directed behaviour. It delineates how voluntary action emerges through the automatic acquisition of bilateral associations between cognitive codes of movement patterns and sensory movement effects. Once acquired, these associations can be used to choose movement patterns by activating codes of intended outcomes (the Lotze–Harleß principle). Actions are planned by specifying the intended outcomes, binding the activated codes, and integrating them with the anticipated trigger stimuli. Integrated action plans are then carried out automatically as soon as the trigger stimulus is encountered.

1   Defining voluntary action

William James (1890), one of the grand old men in cognitive psychology, was not particularly enthusiastic about definitions. A good (though not the best-known) example is the way he introduces the readers of his famous *Principles of Psychology* into Chapter XXVI on the will: 'Desire, wish, will', he wrote, 'are states of mind which everyone knows, and which no definition can make plainer' (Vol. 2, p. 486). However, he goes on to provide further detail:

> We desire to feel, to have, to do, all sorts of things that at the moment are not felt, had, or done. If with the desire there goes a sense that attainment is not possible, we simply wish; but if we believe that the end is in our power, we will that the desired feeling, having, or doing shall be real; and real it presently becomes, either immediately upon the willing or after certain preliminaries have been fulfilled. (James, 1890, Vol. 2, p. 486)

As far as cognitive psychology is concerned, these terms are outdated and no longer in use, as are other terms so obviously tied to introspective experience. However, James' basic approach to understanding voluntary action as goal-orientated movement, directed toward anticipated action effects, is perfectly consistent with the perspective of more recent authors. For example, according to Ach (1910, p. 256), a voluntary action 'represents the realization of the anticipated concrete content of an act of will' (translated by the author); Miller *et al.* (1960) describe voluntary action as movements that are steered towards anticipated goals by super-ordinate plans; Heckhausen (1991, p. 12) believes that 'an action comprises all activities which pursue the same "goal idea" '—and many more examples of this sort can be found in Pongratz (1984) and Hoffmann (1993).

In contrast to James, however, later authors often did not require goals or anticipated action effects to be conscious. Tolman (1932) already argued that, if diagnosed objectively, rats—not commonly suspected of enjoying conscious experiences—can show purposive behaviour as well as humans can. In the same vein, Frith (1992) has argued that some typical delusions exhibited by schizophrenics might reflect a tendency to attribute their own (voluntary) actions to external forces, suggesting that one does not need to be conscious of one's action goal to act voluntarily.

All in all, an acceptable working definition of voluntary action within the domain of cognitive psychology seems to require the concept of an *action goal*, i.e. of some anticipatory cognitive (not necessarily conscious) representation of an intended event that somehow mediates the organization and execution of appropriate movements. The following concentrates on the 'somehow' in this definition. It begins by pointing out that performing a voluntary action presupposes knowledge about action–effect relationships and describes how this knowledge might be acquired. It then describes this in more detail and in which sense action control is anticipatory, before going on to consider how people actually control their actions, then concludes with some critical arguments regarding the usefulness of voluntary action as a scientific concept.

2   Acquisition of action effects

According to our working definition, a voluntary action is a goal-directed activity and, therefore, necessarily orientated towards a future event. Logically, this implies some kind of anticipatory representation of the intended action outcome and some movement pattern carried out to actually produce the outcome. The emergence of outcome representations is easy to understand. We may simply remember a previous event that we have liked and that we now want to enjoy a second time. However, as James (1890) pointed out, a desire without appropriate action remains a wish, which poses the question of how one knows which action is required to attain a particular goal. This is not just a problem with ambitious and complex goals, such as the desire to get rich and be famous, but also of relevance with most common activities, such as reaching for a cup of coffee or tying a shoe—just try to explain in detail *how* you do it! So, the crucial question is, given a particular goal, how do we select the appropriate movement pattern? Put differently, how do we know what a particular movement is good for?

Lotze and Harleß suggested some interesting answers to these questions. In Lotze's (1852) view, the will has no direct access to the motor system and, therefore, cannot select particular movements directly. All it can do is to register the relationship between a given movement and those internal states of the central nervous system that accompany and/or follow it. Once knowledge about these relationships has been acquired, an intended movement can be chosen by re-activating the internal state that is known to be associated with it.

Harleß (1861) followed the same line of reasoning, but presented a more detailed model of how movement-related knowledge is acquired, stored, and used later on. He postulates two stages in the emergence of voluntary action. The first stage consists of the acquisition of bilateral links between movement codes and those sensory codes that are activated as a consequence of performing the movement. That is, the very fact that a sensory code s is activated at about the same time as a motor code m leads to a bilateral association between the two $m \leftrightarrow s$. Obviously, this associative structure represents the knowledge that performing m produces s, a simple form of knowledge about possible means and associated ends. According to Harleß it is these associative structures that underlie voluntary action that, at a second stage, makes intentional, goal-directed use of the collected knowledge. Indeed, as the associations are assumed to be bi directional, re-activating the representation of a particular action effect results in the automatic activation of the associated movement pattern, so that merely 'imagining' an intended action effect invokes the movement capable of producing it without (much) further ado.

This is no doubt a very simplified picture. For instance, it neglects the possibility that performing the same movement under different circumstances produces different effects, such as kicking with the foot against a ball versus kicking against a stone of the same size. To be useful, knowledge about possible actions needs to incorporate not only information about movements and effects, but about contextual conditions as well (Hoffmann, 1993), an issue I will get back to later. Moreover, Lotze and Harleß were mainly concerned with very simple actions like moving one's finger or hand, which produce effects that are mostly body-related (proximal) and immediate, such as kinaesthetic and tactile feedback. However, more complex actions often produce effects that are much more distant in terms of both space (distal) and time—just think of preparing a meal or making a trip. This suggests that action representations include information about all kinds of action effects (proximal *and* remote, immediate *and* delayed), i.e. codes of any event that an actor has experienced as following from particular actions (Hommel, 1997, 1998a).

The assumption that all kinds of action effects are functionally equivalent gives us the opportunity to study the acquisition of knowledge about means and ends even in adults and in the laboratory. For instance, Hommel (1996) had people perform simple key pressing actions that were followed by tones of a particular frequency, such as a single key press followed by a low tone and a double press followed by a high tone. According to the framework of Lotze and Harleß the repeated experience of a tone s following a motor pattern m (responsible for the key press response) should lead to a bilateral association $m \leftrightarrow s$, so that Hommel's (1996) subjects should have acquired two such associations, $m1 \leftrightarrow s1$ and $m2 \leftrightarrow s2$. If so, and if those associations are actually bilateral, there should be a way to activate the motor pattern m by activating the sensory code s. This is what we did in the study: After participants had gained some experience with the key press–tone relationships, tones were presented not only as effects (i.e. after the key press), but also as primes (i.e. briefly before the visual stimulus flashed). There are two possible conditions:

- a *congruent* one in which the prime consists of the same tone as the effect (e.g. high tone → double press → high tone);
- an *incongruent* condition where prime and effect tones are different (e.g. low tone → double press → high tone).

We expected that presenting a tone as a prime would lead to some activation of the (presumably) associated movement, which would speed up response selection in congruent conditions, but impair performance in incongruent conditions. Indeed, we obtained such congruence effects across a number of different versions of this task, supporting the idea of automatic acquisition of bilateral associations between movement codes and codes of their effects—even if these effects are completely arbitrary.

The same conclusion can be drawn from a study of Elsner & Hommel (2001). Again, people were confronted with arbitrary, but consistent relationships between their key pressing actions and key press contingent tones. Then, in a second phase, they were asked to perform free-choice responses to tone stimuli. That is, they heard a randomly determined tone and pressed a deliberately chosen left or right key. As expected, the choice was not random, but depended systematically on the type of tone. For instance, if previously the left key produced a low tone and the right key a high tone, hearing a low tone made the subjects more likely to press the left than the right key, and vice versa. This was true even when the free-choice task was performed under high time pressure and under heavy workload from a secondary task, which rules out the response bias resulting from a strategy. If we manage to induce experimentally some activation of an internal representation of a possible action effect, this leads to some activation of the motor pattern that is known to produce this effect. This does not yet prove that action effect representations play a crucial role in everyday voluntary action (an issue dealt with in the next section), but it demonstrates that action–effect relations are automatically acquired, and suggests that the acquired knowledge includes bilateral associations between codes of movements and their perceivable effects.

The automatic acquisition of action effects is not restricted to simple binary-choice tasks. For instance, Sebald et al. (1999) investigated the role of action effects in a serial learning task, where subjects were to acquire complex sequences of key presses. When each key press produced a particular tone, sequence learning proceeded much faster than in control conditions without artificial action effects. Apparently, the subjects were able to integrate their responses with the tones and then simply learned the 'melody' they produced. Further evidence for an important role of action effects in serial learning has been reported by Zießler (1998).

One limitation of the studies discussed so far is that, with one exception (Zießler, 1998), they all used auditory effects only. The obvious reason is that the manipulated action effects were task-irrelevant and, thus, could have been simply overlooked if presented in a less salient modality such as vision. However, there are reasons to believe that action effects of other modalities can be acquired as well. Apart from demonstrations with visual effects (Hommel, 1993; Zießler, 1998), a recent study of Beckers et al. (2002) shows that electrocutaneous action effects are also learned. In a study phase, they had subjects move a switch up or down in response to the grammatical category (verb versus noun) of neutral words. One of the two responses was consistently followed by a mild electric shock, thus creating an emotionally neutral (no shock) and an unpleasant (shock) action effect. In the test phase, the task was the same, but the stimuli were now words with positive or negative emotional valence. As expected, people responded more quickly if the valence of the stimulus matched the (apparently acquired) valence of the response. Hence, negative words were responded to more quickly with the response followed by a shock, while the opposite was true for positive words. This means that actions acquire the emotional valence of their consequences. The same conclusion can be drawn from a study of Van der Goten et al. (2002). In one experiment of that study, subjects performed two key pressing tasks in a row, with the second key press triggering the visual presentation of a smiley or a grumpy (each mapped onto one of two keys). As it turned out, preparing the smiley-producing key press facilitated the processing of emotionally positive words in the other task, whereas preparing the grumpy-producing response primed words with a negative valence. Again, this suggests that the representations of movements are integrated with codes of the effects they produce.

The extension of the Lotze–Harleß principle into the domain of emotions has particularly interesting theoretical implications in showing that the principle is consistent with, and can be applied to, both cognitive, rationalistic action theories and more motivationally-based pleasure-and-pain approaches. That is, whether we see action as being directed towards rational goals or as driven by a hunger for lust, the underlying cognitive mechanism may be exactly the same. In either case, the first step in the emergence of voluntary action would be the acquisition of associations between movement patterns and their consequences—be they sensory or emotional, if one wishes to make this difference at all. [Indeed, even if we accepted a motivational (e.g. behaviouristic) point of view, it is difficult to tell whether individuals maximize their pleasure (whatever this may be) or their *perception* of pleasure. In the latter case, one would have a hard time to explain why the perception of pleasure—the cognitive representation of input from the autonomous nervous system—should fall into a completely different theoretical category than the cognitive representation of input from other, sensory systems. This is especially obvious in the case of perceiving the presence or absence of pain.]

3 Anticipatory control of voluntary action

According to our considerations, the automatic acquisition of movement-effect associations is a necessary precondition for voluntary action to occur, as they make the anticipation of action outcomes possible and, thus, enable the actor to select movement patterns with respect to intended action goals. Indeed, the available evidence strongly suggests that codes of movements and of their perceived consequences are linked in a bilateral fashion. However, the mere availability of such associations is by no means sufficient, nor does their mere existence prove that they are, indeed, used and functional in everyday action control. So, how can we know that voluntary action is actually selected and controlled by integrated action-effect structures?

One piece of evidence comes from a study on the so-called Simon effect (Hommel, 1993). Subjects responded to low- and high-pitched tones by pressing a left- versus right-hand key. The location of the tone was not relevant, but tones appeared randomly to the left or right of the subject. Conditions like that are known to yield better performance (faster and less error-prone responses) if stimulus and response correspond, hence if the tone signalling the left response appears on the left or if the tone signalling the right response appears on the right side—the Simon effect (for an overview, see Lu & Proctor, 1995). According to the action–effect framework this should be so because the in this case spatial features of the stimulus overlap with those of the action effect. As any action, a key press should be cognitively represented by codes of its sensory consequences: kinesthetic feelings in the active arm and index finger, visual impressions from the moving finger, auditory input from the moved key, and so forth. In case of a left-hand response, many or all of these events take place to the left of the subject, so that their cognitive representations share the feature LEFT. If then the actor perceives a stimulus on the left side, its representation also shares the feature LEFT and thereby partly specifies, in a sense, the appropriate action goal (i.e. the intended action effect). However, if the stimulus appears on the right side, the goal of the incorrect (RIGHT) response would be specified. This leads to response conflict, hence the Simon effect.

If this scenario is a correct description of how action planning works, one should be able to modify the Simon effect by changing the actor's action goal and this was the aim of the Hommel (1993) study. In two experimental groups, each key was connected to a red light on the *opposite* side, so that pressing the left key caused a brief light flash on the right side and pressing the right key produced a flash on the left side. Although the two groups performed exactly the same task with identical stimulus–response and response–light mappings, their instructions differed. One group of subjects was asked to 'press the left/right key' in response to the low/high tone (the *key instruction*), whereas the other group was instructed to 'flash the right/left light' accordingly (the *light instruction*). The idea was that people with a key instruction would specify their action goals in terms of key location, whereas people with a light instruction would specify their goals in terms of light location. As these locations were always opposite to each other, the Simon effect should be completely reversed: a left-side stimulus, say, should facilitate left-hand key presses under key instruction, but right-hand key presses under light instruction—simply because with light instruction the goal of a right-hand key press should be flashing a left-side light. In other words, not the spatial congruence between stimulus and physical action should matter, but that between stimulus and intended action effect. This is exactly what happened. While people in the key group produced a typical Simon effect (i.e. better performance with stimulus-key correspondence) the light instruction completely reversed the result pattern. Obviously, people not only pick up relationships between their movements and movement-contingent sensory events, but they also make use of these relationships to formulate their action goals and select the appropriate action. How they make use of them can be manipulated by the way an action is presented and described, suggesting that the usage is controlled by and thus reflects the actor's intentions.

Further evidence for the intentional use and the functional role of action-effect representations in voluntary action planning comes from a study of Kunde (2001). In Kunde's experiments subjects prepared, in each trial, one of four possible key press responses, which were all followed by a particular tone (i.e. each of two tones was mapped onto two responses). When the stimulus then signalled the already prepared response, reaction times were faster as compared to unprepared conditions. More interesting, however, were the trials where the stimulus signalled another, unprepared response. Although responding was generally slower, the slowing was much reduced when the required response shared its effect tone with the prepared response. This means that preparing a response must have been associated with an activation of the just acquired effect-tone representation, which again produced some priming of the other response associated with this effect tone.

4   Mechanisms of action control

Up to now we have seen that people not only acquire bilateral associations between movement and effect codes, but also actively use these associations to control their voluntary actions. How do they actually do that, and what are the mechanisms that transform knowledge about possible means and ends into goal-directed action? In the following, I will deal with this question in three steps. First, I will set the stage for discussing possible mechanisms by addressing the '*when*' of action planning. It is commonly assumed that action-planning processes intervene between perceiving a stimulus that triggers the planning, on the one hand, and response execution, on the other. This perspective leads to the view of intentional processes or the will as a rational instance, which, in a way, decouples actors from their environment to make their behaviour less stimulus-driven. However, I will argue that this view is probably incorrect and misleading. Secondly, I will describe in further detail how action goals are specified and, thirdly, how they are transformed into overt action. Finally, I will outline how intentional processes prepare the cognitive system for voluntary action by the binding of action plans to trigger conditions. I hasten to add that the emerging picture should be treated as a first, preliminary sketch only, based on some, as yet insufficient empirical evidence.

4.1   Planning an action

According to a common conception in cognitive psychology, human information processing starts with some stimulus information, which is transmitted to increasingly complex processing stages before, eventually, some appropriate response is computed. Although this view has been shown to be enormously successful in generating a whole wealth of empirical findings, it more or less directly takes over the behaviouristic scheme of action as stimulus-triggered *re*-action, which again does not seem to provide an apt characterization of what higher animals really do (Dewey, 1896; Hommel, 1998a, 2000). One possibility to account for the fact that actions are commonly *not* fully determined by our environment, is to have some instance intervene between perception and action. In earlier approaches it was the job of the *will* to evaluate the products of perceptual processing and to select the appropriate response (e.g. Donders, 1868), whereas modern approaches prefer terms like *central executive* (e.g. Baddeley, 1986) or *supervisory attentional system* (e.g. Norman & Shallice, 1986). However, apart from terminological preferences, the question is whether intentional processes actually accompany voluntary action and control it on-line, so to speak.

An alternative concept was suggested some time ago by Sigmund Exner (1879). In his chapter on attention, he reports some introspective observations while making a hand movement in response to the onset of a visual stimulus. Exner noticed that long before the stimulus occurred, he had already set himself into some kind of state that ensured the response would be carried out efficiently and as intended. Evoking that state is a voluntary act requiring attention, so he argues, but once the state is created, the response is actually involuntary, i.e. no further effort of will is needed to translate the forthcoming stimulus into the response. Thus, what makes an action voluntary would not be the intervention of the will between stimulus perception and response preparation, but the intentional preparation of the cognitive system to respond to a particular situation in a particular way. In a sense, while being carried out even the most voluntary action would be involuntary (i.e. governed by previously enabled automatic processes)—the cognitive system works like a prepared reflex (Hommel, 2000).

Exner was not the only one to challenge the idea that the will intervenes between stimulus processing and response execution. In a series of reaction time experiments,

Münsterberg (1889) observed that, even with unpracticed tasks, motor responses often begin before their stimulus is completely identified and consciously perceived—an assumption that is supported by recent investigations of Neumann & Klotz (1994), as well as Eimer & Schlaghecken (1998). Similar considerations were put forward by Marbe (1901) and his Würzburg colleagues from a more phenomenological perspective. To study acts of response-related decision, Marbe had his subjects respond to all sorts of questions, ranging from weight judgements to arithmetic problems. However, when he asked them to describe the processes that intervene between hearing the question and giving the response, the answers were not very informative: some description of the stimulus or the response, but nothing that would refer to a decision. Among other things, it was this outcome that led adherents of the then-evolving Würzburg school to believe that task instructions are transformed into a cognitive task set before and not as a result of stimulus presentation.

These and other findings suggest that intentional processes make actions voluntary by preparing and binding them to situational conditions, not by cutting them off from environmental information, as the processing-stage framework suggests (Hommel, 2000). In particular, they support the idea that action planning is usually not triggered by, but precedes and often prepares for stimulus perception.

4.2 Specifying the action goal

If action planning precedes the stimulus designated to trigger the planned action, something has to be done before that stimulus arrives. According to the scheme proposed above this something consists in specifying the action goal. An action goal, in this scheme, consists of cognitive codes of the features the intended goal should have. Such a goal might be simple, such as with the intention to press a key at a particular location. In that case, the intended action effect might be described and cognitively represented as the experience of the key being depressed, which again may be mediated by the perception of kinesthetic, tactile, auditory, and/or visual feedback. Codes of these intended sensory action effects would make up the action goal (Hommel, 1993). According to the Lotze-Harleß principle all these codes are associated with the motor patterns from which they typically originate and, as the associations are bi-directional, activating the feature codes leads to the activation of the associated motor codes. It is these activated motor codes that make up what one may call the motor programme (Elsner & Hommel, in press).

Action plans will often be more complex than just pressing a key on a computer keyboard—even though both subjects in psychological experiments and psychologists writing reports about the outcomes spend a lot of time doing exactly this. On the one hand, this brings in a whole number of additional problems. The abstract plan of making a trip needs to be transformed into a sequence of more detailed component plans: the where's, how's, and when's need to be specified, and the plan sequence needs to be carried out in the correct order. On the other hand, however, there is no reason why the underlying mechanisms should differ from those involved in planning a key press. That is, once the sequence of sub-goals of an abstract plan is specified, the planning of each individual sub-goal proceeds by activating the cognitive codes of goal features, which then spread their activation to associated motor patterns.

4.3   Integrating the action goal

At first sight, it may seem that specifying the features of the intended action goal is suffi-cient to prepare an action—after all, according to the Lotze-Harleß principle, feature acti-vation should induce the direct activation of the corresponding motor structures. However, it is not overly realistic to assume that people are involved in only one action at a time. We speak while walking, eat while reading, and make notes while listening to a lec-ture. Now, if it is true that action control consists of activating the features of the intended goal and holding them activated until the action is successfully completed, performing two temporally overlapping actions requires the concurrent activation of the goal features for *both* actions. If the two actions have nothing in common, this does not seem to pose a problem. For instance, it is difficult to see why activating a sequence of articulatory goal features, as when speaking, should have any implication for or impact on planning a grasp-ing movement towards a visible object. Assume, however, that two spatially defined actions are planned or carried out at the same time, e.g. turning the body to the right, while point-ing to the left. Planning these actions would require activating the spatial code LEFT *and* the spatial code RIGHT, theoretically leading to confusion about which movement should go left and which should go right (see Fig. 2.1).

These so-called *binding problems* (see e.g. Singer, 1994; Treisman, 1996) are typical for systems with representations made up of multiple components. One way to solve such problems is to indicate, for each given component, which super-ordinate structure they belong to, e.g. by synchronizing the firing behaviour of the cell populations representing the same event (Singer, 1994). In our context, this means that, in addition to activating the feature codes specifying a particular goal, a mechanism is needed to bind and integrate these codes into a coherent action plan. Indeed, Stoet & Hommel (1999) have shown that

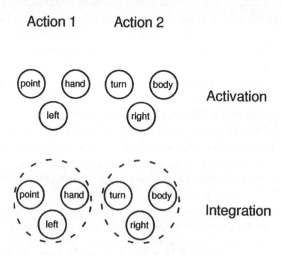

Figure 2.1 If features of more than one action are activated at the same time (see top panel), a feature-binding problem exists. It might be solved by integrating the features belonging to the same action plan (see bottom panel).

planning an action including a particular spatial feature impairs the concurrent planning of actions with overlapping features, suggesting that integrating a feature into one plan makes it temporarily less available for making other plans. Planning an action has even been shown to affect the perception of action-related stimulus events. For instance, Müsseler & Hommel (1997) observed that planning a spatially defined action makes it more difficult to perceive a feature-overlapping stimulus, such as a left-pointing arrow that appears while preparing a left-hand key press. Like the findings of Stoet & Hommel (1999), this suggests that integrating a spatial feature (such as LEFT) into an action plan makes this feature less available for representing other LEFT events.

Apparently, action planning does not only involve the specification of the features the intended action outcome should have, but it also requires the temporary integration of those features into coherent action plans—at least if more than one action plan is in effect at a time. This does not necessarily require additional executive control mechanisms. As shown in Fig. 2.2, feature binding may be an automatic consequence of holding the to-be-bound feature codes active for some minimal time. That is, it may be an inherent property of the cognitive system to bind all the codes whose current activation level reaches a particular integration threshold. As we have seen, this may hold for the integration of movement and effect codes, as well as for action-feature codes that refer to the same action. Evidence discussed in the next section suggests that it is also likely to hold for codes of action features and of context stimuli.

4.4   Contextualizing the action goal

If we assume that action planning commonly precedes the stimulus that triggers the execution of the action, an action plan must include some specification of the context conditions under which it should be carried out—it needs to be *contextualized*. Preliminary ideas of how this might be done have been discussed by several authors. Allport (1980) has

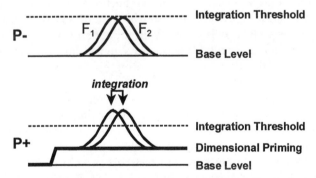

Figure 2.2 A simple integration mechanism. Features are automatically integrated if, and only if, the activation level of their codes reaches an integration threshold. As long as the activation of feature codes (here of codes F_1 and F_2) varies below threshold, no integration occurs (see P-). However, if the dimension of the features gets (e.g. intentionally) primed, the feature codes' base level is temporarily raised (see P+). Accordingly, code activation is more likely to exceed integration threshold, so that the corresponding features will be bound automatically.

argued that actions are controlled by previously set-up condition-action rules or productions in the sense of Anderson (1982)—an assumption that has been taken up by Meyer & Kieras (1997) in working out their EPIC model. Very similarly, Prinz & Neumann (Prinz, 1983; Neumann & Prinz, 1987) proposed that initiating an action is mediated by conditional operations that are intentionally prepared, but automatically performed. Also, most of the now rediscovered interest in task-switching performance (see the overview by Monsell, 1996) is strongly motivated by the idea that processes responsible for implementing task-specific initiation rules can be empirically and theoretically dissociated from the processes applying those rules. Even investigators of long-term planning processes like Gollwitzer (1996) have argued that, once an action plan is formed, it will be re-activated and set in effect automatically if it already includes and thus anticipates the corresponding environmental situation.

Contextualizing an action plan need not require overly complicated mechanisms, as suggested by recent findings (Hommel, 1998b). In each trial of this study, people performed two left-right key pressing responses in a row. The identity of the first response (R1) was signalled by a pre-cue, but the subjects had to withhold responding until the first stimulus (S1) appeared. Although S1 varied in shape, colour, and location, subjects were only to react to the presence of S1, hence all S1 features were irrelevant and could be ignored. A second later another stimulus (S2) would appear, signalling a binary-choice response (R2) to its shape. The important observation was that performance on R2 depended on the relationship between S1 and R1, on the one hand, and between S2 and R2, on the other. For instance, subjects showed better performance if the combination of S1 and R1 either matched that of S2 and R2 (e.g. X → left key, X → left key) or completely mismatched (e.g. O → right key, X → left key), as compared to conditions with a partial match (e.g. O → left key, X → left key). However one accounts for this effect in detail, its existence suggests that the features of S1 and of R1 were bound together in a way that affected the subsequent processing of other stimulus and response features. This is even more interesting as the features of S1 were completely irrelevant, so that binding was not necessary at all. Nevertheless, task relevance did have an indirect influence on S1–R1 binding. Namely, if R2 was signalled by the shape of S2, the relationship between R1 and S1 shape yielded stronger effects than that between R1 and S1 colour, while the opposite was true if R2 was signalled by the colour of S2. In other words, if a particular stimulus dimension was relevant for the task (although only for the second part), features on this dimension were integrated more strongly with response features.

How might these admittedly rather complicated observations of Hommel (1998b) be applied to the issue of plan contextualization? Now, the findings suggest that the features of a stimulus that accompanies a particular response are more or less automatically bound to the features of this response. Apparently, this binding is restricted to features that are of some relevance for the task, irrespective for which part of the task. This again fits well with the simple integration mechanism sketched in Fig. 2.2. If some stimulus or response dimension becomes task-relevant, the base level for features varying on this dimension may be temporarily increased, such as for stimulus shape or colour, and response location in the Hommel (1998b) study. Accordingly, the corresponding features will be automatically integrated if they only occur at about the same time. Once they are integrated, activating the code of one feature will spread activation to the other, as in the case of movement and effect codes. Now, consider what happens during everyday action planning. The prospective actor will, in some way, specify the required features of the intended action effect, such as when imagining oneself going to work. At the same time, the actor will also think of the required trigger conditions, whether they are specified in time ('I have to go at 7 o'clock'), in space ('after leaving the door'), or by preceding events ('after I have finished breakfast'). In terms of cognitive processing, these activities imply that codes of the action-effect features and codes of the trigger-stimulus features are activated at the same time, whether through external stimuli (e.g. when reading a reminder) or internal processes (e.g. when imagining or talking to oneself). As a consequence, the corresponding features will be integrated into a common action plan. If the trigger event occurs, its internal codes will be activated and this activation is spread to the other, action-related components of the action plan. If there is no strong competition through other ongoing plans, the planned action is carried out.

To summarize, planning a voluntary action requires the specification of the action goal (i.e. the features of the event to be produced) and the integration of these features, together with features referring to the trigger conditions. The integration part of this process may be taken care of by rather simple, automatic processes and, thus, is unlikely to require much intellectual works. The same is true for the actual execution, which will often be triggered by anticipated environmental stimuli and context conditions. So, what seems to be really and purely intentional about voluntary action is only the selection of the intended event, the action goal, the activation of which then primes the relevant feature dimensions (which then control integration) and the corresponding motor patterns (by means of movement-effect associations).

5   Voluntary action, a useful concept?

In everyday life, the concept of voluntary action plays an important role. People are attributed less responsibility for bad habits with harmful consequences for everybody, like smoking, when they declare their 'dependence' or 'addiction'. Criminals receive a more favourable judgement, both in the community and before court, when claiming that they 'didn't intend' to commit a given crime. Politicians try to gain a better public opinion by explaining their failures as being 'mistakes'. One can argue about whether we should really think that people are less responsible for their dependence, the circumstances, and their mistakes than for their truly voluntary actions, but my point here is that the common sense concept of voluntary actions works. The question is whether the concept also works scientifically, especially in cognitive psychology, and here I have my doubts.

Let us take the criterion of goal-directedness. Assume, for instance, you are asked to name the colour of stimulus words that happen to consist of colour names, the so-called Stroop test. So, you see the word RED written in green ink and you are expected to say 'green'. Although this task will be manageable, you will make some errors and sometimes say 'red'. Is this an involuntary action? Surely you know that the response was not correct and, in that sense, you 'didn't intend' to say 'red' to a green word. On the other hand, without the intention to respond to colour-related stimuli by saying colour words, you will hardly ever have said 'red' in this context at all. In that sense, your response reflects your intention and it is completely dependent on it. So is it a voluntary action? If you object that this example is artificial and stretched, just think of a robber who 'didn't intend' to shoot the policeman who overwhelmed him during the armed robbery, or consider whether it would be correct to say that smoking or taking other drugs is *not* goal-directed.

The problem I am addressing here is, of course, neither new nor restricted to the concept of voluntary action. As long as psychology was concerned with conscious experiences, as in the days of James, there was some common ground for the laymen and the scientific concept of voluntary action or, for another important example, attention. The commonality laid in the phenomenon—the experience the laymen and the scientist shared—and the explanatory language, while the analytical methods differed. However, modern cognitive psychology is no longer concerned with conscious experience at the explanatory level. Instead, it has become something like functional biology, and explains psychological phenomena in terms of systems and processes, often with reference to the physiological and neuro-anatomical underpinnings. From this perspective it is (and should be) still possible to refer to the laymen concept by trying to explain, at a more basic, functional level, what is going on when a person is said to perform a voluntary action. This is what I have attempted to do here. However, saying that, for instance, process *X* subserves the performance of such an action in such-and-such a way by no means excludes the possibility that the same process does exactly the same thing in the course of an involuntary action, however defined. In fact, we have already seen evidence suggesting that the processes underlying voluntary action subserve involuntary action as well. Action goals can be activated (Hommel, 1993) and even induced by irrelevant stimulus features (Elsner & Hommel, 2001), and feature integration seems to happen automatically (Hommel, 1998b). That is, at the explanatory (i.e., the 'how') level preferred by cognitive psychology volition, just does not make a difference. Therefore, it may be wise to leave the voluntary action concept as it is: a useful everyday word with a fuzzy meaning, but not a scientific term.

References

Ach, N. (1910) *Über den Willensakt und das Temperament.* Leipzig: Quelle & Meyer.

Allport, D.A. (1980) Patterns and actions: cognitive mechanisms are content-specific. In Claxton, G. (ed.), *Cognitive Psychology.* London: Routledge, pp. 26–63.

Anderson, J.R. (1982) Acquisition of cognitive skill. *Psycholog Rev* **89**, 369–406.

Baddeley, A.D. (1986) *Working Memory.* Oxford: Oxford University Press.

Beckers, T., De Houwer, J. & Eelen, P. (2002) Automatic integration of non-perceptual action effect features: the case of the associative affective Simon effect. *Psycholog Res* **66**, 166–73.

Dewey, J. (1896) The reflex arc concept in psychology. *Psycholog Rev* **3**, 357–70.

Donders, F.C. (1868) Over de snelheid van psychische processen. *Onderzoekingen, gedann in het physiologisch laboratorium der Utrechtsche hoogeschool, 2. reeks,* 92–120.

Eimer, M. & Schlaghecken, F. (1998) Effects of masked stimuli on motor activation: behavioural and electrophysiological evidence. *J Exp Psychol: Human Percept Perform* **24**, 1737–47.

Elsner, B. & Hommel, B. (2001) Effect anticipation and action control. *J Exp Psychol: Human Percept Perform* **27**, 229–40.

Elsner, B. & Hommel, B. (in press) Kognitive Neurowissenschaft der Handlungsplanung. In Goschke, T. & Eimer, M. (eds), *Enzyklopädie der Psychologie, Serie Kognition: Kognitive Neurowissenschaft.* Göttingen: Hogrefe.

Exner, S. (1879) Physiologie der Großhirnrinde. In Hermann, L. (ed.), *Handbuch der Physiologie, 2. Band, 2. Theil.* Leipzig: Vogel, pp. 189–350.

Frith, C.D. (1992) *The Cognitive Neuropsychology of Schizophrenia.* Hove: Erlbaum.

Gollwitzer, P.M. (1996) The volitional benefits of planning. In Gollwitzer, P.M. & Bargh, J.A. (eds), *The Psychology of Action: linking cognition and motivation to behaviour.* London: Guilford Press, pp. 287–312.

Harleß, E. (1861) Der Apparat des Willens. *Zeitsch Philosoph philosophische Kritik,* **38,** 50–73.

Heckhausen, H. (1991) *Motivation and Action.* Berlin: Springer-Verlag.

Hoffmann, J. (1993) *Vorhersage und Erkenntnis.* Göttingen: Hogrefe.

Hommel, B. (1993) Inverting the Simon effect by intention. *Psycholog Res* **55,** 270–9.

Hommel, B. (1996) The cognitive representation of action: automatic integration of perceived action effects. *Psycholog Res* **59,** 176–86.

Hommel, B. (1997) Toward an action-concept model of stimulus-response compatibility. In Hommel, B. & Prinz, W. (eds), *Theoretical Issues in Stimulus-response Compatibility.* Amsterdam: North-Holland, pp. 281–320.

Hommel, B. (1998a) Perceiving one's own action—and what it leads to. In Jordan, J.S. (ed.), *Systems Theories and a priori Aspects of Perception.* Amsterdam: North-Holland, pp. 143–79.

Hommel, B. (1998b) Event files: evidence for automatic integration of stimulus-response episodes. *Visual Cognition,* **5,** 183–216.

Hommel, B. (2000) The prepared reflex: automaticity and control in stimulus-response translation. In Monsell, S. & Driver, J. (eds), *Control of Cognitive Processes: Attention & Performance,* Vol. XVIII. Cambridge: MIT Press.

James, W. (1890) *The Principles of Psychology.* New York: Dover.

Kunde, W. (2001) Response-effect compatibility in manual choice-reaction tasks. *J Exp Psychol: Human Percept Perform* **27,** 387–94.

Lotze, R.H. (1852) *Medicinische Psychologie oder die Physiologie der Seele.* Leipzig: Weidmann'sche Buchhandlung.

Lu, C.-H. & **Proctor, R.W.** (1995) The influence of irrelevant location information on performance: a review of the Simon and spatial Stroop effects. *Psychon Bull Rev* **2,** 174–207.

Marbe, K. (1901) *Experimentell-psychologische Untersuchungen über das Urteil.* Leipzig: Engelmann.

Meyer, D.E. & **Kieras, E.D.** (1997) A computational theory of executive cognitive processes and multiple task performance: Part 1, basic mechanisms. *Psycholog Rev* **104,** 3–75.

Miller, G.A., Galanter, E. & **Pribram, K.H.** (1960) *Plans and the Structure of Behaviour.* New York: Holt, Rinehart & Winston.

Monsell, S. (1996) Control of mental processes. In Bruce V. (ed.), *Unsolved Mysteries of the Mind* Hove: Erlbaum, pp. 93–148.

Münsterberg, H. (1889) *Beiträge zur experimentellen Psychologie, Heft 1.* Freiburg: Mohr.

Müsseler, J. & **Hommel, B.** (1997) Blindness to response-compatible stimuli. *J Exp Psychol: Human Percept Perform* **23,** 861–72.

Neumann, O. & **Klotz, W.** (1994) Motor responses to nonreportable, masked stimuli: where is the limit of direct parameter specification? In Umiltà, C. & Moscovitch, M. (eds), *Attention & Performance, Vol. XV: conscious and nonconscious information processing.* Cambridge: MIT Press, pp. 123–150.

Neumann, O. & **Prinz, W.** (1987) Kognitive Antezedenzien von Willkürhandlungen. In Heckhausen, H., Gollwitzer, P.M. & Weinert, F.E. (eds), *Jenseits des Rubikon: Der Wille in den Humanwissenschaften.* Berlin: Springer-Verlag, pp. 195–215.

Norman, D.A. & **Shallice, T.** (1986) Attention to action: willed and automatic control of behaviour. In Davison, R.J., Schwartz, G.E. & Shapiro, D. (eds), *Consciousness and Self-regulation*, Vol. 4. New York: Plenum, pp. 1–18.

Pongratz, L.J. (1984) *Problemgeschichte der Psychologie.* München: Francke.

Prinz, W. (1983) *Wahrnehmung und Tätigkeitssteuerung.* Berlin: Springer-Verlag.

Sebald, A., Hoffmann, J. & **Stöcker, C.** (1999) Learning to produce a sequence of stimuli is easier than learning to respond to a sequence of stimuli (Abstract). In Vandierendonck, A., Brysbaert, M. & Van der Goten, K. (eds), *Proceedings of the 11th Conference of the European Society for Cognitive Psychology.* Gent: Academia Press, p. 213.

Singer, W. (1994) The organization of sensory motor representations in the neocortex: a hypothesis based on temporal coding. In Umiltà, C. & Moscovitch, M. (eds), *Attention & Performance, Vol. XV: conscious and nonconscious information processing.* Cambridge: MIT Press, pp. 77–107.

Stoet, G. & **Hommel, B.** (1999) Action planning and the temporal binding of response codes. *J Exp Psychol: Human Percept Perform* **25**, 1625–40.

Tolman, E.C. (1932) *Purposive Behaviour in Animals and Men.* New York: Appleton-Century-Crofts.

Treisman, A. (1996) The binding problem. *Curr Opin Neurobiol* **6**, 171–78.

Van der Goten, K., Lammertyn, J., De Vooght, G. & **Hommel, B.** (2002) The functional basis of backward-compatibility effects: selecting emotional actions primes the perception of emotional words. Manuscript submitted for publication.

Zießler, M. (1998) Response-effect learning as a major component of implicit serial learning. *J Exp Psychol: Learning, Memory Cognit* **24**, 962–78.

CHAPTER 3

VOLUNTARY ACTION AND COGNITIVE CONTROL FROM A COGNITIVE NEUROSCIENCE PERSPECTIVE

THOMAS GOSCHKE

1 Introduction

The concept of voluntary action is an essential ingredient of our self-conceptualization as autonomous intentional agents, who are capable of deliberate planning and (more or less) rational decision-making, and can thus be held responsible for their actions. [At least, this appears to hold in most Western cultures (for cultural differences in the conceptualization of agency and intentionality, see McCrone, 1999).]

The assumption that we can act voluntarily—at least sometimes—is not only deeply embedded in our common sense psychology, but is constitutive for many cultural, political, and legal institutions and practices. It can make all the difference for our moral evaluation of an act, whether we conceive of it as a willed action or whether we consider it an involuntary response as, for instance, the automatic withdrawal of one's hand when inadvertently touching a hot plate. Interest in the phenomenon of voluntary action is thus not only grounded in scientific curiosity about how our minds and/or brains bring about rational deliberation, conscious choice, and intelligent action, but the way we account for these capacities has profound practical and ethical implications.

However, what does it mean to act voluntarily? What differentiates voluntary actions from involuntary responses? According to one powerful and widely shared intuition, voluntary actions pre-suppose freedom of will. For instance, why do you, at this very moment, read this sentence (rather than doing something different, such as going to the movies, ordering a pizza or listening to your favourite rock band)? Unless you were forced to, the answer is most likely, because you decided to. Could you have done otherwise? Of course you could: had you decided to go to the movies, you could have done so, but—and this is where intuitions sharply diverge—could you have *decided* otherwise?

Whereas for many people it seems self-evident that the answer must, again, be affirmative, a naturalistic perspective rests on the working assumption that everything that happens (including our own deliberations and decisions) is causally determined by antecedent conditions (e.g. the decision to read this chapter was determined by the particular chain of neural processes that was elicited by the particular configuration of internal and external stimuli, which were processed by your nervous system when you pondered your choice, and these processes were, in turn, determined by your previous learning history and genetic predispositions, which in turn were determined by further antecedent conditions, and so on). There is thus a striking discrepancy between our common sense intuition that we are free to choose what we do and scientific attempts to explain all of our actions as causally determined.

This chapter approaches the concept of voluntary action from a decidedly naturalistic perspective, i.e. assuming that voluntary actions are caused by cognitive processes in the brain, and that these processes are open to scientific investigation, using the concepts and methods of experimental psychology and cognitive neuroscience. I will argue that the difference between voluntary actions and involuntary behaviour is not that the former are undetermined, while the latter are causally determined, but that they are determined *in different ways*.

The experimental investigation of the mechanisms underlying voluntary action is at the same time a relatively old and a very recent enterprise. On the one hand, 'willed action' was already a prominent research topic in the early days of experimental psychology (James, 1890; Exner, 1873; Münsterberg, 1889; Ach, 1905; Lewin, 1926). On the other hand, voluntary action has long been neglected as a research topic in 20th century psychology. This was not only true for the behaviourists and their attempt to eliminate any mentalistic terms from psychology, but it also holds for a considerable part of modern cognitive psychology, despite its generous attitude towards mentalistic terms. One reason for this neglect was that the major focus (as well as the main success) of cognitive psychology was the development of information-processing models for isolated tasks like visual search, reading, categorizing, memory retrieval, or motor control. The models typically specify a cascade of (serial or parallel) cognitive operations, which are elicited by a stimulus and which encode, transform, store, and retrieve information and, finally, lead to the selection of a response. However, the question of why a particular sequence of cognitive operations (and not a different one) is elicited by a given stimulus at all, i.e. how intentions or instructions 'configure' the cognitive system for a given task in the first place, was seldom addressed (Monsell, 1996; Neumann & Prinz, 1987). This has changed dramatically in the past two decades, and today topics like cognitive control, executive functions, and volitional self-regulation are major research areas in cognitive, motivational, and social psychology (e.g. Kuhl, 1984, 1996, 2000; Heckhausen *et al.*, 1987; Gollwitzer, 1989; Hershberger, 1989; Allport *et al.*, 1994; Kuhl & Goschke, 1994a; Goschke, 1996a; Monsell, 1996; Kluwe, 1997; Prinz, 1998; Gollwitzer *et al.*, this volume), as well as in the cognitive neurosciences (e.g. Shallice & Burgess, 1998; Monsell & Driver, 2000; Miller & Cohen, 2001; Schubotz & von Cramon, in press). This chapter discusses selected results of this research in an attempt to develop the outlines of a theoretical model of the cognitive processes and neural systems underlying voluntary action. More specifically, I address three empirical questions and will defend three theoretical claims.

1. *How are voluntary actions controlled?* This question concerns the role that intentions play in the causation of voluntary action. Contrary to the widespread view that intentions are the immediate 'triggering' causes of voluntary actions, I will argue that intentions should better be conceived of as *constraints* that modulate the readiness of

responses to become activated by specific stimuli. Rather than causing actions in the way that a billiard ball causes another to move when they collide, I propose that intentions 'configure' perceptual, cognitive, and response systems and thereby bias, which response decision the cognitive system will settle to in a particular situation. Borrowing concepts from dynamical systems theory, one might say that the formation of an intention amounts to a change of the 'attractor landscape' of an organism's state space. I will further argue that the remarkable flexibility with which the human cognitive system can reconfigure 'itself' in response to changing task demands is intimately related to the ability to represent intentions in a linguistic format.

2. *How is the dilemma between persistence and flexibility of voluntary action solved?* Many theories of voluntary action have focused on the ability to shield difficult intentions against distractions and temptations, and to suppress prepotent, but inadequate responses (what may be termed 'will power'). Here, it is argued that the control of voluntary action requires a dynamic balance between antagonistic constraints: to maintain intentions in the face of distractions on the one hand, and to flexibly switch between intentions in order to adapt to changing task demands on the other hand. This *persistence-flexibility dilemma* raises the central, but neglected question of how complementary control processes (serving either the maintenance or switching of intentions) are regulated in a context-sensitive way. I summarize recent findings from our own experiments, which suggest that the mobilization of cognitive control processes, by which intentions are shielded against competing response tendencies, is dynamically adjusted depending on the strength of response conflicts that are elicited by a stimulus.

3. *Who controls voluntary actions?* Contrary to the seductive idea that voluntary actions are controlled by a single 'central executive' at the top of a hierarchy of specialized information-processing systems, I will argue that empirical findings from experimental psychology and cognitive neuroscience leave little headroom for such a unitary control centre. I will sketch an alternative theoretical framework, according to which voluntary action emerges from the interaction of distributed systems, some of which subserve the active maintenance of intentions and the top-down modulation of task-relevant processes, while other serve the complementary function of background-monitoring for potentially significant events outside the current focus.

2   What is voluntary action?

2.1   Philosophical issues

Although the remainder of this chapter is devoted to empirical investigations, a brief digression into philosophical questions will help to make explicit the premises, aims, and boundaries of a naturalistic approach to voluntary action. The philosophical debate about free will and voluntary action is driven by three basic intuitions (Dennett, 1984; Walter, 1998; see also Bieri, 2001). According to the first intuition, voluntary actions are free in the sense of being not determined by antecedent conditions. That is, given exactly the same state of the universe as when we did X, we still could have done Y. According to the second intuition, voluntary actions are rational in the sense that we choose them for good reasons, i.e. voluntary actions are consistent with our beliefs, wishes, and desires. According to the third intuition, voluntary actions are self-determined in the sense that they are chosen, controlled, and initiated by *us*, i.e. we are the agents of our actions.

One extreme position with respect to these intuitions is taken by proponents of a radical libertarianism. For libertarians the idea of free will is incompatible with the assumption that our deliberations, decisions, and actions are causally determined. If seemingly voluntary actions were completely determined by causal antecedents, so the argument goes, these actions, complex and intelligent as they may be, would ultimately be 'nothing else but' sophisticated reflexes, the inevitable result of the mechanistic machinery of brain processes. As a consequence, without metaphysical freedom of choice, i.e. without the possibility that we could have acted otherwise, our subjective impression of free will would be an illusion and we would be preempted of our moral responsibility. As the neurophysiologist Libet (1999) notes, if determinism was true, 'we would be essentially sophisticated automatons, with our conscious feelings and intentions tacked on as epiphenomena with no causal power'.

A radical libertarian position faces a number of problems. First, the assumption that voluntary actions are caused by free 'acts of the will', which are independent from underlying neurological processes (in fact, from *any* antecedent conditions), contradicts the assumption that the physical world is causally closed and determined. This assumption thus forces one to accept *dualism*, and to postulate the existence of two qualitatively different substances or properties in the world, with the will belonging to the realm of the non-physical. This assumption raises the well-known problem of how non-physical and physical events interact, i.e. how mental events (intentions, volitions, acts of the will) can set the physical body in motion. However, even setting aside the issue of dualism, the libertarian position faces a second problem, which takes the form of a dilemma: if voluntary actions are caused by free acts of the will, which are themselves not causally determined by any antecedent events, then voluntary actions would be the result of random, unpredictable, entirely arbitrary decisions. They would thus bear no intelligible relation to *me*, i.e. they would not be explicable in terms of my beliefs, desires, and wishes. As a consequence, precisely the concept of moral responsibility that libertarians want to defend against the challenge of materialism and determinism, seems to lose its meaning. This is also the reason why it is of little help to account for voluntary action in terms of brain processes at the quantum level, as some have tried to do. Even if quantum processes were in a certain sense non-deterministic and influenced our macroscopic behaviour, it is difficult to see how the idea that our actions result from probabilistic fluctuations at the quantum level would make us responsible agents of our actions. The price of rejecting determinism is thus that voluntary actions appear entirely unrelated to the agent's self (for more comprehensive discussions, see Bieri, 2001). In conclusion, it may not be possible to maintain all three intuitions related to the concept of willed action (indeterminacy, rationality, self-determination) simultaneously, because they contradict each other (Walter, 1998). Voluntary action in the sense that it is undetermined, but at the same time rational and related to the self, simply does not exist.

In contrast to libertarian philosophers, *compatibilists* assume that the difference between voluntary and involuntary action is not whether or not an action is causally determined, but rather *how* it is caused (cf. Clark, 1999). The question thus becomes how voluntary actions can be differentiated from involuntary forms of behaviour in non-trivial ways, how the subjective impression of free will emerges, and how concepts like personal responsibility, self-determination, and agency can be conceptualized such that they are compatible with determinism. For instance, consider the difference between, e.g. the reflex-like withdrawal of one's hand from a hot plate and the intentional lifting of one's hand in order to attract a taxi driver's attention. What makes the latter movement—but not the former—a voluntary act is that it rests on a more or less elaborate deliberation of alternative actions, and their anticipated consequences in the light of one's beliefs and desires. To assume that these deliberations are causally determined by the agent's learning history and the current stimulus situation does not call into question that voluntary actions are caused in specific ways that differ in non-trivial ways from the causation of reflexes or automatic responses. The agenda for an empirical science of voluntary action is thus to investigate the cognitive processes and neural systems underlying voluntary action, and it is this agenda to which I now turn.[1]

2.2   Levels of action control

The most fundamental task for any organism is to decide *what to do next*, i.e. to select at any moment from the repertoire of available response alternatives one particular response that can be performed in the current situation, and serves the organism's needs and goals. This selection problem must be solved within a limited time window, on the basis of only partial knowledge about the consequences of alternative behaviour, and in a changing and only partially predictable world (Dörner, 1988). In the course of evolution, organisms have developed different solutions to this fundamental selection problem, which differ with respect to the degree to which the selection of responses is decoupled from the immediate stimulus situation and current need state (Bischof, 1989; Neumann, 1990; Kuhl & Goschke, 1994a; Goschke, 1996a).

   1. *Innate reflexes.* On the most basic level, organisms are endowed with a repertoire of innate, genetically pre-specified response programmes, which are triggered in a fixed manner by specific stimulus conditions and have evolved as adaptations to invariant environmental conditions.

   2. *Procedural learning and habit formation.* Most organisms, however, have developed the capacity to modify behavioural dispositions on the basis of individual experiences. One important source of behavioural adaptation is procedural learning, which consists in the gradual modification of associative connections between perceptual schemata and

---

[1]   There is not enough space to discuss the implications of the debate about free will for the concept of moral responsibility. Suffice it to say that compatibilists—in marked contrast to libertarians—argue that responsibility is not only compatible with, but even *presupposes* causal determinism. According to this view, an individual can be held responsible for an action to the degree that the action was caused by the individual's beliefs, desires, wishes, and deliberations (Dennett, 1984; Bieri, 2001). Likewise, it is not indeterminism, but 'self-determination' that makes individuals responsible agents of their actions. This view, however, raises the problem of whether a meaningful distinction can actually be drawn between causes residing 'within the self' and 'external' forces. For instance, some philosophers have argued that it makes no sense to speak of personal responsibility when all current deliberations and decisions of an individual were already determined by events that occurred before he or she even existed (as radical determinism presupposes).

response programmes, and underlies the acquisition of new habits and skills (Squire, 1992; Goschke, 1996b; Eichenbaum & Cohen, 2001).

3. *Motivated behaviour*. Moreover, most organisms can change their behavioural dispositions on a shorter time scale in response to fluctuating motivational states. Such a need-dependent 'reprogramming' of behavioural dispositions can already be found in comparably simple animals like the blowfly, which, for instance, behaves indifferently to sugar water when satiated, but turns into an efficient sugar detection and ingestion device when in a deprived state. Organisms whose behavioural dispositions are modulated by their current need state can be termed *motivated* and their behaviour can be described as *goal-directed*, although the animal need not have explicit representations of its goals. Importantly, need states do not usually trigger specific responses, but operate like *potentiating signals*, which increase the *readiness* of response programmes to be activated by trigger stimuli (Gallistel, 1985). Although the adaptation of behavioural dispositions to changing needs involves a significant increase of behavioural flexibility, the resulting behaviour is still primarily tied to the immediate internal and external stimulus situation, and consists in the selection of responses that in the past led to the satisfaction of a current need.

4. *Voluntary action*. The crucial step towards voluntary action rests on the ability to form internal representations of desired goal states, i.e. to anticipate *future* effects of one's actions and to select actions on the basis of their anticipated consequences. As William James (1890) noted in his famous chapter on the will, voluntary action is based on an 'anticipation of the movement's sensible effects, resident or remote' (James, 1890, Vol. 2, p. 521; for recent elaborations of this idea, see Prinz, 1998; Hommel, 2000, this volume). Thus, voluntary actions are based on mental representations of *goal states*, which in the course of learning have been associated with *action plans* that are suited to bring about the goal state, given that certain *execution conditions* hold (Kuhl, 1983; Bratman, 1987; Dörner, 1988; Heckhausen, 1989; Hoffmann, 1993; Prinz, 1998). In humans, anticipations of the consequences of an action may range from immediate sensory effects of a single movement (e.g. how it feels like when one's hand touches the handle of a cup of tea) to long-term consequences of actions, including effects on one's own future motivational states (e.g. the anticipated relief when having finished an overdue paper).

This brief description of different forms of behavioural adaptation shows that in the course of evolution the selection of responses has become increasingly flexible. In particular, the ability to anticipate future consequences of actions has led to a radical decoupling of action from the current stimulus situation and one's prevailing motivational state. From this characterization it should not be concluded, however, that more basic forms of behavioural adaptation, like procedural learning or the need-dependent modulation of behavioural dispositions, were abolished with the evolution of 'higher' forms of control. Rather, in humans, different behavioural control systems co-exist and can be considered as adaptive specializations that have evolved in response to partly antagonistic requirements (Kuhl & Goschke, 1994a; Goschke, 1996a, 1997). For instance, while procedural learning is well suited for the gradual acquisition and automation of invariant stimulus-response associations and habits, a qualitatively different type of memory appears to underlie the fast storage of single episodes and arbitrary stimulus-response configurations

(McClelland *et al.*, 1995; Goschke, 1998). Analogously, while the ability to anticipate future motivational states allows humans to decouple the selection of action from their current need state, it would hardly be adaptive if we had the 'will power' to suppress vital needs completely. Rather, even in such 'cognitivistic' organisms like ourselves, emotions and somatic states retain powerful and partly *cognitively impenetrable* control functions (Simon, 1967; Damasio, 1994; Kuhl & Goschke, 1994a).

2.3   Flexibility and persistence as central properties of voluntary action

The ability to anticipate the effects of actions, and to decouple response selection to some degree from the immediate stimulus situation and need state gives rise to two most remarkable properties of voluntary action: *flexibility* and *persistence*. The flexibility of voluntary action shows up in our ability to temporarily couple almost any response to almost any stimulus, even when there are neither innate nor acquired connections between stimulus and response. By forming an intention or receiving an instruction, we can change from one moment to the next—and in almost arbitrary ways—how we will react to the same stimulus. This capacity underlies even the most mundane tasks that participants typically perform in cognitive psychology experiments, as, for instance, naming pictures, pressing a key when a particular word is presented or deciding whether a letter string forms a word. In such tasks responses are not triggered in an obligatory manner by the stimulus, but are produced only because the participant was instructed accordingly and agreed to follow the instructions. Moreover, despite their seeming triviality, even such simple instances of voluntary action require that perceptual, cognitive, and motor systems are co-ordinated from one moment to the next in novel ways, that new connections between stimulus representations and action schemas are established and set into readiness, and that skills are recombined into new behavioural sequences and plans.

No less remarkable is the *persistence* of voluntary action, which shows up in the ability to maintain intentions over time and to persist in a chosen course of action (sometimes for years), even if this requires one to tolerate aversive experiences, to resist emotional temptations, or to suppress strong habits (Mischel, 1974; Kuhl, 1984, 1985; Dörner, 1987).

Flexibility and persistence are both essential for coherent goal-directed action. Without the ability to flexibly reconfigure perceptual, cognitive, and response systems we would be unable to adapt from one moment to the next to changing task-demands. On the other hand, without the ability to maintain intentions and cognitive configurations over time, and to 'shield' them against distracting stimuli or competing response tendencies, we would be driven by strong habits and momentary impulses, unable to perform even relatively simple voluntary acts like concentrating on a passage of prose in the presence of noise from a party in the neighborhood. Adaptive action control thus requires a subtle context-dependent balance between maintaining and switching intentions. The consequences of a breakdown of this balance are dramatically illustrated by tragic cases of neurological patients suffering from lesions of the pre-frontal cortex (Luria, 1973; Duncan, 1986; Stuss & Benson, 1986; Shallice, 1988; Fuster, 1989). On the one hand, such patients often exhibit repetitive behaviour and reduced cognitive flexibility, as demonstrated in the Wisconsin Card Sorting test, which requires one to switch between different categorization rules. On the other hand, pre-frontal patients have been described as suffering from increased distractibility and stimulus-driven behaviour. For instance, some patients show 'utilization behaviour', i.e. they are apparently unable to suppress well-practiced activities in response to common objects, even if they have no respective intention (Lhermitte, 1983). The neuropsychologist Luria has characterized such impairments in terms of an 'inability … to subordinate … movements to the intention expressed in speech, the disintegration of organized programmes, and the replacement of a rational, goal-directed action by the echopraxic repetition of movements or by inert stereotypes …' (Luria, 1973, p. 37).

Such observations have led to the assumption that flexible reconfiguration and stable maintenance of intentions are subserved by a particular class of mechanisms, which are collectively termed 'cognitive control processes', 'executive functions', or 'volitional strategies'. Examples of executive functions are the planning of novel behavioural sequences, the suppression of prepotent, but inadequate responses, or the shielding of a current intention against distracting stimuli or emotional temptations. The mechanisms underlying these capacities are often considered as 'higher-level' or metacognitive processes, because their function is to co-ordinate more specialized subsystems involved in perception, memory retrieval, or motor control in the light of a current goal (Kuhl, 1996; Miller & Cohen, 2001; Goschke, 2002).

3   How are voluntary actions controlled?

3.1   Intention and information: automatic versus controlled processes

In cognitive psychology, the distinction between voluntary action and involuntary forms of behaviour finds it counterpart in an influential distinction between *automatic* and *controlled* processes (e.g. Posner & Snyder, 1975; Neely, 1977; Shiffrin & Schneider, 1977; Logan, 1985). According to the original definition, automatic processes:

*   do not interfere with concurrent processes;
*   are not controlled (or controllable) by intentions, but are triggered in an obligatory manner by stimuli;
*   are fast, parallel, effortless, unconscious, and difficult to modify.

In contrast, controlled processes were said to:

*   depend on intentions;
*   require limited processing capacity;
*   operate in a slow, serial, and conscious, but flexible manner.

While it is tempting to regard the distinction between automatic and controlled processes as a categorical dichotomy between two qualitatively different forms of mental processes (those triggered by a stimulus and those controlled by intentions), it soon became clear that the interplay of the two kinds of processes is more complex than a simple either- or distinction would suggest (for reviews, see Kahneman & Treisman, 1984; Neumann, 1984; Allport, 1989; Bargh, 1989).

3.1.1 Automatic processes are modulated by intentions

One source of discomfort with the neat separation of automatic and controlled processes was the observation that many allegedly automatic processes are, in fact, modulated by intentions. As an example, consider the Stroop colour-word interference task (Stroop, 1935), in which participants have to name the print colour of words, which themselves denote colours. When the print colour and the word meaning are incongruent (e.g. the word 'red' printed in green), participants produce longer response times as compared with when the word and the colour are congruent (e.g. the word 'red' printed in red; for review, see MacLeod, 1991). The fact that the word partly activates an interfering naming response, although participants try to ignore it, was interpreted as evidence that the word meaning is processed automatically. However, subsequent studies showed that this allegedly automatic activation of a competing response is not independent of the subject's conscious intentions and expectations. For instance, the Stroop interference effect becomes larger when participants pay attention to the irrelevant stimulus dimension (Francolini & Egeth, 1980; Kahneman & Henik, 1981), while the effect is reduced when participants are instructed not to read the words, but to treat them as meaningless letter strings (Henik et al., 1983; see also Dyer & Severance, 1973; Goolkasian, 1981). Moreover, Stroop interference effects were larger when participants expected mostly congruent stimuli, which indicates that participants were able to change their processing strategy depending on whether they expected to encounter a response conflict (Logan & Zbrodoff, 1979; Logan et al., 1984; see Neumann, 1984, for a thoughtful review of such findings). Similar conclusions were drawn with respect to the phenomenon of *semantic priming*, which denotes the facilitation of processing a word when it is preceded by a semantically related word (e.g. BREAD—BUTTER; Meyer & Schwaneveldt, 1971; Neely, 1977). While this facilitation was initially considered to reflect automatic spread of activation in semantic memory, further studies showed that the size of the priming effect depends on participants' conscious expectations and strategies (Tweedy et al., 1977; Smith, 1979; Smith, Theodor & Franklin, 1983). As was concluded by Logan (1988, p. 64): '… automatic processing is strongly influenced by intention and attention'.

3.1.2 Voluntary actions can be activated automatically

A second, complementary complication for the assumption of a strict dichotomy between automatic and controlled processes stems from the observation that voluntary responses, which clearly depend on prior intentions, can (under certain circumstances) be activated automatically by a stimulus. As early as 1889, Münsterberg concluded from introspective reports of his subjects that between the presentation of a stimulus and a voluntary response no further conscious contents intervene, but that the intended response simply 'occurs' as soon as the stimulus is identified. Consistent with this observation, recent experiments have shown that even stimuli that are not consciously perceived at all, can activate responses that depend on a prior instruction. For instance, Neumann & Klotz (1994) instructed their subjects to respond with a left or right key press to different geometric forms (e.g. a square and a diamond). Unbeknownst to the subjects, shortly before the presentation of the imperative stimuli either the same or the other form was presented, but so briefly that subjects were unable to recognize it better than by chance. Nevertheless, when the consciously perceived stimulus (e.g. a square) was preceded by an incongruent subliminal prime stimulus (e.g. a diamond), subjects produced longer response times than in the case of congruent primes (see also Eimer & Schlaghecken, 1998). Together with the results of several additional experiments, this finding suggests that the unconsciously processed prime stimulus activated a response that clearly depended on the prior task instruction. These results suggest that—at least in situations, in which all parameters of an intended response are fully specified by the available stimulus information—'the step from the encoding of information to the initiation of the motor response can occur without the intervention of a conscious act of the will' (Neumann & Prinz, 1987, p. 206; author's translation; cf. Hommel, 2000). While the limits of the unconscious activation of 'voluntary' responses remain to be explored, it is noteworthy that such effects appear not to be limited to simple choice-reaction tasks. Rather, recent research in social psychology indicates that unconscious activation of goals and actions can also be demonstrated for more complex forms of behaviour (Bargh *et al.*, 2001; Gollwitzer, Bayer & Ferguson, this volume).

3.2   Action control as multiple-constraint satisfaction in parallel-distributed networks

Empirical findings in concert with theoretical criticisms increasingly undermined the simple view that automatic and controlled processes constitute a categorical 'either-or' distinction (e.g. Kahneman & Treisman, 1984; Neumann, 1984, 1992; Bargh, 1989; Allport, 1993). On the one hand, allegedly automatic processes are modulated by conscious intentions; on the other hand, voluntary responses, which clearly depend on prior intentions, can—at least under certain circumstances—be triggered automatically by a stimulus. For our present topic, the most important implication of these results concerns the causal role of intentions in the control of voluntary action. According to one widespread view intentions are the immediate causal antecedents of voluntary actions and intervene between the perception of a stimulus and the initiation of the intended action. For instance, when a person is instructed to respond to the letter 'A' by pressing a key, the intention operates somehow like a switch that channels input information (e.g. that an 'A' is presented) to particular behavioural programmes (e.g. pressing a key). In contrast, the empirical findings reviewed above suggest that intentions are not immediate triggering causes of voluntary actions, but play a more indirect role in the control of voluntary action. More specifically, I have proposed that we conceive of intentions as *constraints* that 'set the stage' for later processing, by configuring processing systems, increasing the sensitivity of processing pathways, and modulating the readiness of action schemas to be activated by subsequent stimuli (Goschke, 1996a, 1997; for related views see Norman & Shallice, 1986; Neumann & Prinz, 1987; Juarrero, 1999; Hommel, 2000; Miller & Cohen, 2001). This perspective echoes a view that was formulated as early as 1873 by Exner:

> What brings about that the response actually follows the stimulus, (...)
> consists in a central change that has already occurred before the
> stimulus is presented. It is this change which is brought about
> 'voluntarily' (author's translation, p. 616).

A theoretical framework that is particularly suited to implement the idea of intentions as internal constraints is provided by connectionist or parallel-distributed processing (PDP) models. In this chapter I can give only a non-technical description of connectionist models in order to illustrate how the effects of intentions can be modelled in such networks (for excellent introductions, see Rumelhart, McClelland & the PDP Research Group, 1986; O'Reilly & Munakata, 2000). Connectionist networks consist of simple processing units, which can be considered as formal models of neurons (although they abstract from many properties of real biological neurons). Units receive activation from other units via weighted connections (which corresponds to the synaptic transmission of nerve signals) and transform this net input into a new output (usually according to some non-linear activation function). Networks often consist of several layers, with stimuli being encoded as activation patterns over units of an input layer and responses being coded as activation patterns over output units. Between input and output layers, there can be additional layers of so-called hidden units, which generate internal representations of input patterns (Goschke & Koppelberg, 1991) and enable networks to compute arbitrarily complex input–output functions. Connectionist representations are often *distributed*, i.e. a particular entity is not represented by the activation of a single unit, but by *patterns of activation* over several units. Distributed representations make processing noise tolerant and support generalization, and completion of partial patterns.

3.2.1   Response selection as constraint satisfaction

One particular strength of PDP models is their ability to take into account a large number of partially incompatible pieces of information simultaneously and to search for an activation state that satisfies as many constraints as possible. To understand *multiple constraint satisfaction* it is instructive to conceive of units as 'representing' *hypotheses*, of the activation of units as the degree of *confidence* in a given hypothesis and of connections as learnt *contingencies* between hypotheses (Smolensky, 1988). For instance, activation of a particular input pattern may represent the hypothesis that a certain feature is present in the stimulus (e.g. the colour red), activation of an output pattern may indicate the hypothesis that a certain response should be produced (a left key press), and strong excitatory connections between the two groups of units represent the learnt constraint that the left key should be pressed in response to the colour red. Conversely, an inhibitory connection between two units can be interpreted as the constraint that two pieces of information are incompatible (e.g. that the same stimulus cannot simultaneously be a circle and a triangle). Different activation states of the network will satisfy constraints to different degrees. For instance, in our simple example simultaneous activation of the units encoding the feature 'red' and the units encoding a 'left response' satisfies the constraint imposed by the excitatory connections between the two groups of units. By contrast, if the 'red units' are highly activated, but the 'left response units' are inhibited, the constraint is violated. More generally, each possible state of a network (that is, each point in the network's *state space*) is associated with a particular degree to which all constraints are simultaneously violated (this measure is termed *energy*; for details see Rumelhart *et al.*, 1986). Under certain assumptions PDP networks gradually approach stable states in which as many constraints as possible are satisfied simultaneously (these stable states can be conceived of as *attractors* in the network's state space).

The important point for our topic is that the selection of a response can likewise be modelled as a process of multiple constraint-satisfaction. Constraints for response selection derive from two major sources. *Structural constraints* are imposed by the network's connection weights (its 'long-term memory'), which reflect the frequency with which certain stimulus-response mappings were practiced in the past. Learning is based on small changes of connection weights, which occur as a by-product of each processing episode. These small changes gradually accumulate, such that the resulting connectivity increasingly captures regularities in a set of input patterns or in the mapping from input to output patterns. As a result new attractor states evolve in the network's state space, such that a given input pattern causes the network to produce a desired response.

The second class of constraints is *activation-based constraints*. Activation-based constraints are imposed by *input patterns*, which encode a current stimulus, as well as by *context patterns*, which may represent an activated goal or task instruction. As an illustration, consider a connectionist model developed by Cohen *et al.* (1990) to account for empirical findings from the Stroop task, which was described earlier. In their network separate groups of input units encode information about words and colours. Word and colour units project via separate pathways to separate groups of hidden units, which in turn project to output units representing different responses. Connection weights in the word pathway are larger than in the colour pathway, in order to capture the fact that word reading is a much more practiced task than colour naming. As a consequence, by default the network responds more strongly to words than to colours (one might say it falls back to a strong 'habit'). To enable the network to respond to the 'weaker' colour-naming task, the model contains additional 'context' or 'task-demand' units, which encode the current task (that is, the two tasks 'word reading' and 'colour naming' are represented as different activation patterns over the context units). Context units are connected to the hidden units in the task-specific pathways, such that the current task representation can modulate processes within the task-specific pathways. In particular, input from the context units has the effect of increasing the responsivity of hidden units in the task-relevant pathway. Due to local competition between the colour and the word pathway, increasing the responsivity in the colour pathway has the side effect of partly suppressing processing in the word pathway. As a result, processing in task-specific pathways is biased towards task-relevant stimulus features. In this way, the network succeeds in responding to the colour and manages to override the otherwise prepotent response elicited by the word pathway. Like human subjects, however, the network takes longer to produce a correct response when the colour and word inputs are incongruent (e.g. the word RED printed in green), because processing in the word pathway is not completely suppressed by the context input.

Ignoring technical details as to the way in which the biasing effect of context representations is implemented, the more general point of this simple example is that task instructions or goals can be conceived of as *activation-based constraints*, which modulate to which attractor state the network settles in response to a given stimulus. Such activation-based constraints need not necessarily result from external inputs (e.g. instructions or task-cues), but can also consist of *internally* generated activation patterns, which derive from higher-level goal representations. Admittedly, at present, connectionist models of cognitive control address relatively simply tasks, and it remains to be seen how well they can account for more complex tasks involving hierarchical goal structures and sequentially organized actions. Nevertheless, these models demonstrate how in principle intentions can be conceived of as activation-based constraints, which modulate the attractor landscape of the network's state space on a fast time scale, and thereby bias the local competition within and between task-specific processing modules according to a current goal or task (Miller & Cohen, 2001; Desimone & Duncan, 1995). [In the present discussion I focus on *effects* of intentions on response selection. A complete account of voluntary action would have to include a model of how intentions are selected or generated on the basis of motivational processes, which are beyond the scope of this chapter. Moreover, I refer to connectionist models mainly to illustrate the general idea of intentions as modulatory constraints and cannot discuss how well particular models account for empirical results from specific tasks.]

The conceptualization of intentions as constraints sheds a new light on the distinction between automatic and controlled processes (Cohen *et al.*, 1990; Goschke, 1996a; O'Reilly *et al.*, 1999). The difference between the two kinds of processes is not so much that the former are triggered exclusively and in an obligatory manner by stimuli, while the latter are directly triggered by intentions, but in most cases stimulus information and intentions simultaneously impose constraints on the network dynamics and thus jointly modulate, to which response decision the network settles. The constraint-satisfaction framework thus accounts for the obvious fact that even highly practiced actions are seldom triggered in an obligatory way by a stimulus, but are modulated by or even depend on intentions. As an example, even in an highly skilled expert piano player the sight of a sheet of music does not trigger finger movements in a reflex-like way, but only if she *intends* to play the piece. Within this framework, processing can be considered *automatic* to the degree that an intention can be realized by strong pre-existing connections between perceptual patterns and response programmes that were established by prior practice. Processing can be considered *controlled*, when (a) the selection of an intended response requires active maintenance of a representation of the current task or intention, because prepotent, but inadequate responses must be overridden, or when (b) completely new stimulus-response bindings must be established (cf. O'Reilly *et al.*, 1999). In the next section, we turn to the latter aspect and address the question of how to account for the flexibility of voluntary action.

4 Flexibility of voluntary action

So far, I have described in general terms how the role of intentions in the selection of voluntary responses may be modelled in terms of constraint satisfaction processes. The simple, yet powerful idea is to let activation patterns, which represent the current task or goal, modulate or bias processing within task-relevant subsystems. In contrast to the slow, gradual acquisition of stimulus-response connections by procedural learning, such an *activity-dependent* pathway modulation allows rapid reconfiguration of response dispositions and the overriding of prepotent response tendencies.[2]

---

[2] One unresolved problem of this framework should be mentioned. The reader may wonder how a network 'knows' which processing pathways are relevant for a given task. In other words, how does the network *learn*, which task-specific units should receive a biasing top-down input in a given task? A possible solution to this problem rests on the idea that the network first learns to associate output patterns (responses) with the effects they produce, and then uses these response-effect-associations to adjust top-down connections from units representing desired effects (i.e. goals) to task-specific units (Hommel, this volume; Prinz, 1998). However, while conceivable in principle, this sketch raises several non-trivial problems, for instance, how temporally *delayed* effects of responses are learnt (cf. O'Reilly & Munakata, 2000)?

Simulation models based on these principles have been fairly successful in accounting for a variety of empirical findings (Cohen *et al.*, 1990; Cohen & Huston, 1994; O'Reilly & Munakata, 2000). However, one limitation of these models—at least in their simple form— is that they cannot account for one central property of voluntary action: the ability to establish completely new and arbitrary stimulus-response mappings, when a task is performed for the first time. For instance, if you are instructed to press a left key when a triangle is presented, you can easily perform this task, even when you perform it for the first time, and thus have not yet acquired associations between triangles and key presses that could be 'biased' or 'set into readiness'. The problem of how entirely new stimulus-response couplings are established on the fly has received relatively little treatment within connectionist models (but see O'Reilly & Munakata, 2000, Chapter 11). In this section, I argue that part of the solution to this problem lies in our ability to represent intentions in a linguistic format.

4.1   Learning to instruct oneself: the role of language in voluntary action

The performance of tasks involving new and arbitrary stimulus-response mappings requires, in addition to the top-down modulation of task-specific processing modules:

- a memory system that is capable of rapidly storing novel information (e.g. task rules) and retrieving them in response to cues;
- a representational format that allows the encoding of arbitrary relations between stimulus conditions and action schemas.

The first requirement is subserved by what is commonly called *episodic* or *declarative memory*, which underlies the rapid storage of facts and episodes in a spatio-temporal context, and supports flexible access to and retrieval of this knowledge by different cues (Tulving, 1983). Consistent with the idea that episodic memory and the gradual acquisition of habits and skills are characterized by qualitatively different functional properties (McClelland *et al.*, 1995; Goschke, 1998), there is neuropsychological evidence that the two types of memory, in fact, depend on separable brain systems. In particular, episodic memory, but not procedural learning, appears to depend on the hippocampus and adjacent structures in the medial-temporal lobe (for reviews, see Squire, 1992; Schacter & Tulving, 1994; Goschke, 1996b, 1998; Eichenbaum & Cohen, 2001).

A plausible candidate for a representation system that fulfills the second requirement is *language*: it is flexible, generative, and allows the expression of arbitrary relationships between stimuli and responses (including the more or less meaningless instructions typically given to participants in psychological experiments). In fact, it may be no accident that most of our intentions in everyday life, especially when they must be postponed until an adequate opportunity occurs, are represented in terms of verbal self-instructions (e.g. 'I must buy bread before closing time' or 'I must make this phone call at 3 p.m.'). The significant role of linguistic representations of intentions for the control of voluntary action has long been stressed by Russian psychologists like Luria (1961) and Vygotski (1962), who considered the internalization of verbal instructions as a crucial step in the development of intentional self-control. While verbal regulation initially takes place in social interactions with parents and caregivers, children gradually begin to comment on their own actions with verbal utterances, and later start to instruct themselves to do something. (For a recent overview of the functions of private speech, see Diaz & Berk, 1992). According to this view, by gradually learning to represent their own procedural action schemas in a verbal format (Karmiloff-Smith, 1992), children not only vastly increase their behavioural flexibility, but also acquire the ability to maintain intentions over time and pursue long-term goals (Luria & Yudovich, 1959).[3]

However, while language may provide a versatile medium for representing arbitrary intentions, it is a by and large unresolved problem of how verbally represented intentions gain the power to actually *reconfigure* response dispositions (cf. Logan, 1995) and how verbal task representations are transformed into specific movements (cf. Prinz, 1984, 1990a). As Byrne & Anderson (1998), in a recent synopsis of symbol-processing models of higher-level cognition concede, 'theories of cognition have typically neglected the perception and action side of our everyday experience' (p. 167). One attempt to address this problem relies on a tempting analogy between verbally represented intentions and symbolic instructions in a high-level computer language, which must be translated ('compiled') into a 'machine code' in order to 'run' on an actual machine. However, one problem with this analogy is that the verbal representation of an intention usually refers to the distal goal of a movement and does not specify any details or specific parameters of the actual movement (Neumann & Prinz, 1987). The transformation of intentions into movements can thus not—at least not literally—be a *translation* of one language into another.

An alternative, mainly programmatic proposal has been suggested by connectionist theorists. Following Vygotskian ideas, flexible intentional control is seen as emerging from the *internalization* of external instructions (Rumelhart *et al.*, 1986; cf. Clark, 1998; Goschke & Koppelberg, 1991). That is, rather than to presuppose a rich internal representation system that already possesses language-like properties, this proposal assumes that a non-symbolic connectionist network learns to respond to verbal instructions couched in an *external* symbolic code, by the same pattern-matching and learning mechanisms by which it learns to respond to any other input patterns. Subsequently, the network may simulate internally the pattern-matching and symbol-manipulating operations that were initially performed over *external* symbols. As Rumelhart *et al.* (1986, p. 47) suggest:

> Responding to instructions can be viewed simply as responding to some environmental event. We can also remember such an instruction and 'tell ourselves' what to do. We have, in this way, internalized the instruction. We believe that the process of following instructions is essentially the same whether we have told ourselves or have been told what to do.

---

[3] Whereas Miller *et al.* (1960), in their early manifesto of the emerging cognitive science, even considered the ability for inner speech as the '... material from which our will is made' (p. 102), it is noteworthy that the majority of subsequent models in cognitive science accounted for the flexibility of human cognition and action *not* in terms of our ability to use external languages, but rather by postulating an *internal* symbolic representation system (a 'language of thought'; Fodor 1975; Pylyshyn, 1984; Fodor & Pylyshyn, 1988). Influenced by the successes (and even more by the grand promises) of early research in artificial intelligence, higher-level cognition was conceived of as the rule-governed manipulation of mental symbols, which support flexible variable-binding and the construction of complex representations from simple constituents (for criticisms of this view, see Smolensky, 1988; Clark, 1989; Goschke & Koppelberg, 1991).

The step from external control to self-control thus consists in the internalization of external symbolic instructions and the ability to generate the same activation patterns endogenously that were initially evoked by external instructions. In this sense, learning to use a language endows connectionist systems with the combinatorial structures that are essential for representing arbitrary stimulus-response mappings. While it remains to be seen how successfully this proposal will be implemented in specific, testable models of verbally mediated self-control, it highlights the prominent role that the cultural transmission of external symbol systems presumably plays in the development of voluntary action (Prinz, 2000; Tomasello, 1999).

4.2   Empirical evidence for verbal self-instructions in task-set reconfiguration

After this admittedly speculative outline of a theoretical framework of the role of intentions in the control of voluntary action, I now turn to empirical investigations of the processes (including verbal self-instructions) that underlie the flexible reconfiguration of behavioural dispositions. One popular technique for studying these processes is *task-set switching*. The rationale of task-switching experiments is as simple as it is ingenious: Participants are instructed to switch between two or more different tasks (e.g. between reading words and naming the print colour of the words), and their performance in a condition (or on trials) that involve such a task-switch is compared with a control condition (or control trials) in which the same task is performed repeatedly. As was discovered by Jersild (1927) switching between different tasks usually produces increased response times compared with repeating the same task (the 'switch cost' effect). While this basic effect has recently been replicated with a variety of different procedures (e.g. Spector & Biederman, 1976; Allport et al., 1994; Rogers & Monsell, 1995; Meiran, 1996; Kluwe, 1997; De Jong, 2000; Goschke, 2000; Mayr & Keele, 2000; Meiran et al., 2000; Wylie & Allport, 2000), it is a matter of ongoing controversy what processes underlie the switch cost.

One account of the switch cost is that it reflects executive control processes that are required to (re)configure the cognitive system for a new task. This hypothesis predicts that if subjects are given enough time to perform the required executive processes *before* the imperative stimulus appears, the switch cost should become smaller or even disappear. Consistent with prediction, the switch cost is usually reduced substantially (albeit not eliminated), when participants are given sufficient time to prepare for the new task prior to the stimulus (Allport et al., 1994; Rogers & Monsell, 1995, Exp. 3; Meiran, 1996; De Jong, 2000; Goschke, 2000; Meiran et al., 2000). While this indicates that participants were able to (partly) prepare for the new task, it raises the question of what processes underlie this preparation effect. In line with the theoretical discussion in the previous section, I have suggested that the reconfiguration of task-sets involves the retrieval of a *verbal task-representation* prior to the stimulus (Goschke, 2000). Verbal self-instructions should be particularly important, when subjects must switch between novel, unpracticed tasks with arbitrary stimulus-response-mappings (e.g. pressing keys in response to colours). Such tasks cannot be performed by biasing pre-existing stimulus-response connections. Rather, switching between such tasks requires that a (presumably verbal) task representation is retrieved from memory before a response can be selected (for a related view see Mayr & Kliegl, 2000). Support for this hypothesis stems from experiments (Goschke, 2000) in which participants had to switch between tasks with arbitrary and unpracticed stimulus-response rules. On each trial, a letter (A or B) was presented in one of two colours (red or green) and participants had to respond either to the identity or to the colour by pressing one of two response keys. In task-repeat blocks subjects responded constantly to the same stimulus attribute (e.g. colour), whereas in task-switch blocks they had to alternate between the colour and letter tasks. The critical manipulation concerned the preparation interval between each response and the next stimulus. When this interval was only 14 ms, such that participants could not prepare in advance for the next task, switching between the two tasks incurred a large switch cost of about 300 ms as compared with when they repeatedly performed the same task. By contrast, when the preparation interval was increased to 1200 ms and subjects were instructed to verbalize the next task (i.e. say 'colour' or 'letter') before the stimulus appeared, the switch cost was markedly reduced. Most important, in a third condition, in which the preparation interval was also 1200 ms, but retrieval of a verbal task-representation was prevented by a distractor task (subjects had to say irrelevant words like 'Monday' and 'Tuesday' during the response-stimulus interval), the switch cost was as high as in the condition with the short preparation interval. This clearly shows that retrieval of a task representation (i.e. 'self-instruction') is an important component of task-set reconfiguration, at least for tasks with unpracticed stimulus-response mappings. Consistent with this interpretation, in a recent neuropsychological study Mecklinger *et al.* (1999) found that patients with left brain damage suffering from central speech disorders showed disproportionally large switch costs as compared with patients without speech disorders. The authors suggest that articulatory processes may be important for suppressing previously activated task-sets. Also consistent with the role of verbal task representations in performing novel tasks are findings from recent brain-imaging studies, in which tasks requiring the manipulation of information in working memory activated Broca's area, a region in the left frontal cortex involved in verbal rehearsal and inner speech, (e.g. Braver *et al.*, 1997; Paulesu *et al.*, 1993; Smith *et al.*, 1998).

5   Persistence of voluntary action

Having discussed some of the processes underlying the flexible reconfiguration of task sets and response dispositions, I now turn to the second central property of voluntary action: *persistence*. The ability to maintain intentions over time and in the face of distracting stimuli, strong habits, or emotional temptations, is essential for coherent goal-directed action. This holds both on short- and long-term time scales. On a short-term scale, many cognitive tasks require that current goals and task-relevant information is maintained in a highly accessible state, in which it can modulate ongoing processing and is shielded against distractions (multiplying 34×23 without resorting to external aids will give you a concrete idea of these requirements). These functions are usually subsumed under the term working memory (Baddeley, 1986; Gruber, 2000; Miyake & Shah, 1999). In the constraint-satisfaction framework outlined above, short-term maintenance can be implemented by networks of units with strong recurrent bi-directional connections. Such networks have the property of supporting self-stabilizing activation patterns that remain active in the absence of external input (O'Reilly *et al.*, 1999).

With respect to longer time scales, an important function of intentional persistence is to reduce the need to reconsider all possible alternative actions and their consequences before each single act. In most real-life situations it is not possible to weigh exhaustively the probabilities and values associated with the expected outcomes of all possible action alternatives. Rather, because of limited time, information, and processing resources, decision-making must terminate at some point and one must commit oneself to a particular course of action, even at the risk of selecting a sub-optimal alternative (Kuhl, 1983, p. 310). Likewise, it would not be adaptive to change one's commitment in response to every minor change in the environment or one's motivational state. As the action theorist Bratman (1987, p. 16) has noted, intentions should to some degree 'resist reconsideration' and exhibit a 'characteristic *stability* or *inertia*'. This fits with the present characterization of intentions as *constraints* for the later selection of actions.

5.1 Empirical evidence for persisting activation of intentions

Persistence has long been considered a prominent property of intentions. Lewin (1926), in a seminal paper on 'Intention, Will, and Need', conceived of intentions as *tension systems* that attach valences and affordances to objects in the environment and have an inherent tendency to persist until goal attainment. More recently, several action theorists have suggested that uncompleted intentions are 'shielded' against distracting stimuli or competing response tendencies by specific volitional strategies that serve to focus attention on intention-related information (Kuhl, 1983, 1984, 1996; Gollwitzer, 1989; Heckhausen, 1989; Kuhl & Goschke, 1994a; Kuhl & Fuhrmann, 1998; Rothermund, 1998; Goschke, 2002). Likewise, many recent theories in cognitive psychology consider stable goal representations as essential for coherent action. For instance, Prinz (1990b) postulates that 'relevance markers' are tagged to representations of the execution conditions of intentions in long-term memory, which facilitates the detection of intention-relevant cues. Similarly, in Anderson's (1983) influential ACT-theory, goals are conceived of as sources 'of high and constant activation' (p. 156), 'that sustain activation without rehearsal' (p. 118), and exert an enduring bias on memory retrieval and processing.

In a series of experiments, Goschke & Kuhl (1993, 1996, 2002; Kuhl & Goschke, 1994b) made an attempt to obtain direct evidence for a special dynamic status of representations of intentions in long-term memory. Our participants memorized pairs of short texts describing two action sequences (e.g. setting a dinner table and clearing a desk). After the study phase they were instructed that they would have to execute *one* of the action sequences later, whereas the second activity was only to be remembered and served as a control. Prior to the execution of the intended activity, participants received a recognition test, in which a list of test words was presented, which were either taken from the to-be-executed or from the neutral control script (old words), or which had appeared in neither script (new words). Participants had to decide as fast as possible for each test word, whether or not it had appeared in one of the study scripts. Response times for the recognition judgments were interpreted as a measure of the activation level of items in long-term memory. Our main finding was that words from the to-be-executed activity were recognized significantly faster than words from an (equally well-learnt) control activity. This *intention-superiority effect* indicates that representations of uncompleted intentions persist in a state of heightened sub-threshold activation in memory, which makes them more accessible than other contents (see also Marsh *et al.*, 1998, for a replication and extension of these findings).

Further experiments showed that the intention-superiority effect is specific for actions that participants intend to perform themselves, but does not occur when they are instructed to merely *observe* someone else performing an action. Moreover, an intention-superiority effect occurred even when subjects were prevented from selectively rehearsing the to-be-executed script. Finally, the effect was also obtained in an *implicit* or *indirect* memory test, in which participants were not instructed at all to think of or recall intention-related items (Goschke & Kuhl, 1996, 2002; Marsh *et al.*, 1998). For instance, when we asked participants to complete word-fragments (-AB--) with the first word that comes to mind, words from a later to-be-executed script came to mind as solutions more often than words from an equally well-learnt control script. Taken together, these findings suggest that intention-related contents persist automatically in a state of increased activation and/or accessibility in long-term memory, even when voluntary rehearsal strategies or deliberate retrieval attempts are discouraged. This conclusion supports an earlier proposal by Ach (1935), who assumed that intentions establish *determining tendencies* that facilitate subsequent processing of goal-related information even in the absence of a conscious recollection of the task or the instruction.

5.2   The cost of persistence

While the tendency of intentions to persist in a state of high activation in memory promotes the maintenance of intentions in the face of distractions or competing action tendencies, persistence can also incur a cost, especially when one must flexibly switch from one task to another or when one must disengage from a previous intention (Kuhl & Goschke, 1994a,b). As I noted earlier, the response time cost that is incurred when subjects switch between different tasks is substantially reduced when subjects have time to prepare for a new task prior to the stimulus. However, in the majority of experiments a significant *residual switch* cost was obtained even after long preparation intervals (Allport *et al.*, 1994; Rogers & Monsell, 1995; Meiran, 1996; Goschke, 2000; Mayr & Keele, 2000). This is a counter-intuitive finding: why should there be a residual switch cost, even if the time to prepare for the next task was several times as long as the switch cost itself? According to one possible explanation, this residual cost reflects involuntary carry-over effects of previously executed, but not completely de-activated intentions (Allport *et al.*, 1994; Goschke, 2000). To the degree that a previously executed intention still persists in a state of residual activation, it may impose conflicting constraints on response selection and thus prolong the time the system needs to settle to a coherent response decision. Consistent with this hypothesis, I found that the reaction time cost incurred by a switch from one task to another was larger when the previously performed (but now irrelevant) task activated responses were incompatible with the response required by the new task (Goschke, 2000). While this study was concerned with short-term effects of recently performed tasks on the execution of a new task, there is also evidence for relatively long-lasting carry-over effects from previously activated task sets. For instance, Allport *et al.* (1994, Exp. 4) found that performing two tasks (e.g. reading words and naming the colours in which the words were printed) across several blocks of trials produced marked interference in a subsequent block of trials that occurred several minutes later and required subjects to perform two different tasks with the same stimuli (see also Wylie & Allport, 2000).

A different line of evidence for detrimental consequences of an excessive or context-insensitive tendency to maintain intentions in a highly activated state stems from studies of individual differences in action control. For instance, the intention-superiority effect described in the previous section is usually stronger for individuals scoring high on a personality disposition termed *state-orientation*, which is characterized by frequent intrusive thoughts and ruminations about uncompleted intentions (Goschke & Kuhl, 1993; Kuhl & Beckmann, 1994; Kuhl & Goschke, 1994b). At the same time, state-orientated individuals show impaired performance in tasks that require them to interrupt an ongoing activity, and to switch to a different task or goal, especially when such a goal switch is not triggered by external cues, but must be self-initiated (Dibbelt, 1996; Kuhl & Goschke, 1994b). An overly strong tendency to maintain intentions in an active state may thus lead to perseverative behaviour and an impaired ability to switch between goals (Kuhl & Goschke, 1994a). This conclusion is further supported by the finding that individuals suffering from depression (which is positively correlated with state-orientation) show an increased tendency to maintain uncompleted intentions in a highly activated state in memory (Kuhl & Helle, 1986; Johnson *et al.*, 1983), while on the other hand exhibiting reduced cognitive flexibility and behavioural initiative (Kuhl, 2000).

In conclusion, there is clear evidence that previously executed intentions, which are not completely de-activated, may interfere with the execution of a current task and contribute to the residual switch cost (Rogers & Monsell, 1995; Wylie & Allport, 2000). Moreover, there is evidence that the degree to which intentions persist in an activated state is moderated by personality dispositions and affective states (Kuhl, 2000; Kuhl & Goschke, 1994b). These considerations raise the question of whether—in addition to processes serving the maintenance of intentions—there are also control processes that serve the complementary function of inhibiting to-be-abandoned intentions or task sets (Kuhl, 2000; Goschke, 1996a). Evidence that this is, in fact, the case was obtained by Mayr & Keele (2000), who found that switching to a task that had been performed two trials before (e.g. A–B–A) produced a larger reaction time than switching to a new task (e.g. A–B–C). Mayr & Keele interpreted this finding as evidence for a process of 'backward inhibition' by which to-be-abandoned task sets are suppressed in order to reduce pro-active interference. Analogous findings were reported by Marsh *et al.* (1998), who showed that the intention-superiority effect found by Goschke & Kuhl (1993) was reversed *after* the intended activity had been executed, i.e. words related to the executed activity produced even *slower* response times than control words (see also Li *et al.*, 2000).

6   Control dilemmas: complementary constraints on action control

At first sight, some of the results reviewed in the previous section appear to show that the human cognitive system is sub-optimally designed, because it is prone to various kinds of interference from distracting stimuli, competing responses, and previously activated intentions. However, in contrast to this interpretation, I suggest that these seemingly dysfunctional features are manifestations of a competition between complementary control processes, which have evolved in response to antagonistic requirements or *control dilemmas*, and which either serve the stable maintenance or the flexible switching of intentions (Goschke, 1996a, 1997, 2000).

6.1   Control dilemmas

6.1.1   The plasticity-stability dilemma

On the one hand, organisms should gradually acquire strong stimulus-response connections in order to respond with well-established habits to invariant or recurrent situations (Goschke, 1998). On the other hand, the system should be able to establish new and arbitrary stimulus-response-dispositions 'on the fly'. A large body of evidence indicates that these two forms of behavioural adaptation impose incompatible functional requirements on learning mechanisms and have therefore promoted the evolution of separate procedural (implicit) and declarative (explicit) memory systems (Sherry & Schacter, 1987; McClelland *et al.*, 1995; Goschke, 1998; Eichenbaum & Cohen, 2001).

6.1.2   The maintenance-switching dilemma

On the one hand, intentions must be shielded against competing action tendencies in order to promote behavioural stability and persistence in the pursuit of long-term goals, while on the other, an organism must be able to interrupt an ongoing action at any time and to switch to a different action in response to significant changes of the situation. Animals incapable of responding to the sudden appearance of, say, a predator, with a fast switch from the ongoing activity (e.g. eating) to a very different behaviour (e.g. flight), are unlikely to be found among our evolutionary ancestors. As was discussed in previous sections, there is evidence that maintenance and switching of intentions may be mediated by complementary processes (e.g. persisting activation versus backward inhibition).

6.1.3   The selection-monitoring dilemma

In order to produce coherent goal-directed action, organisms must select information relevant for the ongoing action, while inhibiting distracting stimuli to prevent interference and cross-talk. On the other hand, it is equally important to monitor the environment continuously for potentially significant information, even if this information is not directly relevant for the current task. It would not be adaptive if attentional selection operated so efficiently as to suppress task-irrelevant information completely. Rather, ignored information should be processed to a level at which its significance for an organism's 'latent' goals or vital needs can be recognized. As an example, ignoring noise from a party in the neighbourhood, while writing a paper is adaptive only to the degree that it does not prevent one from responding to a fire alarm. Again, complementary mechanisms have presumably evolved for the intentional top-down control of attentional selection, on the one hand, and the involuntary stimulus-driven capture of attention by significant stimuli outside the current attentional focus, which is triggered by the postulated background-monitoring process, on the other hand (Goschke, 1996a; Kuhl, 2000; Prinz, 1990b).

An analysis of these control dilemmas shows that adaptive action control involves a trade-off between antagonistic constraints, which afford a dynamic, context-sensitive regulation of complementary control processes (Goschke, 1996a, 1997, 2000; for related ideas, see also Rothermund, 1998; O'Reilly *et al.*, 1999; Kuhl, 2000; Mayr & Keele, 2000). A fixation at any one pole of a control dilemma will usually have dysfunctional consequences. While stable maintenance of the current intention and inhibition of distracting information supports behavioural stability and reduces interference, it incurs a cost when flexible switching or the detection of task-irrelevant, but significant stimuli is required. Conversely, while sensitivity for irrelevant stimuli or a readiness to switch to different tasks supports flexibility, it may incur a cost in the form of increased cross-talk and distractibility. In fact, the seemingly paradoxical combination of increased distractibility and rigid perseverance that has been observed in patients with lesions of the pre-frontal cortex, can be interpreted in terms of a pathological dysregulation of control dilemmas (Goschke, 1996a; Luria, 1973; Norman & Shallice, 1986).

This analysis raises two fundamental, yet neglected questions for theories of cognitive control: First, what are trigger conditions for the mobilization of specific control processes (e.g. under which conditions is a current intention shielded against distractions)? Second, how is the tradeoff between the complementary requirements of maintaining and switching task-sets regulated dynamically? These questions have received relatively little attention. Persistence and flexibility were often studied as separate research topics, and many prominent theories of volition focus primarily on processes that serve to shield intentions against distractions, rather than on the question of how the balance between maintaining and switching of intentions is regulated (but see Rothermund, 1998; Brandtstädter *et al.*, 1999; O'Reilly *et al.*, 1999; Mayr & Keele, 2000; Kuhl, 2000; Botvinick *et al.*, 2001).

6.2 Conflict and control: dynamic adjustment of complementary control processes

With respect to the question under which conditions cognitive control processes are triggered, it has been suggested that processes supporting the maintenance of intentions and the suppression of competing responses are mobilized specifically by the presence of response conflicts (Botvinick *et al.*, 2001; Goschke, 2000, in preparation). A precursor of this *conflict-triggered control* hypothesis can be found in Ach's (1935) 'difficulty law of motivation', which states that volitional effort increases in response to unexpected task difficulties. This idea was elaborated in Kuhl's (1983, 1984) theory of action control, according to which volitional strategies that serve to 'shield' a current intention against competing response tendencies, are mobilized specifically when conflicts between incompatible action tendencies are encountered (see also Rothermund, 1998). Such context-sensitive adjustments of top-down control do not necessarily reflect conscious changes of processing strategies, but can occur remarkably fast and in a presumably automatic way. This was shown in recent task-switching experiments (Goschke, 2000), in which participants had to respond either to the identity or to the colour of letters (e.g. an 'A' printed in green). Some of the stimuli elicited a response conflict, because the letter and the colour were mapped to incompatible responses (e.g. the colour required a left response, but the letter required a right response), whereas for the remaining stimuli both stimulus dimensions were mapped to the same response. I assumed that on trials involving a response conflict, the distracting stimulus dimension would be selectively inhibited in order to shield the current intention from competing response tendencies. This hypothesis predicts that it should be more difficult to switch from one task to the other, when the new task requires responding to a stimulus dimension, which on the immediately preceding trial elicited a response conflict. For instance, when on trial N one has to respond to the identity of the letter, while the colour of the letter activates a conflicting response, it should be more difficult to respond on the next trial $N+1$ to the colour, because the colour dimension should have been inhibited on trial N. Consistent with this prediction, response times on task-switch trials were significantly larger, when the preceding trial involved a response conflict as compared with when the stimulus on the preceding trial was response-congruent. As one should expect, this effect was restricted to task-switch trials, but did not occur when the same task was repeated. These findings indicate that, quite remarkably, within a few hundred milliseconds after the presentation of a stimulus the cognitive system evaluates the strength of response conflicts and eventually mobilizes compensatory control processes. Thus, the degree to which a current intention is shielded against competing task sets appears to be adjusted 'online' and in a relatively automatic way, depending on the degree of local competition between currently activated responses.

7   Who controls voluntary actions? From the 'central executive' to complementary control systems

So far I have tried to convey two main messages. First, I have argued that intentions are not immediate triggering causes of action, but are better conceived of as constraints that modulate to which attractor state the system settles in response to stimuli. Secondly, I have argued that in controlling voluntary actions the cognitive system must achieve a dynamic balance between the stable maintenance and flexible switching of intentions. In this final section I address the third question posed in the introduction, i.e. what brain systems underlie voluntary action and cognitive control.

7.1   The concept of a central executive

One straightforward answer to the question of 'who' controls voluntary action is, of course, 'the person'. For instance, in their original definition of controlled processing Posner & Snyder (1975) state that controlled strategies '... are under the conscious control of the subject' (1975, p. 73). In a similar vein, Shiffrin & Schneider (1977, p. 156) note that controlled processing is based on the activation of memory contents 'under control of, and through attention by, the subject'. However, these formulations are either trivially true or conceptually incoherent (what could it mean that a *person* controls the component systems, out of which she is composed? For thoughtful criticisms of this way of speaking see Allport, 1980, 1989; Neumann, 1992). One particularly seductive attempt to avoid this category mistake has been to postulate some 'control centre' inside the person's mind or brain that controls the rest of the system. Inspired by the central processing unit in conventional computers, early versions of this view postulated a kind of *mental central processor*. For instance, according to Bobrow & Norman (1975, p. 147), '... the system [is] guided from the top by a single central mechanism ... this central conscious mechanism controls the process that schedules resources, initiates actions ...'. Subsequently, the idea of a central control system underwent several transitions and the all too simple computer analogy was replaced with somewhat more realistic concepts. For instance, it has been suggested that cognitive control functions are subserved by a 'central executive' that does not directly control lower-level systems, but functions more like an 'operating system' at the top of the hierarchy' that 'sets goals for lower level processors and monitors their performance' (Johnson-Laird, 1988, p. 356). Similar ideas have been extremely popular throughout the last two decades, as exemplified by the widespread reference to some kind of central executive, supervisory system, or volitional system in models of human cognition (e.g. Reason, 1984; Logan & Cowan, 1984; Baddeley, 1986; Norman & Shallice, 1986; Umiltà, 1988). Such concepts presumably derive part of their appeal from the fact that they merge two domains of discourse:

- by evoking the image of a central perceiver, decider, and controller they do justice to our introspective intuition of a conscious self;

- by exploiting technomorphic analogies to the central processing unit or operating system of a digital computer they promise to provide a mechanistic account of intentional control.

However, most researchers would probably agree that the central executive is primarily a convenient label for something *to be explained*, rather than an explanation of cognitive control. A serious theory of cognitive control will thus have to specify the mechanisms that underlie the various functions ascribed to the 'executive', like planning of action sequences, suppression of inadequate responses, and co-ordination of subsystems according to a common goal (Allport, 1989; Neumann, 1992; Goschke, 1996a, 1997; Kuhl, 1996; Monsell, 1996; Kuhl & Fuhrmann, 1998).

The question of whether different executive functions are actually subserved by a unitary system is reflected in an ongoing debate in neuropsychology about the functional unity versus heterogeneity of the pre-frontal cortex. While the pre-frontal cortex has long been assumed to be involved in executive control functions and has even been considered the 'anatomical substrate of the will' (Stuss & Benson, 1986, p. 244; cf. Luria, 1973; Milner, 1982; Duncan, 1986; Fuster, 1989), it is still unclear to what degree different frontal areas subserve separable control functions. Correlations between tasks supposed to tap different control operations like planning, active maintenance, inhibition of prepotent responses, or cognitive set shifting are usually positive, but relatively low and often statistically insignificant (e.g. Duncan *et al.*, 1997; Miyake *et al.*, 2000). While this suggests that cognitive control involves a number of separable processes, the interpretation of these results is, however, compromised by methodological problems (see Miyake *et al.*, 2000; Goschke, in press). Converging evidence for separable executive functions stems from studies of patients suffering from lesions of the frontal lobe, which have also yielded some evidence for dissociations between different executive functions like active maintenance, inhibition, planning, or task-set switching (for reviews, see Fuster, 1989; McCarthy & Warrington, 1990; Della Sala & Logie, 1993; Goldman-Rakic, 1996; Goschke, 2002; Shallice & Burgess, 1998; Robbins, 1998). There is, however, an ongoing debate as to whether different areas of pre-frontal cortex differ primarily with respect to the type of information that is processed (e.g. spatial versus object information; Goldman-Rakic, 1996), or whether functional specialization concerns the type of processing operations performed by different areas (e.g. maintenance versus manipulation of information in working memory). Finally, a third line of evidence for functional specialization within pre-frontal cortex stems from neuro-imaging studies, in which brain activity in human volunteers is measured with positron-emission tomography (PET) or functional magnetic resonance imaging (fMRI), while they perform tasks requiring executive control operations. For instance, a recent meta-analysis of neuro-imaging studies of working memory (D'Esposito *et al.*, 1998) supports the conclusion that ventrolateral pre-frontal areas are primarily involved in the maintenance of information over short delays, while dorsolateral areas are activated by tasks, which require the monitoring, manipulation, and updating of information in working memory. A typical example for a task requiring continuous monitoring and updating of working memory is the *n-back task*, in which participants are presented a series of stimuli and have to press a key whenever the current stimulus is identical to the stimulus that was presented 1, 2, or 3 trials back (Cohen *et al.*, 1997).

In summary, there is, at least suggestive evidence for a certain degree of functional specialization within pre-frontal cortex. This fits with the above analysis of control dilemmas, which also suggests that complementary control functions involve a distributed network of separable subsystems. In the final sections I will focus on the neural basis of two specific control functions that were discussed in some detail in previous sections:

• the *maintenance* of goal representations and the *top-down modulation* of task-specific processes by such goal representations;

• the *monitoring* of response conflicts.

7.2   Pre-frontal cortex, goal maintenance, and top-down modulation

According to the theoretical framework developed in this chapter, intentional control of action rests crucially on the activation-based modulation of task-specific processes by representations of current goals and task demands. This presupposes a system with the following three features:

• *Arbitrary binding and flexible switching.* The system should be able to establish novel associations between stimulus features, responses, and other task-relevant information, and to flexibly update these associations in the face of changing goals or task demands.

• *Maintenance.* The system should support the maintenance of representations of goals and task rules over time and in the face of distracting information or competing responses.

• *Global modulation and accessibility.* The postulated system should be able to modulate processing in a large variety of task-specific processing systems, such that the operation of these specialized systems can be coordinated and constrained by higher-level goal representations.

A system with these features has been usually been termed *working memory* (Baddeley, 1986; Miyake & Shah, 1999), *context memory* (Miller & Cohen, 2001), or *global workspace* (Baars, 1988; Goschke, 1996a; Dehaene *et al.*, 1998). There is converging evidence that areas of the lateral pre-frontal cortex are involved in such a system. First, a unique feature of the pre-frontal cortex is that it receives afferent input from almost all cortical association areas, as well as from sub-cortical structures like the basal ganglia, the cerebellum, the amygdala, and the hippocampus (Fuster, 1989; Goldman-Rakic, 1996). Moreover, pre-frontal cortex has reciprocal efferent connections to most regions, from which it receives afferent inputs. The pre-frontal cortex is in an ideal anatomical position to integrate information from various perceptual, as well as motivational systems, and to modulate processes in a large variety of cortical and sub-cortical systems.

Secondly, neurophysiological studies in which the activity of single cells was recorded, have shown that neurons in the dorsolateral pre-frontal cortex of monkeys show sustained activity in so-called delayed-response tasks, in which the animal must maintain a representation of a stimulus over a delay, during which the stimulus is no longer visible (Fuster, 1989; Goldman-Rakic, 1996). These cells have been shown to sustain activity even in the face of intervening distracting stimuli (Miller, 2000) and may thus be the neuronal substrate of the active maintenance of task-relevant information in terms of self-stabilizing activation patterns. Consistent with this interpretation, neuro-imaging studies with humans have shown activation of areas in pre-frontal cortex in tasks, which required subjects to maintain or manipulate information in working memory (for a review see D'Esposito et al., 1998). Most interestingly, recent results from single-cell recordings suggest that a considerable proportion of neurons in lateral pre-frontal cortex not only maintain representations of task-relevant stimuli or anticipated responses, but seem to code arbitrary stimulus-response-mappings or task rules (Miller, 2000). For instance, Asaad et al. (2000) found that more than half of the recorded neurons in lateral pre-frontal cortex showed task-specific activation, i.e. they responded to a given stimulus only when a particular task, but not when other tasks had to be performed. These neurons may thus be involved in the representation of novel and arbitrary stimulus-response mappings (Miller & Cohen, 2001).

Finally, there is evidence both from single-cell recordings and neuro-imaging studies that dorsolateral pre-frontal cortex is involved in the top-down modulation of processing in posterior association areas (e.g. Corbetta et al., 1990; Kastner & Ungerleider, 2000; Miller, 2000; Pollmann et al., 2000; Posner & DiGirolamo, 1998; Postle et al., 2000). In particular, increased activation in dorsolateral pre-frontal cortex has been found in tasks requiring suppression of prepotent, but inadequate responses, like the Stroop task (D'Esposito et al., 1999; Pardo et al., 1990). Interestingly, activation in pre-frontal cortex has been shown to diminish when a task becomes routinized as a result of practice (Raichle et al., 1994).

In conclusion, there is converging evidence that dorsolateral pre-frontal cortex is involved in the maintenance of goals and task-relevant information, and in the top-down modulation of processing in task-specific representation systems. It should be noted that the postulated maintenance function is not simply a terminological disguise for a 'central executive'. In contrast to an omnipotent central control system, in the present framework working or context memory is conceived of simply as a system that imposes stable constraints on task-specific processes by maintaining goal representations. Which contents gain access to this system, however, entirely depends on the continuous interaction and competition of many different kinds of constraints, which are imposed by external stimuli, currently activated contents in long-term memory, 'latent' goals, or prevailing motivational states (Baars, 1988; Goschke, 1996a).

7.3   Conflict-monitoring and online adjustment of control

A second important aspect of voluntary control that has been discussed in this chapter concerns the dynamic 'online' adjustment of control processes depending on the strength of response conflicts. It has recently been suggested that the anterior cingulate cortex (ACC), a region on the medial surface of the frontal lobe, may be part of neural network involved in error detection and conflict monitoring (Botvinick *et al.*, 2001). Unfortunately (at least for cognitive neuroscientists), this brain region is activated by a remarkably wide range of tasks presumably requiring executive control, which makes it difficult to attribute a specific function to it. However, two main hypotheses have emerged to account for the activation of the ACC in these tasks. On the one hand, the ACC is considered a structure involved in strategic processes that resolve response conflicts, reduce cross-talk, and mediate the intentional selection of action (e.g. Posner & DiGirolamo, 1998). On the other hand, it has been suggested that the ACC is primarily involved in the *monitoring* of response conflicts and the generation of signals for the mobilization of control processes (Botvinick *et al.*, 2001). Evidence for the latter view stems from a recent study in which brain activity of participants was measured with event-related functional magnetic resonance imaging (fMRI), while they performed a Stroop colour-word interference task (Carter *et al.*, 2000). It was found that the ACC was more strongly activated in a condition that was associated with a relatively low engagement of control processes, but strong interference, compared with a condition with a high engagement of control processes and less interference. The authors concluded that the ACC is responsible for monitoring conflicts and signalling the demand for control processes, rather than for implementing control. Further support for this interpretation stems from another recent neuro-imaging study by MacDonald *et al.* (2000). Participants performed a Stroop task, and had to switch between reading words (which were colour names) and naming the printed colour of the words. An area in the left dorsolateral pre-frontal cortex was more active, when subjects prepared for the (weak) colour-naming task as compared with when they prepared for the (strong) word reading task. By contrast, the ACC was more active for incongruent compared with congruent stimuli. Again, this suggests that the ACC is involved in monitoring response conflicts and signalling the demand for control, while the dorsolateral pre-frontal cortex appears to be involved in implementing control operations.

8   Open issues and future prospects

In this chapter I have proposed a theoretical framework in which voluntary action is regarded as an optimization problem, which requires a dynamic, context-sensitive balance between antagonistic constraints, in particular, maintenance versus switching of intentions. To the degree that these constraints pose functionally incompatible demands, they presumably promoted the evolution of a cognitive architecture in which different control operations are subserved by complementary systems, rather than being controlled 'from the top' by a unitary central executive. Although many aspects of this framework are still speculative, it is consistent with a wide variety of findings from studies of intention memory, task-set switching, impairments of cognitive control in neurological patients, and neuro-imaging of executive functions. One important aim for future research will be to implement the general constraint-satisfaction framework outlined in this chapter in explicit computational models, which can be directly tested against empirical data from specific tasks. A second aim will be to study in more detail the dynamic interaction between complementary control systems by combining tasks, which allow the separation of different control operations, with neuro-imaging techniques. Finally, a neglected, but particularly fascinating question concerns the influence of *global system parameters* on the dynamic modulation of cognitive control systems. While in this chapter I have mainly focused on *micro-level* adjustments of cognitive control in response to conflicts, the dynamic regulation of complementary control processes presumably depends in addition on *global, macro-level parameters*. To give but one example: how efficient a current intention is shielded against distractions, and how sensitive the cognitive system remains for potentially significant information outside the current focus of attention, depends critically on the activation threshold that must be exceeded by stimuli to gain access to working memory. When this threshold is low, the contents of working memory will be updated rapidly and frequently, which should enhance vigilance and flexibility, but also produces increased distractibility. Conversely, a high threshold will support efficient shielding of the current intention, but may also lead to perseverance and impaired background-monitoring. One central question for future investigations will be how these global, content-unspecific parameters are themselves regulated. One interesting possibility, which attracts increasing attention, is that emotional states (Damasio, 1994; Kuhl & Kazén, 1999; Kuhl, 2000; A. Bolte, T. Goschke & J. Kuhl, in preparation), as well as sub-cortical neuromodulatory systems involved in basic affective responses to reward and punishment play an important role in the regulation of global control parameters (cf. Braver & Cohen, 2000; Roth, this volume). Contrary to the time-honoured view that emotions are antagonists of the will, further investigations of the dynamic regulation of cognitive control may thus reveal that emotions are essential for voluntary action.

Acknowledgments

Part of the research reported in this chapter was supported by the German Research Council (DFG) and the Max Planck Society. I wish to thank Julius Kuhl for many years of continuous support, fruitful collaboration, and inspiring discussions, which have substantially shaped the ideas expressed in this chapter. This chapter was written while I was a visiting scholar at the Max Planck Institute for Psychological Research in Munich, and I would like to thank Wolfgang Prinz for providing an exceptionally stimulating intellectual environment. Alan Allport, Oliver Gruber, Uli Mayr, Steve Keele, and the members of the 'Executive Control Discussion Group' at the Max Planck Institute, in particular Annette Bolte, Günther Knoblich, Iring Koch, and Florian Waszak provided valuable comments on the topics discussed in this chapter.

References

Ach, N. (1905) *Über die Willenstätigkeit und das Denken.* Göttingen: Vandenhoeck & Ruprecht.

Ach, N. (1935) Analyse des Willens. In Abderhalden, E. (ed.), *Handbuch der biologischen Arbeitsmethoden*, Vol. 6. Berlin: Urban & Schwarzenberg.

Allport, D.A. (1980) Attention and performance. In Claxton, G. (ed.), *Cognitive Psychology: new directions*. London: Routledge & Kegan Paul, pp. 112–153.

Allport, D.A. (1989) Visual attention. In Posner, M.I. (ed.), *Foundations of Cognitive Science*. Cambridge: MIT Press, pp. 631–682.

Allport, D.A. (1993) Attention and control: have we been asking the wrong questions? A critical review of twenty-five years. In Meyer, D.E. & Kornblum, S. (eds), *Attention & Performance, Vol. XIV: synergies in experimental psychology, artificial intelligence, and cognitive neuroscience*. Cambridge: MIT Press, pp. 183–218.

Allport, D.A., Styles, E. & Hsieh, S. (1994) Shifting intentional set: exploring the dynamic control of tasks. In Umiltà, C. & Moscovitch, M. (eds), *Attention & Performance, Vol. XV: conscious and nonconscious information processing*. Cambridge: MIT Press, pp. 421–452.

Anderson, J.R. (1983) *The Architecture of Cognition*. Cambridge: Harvard University Press.

Asaad, W.F., Rainer, G. & Miller, E.K. (2000) Task-specific neural activity in the primate pre-frontal cortex. *J Neurophysiology* 84, 451–59.

Baars, B.J. (1988) *A Cognitive Theory of Consciousness*. Cambridge: Cambridge University Press.

Baddeley, A. (1986) *Working Memory*. Oxford: Clarendon Press.

Bargh, J. (1989) Conditional automaticity: varieties of automatic influences in social perception and cognition. In Uleman, J.S. & Bargh, J.A. (eds), *Unintended Thought*. New York: Guildford Press, pp. 3–51.

Bargh, J.A., Gollwitzer, P.M., Lee-Chai, A., Barndollar, K. & Trötschel, R. (2001) The automated will: nonconscious activation and pursuit of behavioural goals. *J Personality Soc Psychol* 81, 1014–27.

Bieri, P. (2001) *Das Handwerk der Freiheit*. München: Hanser Verlag.

Bischof, N. (1989) Emotionale Verwirrungen Oder: Von den Schwierigkeiten im Umgang mit der Biologie. *Psycholog Rundsc* 40, 188–205.

Bobrow, D.G. & Norman, D.A. (1975) Some principles of memory schemata. In Bobrow, D.G. & Collins, A. (eds), Representation and Understanding. New York: Academic Press, pp. 131–49.

Botvinick, M.M., Braver, T.S., Carter, C.S., Barch, D.M. & Cohen, J.C. (2001) Evaluating the demand for control: anterior cingulate cortex and crosstalk monitoring. *Psycholog Rev* 108, 624–52.

Brandtstädter, J., Wentura, D. & Rothermund, K. (1999) Intentional self-development through adulthood and later life: tenacious pursuit and flexible adjustment of goals. In Brandtstädter, J. & Lerner, R.M. (eds), *Action and Self-development: theory and research through the life-span*. Thousand Oaks: Sage, pp. 373–400.

Bratman, M.E. (1987) *Intention, Plans, and Practical Reason*. Cambridge: Harvard University Press.

Braver, T.S. & Cohen, J.D. (2000) On the control of control: the role of dopamine in regulating pre-frontal function and working memory. In Monsell, S. & Driver, J. (eds.), *Control of Cognitive Processes: attention & performance, Vol. XVIII*. Cambridge: MIT Press, pp. 713–37.

Braver, T S., Cohen, J.D., Nystrom, L.E., Jonides, J., Smith, E.E. & Noll, D.C. (1997) A parametric study of pre-frontal cortex involvement in human working memory. *Neuro-image* 5, 49–62.

Byrne, M.D. & Anderson, J.R. (1998) Perception and action. In Anderson, J.R. & Lebière, C. (eds), *The Atomic Components of Thought*. Mahwah: Erlbaum, pp. 167–200.

Carter, C.S., MacDonald, A.M., Botvinick, M., Ross, L.L., Stenger, A., Noll, D. & Cohen, J.D. (2000) Parsing executive processes: strategic vs. evaluative functions of the anterior cingulate cortex. *Proc Nat Acad Sci* 97, 1944–8.

Clark, A. (1989) *Microcognition: philosophy, cognitive science, and parallel distributed processing*. Cambridge: MIT Press.

Clark, A. (1998) Magic words: how language augments human computation. In Carruthers, P. & Boucher, J. (eds), *Language and Thought*. Cambridge: Cambridge University Press, pp. 162–83.

Clark, T.W. (1999) Fear of mechanism: a compatibilist critique of 'The Volitional Brain'. *J Consciousness Stud* 6, 279–93.

Cohen, J.D. & Huston, T.A. (1994) Progress in the use of interactive models for understanding attention and performance. In Umiltà, C. & Moscovitch, M. (eds), *Attention & Performance, Vol. XV: conscious and nonconscious information processing*. Cambridge: MIT Press, pp. 453–76.

Cohen, J.D., Dunbar, K & McClelland, J.L. (1990) On the control of automatic processes: a parallel distributed processing account of the Stroop effect. *Psycholog Rev* 97, 332–61.

Cohen, J.D., Perlstein, W.M., Braver, T.S., Nystrom, L.E., Noll, D.C., Jonides, J. & Smith, E.E. (1997) Temporal dynamics of brain activation during a working memory task. *Nature* 386, 604–8.

Corbetta, M., Miezin, F.M., Dobmeyer, S., Shulman, G.L. & Petersen, S.E. (1990) Attentional modulation of neural processing of shape, colour, and velocity in humans. *Science* 248, 1556–9.

Damasio, A.R. (1994) *Descartes' Error*. New York: Grosset/Putnam.

D'Esposito, M., Aguirre, G.K., Zarahn, E., Ballard, D., Shin, R.K. & Lease, J. (1998) Functional MRI studies of spatial and nonspatial working memory. *Cognitive Brain Res* 7, 1–13.

D'Esposito, M., Postle, B.R., Jonides, J. & Smith, E.E. (1999) The neural substrate and temporal dynamics of interference effects in working memory as revealed by event-related functional MRI. *Proc Nat Acad Sci USA* 13, 7514–19.

Dehaene, S., Kerszberg, M. & Changeux, J-P. (1998) A neuronal model of a global workspace in effortful cognitive tasks. *Proc Nat Acad Sci USA* 95, 14529–34.

De Jong, R. (2000) An intention-activation account of residual switch costs. In Monsell, S. & Driver, J. (eds), *Attention & Performance, Vol. XVIII: control of cognitive processes*. Cambridge: MIT Press.

Della Sala, S. & Logie, R.H. (1993) When working memory does not work: the role of working memory in neuropsychology. In Boller, F. & Grafman, J. (eds), *Handbook of Neuropsychology*, Vol. 8. Amsterdam: Elsevier, pp. 1–61.

Dennett, D.C. (1984) *Elbow Room: the varieties of free will worth wanting*. Oxford: Clarendon Press.

Desimone, R. & Duncan, J. (1995) Neural mechanism of selective visual attention. *Ann Rev Neurosci* 18, 193–222.

Diaz, R.M. & Berk, L.E. (1992) *Private Speech: from social interaction to self-regulation*. Hillsdale: Erlbaum.

Dibbelt, S. (1996) *Wechseln und Beibehalten als Grundfunktionen der Handlungskontrolle*. Unpublished dissertation, University of Osnabrück, Germany.

Dörner, D. (1987) Denken und Wollen: Ein systemtheoretischer Ansatz. In Heckhausen, H., Gollwitzer, P.M. & Weinert, F.E. (eds), *Jenseits des Rubikon: Der Wille in den Humanwissenschaften*. Berlin: Springer-Verlag, pp. 238–50.

Dörner, D. (1988) Wissen und Verhaltensregulation: Versuch einer Integration. In Mandl, H. & Spada, H. (eds), *Wissenspsychologie*. Weinheim: Psychologie Verlags Union, pp. 265–79.

Duncan, J. (1986) Disorganization of behaviour after frontal lobe damage. *Cognitive Neuropsychol* 3, 271–90.

Duncan, J., Johnson, R., Swales, M. & Freer, C. (1997) Frontal lobe deficits after head injury: unity and diversity of function. *Cognitive Neuropsychol* 14, 713–41.

Dyer, F.N. & Severance, L.J. (1973) Stroop interference with successive presentations of separate incongruent words and colours. *J Exp Psychol* 98, 438–9.

Eichenbaum, H. & Cohen, N.J. (2001) *From Conditioning to Conscious Recollection. Memory Systems of the Brain*. Oxford: Oxford University Press.

Eimer, M. & Schlaghecken, F. (1998) Effects of masked stimuli on motor activation: behavioural and electrophysiological evidence. *J Exp Psychol: Human Percept Perform* 24, 1737–47.

Exner, S. (1873) Experimentelle Untersuchungen der einfachsten psychischen Processe. Erste Abhandlung: Die persönliche Gleichung. *Arch gesam Physiol Menschen Thiere* 7, 601–60.

Fodor, J.A. (1975) *The Language of Thought*. Cambridge: Harvard University Press.

Fodor, J.A. & Pylyshyn, Z.W. (1988) Connectionism and cognitive architecture: a critical analysis. *Cognition* 28, 3–71.

Francolini, C.M. & Egeth, H.A. (1980) On the nonautomaticity of 'automatic' activation: evidence of selective seeing. *Percept Psychophys* 27, 331–42.

Fuster, J. M. (1989) *The Pre-frontal Cortex: anatomy, physiology and neuropsychology of the frontal lobe*, 2nd edn. New York: Raven Press.

Gallistel, C.R. (1985) Motivation, intention, and emotion: goal-directed behaviour from a cognitive-neuroethological perspective. In Frese, M. & Sabini, J. (eds), *Goal-directed Behaviour: the concept of action in psychology*. Hillsdale: Erlbaum, pp. 48–66.

Goldman-Rakic, P.S. (1996) The pre-frontal landscape: implications of functional architecture for understanding human mentation and the central executive. *Philosoph Trans Roy Soc Lond Ser B* 351, 1445–53.

Gollwitzer, P. (1989) Action phases and mind-sets. In Higgins, E.T. & Sorrentino, R.M. (eds) *Handbook of Motivation and Cognition: foundations of social behaviour*, Vol.2. New York: Guildford Press, pp. 53–92.

Goolkasian, P. (1981) Retinal location and its effect on the processing of target and distractor information. *J Exp Psychol: Human Percept Perform* 7, 1247–57.

Goschke, T. (1996a) Wille und Kognition. Zur funktionalen Architektur der intentionalen Handlungssteuerung. In Kuhl, J. & Heckhausen, H. (eds), *Enzyklopädie der Psychologie Serie IV, Band 4: Motivation, Volition und Handeln*. Göttingen: Hogrefe, pp. 583–663.

Goschke, T. (1996b) Lernen und Gedächtnis: Mentale Prozesse und Gehirnstrukturen. In Roth, G. & Prinz, W. (eds), *Kopf-Arbeit: Gehirnfunktionen und kognitive Leistungen*. Heidelberg: Spektrum, pp. 359–410.

Goschke, T. (1997) Zur Funktionsanalyse des Willens: Integration kognitions-, motivations- und neuropsychologischer Perspektiven. *Psycholog Beitr* 39, 375–412.

Goschke, T. (1998) Implicit learning of perceptual and motor sequences: evidence for independent learning systems. In Stadler, M. & Frensch, P. (eds), *Handbook of Implicit Learning*. Thousand Oaks: Sage Publications, pp. 401–44.

Goschke, T. (2000) Involuntary persistence and intentional reconfiguration in task-set switching. In Monsell, S. & Driver, J. (eds), *Attention & Performance, Vol. XVIII: control of cognitive processes*. (pp. 331–56). Cambridge: MIT Press.

Goschke, T. (2002) Volition und Kognitive Kontrolle. In Müsseler, J., Prinz, W. & Maasen, S. (eds), *Allgemeine Psychologie*. Heidelberg: Spektrum, pp. 271–335.

Goschke, T. & Koppelberg, D. (1991) The concept of representation and the representation of concepts in connectionist models. In Ramsey, W., Rumelhart, D.E. & Stich, S. (eds), *Philosophy and Connectionist Theory*. Hillsdale: Erlbaum, pp. 129–62.

Goschke, T. & Kuhl, J. (1993) The representation of intentions: persisting activation in memory. *J Exp Psychol: Learning, Memory Cognition* 19, 1211–26.

Goschke, T. & Kuhl, J. (1996) Remembering what to do: explicit and implicit memory for intentions. InBrandimonte, M., Einstein, G. & McDaniel, M. (eds), *Prospective Memory: theory and applications*. Hillsdale: Erlbaum, pp. 53–91.

Goschke, T. & Kuhl, J. (2002) *Priming of Intention-related Information in Implicit Memory*. Manuscript submitted for publication.

Gruber, O. (2000) Two different brain systems underlie phonological short-term memory in humans. *Neuro-image*, 11, 407.

Heckhausen, H. (1989) *Motivation und Handeln*, 2nd edn. Berlin: Springer-Verlag.

Heckhausen, H., Gollwitzer, P.M. & Weinert, F.E. (eds) (1987) *Jenseits des Rubikon. Der Wille in den Humanwissenschaften*. Berlin: Springer-Verlag.

Henik, A., Friedrich, F.J. & Kellogg, W.A. (1983) The dependence of semantic relatedness effects on prime processing. *Memory Cognition* 11, 366–73.

Hershberger, W.A. (1989) *Volitional Action. Conation and Control*. Amsterdam: North Holland.

Hoffmann, J. (1993) *Vorhersage und Erkenntnis*. Göttingen: Hogrefe.

Hommel, B. (2000) The prepared reflex: automaticity and control in stimulus-response translation. (pp. 247–73). In Monsell, S. & Driver, J. (eds), *Control of Cognitive Processes: attention & performance*, Vol. XVIII. Cambridge: MIT Press.

James, W. (1890) *The Principles of Psychology*. New York: Holt.

Jersild, A.T. (1927) Mental set and shift. *Arch Psychol* Issue 89.

Johnson, J.E., Petzel, T.P., Hartney, L.M. & Morgan, L.M. (1983) Recall and importance ratings of completed and uncompleted tasks as a function of depression. *Cognitive Ther Res* 7, 51–6.

Johnson-Laird, P.N. (1988) *The Computer and the Mind*. Cambridge: Harvard University Press.

Juarrero, A. (1999) *Dynamics in Action. Intentional Behaviour as a Complex System*. Cambridge: MIT Press.

Kahneman, D. & Henik, A. (1981) Perceptual organization and attention. In Kubovy, M. & Pomerantz, J. (eds), *Perceptual Organization*. Hillsdale: Erlbaum, pp. 181–211.

Kahneman, D. & Treisman, A. (1984) Changing views of attention and automaticity. In Parasuraman, R. & Davies, R. (eds), *Varieties of Attention*. New York: Academic Press, pp. 29–61.

Karmiloff-Smith, A. (1992) *Beyond Modularity: a developmental perspective on cognitive science*. Cambridge: MIT Press.

Kastner, S. & Ungerleider, L.G. (2000) Mechanisms of visual attention in the human cortex. *Ann Rev Neurosci* 23, 315–41.

Kluwe, R. (1997) Intentionale Steuerung kognitiver Prozesse. *Kognitionswissenschaft* 6, 1–17.

Kuhl, J. (1983) *Motivation, Konflikt und Handlungskontrolle*. Berlin: Springer-Verlag.

Kuhl, J. (1984) Volitional aspects of achievement motivation and learned helplessness: toward a comprehensive theory of action-control. In Maher, B.A. (ed.), *Progress in Experimental Personality Research*, Vol. 13. New York: Academic Press, pp. 99–171.

Kuhl, J. (1985) Volitional mediators of cognitive-behaviour consistency: self-regulatory processes and actions versus state orientation. In Kuhl, J. & Beckmann, J. (eds), *Action Control: from cognition to behaviour*. Berlin: Springer-Verlag, pp. 101–28.

Kuhl, J. (1996) *Wille und Freiheitserleben. Formen der Selbststeuerung*. In Kuhl, J. & Heckhausen, H. (eds), *Enzyklopädie der Psychologie Serie IV, Band 4: Motivation, Volition und Handlung*. Göttingen: Hogrefe.

Kuhl, J. (2000) A functional-design approach to motivation and self-regulation: the dynamics of personality systems interactions. In Boekaerts, M., Pintrich, P.R. & Zeidner, M. (eds), *Handbook of Self-regulation*. New York: Academic Press, pp. 111–69.

Kuhl, J. & **Beckmann, J.** (eds) (1994) *Volition and Personality: action versus state orientation.* Göttingen: Hogrefe.

Kuhl, J. & **Fuhrmann, A.** (1998) Decomposing self-regulation and self-control: the volitional components checklist. In Heckhausen, J. & Dweck, C. (eds), *Life Span Perspectives on Motivation and Control.* Hillsdale: Erlbaum, pp. 15–49.

Kuhl, J. & **Goschke, T.** (1994a) A theory of action control: mental subsystems, modes of control, and volitional conflict-resolution strategies. In Kuhl, J. & Beckmann, J. (eds), *Volition and Personality: action versus state orientation.* Göttingen: Hogrefe, pp. 93–124.

Kuhl, J. & **Goschke, T.** (1994b) State orientation and the activation and retrieval of intentions from memory. In Kuhl, J. & Beckmann, J. (eds), *Volition and Personality: action versus state orientation.* Göttingen: Hogrefe, pp. 127–54.

Kuhl, J. & **Helle, P.** (1986) Motivational and volitional determinants of depression: the degenerated-intention hypothesis. *J Abnormal Psychol* **95**, 247–51.

Kuhl, J. & **Kazén, M.** (1999) Volitional facilitation of difficult intentions: joint activation of intention memory and positive affect removes Stroop interference. *J Exp Psychol: General* **128**, 382–99.

Lewin, K. (1926) Vorsatz, Wille und Bedürfnis (Intention, will, and need). *Psycholog Forsch* **7**, 330–85.

Lhermitte, F. (1983) 'Utilization behaviour' and its relation to lesions of the frontal lobes. *Brain* **106**, 237–55.

Li, K.Z.H., Lindenberger, U., Ruenger, D. & **Frensch, P.A.** (2000) The role of inhibition in the regulation of sequential action. *Psycholog Sci* **11**, 343–7.

Libet, B. (1999) Do we have free will? *J Consciousness Stud* **6**, 47–57.

Logan, G.D. (1985) Executive control of thought and action. *Acta Psycholog* **60**, 193–210.

Logan, G.D. (1988) Toward an instance theory of automatization. *Psycholog Rev* **95**, 492–527.

Logan, G.D. (1995) Linguistic and conceptual control of visual spatial attention. *Cognitive Psychol* **28**, 103–74.

Logan, G.D. & **Cowan, W.B.** (1984) On the ability to inhibit thought and action: a theory of an act of control. *Psycholog Rev* **91**, 295–327.

Logan, G.D. & **Zbrodoff, N.J.** (1979) When it helps to be misled: facilitative effects of increasing the frequency of conflicting stimuli in a Stroop-like task. *Memory Cognition* **7**, 166–74.

Logan, G.D., Zbodroff, N.J. & **Williamson, J.** (1984) Strategies in the colour-word Stroop task. *Bull Psychonom Soc* **22**, 135–8.

Luria, A.R. (1961) *The Role of Speech in Regulation of Normal and Abnormal Behaviour.* London: Pergamon.

Luria, A.R. (1973) *The Working Brain.* London: Penguin Books.

Luria, A.R. & **Yudovich, F.I.** (1959) *Speech and the Development of Mental Processes in the Child.* Harmondsworth: Penguin.

MacDonald, A.W., Cohen, J.D., Stenger, V.A. & **Carter, C.S.** (2000) Dissociating the role of the dorsolateral pre-frontal and anterior cingulate cortex in cognitive control. *Science* **288**, 1835–8.

MacLeod, C.M. (1991) Half a century of research on the Stroop effect: an integrative review. *Psycholog Bull* **109**, 163–203.

Marsh, R.L., Hicks, J.L. & **Bink, M. L.** (1998) Activation of completed, uncompleted, and partially completed intentions. *J Exp Psychol: Learning, Memory Cognition* **24**, 350–61.

Mayr, U. & **Keele, S.W.** (2000) Changing internal constraints on action: the role of backward inhibition. *J Exp Psychol: General* **129**, 4–26.

Mayr, U. & Kliegl, R. (2000) Task-set switching and long-term memory retrieval. *J Exp Psychol: Learning, Memory Cognition* **26**, 1124–40.

McCarthy, R.A. & Warrington, E.K. (1990) *Cognitive Neuropsychology. A Clinical Introduction.* San Diego: Academic Press.

McClelland, J.L., Naughton, B.L. & O'Reilly, R.C. (1995) Why there are complementary learning systems in the hippocampus and neocortex: insights from the successes and failures of connectionist models of learning and memory. *Psycholog Rev* **102**, 419–57.

McCrone, J. (1999) A bifold model of freewill. *J Consciousness Stud* **6**, 241–59.

Mecklinger, A., von Cramon, D.Y., Springer, A. & Matthes-von Cramon, G. (1999) Executive control functions in task switching: evidence from brain injured patients. *J Clin Exp Neuropsychol* **21**, 606–19.

Meiran, N. (1996) Reconfiguration of processing mode prior to task performance. *J Exp Psychol: Learning, Memory, Cognition* **22**, 1423–42.

Meiran, N., Chorev, Z. & Sapir, A. (2000) Component processes in task switching. *Cognitive Psychol* **41**, 211–53.

Meyer, D.E. & Schwaneveldt, R.W. (1971) Facilitation in recognizing pairs of words: evidence of a dependence between retrieval operations. *J Exp Psychol* **90**, 227–34.

Miller, E. (2000) The neural basis of top-down control of visual attention in the pre-frontal cortex. In Monsell, S. & Driver, J. (eds), *Control of Cognitive Processes: attention & performance*, Vol. XVIII. Cambridge: MIT Press, pp. 511–34.

Miller, E. & Cohen, J. (2001) An integrative theory of pre-frontal cortex function. *Ann Rev Neurosci* **24**, 167–202.

Miller, G.A., Galanter, E. & Pribram, K.H. (1960) *Plans and the Structure of Behaviour.* New York: Holt, Rinehart & Winston.

Milner, B. (1982) Some cognitive effects of frontal-lobe lesions in man. *Philosoph Trans Roy Soc Lond B* **298**, 211–26.

Mischel, W. (1974) Processes in delay of gratification. In Berkowitz L. (ed.), *Advances in Experimental Social Psychology*, Vol. 7. New York: Academic Press, pp. 249–92.

Miyake, A. & Shah, P. (eds) (1999) *Models of Working Memory: mechanisms of active maintenance and executive control.* Cambridge: Cambridge University Press.

Miyake, A., Friedman, N.P., Emerson, M.J., Witzki, A.H., Howerter, A. & Wager, T.P. (2000) The unity and diversity of executive functions and their contributions to complex 'frontal lobe' tasks: a latent variable analysis. *Cognitive Psychol* **41**, 49–100.

Monsell, S. (1996) Control of mental processes. In Bruce V. (ed.), *Unsolved Mysteries of the Mind.* Hove: Erlbaum.

Monsell, S. & Driver, J. (eds) (2000) *Attention & Performance, Vol. XVIII: control of cognitive processes.* Cambridge: MIT Press.

Münsterberg, H. (1889) *Beiträge zur experimentellen Psychologie, Heft 1.* Freiburg: Mohr.

Neely, J.H. (1977) Semantic priming and retrieval from lexical memory: roles of inhibitionless spread of activation and limited-capacity attention. *J Exp Psychol: General* **106**, 226–54.

Neumann, O. (1984) Automatic processing: a review of recent findings and a plea for an old theory. In Prinz, W. & Sanders, A.F. (eds), *Cognition and Motor Processes.* Berlin: Springer-Verlag, pp. 255–94.

Neumann, O. (1990) Visual attention and action. In Neumann, O. & Prinz, W. (eds), *Relations Between Perception and Action: current approaches.* Berlin: Springer-Verlag, pp. 227–67.

Neumann, O. (1992) Theorien der Aufmerksamkeit: Von Metaphern zu Mechanismen. *Psycholog Rundsch* **43**, 83–101.

Neumann, O. & Klotz, W. (1994) Motor responses to nonreportable, masked stimuli: where is the limit of direct parameter specification? In Moscovitch, M. & Umiltà, C. (eds), *Attention & Performance, Vol. XV: conscious and unconscious information processing*. Cambridge: MIT Press, pp. 123–50.

Neumann, O. & Prinz, W. (1987) Kognitive Antezedenzien von Willkürhandlungen. In Heckhausen, H., Gollwitzer, P.M. & Weinert, F.E. (eds), *Jenseits des Rubikon: Der Wille in den Humanwissenschaften*. Berlin: Springer-Verlag, pp. 195–215.

Norman, D.A. & Shallice, T. (1986) Attention to action: willed and automatic control of behaviour. In Shallice, T. & Norman, D.A. (eds), *Consciousness and Self-regulation*. New York: Plenum Press.

O'Reilly, R.C. & Munakata, Y. (2000) *Computational Explorations in Cognitive Neuroscience*. Cambridge: MIT Press.

O'Reilly, R.C., Braver, T.S. & Cohen, J.D. (1999) A biologically based computational model of working memory. In Miyake, A. & Shah, P. (eds), *Models of Working Memory: mechanisms of active maintenance and executive control*. New York: Cambridge University Press, pp. 375–411.

Pardo, J.V., Pardo, P., Janer, K.W. & Raichle, M.E. (1990) The anterior cingulate cortex mediates processing selection in the Stroop attentional conflict paradigm. *Proc Nat Acad Sci USA* **87**, 256–9.

Paulesu, E., Frith, C.D. & Frackowiak, R.S.J. (1993) The neural correlates of the verbal component of working memory. *Nature* **362**, 342–5.

Pollmann, S., Weidner, R., Müller, H.J. & von Cramon, D.Y. (2000) A fronto-posterior network involved in visual dimension changes. *J Cognitive Neurosci* **12**, 480–94.

Posner, M.I. & DiGirolamo, G.J. (1998) Executive attention: conflict, target detection and cognitive control. In Parasuraman, R. (ed.), *The Attentive Brain*. Cambridge: MIT Press, pp. 401–23.

Posner, M.I. & Snyder, C.R. (1975) Attention and cognitive control. In Solso, R.L. (ed.), *Information Processing and Cognition*. Hillsdale: Erlbaum, pp. 55–85.

Postle, B.R., Stern, C.E., Rosen, B.R. & Corkin S. (2000) An fMRI investigation of cortical contributions to spatial and nonspatial visual working memory, *Neuro-image* **11**, 409–23.

Prinz, W. (1984) Modes of linkage between perception and action. In Prinz, W. & Sanders, A.F. (eds), *Cognition and Motor Processes*. Berlin: Springer-Verlag, pp. 185–94.

Prinz, W. (1990a) A common-coding approach to perception and action. In Neumann, O. & Prinz, W. (eds), *Relations Between Perception and Action. Current Approaches*. Berlin: Springer-Verlag, pp. 167–201.

Prinz, W. (1990b) Wahrnehmung. In Spada, H. (ed.), *Lehrbuch Allgemeine Psychologie*. Bern: Huber, pp. 25–114.

Prinz, W. (1998) Die Reaktion als Willenshandlung. *Psycholog Rundsch* **49**, 10–20.

Prinz, W. (2000) Kognitionspsychologische Handlungsforschung. *Zeitschr Psychol* **208**, 32–54.

Pylyshyn, Z.W. (1984) *Computation and Cognition. Towards a Foundation for Cognitive Science*. Cambridge: MIT Press.

Raichle, M.E., Fiez, J.A., Videen, T.O., MacCleod, A.K., Pardo, J.V., Fox, P.T. & Petersen, S.E. (1994) Practice-related changes in human brain functional anatomy during nonmotor learning. *Cerebral Cortex* **4**, 8–26.

Reason, J.T. (1984) Lapses of attention. In Parasuraman, R. & Davies, D. (eds), *Varieties of Attention*. New York: Academic Press, pp. 515–50.

Robbins, T.W. (1998) Dissociating functions of the pre-frontal cortex. In Roberts, A.C., Robbins, T.W. & Weiskrantz, L. (eds), *The Pre-frontal Cortex: executive and cognitive functions*, pp. 117–30. Oxford: Oxford University Press.

Rogers, R.D. & Monsell, S. (1995) Costs of a predictable switch between simple cognitive tasks. *J Exp Psychol: General* **124**, 207–31.

Rothermund, K. (1998) *Persistenz und Neuorientierung. Mechanismen der Aufrechterhaltung und Auflösung zielbezogener kognitiver Einstellungen.* Unpublished dissertation, University of Trier, Germany.

Rumelhart, D.E., McClelland, J.L. & PDP Research Group (1986) *Parallel Distributed Processing: explorations in the microstructure of cognition*, Vol. 1. Cambridge: MIT Press.

Rumelhart, D.E., Smolensky, P., McClelland, J.L. & Hinton, G.E. (1986) Schemata and sequential thought processes in PDP models. In McClelland, J.L. & Rumelhart, D.E. (eds), *Parallel Distributed Processing. Explorations in the Microstructure of Cognition*, Vol. 2. Cambridge: MIT Press, pp. 7–57.

Schacter, D.L. & Tulving, E. (eds) (1994) *Memory Systems.* Cambridge: MIT Press.

Schubotz, R. & von Cramon, D.Y. (in press) Exekutive Funktionen. In Goschke, T. & Eimer, M. (eds), *Kognitive Neurowissenschaft. Enzyklopädie der Psychologie.* Göttingen: Hogrefe.

Shallice, T. & Burgess, P. (1998) The domain of supervisory processes and the temporal organization of behaviour. In Roberts, A.C., Robbins, T.W. & Weiskrantz, L. (eds), *The Pre-frontal Cortex. Executive and Cognitive Functions.* Oxford: Oxford University Press, pp. 22–35.

Shallice, T. (1988) *From Neuropsychology to Mental Structure.* Cambridge: Cambridge University Press.

Sherry, D.F. & Schacter, D.L. (1987) The evolution of multiple memory systems. *Psycholog Rev* **94**, 439–54.

Shiffrin, R.M. & Schneider, W. (1977) Controlled and automatic human information processing: II. Perceptual learning, automatic attending, and a general theory. *Psycholog Rev* **84**, 127–90.

Simon, H.A. (1967) Motivational and emotional controls of cognition. *Psycholog Rev* **74**, 29–39.

Smith, E.E., Jonides, J., Marshuetz, C. & Koeppe, R.A. (1998) Components of verbal working memory: evidence from neuro-imaging. *Proc Nat Acad Sci USA* **95**, 876–82.

Smith, M.C. (1979) Contextual facilitation in a letter search task depends on how the prime is processed. *J Exp Psychol: Human Percept Perform* **5**, 239–51.

Smith, M.C., Theodor, L. & Franklin, P.E. (1983) The relationship between contextual facilitation and depths of processing. *J Exp Psychol: Learning, Memory, Cognition* **9**, 697–712.

Smolensky, P. (1988) On the proper treatment of connectionism. *Behav Brain Sci* **11**, 1–74.

Spector, A. & Biederman, I. (1976) Mental set and mental shift revisited. *Am J Psychol* **89**, 669–79.

Squire, L.R. (1992) Memory and the hippocampus: a synthesis from findings with rats, monkeys, and humans. *Psycholog Rev* **99**, 195–231.

Stroop, J.R. (1935) Studies of interference in serial verbal reactions. *J Exp Psychol* **18**, 643–62.

Stuss, D.T. & Benson, D.F. (1986) *The Frontal Lobes.* New York: Raven Press.

Tomasello, M. (1999) *The Cultural Origins of Human Cognition.* Cambridge: Harvard University Press.

Tulving, E. (1983) *Elements of Episodic Memory.* New York: Oxford University Press.

Tweedy, J.R., Lapinski, R.H. & Schwaneveldt, R.W. (1977) Semantic context effects on word recognition: influence of varying the proportion of terms presented in an appropriate context. *Memory Cognition* **5**, 84–98.

Umiltà, C. (1988) The control operations of consciousness. In Marcel, A.J. & Bisiach, E. (eds), *Consciousness in Contemporary Science*. Oxford: Clarendon Press, pp. 334–56.

Vygotski, L.S. (1962) *Thought and Language*. Cambridge: MIT Press.

Walter, H. (1998) *Neurophilosophie der Willensfreiheit*. Paderborn: Schöningh.

Wylie, G. & Allport, D.A. (2000) Task switching and the measurement of 'switch costs'. *Psycholog Res* **63**, 212–33.

CHAPTER 4

VOLUNTARY ACTION FROM THE PERSPECTIVE OF SOCIAL-PERSONALITY PSYCHOLOGY

U. C. BAYER, M. J. FERGUSON, AND P. M. GOLLWITZER

1 Introduction

Social-personality psychologists have traditionally devoted little attention to the theoretical and empirical analysis of the issue of voluntary action. We see two different reasons for this:

1 According to the behaviourist perspective (e.g. Tolman, 1925), purposeful or goal-directed behaviour was solely used as a descriptive category to refer to behaviour that was performed in a certain way (e.g. with great persistence).

2 Motivational theories prevalent in traditional social and personality psychology (e.g. Murray, 1938) conceptualized humans as being mechanically driven by basic needs and instincts, thus preventing an analysis of human action in terms of volition.

The issue of volition only began to receive more attention in the seventies, when humans were perceived as agentic according to social-cognitive theories of personality (Mischel, 1973; Bandura, 1977). In recent years, the issue of volition has been kindled in research on self-regulation, wherein a host of theories on goal setting and goal striving have emerged (reviewed by Oettingen & Gollwitzer, 2001). Voluntary action also became an important issue in research on person perception, as it matters whether an action is perceived as voluntary or not when inferences are made on a person's dispositions (Heider, 1958). Only very recently, however, has research begun to systematically examine the determinants of intentionality judgments with respect to others' and one's own behaviour (Malle *et al.*, 2001). Finally, social psychologists have now addressed the issue of the causal impact of the phenomenal will by asking the question of whether it might simply be an illusion (Wegner & Wheatley, 1999).

In the present chapter, we present and discuss these different lines of research. We begin with delineating different types of goal theories by pointing to the kind of self-regulatory problems they attempt to account for. We then turn to analysing the importance of the concept of intention for interpreting and understanding the behaviour of others. Finally, we address the question of what kind of psychological variables determine the experience of voluntary action (i.e. the phenomenal will).

2   Voluntary action as the pursuit of goals

The cognitive revolution in social and personality psychology (Mischel, 1973; Bandura, 1977) has suggested a number of important cognitive variables: expectancies, control beliefs, competence judgments, self-regulatory plans, and goals. It is the latter concept that is the most relevant to the analysis of voluntary action. A person who has set herself a goal has decided to reach a desired outcome or to perform a respective instrumental behaviour. Social-personality psychologists explicate the issue of goal pursuit in terms of Kurt Lewin's (Lewin *et al.*, 1944) distinction between goal setting and goal striving. 'Goal setting' addresses the question of what goals a person will choose (i.e. what kind of end states a person finds attractive and feasible, and commits herself or himself to attain). 'Goal striving', on the other hand, is behaviour directed toward existing goals and thus addresses questions of moving toward the chosen goal. In recent personality and social-psychology research, many different lines of research exploring issues of goal setting and goal striving have developed.

2.1   Goal setting

The analysis of goal setting can focus either on the determinants of what kind of goals a person sets (e.g. beliefs about the malleability versus stability of intelligence lead to different types of set goals) or on the psychological processes (e.g. contrasting one's noncommittal wishes with reality) that facilitate the setting of binding goals.

2.1.1   Determinants of goal setting

With respect to the determinants of goal setting it has been recognized that goals are often *assigned* by others (e.g. teachers, parents, employers, editors). It matters who assigns goals to whom and how the persuasive message is framed. Relevant variables may include attributes of the source, the recipient, and the message (McGuire, 1969). Locke & Latham (1990) report that source variables, such as legitimacy and trustworthiness, play an important role in the transformation of an assigned goal into a personal goal. For recipients of such assignments, perception of the goal as desirable and feasible, personal redefinition of the goal, and integration with other existing goals are important (Cantor & Fleeson, 1994). Finally, relevant message variables may be the discrepancy between the suggested goal and the recipient's respective current goal (e.g. when a very low-calorie diet is suggested to a person with a moderate dieting goal) and whether fear appeals are used (e.g. information on the dramatic medical consequences of health damaging behaviour is provided). Effective sellers of goals must also consider the processing ability and motivation of the recipient as a moderator of the effects of source, recipient, and message variables on accepting assigned goals as personal goals (Petty & Cacioppo, 1986; Chaiken, 1987).

Goals do not need to be assigned as people also set goals on their own. People prefer to choose goals that are desirable and feasible (Ajzen, 1985; Gollwitzer, 1990; Locke & Latham, 1990; Heckhausen, 1991). Desirability is determined by the estimated attractiveness of likely short- and long-term consequences of goal attainment. Such consequences may pertain to anticipated self-evaluations, evaluations by significant others, progress toward some higher order goal, external rewards of having attained the goal, and the joy/pain associated with moving towards the goal (Heckhausen, 1977). Feasibility depends upon people's judgments of their capabilities to perform relevant goal-directed behaviour (i.e. self-efficacy expectations; Bandura, 1997), their belief that this goal-directed behaviour will lead to the desired outcome (i.e. outcome expectations; Bandura, 1997), or the judged likelihood of attaining the desired outcome (i.e. generalized expectations; Oettingen, 1996) or desired events in general (general optimism; Scheier & Carver, 1985). The information source for efficacy expectations, outcome expectations, generalized expectations, and optimism is past experiences: one's own past performances, the observed performances of others, received relevant persuasive messages, and one's previous physiological responses to challenge (Bandura, 1997). Proper assessment of the feasibility and desirability of a potential goal also requires seeing the goal in relation to other potential goals. A goal associated with many attractive consequences may suddenly appear less desirable in light of a superordinate goal or it might seem more feasible in connection with other compatible goals (Cantor & Fleeson, 1994; Gollwitzer, 1990).

Set goals may differ in structural features (e.g. abstract versus concrete) and in content (e.g. materialistic versus social integrative). People generally prefer to set themselves abstract goals, and adopt concrete goals only when they run into problems attaining an abstract goal. According to action identification theory (Vallacher & Wegner, 1987), people conceive of their actions in rather abstract terms (e.g. cleaning the apartment) and only drop down to lower, concrete levels (e.g. vacuuming the carpet) when difficulties in carrying out the activity as construed at the higher level arise. Some people typically think of their actions in low-level terms, whereas others prefer high-level identifications (Vallacher & Wegner, 1989). This general preference for either an abstract or a concrete level of identifying actions should be reflected in the choice of abstract versus concrete goals.

Goals can be framed with a positive or negative outcome focus (i.e. goals that focus on establishing and keeping positive outcomes as compared with avoiding and ameliorating negative outcomes). Higgins (1997) argues that people may construe their self either as an ideal self that they intrinsically desire to be, or as an ought self that they feel compelled to be. The former orientation focuses on promotion, whereas the latter focuses on prevention. Part of the promotion orientation is a predilection for setting goals geared at accomplishing positive outcomes and terminating negative ones, whereas part of the prevention orientation is a predilection for setting goals geared at avoiding negative outcomes and keeping positive ones.

Goals can also be framed as performance versus learning goals (Dweck, 1996), also referred to as performance versus mastery goals (Ames & Archer, 1988) or ego involvement versus task involvement goals (Nicholls, 1979). Goals in the achievement domain can either focus on finding out how capable one is (performance goals) or on learning how to carry out the task (learning goals). Dweck (1996) reports that implicit theories on the nature of ability determine the preference for performance versus learning goals. If people believe that ability is fixed and cannot be easily changed (i.e. hold an entity theory of ability), they prefer performance goals. However, if people believe that ability can be improved by learning (i.e. hold an incremental theory of ability), they prefer learning goals. Similar implicit theories concerning the malleability of moral character affect the selection of punitive versus educational correctional goals.

Whenever goals are formed on a high level of abstraction (e.g. to become a physician), they determine the content of lower order goals. The content of such 'Be' goals determine the content of respective 'Do' goals, which in turn determine the content of respective 'motor-control' goals (Carver & Scheier, 1998, p. 72). 'Be' goals have been described by terms such as current concerns (Klinger, 1977), self-defining goals (Wicklund & Gollwitzer, 1982), personal projects (Little, 1983), personal strivings (Emmons, 1996), and (individualized) life tasks (Cantor & Fleeson, 1994). Whereas choosing higher order 'Be' goals should be determined by their perceived desirability and feasibility (Klinger, 1977), choosing the respective lower order 'Do' goals also depends on the commitment to the respective 'Be' goals (Gollwitzer, 1986). The issue of higher order goals affecting lower order goal-directed activity is also raised by Joëlle Proust's (this volume) discussion (based on Bach, 1978; Frankfurt, 1988; Jeannerod, 1997) of the voluntary control of minimal actions.

2.1.2 Processes of goal setting

Social-personality researchers have not only analysed the determinants of goal setting, but also the psychological processes that facilitate goal setting. Bandura (1997) suggests that having successfully achieved a set goal stimulates the setting of ever more challenging goals, due to a person's heightened sense of efficacy that is based on having successfully attained the prior goal. Others have pointed out that the core processes of goal setting involve committing oneself to achieving a certain incentive (Klinger, 1977). Heckhausen & Kuhl (1985) argued that the lowest degree of commitment to an incentive is a mere wish to attain it. A wish that is tested for feasibility becomes a want that carries a higher degree of commitment. To develop a full goal commitment (i.e. to form the intention or goal to achieve the incentive), a further relevance check must be carried out relating to necessary means, opportunities, time, relative importance, and urgency.

In their *Rubicon model of action phases*, Heckhausen & Gollwitzer (1987; Gollwitzer, 1990; Heckhausen, 1991) assume that people entertain more wishes than they have time or opportunities to realize. Therefore, they must select between wishes in order to accomplish at least some of them. The criteria for selection are feasibility and desirability. Wishes with high feasibility and desirability have the best chance to become goals. The transformation of wishes into goals is a resolution, resulting in a feeling of determination to act. Through this resolution the desired end state specified by the wish becomes an end-state that the individual feels committed to achieve. To catch the flavour of this transition from wishing to willing, the metaphor of crossing the Rubicon is used.

What are the preliminaries of crossing the Rubicon? The model of action phases (Gollwitzer, 1990; Heckhausen, 1991) states that the realization of a wish demands the completion of four successive tasks:

- deliberating between wishes to select appropriate ones (pre-decision phase);
- planning the implementation of chosen wishes (i.e. goals or intentions) to get started with goal-directed behaviour (pre-action phase);
- monitoring goal-directed behaviour to bring it to a successful ending (action phase);
- evaluating what has been achieved as compared with what was desired to terminate goal pursuit or to restart it (evaluation phase).

People decide to 'cross the Rubicon' (i.e. move from the pre-decision phase to the pre-action phase) when they sense that the feasibility and desirability of a wish is not only acceptably high, but has been exhaustively deliberated and correctly assessed. Gollwitzer, Heckhausen, and Ratajczak (1990) observed that undecided people more readily formed goals when they had been asked to judge the likelihood of wish fulfilment, and to list likely positive and negative, short- and long-term consequences. In addition, when undecided people were lured into planning the implementation of the wish by simply connecting anticipated opportunities with intended goal-directed behaviour, they also showed a greater readiness to cross the Rubicon. Apparently, when undecided people feel that the task of assessing the feasibility and desirability of a given wish is completed, they show a greater readiness to move on and set themselves the respective goal.

A recent *theory of fantasy realization* (Oettingen, 1996) analyses goal setting by delineating different routes to goal formation. The theory distinguishes between two forms of thinking about the future, expectations and free fantasies. Expectations are judgements of the likelihood that a certain future behaviour or outcome will occur. Free fantasies about the future, on the contrary, are thoughts and images of future behaviour or outcomes in the mind's eye, independent of the likelihood that these events will actually occur. For example, despite perceiving low chances of successfully resolving a conflict with a partner, people can indulge in positive fantasies of harmony.

Fantasy realization theory specifies three routes to goal setting that result from how people deal with their fantasies about the future. One route is expectancy-based, while the other two are independent of expectations. The expectancy-based route rests on mentally contrasting positive fantasies about the future with aspects of impeding reality. This mental contrast ties free fantasies about the future to the here and now. Consequently, the desired future appears as something that must be achieved and the impeding reality as something that must be changed. A necessity to act is experienced and, as a consequence, expectations of success become activated and used. If expectations of success are high, a person will commit to the goal of fantasy attainment.

The second route to goal setting stems from merely indulging in positive fantasies about the desired future, thereby disregarding impeding reality. This indulgence seduces one to consummate and consume the desired future envisioned in the mind's eye. Accordingly, no necessity to act is experienced, and relevant expectations of success are not activated and used. Commitment to act towards fantasy fulfilment reflects solely the implicit pull of the desired events imagined in one's fantasies. It is moderate and independent of a person's perceived chances of success (i.e. expectations). As a consequence, the level of goal commitment is either too high (when expectations are low) or too low (when expectations are high). The third route is based on merely dwelling on the negative aspects of impeding reality, thereby disregarding positive fantasies about the future. Again, no necessity to act is experienced, this time because nothing points to a direction in which to act. Commitment to act therefore does not reflect expectations, but merely the implicit push of the negative aspects of impeding reality. Similar to indulgence in positive fantasies about the future, dwelling on the negative reality leads to a moderate, expectancy independent level of commitment, which is either too high (when expectations are low) or too low (when expectations are high). Fantasy realization theory is supported by various experimental studies in the inter-personal and achievement domain (Oettingen, 1999, 2000; Oettingen *et al.*, 2001).

Goal setting does not have to be a product of reflective processes, but can also be a result of reflexive processes. Bargh's (1990) *automotive theory* suggests that strong mental links develop between the cognitive representation of situations and the goals the individual chronically pursues within them. As a consequence of repeated and consistent pairing, these goals are activated automatically when the person enters the critical situation. The automatically activated goal then guides behaviour within the situation without choice or intention. Reflective choice, originally crucial, is now by-passed. Bargh *et al.* (2001) tested the assumption of direct goal activation in several experiments by assessing whether directly activated goals lead to the same behavioural consequences as reflectively set goals. Indeed, non-conscious priming of an achievement goal caused participants to perform better on an intellectual task than a non-primed control group. Moreover, non-consciously primed achievement goals led to increased persistence and a higher frequency of task resumption. By applying a dissociation paradigm, it could be ruled out that these effects were based on the mere priming of the semantic concept of achievement.

The processes described by Bargh and colleagues are based on reflective goal setting at an earlier point in time. Automation relates only to the activation of an already existing goal in a given situation (for related perspectives see Hommel and Prinz, both this volume). It seems possible, however, that behaviour that carries features of goal-directedness can also emerge in the absence of previously or *ad hoc* set goals. Kelso's (1995) theory on dynamic systems suggests that complex goal-directed behaviour can emerge without mental representations of goals. Moreover, robotics research (Brooks, 1991; Maes, 1994) finds that robots can be programmed to perform rather complex, goal-directed behaviour without having to install goal concepts. Connectionist theories are also wary of the goal concept. Some connectionist theories completely abolish the goal concept, while others try to replace the reflective processes of goal choice by suggesting parallel constraint satisfaction models (Read *et al.*, 1997).

Finally, Carver & Scheier (1999) point out that there might be two kinds of goal-related automation. The first is described by Bargh (1990) in his automotive model, and relates to automation through repeated and consistent pairing of a goal with a situational context. The second relates to primitive built-in behavioural tendencies that are present also in non-human species. Carver and Scheier describe this type of automation as an intuitive, crudely differentiated 'quick and dirty' way of responding to reality that provides a default response. One does not wait to form an intention, but responds immediately. This mode of behaving is reminiscent of what McClelland and his colleagues (McClelland *et al.*, 1989) describe as behaviour based on implicit motives. Implicit motives are believed to be biologically based, directly guiding behaviour through natural incentives.

It appears then that (as behaviourists have long asserted) behaviour-carrying features of goal-directedness do not necessarily require subjective goal setting based on reflective thought or the activation of a mental representation of an existing goal. Although some theorists may question the existence and relevance of reflective goal setting or of mental representations of goals, the more challenging research question for the future seems to us, How do the reflective and reflexive systems interact?

2.2 Goal striving

The rate of goal attainment is strongly affected by what kinds of goals people have set for themselves (e.g. learning goals lead to higher rates than performance goals) and how skilfully they cope with implemental problems that arise on the way to goal attainment (e.g. planning in advance).

2.2.1   Determinants of goal striving

Goal contents vary in structural features. They may be challenging or modest, specific or vague, abstract or concrete, proximal or distal, framed with a negative or positive outcome focus, and so forth. As well, goals differ thematically. All of these differences affect the success of goal striving. Locke & Latham (1990) demonstrated that challenging goals spelled out in specific terms are superior to modest specific goals, as well as to challenging, but vague (i.e. do your best) goals in facilitating goal attainment. Bandura & Schunk (1981) observed that proximal goals are more easily attained then distal goals. However, Cochran & Tesser (1996) demurred that the goal proximity effect is reversed for goals framed in terms of preventing failures. Also, learning goals and performance goals have different effects on performance (Dweck, 1996). Learning goals lead to better achievements than performance goals because the former allow for a more effective coping with failure than the latter. For people with performance goals, failure signals a lack of ability and thus causes the reaction of giving up. People with learning goals, on the other hand, view setbacks as cues to focus on new strategies. Accordingly, their behaviour is orientated toward mastering the causes of the setback, ultimately furthering goal attainment. However, Elliot & Church (1997) objected that performance goals are less detrimental when they are framed as approach goals (e.g. I want to get good grades), rather than avoidance goals (e.g. I do not want to get bad grades).

With respect to the thematic content of goals, Ryan *et al.* (1996) suggest that goals of autonomy, competence, and social integration lead to greater creativity, higher cognitive flexibility, greater depth of information processing, and more effective coping with failure. Goals based on autonomy, competence, and social integration needs are also associated with higher well-being and life satisfaction. Recently, Brunstein *et al.* (1999) pointed out that the effects of goals on emotional well-being are also influenced by how well people's goals match their needs or implicit motives (McClelland, 1985). People with strong achievement and power needs, and goals of the same theme—as well as people with strong affiliation and intimacy needs, and goals of the same theme—report higher emotional well-being than those whose needs and goals do not match.

2.2.2   Processes of goal striving

Experience tells us that it is often a long way from goal setting to goal attainment. Having set a goal is just a first step, usually followed by a host of implemental problems that must be successfully solved. In the section above, we described research that predicts successful goal attainment on the basis of structural and thematic properties of the set goals. Process-related research focuses on how the problems of goal pursuit are solved by the individual. To effectively solve problems of initiating goal-directed actions and bringing them to a successful ending, one needs to seize good opportunities to act, ward off distractions, flexibly step up efforts in the face of difficulties, by-pass barriers, compensate for failures and shortcomings, and negotiate conflicts between goals. Various theories address how the individual effectively solves these problems of goal implementation.

The *model of action phases* (Gollwitzer, 1990; Heckhausen, 1991; Heckhausen & Gollwitzer, 1987) understands successful goal pursuit in terms of solving a series of successive tasks: deliberating wishes (potential goals) and choosing between them, planning goal-directed actions and getting started, bringing goal pursuit to a successful end, and evaluating its outcome. The task notion implies that people can promote goal pursuit by developing respective mindsets, which in turn facilitate task completion (Gollwitzer, 1990). Studies conducted on the mindsets associated with either deliberating between wishes (i.e. deliberative mindset) or with planning goal-directed actions (i.e. implemental mindset) support this idea.

When participants are asked to plan the implementation of a set goal, an *implemental mindset* with the following attributes originates (Gollwitzer, 1990; Gollwitzer & Bayer, 1999): participants' minds become closed in that they are no longer distracted by irrelevant information. However, information related to goal implementation is processed very effectively (e.g. information on the sequencing of actions), desirability-related information is processed in a partial manner favouring pro's over con's, and feasibility-related information is analysed in a manner that favours illusory optimism. This optimism extends to an illusion of control over uncontrollable outcomes, and even holds for depressed individuals. Self-perception of important personal attributes (e.g. cheerfulness, smartness, social sensitivity) is strengthened, while perceived vulnerability to both controllable and uncontrollable risks is lowered (e.g. developing an addiction to prescription drugs or losing a partner to an early death, respectively). The implemental mindset favours goal attainment by helping the individual to effectively cope with classic problems of goal striving, such as becoming distracted, doubting the attractiveness of the pursued goal, or being pessimistic about its feasibility.

Set goals commit an individual to attaining the specified desired future, but they do not commit the individual to when, where, and how she intends to act. Such additional commitments can be added by planning goal pursuit via *implementation intentions* with the format of 'If situation *x* is encountered, then I will perform the goal-directed behaviour *y*!'. Gollwitzer (1993) argued that implementation intentions are a powerful self-regulatory strategy for overcoming problems of getting started with goal-directed actions (e.g. when people are tired, absorbed with some other activity, or lost in thoughts, and thus miss good opportunities to act). In support of this hypothesis, it was observed in numerous studies (for summary, see Gollwitzer, 1999) that difficult to reach goals benefit greatly from being furnished with implementation intentions. This effect extends to projects such as resolving important inter-personal conflicts, performing a medical self-examination, regular intake of a vitamin supplement, eating healthy foods, and doing vigorous exercise. It also holds true for people who have problems turning goals into action, such as opiate addicts under withdrawal or schizophrenic patients.

Because implementation intentions spell out links between situational cues and goal-directed behaviour, it is assumed (Gollwitzer, 1993) that by forming such intentions people delegate the control of behaviour to situational cues, thus facilitating the initiation of goal-directed actions. The mental representations of the specified situational cues become highly activated, making these cues more accessible. Various experiments demonstrate that situational cues specified in implementation intentions are more easily detected and remembered, as well as more readily attended to than comparable unintended situations. Moreover, implementation intentions create strong associative links between mental representations of situations and actions, which otherwise are achieved only through consistent and repeated pairing. As a consequence, action initiation becomes automatized. Various experiments demonstrate that the goal-directed behaviour specified in implementation intentions is initiated swiftly and effortlessly (Brandstätter *et al.*, 2001) in the presence of the critical situation. Moreover, the subliminal presentation of the critical situation suffices to activate cognitive concepts and knowledge relevant to the efficient initiation of the intended behaviour. Finally, patients with a frontal lobe injury, who have severe deficits in the conscious and effortful control of behaviour, while remaining unaffected in performing automatized behaviour, benefit greatly from forming implementation intentions (Lengfelder & Gollwitzer, 2001).

Implementation intentions ameliorate not only problems of the initiation of goal-directed behaviour, but also other problems of goal striving (Gollwitzer & Schaal, 1998). In a series of studies, implementation intentions created resistance to tempting distractions, while solving tedious arithmetic problems. Moreover, goals set to escape unwanted habitual responses (i.e. stereotypical beliefs and prejudicial feelings) are more successfully attained when furnished with implementation intentions.

In summary, implementation intentions create a type of behavioural automation that does not originate from laborious practice requiring much effort. Rather, people strategically delegate their control over goal-directed behaviour to anticipated critical situational cues. This easily accessible self-regulatory strategy of forming implementation intentions can be used to increase tenacity in initiating goal-directed action. At the same time, it helps to increase flexibility in escaping unwanted habits of thinking, feeling, and behaving.

There are other effective types of planning besides forming implementation intentions. Planning can be approached in a more reflective way as in *mental simulations* exploring possible ways to achieving a goal. Taylor *et al.* (1998) term such mental simulations 'process simulations'. If applied repeatedly, they further goal attainment, such as achieving good grades in academic exams. Apparently, repeated mental simulations of how to achieve a goal also result in firm plans.

Competing goal pursuits are paid particular attention in Kuhl's *action control theory* (for summary, see Kuhl & Beckmann, 1994). For an ordered action sequence to occur, a current guiding goal must be shielded from competing goal intentions (e.g. the goal of making a phone call from the competing intention to tidy one's desk). Kuhl calls this shielding mechanism action control and differentiates a number of control strategies, such as attention control, emotion control, and environment control. Through environment control, for example, the individual prevents the derailing of an ongoing goal pursuit by removing competing temptations from the situation.

Whether and how effectively these strategies are used depends on the current control mode of the individual. An action-orientated person concentrates on planning and initiating goal-directed action, responds flexibly to situational demands, and uses control strategies effectively. A state-orientated person, in contrast, cannot disengage from incomplete goals and is caught up in uncontrollable perseverance of thoughts related to aversive experiences or in dysfunctional thoughts about future successes. Action and state orientation may be induced by situational variables (e.g. a surprising event, persistent failure), but is founded in a personal disposition.

Recent experimental research on state orientation has discovered a further volitional handicap. State-orientated individuals readily misperceive assigned goals as self-generated. These findings have stimulated a new theoretical perspective (Kuhl, 2000), which sees the volitional control of action as a result of the cooperation of various mental subsystems (i.e. intention memory, extension memory, intuitive behaviour control, and object recognition). Action versus state orientation is understood as a parameter that modulates co-operation between these systems thus leading to a different kind of volitional control of action with different outcomes.

Higher order goals (e.g. to become popular) offer multiple routes to approach them. If one pathway is blocked, an individual can approach the goal another way. *Self-completion theory* (Wicklund & Gollwitzer, 1982) addresses this issue of compensation by analysing self-defining goals. Such goals specify as the desired end state an identity, such as scientist, mother, or a political liberal. As many different things indicate the possession of such identities, the striving for an identity is a process of collecting these indicators (or self-defining symbols). These indicators extend from relevant material symbols (e.g. books and awards for a scientist) to relevant self-descriptions (e.g. using titles) and performances (e.g. accomplishing important research). Whenever shortcomings in one type of symbol are encountered, an individual will experience self-definitional incompleteness, which in turn leads to compensatory self-symbolising efforts. These may take the form of pointing to the possession of alternative symbols or acquiring new symbols.

Research on self-completion has discovered that effective self-symbolising requires a social reality. Compensatory efforts are particularly effective when other people notice them. This, however, has costs. Compensating individuals see others only in terms of their capability to notice compensatory efforts and thus lack social sensitivity. Also, when people make public their intention to acquire a certain self-definitional indicator (e.g. studying hard), actual effort will be reduced, as the proclamation alone produces self-definitional completeness (Gollwitzer *et al.*, 1999).

People may promote goal achievement by compensating for failures, but they also try to avoid committing errors in the first place. Warding off failure becomes a pressing issue whenever difficulties mount. Brehm and Wright's (Brehm & Self, 1989; Wright, 1996) *energization theory* of motivation assumes that the readiness to exert effort is directly determined by the perceived difficulty of a task. As perceived difficulty increases, so does effort expenditure, unless the task is recognized to be irresolvable. There is, however, a second limit to the increase of effort in response to heightened task difficulty: potential motivation. Potential motivation is fed by desirability-related variables (i.e. strength of the related need or higher order goal, the incentive value of the task, and the instrumentality of task completion for satisfaction or attainment of super-ordinate goals). If potential motivation is low, people do not find it worthwhile to expend more effort when an easy task becomes more difficult. The upper limit of effort expenditure is low and quickly reached. If potential motivation is high, however, an increase in difficulty is matched by investment of effort up to high levels of difficulty. In this case, the upper limit of effort expenditure is high and is reached only after much effort expenditure has occurred.

The goal striving theories discussed so far implicitly or explicitly view goals as something attractive that the individual wants to attain. Goals are not simply 'cold' mental representations that specify standards or reference points, but cognitively explicated and elaborated incentives. Such motivational goal theories are rivalled by a more cognitive view that sees goals as solely specifying performance standards. For instance, according to Bandura (1997), goals have no motivational consequences *per se*. They only specify the conditions that allow a positive or negative self-evaluation. If the set goal is attained, positive self-evaluation prevails, whereas staying below one's goal leads to negative self-evaluation. The individual is pushed by the negative self-evaluation associated with the discrepancy, and pulled by the anticipated positive self-evaluation linked to closing the gap between the status quo and the goal. Accordingly, goals stimulate effortful action in particular when people notice a discrepancy between the status quo and the set goal. However, they will try to reduce this discrepancy only when they feel self-efficacious with respect to performing the necessary goal-directed actions.

Carver & Scheier (1998) propose a different *discrepancy reduction theory of goal pursuit*. Based on cybernetic control theory, the central concept of their analysis is the negative feedback loop. They highlight the hierarchical structure of goal pursuits and assume a cascading loop structure. Goal-directed behaviour is regulated at the middle level ('Do-goals') with actions at higher levels ('Be-goals') suspended until the individual becomes self-aware. Discovery of discrepancies on the 'Be-level' or the 'Do-level' triggers lower level goals or behaviour aimed at discrepancy reduction, respectively. An individual tries to close discrepancies only when outcome expectations are high. However, a positive affective response as a consequence of goal attainment is not assumed, nor is the detection of a discrepancy associated with negative affect. Rather, the source of positive or negative feelings in goal pursuit is the speed of discrepancy reduction. The intensity of these feelings is regulated again in a negative feedback loop. If the speed meets a set criterion, positive feelings result, whereas negative feelings are experienced with a speed that stays below this criterion.

The discrepancy notions discussed above construe goals as 'cold' mental representations of performance standards with no links to needs or incentives. This conceptualization of goals makes it difficult to explain why motivation (see Brehm and Wright's notion of potential motivation) moderates the relationship between task difficulty and effort. Moreover, according to discrepancy theory, an increase in task difficulty should reduce efforts at task completion, because an experienced increase in task difficulty should lead to reduced self-efficacy and less positive outcome expectations. As Brehm and Wright have repeatedly demonstrated, however, high potential motivation makes it worthwhile for people to mobilise additional effort whenever heightened task difficulty threatens task completion. Finally, Carver & Scheier's construal of the regulation of the speed of discrepancy reduction assumes that positive discrepancies (i.e. moving towards the goal too fast) are reduced as readily as negative discrepancies (i.e. moving towards the goal too slowly). However, from the perspective that goals represent a desired outcome, a person should be less motivated to reduce positive discrepancies than negative discrepancies (Gollwitzer & Rohloff, 1999).

3   Folk explanations of voluntary action

Beyond the various theories that address how goals are set and attained, social-personality psychologists have traditionally been concerned with questions of how people infer whether someone is *consciously* or *purposefully* engaging in goal-relevant behaviour. That is, researchers have long explored how and when people infer the intention behind others' behaviour or the extent to which a person's behaviour is voluntary (James, 1890; Heider, 1958).

Early theorists such as James (1890) and Heider (1958), and many theorists since (e.g. Jones & Davis, 1965; Kelley, 1967, 1973; Kunda, 1999; Weiner, 1986), recognized that by knowing whether an actor's behaviour was purposefully performed, one can anticipate the actor's future actions, and can thus plan one's own future actions toward the actor accordingly. Purposeful behaviour in a given situation points to the actor's general behavioural tendencies or dispositional characteristics. Dispositional information enables one to make predictions about an actor's behaviour *across* situations. As Heider (1958) states in his seminal treatise concerning the psychology of understanding others, knowing the reasons for someone's behaviour indicates something about the essence of that person: '... dispositional properties are the invariances that make possible a more or less stable, predictable, and controllable world' (p. 80).

3.1 Early theoretical and empirical work

Given that there are potentially numerous and sometimes invisible possible causes of complex and even simple behaviour, how and when do people decide that an actor behaved voluntarily? Heider (1958) was one of the first in psychology to systematically unpack the possible components underlying such judgements. He proposed that there are two necessary and sufficient conditions that need to be met in order to conclude that an actor purposefully behaved. The first component is referred to by Heider as *can*. The concept of *can* refers to both the actor's capability with regard to the action, as well as the difficulty introduced by the contingent environmental conditions. The question of capability refers to whether the actor is able to perform the action, which is then integrated with a consideration of the difficulty of performing the action due to the physical surroundings.

In addition to having to analyse the component of *can* when attempting to understand whether an action was voluntary, Heider posited a second component called *try*. The concept of *try* entails both the aspect of intention, as well as exertion. When an act is intentional, the actor is purposively trying to accomplish some goal. The degree to which someone intended to perform an action is combined with how much they exerted themselves while performing. According to Heider, the greater the exertion, the greater the extent to which the actor was trying to perform the action.

After a perceiver figures out the degree to which an actor *could* have performed the action and *tried* to perform it, an assessment of voluntary action, or the extent to which the action was purposive, can theoretically be reached. These two conditions are informative because they yield predictions about the actor's future possible behaviour. If an athlete attempts to finish a marathon, but fails, we gain a lot of information by knowing whether he was able to finish it, as well as whether he tried to win it. If he was clearly able to win it, we can assume that he did not try hard enough. If he tried to win it, but did not, we can assume that he was not capable of doing so.

Although Heider's (1958) discussion of the constructs of *can* and *try* was mostly geared toward understanding whether an action was caused by the person versus other forces (such as environmental factors), it included the intentionality of the behaviour as a central component in the analysis. His theoretical work served as a useful foundation for later empirical work on the attribution of causes of a behaviour (e.g. Beike & Sherman, 1994; Gilbert, 1998; Jones & Davis, 1965; Weiner, 1985), which also addressed notions of intention. For instance, in their correspondent inference theory, Jones & Davis (1965) postulated that the behaviour of others' is more likely to be interpreted as intentional if it is freely chosen and the effects or consequences are uncommon (i.e. are unexpected). Moreover, acts that produce many desirable outcomes do not reveal a person's specific intention as clearly as acts that produce only a single desirable outcome (Newton, 1974).

Although there is a vast body of literature about attributions of dispositional versus situational causes of behaviour, there is a subtle difference between attributing a particular behaviour pattern to a dispositional cause and deciding that the behaviour was intentional. Deciding that an actor's behaviour was dispositionally caused does not necessarily mean that the actor (consciously) intended to perform the behaviour. Much research, some of which has already been described, demonstrates that people can behave in an automatic fashion, without intention, effort, awareness, or control (Bargh, 1994, 1997; Bargh & Ferguson, 2000). Because of this possibility, it is not necessarily the case that a dispositionally caused behaviour is also an intended one. In line with this distinction, recent work has directly examined the degree to which people infer intentionality for another's behaviour.

3.2   Recent experimental work on inferring intentionality

Malle & Knobe (1997) provided a differentiated model of the concept of intentionality and they conducted a series of studies demonstrating how people typically use the concept of intentionality. In a preliminary study, they investigated whether people ascribe to a common idea of intentionality. They asked research participants to rate the intentionality of 20 different verbally-described kinds of behaviour. The average intercorrelation between any two people in the study turned out to be $r = 0.64$. Participants rated sweating and yawning as unintentional, but inviting a friend to lunch and watering the plants as intentional. These findings suggest that people seem to ascribe to one general understanding of intentionality when judging behaviour.

The authors also explored the determinants of the concept of intentionality by asking participants to define intentionality. In terms of the necessary ingredients for a judgment of intentionality, 51% of participants mentioned answered that the intention (i.e. the decision to perform the action) is a necessary condition, 39% referred to beliefs (i.e. thoughts about the action and its effects), 27% reported desires (i.e. hopes of attaining desired results), and 23% pointed to awareness (i.e. the knowing of doing). In subsequent studies it was demonstrated that skills were also mentioned, thus people seem to base their intentionality judgments on the presence of desire, belief, intention, awareness, and skill.

In our research concerning the perception of intentionality (Bayer, 2000), we extended Malle & Knobe's model by adding aspects described in the Rubicon model of action phases (see above). The five components of Malle & Knobe's (1997) folk concept of intentionality (i.e. desire, beliefs, intention, skills, and awareness) can be incorporated into the deliberation phase (i.e. desire and beliefs) and the action phase (i.e. awareness and skills) of the Rubicon model, and the decision to realise a given wish (i.e. the intention). Still, the Rubicon model points to a further important component that pertains to the planning phase. Planning the implementation of goal-directed behaviour should further enhance judgments of intentionality, as a planned action should be more readily perceived as an intended action.

To test this hypothesis, we ran two experiments using the same procedure. First, the participants read various stories about different persons who performed an unlawful act (i.e. stole a watch) by exploiting an unexpected good opportunity (i.e. low risk to be detected). For each described person, we asked the participants to indicate the degree to which the behaviour was performed intentionally. In the first study, the participants read seven scenarios. Each scenario described a different theft whereby the value of the stolen object was always around $500. The characters in the various scenarios differed in respect to whether they had deliberated the crime, had decided to perform a crime, and had planned how to perform the crime. The number of components (deliberating, deciding, planning) varied between one and three, with all possible combinations of two of the three components, making up seven different stories altogether.

Results indicate that judged intentionality increased as a function of the number of components present in the descriptions. In other words, less intentionality was inferred when only one component was present compared with (all combinations of) two components and, again, more intentionality was inferred when three components were present compared with (any combination of) only two components. This result is in line with the findings of Malle & Knobe (1997) insofar as wishes and beliefs (deliberating), as well as the component of intention (making a decision) enhanced intentionality judgments. Our findings go beyond Malle & Knobe's work by demonstrating that planning also increases intentionality judgments. Apparently, planning represents a further distinct component in the perception of intentionality.

In a second study, we tried to replicate these findings by presenting participants with descriptions of a more severe crime. In these descriptions, the criminal character wanted to rob another person and to shoot him afterwards to ensure that the victim would not contact the police. Four versions of this story were constructed in which the criminal character either (a) deliberated, (b) planned, (c) deliberated and planned, or (d) deliberated, decided, and planned the crime. When we asked the participants to rate the degree of intentionality with which the described character performed the criminal action, characters who planned were perceived as performing the crime with higher intentionality than characters who only deliberated. Moreover, characters who deliberated and planned received higher intentionality ratings than characters who only deliberated. Finally, characters who deliberated, decided, and planned did not receive higher intentionality ratings than characters who only deliberated and planned. This overall pattern of data suggests that learning that another person planned the performance of an action has a particularly strong influence on intentionality judgments, more so than finding out that the other person deliberated or decided on the action.

4 Causal impact of volition on behaviour

Recent work on inferring intentionality (Malle & Knobe, 1997; Malle, 1999; Malle, Moses, & Baldwin, 2001) focuses on the circumstances under which people decide that an actor behaved intentionally. The underlying assumption in that research is that people have implicit theories that intended behaviour in a given situation causally impacts on how the actor thinks and feels. Although much research suggests that people rely on the notion of volition as an influential factor in understanding themselves and others, philosophers and psychologists have questioned whether it is possible for mental events, such as intentions, to cause physical events, such as behaviour (e.g. Christensen & Turner, 1993). There is a long history of discussion in philosophy about the possibility of interaction between the mental and the physical, starting with Descartes and his notion of the duality of mind/body (e.g. Block *et al.*, 1997). Several social psychologists have recently joined this debate and have reiterated the possibility that the apparent causal importance of volition is merely an illusion.

4.1 Empirical versus phenomenal will

For example, Wegner and colleagues (e.g. Wegner & Wheatley, 1999) have developed a line of research in which they assume that volition (what they refer to as conscious will) can be broken down into the *empirical will* and the *phenomenal will*. Wegner and Wheatley argue that the *empirical will* has a veritable causal impact on a persons' conscious thought processes and subsequent behaviour. Researchers in psychology proper have traditionally explored such causal connections and the authors assert that this relation must be assessed within the usual scientific paradigm of observing the degree to which a behaviour can be performed with versus without the precursor of conscious intention or will (see the first section on goal setting and goal striving of the present chapter).

The *phenomenal will*, on the other hand, entails the subjective experience of personally and independently (i.e. with no help from other causal factors) causing a particular action. This self-attribution of causality is so ubiquitous that we also insist on inferring the degree to which other people intend their assorted actions. We believe that we can intentionally perform certain behaviour and so we assume that others can as well. However, despite such popularity and apparent utility of the folk concept of volition, or the phenomenal will, Wegner & Wheatley (1999) argue that there is no basis upon which to use such subjective experience of will as evidence for the actual causal impact of wilfulness on subsequent behaviour. As others in social psychology have demonstrated (Nisbett & Wilson, 1977), people's introspective testament concerning the proceedings of their own mental lives can be misguided. Just as someone may be unable to tell the experimenter why she chose the pair of stockings on the right, rather than one of the other three identical pairs, someone may mistakenly believe that her conscious intention to water the plants actually caused her to do so.

Wegner and Wheatley provide an explanation of how the experience of phenomenal will can arise. They postulate that people tend to attribute causal status to an intention when the intention is temporally *prior* to the behaviour, when it is *consistent* with the behaviour, and when the behaviour could not have been obviously caused by other factors, but is seen as *exclusively* determined by the intention. As long as the intention occurs according to these conditions, one is likely to experience the intention as causal for the subsequent, respective behaviour.

The argument that conscious will arises from identifiable sources that are themselves accounted for in various causal chains is not a trivial one. It challenges the long cherished view of free will that wilfulness somehow springs forth from some special uncaused place and constitutes the essence of human capacity for freely chosen actions (Prinz, this volume;

Sappington, 1990). If one's conscious will itself is caused, then it is impossible to say that one made the decision *oneself,* without any causal impact from other sources. In other words, people are not freely able to intend if those intentions are caused by factors other than some special personal invocation of agency. Wegner and Wheatley argue that this perspective is appropriate given the emphasis that scientists place on causal mechanisms and the idea that the mental lives of people must follow the same laws and mechanistic processes as physical stimuli.

4.2   Will as caused versus will as causal

Accordingly, Wegner & Wheatley (1999) assert that the experience of will can be a mere perception, resulting from an attribution based on factors of priority, consistency, and exclusivity. They then argue that, because of this, experiential will may not actually be a psychological force that causes action. As evidence for this claim, the authors cite research by Libet (1985) showing that the intention to move one's finger (a simple exercise of 'free choice') is preceded by non-conscious brain activity associated with pre-motor preparation (measured by readiness potentials). Wegner & Wheatley conclude that these '... findings are compatible with the idea that brain events cause intention and action, while conscious intention itself may not cause action' (p. 3).

The authors suggest, on the basis of their analysis of priority, consistency, and exclusivity, as well as empirical research, that intention is itself caused, and that therefore it may be that intention and action may both be caused by some 'third variable,' (e.g. non-conscious processes), and that intention is not causally impacting upon action. However, the assertion that it is possible to delineate the causal chain that leads to conscious will needs to be distinguished from the claim that such conscious thoughts are therefore causally irrelevant for subsequent behaviour. It is not clear why one would have to assume that a conscious intention that is itself caused by nameable factors can have no causal bearing for the subsequent, relevant behaviour. That is, if one argues that conscious will is itself caused (based on a mechanistic perspective), then it seems inconsistent to, in turn, argue that conscious will should only sometimes have a causal impact on the following behaviour. This would be tantamount to only sometimes endorsing such a mechanistic perspective.

4.3   Causal will versus unwilled behaviour

One might argue that a wide array of findings suggests that conscious, intentional thought is actually *not* necessary for a particular behaviour to occur. Indeed, numerous studies demonstrate how people can negotiate the environment nonconsciously (Bargh, 1997; Bargh & Ferguson, 2000). For example, people can form inferences about social behaviour both intentionally and unintentionally (Uleman, 1999). One might suppose then, on the basis of this research, that the intention to generate an inference is not what is actually causing the subsequent inferential thinking; instead it might be various, underlying nonconscious processes.

However, although many studies demonstrate that an action can occur with *and* without prior intentional thought, this does not mean that the intentional thought had no causal bearing on that action, even if such impact was not crucial for the observation of the action, or central to the definition of the action. For instance, the inferential thinking (Uleman, 1999) that occurs after the intention to do so might be qualitatively different from that which occurs when the perceiver does not intend to do so. Although the 'act of inferential thinking' takes place regardless of a preceding intention, the *unintended* inferential process might depend upon different patterns of activation in the brain, deliver different emotional and cognitive consequences, and bear different implications for the person in a host of ways compared with intentional inferential thinking. The two processes both qualify as inferential thinking and may even bear some similarities, but this loose similarity does not preclude deeper, perhaps unobserved or even unobservable differences from existing.

Although we understandably identify behaviour in a loose sense in order to be able to categorise it (at a very detailed level, no two acts of inferential thinking are the same, just as it is impossible to step into the same river twice), such looseness should not mislead us into thinking that an action that can occur with and without conscious intent serves as evidence that the intent was causally irrelevant for the subsequent action. Maybe conscious intent does not influence the behaviour *that is measured*, but to suggest that it sometimes does not causally impact the person in some (perhaps unobserved) way requires one to assume dualist notions concerning the separability of mental and physical phenomena.

In summary, the belief that conscious will is the *first* and *only* causal impetus behind an action is clearly an illusion, and Wegner & Wheatley (1999) provide a clear and valuable exposition of the development of this illusion. Furthermore, although volition might sometimes not be necessary for the occurrence (i.e. measurement) of a related, subsequent behaviour, we presume, in line with non-dualist, scientific perspectives of causality, that such volition always has causal implications for subsequent thought and behaviour, albeit possibly unobserved or subtle.

5   Conclusion

Social and personality psychologists generally adopt a perspective on voluntary action that allows for the possibility that conscious intending has discernable effects on a person's thoughts, feelings, and actions. In line with this perspective, research on goal setting and goal striving has demonstrated that the kind of intentions people form, and also how they regulate the implementation of those intentions, impacts subsequent experience and behaviour. Furthermore, the degree of intentionality that people ascribed to others impacts how people think, feel, and act toward others. In other words, different kinds of intending as well as ascriptions of intentionality lead to different kinds of effects on people's thoughts, feelings, and actions. This is a discovery that represents an important cornerstone to the theoretical and empirical analysis of volition. Furthermore, this discovery has important applied implications when it comes to answering questions whether people should try to influence their own thoughts, feelings, and actions via forming intentions.

Importantly, social and personality psychologists' perspective on voluntary action also allows for the possibility that voluntary action can proceed without accompanying conscious intending. As recent research demonstrates, thoughts, feelings, and behaviour that carry features of goal-directedness can emerge directly without a person's conscious intent. The same is true for making inferences about the intentionality of others' thoughts, feelings, and behaviour.

Recognizing that voluntary thoughts, feelings, and behaviour can be guided by conscious intentions, but may also occur without such guidance allows one to move ahead and raise intriguing questions that place the two forms of volition in relation to each other (e.g. How does consciously guided voluntary action differ from automatic voluntary action? How can consciously guided voluntary action moderate automatic voluntary action or vice versa?). It is these types of questions social-personality psychologists have just started to address and will be concerned with in the years to come.

References

Ajzen, I. (1985) From intentions to actions: a theory of planned behaviour. In Kuhl, J. & Beckmann, J. (eds), *Action control: from cognition to behaviour*. Heidelberg: Springer-Verlag, pp. 11–39.

Ames, C. & Archer, J. (1988) Achievement goals in the classroom: students' learning strategies and motivation processes. *J Educat Psychol* **80**, 260–7.

Bach, K. (1978) A representation theory of action. *Philosoph Stud* **34**, 361–79.

Bandura, A. (1977) Self-efficacy: toward a unifying theory of behavioural change. *Psycholog Rev* **84**, 344–58.

Bandura, A. (1997) *Self-efficacy: the exercise of control.* New York: Freeman.

Bandura, A. & Schunk, D.H. (1981) Cultivating competence, self-efficacy and intrinsic interest through proximal self-motivation. *J Personality Soc Psychol* **41**, 586–98.

Bargh, J.A. (1990) Auto-motives: pre-conscious determinants of social interaction. In Higgins, E.T. & Sorrentino, R.M. (eds), *Handbook of Motivation and Cognition*, Vol. 2. New York: Guilford, pp. 93–130.

Bargh, J.A. (1994) The four horsemen of automaticity: Awareness, intention, efficiency, and control in social cognition. In R.S. Wyer Jr. & T.K. Srull (eds.), *Handbook of social cognition*. Vol. 1: Basic processes; Vol. 2: Applications (2nd ed., pp. 1–40). Hillsdale, NJ: Lawrence Erlbaum Associates.

Bargh, J.A. (1997) The automation of everyday life. In Wyer, R.S., Jr (ed.), *Advances in Social Cognition*, Vol. 10. Mahwah: Erlbaum, pp. 1–62.

Bargh, J.A. & Ferguson M.J. (2000) Beyond behaviourism: on the automation of higher mental processes. *Psycholog Bull* **126**, 925–45.

Bargh, J.A., Gollwitzer, P.M., Lee Chai, A, Barndollar, K. & Trötschel, R. (2001) Automating the will: nonconscious activation and pursuit of behavioural goals. *J Personality Soc Psychol* **81**, 1014–27.

Bayer, U.C. (2000) *Intentionalitätsurteile und seine Determinanten.* Talk held at the workshop "Voluntary action" at Delmenhorst, March 2000.

Beike, D.R. & Sherman, S.J. (1994) Social inference: Inductions, deductions, and analogies. In R.S. Wyer Jr. & T.K. Srull (eds.), *Handbook of social cognition*. Vol. 1: Basic processes; Vol. 2: Applications (2nd ed., pp. 209–85). Hillsdale, NJ: Lawrence Erlbaum Associates.

Block, N., Flanagan, O. & Güzeldere, G. (Eds) (1997) *The Nature of Consciousness: philosophical debates.* Cambridge: MIT Press.

Brandstätter, V., Lengfelder, A. & Gollwitzer, P. M. (2001) Implementation intentions and efficient action initiation. *J Personality Soc Psychol* **81**, 946–60.

Brehm, J.W. & Self, E.A. (1989) The intensity of motivation. *Ann Rev Psychol* **45**, 560–70.

Brooks, R.A. (1991) New approaches to robotics. *Science* **253**, 1227–32.

Brunstein, J.C., Schultheiss, O.C. & Maier, G.W. (1999) The pursuit of personal goals: a motivational approach to well-being and life adjustment. In Brandtstädter, J. & Lerner, R.M. (eds), *Action and Self-development: theory and research through the life span.* Thousand Oaks: Sage, pp. 169–96.

Cantor, N. & **Fleeson, W.** (1994) Social intelligence and intelligent goal pursuit: a cognitive slice of motivation. In Spaulding, W. (ed.), *Nebraska Symposium on Motivation*, Vol. 41. Lincoln: University of Nebraska Press, pp. 125–80.

Carver, C.S. & **Scheier, M.F.** (1998) *On the Self-regulation of Behaviour.* New York: Cambridge University Press.

Carver, C.S. & **Scheier, M.F.** (1999) Themes and issues in the self-regulation of behaviour. In Wyer, R.S. (ed.), *Advances in Social Cognition.* Mahwah: Erlbaum, pp. 1–105.

Chaiken, S. (1987) The heuristic model of persuasion. In Zanna, M.P., Olson, J.M. & Herman, C.P. (Eds), *Social Influence: the Ontario symposium*, Vol. 5. Hillsdale: Erlbaum, pp. 3–39.

Christensen, S.M. & **Turner, D.R.** (1993) *Folk Psychology and the Philosophy of Mind.* Hillsdale: Erlbaum.

Cochran, W. & **Tesser, A.** (1996) The 'what the hell' effect: some effects of goal proximity and goal framing on performance. In Martin, L. L. & Tesser, A. (eds), *Striving and Feeling.* Mahwah: Erlbaum, pp. 99–120.

Dweck, C.S. (1996) Implicit theories as organizers of goals and behaviour. In Gollwitzer, P.M. & Bargh, J.A. (eds), *The Psychology of Action: linking cognition and motivation to behaviour.* New York: Guilford, pp. 69–90.

Elliot, A.J. & **Church, M.A.** (1997) A hierarchical model of approach and avoidance achievement motivation. *J Personality Soc Psychol* **72**, 218–32.

Emmons, R.A. (1996) Striving and feeling: personal goals and subjective well-being. In Gollwitzer, P.M. & Bargh, J.A. (Eds), *The Psychology of Action: linking cognition and motivation to behaviour.* New York: Guilford Press, pp. 313–37.

Frankfurt, H. (1988) *The Importance of What we Care About.* Cambridge: Cambridge University Press.

Gilbert, D.T. (1998) Ordinary personology. In D.T. Gilbert & S.T. Fiske (eds.), *The Handbook of social psychology* (Vol. 2, 4th ed., pp. 89–150). New York, NY: McGraw-Hill.

Gollwitzer, P.M. (1986) The implementation of identity intentions. In Halisch, F. & Kuhl, J. (eds), *Motivation, Intention, and Action.* Heidelberg: Springer-Verlag, pp. 349–69.

Gollwitzer, P.M. (1990) Action phases and mind-sets. In Higgins, E.T. & Sorrentino, R.M. (Eds), *Handbook of Motivation and Cognition*, Vol. 2. New York: Guilford, pp. 53–92.

Gollwitzer, P.M. (1993) Goal achievement: the role of intentions. In Stroebe, W. & Hewstone, M. (eds), *European Review of Social Psychology*, Vol. 4. Chichester: John Wiley, pp. 141–85.

Gollwitzer, P.M. (1999) Implementation intentions: strong effects of simple plans. *Am Psycholog* **54**, 493–503.

Gollwitzer, P.M. & **Bayer, U.** (1999) Deliberative versus implemental mindsets in the control of action. In Chaiken, S. & Trope, Y. (eds), *Dual Process Theories in Social Psychology.* New York: Guilford, pp. 403–22.

Gollwitzer, P.M. & **Rohloff, U.** (1999) The speed of goal pursuit. In Wyer R. S. (ed.), *Advances in Social Cognition*, Vol. 12. Hillsdale: Erlbaum, pp. 147–59.

Gollwitzer, P.M. & **Schaal, B.** (1998) Metacognition in action: the importance of implementation intentions. *Personality Soc Psychol Rev* **2**, 124–36.

Gollwitzer, P.M., Heckhausen, H. & **Ratajczak, H.** (1990) From weighing to willing: approaching a change decision through pre- or postdecisional mentation. *Organizat Behav Human Decision Processes* **45**, 41–65.

Gollwitzer, P.M., Bayer, U., Scherer, M. & **Seifert, A.E.** (1999) A motivational-volitional perspective on identity development. In Brandtstädter, J. & Lerner, R.M. (Eds), *Action and Self-development.* Thousand Oaks: Sage, pp. 283–314.

Heckhausen, H. (1977) Achievement motivation and its constructs: a cognitive model. *Motiv Emotion* **1**, 283–329.

Heckhausen, H. (1991) *Motivation and Action.* Heidelberg: Springer-Verlag.

Heckhausen, H. & **Gollwitzer, P.M.** (1987) Thought contents and cognitive functioning in motivational versus volitional states of mind. *Motiv Emotion* **11**, 101–20.

Heckhausen, H. & **Kuhl, J.** (1985) From wishes to action: the dead ends and short cuts on the long way to action. In Frese, M. & Sabini, J. (eds), *Goal-directed Behaviour: the concept of action in psychology.* Hillsdale: Erlbaum, pp. 134–59.

Heider, F. (1958) *The Psychology of Interpersonal Relations.* New York: Wiley

Higgins, E. T. (1997) Beyond pleasure and pain. *Am Psychol* **52**, 1280–300.

James, W. (1890/1950) *Principles of Psychology*, 2 vols. New York: Dover.

Jeannerod, M. (1997) *The Cognitive Neuroscience of Action.* Oxford: Basil Blackwell.

Jones, E.E. & **Davis, K.E.** (1965) From acts to dispositions: the attribution process in person perception. In Berkowitz, L. (ed.), *Advances in Experimental and Social Psychology*, Vol. 2. New York: Academic Press, pp. 219–66.

Kelley, H.H. (1967) Attribution theory in social psychology. *Nebraska Symp Motiv* **14**, 192–241.

Kelley, H.H. (1973) The process of causal attribution. *Am Psychol* **28**, 107–28.

Kelso, J.A.S. (1995) *Dynamic Patterns: the self-organization of brain and behaviour.* Cambridge: MIT Press.

Klinger, E. (1977) *Meaning and Void.* Minneapolis: University of Minnesota Press.

Kuhl, J. (2000) A functional-design approach to motivation and self-regulation: the dynamics of personality systems interactions. In Boekaerts, M., Pintrich, P.R. & Zeidner, M. (eds), *Self-regulation: directions and challenges for future research.* New York: Academic Press, pp. 111–69.

Kuhl, J. & **Beckmann, J.** (1994) *Volition and Personality.* Göttingen: Hogrefe.

Kunda, Z. (1999) *Social Cognition. Making Sense of People.* Cambridge: MIT Press.

Lengfelder, A. & **Gollwitzer, P.M.** (2001) Reflective and reflexive action in frontal lobe patients. *Neuropsychol* **15**, 80–100.

Lewin, K., Dembo, T., Festinger, L.A. & **Sears, P.S.** (1944) Level of aspiration. In Hunt J. (ed.), *Personality and Personal Disorders.* New York: Ronald Press, pp. 333–78.

Libet, B. (1985) Unconscious cerebral initiative and the role of conscious will in voluntary action. *Behav Brain Sci* **8**, 529–66.

Little, B.R. (1983) Personal projects: a rationale and methods for investigation. *Environ Behav* **15**, 273–309.

Locke, E.A. & **Latham, G.P.** (1990) *A Theory of Goal Setting and Task Performance.* Englewood Cliffs: Prentice Hall.

Maes, P. (1994) Modeling adaptive autonomous agents. *Artific Life* **1**, 135–62.

Malle, B.F. (1999) How people explain behaviour: a new theoretical framework. *Personality Soc Psychol Rev* **3**, 23–48.

Malle, B.F. & **Knobe, J.** (1997) The folk concept of intentionality. *J Exp Soc Psychol* **33**, 101–21.

Malle, B.F., Moses, L.J. & **Baldwin, D.A.** (Eds) (2001) *Intentions and Intentionality: foundations of social cognition.* Cambridge: MIT Press.

McClelland, D.C. (1985) *Human Motivation.* Glenview, IL: Scott, Foreman.

McClelland, D.C., Koestner, R. & **Weinberger, J.** (1989) How do self-attributed and implicit motives differ? *Psycholog Rev* **96**, 690–702.

McGuire, W.J. (1969) The nature of attitudes and attitude change. In Lindzey, G. & Aronson, E. (eds), *Handbook of Social Psychology*, Vol. 3, 2nd edn. Reading: Addison-Wesley, pp. 136–314.

Mischel, W. (1973) Toward a cognitive social learning reconceptualization of personality. *Psycholog Rev* **80**, 252–83.

Murray, H. A. (1938) *Explorations in Personality*. New York: Oxford University Press.

Newton, D. (1974) Dispositional inference from effects of actions: effects chosen and effects foregone. *J Exp Soc Psychol* **10**, 487–96.

Nicholls, J.G. (1979) Quality and equality in intellectual development: the role of motivation in education. *Am Psychol* **34**, 1071–84.

Nisbett, R.E. & Wilson, T.D. (1977) Telling more than we can know: verbal reports on mental processes. *Psycholog Rev* **83**, 231–59.

Oettingen, G. (1996) Positive fantasy and motivation. In Gollwitzer, P.M. & Bargh, J.A. (eds), *The Psychology of Action: linking cognition and motivation to behaviour*. New York: Guilford, pp. 236–59.

Oettingen, G. (1999) Free fantasies about the future and the emergence of developmental goals. In Brandtstädter, J. & Lerner, R.M. (eds), *Action and Self-development: theory and research through the life span*. Thousand Oaks: Sage, pp. 315–42.

Oettingen, G. (2000) Expectancy effects on behaviour depend on the mode of thinking about the future. *Soc Cognit* **18**, 101–29.

Oettingen, G. & Gollwitzer, P.M. (2001) Goal setting and goal striving. In Tesser, A. & Schwarz, N. (eds), Intraindividual processes, *Blackwell Handbook of Social Psychology*, Vol. 1. Oxford: Blackwell, pp. 329–49.

Oettingen, G., Pak, H. & Schnetter, K. (2001) Self-regulation of goal-setting: turning free fantasies about the future into binding goals. *J Personality Soc Psychol* **80**, 736–53.

Petty, R.E. & Cacioppo, J.T. (1986) *Communication and Persuasion: central and peripheral routes to attitude change*. Berlin: Springer-Verlag.

Read, S.J., Vanman, E.J. & Miller, L.C. (1997) Connectionism, parallel constraint satisfaction processes, and Gestalt principles: (re)introducing cognitive dynamics to social psychology. *Rev Personality Soc Psychol* **1**, 26–53.

Ryan, R.M., Sheldon, K.M., Kasser, T. & Deci, E.L. (1996) All goals are not created equal: an organismic perspective on the nature of goals and their regulation. In Gollwitzer, P.M. & Bargh, J.A. (eds), *The Psychology of Action: linking cognition and motivation to behaviour*. New York: Guilford, pp. 7–26.

Sappington, A.A. (1990) Recent psychological approaches to the free will versus determinism issue. *Psycholog Bull* **108**, 19–29.

Scheier, M.F. & Carver, C.S. (1985) Optimism, coping, and health: assessment and implications of generalized outcome expectancies. *Hlth Psychol* **4**, 219–47.

Taylor, S.E., Pham, L.B., Rivkin, I.D. & Armor, D.A. (1998) Harnessing the imagination. *Am Psycholog* **53**, 429–39.

Tolman, E.C. (1925) Purpose and cognition: the determinants of animal learning. *Psycholog Rev* **32**, 285–97.

Uleman, J.S. (1999) Spontaneous versus intentional inferences in impression formation. In Chaiken, S. & Trope, Y. (eds), *Dual Process Theories in Social Psychology*. New York: Guilford, pp. 141–60.

Vallacher, R.R. & Wegner, D.M. (1987) What do people think they're doing? Action identification and human behaviour. *Psycholog Rev* **94**, 3–15.

Vallacher, R.R. & **Wegner, D.M.** (1989) Levels of personal agency: individual variation in action identification. *J Personality Soc Psychol* **57**, 660–71.

Wegner, D.M. & **Wheatley, T.P.** (1999) Why it feels as if we're doing things: sources of the experience of will. *Am Psychol* **54**, 480–92.

Weiner, B. (1985) 'Spontaneous' causal thinking. *Psycholog Bull* **97**, 74–84.

Weiner, B. (1986) *An Attributional Theory of Motivation and Emotion*. New York: Springer-Verlag.

Wicklund, R.A. & **Gollwitzer, P.M.** (1982) *Symbolic Self-completion*. Hillsdale: Erlbaum.

Wright, R.A. (1996) Brehm's theory of motivation as a model of effort and cardiovascular response. In Gollwitzer, P. M. & Bargh, J.A. (eds), *The Psychology of Action: linking cognition and motivation to behavior*. New York: Guildford, pp. 424–53.

SECTION II

BETWEEN CORTEX AND THE BASAL GANGLIA: NEUROSCIENTIFIC ACCOUNTS OF VOLUNTARY ACTION

GERHARD ROTH

The study of voluntary action has a long tradition in neurobiology and neurology, especially because of the consequences of impairment in the motor system, such as in Parkinson's disease or in Chorea Huntington. Usually, voluntary actions are experienced consciously and are accompanied by the feeling that they originate from within ourselves—as opposed to being a reflex. In more neurological and neurobiological terms, voluntary actions include all kinds of behaviour that can be started, restrained, or changed during its course and can vary in intensity. They can typically improve through practice, as in the case of driving a car, cycling, or playing the piano. Characteristically, they first require conscious control in the form of attention and concentration, and an explicit act of will, but the more they are perfected and stereotyped, the less they require conscious control, including an act of will. Interestingly—despite this process of automation and decoupling from consciousness—we still attribute these movements to ourselves.

Voluntary actions have long been viewed as being the exclusive product of the activity of the cortical *pyramidal system*, as opposed to the *extra-pyramidal system* comprising subcortical motor centres. The pyramidal system includes the primary motor, pre-motor, and supplementary motor cortex (SMA and pre-SMA), the posterior parietal cortex, and the pre-frontal cortex in ascending order of importance. Willed actions were understood as being prepared and initiated by the pre-frontal cortex as the highest control centre for planning and decisions, co-operating with the posterior parietal cortex responsible for the adaptation of planned actions to a given spatial context and the co-ordination between eye, arm, hand, and finger movements. Neural signals from these two executive centres are sent to the supplementary and pre-motor areas responsible for the global setting of more internally or more externally driven actions, respectively. These areas, in turn, activate the primary motor area responsible for controlling single muscles via the pyramidal tract (hence, pyramidal system), which descends from cortex to motor nuclei in the lower brainstem, and to motor segments within the spinal cord that serve specific sets of muscles.

The extra-pyramidal system, in the traditional sense, comprises the basal ganglia (putamen, nucleus caudatus, globus pallidus, substantia nigra, subthalamic nucleus), which activate brainstem and spinal motor centres through fibre tracts running outside the pyramidal tract (hence *extra-pyramidal system*). This system was believed to guide reflexive and instinct-driven movements that can occur without conscious control. Therefore, the traditional opposition between willed, conscious, flexible, cortically initiated and controlled versus unwilled, unconscious, subcortically-driven stereotyped movements.

More recently, however, this sharp distinction between the two systems has been abandoned. It has become increasingly clear that a close interaction between cortical and subcortical executive, pre-motor and motor centres is indispensable for executing voluntary actions. One reason for this conceptual change was the acknowledgement of the fact that many if not most of our daily movements are executed more or less automatically, either without any or with only accompanying awareness (i.e. I am aware of the fact that I just moved my arm to reach for a cup of coffee or to shift gears of my car—movements I did not consciously initiate and control). Nevertheless, these movements can be quite flexible and detailed and always involve the activity of the primary motor cortex necessary for fine motor control. Despite the low degree of awareness and the absence of an explicit act of will, we—upon being asked—attribute these movements to ourselves. If I miss the cup and spill the coffee, then I will be blamed (and will blame myself) for that mistake.

On the other hand, I may have a strong act of will to exert a certain action—but nothing happens. This can occur (as already discussed by William James) on a dark, cold morning when I actually need to get up early, but my limbic centres insist on continuing to sleep. Likewise, patients suffering from Parkinson's disease have the explicit will to rise from their seat or to walk, but are unable to do so—at least in the late stages of the disease. This demonstrates that a conscious act of will alone does not automatically lead to movement initiation. Importantly, in Parkinson patients, the 'defect' responsible for the inability to initiate voluntary movements is not located within the cortical executive and motor system, but subcortically in the basal ganglia, as part of the extra-pyramidal system.

From this it follows that the pre-frontal cortex, where plans of those actions emerge, is by itself incapable of sufficiently activating the cortical supplementary pre-motor and motor areas to generate the so-called readiness potential (German: *Bereitschaftspotential*). This negative potential was discovered by Kornhuber & Deecke in the sixties (Kornhuber & Deecke, 1965). Using standard EEG technique, it can best be recorded above the pre-motor and supplementary (including pre-SMA) motor area, and precedes any voluntary movement by 1–2 s. It consists of a first part that can be recorded on both sides of the cerebral hemispheres (called the *symmetrical* readiness potential) and a second one, best recorded on the hemisphere opposite to the moved limbs (the *lateralized* readiness potential). According to the present view, additional activity running from the basal ganglia to the supplementary and pre-motor cortex via thalamic relay nuclei is needed in order to build up a full readiness potential; accordingly, an effective readiness potential is generated only by combined cortical and subcortical activity.

It was the occurrence of the readiness potential 1–2 s before the onset of a voluntary movement that led the American neurobiologist Benjamin Libet to run his famous experiment on the 'free will' (Libet *et al.*, 1983), which stimulated much discussion and criticism afterwards. These experiments and their surprising outcome—that subcortical centres 'decided' about the initiation of a movement half a second before our 'willed' conscious decision—have been described in detail elsewhere (cf. Jeannerod, this volume). Because of much methodological criticism, Libet's experiments have been repeated recently by Haggard & Eimer (1999), essentially confirming the Libet *et al.*'s findings (1983). One crucial modification was that Haggard & Eimer used the more reliable lateralized readiness potential instead of the symmetrical readiness potential; another was the introduction of a 'free' choice between left and right side movements.

There is still much debate about the conclusions regarding the true nature of 'free will' that may or may not be drawn from these experiments. Nonetheless, the experimental findings by Libet *et al.* (1983) and Haggard & Eimer (1999) are fully consistent with the neurobiological and neurological knowledge that has accumulated as to the interaction between cortical and subcortical executive, pre-motor, and motor centres. In this sense, movements become 'willed' only if combined cortical and subcortical activity passes a certain threshold inside the supplementary motor area (more precisely pre-SMA). This is consistent with another finding by Libet, which showed that cortical activation must have a sufficient amplitude and duration in order to generate consciousness (Libet, 1990).

Despite these new findings being undisputed among neuroscientists, there are still differences in the emphasis placed on the role of either cortical or subcortical executive, pre-motor, and motor centres, as will become evident in the three chapters in Section II. In his article, Gerhard Roth admits that it is the (evolutionarily-speaking 'younger') prefrontal cortex, where plans of those actions emerge that are not sufficiently automatized, because they pose certain new problems and difficulties. Those plans, however, must pass subcortical censorship of the basal ganglia, which are in turn controlled by the limbic experiential memory (mainly the amygdala and hippocampal formation). The latter are to ensure that the action is in accordance with the stored evaluations of previous actions by the limbic system. This is to say, whether or not voluntary actions are actually carried out is subject to the 'decision' of subcortical brain regions, inaccessible to consciousness. This might offend our intuitions of rational, deliberating selves because they (i.e. their prefrontal cortex) do not have the final say in volition. From an evolutionary point of view, this appears to be highly functional: conscious plans need to check back with the limbic memory containing all our conscious and unconscious memories since our foetal life.

Rüdiger Seitz, in his article, emphasizes the role of cortical executive, pre-motor, and motor areas. As the emergence of volition is intimately connected to the evolutionary augmentation of the frontal lobe, the latter is likely to comprise the relevant processing cortical nodes subserving the generation of voluntary action. After description of the various methodological tools (PET, fMRI, EEG, MEG), Seitz asks how physical action can emerge from mental volition. For him, neuro-imaging data show that conscious motor behaviour engages the entire cortical circuitry related to movement performance inclusive of motor, pre-motor, and parietal cortex, as well as the supplementary motor area (SMA and pre-SMA) and the adjacent cingulate cortex. The processes related to the control of action—be it in relation to instruction, selection, or processing of imposed behavioural challenges—involves the dorso-lateral pre-frontal cortex. Clinical studies with patients suffering from frontal brain lesions (e.g. motor hemi-neglect) demonstrate this and how brain lesions interfere with voluntary actions. They do so by way of showing the modular organization of the brain and the multiplicity of subfunctions required for proper generation and execution of voluntary action. Seitz concludes with a hypothetical scheme of human sensorimotor control, according to which a medial initiation system (i.e. SMA, pre-SMA) mediates processing of information reflecting the subject's drive to act voluntarily, whereas the lateral evaluation system mediates processing of information external to the subject.

Marc Jeannerod in his chapter states: 'Voluntary actions are consciously represented actions'. He tries to specify the content of this sentence in the light of new research. Most endogenously produced motor representations are actually unconscious and have to be attributed to the agent afterwards by a slower system. This means that the role of consciousness in actions that are highly automatized is *monitoring*. However, whenever an obstacle in movement execution arises, this produces a shift to another type of action, namely from an automatic transfer of a representation, into execution, to a consciously performed action. Consciousness of an action, according to that view, occurs as a consequence of lack of completion or failure of an action. The price to be paid for conscious control (and correction) is that consciously monitored actions are much cruder and generally more inaccurate than automatized movements. Jeannerod refers to the experiments with schizophrenics as an example of what happens when that monitoring breaks down. To be capable of attributing actions to oneself, ultimately, seems to amount to the knowledge that one is the author of intentions and may correct undue courses of actions. If one cannot detect oneself as the author of an intention, the latter must pertain to somebody else (either in reality or because of a delusion).

Despite all progress in elucidating the neural basis of voluntary actions, much remains to be studied. For example, the exact way in which limbic centres (hippocampus, amygdala, ventral tegmental area, basal forebrain) influence the basal ganglia is basically still unclear. Do they simply give 'go–no go' commands, or do they select between the very many movement patterns assumed to be stored in the basal ganglia? The same questions hold for the meaning (instructive? permissive?) of the dopamine signal sent by the substantia nigra to the striatum, without which no voluntary movement can occur. Also, it is unknown how the basal ganglia, via thalamic relay nuclei, act upon the cortical supplementary and premotor areas such that a sufficiently strong readiness potential forms. Do they increase the firing rates of neurons within these areas or do they assist to synchronize them? Last, but not least, it remains enigmatic how the conscious act experienced as 'act of will' (be it a necessary step in the control of voluntary actions or an epiphenomenon) arises from the activity of cortical networks. In other words, much work remains to be done in close collaboration between neuroscientists, psychologists, and even philosophers and social scientists.

References

Haggard, P. & **Eimer, M.** (1999) On the relation between brain potentials and the awareness of voluntary movements. *Exp Brain Res* **126**, 128–33.

Kornhuber, H.H. & **Deecke L.** (1965) Hirnpotentialäderungen bei Willkürbewegungen und passiven Bewegungen des Menschen: Bereitschaftspotential and reafferente Potentiale. *Pflügers Archiv für Gesamte Physiologie* **284**, 1–17.

Libet, B. (1990) Cerebral processes that distinguish conscious experience from unconscious mental functions. In: J.C. Eccles und O.D. Creutzfeldt (Hrsg.), The principles of design and operation of the brain. *Pontificae Academiae Scientiarum Scripta Varia* **78**, 185–202.

Libet, B., Gleason, C.A., Wright, E.W. & **Pearl, D.K.** (1983) Time of conscious intention to act in relation to onset of cerebral activity (readiness potential): the unconscious initiation of a freely voluntary act. *Brain* **106**, 623–42.

CHAPTER 5

THE INTERACTION OF CORTEX AND BASAL GANGLIA IN THE CONTROL OF VOLUNTARY ACTIONS

GERHARD ROTH

1 Introduction

Voluntary actions are accompanied by the feeling that they come from within ourselves—as opposed to being reflexes. When I am reaching for a cup of coffee, I have the strong impression that it is *me* who planned and executed this action, and even when I did this while concentrating on the interesting talk going on, I nevertheless attribute the action to me and I will feel responsible for the possible consequences of the action (e.g. when I failed to grasp the cup and the coffee spills over the table). However, when my body executes reflexes (e.g. eye blink reflex, knee-jerk reflex), I will usually say that this was not me, but my eyelid or my knee, and usually I do not feel and am not regarded as responsible for such reflex actions.

Neurobiologically, voluntary actions in the above sense are controlled by the complex interaction of cortical areas, traditionally designated the *pyramidal system*, and subcortical centres, traditionally called the *extra-pyramidal system*. Both systems used to be contrasted functionally in the sense of conscious versus unconscious control of actions. The traditional view is that the cerebral cortex and, above all, the pre-frontal cortex—as the 'seat' of conscious planning and control of action—are the 'central executor' of willed actions (cf. Goschke, this volume). As we will see, however, this view is incorrect, because both systems—the pyramidal and the extra-pyramidal system—work together very closely in both kinds of action control. Inside the brain, there is no such thing as a single 'central executor'.

The following presents recent findings as regards the function of those diverse areas and the interaction between them. It shows that cortical areas do not have the final word in volition, but have to check back, in a complex manner, with the limbic experiential memory, which is itself inaccessible to consciousness.

2 Cortical motor and executive areas

According to current knowledge, the following areas participate in the preparation and execution of voluntary actions (e.g. eye, lip, head, hand, or limb movements): The *primary motor cortex* (Brodmann Area BA 4), the *dorso-lateral pre-motor cortex* (BA 6), the *medial pre-motor cortex* consisting of the *supplementary motor area proper* (SMA), and the *pre-SMA* rostral to SMA (both part of BA 6), and the *rostral* and *caudal cingulate motor area* (*rCMA, cCMA*). Eye movements are controlled by the *frontal eye field, FEF* (part of BA 8), and the *supplementary eye field, SEF* (part of BA 6), (Creutzfeldt, 1983; Jeannerod, 1997; Passingham, 1993; see Figs 5.1 and 5.2).

The primary motor cortex is located directly in front of the central sulcus of the cerebral cortex (Fig. 5.1). It regulates individual muscles (except the eye muscles), especially the so-called distal muscles (e.g. those of the fingers) of the contralateral body side. It is soma-totopically organized ('motor homunculus') in the sense that the muscles of the body are represented in a spatially systematic fashion, albeit 'upside down' from the dorso-medial (i.e. upper inner) portion of the primary motor cortex (foot, leg) to its ventrolateral (i.e. lower outer) portion (mouth region, lips, and tongue; Fig. 5.3).

In front of the primary motor cortex we find the dorso-lateral pre-motor cortex. It controls the 'proximal' musculature of the limbs (i.e. those close to the torso), the head, and the torso, as well as arm-hand-eye co-ordination (Rizzolatti *et al.*, 2000). This area has to do with the planning and selection of learned kinds of movement. Here, we find cells in monkeys that fire when the animal is preparing a movement. Cells are also active when the animal has a visual-motor task to learn (e.g. to operate a certain lever under certain conditions). As a whole, the lateral pre-motor cortex is more likely to be active when an *externally stimulated* behaviour is being planned and/or prepared.

On the inner side of the cerebral cortex is the medial pre-motor cortex, that is, the supplementary motor areas (SMA proper and pre-SMA) and the cingulate motor areas (rCMA, cCMA; Fig. 5.2). SMA proper and pre-SMA are also involved in the planning and selection of movements. While previously SMA was considered to control *internally generated* (e.g. memory-guided), motivationally-driven and imagined movements (Roland *et al.*, 1980), today this function is ascribed to pre-SMA only (Decety *et al.*, 1994) and SMA proper is believed to be active at real movements only. SMA proper is connected to the primary motor cortex, while pre-SMA is connected to the pre-frontal cortex (Rizzolatti *et al.*, 1996). Furthermore, the two areas receive different thalamic inputs: SMA proper from the ventrolateral thalamic nucleus, which exerts motor functions, and pre-SMA from the dorso-medial and anteroventral thalamic nuclei, which have executive and limbic-motivational functions. These differences in cortical and subcortical inputs support the assumption that SMA proper is a pre-motor region, while pre-SMA has executive and motivational functions. (The position and function of the rostral and caudal cingulate motor areas are debated and are not further considered here.)

The posterior parietal cortex (BA 5, BA 7; Fig. 5.1) is closely connected with the lateral pre-motor cortex. It is involved in bodily sensations, spatial perception, and orientation, with visual spatial attention, arm-hand-eye co-ordination, and generally in the planning and preparation of actions, especially the preparation of reaching and grasping movements (Jeannerod, 1997; Passingham, 1993; Rizzolatti *et al.*, 2000). Lesions in the ventral posterior parietal cortex lead to sustained disturbances of the design of movements, known as *ideatoric* and *ideomotor apraxia* (Freund, 1995).

Of particular importance for the planning of actions is the pre-frontal cortex in the broader sense. Anatomically, it is divided into two parts: the *dorso-lateral* PFC or *PFC*

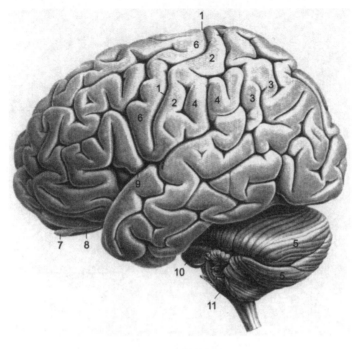

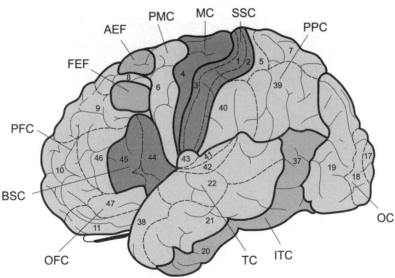

Figure 5.1 Lateral (left) view of the human brain showing lateral cortical areas and the cerebellum. Numbers in lower figure refer to cytoarchitectonic cortical fields according to Brodmann. *Abbreviations*: AEF = anterior eye field; BSC = Broca's speech centre; FEF = frontal eye field; ITC = inferotemporal cortex; MC = primary motor cortex; OC = occipital cortex; OFC = orbito-frontal cortex, PFC = pre-frontal cortex; PMC = dorso-lateral premotor cortex; PPC = posterior parietal cortex; SSC = somatosensory cortex; TC = temporal cortex (from Nieuwenhuys *et al.*, 1989, modified).

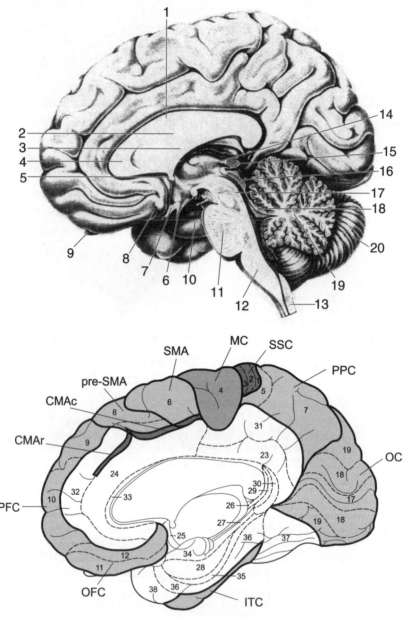

Figure 5.2 Medial view of the human brain showing medial cortical areas. Numbers in upper figure refer to cyto-architectonic cortical fields according to Brodmann. *Abbreviations*: CMAc = caudal cingulate motor area; CMAr = rostral cingulate motor area; ITC = inferotemporal cortex; MC = motor cortex; OC = occipital cortex; OFC = orbito-frontal cortex; pre-SMA = pre-supplementary motor area; PFC = pre-frontal cortex; PPC = posterior parietal cortex; SMA = supplementary motor area; SSC = somatosensory cortex (from Nieuwenhuys *et al.*, 1989, modified).

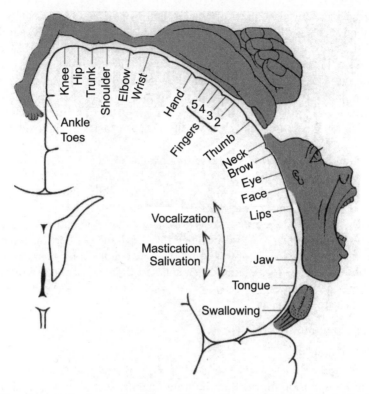

Figure 5.3 Motor homunculus. See text for further explanation (from Benninghoff, 1994; after Penfield & Rasmussen, 1950; modified).

proper (BA 9, 10, and 46), and the orbito-frontal cortex, *OFC* (BA 11, 12, 13, and 14; Fig. 5.1), each of which has different inputs and functions. The PFC proper, in turn, is divided into a dorsal and a lateral-ventral portion. The dorsal portion of the PFC receives cortical inputs primarily from the posterior parietal cortex mediating information about head, neck, face, body, and eye movements, as well as about the location of the body and of action-relevant objects in space. Correspondingly, it is assumed that the dorsal PFC has to do with the planning of movements in space, with spatial learning, with the temporal analysis of events relevant to actions, and with 'strategic' thought (Kim & Shadlen, 1999; Petrides, 2000). The lateral-ventral portion of the PFC receives its major cortical input from the temporal lobe mediating information about complex auditory and visual perception, for instance, recognition of objects and scenes (Wilson *et al.*, 1993). The lateral-ventral PFC is more involved in the comparison and evaluation of events, decisions upon actions, and the preparation of actions (Passingham *et al.*, 2000; Petrides, 2000).

The orbito-frontal cortex, OFC, is the only isocortical (i.e. six-layered) part of the limbic system. It receives—among others—input from the perirhinal and parahippocampal cortex (involved in the organization of declarative memory), as well as from other limbic centres, such as the amygdala, the ventral tegmental area (VTA), and the 'limbic' anterior and medial nuclei of the thalamus. In contrast to the PFC proper, the OFC has to do with emotional and motivational aspects, and the conscious evaluation of positive and negative consequences of behaviour. Lesions in the OFC lead to the loss of conscious emotions, of the recognition of consequences of particular actions, and of the ability to comprehend socially communicative contexts, such as the meaning of represented scenes of facial expressions. Patients with damage to the OFC are incapable of acting according to their knowledge about the consequences (especially negative ones) of their own behaviour (Bechara *et al.*, 1997).

Closely connected to the OFC is the anterior cingulate cortex (BA 24; Fig. 5.2). It has an important mediating role between cortical-cognitive and limbic-emotional functions, particularly regarding attention, the sensation of pain, error monitoring, and error correction (Carter *et al.*, 1998; Gehring & Knight, 2000).

The cortical motor and pre-motor areas listed above have one output in the pyramidal tract (*tractus cortico-spinalis*), which includes 15% of the entire cortical motor output; hence, the name pyramidal motor system. The pyramidal tract consists of roughly 2 million fibres and runs to the motor segments in the spinal cord that innervate distal muscles of the limbs. However, the majority of cortical motor output runs to subcortical motor centres, namely:

- the corpus striatum;
- thalamic relay nuclei;
- the nucleus ruber ('red nucleus') situated in the midbrain and (via projections to the spinal cord) responsible for rhythmic body movements, such as walking and swimming;
- relay nuclei in the pons (and from there to the cerebellum) and in the medulla oblongata (and from there to the spinal cord);
- to the inferior olive in the medulla oblongata (and from there to the cerebellum).

Contrary to common belief mentioned above, the cortical areas including the 'executive' pre-frontal cortex, alone are *not* able to elicit voluntary actions. More precisely, they cannot sufficiently activate the pre-motor and motor area such that the intended actions can occur. This is most clearly seen in patients with Parkinson's disease. These patients are characterized by tremor, muscular rigidity and difficulty, and eventually the inability to initiate voluntary actions. Their primary, action-specific deficit does *not* concern cortical, but rather subcortical motor centres, more precisely, the basal ganglia. From this and other facts it is evident that cortical motor and pre-motor areas require the assistance of the basal ganglia to execute voluntary actions.

3   Subcortical motor centres relevant for the execution of voluntary actions

Our daily life consists of a large number of actions that are highly automatized and executed without specific planning and decisions, and without paying attention to it. These automatized kinds of actions are generated by the joint action of the pre-motor and

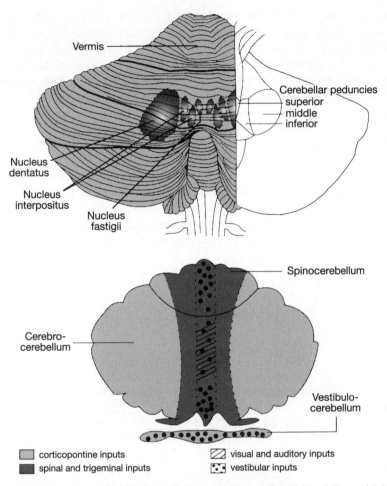

Figure 5.4 (Above) Dorsal view of the human cerebellum, with the so-called deep cerebellar nuclei. (Below) Schematic drawing of the functional organization of the cerebellum (after Kandel *et al.*, 1991, modified).

primary motor cortex and the *cerebellum* (Figs 5.1 and 5.4). The cerebellum, more precisely the lateral hemispheres of the cerebellum (the *cerebro-cerebellum*), influences the motor and pre-motor cortex areas via the 'deep' cerebellar nucleus dentatus and the ventrolateral thalamic nucleus. The cerebellum plays an important role in sequencing and 'smoothing' motor reactions, and in motor learning, especially for actions that are automatized with increasing practice. This is also the case for linguistic reactions such as quick answers to keywords (Leiner *et al.*, 1995; Ivry & Fiez, 2000).

However, many other actions in our daily life require some (although often trivial) selection and decision—be those conscious or unconscious (rising from a chair now and not a minute later; reaching for the sugar first and then for the milk at coffee-drinking). Such decision-bound actions require the activity of the *basal ganglia*.

The basal ganglia include the dorsal *corpus striatum* ('striped body') the dorsal *globus pallidus* ('pale sphere'), the *substantia nigra* ('black substance'), and the *nucleus subthalamicus* ('nucleus below the thalamus'). It was long assumed that the basal ganglia constitute a kind of primitive motor system to control the motor functions of bodily posture; later it was believed that they are responsible for automatized movement processes, such as 'instinct-driven' actions. Today, the basal ganglia are regarded as a system that, along with the cortical pyramidal system, is indispensable for any kind of voluntary actions that are *not* highly automatized. Their special role consists in the control of voluntary actions by selecting appropriate motor actions, and by comparing the action's goal and course with previous experience (see below).

The corpus striatum (usually called 'striatum') is located deep inside the telencephalon and consists of the nucleus caudatus and the putamen. It represents the largest subcortical cell mass containing about 100 million neurons (Fig. 5.5). Most of them are medium-sized, have dendrites covered with spines, and use the inhibitory transmitter GABA (gamma-amino-butyric acid). Nucleus caudatus and putamen are identical in structure,

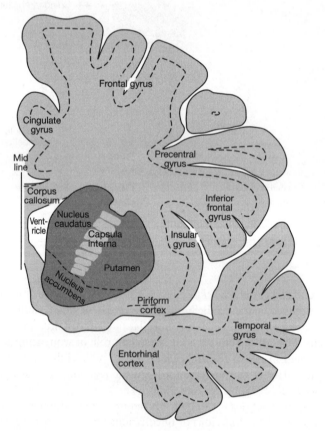

Figure 5.5 Cross-section through one hemisphere of the telencephalon at the level of the dorsal striatum (i.e. nucleus caudatus and putamen) and the ventral striatum/nucleus accumbens (after Mai *et al.*, 1997, modified).

but receive different cortical input (see below). The globus pallidus (mostly called 'pallidum') is part of the diencephalon, but situated in close proximity to the striatum. The pallidum contains about 600,000 neurons, and consists of a medial portion called *globus pallidus internus* and a lateral portion called *globus pallidus externus*, which in primates, including man, are separated by the lamina medullaris medialis and receive different inputs from the striatum (see below). The large-celled nucleus subthalamicus is situated in the caudal diencephalon and is in close contact with the substantia nigra situated in the ventral midbrain (tegmentum). The substantia nigra consists of a dorsal, cell-rich portion, the *pars compacta*, and a ventral portion, the *pars reticulata*, containing relatively few cells. The substantia nigra pars compacta contains neurons that synthesize the neurotransmitter (neuromodulator) dopamine and project to the dorsal striatum. The specific role of these neurons will be described below.

4   Pathways between cortex and basal ganglia

With regard to the control of voluntary action, the basal ganglia are linked to the cerebral cortex via a number of separate, parallel loops (Alexander *et al.*, 1990; Nieuwenhuys *et al.*, 1989; Fig. 5.6A–C).

In the first loop (part of the so-called dorsal loop; Fig. 5.6A), the anterior portion of the posterior parietal cortex (aPPc), the frontal eye field (FEF), the dorso-lateral pre-frontal cortex (dlPFC), and pre-SMA, which are all involved in action planning and preparation, project to the central portion of the striatum (i.e. medial putamen, mPU), which via the central portion of the pallidum (cGP) projects to the ventral anterior thalamic nucleus (VA) and the parvocellular ('small-celled') portion of the mediodorsal thalamic nucleus (pMD), and from there back to the cortical areas of origin.

In the second loop (another part of the *dorsal* loop; Fig. 5.6B), the motor cortex (MC), the dorso-lateral pre-motor (dlPMC) and medial pre-motor cortex (SMA proper), and the posterior portion of the posterior parietal cortex (pPPC), which all have to do with the execution of movements, project to the lateral striatum (i.e. the lateral portion of the putamen, lPU) and via the lateral pallidum (lGP) to the ventrolateral thalamic nucleus (VL), and back to the cortical areas of origin.

The third loop (also called *ventral* loop; Fig. 5.6C) is formed in the way that the orbito-frontal (OFC), anterior cingulate (AC), and inferior temporal cortex (ITC), which are involved in complex cognitive, emotionally, and motivationally relevant information, project to the medial portion of the striatum (i.e. nucleus caudatus, NC), as well as to the ventral striatum/nucleus accumbens (NA) and from there to the dorso-medial pallidum (dmGP). This nucleus projects to the magnocellular ('large-celled'), ventromedial portion of the mediodorsal thalamic nucleus (mMD), which in turn projects back to the orbito-frontal, anterior cingulate, and inferior temporal cortex.

All these pathways from the above-mentioned cortical areas to the basal ganglia are excitatory using glutamate as transmitter.

Within the basal ganglia, a complicated process arises from the interplay between inhibition and excitation (Fig. 5.7). The striatum exerts an *inhibitory* influence (via GABAergic neurons) both on the substantia nigra pars reticulata and the globus pallidus internus, and these structures, in turn, inhibit the nucleus ventralis anterior, the nucleus

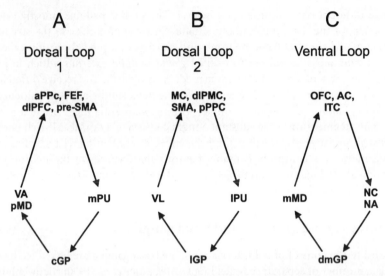

Figure 5.6 Schematic diagram of loops between cortex, basal ganglia, and thalamic relay nuclei. (A) Dorsal loop between posterior parietal cortex, frontal eye field, dorso-lateral pre-frontal cortex, pre-SMA, central striatum, central pallidum, ventral anterior, and parvocellular mediodorsal thalamic nucleus. (B) Dorsal loop between motor cortex, dorso-lateral pre-motor cortex, SMA proper, posterior parietal cortex, (C) ventral loop between orbito-frontal , anterior cingulate and inferior temporal cortex, medial striatum (i.e. nucleus caudatus), ventral striatum/nucleus accumbens, ventral pallidum, and magnocellular mediodorsal thalamic nucleus. *Abbreviations*: AC = anterior cingulate cortex; aPPC = posterior parietal cortex; cGP = central portion of the globus pallidus; dPMC = dorso-lateral pre-motor cortex; dlPFC = dorso-lateral pre-frontal cortex; dmGP = dorso-medial globus pallidus; FEF = frontal eye field; ITC = inferior temporal cortex; lGP = lateral globus pallidus; lPU = lateral portion of the putamen; MC = motor cortex; mDM = magnocellular portion of the mediodorsal thalamic nucleus; NC = nucleus caudatus; OFC = orbito-frontal cortex; pMD = parvocellular portion of the mediodorsal thalamic nucleus; pPPC = posterior portion of the posterior parietal cortex; pre-SMA = pre-supplementary motor area; SMA = supplementary motor area; VA = ventral anterior thalamic nucleus; VL = ventrolateral thalamic nucleus.

ventralis lateralis, and the nucleus dorso-medialis (parvocellular section) of the thalamus. These send *excitation* (via glutamate) back to the cortex—more specifically, the nucleus dorso-medialis (parvocellular section) to the PFC, and the nucleus ventralis anterior and lateralis, to the SMA/pre-SMA and PMC. Simultaneously, the striatum inhibits the globus pallidus externus. This centre inhibits the globus pallidus internus, as well as the substantia nigra pars reticulata. The globus pallidus internus, just as the substantia nigra pars reticulata, inhibits the mentioned thalamic nuclei. Thus, we have a system of pathways here that consists of an excitatory segment (cortex), an inhibitory segment (striatum), a second inhibitory segment (globus pallidus externus), a third inhibitory segment (globus pallidus internus and substantia nigra), and finally a second excitatory segment (thalamus).

These loops inside the basal ganglia incorporate two supplementary loops. In the first of these the striatum inhibits the substantia nigra pars compacta, which reacts back via dopaminergic neurons on the striatum and influences inhibitory output neurons of the

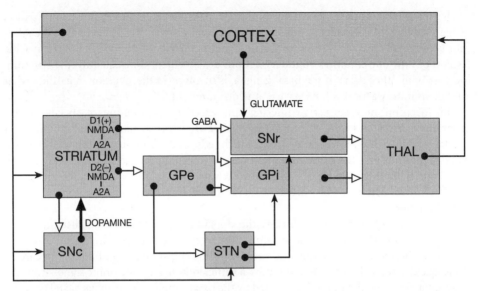

Figure 5.7 Pathways among the components of basal ganglia, their afferents from the cortex and their efferents to the thalamus and cortex. Excitatory pathways mediated by the transmitter glutamate are represented by black arrowheads, inhibitory pathways mediated by the transmitter GABA are represented by white arrowheads. The striatum receives a dopaminergic input (thick black arrow) from the substantia nigra pars compacta.
Abbreviations: A2A = adenosine receptors; D1/D2 = dopaminergic receptor types; GPe = globus pallidus, outer part; GPi = globus pallidus, inner part; NMDA = glutamatergic receptor type; SNc = substantia nigra, pars compacta; SNr = substantia nigra, pars reticulata; STN = nucleus subthalamicus; THAL = thalamus. See text for details.

striatum that send their fibres to the substantia nigra pars reticulata and the globus pallidus internus and externus (see above). These inhibitory neurons have two different receptors ('docking points') for the neuromodulator *dopamine*: one through which dopamine *excites* (the D1 receptor) and another (the D2 receptor) through which dopamine inhibits the inhibitory striatal output neurons. Consequently, through dopamine via D1 receptors, the inhibiting effect of the striatum output neurons on the substantia nigra pars reticulata and the globus pallidus internus is intensified, while via the D2 receptors their inhibiting effect is reduced.

The second supplementary loop results as the globus pallidus externus inhibits the nucleus subthalamicus, which, in turn, excites (via glutamate) the globus pallidus internus and the substantia nigra pars reticulata resulting in an intensification of their inhibitory effect on the thalamic relay nuclei.

The entire information flow associated with planning and controlling actions through the basal ganglia is thus determined by an extraordinarily complex interplay between excitatory (glutamatergic) and inhibitory (GABAergic) input, in which dopamine intervenes as a *modulator*, that is, increasing or decreasing the inhibitory effect of GABAergic striatal output neurons. Increased dopamine secretion into the striatum through neurons of the substantia nigra pars compacta ultimately results in a *dis*-inhibition of the thalamic nuclei, which project back to the cerebral cortex, and thus leads to an increase of cortical motor activity.

The linkage of numerous, primarily inhibitory paths allows extremely fine co-ordination of the 'enabling' of voluntary actions within the basal ganglia. It is believed that the striatum is essentially involved in motor learning and is the site of memories for the specific fashion of how our countless voluntary actions are executed. Consequently, the striatum, together with other parts of the basal ganglia, is involved in the 'decision' regarding what kind of voluntary action will be started at which moment.

This 'decision' may consist in filtering and selective disinhibiting of specific action programmes situated in the striatum (Graybiel et al., 1994). It requires the inhibition of striatal inhibitory D2-projection neurons, which reduces the inhibitory effect of the globus pallidus internus and the substantia nigra pars reticulata upon the thalamic relay nuclei. These nuclei are then capable of sufficiently exciting the pre-motor and motor areas such that a voluntary action can be started. As mentioned before, these areas alone are unable to start the action.

In patients with Parkinson's disease, the dopaminergic cells in the substantia nigra pars compacta that project to the striatum are largely degenerated (the disease becomes manifest, when 80% of dopaminergic neurons in the substantia nigra have disappeared). Consequently, the striatum does not receive a sufficiently strong 'dopamine signal' from the substantia nigra and the inhibition exerted by the basal ganglia on the thalamic relay nuclei is not removed. The patients have the *will* to initiate a voluntary action (e.g. to rise from a seat or walk), but are unable to do so. Only after administration of *Levodopa*—a precursor that will be metabolized in the brain into dopamine—are the patients temporarily capable of initiating and executing voluntary actions.

It is still unclear what the precise role of the dopamine signal from the substantia nigra to the striatum is. It could have a permissive function allowing, so to speak, striatal networks to execute programmes that have already been chosen or it could play an 'instructive' role by participating more specifically in the 'decision' (Graybiel et al., 1994).

5   The readiness potential

This necessity of sufficient activation of cortical pre-motor and motor areas by the basal ganglia (via thalamic relay nuclei) is best seen in the so-called readiness potential (Fig. 5.8). This slow negative cortical potential, which is filtered out from the electroencephalogram (EEG) was discovered and first described by Kornhuber & Deecke (1965; cf. also Lang et al., 1991; Cunnington et al., 1997; Brunia & van Boxtel, 2000). Slow negative cortical potentials are interpreted as activation of cortical neuronal networks. The readiness potential consists of two components. The first is a *symmetrical* component, that is, one that is equally strong in the left and right cerebral hemisphere, and is best recorded from the scalp above SMA and pre-SMA. It starts 1–2 s before the onset of motor activity (e.g. arm or finger movement). The second component is the *lateralized* readiness potential. It is strongest in the cerebral hemisphere opposite (contralateral) to the part of the limbs to be moved (note that the right limbs are controlled by the left cerebral hemisphere and vice versa). It is best recorded above the lateral pre-motor and the primary motor area. It starts 700–500 ms before the onset of motor activity and is the direct predictor of that activity.

It is now widely assumed that both the symmetrical and lateralized readiness potential reflect the synchronized activity of neurons in SMA/pre-SMA, and in the dorso-lateral pre-motor and motor cortex, respectively. The symmetrical readiness potential is essentially driven by the neuronal activity coming from the basal ganglia via the thalamic relay neurons. Accordingly, it is weak or absent in patients with Parkinson's disease (Cunnington *et al.*, 1997; Brunia & van Boxtel, 2000).

6   The function of the 'ventral' loop and of the limbic system

As shown, the execution of voluntary actions largely depends on whether or not the parts of the basal ganglia described 'enable' the action to be performed. Here, the release of dopamine through cells in the substantia nigra pars compacta plays an essential role. The question remains, what occasions the substantia nigra to secrete dopamine. The substantia nigra pars compacta by itself does not possess any known higher cognitive, emotional, motivational, or memory functions that would enable it to contribute to the 'decision' about which voluntary action will be executed at which moment and in what manner. Apparently, this must occur through a different system that mediates those complex functions.

This system is represented by the so-called *ventral* or *limbic loop* between the cortex and centres of the limbic system, above all the ventral striatum/nucleus accumbens, the ventral pallidum. As already described above, at cortical levels, this 'ventral' loop originates in both the orbito-frontal cortex and the anterior gyrus cinguli, both of which project to the

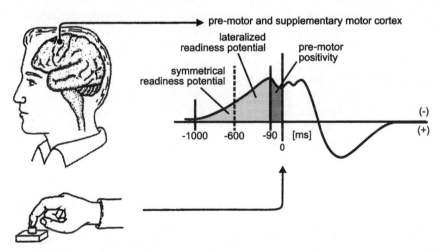

Figure 5.8 Origin of the readiness potential ('Bereitschaftspotential') neurons in the dorso-lateral and supplementary motor cortex become active about 1000 ms before the onset of a voluntary finger movement. The first to appear is the symmetrical readiness potential; about 600 ms before the onset of movement, the lateralized readiness potential begins to be built up. The motor neurons initiating the motor action fire about 90 ms before the onset of movement (time 0). See text for details (after Kandel *et al.*, 1991, modified).

ventral striatum/nucleus accumbens. The nucleus accumbens, in turn, projects to the ventral pallidum, which, in partial 'co-operation' with the substantia nigra pars reticulata, projects to the mediodorsal thalamic nucleus (magnocellular and parvocellular portion), and this nucleus projects back to the orbito-frontal cortex and to the anterior gyrus cinguli. This closes the 'ventral loop'.

The nucleus accumbens, together with the VTA and the lateral hypothalamus, comprises the *meso-limbic system*. This system dominates the registration and processing of natural rewarding events and apparently represents the cerebral reward system, or at least an important part of this system (Panksepp, 1998; Schultz, 1998; Rolls, 1999; Tremblay & Schultz, 1999). Intra-cranial self-stimulation leads to conditions marked by strong pleasure in rats and humans, but only when an organism is in a condition of *need*. It also serves as the location of drug activity, including alcohol and psychedelic drugs. The latter raise the dopamine level in the VTA or the nucleus accumbens. However, according to recent research, it appears that raising the dopamine level is necessary only for the *development* of addiction, but not for its maintenance, which appears to be mediated by glutamatergic mechanisms. In the light of these findings, dopamine seems to function more as a signal or predictor for the association of rewards and certain events, rather than as a 'reward substance' itself. Such reward substances apparently are the opium-like endorphins and enkephalins produced by the brain (Spanagel & Weiss, 1999).

Important in this context is the fact that the nucleus accumbens, as a major centre of the 'ventral' loop, receives input not only from the orbito-frontal and cingulate cortex, but also from the ventral tegmental area, from the hippocampus, the entorhinal, perirhinal, and parahippocampal cortex (EPPC), and the amygdala. Hippocampus and EPPC are regarded as the 'organizers' of the declarative (i.e. episodic and semantic) memory. The task of organizing the episodic memory is assigned to the hippocampus, that of the semantic memory to the EPPC (Tulving & Markowitsch, 1998; Aggleton & Brown, 1999; Markowitsch, 2000). The *amygdala* plays a central role in the production and control of emotions. It is considered the core region of the *evaluation of behaviour directed by fear and anxiety*. Lesions of the amygdala lead to the omission of the fear or anxiety components of events (Aggleton, 1992, 1993; Bechara *et al.*, 1995; LeDoux, 1996, 2000).

Another important section of the ventral loop is the ventral pallidum, which not only receives inputs from the ventral striatum/nucleus accumbens, as mentioned above, but also directly from the amygdala, from the EPPC, the VTA, the substantia nigra and parts of the basal forebrain (septum, nucleus basalis Meynert, nucleus of the diagonal band of Broca). The ventral pallidum projects within the ventral loop to the mediodorsal nucleus of the thalamus, which projects to the pre-frontal and cingulate cortex, as well as to the amygdala and the VTA.

As a whole, the meso-limbic system (VTA, nucleus accumbens, lateral hypothalamus), the amygdala, and the declarative memory system (hippocampus and EPPC) represent the *experiential memory*, which functions largely unconsciously, evaluating everything the body has done at the brain's bidding since the womb in terms of *good/pleasant/advantageous* or *bad/unpleasant/disadvantageous*, and then storing these evaluations along with the concrete conditions and consequences of the action. It is believed that hippocampus and EPPC process and organize information about details and the context of events in a rather 'unemotional' fashion, whereas the amygdala and the meso-limbic system are mainly involved in the *emotional* aspects of events (especially with respect to good or bad consequences), but are poor at recognizing details. Thus, only the combined information from hippocampus/ EPPC and from the limbic centres yields a full, detailed and emotionally laden picture of a situation.

This experiential declarative and emotional memory works via the ventral loop to influence the dorsal loop for the planning and control of voluntary actions. The most important convergence centres of dorsal and ventral loops at the cortical-conscious level are the orbito-frontal cortex and at the subcortical, unconscious level the substantia nigra and the dorso-medial thalamic nucleus.

7   Conclusions

What do all of these findings mean for the issue of controlling voluntary actions? Put simply, it seems that for internally-guided voluntary actions, which are not sufficiently automatized, the pre-frontal and orbito-frontal cortex (in co-operation with other cortical areas) plans, and prepares a certain action. This already happens under strong influence of the unconscious limbic-emotional centres (above all amygdala and meso-limbic/ meso-cortical system) via the limbic loop. Interestingly, our conscious brain is unaware of the subcortical origin of many, if not most of our wishes; they seem to come from 'nowhere'.

Before being eventually realized, these wishes and plans must pass through the dorsal loop for a second subcortical 'censorship' before the cortex can influence the pre-motor and motor centres of the cerebral cortex, so that these determine the actions in detail and induce them. This censorship of the basal ganglia is, in turn, controlled via the ventral loop by the experiential declarative and emotional memory contained in the limbic system.

It appears that the censorship of the basal ganglia is essentially concerned with two questions:

1   Whether *in the light of previous experience* the planned action should really be carried out rather than another action.

2   Whether the intended action is *appropriate* to the situation.

Only when both questions are answered affirmatively do the basal ganglia activate the pre-motor and motor cortex via the thalamus (more precisely, they reduce or abolish the inhi-bition of the thalamic nuclei). This happens via the 'dopamine signal', which in turn is under the control of the unconscious emotional-experiential memory.

This means that the 'final word' about whether voluntary actions are actually carried out comes from brain centres that are inaccessible to consciousness, namely the basal ganglia, the amygdala, the meso-limbic system, and the limbic thalamic nuclei. This assumption is further corroborated by studies determining the temporal relationship between the onset of the symmetrical and lateralized readiness potential on the one hand, and the moment of the subjectively felt 'act of will' (Libet *et al.*, 1983; Haggard & Eimer, 1999). These studies demonstrate that the 'act of will' occurs several hundred seconds after the onset of the symmetrical and lateralized readiness potential. This means that the 'act of will' cannot cause voluntary actions and that freedom of the 'act of will' is an illusion. This may insult our understanding of ourselves, for the thinking, feeling, and planning self is a product of the associative, especially the pre-frontal cortex, and belief itself is the cause of all voluntary actions, as 'lord of the manor'.

However, psychological studies reveal that *human beings feel free when they do what they want.* As many, if not most of their wishes and plans originate in the subcortical, unconscious limbic system, the impression of acting freely arises when our conscious intentions are in harmony with the unconscious ones. In this way, it is guaranteed that only those plans of the conscious brain (i.e. the associative areas of the cerebral cortex), which agree with the limbic experiential memory, will in fact be carried out.

References

Aggleton, J.P. (1992) *The Amygdala: neurobiological aspects of emotion, memory, and mental dysfunction.* New York: Wiley-Liss.

Aggleton, J.P. (1993) The contribution of the amygdala to normal and abnormal emotional states. *Trends Neurosci* **16**, 328–33.

Aggleton, J.P. & **Brown, M.W.** (1999) Episodic memory, amnesia, and the hippocampal-anterior thalamic axis. *Behav Brain Sci* **22**, 425–89.

Alexander, G.E., Crutcher, M.D. & **DeLong, M.R.** (1990) Basal ganglia-thalamocortical circuits: parallel substrates for motor, oculomotor, 'pre-frontal', and 'limbic' functions. In Uylings, H.B.M., van Eden, C.G., de Bruin, J.P.C., *et al.* (eds), *The pre-frontal cortex: Its structure, function and pathology* (pp. 119–146) Amsterdam, New York: Oxford.

Bechara, A., Tranel, D., Damasio, H., Adolphs, R., Rockland, C. & **Damasio, A.R.** (1995) Double dissociation of conditioning and declarative knowledge relative to the amygdala and hippocampus in humans. *Science* **269**, 1115–18.

Bechara, A., Damasio, H., Tranel, D. & **Damasio A.R.** (1997) Deciding advantageously before knowing the advantageous strategy. *Science* **275**, 1293–1295.

Brunia, C.H.M. & **van Boxtel, G.J.M.** (2000) Motor preparation. In Caccioppo, J.T., Tassinary, L.G. & Berntson, G.G. (eds), *Handbook of Psychophysiology*, 2nd edn. Cambridge: Cambridge University Press, pp. 507–32.

Carter, C.S., Braver, T.S., Barch, D.M., Botvinick, M.M., Noll, D. & **Cohen, J.D.** (1998) Anterior cingulate cortex, error detection, and the online monitoring of performance. *Science* **280**, 747–9.

Creutzfeldt, O.D. (1983) *Cortex Cerebri: Leistung, strukturelle and funktionelle Organisation der Hirnrinde.* Berlin: Springer-Verlag.

Cunnington, R., Iansek, R., Johnson, K.A. & **Bradshaw, J.L.** (1997) Movement-related potentials in Parkinson's disease. *Brain* **120**, 1339–53.

Decety, J., Perani, D., Jeannerod, M., Bettinardi, V., Tadary, B., Woods, R., Mazziotta, J.C. & **Fazio, F.** (1994) Mapping motor representations with positron emission tomography. *Nature* **371**, 600–2.

Drenckhahn, D., & **Zenker, W.** (eds.) (1994) Urban and Schwarzenberg, München-Wien-Baltimore. Benninghoff Anatomie Vol. 2.

Freund, H-J. (1995) The apraxias. In Kennard, C. (ed.), *Recent Advances in Clinical Neurology.* New York: Churchill Livingstone, pp. 29–49.

Gehring, W.J. & Knight, R.T. (2000) Pre-frontal-cingulate interactions in action monitoring. *Nature Neurosci* **3**, 516–20.

Graybiel, A.M., Aosaki, T., Flaherty, A.W. & Kimura, M. (1994) The basal ganglia and adaptive motor control. *Science* **265**, 1826–31.

Haggard, P. & Eimer, M. (1999) On the relation between brain potentials and the awareness of voluntary movements. *Exp Brain Res* **126**, 128–33.

Ivry, R. and Fiez, Markowitsch, H., Rizzolatti G., *et al.* (all 2000). M.S. Gazzaniga (editor-in-chief)

Ivry, R.B. & Fiez, J.A. (2000) Cerebellar contributions to cognition and imagery. In Gazzaniga, M.S. *et al.* (eds), *The New Cognitive Neurosciences*, 2nd edn. Cambridge: MIT Press, pp. 999–1011.

Jeannerod, M. (1997) *The Cognitive Neuroscience of Action.* Oxford: Blackwell.

Kandel, E.R., Schwartz, J.H. & Jessell, T.M. (1991) Principles of Neural Science (3rd edn). Elsevier, New York, Amsterdam, London, Tokyo.

Kim, J-N. & Shadlen, M.N. (1999) Neuronal correlates of a decision in the dorso-lateral pre-frontal cortex of the macaque. *Nature Neurosci* **2**, 176–85.

Kornhuber, H.H. & Deecke, L. (1965) Hirnpotentialänderungen bei Willkürbewegungen und passiven Bewegungen des Menschen: Bereitschaftspotential und reafferente Potentiale. *Pflüg Arch Gesamte Physiol* **284**, 1–17.

Lang, W., Cheyne, D., Kristeva, R., Beisteiner, R., Lindinger, G. & Deecke, L. (1991) Three-dimensional localization of SMA activity preceding voluntary movement. *Exp Brain Res* **87**, 688–95.

LeDoux, J. (1996) *The Emotional Brain: the mysterious underpinnings of emotional life.* New York: Simon & Schuster.

LeDoux, J. (2000) Emotion circuits in the brain. *Ann Rev Neurosci* **23**, 155–84.

Leiner, H.C., Leiner, A.L. & Dow, R.S. (1991) The human cerebro-cerebellar system: its computing, cognitive, and language skills. *Behav Brain Res* **44**, 113–28.

Libet, B., Gleason, C.A., Wright, E.W. & Pearl, D.K. (1983) Time of conscious intention to act in relation to onset of cerebral activity (readiness-potential). *Brain* **106**, 623–42.

Mai, J.K., Assheuser, J. & Paxinos, G. (1997) *Atlas of the Human Brain.* Academic Press, San Diego.

Markowitsch, H.J. (2000) The anatomical bases of memory. In Gazzaniga, M.S. *et al.* (eds), *The New Cognitive Neurosciences*, 2nd edn. Cambridge: MIT Press, pp. 781–95.

Nieuwenhuys, R., Voogd, J. & van Huijzen, C. (1989) *The Human Central Nervous System.* New York: Springer-Verlag.

Penfield, W. & Rasmussen, T. (1950) The Cerebral Cortex of Man. MacMillan, New York.

Panksepp, J. (1998) *Affective Neuroscience: the foundations of human and animal emotions.* Oxford: Oxford University Press.

Passingham, R. (1993) *The Frontal Lobes and Voluntary Action.* Oxford: Oxford University Press.

Passingham, R.E., Toni, I. & Rushworth, M.F.S. (2000) Specialisation within the pre-frontal cortex: the ventral pre-frontal cortex and associative learning. *Exp Brain Res* **133**, 103–13.

Petrides, M. (2000) The role of the mid-dorso-lateral pre-frontal cortex in working memory. *Exp Brain Res* **133**, 44–54.

Rizzolatti, G., Fadiga, L., Fogassi, L. & Gallese, V. (1996) Pre-motor cortex and the recognition of motor actions. *Cognitive Brain Res* **3**, 131–41.

Rizzolatti, G., Fogassi, L. & Gallese, V. (2000) Cortical mechanisms subserving object grasping and action recognition: a new view on the cortical motor functions. In Gazzaniga, M.S. *et al.* (eds), *The New Cognitive Neurosciences*, 2nd edn. Cambridge: MIT Press, pp. 539–52.

Roland, P.E., Larsen, B., Lassen, N.A. & Skinhut, E. (1980) Supplementary motor area and other cortical areas in organization of voluntary movements in man. *J Neurophysiol* **43**, 118–36.

Rolls, E.T. (1999) *The Brain and Emotion*. Oxford: Oxford University Press.

Schultz, W. (1998) Predictive reward signals of dopamine neurons. *J Neurophysiol* **80**, 1–27.

Spanagel, R. & Weiss, F. (1999) The dopamine hypothesis of reward: past and current status. *Trends Neurosci* **22**, 521–7.

Tremblay, L. & Schultz, W. (1999) Relative reward preference in primate orbitofrontal cortex. *Nature* **398**, 704–8.

Tulving, E. & Markowitsch, H.J. (1998) Episodic and declarative memory: role of the hippocampus. *Hippocampus* **8**, 198–204.

Wilson, F.A.W., Scalaidhe, S.P.O. & Goldman-Rakic, P.S. (1993) Dissociation of object and spatial processing domains in primate pre-frontal cortex. *Science* **260**, 1955–8.

CHAPTER 6

HOW DO WE CONTROL ACTION?

RÜDIGER J. SEITZ

Abstract

The aim of this contribution is to provide an outline of the neural correlate underlying the control of voluntary action from the perspective of clinical neurology and systems physiology. Voluntary action has been defined as a consciously initiated process underlying goal-directed movement control. Based on evidence from functional neuro-imaging and from neurological syndromes, such as akinesia, neglect, and apraxia, a distributed model of information processing is proposed that describes the central position of action between the individual's behaviour and the single movement. It will be argued that an initiation system in the medial part and an evaluation system on the lateral aspect of the human brain represent anatomically distinct, but highly interconnected circuits that underlie free, person-specific and simultaneously flexible behaviour.

1 Introduction

Voluntary action has been defined as the process of doing things by will (*The Concise Oxford Dictionary of Current English*, Oxford 1990). Volition is the power of using one's own will for choosing and making a decision (ibid). In systems physiology, voluntary action has been conceptualized as the individual's ability to initiate goal-directed bodily activity. Accordingly, the acting subject has a motive to do something by his will with his full individual responsibility. The prerequisite of being able to act voluntarily in order to achieve an intended goal or to reach a decision, is consciousness, including alertness and full orientation as to place, time, and one's own personality. Furthermore, when intending to perform an action, the acting subject has to be aware of the situational context and of the particular goal requirements. Usually, such an intended activity evolves in the context of externally imposed challenges. Therefore, early during action generation, there is the need to direct one's attention to an external object or event. The range of possible voluntary actions may be restricted by the number of possible choices given by the context. Thus, action selection includes the cognitive evaluation of cues in the external world and of the subject's own behaviour. That is, a plan for action stored in memory will be subjected to flexible and anticipatory adjustments according to ongoing feedback or prior experience, as reviewed by Fuster (2000). This information allows for spatial and temporal specification of the selected goal-directed action utilizing conscious control.

It is clear from what has been stated so far that voluntary actions require consciousness, implying responsibility of the actor. Nevertheless, the rationality of one's action may be questioned by another individual, since he or she may experience the contextual demands or limitations differently, and thus may choose to act differently. Human behaviour, however, is not restricted to voluntary actions, but usually also comprises actions that are not controlled by volition. For example, non-voluntary actions lack intention or are not reachable for voluntary modulation. This is the case with brain diseases, such as focal epilepsy, ballism, and dystonia. An example of less voluntary actions is the failure of the acting subject to control his temper, which may result in the execution of unintended and possibly even criminal actions. In this situation, there is the voluntary initiation of action, but the lack of modulation due to negligence of anticipation of possible consequences. It will be described in this chapter that the subject's behaviour is composed of a large variety of actions, which themselves become manifest by a large number of different single movements.

Operationally for laboratory and clinical testing of voluntary action, subjects are required to execute a response to an instruction in an expected but for the subject ambiguous manner. In such laboratory situations, forced-choice paradigms are potent means to restrict the subject's response space. That is, a subject is required to perform a voluntary action, while the modulation of that action by instruction through the experimenter or feedback perceived by the subject is in the focus of investigation. Perspectives on this topic will be given. In particular, it will be discussed how functional neuro-imaging studies can identify topographic representations in the human brain or can be used for hypothesis testing of cerebral circuits regarding movement execution, sensory perception, and cognitive problem-solving inclusive of action control. During the last decade functional neuro-imaging has developed into a powerful tool to investigate cerebral activity in terms of localization and temporal evolution in the different parts of the human brain (for a survey, see Mazziotta *et al.*, 2000). Specifically, neuro-imaging technology allows identification of the cerebral areas of the human brain engaged in movement execution, sensory perception, cognitive problem solving, and in the production of voluntary action. By cognitive subtraction, the images obtained during a control task will be subtracted from those obtained during a more complex task, thus allowing to identify the brain areas engaged with the different aspects of voluntary action. Likewise, brain areas can be identified that are engaged in the purely mental process of consciously conceptualizing and perceiving an action in absence of any overt action.

Functional neuro-imaging studies show the positive evidence for a specific engagement of certain brain areas as compared to the negative evidence obtained from the functional impairment following a brain lesion in clinical neurology. Since the advent of structural neuro-imaging, brain lesions can be identified and mapped *in vivo*, while functional neuro-imaging allows also for assessing secondary functional effects of brain lesions on distant brain areas indicating the interference of a certain brain area in a circuit that sub-serves a certain function (for a survey, see Mazziotta *et al.*, 2000). The concerted approach of both neurophysiology employing the different functional neuro-imaging methods and neurology employing structural imaging of brain lesions bears a great promise for improved understanding of human brain functioning. With this armature the different cerebral processes underlying voluntary action can also be disentangled by appropriate behavioural assessment and ascribed to a temporally organized structure of distributed topographic implementations in the human brain. As the emergence of volition is intimately connected with the evolutionary augmentation of the frontal lobe (Fuster, 2000), the human frontal lobe is expected to comprise the relevant processing nodes subserving the generation of voluntary action. It will be argued that an initiation system in the medial part and an evaluation system on the lateral aspect of the human brain represent anatomically distinct, but highly interconnected circuits underlying free, person-specific and simultaneously flexible behaviour.

Before discussing this topic from the perspective of clinical neurological and systems physiology, an overview of investigation is given. At the end of the chapter, recent studies that investigated social and cultural impact on brain function will be discussed.

2 Methodological tools

Neuro-imaging has been increasingly seen as a powerful technology for mapping of human brain function (Fox, 1997; Seitz et al., 2000b). There is the approach of mapping brain lesions using computed tomography (CT) or magnetic resonance imaging (MRI). In these studies on the topography of brain damage, brain lesions can be mapped into a stereotactic reference system (Talairach & Tournoux, 1988). This allows for determining the critical node that induces the specific neurological deficit and between patient comparisons by spatial superimposition of the lesions of different subjects. In addition, functional changes induced by a brain disease can be mapped, providing the means to identify the brain areas that are directly or indirectly affected by a brain disease or lesion. Most often depressions of regional cerebral metabolism, as measured with positron emission tomography (PET), have been reported as disease-related abnormalities of human brain function (see Fig. 6.1). This figure shows the wide distribution of significant metabolic depressions in patients with motor hemi-neglect. Thus, disease-related functional changes in the brain can be associated with defined neurological deficits. In the example shown here, it is apparent that lateral and medial brain areas—which have been hypothesized to be part of a circuit underlying the normal generation of voluntary action (see Figure on next page)—were functionally impaired in these patients.

In the last decade the functional imaging methods have been developed. They provide means to study brain function in healthy subjects and neurological patients. For this purpose, measurements of stimulation-related haemodynamic changes are most widely used. These changes can be assessed with measurements of the regional cerebral blood flow (rCBF) using PET and of the blood oxygenation level-dependent changes (BOLD) with functional magnetic resonance imaging (fMRI). These tomographic imaging tools can localize brain-activity changes induced by a certain type of brainwork allowing for a spatial resolution of approximately 5–9 mm (Roland, 1993; Frackowiak, 1994; Calamante et al., 1999), which is good given a diameter of 3–5 mm of the human cerebral cortex. The temporal resolution of fMRI and PET, however, is relatively poor, being in the range of approximately 6 s to 1 min due to the slow haemodynamic response characteristics and tracer kinetics, respectively. In contrast, bio-electric neural activity has a time-course in the range of some milliseconds, thus exceeding the haemodynamic measures by three orders of

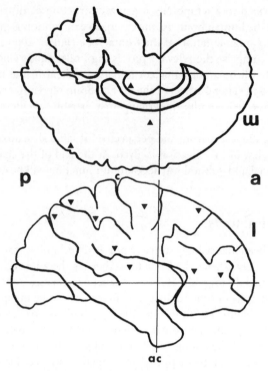

Figure 6.1 Topography of the distributed depressions of the regional cerebral metabolism in patients with motor hemi-neglect as compared to healthy controls. Shown are the lateral (l) and medial (m) views of the standard human brain in the stereotactic coordinate system. Indicated are the horizontal and vertical line through the anterior commissure (ac). a = Anterior; p = posterior pole of the brain; c = central sulcus. Adapted from von Giesen *et al.* (1994).

magnitude. Nevertheless, the reconstructed tomographic image data allows detection of activity changes that occur simultaneously in different parts of the brain including the different parts of the cerebral cortex, subcortical structures as the basal ganglia, thalamus, and the cerebellum. Most widely used are systems that allow estimation the activations on a pixel-by-pixel basis after spatial image standardization (Fox *et al.*, 1988; Evans *et al.*, 1988; Seitz *et al.*, 1990; Worsley *et al.*, 1992; Friston *et al.*, 1994; Roland *et al.*, 1997). It should be borne in mind, however, that the observed haemodynamic changes represent only indirect measures of brain activity. Because, under physiological conditions, there is a tight coupling of activation-related metabolic and haemodynamic changes to increases in neural activity (Fox & Raichle, 1984; Blomqvist *et al.*, 1994; Bandettini *et al.*, 1997; Buxton & Frank, 1997; Hoge *et al.*, 1999), one of the assumptions underlying functional imaging with PET and fMRI is that a state of activation has to be kept constant over a sufficiently long period of time to capture functional changes in the different parts of the brain during a steady-state-like condition. Figure 6.2 summarizes the cerebral activations in a number of recent studies exploring cognitive aspects of action control using standard

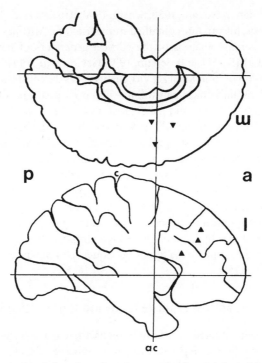

Figure 6.2 Common activations in lateral pre-frontal cortex related to verbal, spatial, and perceptuo-motor problem-solving in healthy volunteers [adapted from Duncan *et al.* (2000) and Stephan *et al.* (2002)]. On the mesial surface the significant activations related to the conception of action are shown [adapted from Seitz *et al.* (1997) and Binkofski *et al.* (2000)]. Note the non-overlapping distribution of the activation sites shown here as compared to the metabolic depressions in motor neglect shown in Fig. 6.1; the only exception is the cingulate gyrus, probably reflecting the initiation problem in motor neglect.

acquisition and categorical image subtraction protocols (see above for the physiological task conditions).

Bioelectric activity of the human brain can be recorded from the surface of the head using electroencephalography (EEG) and magneto-encephalography (MEG), the latter measuring the magnetic fields induced by electrical current flow. Temporal resolution of these techniques lies in the range of milliseconds optimally reflecting the dynamics of brain activity (Hari & Lounasmaa, 1989; Näätänen *et al.*, 1994). Spatial resolution of these techniques, however, is relatively poor being determined by the number and distribution of the recording electrodes or sensors covering the head. The most widely used MEG systems are equipped with 128 sensors covering the entire head. The electrical potentials or magnetic fields recorded with EEG and MEG, respectively, on the surface of the head, however, do not reflect the localization of the underlying electrical activity changes in the brain, because the regionally varying degrees of volume conductance in the cerebrospinal fluid compartment, the meninges, and especially in the skull severely distort the data recorded. Therefore, spatial analysis is based on biomathematical models, which statistically explain the data recorded from the surface of the brain by intra-cerebral sources

(Wood *et al.*, 1985; Romani & Rossini, 1988; Scherg, 1990; Kristeva *et al.*, 1991; Snyder, 1991). To improve data analysis, information obtained from structural MRI has been used to create realistic head models for the analysis of the cortical generators of bioelectric activity as recorded with EEG and MEG (Dale & Sereno, 1993; Gevins *et al.*, 1994; Marin *et al.*, 1998). More recently, localization of functional activity changes—as demonstrated by rCBF or fMRI measurements, as well as anatomical constraints—has been used for both interpreting and restricting the search space in EEG and MEG recordings (Heinze *et al.*, 1994; George *et al.*, 1995; Gerloff *et al.*, 1996; Korvenoja *et al.*, 1999). Nevertheless, the basic assumption underlying these measures is that the task-specific, regional neuronal activity is reliable across subsequent trials during the repetitive event-related recordings of EEG and MEG.

Most recently, fMRI has been developed further to accommodate activity recordings in an event-related fashion (D'Esposito *et al.*, 1998; Buckner *et al.*, 1998; Friston *et al.*, 1998). These measurements capitalize on the high image-acquisition capacity of fMRI, which allows monitoring the evolution of the activation-related haemodynamic response. Thus, event-related fMRI combines high spatial with high temporal resolution (Menon & Kim, 1999), with the potential to capture the temporal sequence of the different neural events in the human brain.

3   How can physical action emerge from mental volition?

Preceding all kinds of self-initiated actions in humans, there is a surface-negative potential, which has been termed *Bereitschaftspotential* (Kornhuber & Deecke, 1964). It emerges about 1–2 s before complex and even simple finger movements over the frontal midline of the head. Thus, the medial parts of the human brain subserve the initiation of action from the internal world of the acting subject. As known from anatomical and electrophysiological studies in non-human primates and from imaging studies in man, the dorsal medial pre-motor subareas F6 and F7 (supplementary motor area, SMA, and pre-supplementary motor area) are engaged during selection and generation of motor acts before movement onset (Kurata & Wise, 1988; Lang *et al.*, 1988; Deiber *et al.*, 1991; Rao *et al.*, 1997). While the SMA is concerned with executive aspects of motor performance including postural limb coordination (Rizzolatti *et al.*, 1996; Kazennikov *et al.*, 1998; Stephan *et al.*, 1999a), the pre-SMA—due to its massive input from the pre-frontal cortex (Luppino *et al.*, 1990)—mediates the initiation and selection of movement and sustains the readiness to act (Deiber *et al.*, 1991; Humberstone *et al.*, 1997; Haxby *et al.*, 2000). Thus, the initiative route is continuously influenced by information from the external world that allows for strategic and goal-directed, for instance, flexible selection of action.

Furthermore, neuro-imaging studies showed that even the conception of movements activates the dorsal fronto-mesial cortex and the adjacent anterior cingulate gyrus (Roland *et al.*, 1980; Decety *et al.*, 1994; Stephan *et al.*, 1995; Binkofski *et al.*, 2000). These data suggest that the conception of an action involves attention for error detection and action specification from the broad variety of possibilities, as shown by the anterior cingulate activation in divided attention tests and high attention load (Pardo *et al.*, 1990; George *et al.*, 1995; Carter *et al.*, 1998). Similar anterior cingulate activations during speech production (Petersen *et al.*, 1988) underscores the general applicability of this mechanism for specification of action. Since positive, rewarding attributions of external stimuli and emotions are processed by the fronto-orbital cortex (Rolls, 2000a,b; Northoff *et al.*, 2000), it is tempting to speculate that motivation for action is coded down the line in the pre-frontal cortex. Finally, in the dorsal fronto-mesial cortex the go-signal is coded for specific actions. It can be disrupted by applying trains of interfering stimulation by trans-cranial magnetic stimulation over the dorsal fronto-mesial cortex (Gerloff *et al.*, 1997). Thus, the internal drive reflects the subject's readiness to do something spontaneously. It is the 'what' aspect of movement generation (Brooks *et al.*, 1995).

For comparison, in the dorso-lateral pre-frontal cortex, cognitive aspects of action control are processed. Delayed response tasks show that specific target actions are generated in relation to external cues that have been recognized as appropriate previously implying long- and short-term memory in this process (Rainer *et al.*, 1999; Goldman-Rakic, 2000). In the primate, the most critical area for this process is situated around the principal sulcus (Levy & Goldman-Rakic, 2000). Stimuli that signify to the primate not to act elicit a recognizable potential over the lateral frontal cortex, which has been termed the 'no-go' potential (Sasaki & Gemba, 1986). These potentials are most heavily pronounced in the dorsal bank of the principal sulcus reflecting the differential role of pre-frontal cortex on action generation. The role of the pre-frontal cortex for mediating pre-movement planning and online monitoring of actions in humans was highlighted in a meta-analysis of a broad series of imaging studies on different types of working-memory studies (Duncan & Owen, 2000). Specifically, it was found that spatial, visuo-spatial and verbal working-memory studies produced distributed patterns of overlapping activation foci within the dorso- and ventro-lateral pre-frontal cortex, which make distinct executive contributions to action control analogous to different short-term memory processes. Recently, it has been shown in a response-selection paradigm that high-level as compared to low-level cognitive problem solving activated the dorso-lateral pre-frontal cortex irrespective of the process-ing system involved (Duncan *et al.*, 2000). Moreover, a similar region was also involved for high-level as compared to low-level temporal movement coordination (Stephan *et al.*, 2002; Fig. 9.2). These data are extended by the observation that the dorso-lateral pre-frontal cortex is not involved in maintaining movement-relevant information online, but in relation to free selection of items from working memory (Rowe *et al.*, 2000). In addition, the ventro-lateral pre-frontal cortex is critically involved in learning visual associations (Passingham *et al.*, 2000). As soon as explicit learning of a motor act is accom-plished, pre-frontal engagement shifts to pre-motor, posterior parietal, and cerebellar regions (Jenkins *et al.*, 1994; Shadmehr & Holcomb, 1997). In a broader view, it is suggested that conscious behaviour is accompanied by the processing of external information origi-nating from the situational circumstances and internal information of the ongoing body movements. Thus, sensory information is being processed at different levels, with the high-est level of abstraction in the pre-frontal cortex allowing for influence on free, conscious behaviour. Future studies will have to parcellate the pre-frontal cortex further, since there is evidence that a separation of activation in dorso-lateral pre-frontal cortex can be achieved in similar tasks engaging different modalities employed for action (Hyder *et al.*, 1997).

The caudally adjacent pre-motor cortex in the lateral frontal cortex is concerned with movement-relevant aspects of motor control (Rizzolatti *et al.*, 1996). Due to its massive input from the parietal cortex it transposes representations of action into the appropriate motor commands. In particular, the lateral pre-motor cortical areas code the mode of action in response to perceptual cues and the specific kind of action in relation to cue-movement associations (Halsband & Freund, 1990; Jeannerod *et al.*, 1995). Furthermore, the inferior lateral frontal cortex including the so-called pre-motor cortex mediates the encoding of movement during motor learning and movement recognition (Seitz & Roland, 1992; Bonda *et al.*, 1995; Parsons *et al.*, 1995; Rauch *et al.*, 1995; Binkofski *et al.*, 2000). These pre-motor cortical activations are accompanied by task-specific, topographically organized parietal lobe activations (Kawashima *et al.*, 1994; Grafton *et al.*, 1996; Seitz *et al.*, 1997; Binkofski *et al.*, 1999b). This indicates the presence of highly organized and tightly interconnected fronto-parietal circuits engaged for coding of goal-directed action in the human brain, too (Rizzolatti *et al.*, 1996). In implicit compared with explicit motor learning, the pre-motor areas are not active (Seitz & Roland, 1992; Hazeltine *et al.*, 1997), suggesting that the pre-motor cortex specifies movement synergies with enormous flexibility, particularly, in relation to externally imposed task requirements. The processing nodes in pre-motor and parietal cortex are functionally inhibited in motor neglect as evident from spatial overlap of these activation areas during movement processing with the depressions of regional cerebral metabolism in patients with motor hemi-neglect (Fig. 6.1).

Finally, motor cortex mediates differentiated and powerful limb movements in a strict temporal and spatial relation to the involved groups of muscles (Schieber & Hibbard, 1993; Sanes *et al.*, 1995). The inherent aspects of permanency and flexibility of cerebral representations of function as well as the consequences of reorganization secondary to physiological learning and to post-lesional deficit compensation on these representations have been discussed in detail elsewhere (Seitz & Azari, 1999; Seitz *et al.*, 2000a). Here, it is emphasized that movement activity elicits coherent activity of motor and pre-motor cortex with inter-hemispheric distribution even in simple unilateral movements (Gerloff *et al.*, 1998), thus arguing for a system of distributed representations for movement generation.

Most importantly, the conception of action involves the entire pre-motor-parietal circuitry engaged during movement execution even in the absence of movements, as evident from motor imagery and mental training (Jeannerod, 1995). For example, it was shown that imagery of gestures and of abstract motion, as well as the generation of action words activate the lateral pre-motor and parietal cortex with a specific topography for particular task requirements (Bonda *et al.*, 1995; Martin *et al.*, 1995; Parsons *et al.*, 1995; Decety *et al.*, 1997; Binkofski *et al.*, 2000). By contrast, neuro-imaging methods failed to reveal activity changes in the motor cortex of comparable magnitude (Porro *et al.*, 1996; Roth *et al.*, 1996; Seitz *et al.*, 1997; Binkofski *et al.*, 2000). Conversely, magneto-encephalography and evoked potential recordings provided evidence for the involvement of motor cortex in motor imagery (Schnitzler *et al.*, 1995; Stephan & Frackowiak, 1996). Specifically, these studies showed a lowered excitability threshold in motor cortex during imagery, but no change in the evoked potentials, arguing for the participation of the entire cortical motor system for mental volition of action. Moreover, recent evidence suggests that the dorsal fronto-mesial and cingulate cortex participate in the mental conception of action (Binkofski *et al.*, 2000). These authors demonstrated that different motor-imagery tasks reflexive on the acting subject resulted in activation of these areas, while imagery of abstract motion not involving the subjects' body part did not.

In conclusion, neuro-imaging data show that conscious motor behaviour engages the entire cortical circuitry related to movement performance inclusive of motor, pre-motor, and parietal cortex, as well as the supplementary motor area and the adjacent cingulate cortex. In addition, the processes related to control of action—be it in relation to instruction and selection, and to processing of imposed behavioural challenges—involve the dorso-lateral pre-frontal cortex.

4   The problem of voluntary action in neurology

Brain lesions interfere with voluntary actions. Freund (1987) provided a comprehensive review of the effect of cortical lesions on motor behaviour. Here, specific aspects shall be highlighted inasmuch they are relevant for action control.

Fronto-mesial lesions induce akinesia and mutism in the presence of an intact motor output system (Feinberg et al., 1992). That is, the patients do not move spontaneously nor do they respond upon command. Even the facial expression is motionless and does not reflect emotional sway. Interestingly, some patients experience their own limbs contralateral to the lesion as alien, not belonging to themselves. Although the patients have a viable motor system, they fail to act spontaneously or to react upon command, but do so when subjected to heavy or painful stimulation (Heilman et al., 1985). The inability to act in response to stimuli and to recognize the contra-lesional limb as their own is by no means lesion-specific, but can also occur in apraxia after parietal lobe lesions (Sirigu et al., 1999; Bundick & Spinella, 2000). In certain posterior lesions of the brain involving the angular gyrus, patients are well able to move their arms, but are not capable of transforming the mirror space in movement-relevant co-ordination (Binkofski et al., 1999a). Consequently, the affected arm is alien in the co-ordinate system of body space. These studies demonstrated that focal brain lesions are able to interfere with specific aspects of voluntary generation of action, emphasizing the role of the parietal lobe for the conception of goal-directed movement. In patients with parietal lobe lesions presenting clinically as apraxia this ability is impaired. Thus, the patients cannot imitate movements, or recognize or pantomime gestures, while hand and arm movements can well be performed. In the most severe cases, such patients may even lose their ability to use tools and thus become completely helpless and dependent (Freund, 1987). Most interestingly, detailed clinical-anatomical correlations revealed differentiated patterns of disturbed subfunctions of goal-directed forelimb actions in those patients revealing a relation of a modular distribution of lesion-induced deficits in anatomically defined locations within the posterior parietal lobe (Binkofski et al., 1998, 1999a, 2001). Thus while frontal, and in particular fronto-mesial, lesions interfere with movement initiation, parietal brain lesions severely distort movement execution. Interestingly, the neurological deficits after parietal lesions are quite persistent, while similar neurological deficits after lesions of lateral pre-motor cortex, such as limb kinetic apraxia usually resolve shortly after occurrence of the lesion (Freund & Hummelsheim, 1985; Freund, 1987; Feinberg et al., 1992).

A critical demonstration of impaired sensorimotor integration was evident in patients with focal brain lesions of different location, who all suffered from motor hemi-neglect (von Giesen et al., 1994). Functional neuro-imaging revealed that this disorder was associated with a disturbance in a widespread network of cortical and subcortical brain areas underlying movement control as illustrated in Fig. 6.1. It is apparent that significant metabolic depressions occurred in the lateral pre-motor and parietal cortex, which have been ascribed to the integrative system of sensorimotor control. In addition, the involvement of the anterior cingulate cortex underscores the importance of the medial initiative system of sensorimotor control. Note that also subcortical relay nodes such as the basal ganglia and thalamus were affected reflecting the cortico-subcortical information exchange in sensorimotor control. These data underscore that conscious motor control involves a network of distributed representations showing that lesion of each of them can result in lesion-specific deficits. In addition, there are accompanying non-specific abnormalities that interfere with action that can be identified by appropriate kinematic assessments. Similarly, networks of multi-nodal processing units in cerebral cortex and in subcortical structures have been proposed also for cognitive functions such as attention, language, and memory (Mesulam, 1990). Interference of brain function with transcranial magnetic stimulation and lesion studies relying on mapping of structural lesions related to defined functional consequences provide probes to reveal the critical nodes involved for generating a certain action. They provide insight into the modular organization of the human cortex (Binkofski *et al.*, 1998; Kosslyn *et al.*, 1999; Stephan *et al.*, 1999) showing the multiplicity of distinct subfunctions that are required for proper generation and execution of voluntary action.

5   A perspective on the neural correlate of human behaviour

As was described above, activation studies in healthy subjects and lesion studies in neurological patients with well-defined clinical deficits elucidate the neural correlate of behaviour in the human brain. Common to the different approaches of human brain research is the fundamental idea that brain functioning can be mapped in temporally structured, topographically distributed processing nodes. Thus, a physiological map of the different brain functions including voluntary action appears feasible. Based on the results presented, brain functions can be conceived as being organized in systems of concertedly working areas, each of which performs its role in functional subsystems. These systems include the different sensory

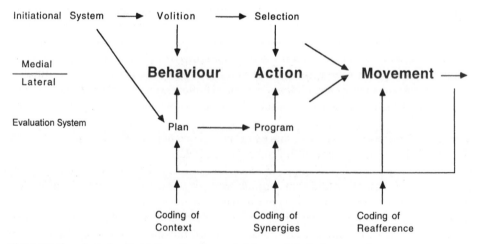

Figure 6.3 Flow chart of cortical information flow underlying control of voluntary action.

modalities providing the brain with external information, the motor system allowing for physical activity and the so-called higher cortical areas subserving cognition.

Figure 6.3 summarizes the relation of behaviour, action, and movement in the framework of a hypothetical and simplistic scheme of human sensorimotor control. It is suggested that a medial initiation system mediates processing of information reflecting the subject's drive to act voluntarily, whereas the lateral evaluation system mediates processing of information that is external to the subject. These systems are co-active in channelling information from the broad range of behaviour to progressively more specific subunits, meaningful or goal-directed actions, and ultimately to defined single limb movements. One should bear in mind that anatomical afferents and efferents converge at the cortical node points described above, allowing information arising from different and distributed source nodes to be processed. For reasons of clarity, this scheme shows cortical circuits only, although intensive cortico-subcortical circuits involving the basal ganglia, thalamus, cerebellum, and amygdala have been identified, and ascribed to automatic, co-ordinated, cognitive, and emotional aspects of action control (Allen & Tsukahara, 1970; Alexander *et al.*, 1986; Mink & Thach, 1993; Schwarz & Thier, 1999; Chua & Dolan, 2000). A number of these circuits have been identified in animal research and are in the focus of current research. A perspective of the cortical–subcortical interplay for human brain function is provided by Roth (this volume).

The view of a task-related assembly of cerebral networks at different critical processing nodes is also compatible with the view that physiological learning and adaptation to pathological conditions is mediated by plastic topographical and temporal reorganization of the human brain. Indeed, functional neuro-imaging provided evidence for a differential recruitment of brain areas in relation to the stage of acquisition of a task or proficiency of performance (reviewed by van Mier, 2000). Similar mechanisms have been advocated for the processes underlying recovery from neurological diseases. A review on cerebral reorganization underlying the restoration of motor functions after brain lesions has been given elsewhere (Seitz, 1997). As a consequence, changes in human behaviour are likely to be reflected by the emergence of cerebral activation patterns that deviate from the naive state.

Most intriguing for this chapter is the question whether functional neuro-imaging studies are also capable of addressing the relation of the social and cultural environment on human brain function. Conversely, one may ask whether neuro-imaging may provide evidence for the notion that brain activity creates the mental representation of perception inclusive of the generation of voluntary action in the social environment. Indeed, there are a few recent studies supporting both views.

There is evidence from functional neuro-imaging that perception is critically connected with activation of the medial posterior parietal cortex (e.g. the precuneus). It was found that the recall of words with highly imaginable context (such as 'car' and 'truck') was associated with activation of the precuneus (Fletcher *et al.*, 1995). Also, the perception of faces from impoverished cartoons specifically involved the precuneus (Dolan *et al.*, 1997). These data render the precuneus a key node for the mental representation of the nature of external objects. Also, purely mental activity was mapped in the human brain. Specifically, it was shown that mathematical thinking involves large-scale circuits in the human brain that differ depending on whether exact calculation or approximation was required (Dehaene *et al.*, 1999). While exact arithmetic calculation predominantly involved the left pre-frontal cortex, left angular gyrus, and left precuneus, numerical approximation involved predominantly the cortex lining the intra-parietal sulcus bilaterally and the right precuneus. That is in exact calculation areas known to be involved in language processing became activated, while the intra-parietal sulcus has been found to play an important role in fine finger-movement control (Binkofski *et al.*, 1998, 1999b). The latter observation is of particular interest with respect to the interaction of mental activity and the representation of action, because fingering is known to be crucial in infantile acquisition of mathematical calculations.

An important cultural achievement is the creation of languages with their spoken and written expressions. Clearly, the study of language perception and generation provides clues about the neural implementation of speech in the human brain (reviewed by Indefrey & Levelt, 2000). Of interest in the framework of this chapter is whether different languages may involve similar or dissimilar areas in the human brain. Again, it turned out that skill acquisition greatly influenced the cerebral activation pattern. In fluent Mandarin-English bilingual subjects, single-word generation involved the same cortical areas for either language. These areas included, in the frontal lobe, the left middle and inferior frontal gyrus, the supplementary motor area for both languages (Chee *et al.*, 1999). In contrast, in late bilinguals the activation was shown to be different for the first and second language in the left inferior frontal activation, which is assumed to represent the motor-speech area (Kim *et al.*, 1997). In contrast, there was activation overlap in the posterior superior temporal gyrus, which is thought to be the site of the sensory speech area. Thus, perception occurred in the same area, but speech production differed. Furthermore, language perception may be different in relation to the orthographic system. In Japanese there are two orthographic systems, with Kanji representing word morphology and Kana representing syllables. The left inferior temporal gyrus was found to be activated in Kanji writing as compared to the left angular gyrus in Kana writing (Tokunaga *et al.*, 1999). It was argued that the left posterior inferior temporal cortex plays an important role in writing Kanji through retrieval of their visual graphic images, suggesting language-specific cerebral organization of writing (Nakamura *et al.*, 2000). Similarly, Italians showed faster word and non-word reading than English subjects, which was associated with a greater activation in left superior temporal regions during phoneme processing in Italians. In contrast, English readers showed greater activation in left posterior inferior temporal gyrus and anterior inferior frontal gyrus areas associated with word retrieval during reading and naming tasks (Paulesu *et al.*, 2000). These data support the notion that interpretation of stimuli in the outside world is acquired by education during childhood development in a given cultural environment. Since many human actions are performed in response to external cues in general and to language in particular, culture apparently plays an important role for action control.

The cultural influence on brain function can be appreciated further from studies on the theory of mind. Specifically, interpretation of cartoons and stories showed overlapping activation in the inferior medial pre-frontal cortex including the paracingulate cortex (Gallagher *et al.*, 2000). Processing of cartoons also involved activation of the precuneus. These results were suggested to provide evidence that the ability to attribute mental states is mediated by a highly circumscribed brain system, which is independent of modality. It is interesting to note that viewing pictures of people one loves activates completely different brain areas, such as the medial insula, anterior cingulate, caudate nucleus, and putamen, and de-activates areas shown to play an important role in cognition, for instance, the posterior cingulate, dorsal pre-frontal, parietal, and middle temporal cortex (Bartels & Zeki, 2000).

Most recently, the neural correlates of a religious experience were investigated using functional neuro-imaging. During religious recitation, self-identified religious subjects activated a frontal-parietal circuit, composed of the dorso-lateral pre-frontal, dorso-medial frontal, and medial parietal cortex (Azari *et al.*, 2001). Thus, it was suggested that religious experience may be a cognitive process, mediated by a pre-established neural circuit, involving dorso-lateral pre-frontal, dorso-medial frontal, and medial parietal cortex. Since religious attributions are made in anomalous or ambiguous situations, when a person does not know what to expect or do, yet actively and persistently seeks a solution, a persistent, internally generated 'readiness' emerges, which subsequently serves to re-activate the religious schema in the presence of salient religious cues (Azari *et al.*, 2001). This 'readiness' is probably mediated by the dorso-medial frontal cortex, leading to the commonly reported immediacy of religious experience. Also the cognitive process of religious experience most likely involves the dorso-lateral pre-frontal and medial parietal cortex (Partiot *et al.*, 1995; Fletcher *et al.*, 1995).

Based on a biological view, everybody will agree that the thoughts, ideas, beliefs, and emotions of each human being are brought about by the human brain. Yet, the mental events intuitive to the individual are only potentially communicable. Until recently, human brain research has failed to bridge this gap between brain and mind, leaving the answers to this dualistic world embedded in the social and cultural background of each community, and ultimately personal. We are now at the edge of understanding how cognition is transformed into action.

References

Alexander, G.E., DeLong, M.R. & Strick, P.L. (1986) Parallel organization of functionally segregated circuits linking basal ganglia and cortex, 2. *Ann Rev Neurosci* **9**, 357–81.

Allen, G.I. & Tsukahara, N. (1970) Cerebrocerebellar communication systems. *Physiolog Rev* **54**, 957–1006.

Allen, R.E. (ed.) (1990) The concise Oxford dictionary of current English. 8th Edition, Clarendon Press, Oxford, UK.

Azari, N.P., Nickel, J., Wunderlich, G., Niedeggen, M., Hefter, H., Tellmann, L., Herzog, H., Stoerig, P., Birnbacher, D. & Seitz, R.J. (2001) The neural correlate of religious experience. *Eur J Neurosci* **13**, 1649–53.

Bandettini, P.A., Kwong, K.K., Davis, T.L., Tootell, R.B., Wong, E.C., Fox, P.T., Belliveau, J.W., Weisskoff, R.M. & Rosen, B.R. (1997) Characterization of cerebral blood oxygenation and flow changes during prolonged brain activation. *Human Brain Mapping* **5**, 93–109.

Bartels, A. & Zeki, S. (2000) The neural basis of romantic love. *Neuroreport* **11**, 3829–34.

Binkofski, F., Dohle, C., Posse, S., Stephan, K.M., Hefter, H., Seitz, R.J. & Freund, H-J. (1998) Human anterior intraparietal area subserves prehension: a combined lesion and functional MRI activation study. *Neurol* **50**, 1253–9.

Binkofski, F., Buccino, G., Dohle, C., Seitz, R.J. & Freund, H-J. (1999a) Mirror agnosia and mirror ataxia constitute different parietal lobe disorders. *Annl Neurol* **46**, 51–61.

Binkofski, F., Buccino, G., Posse, S., Seitz, R. J., Rizzolatti, G. & Freund, H-J. (1999b) A fronto-parietal circuit for object manipulation in man: evidence from an fMRI-study. *Eur J Neurosci* **11**, 3276–86.

Binkofski, F., Amunts, K., Stephan, K.M., Posse, S., Schormann, T., Zilles, K. & Seitz, R.J. (2000) Broca's area subserves imagery of motion: a combined cytoarchitectonic and MRI study. *Human Brain Mapping* 11, 273–85.

Binkofski, F., Seitz, R.J., Hackländer, T., Pawelec, D., Mau, J. & Freund, H-J. (2001) The recovery of motor functions following hemiparetic stroke: a clinical and MR-morphometric study. *Cerebrovasc Dis* 11, 273–81.

Blomqvist, G., Seitz, R.J., Sjogren, I., Halldin, C., Stone-Elander, S., Widen, L., Solin, O. & Haaparanta, M. (1994) Regional cerebral oxidative and total glucose consumption during rest and activation studied with positron emission tomography. *Acta Physiolog Scandin* 151, 29–43.

Bonda, E., Petrides, M., Frey, S. & Evans, A. (1995) Neural correlates of mental transformations of the body-in-space. *Proc Nat Acad Sci USA* 92, 11180–4.

Brooks, V., Hilperath, F., Brooks, M., Ross, H.G. & Freund, H-J. (1995) Learning 'what' and 'how' in a human motor tasks. *Learn Memory* 2, 225–42.

Buckner, R.L., Goodman, J., Burock, M., Rotte, M., Koutstaal, W., Schacter, D., Rosen, B. & Dale, A.M. (1998) Functional-anatomic correlates of object priming in humans revealed by rapid presentation event-related fMRI. *Neuron* 20, 285–96.

Bundick, T., Jr & Spinella, M. (2000) Subjective experience, involuntary movement, and posterior alien hand syndrome. *J Neurol Neurosurg Psychiat* 68, 83–5.

Buxton, R.B. & Frank, L.R. (1997) A model for the coupling between cerebral blood flow and oxygen metabolism during neural stimulation. *J Cereb Blood Flow Metab* 17, 64–72.

Calamante, F., Thomas, D. L., Pell, G. S., Wiersma, J. & Turner, R. (1999) Measuring cerebral blood flow using magnetic resonance imaging techniques. *J Cereb Blood Flow Metab* 19, 701–35.

Carter, C.S., Braver, T.S., Barch, D.M., Botvinick, M.M., Noll, D. & Cohen, J.D. (1998) Anterior cingulate cortex, error detection, and the online monitoring of performance. *Science* 280, 747–9.

Chee, M.W., Tan, E.W. & Thiel, T. (1999) Mandarin and English single-word processing studied with functional magnetic resonance imaging. *J Neurosci* 19, 3050–6.

Chua, P. & Dolan, R.J. (2000) The neurobiology of anxiety and anxiety-related disorders: a functional neuro-imaging perspective. In Mazziotta, J.C., Toga, A.W. & Frackowiak, R.S. (eds), *Brain Mapping: the disorders*. San Diego: Academic Press, pp. 509–22.

Dale, A.M. & Sereno, M.I. (1993) Improved localization of cortical activity by combining EEG and MEG with MRI cortical surface reconstruction: a linear approach. *J Cognit Neurosci* 5, 162–76.

Decety, J., Perani, D., Jeannerod, M., Bettinardi, V., Tadary, B., Woods, R., Mazziotta, J.C. & Fazio, F. (1994) Mapping motor representations with positron emission tomography. *Nature* 371, 600–2.

Decety, J., Grèzes, J., Costes, N., Perani, D., Jeannerod, M., Procyk, E., Grassi, F. & Fazio, F. (1997) Brain activity during observation of actions: influence of action content and subject's strategy. *Brain* 120, 1763–77.

D'Esposito, M., Aguirre, G.K., Zarahn, E., Ballard, D., Shin, R.K. & Lease, J. (1998) Functional MRI studies of spatial and nonspatial working memory. *Cognit Brain Res* 7, 1–13.

Dehaene, S., Spelke, E., Pinel, P., Stanescu, R. & Tsivkin, S. (1999) Sources of mathematical thinking: behavioral and brain-imaging evidence. *Science* 284, 970–4.

Deiber, M.P., Passingham, R.E., Colebatch, J.G., Friston, K.J., Nixon, P.D. & Frackowiak, R.S. (1991) Cortical areas and the selection of movement: a study with positron emission tomography. *Exp Brain Res* 84, 393–402.

Dolan, R.J., Fink, G.R., Rolls, E., Booth, M., Holmes, A., Frackowiak, R.S. & Friston, K.J. (1997) How the brain learns to see objects and faces in an impoverished context. *Nature* 389, 596–9.

Duncan, J. & Owen, A. (2000) Dissociative methods in the study of frontal lobe function. In S. Monsell & J. Driver (eds), *Attention and Performance*, Vol. XVIII. Cambridge: MIT Press, pp. 567–76.

Duncan, J., Seitz, R.J., Kolodny, J., Bor, D., Herzog, H., Ahmed, A., Newell, F. & Emslie, H. (2000) A neural basis for general intelligence. *Science* **289**, 457–60.

Evans, A.C., Beil, C., Marrett, S., Thompson, C.J. & Hakim, A. (1988) Anatomical-functional correlation using an adjustable MRI-based region of interest atlas with positron emission tomography. *J Cereb Blood Flow Metab* **8**, 513–30.

Feinberg, T.E., Schindler, R.J., Flanagan, N.G. & Haber, L.D. (1992) Two alien hand syndromes. *Neurol* **42**, 19–24.

Fletcher, P.C., Frith, C.D., Baker, S.C., Shallice, T., Frackowiak, R.S. & Dolan, R.J. (1995) The mind's eye: precuneus activation in memory-related imagery. *Neuro-image* **2**, 195–200.

Fox, P.T. (1997) The growth of human brain mapping. *Human Brain Mapping* **5**, 1–2.

Fox, P.T. & Raichle, M.E. (1984) Stimulus rate dependence of regional cerebral blood flow in human striate cortex, demonstrated by positron emission tomography. *J Neurophysiol* **51**, 1109–20.

Fox, P.T., Mintun, M.A., Reiman, E.M. & Raichle, M.E. (1988) Enhanced detection of focal brain responses using intersubject averaging and change-distribution analysis of subtracted PET images. *J Cereb Blood Flow Metab* **8**, 642–53.

Frackowiak, R.S. (1994) Functional mapping of verbal memory and language. *Trends Neurosci* **17**, 109–15.

Freund, H-J. (1987) Abnormalities of motor behavior after cortical lesions in humans. In Plum, F. (ed.), *Handbook of Physiology, V: the nervous system*. Bethesda: American Physiological Society, pp. 763–810.

Freund, H-J. & Hummelsheim, H. (1985) Lesions of pre-motor cortex in man. *Brain* **108**, 697–733.

Friston, K.J., Holmes, A., Worsley, K., Poline, J.B., Frith, C.D. & Frackowiak, R.S.J. (1994) Statistical parametric maps in functional imaging: a generalized linear approach. *Human Brain Mapping* **2**, 189–210.

Friston, K.J., Fletcher, P., Josephs, O., Holmes, A., Rugg, M.D. & Turner, R. (1998) Event-related fMRI: characterizing differential responses. *Neuro-image* **7**, 30–40.

Fuster, J.M. (2000) Executive frontal functions. *Exp Brain Res* **133**, 66–70.

Gallagher, H.L., Happe, F., Brunswick, N., Fletcher, P.C., Frith, U. & Frith, C.D. (2000) Reading the mind in cartoons and stories: an fMRI study of 'theory of mind' in verbal and nonverbal tasks. *Neuropsychol* **38**, 11–21.

George, J.S., Aine, C.J., Mosher, J.C., Schmidt, D.M., Ranken, D.M., Schlitt, H.A., Wood, C.C., Lewine, J.D., Sanders, J.A. & Belliveau, J.W. (1995) Mapping function in the human brain with magnetoencephalography, anatomical magnetic resonance imaging, and functional magnetic resonance imaging. *J Clin Neurophysiol* **12**, 406–31.

Gerloff, C., Grodd, W., Altenmüller, E., Kolb, R., Naegele, T., Klose, U., Voigt, K. & Dichgans, J. (1996) Coregistration of EEG and fMRI in a simple motor task. *Human Brain Mapping* **4**, 199–209.

Gerloff, C., Corwell, B., Chen, R., Hallett, M. & Cohen, L.G. (1997) Stimulation over the human supplementary motor area interferes with the organization of future elements in complex motor sequences. *Brain* **120**, 1587–602.

Gerloff, C., Richard, J., Hadley, J., Schulman, A.E., Honda, M. & Hallett, M. (1998) Functional coupling and regional activation of human cortical motor areas during simple, internally paced and externally paced finger movements. *Brain* **121**, 1513–31.

Gevins, A., Cutillo, B., DuRousseau, D., Le, J., *et al.* (1994) Imaging the spatiotemporal dynamics of cognition with high-resolution evoked potential methods. *Human Brain Mapping* **1**, 101–16.

Goldman-Rakic, P. (2000) Localization of function all over again. *Neuro-image* **11**, 451–7.

Grafton, S.T., Fagg, A.H., Woods, R.P. & Arbib, M.A. (1996) Functional anatomy of pointing and grasping in humans. *Cereb Cortex* **6**, 226–37.

Halsband, U. & Freund, H-J. (1990) Pre-motor cortex and conditional motor learning in man. *Brain* **113**, 207–22.

Hari, R. & Lounasmaa, O.V. (1989) Recording and interpretation of cerebral magnetic fields. *Science* **244**, 432–6.

Haxby, J.V., Petit, L., Ungerleider, L.G. & Courtney, S.M. (2000) Distinguishing the functional roles of multiple regions in distributed neural systems for visual working memory. *Neuro-image* **11**, 145–56.

Hazeltine, E., Grafton, S.T. & Ivry, R. (1997) Attention and stimulus characteristics determine the locus of motor- sequence encoding. A PET study. *Brain* **120**, 123–40.

Heilman, K.M., Valenstein, E. & Watson, R.T. (1985) The neglect syndrome. In Frederiks, J.A.M. (ed.), *Clinical Neuropsychology.* Amsterdam: Elsevier, pp. 153–83.

Heinze, H.J., Mangun, G.R., Burchert, W., Hinrichs, H., Scholz, M., Munte, T.F., Gos, A., Scherg, M., Johannes, S. & Hundeshagen, H. (1994) Combined spatial and temporal imaging of brain activity during visual selective attention in humans. *Nature* **372**, 543–6.

Hoge, R.D., Atkinson, J., Gill, B., Crelier, G.R., Marrett, S. & Pike, G.B. (1999) Linear coupling between cerebral blood flow and oxygen consumption in activated human cortex. *Proc Nat Acad Sci USA* **96**, 9403–8.

Humberstone, M., Sawle, G.V., Clare, S., Hykin, J., Coxon, R., Bowtell, R., Macdonald, I.A. & Morris, P.G. (1997) Functional magnetic resonance imaging of single motor events reveals human presupplementary motor area. *Annl Neurol* **42**, 632–7.

Hyder, F., Phelps, E.A., Wiggins, C.J., Labar, K.S., Blamire, A.M. & Shulman, R.G. (1997) 'Willed action': a functional MRI study of the human pre-frontal cortex during a sensorimotor task. *Proc Nat Acad Sci USA* **94**, 6989–94.

Indefrey, P. & Levelt, W.J.M. (2000) The neural correlates of language production. In Gazzaniga, M. (ed.), *The Cognitive Neurosciences,* 2nd edn. Cambridge: MIT Press, pp. 845–65.

Jeannerod, M. (1995) Mental imagery in the motor context. *Neuropsychol* **33**, 1419–32.

Jeannerod, M., Arbib, M. A., Rizzolatti, G. & Sakata, H. (1995) Grasping objects: the cortical mechanisms of visuomotor transformation. *Trends Neurosci* **18**, 314–20.

Jenkins, I.H., Brooks, D.J., Nixon, P.D., Frackowiak, R.S. & Passingham, R.E. (1994) Motor sequence learning: a study with positron emission tomography. *J Neurosci* **14**, 3775–90.

Kawashima, R., Roland, P.E. & O'Sullivan, B.T. (1994) Fields in human motor areas involved in preparation for reaching, actual reaching, and visuomotor learning: a positron emission tomography study. *J Neurosci* **14**, 3462–7.

Kazennikov, O., Hyland, B., Wicki, U., Perrig, S., Rouiller, E.M. & Wiesendanger, M. (1998) Effects of lesions in the mesial frontal cortex on bimanual co-ordination in monkeys. *Neurosci* **85**, 703–16.

Kim, K.H., Relkin, N.R., Lee, K.M. & Hirsch, J. (1997) Distinct cortical areas associated with native and second languages. *Nature* **388**, 171–4.

Kornhuber, H.H. & Deecke, L. (1964) Brain potential changes with voluntary movements and passive movements of mean: Readiness potential and reafferent potential. *Pflüg Arch Physiol* **284**, 1–17.

Korvenoja, A., Huttunen, J., Salli, E., Pohjonen, H., Martinkauppi, S., Palva, J.M., Lauronen, L., Virtanen, J., Ilmoniemi, R.J. & Aronen, H.J. (1999) Activation of multiple cortical areas in response to somatosensory stimulation: combined magneto-encephalographic and functional magnetic resonance imaging. *Human Brain Mapping* **8**, 13–27.

Kosslyn, S.M., Pascual-Leone, A., Felician, O., Camposano, S., Keenan, J.P., Thompson, W.L., Ganis, G., Sukel, K.E. & Alpert, N.M. (1999) The role of area 17 in visual imagery: convergent evidence from PET and rTMS [published erratum in Science 1999, 284, 197]. *Science* **284**, 167–70.

Kristeva, R., Cheyne, D. & Deecke, L. (1991) Neuromagnetic fields accompanying unilateral and bilateral voluntary movements: topography and analysis of cortical sources. *Electroencephal Clin Neurophysiol* **81**, 284–98.

Kurata, K. & Wise, S.P. (1988) Pre-motor and supplementary motor cortex in rhesus monkeys, *Exp Brain Res* **72**, 237–48.

Lang, W., Lang, M., Uhl, F., Koska, C., Kornhuber, A. & Deecke, L. (1988) Negative cortical DC shifts preceding and accompanying simultaneous and sequential finger movements. *Exp Brain Res* **71**, 579–87.

Levy, R. & Goldman-Rakic, P.S. (2000) Segregation of working memory functions within the dorso-lateral pre-frontal cortex. *Exp Brain Res* **133**, 23–32.

Luppino, G., Matelli, M. & Rizzolatti, G. (1990) Cortico-cortical connections of two electrophysio-logically identified arm representations in the mesial agranular frontal cortex. *Exp Brain Res* **82**, 214–18.

Marin, G., Guerin, C., Baillet, S., Garnero, L. & Meunier, G. (1998) Influence of skull anisotropy for the forward and inverse problem in EEG: simulation studies using FEM on realistic head models. *Human Brain Mapping* **6**, 250–69.

Martin, A., Haxby, J.V., Lalonde, F.M., Wiggs, C.L. & Ungerleider, L.G. (1995) Discrete cortical regions associated with knowledge of color and knowledge of action. *Science* **270**, 102–5.

Mazziotta, J.C., Toga, A.W. & Frackowiak, R.S.J. (2000) *Brain Mapping: the disorders.* San Diego: Academic Press.

Menon, R.S. & Kim, S.G. (1999) Spatial and temporal limits in cognitive neuro-imaging with fMRI. *Trends Cognit Sci* **3**, 207–16.

Mesulam, M.M. (1990) Large-scale neurocognitive networks and distributed processing for attention, language, and memory. *Annl Neurol* **28**, 597–613.

Mink, J.W. & Thach, W.T. (1993) Basal ganglia intrinsic circuits and their role in behavior. *Curr Opin Neurobiol* **3**, 950–7.

Näätänen, R., Ilmoniemi, R.J. & Alho, K. (1994) Magnetoencephalography in studies of human cognitive brain function. *Trends Neurosci* **17**, 389–95.

Nakamura, K., Honda, M., Okada, T., Hanakawa, T., Toma, K., Fukuyama, H., Konishi, J. & Shibasaki, H. (2000) Participation of the left posterior inferior temporal cortex in writing and mental recall of kanji orthography: a functional MRI study. *Brain* **123**, 954–67.

Northoff, G., Richter, A., Gessner, M., et al. (2000) Functional dissociation between medial and lateral pre-frontal cortical spatiotemporal activation in negative and positive emotions: a combined fMRI/MEG study. *Cereb Cortex* **10**, 93–107.

Pardo, J.V., Pardo, P.J., Janer, K.W. & Raichle, M.E. (1990) The anterior cingulate cortex mediates processing selection in the Stroop attentional conflict paradigm. *Proc Nat Acad Sci USA* **87**, 256–9.

Parsons, L.M., Fox, P.T., Downs, J.H., Glass, T., Hirsch, T.B., Martin, C.C., Jerabek, P.A. & Lancaster, J.L. (1995) Use of implicit motor imagery for visual shape discrimination as revealed by PET. *Nature* **375**, 54–8.

Partiot, A., Grafman, J., Sadato, N., Wachs, J. & Hallett, M. (1995) Brain activation during the generation of non-emotional and emotional plans. *Neuroreport* 6, 1397–400.

Passingham, R.E., Toni, I. & Rushworth, M.F. (2000) Specialisation within the pre-frontal cortex: the ventral pre-frontal cortex and associative learning. *Exp. Brain Res* 133, 103–13.

Paulesu, E., McCrory, E., Fazio, F., *et al.* (2000) A cultural effect on brain function. *Nature Neurosci* 3, 91–6.

Petersen, S.E., Fox, P.T., Posner, M.I., Mintun, M. & Raichle, M.E. (1988) Positron emission tomographic studies of the cortical anatomy of single-word processing. *Nature* 331, 585–9.

Porro, C.A., Francescato, M.P., Cettolo, V., Diamond, M.E., Baraldi, P., Zuiani, C., Bazzocchi, M. & di Prampero, P.E. (1996) Primary motor and sensory cortex activation during motor performance and motor imagery: A functional magnetic resonance imaging study. *J Neurosci* 16, 7688–98.

Rainer, G., Rao, S.C. & Miller, E.K. (1999) Prospective coding for objects in primate pre-frontal cortex. *J Neurosci* 19, 5493–505.

Rao, S.M., Harrington, D.L., Haaland, K.Y., Bobholz, J.A., Cox, R.W. & Binder, J.R. (1997) Distributed neural systems underlying the timing of movements. *J Neurosci* 17, 5528–35.

Rauch, S.L., Savage, C.R., Brown, H.D., Curran, T., Alpert, N.M., Kendrick, A., Fishman, A.J. & Kosslyn, S.M. (1995) A PET investigation of implicit and explicit sequence learning. *Human Brain Mapping* 3, 271–86.

Rizzolatti, G., Luppino, G. & Matelli, M. (1996) The classic supplementary motor area is formed by two independent areas. *Adv Neurol* 70, 45–56.

Roland, P.E. (1993) *Brain Activation*. New York: Wiley.

Roland, P.E., Larsen, B., Lassen, N.A. & Skinhoj, E. (1980) Supplementary motor area and other cortical areas in organization of voluntary movements in man. *J Neurophysiol* 43, 118–36.

Roland, P.E., Geyer, S., Amunts, K., Schormann, T., Schleicher, A., Malikovic, A. & Zilles, K. (1997) Cytoarchitectural maps of the human brain in standard anatomical space. *Human Brain Mapping* 5, 222–7.

Rolls, E.T. (2000a) The orbitofrontal cortex and reward. *Cereb Cortex* 10, 284–94.

Rolls, E.T. (2000b) Memory systems in the brain. *Ann Rev Psychol* 51, 599–630.

Romani, G.L. & Rossini, P. (1988) Neuromagnetic functional localization: principles, state of the art, and perspectives. *Brain Topogr* 1, 5–21.

Roth, M., Decety, J., Raybaudi, M., Massarelli, R., Delon-Martin, C., Segebarth, C., Morand, S., Gemignani, A., Decorps, M. & Jeannerod, M. (1996) Possible involvement of primary motor cortex in mentally simulated movement: a functional magnetic resonance imaging study. *Neuroreport* 7, 1280–4.

Rowe, J.B., Toni, I., Josephs, O., Frackowiak, R.S. & Passingham, R.E. (2000) The pre-frontal cortex: response selection or maintenance within working memory? *Science* 288, 1656–60.

Sanes, J.N., Donoghue, J.P., Thangaraj, V., Edelman, R.R. & Warach, S. (1995) Shared neural substrates controlling hand movements in human motor cortex. *Science* 268, 1775–7.

Sasaki, K. & Gemba, H. (1986) Electrical activity in the pre-frontal cortex specific to no-go reaction of conditioned hand movement with colour discrimination in the monkey. *Exp Brain Res* 64, 603–6.

Scherg, M. (1990) Fundamentals of dipole source potential analysis. In Grandori, F., Hoke, M. & Romani, G.L. (eds), *Auditory Evoked Magnetic Fields and Electrical Potentials*. Basel: Karger, pp. 40–69.

Schieber, M.H. & Hibbard, L.S. (1993) How somatotopic is the motor cortex hand area? *Science* 261, 489–92.

Schnitzler, A., Witte, O.W., Cheyne, D., Haid, G., Vrba, J. & Freund, H-J. (1995) Modulation of somatosensory evoked magnetic fields by sensory and motor interferences. *Neuroreport* **6**, 1653–8.

Schwarz, C. & Thier, P. (1999) Binding of signals relevant for action: towards a hypothesis of the functional role of the pontine nuclei. *Trends Neurosci* **22**, 443–51.

Seitz, R.J. (1997) Recovery of executive motor functions. In Boller, F. & Grafman, J. (eds), *Handbook of Neuropsychology*, Vol. 11. Amsterdam: Elsevier, pp. 185–207.

Seitz, R.J. & Azari, N.P. (1999) Postlesional neuroplasticity in man. In Stefan, H., Andermann, F., Shorvon, S. & Chauvel, P. (eds), *Plasticity and Epilepsy*. Philadelphia: Lippincott-Raven, pp. 37–47.

Seitz, R.J. & Roland, P.E. (1992) Learning of finger movement sequences: a combined kinematic and positron emission tomography study. *Eur J Neurosci* **4**, 154–65.

Seitz, R.J., Bohm, C., Greitz, T., Roland, P.E., Eriksson, L., Blomqvist, G., Rosenqvist, G. & Nordell, B. (1990) Accuracy and precision of the computerized brain atlas programme for localization and quantification in positron emission tomography. *J Cereb Blood Flow Metab* **10**, 443–57.

Seitz, R.J., Canavan, A.G., Yaguez, L., Herzog, H., Tellmann, L., Knorr, U., Huang, Y. & Homberg, V. (1997) Representations of graphomotor trajectories in the human parietal cortex: evidence for controlled processing and automatic performance. *Eur J Neurosci* **9**, 378–89.

Seitz, R.J., Stephan, K.M. & Binkofski, F. (2000a) Control of action as mediated by the human frontal lobe. *Exp Brain Res* **133**, 71–80.

Seitz, R.J., Volkmann, J. & Witte, O. W. (2000b) Functional mapping of the human brain. *Neuroscientist* **6**, 75–6.

Shadmehr, R. & Holcomb, H.H. (1997) Neural correlates of motor memory consolidation. *Science* **277**, 821–5.

Sirigu, A., Daprati, E., Pradat-Diehl, P., Franck, N. & Jeannerod, M. (1999) Perception of self-generated movement following left parietal lesion. *Brain* **122**, 1867–74.

Snyder, A.Z. (1991) Dipole source localization in the study of EP generators: a critique. *Electroencephalogr Clin Neurophysiol* **80**, 321–5.

Stephan, K.M., Binkofski, F., Halsband, U., et al. (1999) The role of ventral medial wall motor areas in bimanual co-ordination. A combined lesion and activation study. *Brain* **122**, 351–68.

Stephan, K.M., Fink, G.R., Passingham, R.E., Silbersweig, D., Ceballos-Baumann, A.O., Frith, C.D. & Frackowiak, R.S. (1995) Functional anatomy of the mental representation of upper extremity movements in healthy subjects. *J Neurophysiol* **73**, 373–86.

Stephan, K.M. & Frackowiak, R.S. (1996) Motor imagery: anatomical representation and electro-physiological characteristics. *Neurochem Res* **21**, 1105–16.

Stephan, K.M., Thaut, M.H., Wunderlich, G., Schicks, W., Tian, B., Tellmann, L., Schmitz, T., Herzog, H., McIntosh, G.C., Seitz, R.J. & Hömberg, V. (2002) Conscious and subconscious sensorimotor synchronization—prefrontal cortex and the influence of awareness. *Neuroimage* **15**, 345–52.

Talairach, J. & Tournoux, P. (1988) *Co-planar Stereotaxic Atlas of the Human Brain*. Stuttgart: Thieme.

Tokunaga, H., Nishikawa, T., Ikejiri, Y., Nakagawa, Y., Yasuno, F., Hashikawa, K., Nishimura, T., Sugita, Y. & Takeda, M. (1999) Different neural substrates for Kanji and Kana writing: A PET study. *Neuroreport* **10**, 3315–19.

van Mier, H. (2000) Human learning. In Toga, A.W. & Mazziotta, J.C. (eds), *Brain Mapping: the systems*. San Diego: Academic Press, pp. 605–20.

von Giesen, H.J., Schlaug, G., Steinmetz, H., Benecke, R., Freund, H-J. & Seitz, R.J. (1994) Cerebral network underlying unilateral motor neglect: evidence from positron emission tomography. *J Neurolog Sci* **125**, 29–38.

Wood, C.C., Cohen, D., Cuffin, B.N., Yarita, M. & Allison, T. (1985) Electrical sources in human somatosensory cortex: identification by combined magnetic and potential recordings. *Science* **227**, 1051–3.

Worsley, K.J., Evans, A.C., Marrett, S. & Neelin, P. (1992) A three-dimensional statistical analysis for CBF activation studies in human brain [see comments]. *J Cereb Blood Flow Metab* **12**, 900–18.

CHAPTER 7

SELF-GENERATED ACTIONS

MARC JEANNEROD

1 Introduction

Voluntary actions are consciously represented actions. However, this far too simple definition does not specify when consciousness is supposed to occur: is it prior to execution (i.e. at the representational stage), or during execution or even after the action is completed? In order to clarify some aspects of this problem, I will first examine the basic notion of a representation for action, and subsequently try to understand its role in ultimately generating a conscious intention and a voluntary action.

In the last 40 years or so, a new set of concepts has been elaborated concerning the factors allowing a goal-directed movement to be produced. The crude input–output system holding for reflexes was replaced by open-loop systems bearing some autonomy with respect to the environment. In this type of systems, behaviour was thought, when properly triggered, to unfold by itself until the goal corresponding to the stimulus was reached. This concept of an endogenous organization of action was prompted by experiments demonstrating the ability of animals and human subjects to generate and execute actions without intervention of sensory afferences. In monkeys, de-afferentation experiments by Bizzi and colleagues showed (by section of the dorsal roots, Bizzi *et al.*, 1971) that the entire structure of a pointing movement could be predetermined centrally, including not only its initial, ballistic phase, but also its low-velocity phase and its endpoint. These results led to a minimalist formulation of the motor representation—the equilibrium point model— where the position of a joint was described as a single equilibrium point determined by the degree of stiffness of the muscles attached to that joint. A simple change in equilibrium point produced a rotation of the joint and a new position of the limb. Clinical observation of subjects with de-afferented limbs led to similar conclusions (e.g. Lashley, 1917).

This sort of model, however, only accounted for the programming stage of the representation, thus neglecting earlier and perhaps more interesting stages. In this chapter, I will use the term of representation to include the whole set of central, covert, events that are supposed to take place before an action begins (e.g. Saltzman, 1979). According to this definition, representation should include the neural coding of the goal of the action, a prediction of its potential consequences, and the commands necessary to achieve that action.

The notion that actions are internally generated, which is critical for the concept of motor representation, was accepted only with difficulty and met strong oppositions. The core of the debate was about the degree of autonomy of the central part of a physiological executive system with respect to the external environment. Several modalities of functioning for such systems will be examined, ranging between completely 'closed' systems without autonomy of the central stage and 'open' systems with different degrees of independence with respect to the external milieu.

2   Motor representations in historical perspective: the notion of reference for guiding behaviour

One of the first conceptions of the central stage of an executive system comes from devices used for controlling machines. This notion was already familiar to engineers during the early nineteenth century. Regulation of steam engines (by Maxwell's 'governors') implied a reference state that the system was supposed to reach and maintain. Biological systems soon appeared to be liable to the same mode of functioning. Claude Bernard made the point that systemic regulations were circular mechanisms aimed at maintaining 'constancy' of the internal milieu. Regulation of blood glucose, for instance, was based on constancy of glycaemia (the reference state) at a level corresponding to tissue metabolic needs. When glycaemia dropped below its reference value, processes were activated to restore the reference state. This mode of regulation can therefore be schematized as a genetically determined system with an input stage (receptors), an output stage (effectors), and a central stage (the reference), which detects errors between reference and input, and activates or deactivates the effectors. One of the important points in Claude Bernard's description was that such self-regulating (later called homeostatic) systems proceeded from a teleonomic functioning driven by a predetermined representation of their reference state. Homeostatic systems are classically considered to be closed-loop systems aimed at maintaining a fixed inbuilt reference. Their activation is thus automatically related to the monitoring of a mismatch between their input and central stages, a design that implies a lack of decision processes, and little or no influence of intervening factors. Interestingly, these characteristics were applied to the regulation of motor reflexes. It was Pflüger who first expressed the idea that spinal reflexes in spinal animals were 'purposive', in the sense that they were apparently organized so as to preserve the integrity of the animal organism in response to aggressions (for references, see Jeannerod, 1990).

It is a matter of discussion whether this mode of control, which seems valid for reflexes, can also apply to individual voluntary movements. Bernstein (1967) considered that, in actions like prehension, a required position of the limb was established by the command apparatus and compared during execution to its factual position, as detected by the sensory receptors. The discrepancy between the factual and the required values was used as a driving signal to the muscles until the system self-stabilized. This model was similar to that Craik (1947) had designed for actions like tracking a moving target by hand. In such situations, according to Craik, the human operator behaves as an intermittent correction servo, where errors with respect to reference are corrected by small ballistic movements.

It is common sense, however, that voluntary movements should be relatively independent from feedback signals and should be directed at individual goals, rather than be governed by fixed references. The terms 'reference' and 'goal' are used here tentatively to express different degrees of teleonomy and to indicate that, whereas reflex movements are clearly executed in fulfillment of a supra-ordinate function, voluntary movements have a greater autonomy with respect to biological needs and, therefore, to external control.

3 The cognitive content of motor representations

Motor representations are autonomous mental constructs that share the characteristics of representations in other domains of cognitive psychology. An early example was Head's concept of 'schema' (see Bartlett, 1926). Although this concept was first used by its author to account for maintenance and regulation of posture, it was later developed by others as an internal model of the body in action, largely unconscious, and built from sensations and previous responses to external stimuli (for a critical account, see Oldfield & Zangwill, 1942). Craik (1943), as an early proponent of Artificial Intelligence, proposed that the environment had to be represented internally in a symbolic form and that action consisted in retranslating the symbols contained in this representation. At a later stage, hierarchical structures similar to those of computer programmes were used to conceptualize action plans. In structures like computer programmes, actions were represented as sequences of steps involving tests and operations (see Miller *et al.*, 1960).

The computer model of motor representation was strongly influenced by Marr's (1982) concept of levels of functioning in information-processing devices. According to Marr, the top level of the representation of information in such systems was the level of the 'computational theory', which defined the goal of the computation, its appropriateness, and the logic of the strategy by which it could be carried out. The intermediate level was that of the implementation of the computational theory into a representation of the input and output of the system, and into an algorithm for transforming the input into output. The third level was the hardware implementation of the representation and the algorithm.

The Marr theory thus could be seen as a general framework for top-down models of motor representation. Norman & Shallice (1980, p. 5), for instance, assumed that specification of action components was carried out '... by means of numerous memory schemas, some organized into hierarchical or sequential patterns, others in heterarchical or independent parallel (but cooperating) patterns ...'. In this concept, any given action sequence was represented by an organized set of schemas, with one—the source schema—serving as the highest order control and activating the other component schemas for the individual movements of that action. When a given source schema had been selected, component schemas were controlled by horizontal and vertical processing threads. Horizontal threads determined the order of activation of the component schemas and thus specified the structure for the desired action sequence, although vertical threads determined activation values for these schemas.

The Arbib model for sensorimotor representation is another interesting example (Arbib, 1981). This model attributes to the neural ensemble that controls prehension, properties that are directly inferred from the study of real prehension movements. For instance, the fact that prehension involves simultaneously a proximal movement for transporting the hand at the object location, a distal movement for grasping it and possibly other motor components (Jeannerod, 1981), is directly reflected in the model by an equal number of parallel visuomotor channels. These pathways are largely independent from each other in that they are activated by widely different stimuli (e.g. one pathway deals with location of the object in visual space, another one with size and shape of the object, and so forth), and generate different types of movements (e.g. arm or finger movements). Another characteristic of Arbib's model is that the visuomotor channels, independent as they are, share a common gating system that defines the timing of the action of prehension and the co-ordination of its different components. This system seems inherent to the general structure of any model with several parallel pathways (Weiss & Jeannerod, 1998).

4 Motor representations as anticipatory states

Monitoring its own output is a basic principle of functioning of the nervous system. This idea, inherited from the cybernetic era and still operational nowadays, is based on the notion of a comparison of the actual output of the system with the expected or desired output. Let us examine the role of this mechanism in regulating motor output. It is assumed that each time the motor centres generate an outflow signal for producing a movement, a copy of this command (the 'efference copy') is retained. The reafference inflow signals generated by the movement (e.g. visual, proprioceptive) are compared with the copy. If a mismatch between the two types of signals is recorded, new commands are generated until the actual outcome of the movement corresponds to the desired movement.

An essential aspect of this mechanism is its predictive nature. Predictions concerning the interactions of the effector with the environment, and the effects of these interactions in changing the state of the system itself are based on 'internal models' or 'representations' of forthcoming events, which are built from stored knowledge and experience from previous interactions. Recent forward models may even mimic the causal flow of this process by predicting its next state without waiting for the sensory re-afference or even without performing it (Wolpert *et al.*, 1995). Typically, such a mechanism is a combination of two processes: 'The first process uses the current state estimate and motor command to predict the next state by simulating the movement dynamics with a forward model. The second process uses a model of the sensory output process to predict the sensory feedback from the current state estimate. The sensory error—the difference between actual and predicted sensory feedback—is used to correct the state estimate resulting from the forward model' (Wolpert *et al.*, 1995, p. 1881). This is exactly what one would expect from a mechanism accounting for planning and controlling execution of an action.

Goal-directed behaviour implies that the action should continue until the goal has been satisfied. Motor representation must therefore involve not only forward mechanisms for steering and directing the action, but also mechanisms for monitoring its course and for checking its completion. This error-correction mechanism implies a short-term storage of outflow information processed at each level of action generation (Jeannerod, 1997). Since re-afferent signals during execution of a movement are normally delayed with respect to the command signal, the comparator must look ahead in time and produce an estimate of the movement velocity corresponding to the command. The image of this estimated velocity is used for computing the actual position of the limb with respect to the target (Hoff & Arbib, 1993). It is only because the current state of the action is monitored on-line (rather than after the movement terminates), that corrections can be applied without delay as soon as the deviation of the current trajectory from the desired trajectory is detected.

In order to be useful for the comparison process, the re-afferent signals must be compatible with the efferent ones, that is, the two must use the same code for being mutually understandable and for enabling the matching process. The ideal situation would be that where the re-afference is a mirror image of the representation (which is what von

Holst, 1954, suggested by using the analogy of a negative and a positive of the same photograph that cancel each other). This is not physiologically absurd: the discharge of muscle spindles in the agonist muscle during a movement (due to the co-activation of the gamma motor neurons) exactly fulfils the criterion for an efference copy that mimics the motor input to the alpha motor neurons. This signal that is a direct image of the contraction of the muscle, could well be used for comparison with incoming signals resulting from the limb movement (Miles & Evarts, 1979).

It has been proposed that the information stored in the comparator should encode not joint rotations or kinematic parameters, but final configurations (of the body, of the moving segments, etc.) as they should arise at the end of the action. In other words, the goal of the action, rather than the action itself, would be represented. This idea of the representation of a final state of the system (a representation of the state of the organism when the goal has been reached) is appealing: indeed, the difference between the present state (before the action) and the final state (after the action has been completed) *is* the action. This hypothetical mechanism is supported by experimental arguments. Desmurget *et al.* (1995) recorded reach and grasp movements directed at a handle that had to be grasped with a power grip. When the orientation of the handle was suddenly changed at the onset of a movement, the arm smoothly shifted from the optimal configuration initially planned to reach the object to another optimal configuration corresponding to the object in its new orientation. The shift was achieved by simultaneous changes at several joints (shoulder abduction, wrist rotation), so that the final grasp was effected in the correct position.

In addition to matching the movement trajectory to the representation of the intended movement, this mechanism has also other potential functions for the control of movements. The comparison between corollary and incoming signals might be used at a lower level of control to produce a correspondence between the motor command and the amount of muscular contraction, even if the muscular plant is not linear. Non-linearities may also arise from interaction of the moving limb with external forces, especially if it is loaded (for a review, see Weiss & Jeannerod, 1998). This mapping problem, which is a critical factor for producing accurate limb movements, is less important for eye movements, where interactions with the external force field are minimal and where the load of the moving segment is constant. In this case, the pattern of command issued by the saccadic pulse generator should unequivocally reflect the final desired position of the eye, that is, the position where the retinal error is zero.

At a higher level, that of actions aimed at complex and relatively long-term goals, similar processes have been postulated for comparing the representation of the intended action with the actual action and compensating for a possible mismatch between the two. Several studies, using brain-imaging techniques, have focused on identifying neural structures that would fulfill the requirements for a comparator or an error-detecting device. Carter *et al.* (1998) studied the activity of the anterior cingulate gyrus, a region lying on the medial cortical surface of the frontal lobe in a letter detection task designed to increase error rates and manipulate response competition. Activity was found to increase during erroneous responses, but also during correct responses in conditions of high levels of response competition. Hence, their conclusion that the anterior cingular gyrus detects conditions under which errors are likely to occur, rather than errors themselves. This result suggests that action-monitoring mechanisms anticipate the occurrence of errors, by using internal models of the effects of the action on the world. In other words, the sensory consequences of an action are evaluated before they occur, even in conditions where the action may not be executed.

This mechanism can also become a powerful means of determining whether a sensory event is produced by our own action or by an external agent (and, ultimately, if an action is self-produced or not). Blakemore *et al.* (1998) compared brain activity during the processing of externally produced tones and tones resulting from self-produced movements. They found an increase in the right inferior temporal-lobe activity when the tones were externally produced, suggesting that this area would be inhibited by the volitional system in the self-produced condition. This result raises interesting questions about the possible consequences of a dysfunction of such a system. Increased activity in the primary auditory areas in the temporal lobe has been observed during auditory hallucinations in psychotic patients (Dierks *et al.*, 1999). Hence, there is a possibility that a defective self-monitoring system would produce false attribution of one's own speech to an external source.

5 Conscious action monitoring

How do we know that we are the authors of our own movements? How do we distinguish a self-produced movement from a movement imposed from the outside? Is it because we feel self-generated movements as endogenous? If this is the case, on the basis of which signal? To partially answer these questions, some data are reviewed concerning the monitoring of intentions and the nature of the cues that signal the intentional nature of an event.

There are limitations to the monitoring of efferent activity. Several experimental results suggest that intentions for carrying out voluntary action are generated without explicit awareness. Libet *et al.* (1983; see Libet, 1985) instructed subjects to perform *ad libitum* simple hand movements and to report the instant (*W*) at which they became aware of wanting to move (by reporting the clock position of a revolving spot). In addition, readiness potentials were recorded from the subjects skull. EMG was also recorded for measuring the precise onset of the movement. *W* was found to lag the onset of readiness potentials by about 345 ms. In Libet's terms:

> This leads to the conclusion that cerebral initiation ... of a spontaneous voluntary act ... can and usually does begin *unconsciously*.

> The brain 'decides' to initiate or, at least, to prepare to initiate the act before there is any reportable subjective awareness that such a decision has taken place. (Libet, 1985, p. 536)

This interesting result is hardly compatible with the notion of monitoring sensations in relation to voluntary acts, unless one considers that intentions can only be consciously perceived after a certain intensity threshold has been crossed.

An experiment by Nielsen (1963) deals with the same question. He used a paradigm where subjects were unknowingly shown an alien hand in exact concordance with their own hand. They were asked to follow with their (invisible) hand a straight line shown in a mirror. While they were doing so the (visible) alien hand gently deviated to the right. Subjects were consistently found to deviate their own movement to the left, as if they tried to compensate the visually perceived deviation. In addition, almost all subjects (18 out of 20) experienced the notion that the hand they saw was their own hand, and tried to interpret the rightward deviation by inattention or fatigue, or by the action of external forces. In other words, the subjects preferred to rely on visual information, rather than on their own motor outflow.

Comparing conditions where efforts of will are consciously perceived and conditions where they are not (as in Nielsen's experiment) is interesting. It reveals that efforts of will may not be consciously perceived unless action is blocked or grossly impaired. This happens in abnormal situations like paralysis; it may also be the case in conditions of motor imagery where action is purposively inhibited. It remains that, although not being consciously perceived, efferent signals are nonetheless monitored at some point of the system in order to produce corrections, for example. The distinction made by Searle (1983) between 'intention in action' (the implicit step that precedes an overtly executed action) and 'prior intention' (a conscious desire to do something) is quite relevant here. This is because this distinction provides a phenomenological description of two different situations and not because it corresponds to a radical difference between those situations. Consider, for example, the case where the movement of raising my arm is impossible because of paralysis. If I need to raise my arm to catch an object (an intention in action), the movement will not be performed, but I will shortly realize, in seeing my immobile arm, that in fact I intended to raise my arm (a prior intention). The obstacle on movement execution produces a shift from one type of action to another, that is, from an automatic transfer of a representation into execution to a consciously performed action. It has been speculated, based on empirical observations, that consciousness of an action would arise as a consequence of lack of completion or failure of that action (e.g. Jeannerod, 1994). This has been experimentally verified by introducing a delay between the presentation of a target for a grasping movement, for example, and the go signal: the action of grasping, which is normally executed automatically, then becomes a controlled process. The shift from automatic to controlled execution involves a change in the kinematics of the whole movement: movement time increases, maximum grip aperture is larger, and the general accuracy degrades. These changes have been taken as a case for the use of different neural substrates, the dorsal occipitoparietal system for fast visuomotor transformation being substituted by the slower ventral occipitotemporal system (see Milner *et al.*, 1999).

6   Consciousness of the self

In the previous sections we have set the stage for several different modalities of running an action. An action can be run to its completion through an automatic mechanism using an implicit internal model of the desired movement to be achieved and control systems (comparators) for checking completion. Under certain conditions, especially when the automatic mechanism fails, an action can be consciously monitored; that is, it can be changed into a controlled process. However, this automatic/controlled distinction refers to the agent's subjective experience, not to empirically validated conditions. In the present section, new experimental situations are described, where the different degrees of consciousness of action can be disentangled. In addition, the contribution of pathological conditions to this problem is reported.

The key experiment was described by Fourneret & Jeannerod in 1998. In this experiment, subjects were instructed to move a stylus with their unseen hand at a visual target: only the trajectory of the stylus was visible as a line on a computer screen, superimposed on the hand movement. In the perturbed condition, a directional bias was introduced electronically, such that the visible trajectory no longer corresponded to that of the hand. In order to reach the target, the hand-held stylus had to be deviated in a direction opposite to the bias. In other words, although the line on the screen appeared to be directed at the target location, the hand movement was directed in a different direction. The novel aspect of the experiment is that, besides the data concerning subjects' accuracy in automatically correcting for the bias, other data were collected on subjects' judgements about their own performance. At the end of each trial, subjects were asked in which direction they thought their hand had moved (by indicating verbally the line of the corresponding direction on a chart).

This experiment revealed several important points: First, subjects accurately corrected for the bias in tracing a line that appeared visually to be directed to the target. This resulted from an automatic adjustment of the hand movement in a direction opposite to the bias and by the same angle. Secondly, subjects tended to ignore the veridical trajectory of their hand in making a conscious judgement about the direction of their hand. They tended to adhere to the direction seen on the screen and based their report on visual cues, thus ignoring non-visual (e.g., proprioceptive) cues (Fourneret & Jeannerod, 1998). This result suggests that the visuomotor system may appropriately use information for producing accurate corrections, but cannot be accessed consciously.

In another experiment using the same apparatus, the bias was progressively increased from trial to trial (Slachevsky et al., 2001). Although in the previous experiment the bias was randomly presented and was limited to a maximum angle of 10° to the right or to the left, Slachevsky et al. used biases of up to 42°, always presented in the same direction (e.g. to the right). When the bias amounted a mean value of about 14°, normal subjects changed strategy, and began to use conscious monitoring of their hand movement to correct for the bias and to reach the target. In other words, the discrepancy between the seen and felt trajectory became too large to be corrected automatically, and the failure of these corrections was compensated for by conscious deviations of the hand movement in the appropriate direction. This was not true for a group of patients with frontal lesions, who apparently never became fully aware of this discrepancy, and continued to apply the automatic mechanism with the consequence of larger and larger uncorrected errors in attempting to reach the target. The conclusion to be drawn from these results is two-fold. First, failure of the automatic visuomotor system produces error signals that can be consciously monitored and induce a shift to a different strategy. Secondly, pre-frontal areas are likely to be involved in this strategic shift.

In a third version of the same experiment, an additional difficulty was introduced. Visual cues, which were available to the subjects in the first two experiments, were suppressed by placing an opaque mask on the screen, such that subjects could see their trajectory only in the last third of the movement. The bias was fixed at 15° to the right. During the first trials, subjects noticed large errors with respect to the target position when the spot became visible and had to make a correction during the last third of the movement in order to reach the target position. Normal subjects were able to establish a strategy of changing the direction of their hand during the unseen part of the trajectory. Indeed, they consciously monitored their hand movement, by trying to go farther to the left. About 10 trials were needed to obtain this result. In subsequent trials, normal subjects were able to maintain this strategy of systematically deviating their unseen hand from the beginning of the movement (i.e. they did not have to wait for a discrepancy between the visual and the 'motor' trajectories for producing a 'correction'; Fourneret et al., 2001).

This notion of a central monitoring of efferent cues related to motor intentions (which are likely to be used for reaching the target in the absence of visual cues) was the subject of a series of experiments by Malenka et al. (1982) and by Frith (Frith & Done, 1989; Frith, 1992). These authors found that this ability of monitoring one's own intentions was lacking in specific groups of schizophrenic patients. Hence, their claim that schizophrenic patients should no longer be able to monitor efferent signals resulting from their intentions and should therefore have defective functioning of their motor representations, namely the process of comparing between the efferent and the re-afferent signals should no longer be possible. This failure of the 'intention monitor' (Frith & Done, 1989) was proposed as an explanation of why schizophrenics may not be able to keep track of whether an action is produced as the result of a prior intention or whether it was triggered by an external stimulus.

This theory was re-examined by Fourneret et al. (2001) in two groups of schizophrenic patients. One group showed positive—Schneiderian—symptoms (e.g. hallucinations, delusion of influence, etc.), the other group was devoid of such symptoms (i.e. patients presented mostly negative symptoms). A striking finding was that patients essentially behaved like normal controls for what concerned the ability to learn (or adapt to) the visuomotor conflict. In addition, a large proportion of patients explicitly reported a strategy of moving their unseen hand so as to be able to connect the starting point to the target. In addition, the Schneiderian patients were not worse than those with passive symptoms. The reason for the discrepancy between this result and those obtained in previous experiments (e.g. Frith & Done, 1989) remains an open question.

Another result reported in the same experiment (Fourneret et al., 2001) concerns a further level of consciousness of action, namely that which is used to attribute the action to oneself or to another agent. Among the subjects (normal controls and patients) who explicitly reported making corrections behind the mask, only a few were able to determine that the perturbation for which they had to generate a compensatory strategy was of an external origin. First, only half the normal subjects considered that there was an external bias (e.g. introduced by the experimenter) for which they had to compensate. The other half tended to attribute the problem to themselves (e.g. lack of concentration, tiredness, etc.). Secondly and, most importantly, patients massively misattributed the perturbation to themselves. The proportion of self-attributors was higher among the Schneiderian group. This result is to be compared with those reported by Daprati et al. (1997) and Franck et al. (2001), showing misattribution of action in subjects presented with hand movements of an ambiguous origin. Although normal controls showed attribution errors in about 25% of trials, the proportion of self-attributions raised to more than 80% in Schneiderian patients.

7   Conclusion: consciousness of action as a dormant monitor

The results from the above perturbation experiments emphasize the existence of several levels of consciousness of action. First, at the lower level, automatic, non-conscious mechanisms operate for visuomotor adaptation. This level seems to require integrity of basic mechanisms for the control of action. These mechanisms have often been localized in the cerebellum, which operates as a detector of errors between efferent output and re-afferent input. Cerebellar lesions have been shown to impair prism adaptation, for example. There is no reason to believe that this level directly participates in conscious monitoring of action.

Secondly, at a higher level, a mechanism of monitoring 'how to do' seems to operate. Its existence is demonstrated by the shift in strategy that occurs when the automatic system becomes insufficient for correcting the perturbation and large errors persist at the end of the movement. A strategy based on the consciousness of the discrepancy is introduced. Subjects become aware of the perturbation and can efficiently monitor the error correction. The involvement of pre-frontal cortical areas in this mechanism, besides its empirical demonstration by the above experiment of Slachevsky *et al.* (2001), can be explained by a disruption of the role of pre-frontal cortex in executive functions like anticipation of the consequences of an action. Its impairment is likely to affect conscious monitoring of operations needed to influence the course of an action in order to achieve a particular goal.

Finally, at a still higher level, another conscious mechanism comes into play for assigning the perturbation to its real origin. This function requires not only a simulation of the whole action and its consequences on the external world, but also the monitoring of intention-related signals. This is a key mechanism for correctly attributing intentions to their authors. The attribution of intentional states to other people would thus be based on our ability to monitor our own mental states, so that, if an intention is not recognized as ours, it must pertain to someone else. This mechanism is likely to be altered in schizophrenic patients, specifically those who present Schneiderian symptoms. Their inability to disentangle their own mental states (or actions) from those of other people may be at the origin of their symptoms of hallucinations and delusions. Whether a pre-frontal dysfunction could also account for this impairment has been the subject of many studies (see Posada *et al.*, 2001), which typically showed a decreased frontal activity during attribution tasks in schizophrenic patients. In this case, the role of pre-frontal cortex in inhibiting other areas specialized in analysing the consequences of sensory input (e.g. in the parietal and temporal lobes) may become dysfunctional. The dissociation, in schizophrenia, between a preserved monitoring of errors and an impaired monitoring of the source of the perturbation, as shown here, suggests that these two pre-frontal functions may be affected independently from each other. Such a dissociation calls for new experimental paradigms for a more precise localization of the critical pre-frontal zones involved in these respective functions.

Consciousness of action thus has several functions. First, it is used for monitoring the course of an action and the concomitant re-afferent signals for achieving its goal when compensation for perturbations and non-linearities are beyond the possibilities of automatic control. Moreover, it is essential for determining the direction of interactions occurring during communication between several individuals. The fact that consciousness is called into operation when the normal course of action fails and when problems arise is a good argument for attributing to consciousness of action a dormant role in our everyday behaviour. It wakes up when the normally automatic and implicit mode becomes inefficient in coping with the contingencies of the external world.

References

Arbib, M.A. (1981) Perceptual structures and distributed motor control. In Brooks, V.B. (Ed.) *Handbook of Physiology, Section I: The nervous system, Vol. 2: Motor control.* Baltimore: Williams & Wilkins, pp. 1449–80.

Bartlett, F.C. (1926) Aphasia and kindred disorders of speech, by Henry Head (review). *Brain* **49**, 581–7.

Bernstein, N. (1967) *The Coordination and Regulation of Movements.* Oxford: Pergamon Press.

Bizzi, E., Kalil, R.E. & Tagliasco, V. (1971) Eye-head coordination in monkeys. Evidence for centrally patterned organization. *Science* **173**, 452–4.

Blakemore, S.J., Wolpert, D.M. & Frith, C.D. (1998) Central cancellation of self-produced tickle sensation. *Nature Neurosci* **1**, 635–40.

Carter, C.S., Braver, T.S., Barch, D.M., Botvinick, M.M., Noll, D. & Cohen, J.D. (1998) Anterior cingulate cortex, error detection and the online monitoring of performance. *Science* **280**, 747–9.

Craik, K.J.W. (1943) *The Nature of Explanation.* Cambridge: Cambridge University Press.

Craik, K.J.W. (1947) Theory of the human operator in control system, I: the operator as an engineering system. *Br J Psychol* **38**, 56–61.

Daprati, E., Franck, N., Georgieff, N., Proust, J., Pacherie, E., Daléry, J. & Jeannerod, M. (1997) Looking for the agent: An investigation into consciousness of action and self-consciousness in schizophrenic patients. *Cognition* **65**, 71–86.

Desmurget, M., Prablanc, C., Rossetti, Y., Arzi, M., Paulignan, Y., Urquizar, C. & Mignot, J.C. (1995) Postural and synergic control for three-dimensional movements of reaching and grasping. *J Neurophysiol* **74**, 905–10.

Dierks, T., Linden, D.E.J., Jandl, M., Formisano, E., Goebel, R., Lanferman, H. & Singer, W. (1999) Activation of the Heschl's gyrus during auditory hallucinations. *Neuron* **22**, 615–21.

Fourneret, P. & Jeannerod, M. (1998) Limited conscious monitoring of motor performance in normal subjects. *Neuropsychol* **36**, 1133–40.

Fourneret, P., Franck, N., Slachevsky, A. & Jeannerod, M. (2001) Self-monitoring in schizophrenia revisited. *Neuroreport* **12**, 1203–8.

Franck, N., Farrer, C., Georgieff, N., Marie-Cardine, M., Daléry, J., D'Amato, T. & Jeannerod, M. (2001) Defective recognition of one's own actions in schizophrenic patients. *Am J Psychiat* **158**, 454–9.

Frith, C.D. (1992) *The Cognitive Neuropsychology of Schizophrenia.* Hove: Erlbaum.

Frith, C.D. & Done, D.J. (1989) Experiences of alien control in schizophrenia reflect a disorder in the central monitoring of action. *Psycholog Med* **19**, 359–63.

Hoff, B. & Arbib, M.A. (1993) Models of trajectory formation and temporal interaction of reach and grasp. *J Motor Behav* **25**, 175–92.

Holst, E., von (1954) Relations between the central nervous system and the peripheral organs. *Br J Anim Behav* **2**, 89–94.

Jeannerod, M. (1981) Intersegmental coordination during reaching at natural visual objects. In Long, J. & Baddeley, A. (eds), *Attention & Performance,* Vol. IX. Hillsdale: Erlbaum, pp. 153–68.

Jeannerod, M. (1990) The representation of the goal of an action and its role in the control of goal-directed movements. In Schwartz, E.L. (ed.), *Computational Neuroscience.* Cambridge: MIT Press, pp. 352–68.

Jeannerod, M. (1994) The representing brain. Neural correlates of motor intention and imagery. *Behav Brain Sci* **17**, 187–245.

Jeannerod, M. (1997) *The Cognitive Neuroscience of Action.* Oxford: Blackwell.

Lashley, K.S. (1917) The accuracy of movement in the absence of excitation from the moving organ. *Am J Physiol* **43**, 169–94.

Libet, B. (1985) Unconscious cerebral initiative and the role of conscious will in voluntary action. *Behav Brain Sci* **6**, 529–66.

Libet, B., Gleason, C.A., Wright, E.W. & Pearl, D.K. (1983) Time of conscious intention to act in relation to cerebral activities (readiness potential). The unconscious initiation of a freely voluntary act. *Brain* **106**, 623–42.

Malenka, R.C., Angel, R.W., Hampton, B. & Berger, P.A. (1982) Impaired central error-correcting behaviour in schizophrenia. *Arch Gen Psychiat* **39**, 101–7.

Marr, D. (1982) *Vision.* San Francisco: Freeman.

Miles, F.A. & Evarts, E.V. (1979) Concepts of motor organization. *Ann Rev Psychol* **30**, 327–62.

Miller, G.A., Galanter, E. & Pribram, K.H. (1960) *Plans and the Structure of Behaviour.* New York: Holt.

Milner, A.D., Paulignan, Y., Dijkerman, H.C., Michel, F. & Jeannerod, M. (1999) A paradoxical improvement of misreaching in optic ataxia. New evidence for two separate neural systems for visual localization. *Proc Roy Soc Lond B* **266**, 2225–9.

Nielsen, T.I. (1963) Volition: a new experimental approach. *Scand J Psychol* **4**, 225–30.

Norman, D.A. & Shallice, T. (1980) *Attention to action. Willed and automatic control of behaviour. Center for Human Information Processing,* Technical Report 99. University of California at San Diego.

Oldfield, R.C. & Zangwill, O.L. (1942) Head's concept of the schema and its application in contemporary British psychology. *Br J Psychol* **32**, 267–86; **33**, 58–64.

Posada, A., Franck, N., Georgieff, N. & Jeannerod, M. (2001) Anticipating incoming events. An impaired cognitive process in schizophrenia. *Cognition* **81**, 209–25.

Saltzman, E. (1979) Levels of sensorimotor representation. *J Mathemat Psychol* **20**, 91–163.

Searle, J. (1983) *Intentionality. An essay in the philosophy of mind.* Cambridge: Cambridge University Press.

Slachevsky, A., Pillon, B., Fourneret, P., Pradat-Diehl, P., Jeannerod, M. & Dubois, B. (2001) Preserved adjustment but impaired awareness in a sensory-motor conflict following pre-frontal lesions. *J Cognit Neurosci* **13**, 332–40.

Weiss, P. & Jeannerod, M. (1998) Getting a grasp on coordination. *News Physiol Sci* **13**, 70–5.

Wolpert, D.M., Ghahramani, Z. & Jordan, M.I. (1995) An internal model for sensorimotor integration. *Science* **269**, 1880–2.

SECTION III

BETWEEN EPIPHENOMENALISM AND RATIONALITY: PHILOSOPHICAL ACCOUNTS OF VOLUNTARY ACTION

TILL VIERKANT

In our modern world, most people accept that everything ultimately has a physical cause. Thunderstorms are not caused by gods, but by friction, human life is best explained in terms of the operation of DNA sequences, and so on. Voluntary action is an interesting phenomenon because, although people believe the above-mentioned statements, they do believe, as well that they can choose their actions freely. This seems to be impossible should it hold true that ultimately everything, including voluntary actions, has a physical cause. This problem is not a new one (200 years ago it was the point of departure for Kant's philosophy), but it has become even more pressing. In recent times, neuroscientists and psychologists find more and more evidence that, as Gerhard Roth expresses it, consciousness is not the 'lord of the manor' in our brains. We seem to be no more than epiphenomena of our brains, which 'decide' for us what to do. Solutions to this problem appeal to a metaphysical intellectual realm where we are still free, as envisaged by Kant, and Descartes before him, and are not particularly attractive in our materialist-minded times. How else could this seeming paradox be resolved? One solution that is gaining more and more support among scientists is the idea advanced by radical eliminitavists such as the Churchlands. They suggest that folk psychology, including all the discussion surrounding the willing subject, is nothing but a theory that has been proven wrong and should be eliminated in favour of a new language based on scientific evidence.

If one does not find this or similar radical reductionist forms of explanation convincing, then one has to demonstrate two things. First, the very possibility of the causal efficaciousness of mental events has to be shown. The first two chapters in this section (Schröder and Eilan) are therefore concerned with the challenge of epiphenomenalism (i.e. the philosophical position that denies that mental events could be causally efficacious). Secondly, one has to provide an answer to the question of what exactly it is that we mean when we talk about the 'influence of the mental'. Traditionally, one such answer is 'rationality'. Voluntary actions are understood as actions that we perform because we have reasons for them. The second two chapters (Proust and Vossenkuhl) question not only the role of rationality for voluntary action, but also the very concept of rationality itself. The four essays assembled here come from very different philosophical positions, some compatible and some incompatible with physicalism. Nevertheless, they all have a common interest in making the ways in which the scientific explorations that have been the topic of this book understandable can co-exist with a concept of voluntary action that is not formulated in purely physical terms.

It should come as no surprise, then, that the problem of epiphenomenalism is the starting point of the philosophical section. Jürgen Schröder wishes to demonstrate that the content of consciousness is not epiphenomenal. By epiphenomenalism, he means a physicalist or a property epiphenomenalism. Such an epiphenomenalism holds, like Schröder himself, that the mental is no extra substance. Schröder is convinced that mental properties supervene on physical properties, but he is nevertheless not convinced that this has to make them causally idle, although it is precisely this causal idleness that is the claim of the physical epiphenomenalists. Schröder cites Jagwon Kim's supervenience argument that concludes, from the premise of physical closure and the supervenience of the mental, that the mental has to be causally idle. This argument is, in this respect, a new and more sophisticated variant of the old Kantian problem set in a physicalist monist world. Schröder wishes to show that Kim's argument does not succeed. He tries to show that the argument fails because it employs a dubious notion of causality. Causes have to be proportional to the effects they generate. Schröder argues that no physical cause adequately describes why, as he writes in his example, 'Jones drives to the garage'.

If Schröder's argument succeeds, then it can be shown that there is a causal role for consciousness, but this might not be enough to save our everyday life intuitions. It was Ned Block who came up with the distinction between access consciousness and phenomenal consciousness. It might be the case that access consciousness is causally relevant, but that phenomenal consciousness is not. Access consciousness has representational content, which Schröder tried to prove causally relevant. However, psychologists might agree that representational features of consciousness are causally relevant, but nevertheless continue to deny that the phenomenal side of consciousness is causally relevant, too.

It is this epiphenomenalist threat that Naomi Eilan starts with. Her first argument is supposed to show that Block's distinction does not work, and that access consciousness and phenomenal consciousness are not separable. Yet this is still not enough for Eilan, who then identifies another fundamental epiphenomenalist threat. This threat arises because the identity claim between the phenomenal and the representational sides can be read in two ways:

- The identity claim could be read reductively. A reductive reading would agree that phenomenal and representational properties are identical, but it would also claim that we can reduce the phenomenal side to an independently describable representational framework. The second reading would be an interdependent one.

- The interdependence claim denies the possibility of a reductive reading and argues that we can only understand consciousness by using irreducible terms from both domains. Eilan holds that common-sense realism is only compatible with the latter.

Thus, the most puzzling problem for common sense realism is the opinion that ultimately causal explanations have to be independent of perspective. Because this is so, the interdependence claim seems to be incoherent. Eilan's core argument against this incoherence is that objectivity and the 'god's eye view' are not the same thing. In fact, the 'view from nowhere' is not possible. Objectivity essentially includes perspectivity (Nagel).

Schröder and Eilan provide us with reasons why our everyday intuitions might not be wrong when they try to demonstrate that voluntary action is *not* an epiphenomenon of something both more fundamental and physical. This is a very interesting counterpoint to the empirical sections in this book, but it leaves a lot of work to do. They demonstrate the possibility that our everyday intuitions might not be as wrong as it first seems when reading the empirical sections, but this alone does nothing to prove that they are, in fact, right.

Even if we are convinced that voluntary action is no epiphenomenon, do we really know what we mean when we talk about voluntary action? One traditional answer to this question has been the case of rationality. It is simple enough to see why this should be so. Voluntary actions usually seem to be actions that follow from a chain of reasoning. If I am cold and I have the belief that closing the window will make the room warmer, then I will close the window. I act because of a certain rational conclusion that follows from a conscious belief entertained by me. Again, this answer is not a new one and can be found in Descartes and Kant, and even if nobody wants to buy their metaphysical solutions to the problem of epiphenomenalism any more, their suggestions with regard to what might centrally characterize will are still going strong. Rationality is still one of the strongest contenders for the decisive criterion of voluntariness (most notably is the role of reason in Donald Davidson's work, the starting point of most modern discussions on the topic of voluntary action in philosophy). Virtually nobody in philosophy denies that rationality is one important ingredient for voluntariness, but after that the disagreements begin. Is it the only condition? Is it a necessary one? What exactly is rationality? In what way does it influence our actions? The questions about the nature of voluntary action and the role of rationality within it, is a growing field within philosophy today, but even though the literature is growing, this does not necessarily mean that there is more contact with the results of other sciences interested in human action. This is surprising, as some of the traditional intuitions about the relationship between our reasons and actions have been rendered problematic by the results of the cognitive sciences. Neurophysiologists like Jeannerod and psychologists like Prinz (both in this volume), for example, discovered that some of the actions that people describe as voluntary are not only executed by a fast unconscious system of which the people acting are not aware, but they could also show that this system unconsciously corrects wrong ideas of the representative conscious system about what the right method would be for a particular action. This seems to indicate that the relationship between reasons and actions is not as direct as previously assumed. The system does not act because of the consciously entertained belief and the rational reasoning that flows from it, but because of its unconscious knowledge. It is just as well that the system works like this, because consciously entertained beliefs quite often tend to be inaccurate or even wrong, but it shows at the same time that the conscious lord of reason is, indeed, not quite as much in control of its unconscious household as it likes to believe. This holds true, despite the fact that consciousness might not be an epiphenomenon, and raises questions about the necessity of corrections to our intuitions, even if one agrees that they should not be abandoned altogether in favour of more correct scientific language.

Joëlle Proust is a philosopher who tries to integrate the exciting findings from neurophysiology and psychology into a new account of voluntary action. She distinguishes three senses of voluntariness. In the first sense, voluntary action is connected with the *feeling* of wilful action. This means, for an action to be voluntary in this sense it does not have to be conscious. As long as the system does not complain that this was not the movement it initiated, the movement is voluntary. With this sense of voluntariness, Proust tries to do justice to the above-mentioned results of the empirical sciences. Her two other senses of voluntariness attempt to integrate these findings into a philosophical framework.

In the second, classically philosophical sense, reasoned actions are voluntary, but again, Proust includes the psychological knowledge about our system in her claim that reasons can only act as constraints for the execution of the action. The third sense of voluntariness is long-term voluntariness. This type is the voluntariness of Frankfurt's higher order states. Actions are voluntary in this sense if they are in accordance with some long-term principle that the person considers part of her personality, life plan, moral convictions, etc. In this respect, even reflexes can be voluntary. Reflexive ducking, for example, is involuntary in the second sense (because such an action is not constrained by reasons), but voluntary in the third sense, because being hit by a missile is, for most people, not something that is in accordance with their life plans.

Proust tries to understand what our folk psychological notions of voluntary actions might mean in the context of the cognitive sciences. She does not question the structure of some of the most fundamental folk psychological assumptions themselves. The last philosophical contribution is concerned with exactly this problem. Rationality might be a central notion for our understanding of voluntary action (at least if we take Proust's second level of voluntariness), but before we try to find out what its role is, it might be necessary to ask what exactly rationality is.

In his chapter, Wilhelm Vossenkuhl subdivides rationality into wide and narrow rationality. Wide rationality is equivalent to reason, while narrow rationality is the instrumental rationality of game theory. Vossenkuhl is interested in the latter. This is defined by two components:

- mathematical axioms that help to maximize utility;
- the psychological foundations that define what utility is.

This seems to suggest that rationality is the slave of the psychological utility that defines emotion. The prisoner's dilemma is used to render that theory problematic. Even with rational scaffolding, emotional gain-orientated choice remains suboptimal. On the other hand, Vossenkuhl shows that the axiomatic structure of the theory does not describe human behaviour accurately because, for example, the single dimension, required for narrow rationality, does not really guide human behaviour. Vossenkuhl concludes that there is no easy single relationship between reason and passion. This, in turn, leads to the result that the rationality of an action can only be determined externally by its objects and that no action can be intrinsically rational. The theory of action is a large field in philosophy. It ranges from ontology, via the philosophy of mind, to questions of morality and applied ethics. Obviously, this section cannot address all the issues involved in this heterogeneous field. Nevertheless, the two topics selected, epiphenomenalism and rationality, are not only philosophical core topics for the interdisciplinary discourse in cognitive science—they are also at the heart of most of the debates that go on within the discipline of philosophy itself. In this respect, this section is supposed to provide an insight into the way philosophers tackle the problem of voluntary action in their home discipline. Nevertheless, there is something missing: the practical dimension of the problem. The philosophers mainly addressed theoretical problems. Wilhelm Vossenkuhl indicates that deliberations about rationality should have some consequences in ethics, but within the limited space, he concentrates on the more theoretical issues, like the authors before him. This will change in the subsequent section (Section IV). Law and anthropology provide more practical access to the phenomenon. It should be stimulating for the reader of the scientific and philosophical sections to find the theoretical ideas being dealt with in areas like law, where, in practice, they matter most for us all.

CHAPTER 8

MENTAL CAUSATION: THE SUPERVENIENCE ARGUMENT AND THE PROPORTIONALITY CONSTRAINT

JÜRGEN SCHRÖDER

1 Introduction

One central aspect of the mind-body problem traditionally has been the question: 'How can the mind influence the body, and how it is possible that mental items like intentions and beliefs can make a difference to how we act'. By the times of Descartes this question threatened to undermine his substance dualism because it was not at all clear how something immaterial could change the course of the material particles out of which the human body is composed. Later on, when the conservation of energy was discovered, it was thought that a causal influence from an immaterial soul to a material brain would violate this conservation law because any time there is a mental change, energy would disappear from the brain, and any time there is a mentally induced change in the brain, energy would be created. Although this problem did much to weaken the support for substance dualism, there were still those who sought to render mental causation compatible with the conservation of energy by appealing to quantum effects (e.g. Eccles, 1989).

However, even if the majority consensus in the philosophy of mind today is against substance dualism, the problem of mental causation has not gone away. It has changed its outlook. Its new locus is not substances, but properties. The contemporary problem of mental causation is how mental properties can be causally relevant for the instantiation of physical properties.

What are mental properties? In the philosophy of mind there is a distinction between two broad classes. One class comprises phenomenal properties that are the qualities of the various sense modalities like the quality of a colour or a gustatory sensation. The other class is constituted by intentional properties, that is, the various contents of mental representations. Some authors (e.g. Dretske, 1995; Tye, 1995) contend that there is really only one class and that the first is a part of the second.

In this chapter I shall be concerned with intentional properties only without taking a stand towards the claim that phenomenal properties are intentional or representational properties. If the claim is true we do not need to consider the causal relevance of phenomenal properties independently from the causal relevance of intentional properties. If it is false and it turns out that intentional properties are causally idle, then the possibility has to be considered that phenomenal properties are causally relevant for behaviour. Anyway, I will restrict my discussion to intentional properties and try to show that they can be causally relevant for behaviour.

An alternative construal of the relationship between phenomenal and representational properties is proposed by Naomi Eilan (this volume). She argues that phenomenal and representational properties are interdependent and denies that the phenomenal reduces to the representational. In my view, however, her conviction that 'all sides concede a causal role for representational properties' is overly optimistic. Indeed, in what follows we shall see that there is an argument that challenges this optimism.

Over the last years, Jaegwon Kim has argued that the possibility of mental causation is called into doubt by an argument that he called 'the supervenience argument' and which unfolds in three stages (Kim, 1993, 1997). The first stage consists of the principle of causal closure of the physical domain that says, roughly, that for every phenomenon describable in physical terms there is a sufficient cause equally describable in physical terms. When we apply this principle to any case of mental causation it says that for the event to be explained, for instance, a behaviour, there is a physical cause of this behaviour. Now we have a mental and a physical cause for the same behaviour, and the question arises how they are related to each other. The second stage of the argument tries to consider exhaustively the possible candidates for such relationships yielding the result that the mental properties of the cause supervene on its physical properties without being identical or reducible to them. Finally, an exclusion principle is applied which states that if the complete causal work on a given occasion with respect to a property B (of behaviour) is done by a property P of a brain state then anything that is not P is causally superfluous with respect to B on this occasion. Since the result of the second stage is that mental properties only supervene on physical properties without being identical with them, the conclusion follows that mental properties are causally idle.

The first part of this chapter sets forth the premises of Kim's argument suggesting that we provisionally accept its first and second stage. It is the third stage that is flawed because of a misleading analogy between our common sense understanding of work being done by intentional agents and work being done by properties. At the end of the paper it is argued, however, that the premise of causal closure is in a way misleading. While there is a version of it that seems to be true there is another one that cannot be maintained. Besides, it can be argued that Kim's principle of causal inheritance, which is supposed to secure causal relevance to second-order functional properties, cannot be sustained. So functional properties, although physical, have no causal potential at all.

The second part takes Stephen Yablo's proportionality constraint to be the basis of a solution for the problem of mental causation and argue that this constraint not only applies to causal explanations, but to the causal relationship itself.

The third part compares content properties with intrinsic properties of mental representations, which I take to be activation vectors, and argues that the semantic property of a representation is more proportional to an abstract behavioural property than the form of an activation vector. If, however, the explanandum is a set of trajectories of limb movements, then this form is more proportional. For different properties that are instantiated by an event e, different properties of an event c are causally relevant if proportionality is to constrain the relationship of causal relevance. This leads finally to a change in the task for defenders of the supervenience argument: if the proportionality constraint is endorsed they have to show that there are abstract physical properties that are as proportional to the behavioural properties as the semantic properties are. It is argued briefly that, in some cases, physical properties *cannot* be proportional to the behavioural properties, while the semantic ones can always be and that, therefore, the physical properties cannot pre-empt the semantic ones from being causally efficacious.

2   Kim's premises

We have seen that the conclusion of idleness of mental properties is supposed to follow from the principle of causal closure of the physical domain, from the supervenience, non-identity, and non-realization of mental properties with respect to physical properties, and from the exclusion principle. The principle of causal closure assures us of there being an explanation of a behaviour in physical terms, so that we have two causes whose relationship is to be determined. The exclusion of all possible relationships except supervenience leads us to the idea of mental properties as dependent upon, but different from the physical properties of brain states. Finally, the exclusion principle drives home the point that mental properties that are neither functional, nor identical with physical properties, and which are only instantiated if certain physical properties are instantiated, have no causal work to do, and thus seem to be epiphenomenal, contrary to our intuitions as agents.

Kim has presented this argument not in order to convince us of epiphenomenalism, but to state the background against which the possibility of mental causation has to be demonstrated. For him, the reality of mental causation is not in question. Rather, what needs to be done is to show how mental causation is possible in a physical world. If Kim's argument shows why mental causation is not possible and if mental causation is actual, then there must be something wrong with this argument. There must be one or several places that should not stand up to closer inspection.

2.1   Closure, supervenience, and causal inheritance

I suggest that we accept the first stage of the argument, the principle of causal closure. The main reason for accepting it is the past track record of the physical sciences, such as physics proper, physical chemistry, chemistry, biochemistry, etc., which, in order to causally explain any phenomenon in their domain, did not need to make reference to supernatural powers. Of course, there are those phenomena studied by parapsychologists, such as telekinesis and extrasensory perception, but even for those phenomena, people working in this field are suggesting physical explanations (Balanovski & Taylor, 1978; Schmidt, 1982).

Then, there is the possible objection that who knows what physics will be like in a hundred years or so. Perhaps physicists will postulate new properties or theories as in the last century, when Newton's laws of motion and gravitation could not explain the electrical phenomena. However, this objection is clearly overstating the case. What is at stake in mental causation is the causal efficacy[1] of semantic properties and nobody will probably believe that such properties could be introduced into physics in order to explain phenomena that could not be explained before. New properties of elementary particles, perhaps, but meanings, certainly not. In any case, it seems that meanings could not be basic physical properties, that is, properties of fields or particles, because we would simply be unable to say what these meanings could be or what they were for.

When we accept the closure principle vis-à-vis semantic properties, there are two stages left where something might have gone wrong: the exclusion of all other relationships except supervenience and the exclusion principle itself.

I suggest we accept the second stage of Kim's argument, since if a kind of dependence relationship is to be achieved between mental and physical properties, mental properties will not be independently instantiated and so the possibilities of over-determination, of joint sufficiency, and of intermediate links in a chain are ruled out. For semantic properties, identity and realization seem to be ruled out as well. So mental and intrinsic physical properties seem to be distinct properties (no identity), the one not being realized by the other (semantic properties are not functional roles), but the mental depending on the physical.

There is perhaps one point that is controversial in this part of the argument—the claim that semantic properties are not functional roles. This claim has been put deliberately as an identity thesis because, in this form, it is less controversial than as a determination thesis. However, even in this form, the claim that content is not identical with a functional role of brain states may still be controversial. The strategy will therefore be to assume that content *is* identical with functional role and then to show that if it is, contrary to first appearances, it cannot be causally efficacious. Identifying content with functional role would then not be a solution of the problem, but would amount to accepting the truth of epiphenomenalism for mental content. However, even if this argument is successful, the question of whether content *is* functional role or not is still not settled. It could be suggested, however, that arguments such as Fodor's against the adequacy of functional role semantics that concern the compositionality of meanings (Fodor & Lepore, 1996; Fodor, 1998) tend to show that meanings are not functional roles.

Assume for a moment, however, that semantic properties *are* functional roles, that they stand in a realization relationship with intrinsic properties of brain states. In this case, according to Kim, the possibility of mental causation would not be in question. This is because, as functional properties, they would inherit their causal powers from their realizers.

> Functional properties, as second-order properties, do not bring new causal powers into the world: they do not have causal powers which go beyond the causal powers of their first-order realizers. If M has two realizers, P_1 and P_2, each M-instance is either a P_1-instance or P_2-instance, and those M-instances that are P_1-instances have the causal powers of P_1, and, similarly, the M-instances that are P_2-instances have the causal powers of P_2. There is, therefore, no special problem about their causal efficacy either; *they will simply inherit the causal powers of their realizers.* (Kim, 1997, p. 295, emphasis added)

The principle of causal inheritance according to which a functional property inherits the causal powers of its realizer seems to be wrong, however, for the following reason. If the metaphor of inheritance is to be any guide in these abstract matters there must be a heir and a testator, but we only have a testator, the physical property, and no heir. This is because the functional property is second-order. It is not a property on the same footing as the realizer property. Just as a policeman cannot inherit the fortune of Jones if Jones *is* the policeman, that is, if Jones fills the role of a policeman, so it is impossible for a second-order property to inherit the causal powers of its first-order property. If there cannot be any inheritance where there is only a testator but no heir, there is no inheritance of causal powers by functional properties because there is no heir.

The same point can be seen when we think about the second-order property of being a functional role of the first-order property. A functional role is a set of causal powers. The first-order property is said to have this set of causal powers. If the second order property would inherit the causal powers from the first-order property, it would inherit itself, since it *is* what it is supposed to inherit, namely, the set of causal powers. Again, if inheritance requires two distinct entities then we have no instance of inheritance here. If the functional property is second-order, that is, a property of a first- or lower order property, then it does not *have* causal powers, but it *is* causal powers. If you are a set of causal powers you do not have them, that is, the causal powers are not again properties of you. It would be equally wrong to say that the property red has the property of being red. Although the relationship between a thing and its being red is not a relationship between first- and second-order property, we have the same basic relationship in both cases, that between something and one of its properties. In general then, it is wrong to claim that every (higher-order) property has itself as a property. There may be properties for which the claim is true, perhaps the property of being exciting is in itself exciting, but it is wrong for red and it is wrong for sets of causal powers.

It is instructive to have a closer look at the above quote once again. Kim is speaking about *M*- and *P*-instances. There is an ambiguity between the causal powers of a property instance and the causal powers of the property itself. A property instance may have causal powers that the property itself does not have. The property of hitting the windowpane at 12 o'clock is not a causally relevant property for the breaking of the window, but one of the causal powers of the *instance* of the property 'hitting my window pane at 12 o'clock' is that it was able to break my window. It is true then that the *M*-instances that are P_1 have the causal powers of P_1 and that the *M*-instances that are P_2 have the causal powers of P_2, but, and this is the important point, nothing with respect to the *property* M follows. As Kim says, The *M-instance* gets its causal power from the *property P*. He does not say that the *property M* gets its causal powers from P, and as we have seen, it could not get its causal powers from *P* if it is nothing but those powers.

2.2 Exclusion

We have arrived at the third stage of the argument, the exclusion principle that says, since mental properties supervene on physical properties and are not identical with them, they have no causal work to do because this work is already done by the physical properties. I think the basic mistake of the argument is hidden in this principle, which at first sight looks completely innocent and self-evident. What could be more obvious than the fact that if somebody's work is done by somebody else then there is no need any more for anyone to do this work? Yet again, we seem to have a misleading metaphor. When the work to be done is driving a car to a fuel station and filling the tank then if Jones does it Smith need not do it. The work to be done is a concrete event, which may instantiate a variety of properties beside the property that it is driving to the fuel station and tank filling. The agent who does the work has to bring about this event, that is, take the car, drive to the station, etc., *and* he has to make sure that it satisfies the requisite property. He has to make sure that a possible variety of physically different events all satisfy the relevant description. Now, the counterpart of Jones is a physical property of an event that is a cause of the instantiation of another property of another event. However, this property does *not* ensure that a possible variety of physically different events *all* satisfy a certain description.

What the physical property $P1$ makes sure is that another event has a certain property P_2. It does not and it cannot assure that a different property P_3 equally satisfies a certain description B, that is, a behavioural description like 'grasping a cup of tea'. However, this is exactly what Jones does. Jones is able to make sure that a variety of different physical events satisfy the description 'tank filling' because his mental representation of a proper tank filling contains criteria for a physical event's satisfying the description. So it seems that what really accounts for the fact that Jones makes sure that the tank gets filled is the content or certain aspects of the content of his mental representations.

There is always a huge variety of different combinations of muscles to move a limb on a certain path through space and there is also a huge variety of trajectories to achieve a certain goal, to reach for an object, or to get a tank filled. What M_1 (the property of being an intention that the gas tank gets filled) does is to make sure that this goal is achieved and that some P_i, one of the members of the set of goal equivalent behaviours, gets instantiated. It is clearly relevant for the achievement of the goal that if a certain P_i cannot be instantiated another P_j takes its place.

We have seen that mental properties are in a certain respect like agents, whereas the intrinsic physical properties of brain states are not. The analogy between human doings and brain happenings is misleading in yet another respect. What we have considered so far is a counterpart of Jones, namely, a physical property. What is still missing is a counterpart of Smith, the man whose work is done by Jones. If the counterpart of an intentional agent is another intentional agent the counterpart of a mental property should be another mental property, but if it is mental properties that should be substituted for each other then it would be a mistake to substitute a physical for a mental property if the analogy to the case of Jones and Smith is to be preserved. If we take the analogy seriously we would substitute one mental property by another one, for example, the property of being an intention to fill the tank of a car could be substituted by the property of being an intention to fill the tank in a specific way, say by driving to a particular fuel station. Conversely, if we are looking for a counterpart of the relationship between physical and mental properties we find it in the relationship between the properties of being trajectories of limb and car movements, on the one hand, and the property of being a tank filling, on the other hand. Of course, the work that Jones is doing, i.e. to make sure that his and the car's behaviour count as a driving to the fuel station etc., is *not* being done by *any* of the specific physical properties on which the whole action supervenes.

The 'making sure' has to be cashed out somehow and it can be done in the following way. Suppose that, as a result of learning, a variety of motor routines, which have all the same desired effect, have been connected to a certain goal representation. What makes sure that if one of the routines cannot be executed, an alternative is executed, is precisely these connections with the same goal representation. What played a causal role in the process of establishing these connections is the fact that the goal representation has a certain representational content (cf. Dretske, 1988). For every single connection between one goal representation and various equivalent motor representations (equivalent with respect to goal achievement), it is the fact that the goal representation has a certain content that is responsible for the build-up of these connections. However, if content is responsible for the build-up of every connection, then it is responsible for the build-up of the whole structure which connects the goal representation to the various motor representations. It is this whole structure that cashes out what 'making sure' means in this context and underlies the counterfactual claim that if one motor representation failed to be activated, another one would have been activated. What was, however, causally responsible for the build-up of this structure is the content of the goal representation. If the structure makes sure that alternative movements are produced and if content is causally responsible for the build-up of this structure then, I think, it is fair to say that content itself makes sure that alternative movements can be produced if, for some reason, a particular movement cannot be produced. It is such stories that we need in order to justify that a property makes sure that an event of type F occurs.

I conclude that the analogy of work being done is misleading in two respects. First, if we cling to the analogy the work of mental properties could be done by other *mental* properties. Secondly, and more importantly, the work being done in the sense of making sure *could* not be done by subvenient physical properties.

3 Yablo's proportionality constraint

The idea that a property makes sure that an effect occurs that satisfies a certain description interlinks well with a constraint on causation which has been suggested by Stephen Yablo: the proportionality constraint (*PC*; Yablo, 1992, 1997). For any instance of causation, the property of the cause, which is to be causally relevant for the instantiation of a given property of the effect, must be proportional to this property of the effect.

What does it mean when a property is proportional to another property? The respect in which a property A should be proportional to a property B is the degree of abstractness of A. If B has a high degree of abstractness, then A should also have a high degree. If B's level of abstractness is low, i.e. if B contains certain details, then A should contain certain other details as well. To illustrate, if the fact to be causally explained is the breaking of a windowpane without any further details then the property to be cited in a causal explanation would be the momentum of an object hitting the window. If the fact to be explained is the breaking in a certain way, for instance, that it started breaking on a rectangular surface of 20 square inches, then the momentum alone is not sufficient to cause this further property instantiation, but the form and surface of the impacting object may explain why the window started to break in that way. The more detailed the properties to be explained the more detailed have to be the explaining properties. The proportionality constraint works in two directions. On the one hand, and more obviously, it forces explanations to deliver the details that are needed to account for the details of the effect. The fact that (PC) is *always* endorsed in this direction constitutes an argument for (PC). On the other hand, less obviously, it asks for the maximally abstract property, which is able to account for the property of the effect to be explained. If all or most window panes of a certain sort break upon impact of objects with a momentum of more than 5 kgm/s then the property which is proportional to this property of the effect, viz. breaking, is having a momentum of more than 5 kgm/s. Objects with a momentum of 6, 7, or 8 kgm/s lead all to a breaking of the window, but they lead to its breaking in virtue of the same property, namely, having a momentum of more than 5 kgm/s. Therefore, with respect to the breaking alone the more specific properties of having a momentum of 6, 7, or 8 are irrelevant. What is relevant instead is the more abstract property. In order to find out what the proportional properties are we need to apply Mill's method of differences, adding or subtracting detail in the process until deletion of further detail does not produce the effect anymore.

While it is quite clear that the proportionality constraint is always endorsed in the direction of greater specificity it may be questioned if the constraint really works in two directions or whether it is not really a specificity constraint that is endorsed. Differences in causes should be specified in order to explain differences in effects, but is the converse also true? If a momentum of 8 kgm/s caused the breaking of the window on this occasion, was not it *this* momentum that did the breaking? Of course it was this momentum, but the event of impact did not only have this property, it also had other properties. One of them was that the momentum was greater than 5 kgm/s. When we are experimenting with various momenta we will eventually find that all stones with a momentum greater than 5 will lead to a breaking of the window. When we possess this knowledge and ask again what property is responsible for the breaking as such, that is, irrespective of the particular way of breaking we are forced to answer that it is the property of being greater than 5, not the property of being 8, which is responsible for the breaking. The property of having a momentum of 8 may be responsible for the fact that the window broke in a certain fraction of a second or some such property, but it is the property of being greater than 5 which is responsible for the breaking as such.

It is somewhat misleading to say that, on this occasion, it was a momentum of 8, while on that occasion it was one of 6 which led to the breaking of two windows sharing a number of properties, such as thickness, form, and area. It is misleading because either we want to know which properties are causally relevant for certain other properties or we do not. If we do 'then' if the same property is instantiated by the effect on two occasions, *the most parsimonious explanation* is that the same causally responsible property was instantiated by the cause on these occasions. Of course, we could say that, on various occasions, it is various properties that account for the same effect, i.e. the instantiation of the same property. However, then we would have violated the principle of parsimony if there really *is* a property that is equally instantiated by different cause events.

Moreover, assume that there is a common cause of two effects, which are thereby correlated with each other, as in the case of a drop in atmospheric pressure, the onset of bad weather, and a change in the state of a barometer. The change in the barometer does not cause the bad weather nor does the onset of the bad weather cause a change in the barometer. In this case we are not content with the regularity existing between the two kinds of change. We want to know if one is the cause of the other until we finally find out that they both depend on a third kind of change, the drop in atmospheric pressure. Analogously, we should not be content with the regularity that a certain kind of window always breaks when there is an impact with a momentum of 8 kgm/s, but ask whether it is this property which is causally relevant for the breaking as such. To find out whether it is this property or not we have to do certain experiments, and to compare their results with our regularity. If there is a range of momenta that lead to the breaking of a given kind of window then the property we deemed to be causally relevant for the breaking, in fact, is not really relevant for the breaking as such, but for something more specific.

The principle of parsimony and the analogy to what we are doing in cases where there is a common cause both argue in favour of the proportionality constraint. They both suggest that our explanatory practice is, indeed, governed by the second part of the constraint, which says that you should look for the maximally abstract property that is either sufficient for the instantiation of another property or a part of a set of jointly sufficient properties. However, showing that our explanatory practice obeys (PC) is perhaps not sufficient to show that (PC) is a constraint on causation. Proportional properties might be necessary for explanations in the special sciences, but not for the instantiation of the to-be-explained properties themselves. Why should that be? When we are looking for more specific or more abstract properties, what we want to find out is on what properties a given effect really depends, whether the *apparent* dependence on a property P is still to be confirmed when we vary the amount of detail of P. This quest for a property on which the instantiation of another property really depends, seems to argue for the idea that (PC) is a constraint on causation itself, rather than a constraint on causal explanation only. Thus, it belongs to metaphysics, and not only to epistemology and scientific methodology.

If we accept (PC) as a constraint on causation in general, then we are in a position to see what is wrong with the exclusion principle. Instead of exempting the supervenient mental properties of their causal efficacy the subvenient properties, which contain more detail than the supervenient ones, are causally irrelevant with respect to certain properties of the behaviour to be explained. If the property to be explained is one of drinking, then the exact form of the physical state on which the intention to drink supervenes is irrelevant for this property to be instantiated. If, on the other hand, the exact trajectories of the limbs, which achieve the action of drinking on a given occasion, are to be explained, then an intention to drink does not contain enough detail and the form of a physical state in the prefrontal cortex may be proportional to this property of the effect.

The proportionality constraint, counteracting the force of the intuition that sustains commitment to the exclusion principle, equally shows how properties that are mentioned by other special sciences, such as biochemistry, physiology, geology, etc., can be causally efficacious. They can be causally efficacious as proportional properties. Only if they are purely functional properties[2] they cannot have causal powers because then they *are* causal powers. The causal efficacy of the properties singled out and mentioned by the special sciences is *guaranteed*, since they have been accepted by the practitioners of those sciences precisely *because* they are proportional to the effects to be explained.

4 Applying the proportionality constraint to semantic properties

4.1 Content and activation vectors

In order to show now that the semantic properties are more proportional to the relevant property of behaviour it is necessary, first, to say what the properties are on which the semantic properties depend. Usually, not much attention is given to this, but it is assumed that there is a base property P on which another property M supervenes. Normally, nothing more is said about P. Let us assume for the sake of vividness, however, that the base properties are the forms of activation vectors where an activation vector is an n-tuple of activation values of a set of nerve cells (McClelland *et al.*, 1986; Churchland & Sejnowski, 1992; Georgopoulos, 1997). The assumption that representations are activation vectors is neutral with respect to the debate between classicalists and connectionists since activation vectors can be implementations of symbolic representations (cf. Fodor & Pylyshyn, 1988).

If we decide to identify representations in the brain with activation vectors, we have to say how we treat weight vectors because they are also candidates for representations. Weight vectors are n-tuples of weight values of connection weights between nerve cells. Weight vectors determine how activation in a network develops over time. They can be regarded as representing inferential knowledge, knowledge of what to infer from what. Activation vectors, on the other hand, represent the terms of the inferences. When we take intentions for action to be the result of inferences from beliefs and desires they are terms of inferences. This is one reason for choosing the form of activation vectors as the base properties.

A second reason derives from the fact that what we worry about in mental causation is how the content of our *conscious* intentions can be causally efficacious for our behaviour. We would not be worried if the efficacy of our unconscious motives were the only thing in question. However, it does not seem to be unreasonable to identify conscious states with some kind of activation vectors (O'Brien & Opie, 1999). Whether they are identified with *stable* activation vectors or with some other (possibly complex) kind is of minor importance (Schröder, 1999). However, if we adopt a so-called vehicle theory of consciousness[3] and link consciousness to activation vectors, it seems inevitable to consider activation vectors as the vehicles of conscious content.

Let's assume then that the forms of activation vectors are the base properties for content. And let's counterfactually assume for a moment that every vector consisted of the activation of a single cell. Every representational content would be represented by single cells. Not very economic, but clearly not conceptually impossible, assuming, again contrary to fact, that all these cells had the same intrinsic characteristics, i.e. the same input–output functions, the same thresholds, etc. Now, consider one of these cells in the brain of a cat that, say, represents mice, is connected to sensory representations of mice and to motor representations of chasing behaviour. Another cell representing dogs is connected to sensory representations of dogs and to motor representations of fleeing behaviour. In this case, we could substitute the mouse cell for the dog cell without there being any change either in consciousness, or content or behaviour. There is no such change when we concentrate upon the cell that is replaced. At the location where it was a cell is inserted which has the same intrinsic properties standing in the same relationships to other cells and to environmental properties as the previous cell. If consciousness depends on representation (cf. Dretske, 1995; Tye, 1995), the content of consciousness will be the same because the representational content is the same. If it depends on intrinsic properties it will be the same because these properties are the same, too. If we want to explain chasing behaviour we refer to what the cell's activation represents, not to the physical properties of the representation. If the cell had not represented mice, but dogs it would have activated the fleeing behaviour motor assembly. It would have represented dogs if it had been connected to sensory representations of dogs such that its maximal response would have been to dogs and not to mice. I follow common practice in neurobiology when taking the maximal response of a nerve cell as a criterion for the properties in the environment to be represented (cf. Hubel & Wiesel, 1968; Barlow, 1972). Nothing crucial hinges on this assumption. In this case, the base properties do not contain too much detail, but they are not specific enough in order to explain the differences in behaviour since we have assumed that they are intrinsically all the same.

Let us assume now that every cell differed intrinsically from every other cell and had a different content. Would the intrinsic properties then pre-empt the content properties from being causally efficacious? Since virtually all kinds of behaviour can be accomplished in a variety of ways it follows from this fact alone that the intrinsic properties of a cell cannot be proportional to the behavioural property to be explained since there have to be some properties that are causally relevant for the trajectories of limbs. However, the semantic properties are not so relevant because they are not proportional (not specific enough) to the trajectories. Since the semantic properties are not proportional the intrinsic properties must be, but if they are proportional to the trajectories they cannot be proportional to the abstract behavioural property.

Until now we have considered representations being constituted by single cells. If our mental representations were activations of single cells their intrinsic properties would not be proportional to the properties to be explained. Initially, and more realistically, we assumed the bases of content properties to be the forms of activation vectors. Well, does this difference make a difference for our discussion? It does, but the difference is not decisive. First, while in the case of single cells it was possible to have a set of single cells all with the same intrinsic properties and all with different contents in the case of complex activation vectors it is quite implausible that vectors that correspond to different contents can be intrinsically the same. Part of the complexity of the representation is needed for an adequate adjustment of muscles which realizes a certain action so that if this adjustment differs the representation has to differ as well and not only in content, but in its intrinsic properties, for it is these properties which are proportional to the trajectories of limbs. However, even if there are no complex activation vectors corresponding to different contents, while intrinsically being the same the analogy to the single cell situation in which different contents correspond to different intrinsic properties does hold. What is crucial is that there have to be differences in intrinsic properties, which correspond to differences in muscle adjustments and limb trajectories, and that if the intrinsic properties are proportional to the trajectories they cannot be proportional to more abstract behavioural properties. However, the semantic properties can and it is these properties that are causally relevant for the behavioural properties. We may conclude that whether mental representations are constituted by single cells or cell assemblies is a difference that makes almost no difference with respect to the causal efficacy of content properties.

4.2   Proportionality and causal closure

If proportionality is a constraint on causation, where does this leave us with respect to the principle that the physical domain is causally closed? To answer this question, we should distinguish between two versions of the closure principle. In its typical formulation, the principle says that for every physical effect there is a sufficient physical cause. It does not say that physical effects have to be described in a certain way nor does it say that for every physical description of an effect there is a sufficient physical cause. One could, however, strengthen the principle such that it would require that every physical effect under every physical description has a sufficient physical cause:

CPstrong: every physical effect has a sufficient physical cause under *every* physical description.

A different formulation of the principle says that for every physical effect there is *some* description relative to which there is a sufficient physical cause.

CPweak: every physical effect has a sufficient physical cause under *some* physical description.

This formulation is compatible with the situation that there are some physical descriptions of an effect which are so abstract that there are no abstract physical properties of their causes, which are proportional to them. If we take causation to be a relationship between facts then the closure principle should say something about the descriptions relative to which we want to explain an event. However, CP_{strong} is probably too strong because it takes something for granted for which we do not have any evidence—that there are very abstract physical properties of mental representations that are proportional to abstract behavioural properties. For this reason, the principle should be accepted in its weak form only.

It is sometimes said that if the closure principle is violated then this means that physical theory is incomplete or that there are (mental or otherwise) intrusions in physical processes. According to CP_{weak}, however, every concrete event, i.e. every instantiation of some property at some region of space-time, has at least one property for which there is a proportional physical cause. In this sense, there is no incompleteness of physical theory. It covers all events under at least some descriptions. Cases in which there are no proportional physical causes do not challenge the completeness of physics. What they challenge is CP_{strong}, but it would seem to be absurd that the completeness of physics should be understood according to CP_{strong}. If it were so understood we would expect from physics perspicuous explanations of such things as why Jones went to the meeting or why Lisa cancelled her flight. However, we do not expect such explanations from physics, that is, we do not expect explanations, which do not only explain why the elementary particles that are involved in Jones' and Lisa's behaviour came to be distributed in a certain way, but why this distribution instantiated a particular abstract property.

4.3   Proportionality and exclusion

We have tacitly assumed in this discussion that the content of a representation is more proportional to the property of behaviour to be explained than any intrinsic physical or physiological property. However, this assumption may be wrong. Perhaps there are abstract physical properties, which are just as proportional to the behavioural property as the content of a representation is. If there are we could run a variant of Kim's exclusion argument in order to show that content properties are causally idle, since we already have a proportional physical property and since this property is not identical with the semantic property. How are we to respond to this objection?

Suppose we take all those activation vectors that lead to a behaviour that satisfies a certain description from the point of view of the agent, for instance, 'reaching for a cup of tea'. Our task is then to find a physical property being such that all and only those activation vectors, which lead to a behaviour that satisfies the description have this property. What we are looking for are forms of activation vectors corresponding to a given content.

The physical property must be such that it is not simply a disjunction of the different specific forms of vectors because, for one thing, that would render the task trivial and, secondly, this manoeuvre would raise the problem of projectibility, which has been urged by Kim (1992). If we exclude disjunction what could this property be like?

Suppose what is unlikely, but not impossible (with single cells anyway), namely, that two representations have the same intrinsic properties, but different meanings and different connections with the motor cortex. In every such case, the physical property would be too unspecific in order to explain the difference between two behaviours associated with the two representations. That is, it would not meet the proportionality constraint. In such cases, it would be clear that the intrinsic properties are not causally relevant for the instantiation of abstract behavioural properties. However, in the majority of cases there will be differences between intrinsic properties of representations when there are differences between behaviours. We clearly cannot rule out that there may be abstract intrinsic properties corresponding to the behaviour and to the content properties, but, once again, what should they be and, more importantly, *why* should they exist? We have seen no reason yet that requires the existence of such properties. From a purely physical point of view, the grouping together of all those movements that satisfy the description 'grasping a cup of tea' is simply invisible. There are movements and there are physical explanations of these movements. Nothing else shows up in this perspective. Therefore, it seems that, physically speaking, the existence of abstract intrinsic properties is not called for. That means that, from the physical sciences, a reason for the existence of such properties will quite probably not be forthcoming.

It may be possible to construct 'averaged' activation vectors taking all the vectors corresponding to all the movements that satisfy a certain behavioural description. How exactly this averaging might proceed would be a matter of further investigation, but let's suppose we had a specific proposal and it worked, that is, for every set of activation vectors it would yield an 'average' vector. Would this show that there are intrinsic physical properties that are proportional to the behavioural property to be explained? I think it would not, since the average vectors have been artificially constructed and this renders the construction trivial. The construction is artificial because it needed the equivalence class of behaviours to get started. No such equivalence class, no construction. Contrast this with the explanation of a limb trajectory. Here, no help from a description in ordinary behavioural terms is needed. The explanation is completely free standing. Take away the guidance from the equivalence class and the averaging process will not work because you will not know which vectors the process should be based on.

There are cases where averaging procedures are legitimate means for constructing a more abstract property. For example, changes in the mean kinetic energy of molecules in the case of ideal gases are legitimately proportional to various effects, for instance, changes in pressure. However, here there is no question about how to select the analogues of activation vectors, namely, the molecules that go into the averaging. It is simply all the molecules of the gas sample. The question of selection does not arise because there is nothing that corresponds to an equivalence class of behaviours—at least nothing that would be determined by criteria extraneous to physics.

I take these reflections to show that there are legitimate and illegitimate proportional properties for arbitrary effects. Furthermore, in order to maintain Kim's original argument it would be necessary to produce legitimate physical proportional properties for which the prospects seem extremely bleak, in my view, since we do not get at the right equivalence classes with physical concepts alone.

Before the proportionality constraint was put forward as an adequacy condition on causation there was no need to find such properties. It was enough to have *some* physical property, for example, some form of an activation vector or other, being sufficient (among other things) for a certain movement to occur. Of course, to find such physical properties was not difficult at all. With the proportionality constraint in place, however, the task has changed dramatically. In order to run an analogue to Kim's supervenience argument it has to be shown now that there are abstract physical properties that pre-empt the proportional semantic properties from being causally efficacious. Not only has the difficulty of the task changed, but the burden of the argument has changed as well. If someone wants still to argue for epiphenomenalism, they have to show how to construct the requisite abstract physical properties. The properties that are used by cognitive psychology in explanations of certain aspects of actions (cf. Hommel, this issue) are certainly not of the requisite sort. Although these properties are not semantic, but abstract physical properties of a system, the explananda of such explanations are not the same as the explananda of common sense explanations. Semantic properties are supposed to explain the form of a behaviour, e.g. 'Why did she go shopping today?', whereas cognitive psychology seeks answers to questions about the mechanisms that *realize* goal-directed action, such as what mechanisms exploit the combinations of motor patterns and sensory codes. Both explanatory projects are worth pursuing, the scientific one because we want to know the functional organization that underlies our decision process and the common sense one because we want to be able to understand ourselves as agents who are responsible for their actions.

If semantic properties of physical structures are proportional to the behavioural properties in want of an explanation and if no properties describable in purely physical terms are proportional, then the semantic properties are causally relevant for the instantiation of the behavioural properties and the physical properties are not.

I have argued that proportionality is not only a constraint on causal explanations, but on the causal relationship itself. If this is correct, then semantic properties of mental representations seem to have a better claim to causal relevance vis-à-vis certain properties of behaviour than the intrinsic physical properties of these representations. This is not to say that it is impossible to find abstract physical properties that are as proportional to the behaviour to be explained as the semantic properties are. However, I have argued that it is unlikely that such properties will be found because, for example, averaging procedures over activation vectors would be either trivial or cheating. Therefore, it seems that semantic properties stand a better chance to be causally relevant for abstract behavioural properties than intrinsic physical properties.

I have also hinted at the kind of causal relevance semantic properties may have. In the discussion about what it means that semantic properties make sure something it turned out, that the causal relevance of semantic properties for behaviour consists in making sure that one out of a number of equivalent goal-directed movements gets realized. The semantic properties do not make sure that this or that specific movement is realized, but that *some* movement which satisfies the goal description is realized. Semantic properties of a representation can play this role because they are responsible for the build-up of a material structure of connections in the brain, which is the proximate cause of making sure that goal-directed behaviour will be instantiated. However, it is a kind of representational content, namely, the instantiation of properties in the environment, which guides the build-up of this material structure. Per transitivity, this representational content contributes to making sure that behaviour that meets the current goal description will be displayed. This is *how* semantic properties can be causally relevant for the instantiation of behavioural properties while the function of the proportionality constraint is to show *that* they can be so relevant.

However, a problem remains. I have spoken of the instantiation of properties in the environment as the content of mental representations. Some people would object to such an interpretation of content on the grounds that a representational content should be something that can be satisfied or not, true or false, but an instantiation of a property cannot be true or false. So, the objection would be that it has not been shown that semantic properties are causally relevant for behaviour, but only that something similar is.

This objection can possibly be met in the following way. First, what is crucial for causality is proportionality. Secondly, real semantic properties and proto-semantic properties (as we might call them) have the same degree of proportionality. If a proto-semantic property is proportional to a behavioural property, a corresponding real semantic property will also be proportional because they are different only with respect to the capacity of being true or false. Thirdly, what we need in order to vindicate our common sense conception of mental causation is that the content of our intentions is causally relevant for our behaviour, but this content does not have to be construed as something that can be satisfied like a proposition. It may be a part of the world. If, for our common sense conception of mental causation, the difference between real and proto-semantic properties is irrelevant, then it is enough to vindicate this conception based on proto-semantic properties.

Notes

1 Throughout this article I will use 'causal efficacy' and 'causal relevance' interchangeably. Thus, I depart deliberately from a use of these terms by Jackson & Pettit (1988, 1990). According to them, a property may be causally relevant without being causally efficacious. The causal relevance being due to its programming a certain type of effect.

2 A property is *purely* functional if it is the second-order property of being a set of causal powers that is a property of a first-order property. It is, of course, possible to refer to a first-order property via a functional profile. In this case, the property referred to is not functional and thus *can* have causal powers.

3 A vehicle theory says that it is not certain processes a representation has to undergo in order to become conscious, but that the token representation, as such, is sufficient for being conscious of its content.

References

Balanovski, E. & **Taylor J.** (1978) Can electromagnetism account for extrasensory perception? Nature 276, 64–7.

Barlow, H.B. (1972) Single units and sensation: a neuron doctrine for perceptual psychology? *Perception* 1, 371–94.

Churchland, P. & Sejnowski, T. (1992) *The Computational Brain.* Cambridge: MIT Press.

Dretske, F. (1988) *Explaining Behaviour.* Cambridge: MIT Press.

Dretske, F. (1995) *Naturalizing the Mind.* Cambridge: MIT Press.

Eccles, J. (1989) *Evolution of the Brain: creation of the self.* London: Routledge.

Fodor, J.A. (1998) *Concepts.* Oxford: Clarendon Press.

Fodor, J.A. & Lepore, E. (1996) The red herring and the pet fish: why concepts still can't be prototypes. *Cognition* **58**, 253–70.

Fodor, J. & Pylyshyn, Z. (1988) Connectionism and cognitive architecture: a critical analysis. *Cognition* **28**, 3–71.

Georgopoulos, A. (1997) Voluntary movement: computational principles and neural mechanisms. In Rugg, M.D. (ed.), *Cognitive Neuroscience.* Hove: Psychology Press, pp. 131–68.

Hubel, D.H. & Wiesel, T.N. (1968) Receptive fields and functional architecture of monkey striate cortex. *J Physiol* **195**, 215–43.

Jackson, F. & Pettit, P. (1988) Functionalism and broad content. *Mind* **87**, 381–400.

Jackson, F. & Pettit, P. (1990) Program explanation: a general perspective. *Analysis* **50**, 107–17.

Kim, J. (1992) Multiple realization and the metaphysics of reduction. *Philos Phenomenolog Res* **52**, 1–26.

Kim, J. (1993) Mental causation in a physical world. *Philosoph Iss* **3**, 157–76.

Kim, J. (1997) Does the problem of mental causation generalize? *Proc Aristotelian Soc* **97**, 281–97.

McClelland, J.L., Rumelhart, D.E. & the PDP Research Group (1986) *Parallel Distributed Processing,* Vols I and II. Cambridge: MIT Press.

O'Brien, J. & Opie, J. (1999) A connectionist theory of phenomenal experience. *Behav Brain Sci* **22**, 127–96.

Schmidt, H. (1982) Collapse of the state vector and pk effect. *Found Phys* **12**, 565–81.

Schröder, J. (1999) What has consciousness to do with explicit representations and stable activation vectors? *Behav Brain Sci* **22**, 166–7.

Tye, M. (1995) *Ten Problems of Consciousness.* Cambridge: MIT Press.

Yablo, S. (1992) Mental causation. *Philosoph Rev* **101**, 245–80.

Yablo, S. (1997) Wide causation. *Philosoph Perspect* **11**, 251–81.

CHAPTER 9

THE EXPLANATORY ROLE OF CONSCIOUSNESS IN ACTION

NAOMI EILAN

On the view that I will be calling 'common sense realism', conscious experiences have a critical causal role in explaining action. On this view, because of the way a pain feels to me, subjectively, I take steps to stop it; or because a cake seems, phenomenally, to be on my left, I reach out in that direction. During the past two decades, this fundamental ingredient in our everyday psychology has been put under severe pressure, both by philosophers and by psychologists, who for a variety of reasons have claimed that phenomenal consciousness is causally epiphenomenal; it has no causal role at all. To put it very crudely—as far as the *causal* workings of our minds are concerned, we might as well be zombies.

My concern in this paper will be to put pressure on two pervasive lines of reasoning in the philosophical literature for claiming that phenomenal consciousness is causally epiphenomenal, which also, in my view, have influenced psychological and neuroscientific approaches to this question. The first rests on a general understanding of what causal explanation involves. It says that, ultimately, the causal workings of the world require explanations that are perspective-free. In particular, it says that they require ways of thinking which necessarily leave out the kind of perspectival concepts essential for capturing the phenomenal properties of experiences. This kind of argument and reasons for resisting it, will be the concern of parts III and IV.

The second line of reasoning rests on a prevailing view about the relationship between representation and phenomenology. Suppose you want an apple, see it in front of you and reach out to get it. The causal explanation of why you reach in the direction you do will mention how your perception represents the world; in this case, the way in which it represents the location of the apple relative to you. Call the way your experience represents the world its 'representational' properties. The experience also has phenomenal properties— there is a way things are with you, phenomenally speaking, when you have such an experience. It is these properties that have been claimed to be epiphenomenal. The line of reasoning we will be concerned with says that we can give an exhaustive account of the representational properties of your experience without appeal to its phenomenal aspects, and that only such phenomenology-independent properties are relevant to the causation of your action. Arguments for this view, and the reasons it should be dismissed, will be the concern of part II.

Both these lines of reasoning, about the nature of causal explanation in general, and about the relationship between the phenomenal and representational properties of an experience, are not specific to action, although they have immediate bearings on how one thinks consciousness enters into the explanation of action. The third issue I want to raise is specific to action. It is the question of the account we should give of what makes an action conscious. In this paper, I will focus exclusively on the question of what makes environment-directed actions conscious, actions such as reaching for a cup or catching a ball. Here, we find two distinct types of theory. One type, which I will call the 'reflective theory', holds that it is some form of reflection on some aspect of the intention or the action that makes the action conscious. The other type, which I label the 'perceptual theory', says that it is some form of consciousness of the environment that makes the action conscious. The debate between these theories clearly has an impact on the general question of how consciousness comes into the causal explanation of action. This is the issue that will concern us in part I, in which I will argue, briefly and informally, for a particular form of perceptual theory. (For examples of reflective theories, see Jeannerod, this volume, 2002/3; Proust, this volume, 2002/3. For perceptual theories, see Campbell, 2002/3a,b; Roessler, 1999, 2002/3a,b. The sketch proposed here of a perceptual theory owes much to Roessler's treatment of the topic in Roessler, 2002/3.)

The line one takes on all three issues has clear implications for the way one conceives of the role of information-processing theories in furthering our understanding of the role of consciousness in explaining action. In the final brief summary of the paper, in part V, I make a few programmatic remarks on this general and hard question.

I

In everyday usage, the actions we think of as conscious are those actions we perform knowing what we are doing, in some sense. To perform an action consciously and to know what one is doing amount, in this usage, to the same thing. This is the sense of conscious actions that I am concerned with. As noted, my interest here is in environment-directed actions, such as reaching out to a cup in front of one when thirsty. Our question is: 'What has to be true of a subject who performs such an action in order for it to be true that she knows what she is up to, in the minimal sense required for consciousness?'

The reflective theory says that what is required is some kind of second-order representation of the occurrence of the action, and/or of the formation of the intention to act, and/or of the onset of the action, and/or of the movements executed. This is a natural claim to make, but is, in my view, wrong. By way of illustration of what is wrong, it will help to have before us the much discussed pathology of blindsight. Blindsighted subjects are subjects who, following damage to their visual cortex, become 'functionally blind' in particular areas of their visual field; that is, they fail to respond spontaneously, in action or judgement, to stimulation from those areas (for a comprehensive review of such cases, see Weiskrantz, 1986). However, as several neuropsychologists have shown, when induced to guess what is in the functionally blind area, such subjects can do so for quite a wide range of properties, while simultaneously denying that they have any visual experience of the properties about which they are issuing guesses.

Blindsighted subjects can also, under instruction from an experimenter, direct actions towards objects and properties in their blind field. For example, they may be asked to point to a source of light they are told is in that field, or reach out to grasp an object they are told is there. In all such cases we find denial of any experience of anything being there. In many cases, this is coupled with accurate location of the object, source of light, etc., appropriate hand grasps, and so forth.

Consider now a blindsighted subject who is asked to point to a source of light in the blind field or to reach out for an object in that field. Such a subject may be proprioceptively aware of his movements, aware of an intention to move his arm to where he guesses the object is, aware of the onset of the action, and so forth. So we have everything that, for reflective theories, would count as conscious action. Contrast this, now, with the case of smoker who accurately de-ashes into an ashtray, while engrossed in conversation. She may be unaware of her movements or have no second-order thoughts at all about the formation of an intention to de-ash, the onset of action, and so forth. However, she will have something the person with blindsight lacks, which I take as critical for our normal intuitive concept of conscious, environment-directed action. Intuitively, the perception *guides* her action in the way it does not in the blindsight case. It this guidance, intuitively, which yields a basic kind of knowledge of what one is doing that is lacking in blindsight. This is the intuition that underpins the perceptual theory, but what does it come to?

In the normal case, conscious perceptions play two knowledge-yielding roles with respect to action. First, they provide us with knowledge of the targets of the action, the object(s) and place(s) our actions are directed at. Secondly, they normally provide us with the means of assessing our success or failure in performing our intended actions. Now it may appear, and has appeared to many, that only the first role is crucial for knowledge of what one is doing. Thus, when I ask you what you are doing, when I see your hand move, for example, you will normally reply by describing the action in terms of its target, e.g. the cup in front of you which you intend to lift. Whether or not you succeed in lifting it seems to be a separate, additional question, additional, that is, to the description of the intended action. But this cannot be quite right. Imagine that you *never* find out about success or failure. Suppose, for example, that the lights always went out whenever you aimed your ball at a target, or suppose you never got any kind of perceptual input about whether or not you succeed in establishing contact with an object you intend to get hold of. If this were the case, I suggest, you would retreat to claiming that you know what you were *trying* to do, rather than what you were doing. In everyday usage, knowledge of what one is up to spans the successful (or otherwise) completion of the action. Moreover, everyday usage apart, there could, arguably, be no *rational* learning by acting, no learning of how to get it right without such knowledge. It is arguably the case that it is wrong to speak of rationally caused action, and hence action at all, in cases where the possibility of such learning is ruled out.

Let us say, then, that the basic knowledge of what one is doing implicated in conscious, environment-directed action requires both kinds of information. Now, it is generally assumed that the blindsighted subject has both types of information. Yet we agree that he does not know what he is doing or, rather, does not have the kind of knowledge needed for his actions to count as consciousness. What the perceptual theory says can now be put as follows. Knowledge of what one is doing, in the minimal basic sense required for an action to be conscious, requires that the information that specifies the target, and one's success or otherwise in carrying out the action, must itself be conscious. When the perceptual input is conscious it can provide the kind of guidance needed for knowing what one is up to in the case of environment-directed actions. When this is the case, the performance of the action is in the stream of a subject's consciousness. To take this kind of line, in contrast to the line suggested by reflective theories, is not to deny that when actions are conscious in this way one is also capable of self-ascribing them. It is to deny that their consciousness just *consists* in their being self-ascribed. On the perceptual theory, knowledgeable self-ascriptions are, rather, *explained* by the action occupying the subject's stream of consciousness, which in turn is explained by its being guided by conscious perceptual input.

On the perceptual theory, then, the question about the role of consciousness in action explanation is, first and foremost, a question about the explanatory role of the consciousness of the perceptual input to action. Relative to this theory, the charge of epiphenomenalism is, first and foremost, the claim that the consciousness of the perception, *contra* the intuitions underpinning the perceptual theory, in fact plays no role at all in causally explaining the occurrence of the action and the properties it has. One kind of experimental finding that is often cited to make the epiphenomenalist charge, thus put, is this. Imagine you are subjected to an illusion in which it appears to you that a stationary dot has moved (because of the movement of the frame in which it is enclosed). It turns out that if asked to point to it you will point to the correct, rather than the illusory location (Bridgeman *et al.*, 1981). Conversely, if a target is moved during a saccade, while you fail consciously to detect the movement, the perceptual input exploited by your motor system does, and you will, again, point to the right location, rather than the one you are conscious of in perception (for a review of such experiments and others, see Milner & Goodale 1995, Ch. 6).

These cases are like blindsight in that the subject's success in carrying out a set task is causally explained by non-conscious perceptual input. This has been taken to show that the connection between perceptual input and action, in the normal, non-illusory case as well, bypasses perceptual consciousness altogether and, hence, that consciousness is epiphenomenal. On the face of it, though, such experiments show no such thing. In all these cases, the subjects *do not know what they are doing*, in the basic sense. The difference between the experimental set-ups and the blindsight case, is that in the former, subjects have the *illusion* of knowing what their target in acting is, because in these cases there is conscious perpetual input, on which the subject bases a mistaken claim about the target, while in the blindsight case, because there is no conscious input at all, the subject thinks he is merely guessing. However, illusions of knowledge are, precisely, illusions. What is needed for genuine knowledge is that the conscious perceptual inputs causally explain not only the subject's conception of what the target of his action is, but also the actual target of the movement he performs. Only then does the perceptual input supply the subject with reasons for acting as he does and, hence, cause something that can count as a rational action. Mere causation of movement by perceptual input, independently of perceptual consciousness, on the one hand, and mere consciousness of target, independently of causation of movement, on the other, are each, on their own, insufficient for rational action.

On their own, then, such experiments no more show that consciousness is epiphenomenal than does blindsight. On the contrary, they seem to point precisely to justification of what I called common sense realism. What they show, on the face of it, is that perception can play two quite distinct types of causal role in generating an action, one rational, which yields knowledge, and one brutally causal, which does not, depending on whether or not conscious perceptions of the environment play a causal role in generating it. We would need abstract arguments about the nature of consciousness and causation, respectively, to show that this *prima facie* vindication of common sense realism is illusory. Let us now turn to the first of such arguments that we will be considering here.

II

The first objection to this way of appealing to blindsight to justify common sense realism may be familiar to many from the current consciousness literature and can be introduced as follows. There are various aspects of consciousness that are lacking in the blindsight case, and one reason it has been discussed so much is that thinking what is going on in that case serves to bring into relief issues about the relationship between various *a priori* ingredients in our concept of consciousness. In particular, as blindsight is appealed to in discussions of consciousness, it is said to show the possibility of the following combination of states of affairs:

1 The subject has perceptual information about the environment (inferred from his capacity to guess some of the properties in the 'functionally blind' area of the visual field and, when induced, to direct appropriate movements towards them).

2 There is no consciousness of the portion of the environment about which the information is taken to exist. (There is no 'consciousness of' or 'transitive consciousness').

3 The perception is not in the stream of consciousness, not 'in mind'. (There is no 'intransitive consciousness').

4 There is no phenomenal consciousness, no experience.

5 There is no reflective consciousness—there is nothing for the subject to introspect.

6 The perceptions do not provide the basis for rational judgements and rationally guided action. (The subject merely guesses, as the perceptual information provides him with no idea of why what he says is true, if it is, or, in the action case, of why he is doing what he is.)

The first objection to the argument from blindsight to common sense realism claims that the argument rests on conflating different senses of consciousness. In particular, the kind of consciousness that people are interested in when they claim that consciousness is epiphenomenal is what is referred to as 'qualitative' or 'phenomenal' consciousness. This is the kind of consciousness in virtue of which there is a phenomenal feel to the state one is in, a 'what it is like' (4). What is needed for guidance of rational action, on the other hand, is that perceptual information be accessible to the reasoning system. When it is, the perception is access conscious (6). The claims, then, are as follows:

1 These are two wholly distinct kinds of property a state may have.

2 While access consciousness clearly has a causal role in the production of action, to demonstrate a causal role for it is not yet to demonstrate a causal role for phenomenal consciousness, which is what we need for a common sense realism.

3 While normal perceptions have both kinds of consciousness and blindsighted perceptions lack both, we cannot infer from this that phenomenal consciousness has a causal role in normal action. Perhaps its absence causes the absence of access consciousness,

but perhaps it is the other way round. Perhaps it is only when the perception is accessible in a rationalizing way that we get phenomenal consciousness, as a causally inert by-product. Nothing in blindsight tells us which way round it goes.

4   It is only because of the failure to so much as distinguish access from phenomenal consciousness that we think that blindsight demonstrates a causal role for phenomenal consciousness.

This is Ned Block's claim in his paper 'A confusion about the function of consciousness' (Block, 1995) in which he accuses all philosophers and psychologists who argue from blindsight to what I have called common sense realism of confusion. There are various responses one might make to this charge. The one I am interested in focuses on the idea that in the perceptual case, and phenomenal and access consciousness are, indeed, distinct properties. If they are not distinct, then acknowledging a causal role for one suffices, at the same time, to secure a causal role for the other.

In order to show that access and phenomenal consciousness are distinct in the perceptual case, Block gives examples of what he thinks are conceivable circumstances in which we have one and not the other. The example that is of interest to us is the one in which he attempts to show that we can imagine cases of perception where there is access consciousness only, without phenomenal consciousness. It is described as follows. Suppose a blindseer could be trained to guess at will what is in the functionally blind area of his visual field, that is, without being prompted to do so. Call him a 'super-blindseer'. In such a case, says Block, visual information will simply 'pop into mind' in the way solutions to problems do, where the result is that one has a sense of knowing, rather than merely guessing at, the answer. The super-blindseer himself contrasts these kinds of case with his normal perceptual experiences, in which there is, in addition, something it is like, a phenomenal feel. The claim is that in such a case, if we agree it is conceivable, perceptual information will be access conscious without having any phenomenal properties.

The example Block gives concerns the causation of judgement, rather than action, but one can easily imagine an action equivalent. Suppose a super-blindseer is looking for her cigarettes. Then, presumably, she would, on occasion, find herself reaching out to an area in her blind field and would report that it just came to her, out of the blue, that that is where they are in the same way as a solution to a practical question can suddenly pop into the mind, out of the blue, without the perception that causes her to act as she does having any phenomenal properties.

Our question is 'Do these examples succeed in showing that our normal sense of access consciousness, as we apply it to perceptual states when they guide judgement and action, is indeed independent of any appeal to phenomenal aspects of experience?' The most immediate and obvious puzzle the examples raise is the following. As Block himself describes it, the judgement about the world, based on the super-blindsighted events, strikes the subject as coming out of the blue. Similarly, in the action case, there is a sense in which the subject does *not know why* she has reached out in the way she has, to the place she has, and so forth. That is, it does not appear to her to be rationally justified. The contents of perceptual input do not provide the subjects with reasons for their judgement (or, in our case, reason for action). So, as the examples are described, we do not, on the face of it, have here the kind of reason-conferring access Block himself says is connected with our concept of consciousness. Whatever notion of access we have here, it is not the kind we associate with consciousness.

If we ask what is lacking here, one thought is that were the perception in mind, in the stream of the subject's consciousness (3), then such a justification would be forthcoming. So, in the occurrent, perceptual case, we seem to need a notion of access that is such that if a state is accessible it follows that its contents are in mind, in the subject's stream of consciousness. Suppose then we ask: What is needed for the latter? The intuitive answer is that when perceptions yield consciousness of the world (2), this suffices both for both 'in-mindedness', and for rational access. If we ask now 'Why do not the super-blindseer's or the blindseer's perceptions yield awareness of the environment? What do we need in order for there to be in play not merely information about the environment, but awareness of it?' Here, we reach intuitively for the phenomenal consciousness that is lacking in blindsight and super-blindsight. In some way, when phenomenal consciousness is in play, we have consciousness of the world, a presence of the world to the subject, rather than mere information about it. When we have that, in turn, we have everything we need for rationalizing access.

So, in the normal perceptual case, being in the stream of consciousness, consciousness of phenomenology and rationalizing access come together. Let us say that when they do, perceptions *present* the world to the subject as being such and such. It is this presentation of the world to the subject, or its appearance as such and such to the subject that (a) gives the perception its rationalizing status, (b) secures its being in the stream of consciousness, and (c) at the same time yields something it is like for the subject, from her perspective. It is presence of the world to the subject, thus understood, that is lacking in both blindsight and super-blindsight.

How is presence to be explained? In particular, what account should we give of the relationship between the representational content of the experience, which provides the rationalization of the action and the judgement, on the one hand, and the phenomenal properties of the experience, on the other? There are basically two options. One is to introduce non-representational phenomenal properties, which yield a something it is like from the subject's perspective and to say that the *de facto* co-occurrence of non-phenomenal representational properties with non-representational phenomenal properties yields the kind of presence we are after. The other is to say the relevant phenomenal properties are a special kind of representational property.

Suppose, first, that phenomenology is explained exhaustively by appeal to non-representational properties. Then the only justification or reason they could provide for judgements will be indirect. They would function, that is, as indirect evidence for judgements about their possible cause. It is dubious, from discussions of scepticism about the external world, whether such indirect reflective judgements could actually provide an alternative justification, but even when we bracket sceptical doubts and focus exclusively on the notion of presence this suggestion will not work. First, our own perceptions give rise to direct, non-reflective rationalizations of our actions and judgements, and such directness is part of what we mean when we say that perception makes the world present to us. Secondly, reflective, indirect arguments about the world on the basis of sensation can be made, intuitively, while the representational contents of the perceptual state remain wholly non-conscious, that is, wholly outside a subject's stream of consciousness. So, neither the usual rationalizing role of the perpetual input, nor its being in the stream of consciousness are secured by adding non-representational phenomenal properties to representational properties in this way.

The requisite notion of presence cannot be right, then, if we assume that the phenomenal aspect of normal experiences is explained by appeal to non-representational properties. The alternative is to say that what we need is an account of how representational and phenomenal aspects of experience are interwoven with each other in such a way as to yield such presence of the world to the subject, and to treat this as a *sui generis* kind of representational property that perceptual experiences, as opposed to beliefs, for example, can have.

To take this line, however, is to reject the distinction between phenomenal and access consciousness in the perceptual case. For a state is access conscious in virtue of its representational contents and phenomenally conscious in virtue of its phenomenal properties. The upshot of our discussion has been that, in the perceptual case, we must treat the relationship between phenomenal and representational properties as one of identity, if the intuitive notion of presence of the world to the subject is to be explained.

III

On the face of it, we have in these arguments a renewed defence of the idea that blindsight reveals the causal role of phenomenal consciousness. If the relationship between representational and phenomenal properties is one of identity and all sides concede a causal role for representational properties, we seem to have secured a causal role for phenomenal properties as well.

However, this is too quick. In fact, there are two quite different ways of reading the suggestion that phenomenal and representational properties must be identified, and only one of them yields a vindication of common sense realism. It is in spelling out the difference between these two readings that we come to the second, deeper objection to common sense realism. I will first introduce the difference between these two readings and then, using the terms in which the distinction is formulated, go on to state what I take to be the most pervasive and deep objection to common sense realism, namely that it distorts fundamental requirements on causal explanation.

The first reading of the identity between phenomenal and representational properties accepts one half of the two-concept claim, but denies the other. I call this the 'reductive reading'. It denies that we can give an exhaustive account of phenomenal perceptual consciousness without the material we appeal to in accounting for access consciousness, in particular without giving an account of what it is to represent the world. However, it accepts the second half of the claim. It agrees that we can give an exhaustive account of perception considered as a cognitive mediator between environment, judgement, and action without any essential appeal to phenomenology. I call this the 'reductive' reading of the identity claim because it states that we can reduce phenomenal properties to independently described representational properties, and phenomenal consciousness to an independently described access consciousness.

In contrast, the second, more radical rejection of the two-concept approach, which also delivers an identity between phenomenal and representational properties, denies both halves of the two-concept claim. I will call it the 'interdependence claim'. On this view, the phenomenological and representational ingredients in our everyday concept of perception are interdependent. Like the reductive claim, the interdependence claim says that we cannot get the phenomenology right or individuate the phenomenological ingredient in our everyday concept of perception, without essential appeal to the spatial/casual explanatory framework we use in thinking of perception as a representation-delivering process. However, it also says, and here it differs from the previous claim, that we cannot get the causal, representational framework right without essential appeal to the phenomenology.

What does this mean? One of the most robust intuitions about the phenomenal properties of experience is that they must be described from a particular point of view. In particular, a central intuition about phenomenal consciousness, appealed to by both Jackson and Nagel, for example, is that to know what an experience is like one must be capable of having experiences of the relevant kind (Jackson, 1982, 1986; Nagel, 1974, 1986). Thus, it is claimed that knowing a theory of what is involved in the perception of red does not suffice for knowing what it is like to see red (Jackson), and that knowing everything there is to know about the mechanisms involved in echo-location does not suffice for knowing what it is like to echo-locate (Nagel). One must actually have experiences with such phenomenal properties in order to understand the concepts that refer to these properties. Call this the 'experience-dependence claim' about our phenomenal concepts. It reflects a widely held intuition about these concepts, and I will take it as a constitutive claim about the phenomenal concepts we actually use when describing the phenomenology of experiences.

Now, the interdependence claim holds that we cannot get right what perception is, considered a causal representational process, without essential appeal to phenomenology. I shall take this to mean that we cannot get it right without essential use of our phenomenal, experience-dependent concepts. So, applied to the case of echo-location or the experiential representation of redness, the claim will be that one can only give an account of the kind of representations involved in such experiences if one is capable oneself of having experiences that represent the world in the same way. Let us call this kind of understanding of representational contents, 'inside knowledge'. It may be contrasted with 'outside knowledge', which accounts for the nature of representations and the causal processes underpinning them in a way that does not appeal to one's capacities to be in states that represent in the way being described. For example, most work in information-processing psychology explains representations in this way, by appealing to functional organization, syntactic properties, and so forth, and their normal cause. I shall take the reductive claim, as opposed to the interdependence claim, to be saying that we can give an exhaustive account of experiential representations from the outside.

Common sense realism says that thinking of our experiences as we do, using our everyday phenomenal concepts, at the same time commits us to a causal role for phenomenal properties. As I understand it, common sense realism commits us to the interdependence version of the identity claim. That is, it commits us to the view that the correct description of the causally relevant representational properties of the kinds of perceptions that yield conscious action relies, essentially, upon experience-dependent phenomenal concepts. Relative to this, the argument for epiphenomenalism can now be stated as follows. Causation is part of the objective world. Understanding causal processes and giving a full description of them is a matter of locating them in the world, objectively conceived.

Now, on a prevailing account of objectivity, which we find in Nagel, for example, and many others, an objective representation is a representation of the world from no point of view (Nagel, 1986). Anyone can understand and use it, no matter what their *de facto* situation in the world is, no matter what properties they do or do not happen to have, no matter what experiences they have. It presents what has been called the God's-eye view. On this account of objectivity, a full account of perception considered as a causal process of information uptake for the purposes of action and judgements is a matter of describing these processes from no particular point of view. So a full account of perception considered as a causal process requires abandoning precisely those experience-dependent ways of thinking that the interdependence claim says we must use in individuating causal processes in psychology. This is the strongest argument for the reductive claim and, at the same time, for thinking that phenomenology is in some deep sense epiphenomenal.

IV

The idea that thinking causally requires, ultimately, abandoning perspectival ways of thinking is based on the following two ideas. First, scientific thought is thought from no particular point of view. Secondly, our concept of causation derives its legitimacy from scientific thought. Some version of the first claim must be right. The difficulties come in with the second. I will first spell out in somewhat less metaphorical terms what the ideal governing scientific thought is and then go on to use the terms in which this is articulated to raise questions about the second claim.

Imagine entertaining the thought 'This object is square' about an object you can see. The demonstrative concept 'this' expresses a way of thinking of objects that is perspectival in the following sense. In order to succeed in referring to a particular object using this concept, the subject must be in the same space as the object and be causally connected to it (through perception). We can contrast this with a way of thinking about an object that is thinkable by anyone irrespective of where they are and, more generally, irrespective of any idiosyncratic properties the subject may have. For example, thinking of an object as 'the tallest tree that ever existed' can be done by anyone, anywhere. Such a way of thinking is wholly non-perspectival.

The ideal of science as representing the world from no point of view can now be expressed as follows. Science aims to represent the world in wholly non-perspectival concepts. That is, the representations it aims, ultimately, to arrive at are ones that owe nothing to the fact that we are located in and causally connected with the world we are representing. More generally, they owe nothing to any idiosyncratic properties of the users of the concepts. They can, in this sense, be used and understood by anyone, and are, in this sense, objective.

Turning now to phenomenal concepts: the experience-dependence claim, as it is normally understood, says not merely that we happen to think of phenomenal properties using perspectival concepts. This would be consistent with saying they can also be individuated from no particular point of view, can also be individuated scientifically. The claim, at its strongest, is, rather, that they can *only* be singled out using perspectival concepts. That is, only subjects who actually have such properties can know what they are. To say this is to say that they simply disappear from view when we switch to describing the universe from no particular point of view. They are in this sense subjective.

Suppose we accept this way of characterizing a major difference between the concepts science aspires to employ and those we think we use in referring to what our experiences are like. The epiphenomenalism charge we are considering can now be spelled out as follows. First, wherever there is a real causal relationship, the properties in virtue of which this relationship holds can be described in wholly non-perspectival ways. For where there is causation there is, at rock bottom, a purely scientific explanation of it. Secondly, if this is true, we have one of two choices. Either we say that phenomenal properties can, *contra* first appearances, also be captured in non-perspectival terms, which in turn means we should accept the kind of reductive reading of the identity claim described in the previous section. Alternatively, we say they cannot be thus captured and can only be singled out using perspectival concepts. However, if the first claim is granted, then to take this line just is to say they have no causal role. Thirdly, if this is right then the interdependence claim should be seen as trying, illegitimately, to span both options by insisting both that phenomenal concepts are essentially perspectival and that they figure in causal explanations. There is no such middle ground, and this is the middle ground that so-called 'common sense' realism seeks to occupy.

A full discussion and rebuttal of the thinking that underlies this very pervasive reasoning will not be possible in the space we have, but I would like to sketch one kind of argument that might help loosen its grip. It can be broken down into two steps. First, our concept of a physical object and our concept of causation are interdependent. A physical object just is the unit of causal interaction at a time and over time. Indeed, it arguable that once we arrive at a level of scientific physics in which the basic *a priori* laws we apply to an object, e.g. the idea that an object can only be at one place at a time, break down, then our grip on the very notion of causation goes with it (see Salmon, 1984, chapter 9).

The second step raises the question of whether or not our thoughts about physical objects meets the 'no point of view' requirement spelled out as characteristic of science. The short answer is that it doesn't, where the argument for this claim is due to Strawson (Strawson, 1959, Ch. 2). Suppose you attempt to single out an object using wholly non-perspectival concepts, as opposed to demonstratives. You will begin by describing its intrinsic properties, spatial and otherwise. Suppose then someone says that you can imagine that there is another portion of the universe in which there exists an object with exactly the same properties, so your description has not sufficed to single out this particular object, rather than its duplicate. You may go on to add much detail, relating the object to other objects in its vicinity and so forth, but no matter how extensive a description we give of an object in purely general terms, this will not suffice to individuate it, given the possibility that all the properties we refer to might be duplicated in some other portion of the universe. Individuation must rely, ultimately, on demonstratives, which are perspectival. Our thoughts about particular objects are, then, essentially perspectival.

If we accept both claims about the deep interdependence between our concept of a physical object and the idea that reference to particular objects can only be secured by relying on perspectival demonstratives, this suggests that our grip on causation is based on ways of thinking that are not wholly non-perspectival. Even if science does aim for the latter type of representation, insofar as it relies on the concept of causation, it must come back to ways of thinking that essentially exploit the fact that we are located in the world we think about (see Campbell, 2002/3a,b, for an illuminating argument for this claim).

If we take seriously the interdependence between causal thought and reference to particular physical objects, it would appear that common sense realism about phenomenal properties is no worse off than everyday causal thought about the physical world. This is not, on its own, sufficient to vindicate common sense realism about consciousness, but it does serve to shift the burden of proof back onto the epiphenomenalist. In particular, on the face of it, if the argument so far is accepted, an epiphenomenalist must show that there is something other than the perspectivity of our phenomenal concepts that rules them out from figuring in causal explanations.

V

On the perceptual theory, the consciousness of an action is due to the consciousness of the perception that guides it. The two arguments for epiphenomenalism that we have been considering, taken together, can be summarized as follows. Everyone agrees that the representational contents of a perception have a causal role in guiding action, and that there is a sense of consciousness on which a perception is conscious when its contents are accessible to a subject's reasoning system. Justifying common sense realism about the role of consciousness in action, however, is a matter of justifying the claim that it is, in particular, the phenomenal aspects of perceptual input that have a role in guiding actions in a way that makes them yield knowledge of what one is doing. To do so we must show, first of all, that the phenomenal and representational aspects of experiences must be treated as identical if the contents are to rationalize judgement and action. The burden of parts II and III was that this is, indeed, the case. However, this still leaves open the option that we can reduce phenomenal properties to independently described representational properties. The suggestion has been that we should understand the debate between reductive and non-reductive claims as one about whether or not we must appeal to the experience-dependent concepts we normally use when introspecting in order to individuate the representational contents of an experience. The reductive claim is the claim that we can give a full account of the representational contents of the way in which perceptions present the world to the subject using wholly non-perspectival and scientific terms to describe these contents. The anti-reductive, interdependence claim insists that these properties can only be captured using experience-dependent, perspectival concepts. It is the latter claim, in turn, that common sense realism was interpreted as making. The second epiphenomenalist argument was that to be a common sense realist, in this sense, is to falsify the nature of causal explanation. The properties that play a causal role must be describable from no point of view, as all causal explanations are grounded, ultimately, in non-perspectival, scientific explanation. The burden of section (IV) has been that the way in which the concepts of causation and of a physical object are connected suggests, on the contrary, that our causal explanations are grounded in perspectival ways of thinking. If this is so, common sense realism about phenomenal consciousness is no worse off than causal realism about physical objects.

Saying this is not, as noted, anywhere near providing a full-scale defence of common sense realism about phenomenal consciousness, but suppose such a defence were possible, as I believe it is. What would the implications be for the role of information-processing theories in furthering our understanding of consciousness and its role in action explanation? I end with one brief comment on this complex subject.

Underpinning the epiphenomenalist charge is an ideal of cognitive psychology on which we treat what psychologists are up to, and what physicists and biologists are up to under one heading: All are engaged in an enterprise called the brain sciences, where the kinds of explanations aimed for on this level are wholly perspective-independent. If common sense realism is right, and we must avail ourselves of perspectival concepts in order to capture the datum we are seeking to explain, then psychology cannot be roped into the natural sciences in this way. To the extent that it is an empirical investigation of the mechanisms that subserve what we call perception, action, thought, and memory, then to that extent it must be answerable to the perspectival ways we have of identifying mental states. In particular, these mechanisms must be answerable, ultimately, to the subject's perspective, which imposes *a priori* constraints on the kinds of mechanism that will do the explanatory work. If this is right, the gap between psychology and the natural sciences is as big as that between our phenomenal concepts and science.

More specifically, I take it that the kinds of explanations given by information-processing theories of cognition aim, by and large, to be outside explanations, in the sense outlined above. That is, their account of the content of representation does not require inside understanding of such contents. (There is no difference in kind, in this respect, between explanations given of echo-location and human vision). Now the reductive theory we considered earlier says that this is the ultimate level of causal explanation. Inside individuations of properties are, at best, parochial ones, which must be dropped when we go on to do the real causal work. The import of the interdependence claim, in contrast, can be summarized as follows.

To the extent that we are interested in explaining what happens when we act consciously or have a conscious visual experience, for example, the basic causal explanatory framework is given by a network of *a priori* connections that draw, essentially, on inside individuations. As far as information-processing theories are concerned this means two things.

1 The perspective-free causal explanations, to the extent that they reveal the mechanism underpinning conscious perception, action, and the like, should be seen as *abstractions* from the perspective-dependant story, rather than as *replacements* for it.

2 It is a mistake to expect a perspective-free information-processing explanation of what consciousness is. To understand what consciousness is, we should look to the way the contents figure in the *a priori* perspective-dependent explanations we give of the relationship between conscious perception and action or judgement, for example. The perspective-free information-processing story, while it can tell us much that is valuable about how, in fact, we manage to be conscious, does not provide a more fundamental way of understanding what consciousness is.

Acknowledgements

I am much indebted to Johannes Roessler, Christoph Hoerl, and John Campbell, for discussion of the issues raised in this paper, and to the participants in the workshop on Voluntary Action in Delmenhorst, on which this volume is based.

References

Block, N. (1995) On a confusion about a function of consciousness. *Behav Brain Sci* **18**(2), 227–47.

Bridgeman, B., Kirch, M. & Sperling, A., (1981) Segregation of cognitive and motor aspects of visual function using induced motion. *Percept Psychophys* **29**, 336–42.

Campbell, J. (2003) Demonstratives and action. In Roessler, J. & Eilan, N. (eds), *Agency and Self-awareness*. Oxford: Oxford University Press (in press).

Campbell, J. (2002) *Reference and Consciousness*. Oxford: Oxford University Press (in press).

Evans, G. (1980) Things without the mind. In van Straaten (ed.), *Philosophical Subjects: essays presented to P. F. Strawson*. Oxford: Oxford University Press.

Jackson, F. (1982) Epiphenomenal qualia. *Philosoph Quart* **32**, 127–36.

Jackson, F. (1986) What Mary didn't know. *J Philos* **83**, 291–5.

Jeannerod, M. (2003) Consciousness of action and self-consciousness: a cognitive neuroscience approach. In Roessler, J. & Eilan, N. (eds), *Agency and Self-awareness*. Oxford: Oxford University Press.

Milner, D. & Goodale, M.A. (1995) *The Visual Brain in Action*. Oxford: Oxford University Press.

Nagel, T. (1974) What is it like to be a bat? *Philosoph Rev* **83**, 435–50.

Nagel, T. (1986) *The View from Nowhere*. Oxford: Oxford University Press.

Proust, J. (2003) Perceiving intentions. In Roessler, J. & Eilan, N. (eds), *Agency and Self-awareness*. Oxford: Oxford University Press (in press).

Roessler, J. (1999) Perception, introspection and attention. *Eur J Philos* 47–64.

Roessler, J. (2003) Intentional action and self-awareness. In Roessler, J. & Eilan, N. (eds), *Agency and Self-awareness*. Oxford: Oxford University Press (in press).

Roessler, J. & Eilan, N. (eds) (2003) *Agency and Self-awareness*. Oxford: Oxford University Press.

Salmon, W.C. (1984) *Scientific Explanation and the Causal Structure of the World*. Princeton: Princeton University Press.

Strawson, P.F. (1959) *Individuals: an essay in descriptive metaphysics*. London: Methuen.

Weiskrantz, L. (1986) *Blindsight: a case study and implications*. Oxford: Oxford University Press.

CHAPTER 10

HOW VOLUNTARY ARE MINIMAL ACTIONS?

JOËLLE PROUST

This chapter aims at exploring how intentional a piece of behaviour should be to count as an action, and how a minimal view of action, not requiring a richly intentional causation, may still qualify as voluntary.

Knowing what counts as an action is not only a matter of nominal definition. It has important consequences for education and law, as well as ethics. One unresolved question in the domain of action consists in determining which features, if any, are distinctive of human action as contrasted with non-human animal action. The interest in studying what Kent Bach (1978) called 'minimal actions' is that they seem not to presuppose any prior intention, not even any conscious decision. Defining a minimal action as a guided bodily movement (not requiring an intentional belief–desire–causation) will help us to discuss some issues that become easily blurred within the folk psychological approach to full-fledged, richly intentional actions. In the first section, I will first develop the contrast between the two kinds of action and offer reasons for taking the category of minimal action as a functionally relevant one. In the second section, this 'austere' definition of action will be used to test our intuitions about what counts as a voluntary action. In ordinary usage, three different ways of explaining what makes an action voluntary can be found. The first involves the *sense of agency* that normally, but not necessarily, accompanies self-generated bodily movement. The second invokes the fact that the subject *wanted* to act as she did. The third, richer meaning of a voluntary action requires an agent to have a *positive evaluation* of what she did, in the sense that her second-order desires are in agreement with the action taken. We will examine how these three senses may apply to minimal actions. This analysis will hopefully contribute to separating out causal, experiential, and metaphysical considerations on voluntary action.

1   Full-blooded versus minimal actions

Standard philosophical approaches of action define action in terms of a particular psychological state causing a relevant bodily movement. While there is now wide convergence on this causal approach of action, there are disagreements on the kind of psychological state deemed relevant for action. Davidson (1980) holds that what is causal is a *reason to act*, that is, a 'pro-attitude' (desire) relative to some state of affairs, in combination with the relevant belief that such-and-such a movement will bring about the desired condition. Similarly, Goldman (1970) maintains that the psychological states causing behaviour are wants and beliefs. Searle (1983), Bratman (1987), and Mele (1992) claim that *intentions* form an indispensable link between reasons and actions. Intentions have two essential features: they guide behaviour by virtue of their *representational content*, and they move an agent to act by virtue of their *executive* properties.

What is important to note is that, in these various causal theories, an agent is not directly a cause of her actions: her beliefs, or motivational or intentional states are. Also, these theories embed action in a *practical reasoning schema*: an agent has to judge that she desires P and that he believes Q in order to conclude that the action A recommends itself; she also has to assess the relative strength of her various competing reasons for performing an action of type A, rather than of type B. In this way, the causes of an action coincide with the reasons the agent has for acting.

Thus, the reason to act, in these standard theories, is both a *justification* of an action and a *cause* of the corresponding physical behaviour. In the intentional account, for example, a subject acts because she formed and was able to self-ascribe the corresponding intention. Forming an intention of a certain type and self-ascribing the corresponding intention further requires an ability to use the relevant *concepts* in formulating her intentions, in appreciating her preferences, and in performing her practical reasoning from the subject. Many authors would also defend the view that an agent must have a concept of *self* to recognize the corresponding intentions as her own and take responsibility for the developing action. In this account of action, mental events and properties endowed with *conceptual* content play an overwhelming role in the very causation of an action.

Starting with this view of action, there are two ways of relating the conditions for a particular behaviour to qualify as an action. The first consists in disconnecting the causation of action from the appreciation of the reasons that justify the actions; the second consists of questioning the importance of having a specific intention for an action to be triggered. We shall examine, first, why the definition of an action needs to be extended in these two respects.

1.1   Ability in justifying action as a precondition for acting

While it makes sense, biologically, that an organism should use all the knowledge available to it to adequately control its behaviour, it is not clear that the elements of conceptual knowledge offered in rationalizing behaviour should also be a *necessary* pre-condition for triggering an intention and the corresponding action. In other words, it seems plausible to allow a disconnection between performing an action of type A in context C, on the one hand, and rationalizing this performance, on the other hand.

This disconnection may be either radical or graded. In the radical approach, a non-linguistic animal would be attributed agency capacities just in case it performs some goal-directed behaviour based on its prior encounters with similar situations. Such an organism may be said to act if it behaves on the basis of prior learning of what is to be done in context C (C includes endogenous motivational states and exogenous affordances), whether or not it engages in practical reasoning. Learning triggers the behaviour in the sense that an organism exposed to motivating cues in a given context is disposed to perform an action of type A. Nevertheless, learning is nothing else than a set of representations being activated in the control of behaviour; by using the internal indicators whose function is to signal meaningful events and properties (presence of a predator, of food, of a mate), the agent—human or non-human—can develop the adequate motor response. In this radical version of the cause/reason disconnection, an action may well develop without the agent consciously representing the situation in a space of reasons. Indeed, learning can develop outside any conscious access to reasons for acting in this particular way.

The graded approach would simply admit the possibility of a loose connection between acting and rationalizing action. In this view, learning is a case in which reasons for acting might still be offered, although not necessarily by the agent himself. An observer would be allowed to put herself in the place of the agent to explain in which way the chosen course of action conforms to the agent's best interests, given its other epistemic and motivational states. A reason to favour the graded approach has to do with the fact that reinforcement learning, in a way, *instantiates* a piece of practical reasoning. Reinforcement learning could be expressed through the following sequence of representations. Given that certain internal representations have been activated ('This is a predator'), given the established associative links between these representations and highly significant properties ('danger for self and for offspring'), the conclusion reached is that '… flight (or protective attack) should be preferred'. However, the difference between this kind of embodied reasoning and full-blown practical reasoning is that reinforcement does not rely on a general and detached analysis of the facts at hand, as does practical reasoning. It does not need to explore counterfactual events and properties—those which would not be present if the action was not to take place. Although reinforcement learning can be evaluated as a rational way of coping with a stable world, it cannot be equated with a form of practical reasoning because no representation of the alternative courses is needed in the former, while it is essential to the latter.

If the analysis above is on the right track, the very notion that a causal account of action should coincide with justification in terms of reasons to act dissolves. A non-speaking animal or a young child cannot provide a justification for their actions, and cannot even represent to themselves the problem of justifying them. This is not only because they cannot explain what they did to others or to themselves, cannot select the appropriate concepts while communicating the content of their intentions, and therefore cannot rationalize what they did, but also because they cannot represent counterfactual situations, i.e. alternative courses of action available in the same context, with their consequences and their relative motivational strengths. This suggests that the radical view of the disconnection between action and reason-giving is more accurate than the graded view in the case of actions performed by non-speaking animals.

What holds for all kinds of animal or infant actions also holds for an extended set of human adult actions. There are many cases in which an agent has no interest in developing practical reasoning in its full-fledged form. The agent simply acts without conscious thought, and not on the basis of a former representation, however sketchy, of the means–end relationship; he/she accordingly has no explicit reason to act in the way he/she does.

1.2 Intention as a precondition for acting

Another way of weakening the standard account of an action consists of questioning the essential role of intentions in initiating an action. Kent Bach boldly claimed that the supposition that every action should be taken as intentional—or at least, when unsuccessful, to involve an intentional part—is 'unsupported' (Bach, 1978, p. 363). By an *intention*, Bach understands a distinctive conscious act of will, a mental event that could be presented by the agent through the words 'I will do A.' Bach observes correctly that there are types of actions that are performed routinely and unthinkingly, actions for which it cannot be claimed that they were willed in the sense in which one willingly writes a letter or utters a sentence. Examples of these 'minimal' actions are all kinds of postural or pre-attentive movements, such as scratching an itch, doodling, brushing away a fly, avoiding an object (Bach, 1978), shifting a gear, pacing about the room (Searle, 1983), and impulsive or expressive actions, such as tearing a photo into pieces out of rage, jumping for joy (Hursthouse, 1991).

Bach (1978) offers two main reasons for admitting unintentional kinds of actions. First, it seems difficult to reject from voluntary actions all the types of behaviour cited above. They might well be the only kind of actions that infants, patients with executive disorders, and 'animals on the middle rungs of the phylogenetic ladder' are able to perform. Secondly, there is more to an action than its initiation. The way in which an action is carried out seems not to be determined at the level of a prior intention. Although the specific way in which an action is performed requires a form of awareness, the latter seems 'below the level of intentions and reasons'. The level of acting that is left, when (conscious or unconscious) prior intentions are missing corresponds to what Bach calls a 'minimal' action.

One might want to say that John Searle's analysis in his (1983) essay gives an adequate answer to Kent Bach's challenge. First, Searle acknowledges the existence of actions performed *without* prior intentions. In contrast to the situation where an agent forms a priori the intention to do A—an intention reportable by the linguistic form 'I will do A'—Searle claims that one often performs an action with no such prior intention, but rather with an occurrent thought of the linguistic form 'I do A'. When I scratch my back, I do not form the prior intention to the effect that I will scratch my back—I just do it (1983, p. 84), but there is no reason, according to Searle, to conclude that I do it unintentionally, so to speak. This kind of mental state belongs to intentions, because it is constituted—and this is a central point—*by the conscious experience of acting*. According to Searle, it is 'inseparable from action' and for that very reason it is called 'an intention in action' (Searle, 1983, p. 84).

Secondly, intentions in action have another feature that meets Bach's objection that an intention should not only trigger an action, but control its development. When an agent has the intention to drive to her office, she does not form explicitly the prior intention to shift gears from second to third; she does so as a result of her intention in action to shift gears from second to third. Such an intention in action has the function of specifying the details of how an intentional content—the goal of the corresponding action—should be realized. A further question here is to explain *how* this realization of a conceptual intentional content into a non-conceptual concrete behaviour can be made possible. According to Searle, the explanation consists in embedding a second causal link in the intentional chain. The prior intention specifies the goal in conceptual terms; the intention in action consists of an 'experience of acting', which causes the specific bodily movements associated with it. In Searle's view, an experience of acting is a 'presentation of its conditions of satisfaction' (Searle, 1983, p. 88). This ensures that the representational character of the experience will be tightly linked to its distinctive 'feeling': being a *presentation* involves having a specific phenomenological character, an associated feeling of agency; having *conditions of satisfaction* make it a fully intentional state, that is, a state whose function is determined by a relationship between a mental representation and an external state of affairs.

Searle's notion of an intention in action certainly responds in part to Bach's problem. Indeed, it does account for the two essential constraints that make an action minimal. An intention in action has to do with the routine, unplanned ways of coping with the environment, whether physical or social; it also accounts for the specific dynamics of the bodily movements through which an action is being performed.

Still there are features in Searle's analysis that conflict with the demands of minimal actions. First, the *direction of causation* of an intentional action is taken by Searle to be, in all cases, 'mind-to-world' (Searle, 1983, p. 88): An intention in action is a mental experience of trying that causes the bodily movement fitting that very intention, that is, a bodily movement whose adequacy is an objective fact out in the world. In this analysis, an action whose direction of causation is world-to-world is a conceptual impossibility. Such a world-to-world direction of causation seems, however, involved each time an organism simply does what the context prompts him/her to do, that is, each time a piece of goal-directed behaviour is *stimulus-driven*. When, for example, a patient with an *imitation syndrome* (Lhermitte *et al.*, 1986) is performing an action when she sees the same action performed by another agent, she is displaying an intentional behaviour based, presumably, on the formation of intentions in action, but the *causation* of her action is not mind-to-world for that. The world causes her to act and she might be in a position to complain that people use her neurological problem to make her do things she does not approve of. A similar situation occurs in many cases in which normal agents are influenced to act as they do by contingent events in their environment: Babies starting to cry when another baby cries, crowds of people running in panic to the same exit door, any one of us responding to a hand-shake approach by a hand-extension, etc. A last important set of less-than-intentional cases consists in what might be called deferred quasi-intentional behaviour: an agent forms a plan, then forgets subsequently that he did, but nevertheless acts accordingly without a *conscious* intention in action when the context cues him to do so (see Wegner, in Roth *et al.*, 2000, Vol. 2, p. 22 ff.). The case of the post-hypnotic agent executing an action she does not remember having been instructed to perform probably belongs to this category.

What seems to make these cases difficult for Searle is that:

- his concept of an intention in action is tailored to be autonomously causative in action;
- it *essentially* belongs to the family of conscious states
- causation is effected through the very experience that the corresponding intention in action provides.

What happens, then, when an action is performed *without* a conscious experience of doing so, for example, in driving absent-mindedly? Searle admits that

> in such a case the intention in action exists without any experience of acting. The only difference then between them [= between this case and the case in which the action is conscious] is that the experience may have certain phenomenal properties that are not essential to the intention. (Searle, 1983, p. 92)

In thus arguing, he aims explicitly at finding a theoretical status for unconscious intention in action *symmetrical* to the case of unconscious perception in blindsight. A patient with blindsight has no phenomenal experience of seeing P, but can still extract from vision at least some of its intentional properties. Similarly, a distracted person may have no phenomenal experience that he is driving, but rather have a non-congruent experience (listening to his car radio, thinking about the elections, etc.); he may still accomplish the bodily movements that are part of the intentional conditions of satisfaction for driving.

This symmetry between perception and action is more apparent than real, however, and in particular it is easy to see that the parallel with blindsight does not work. For while a visual content can survive the absence of a visual experience, because the external object is what makes the extraction of a specific intentional content possible to begin with (Searle, 1983, p. 47), it does not seem open to us, at least within Searle's theory, to say that the experience of an action can go on causing the corresponding action when it has no phenomenological property. Because in that case there is no independent event—at least no event Searle would be happy to consider—causing both the subjective experience and the bodily movement as is the case in perception (where one can be informationally connected with an object without recognizing it). Given that an intention in action is essentially conscious and is supposed to operate through the image of the action it provides, the notion of an unconscious intention in action remains rather obscure and does not allow an understanding of how it might cause the action as if it had been conscious all along.

A more intelligible theory of the mental cause of an action would follow a functional, rather than an experiential lead. There is, indeed, a mental process causing the action on which the conscious experience of acting partly supervenes: it consists in activating a specific *motor representation*. Such a notion has all the features that make the concept of intention in action attractive, without excluding the possibility of minimal actions. Being both executive in its function and specific in its content, an active motor representation explains how an agent can execute in a concrete and flexible way a general plan; it accounts for the adjustments that the agent has to make to reach the target state (by comparing dynamically the observed result with the anticipated goal). This solution further allows that a representation can be activated without being conscious or susceptible of becoming conscious. Finally, the activation of a motor representation does not presuppose that the source of the representational activation is endogenous, that is, constituted by some particular intention to act. In this general scheme, an action should not be defined in terms of its source, but rather in terms of its specific development from an internal model towards a goal with an appropriately monitored execution. What is pertinent is whether or not the bodily movements tend to be under the agent's guidance' (several theories make this point: Frankfurt, 1988, 72 ff.; Jeannerod, 1997; Proust 1997, 1999a): Whatever the causal antecedents of a specific goal-directed movement may be, what makes it an action is the contribution of the corresponding agent to actively maintain the orientation of his bodily effort towards achieving a target event. In the case of minimal actions, the source of the action, that is, the actual cause that triggers it, may be exogenous (a motivating or 'prepotent' stimulus) as well as endogenous (a forgotten instance of planning, an over learned routine). In this theory, minimal actions become the far end of a wide spectrum of behaviour; the way in which an action is carried out may vary from a purely automatic, unconscious process to a controlled and deliberate monitoring.

It is to the credit of Kent Bach to have sketched such a theory—which he calls Representational Causalism—well before neurophysiological findings could give this theory its empirical credentials (for a review, see Jeannerod, 1994). The central claim of Representational Causalism is that all actions, including minimal ones, '… require "effective" representations for their initiation and execution …' (Bach, 1978, p. 367). In this view, the representational character of the motor instructions permits the guidance to develop over time towards the goal. In other words, acting presupposes the ability to compare the representation of what is to be done with the various feedback representations conveyed by the agent's senses (what Bach calls 'receptive representations'). Effective representations provide the motor commands, whereas the receptive representations correspond to the reafferences used as feedback for corrections or termination of the process. The set of effective and receptive representations, considered independently from their mind-to-world or world-to-mind 'direction of fit', is aptly referred to as *executive representations*. Although Bach does not call his executive representations 'motor representations', he insists that they are not propositional in form and not necessarily linguistically coded; nor do they necessarily imply any intentions or beliefs (Bach, 1978, p. 366). Let us mention two other features that would deserve more attention, but can only be mentioned in the present chapter. Such a set of representations is stored in memory, and thus *allows* recall and mental simulation, as well as an active role in executive feed-forward and feedback. This choice of dispositional aspects of motor representations accounts for the role of imagery in simulation and in preparation of action, and for the fact that imagery, while useful, may also be entirely absent from performance. Furthermore, such representations may be activated in the absence of any conscious control or self-attribution, while again taking part in these processes when certain additional conditions are present.

1.3   Revising the constituents of a minimal action

As John Searle insists, 'The key of Intentionality is conditions of satisfaction. It ought to be a rule in all of these discussions that nobody is allowed to talk about an intentional phenomenon without telling us what its conditions of satisfaction are' (1991, p. 297). Now that we have shown that an action may develop without relying on prior pragmatic reasoning or even on a conscious intention, it is time to make explicit the conditions of satisfaction of a minimal action.

As we have seen, the causation may be world-to-world, as well as mind-to-world; therefore, the *causal origin* of the activation of a specific motor representation should not be part of the definition of a minimal action. *A successful minimal physical action is such that a given motor representation takes control of behaviour and monitors adequately occurrent feedback until its target event is reached.* As in the kind of analysis offered by Searle, this persistent role of the representation in the action, from triggering until completion, can be expressed as a kind of self-reference of the motor representation in the intentional content; the latter can be articulated as *that this very representation cause the appropriate bodily movement.*

The 'appropriateness' here is normally the result of prior learning or, alternatively, of hardwired responses to context, such as a flight induced by spotting a predator. Adequate monitoring is such that it gradually enables a transformation of the world in some expected condition through an appropriate sequence of active bodily movements. Inadequate monitoring would defeat the minimal action just as it defeats a full-fledged one. For example, if a minimal action consists of pacing about a room, tripping on the carpet or stepping on a brittle item would present a failure of the relevant motor representation in monitoring the input–output flow of information; new energy-consuming steps would have to be taken. If by scratching an itch an extension of the itch or an open wound follows, these infelicitous and unexpected consequences lead the agent to cope with a new situation. So minimal actions also have conditions of satisfaction; failing to achieve the latter or achieving them improperly, may interfere with other plans of the same agent.

Whereas a typical failure in full-fledged action consists in missing crucial steps or mistaking the target for another, it is less typical in the case of minimal actions, because they normally involve elementary bodily movements: launching one single automatic process, like walking or scratching, does not seem to lend itself to disruptive interferences, because being more automatic than the rest of the actions, it is likely to be successfully absorbed in the course of the other actions being launched in parallel (e.g. one can scratch an itch while answering the phone). It may, nevertheless, sometimes happen that a minimal action never reaches its goal, maybe for lack of any adequate motor representation (e.g. scratching a part of the back one cannot reach), for lack of time or for lack of other external conditions of satisfaction. Other ways in which a minimal action can fail to succeed is to fail to come to a stop by failing to register that its target event has been reached. This is the case of compulsive scratching or washing, for example, which can be analysed as cases of perseveration.

Let us take stock. What distinguishes executive representations from intentions as used in the standard causal theory is:

- that they are not necessarily conscious;
- that they nevertheless actually guide the course of an action.

The kind of relationship they have to action, in other words, is functional, rather than experiential. However, all these welcome consequences are associated to a less than welcome one: there is now a gap to be bridged between conscious access to intention and action, on the one hand, and the actual representational causation of the action, on the other hand. There is, moreover, no guarantee that bridging this gap will leave our sense of agency unscathed. To understand why, we have to understand how representations become effective, that is, causally efficacious in causing a bodily movement. We will ask this question in the context of a more general question, having to do with the ways in which it is justified— or only tempting, but wrong—to say that a minimal action is voluntary.

2 How voluntary are minimal actions?

There are three senses at least in which an action is ordinarily called voluntary. The first has to do with the *feeling of will* associated with the action; the second has to do with the *causal origin* of the action: an action is called voluntary in the latter sense if its cause is endogenous and can be consciously accessed; the third sense involves *higher order states* of the agent relative to the first-order intentional content of the action. Let us examine, in turn, each notion of will involved in order to evaluate how voluntary minimal actions can be.

2.1   Voluntariness as a feeling of wilful action

Intuitively, speaking of a voluntary action suggests a specific feeling of being in charge, in contrast with cases when a move is triggered by physical forces or social constraints. With minimal actions, an agent may also have a feeling of being in charge, even though she did not deliberate on her doing what she does. She has the sense of doing X voluntarily (jumping for joy, scratching her arm, etc.). How is she aware of this specific quality of her behaviour? A natural response would be to say that an agent gains this awareness on the basis of the specific motor representation presently activated. In this view, the motor representation would carry its own representational status on its sleeve, so to speak. If a representation adequately monitors current behaviour, it would 'tell' the subject *what* she does while she does it. Even in the specific case of minimal actions where no prior intention is involved an agent could recognize that she acts because whatever she does is guided by corresponding motor representations.

There are several reasons, however, to reject the general view that conscious awareness of agency is a by-product of activating executive representations. First, neurological dissociations have been documented between the awareness of having performed a movement and the awareness of thereby performing a specific action. Clinical data from apraxia and schizophrenia, as well as experimental results on normal subjects suggest that a subject may know which action she is performing, while being wrong about the way she is performing it, and vice versa (for example, normal subjects are unaware of a brisk change in the location of a visual target, while pointing correctly to the new location. (Goodale *et al.*, 1986): a subject may know which movement she executes, while being unaware of, or confabulating, the intentional motive of the movement. In other words, she may be able to characterize her goal, but be unable to report on the way she acted towards it; reciprocally, she may be able to copy a particular gesture without being able to extract from it information on the goal that this gesture normally subserves. In echo-praxias, patients may also invent a goal for what seems to be a pure case of stimulus-driven behaviour. More surprisingly, an agent may identify an action through its goal and through the specific movement token that is used to reach it, without being able to identify correctly the author of this action.

One way of testing the ability of a subject to determine whether or not he is the agent of a particular action consists of providing him with an ambiguous visual feedback about the spatial and temporal properties of his actions in a context where agency attributions cannot be easily inferred. This can be done using an experimental paradigm in which the subject looks at his own gloved hand behind a transparent screen. What he considers to be his hand can also be the video-image of a similar, but alien hand. He must carefully compare his own internal representation of the action with the available visual feedback in order to detect possible mismatches. This paradigm was used to investigate the performance of schizophrenic patients in attributing to themselves a token of action on the basis of a visual feedback that can be either veridical (what they see is their own hand) or spurious (they see a similar alien hand; Daprati *et al.*, 1997, Proust, 2000). There were three conditions: The seen hand could be the subject's (condition I) or the experimenter's; in the latter case, the movement of the alien hand could be identical to the subject's response (condition II) or not (condition III). It was found that normal subjects misjudged the alien hand as theirs in condition II only, in roughly 30% of the cases, and never misattributed their own hand movement to the experimenter. Schizophrenic patients had a performance similar to normal subjects in condition I and III, but their error rate increased to 77% (for patients with hallucinations) and 80% (for patients with delusions) in condition II.

What is largely documented in neuropsychological patients is also true for normal people in specific contexts. As every gym teacher knows, normal untrained children and adults are rather poor at reproducing accurately a specific token of a movement. Although they can describe exactly what they see being done, they seem to have trouble identifying the way in which they themselves are moving, in particular in the absence of a target object. In an experiment by Fourneret & Jeannerod (1998), normal subjects are asked to draw a sagittal line on a horizontal plane with a stylus, which they are not allowed to see directly. What they see is an image of their line-drawing on a monitor screen. Unknown to the subjects, the visual image is occasionally biased in deviating more or less from the line they actually produce; the subjects need to deviate their own movement in the opposite direction for achieving a saggital line on the monitor. When asked to reproduce their drawing with eyes closed, right after each trial, the subjects tend to draw a line straight ahead, as suggested by the former visual reafference, in contradiction to any endogenous source of information they might have had during their action.

These data on action awareness might be extended to the case of minimal actions and suggest that, in this case too, the perceptual *experience* of the action-related situation does not directly draw on the motor representation controlling the corresponding behaviour. So it may be asked again: On the basis of what kind of information is a subject aware of her minimal actions as her own?

Usually, any mental or physical activity is perceived as originating in self or in some external event thanks to the information carried by a dedicated signal, telling whether a movement was effected by the individual; when absent, the brain would 'interpret' a movement as unwilled, as when the body is passively subjected to some external force. The relevant signal is supposed to help compare reafferent signals with the signals that are expected on the basis of the current willed movement. It has been suggested that such a signal would be delivered by a mechanism underlying active perceptual activities, named corollary discharge (Sperry, 1950) or efferent copy (von Holst & Mittelstaedt, 1950). This mechanism is required to explain, for example, how ocular saccades can be taken into account and neutralized in interpreting visual input. When no such efferent copy signal is produced, like when sitting in a train, it is much more difficult to say whether one is moving or whether the perceived scene is. In our conscious sense of agency, a major component would thus consist in the *sense of effort* that is the subjective correlate of the corollary discharge of any action.

This sense of effort would account for the general feeling of having executed voluntarily an action, and would be lacking when a bodily movement happens involuntarily (by way of some external force, as when you're pushed by someone). An activation of this signal might certainly tell the agent, generally speaking, whether he is moving in a voluntary way. Yet this does not explain how the agent could become aware that he did such-and-such *specific* type of movement or action.

The answer to this question might be related to the kind of expectations that are prompted to an agent when her behaviour is controlled by a given motor representation. A subject might use the subpersonal information concerning the present input sequence as being actively gained and the feedback expectancies associated to a given motor representation (also activated at a subpersonal level). She would thus be able to perceive the intentional content of her action through the kind of visual feedback and end result that she is able (when her action is successful) to anticipate and experience sequentially in the visual, proprioceptive, or auditory modes. In this view, a subject is able to perceive her own actions by looking directly at the dynamic visual, auditory, properties of the world. Perceiving an action would thus crucially depend upon the very existence of a distinctive sequence of perceptual feedback, in particular of a visual nature. When this feedback is ambiguous or distorted, then the sense of what is done would be distorted accordingly (for a full development of this view, see Proust, in press).

Such a claim seems largely consonant with Daniel Wegner's view, according to which 'we would tend to see ourselves as the authors of an act primarily when we had experienced relevant thoughts about the act at an appropriate interval in advance, and so could infer that our own mental processes had set the act in motion' (Roth et al., 2000, Vol. II, p. 22). The two approaches only seem to diverge on the inferential nature of the whole process. In the present view, while perceiving her own actions, an agent perceives a sequence of objects and properties in her environment, and the transformations contingent to her bodily movements. This kind of perception is of a sensory kind; it may give rise to a perceptual judgment as to the kind of action currently being performed, well before the action is completed. The action may be recognized perceptually through very tenuous cues without having to be inferred (no less than seeing a part of the Eiffel Tower leads one to *inferring* the presence of the Eiffel Tower; the Eiffel Tower is perceived and not inferred).

The fact that a subject can read off her own actions from her perceptual reafferences does not imply, however, that her perception is *reliable* in all circumstances: both the approaches of Wegner's and the present study, converge again on this point. If the reafferences are either entirely unexpected by the agent, for lack of any prior experience or because the environment is very different from the ordinary, the subject may fail to perceive the action as her own (just as any pattern, visual, auditory, etc., cannot be extracted if there is too much 'noise').

If, on the other hand, as is the case with minimal actions, the reafferences are processed in an automatic way, with a diminished awareness, the sense of the action being voluntary should also be diminished. There might be numerous cases in which a subject admits that she executed an action 'without realizing it', and pleads for distraction or even denies having performed the action (as in many delusional states). Our definition, nevertheless, implies that if she exerted a control in performance, then she did perform the action.

One can object to this definition of a voluntary action through perceptual access, however, by claiming that it only emphasizes what is crucial for voluntary *movement*, while being silent about voluntary *action*. A subject can certainly *see* that she herself moved, but finding out that she herself *acted* is more complicated and calls for a second type of analysis.

2.2 Voluntariness as an endogenous causal feature

At least in one sense of action, there is more to voluntary action than there is to voluntary movement. An *action* being voluntary has to be contrasted with a movement being voluntary. I may have moved to the window because I wanted to see whether my friend had arrived; because I was influenced by a previous hypnosis session; because I was ordered to do so; or because I was attracted by light. There is nothing in the signals explored above (efference copy, perceptual reafferences) that can tell the agent whether he has done the action deliberately or not, through his own choice, or under the influence of external cues. The signals in question have the function of helping an agent recognize whether he did move or whether the environment changed independently, but they do not help him recognize whether he *has been made to move* at a 'deeper' causal level. The second sense in which an action is voluntary consists in attributing to the agent's mental states an *active* versus an *instrumental* role in initiating the action.

By an *active role* it is meant that the event that caused the bodily movement is some set of conscious beliefs or of motivations (it should be kept in mind, however, that most internal states and events, such as storing information or producing an emotional response, are *not* themselves voluntary processes). This is the kind of account of action favoured by folk psychology, and it is in this sense that the word *voluntary* is usually applied. In the terms of Prinz (1997) summarizing critically this standard view, '… voluntary actions appear in the world because actors have a certain goal that they want to attain, and because they believe that this goal can be attained with the help of a certain action' (Prinz, 1997b, p. 157).

By an *instrumental role* it is meant that the relevant causal event for triggering the bodily movement in the agent is some sub-personal mechanism harnessed to a particular property in the environment, making the agent directly susceptible to be set to act by that property. For example, an agent sees an object of interest, which triggers an arm extension for taking hold of this object. Similarly, a red traffic light automatically leads the driver to apply the brake.

This sense of a voluntary action allows specifying our question: are minimal actions voluntary in this B-sense. Given that, as we saw, they are by definition not caused by an intention with a specific content, but rather by specific cues in a given context, they obviously *fail to be voluntary in sense B*. Although they feel like something done by the self, in sense A of a voluntary movement, they are not caused by any particular occurring conscious mental state. There is nothing in the awareness that a subject gains of his own 'minimal' action, which allows him to realize that 'he was *not* in charge'. No particular feature in the subject's experience can inform him whether he himself did what he did, or whether he was instead moved to do it by some subpersonal mechanism resonating to some feature out in the world. It is all the more striking that the absence of any distinctive phenomenological property for 'active' versus 'instrumental' agency does not leave, so to speak, a gap in the subject's experience. Each time he *moves* voluntarily, the agent seems disposed to believe that he thereby *acts* voluntarily. There may be wide differences linked to the cultural background of the agent. Ancient Greeks, for example, seemed to attribute to the Gods or to Destiny the causal role in initiating in the agent's behaviour certain kinds of socially relevant actions. Agents engaging in minimal actions, as Wolfgang Prinz observes, 'do not do what they want, but they want what they do' (Prinz, 1997b, p. 155; cf. Roth *et al.*, 2000, Vol. II).

Most authors agree that the causation of an action is not located at the agent's level, but at the level of motivational and epistemic states. A bolder claim, defended among others by Prinz (Roth *et al.*, 2000, Vol. II) and Proust (1996), takes the agent considered to be a person as a late—and maybe optional—construct in human development, with no primary causal role in action, minimal or full-fledged. In contrast, the very belief that one is a person carries a lot of causal potential. People learn first how to act, then strive for being identified and recognized over time by their group fellows as temporally extended responsible persons. This strife leads them to perform actions that they would not have been motivated to do otherwise.

However, this analysis of persons in terms of beliefs should not lead us to the view that an individual human being has no internal states, no goals, and no desires of his own. Indeed, in a system with no such states, no construction of selves could ever occur. What we should rather say is that the motivational and epistemic states have a causal power by themselves, independently of the particular belief in an overwhelming entity or person who would 'own' these states and, so to speak, pilot herself with one part of herself.

The reason why it would be mistaken to claim that all human actions are minimal is that, once we acknowledge that stored information does shape current behaviour, then the capacity of mental states to jointly cause an action has to be admitted. Of course, the stored information has not been *generated* by the agent. The context contained the relevant kind of information the system was able to extract, categorize, and store. Desires were largely generated as a consequence of social interactions and phylogenetic programming. They did not arise as a consequence of purely endogenous events. This granted, a distinction should be made between those episodes where an action is carefully thought over and planned, and those where an agent acts with no conscious, verbally expressible motive. Even if we question the ontological significance of persons in causation of actions, it seems implausible to jump to the claim that all kinds of action are 'arational'.

We have seen above that discovering whether oneself moved or whether the perceived environment moved is a matter of perception. Considering now the sense B of a voluntary action, one might agree that knowing whether one acted voluntarily is a matter of inference. As emphasized by Wegner, the agent relies on the phenomenology of active movement to *infer* that he is also the conscious causal source of his own acts. As the well-known experiments of Nisbett & Wilson (1977) have shown, subjects tend to explain retrospectively their actions by invoking the standard reasons other people give for doing them, even when they, in fact, acted under some external pressure. In other words, they tend to mistake minimal actions for full-fledged ones. As we have seen above, a minimal action is precisely not defined by its having an internal, mental cause. So, whereas, by definition, minimal actions fall in the realm of behaviour that imply a voluntary movement, they fail to imply the property of being voluntary in this deeper sense of having a long-term internal state as their cause.

Let us come back to our former example. Only in the first case ('I moved to the window because I wanted to see whether my friend had arrived') is the agent acting voluntarily, in the sense that she has a specific reason for going to the window. If she goes to the window because she is influenced by a previous hypnosis session, she is certainly not acting voluntarily: she has no reason of her own to make this move; furthermore, she is unaware that her doing so satisfies the intention of someone else (the hypnotist). This contrast warrants making a B distinction between 'acting voluntarily' and 'acting involuntarily'. Some people may move voluntarily while acting in an involuntary way. They are just caused to act by some external agent or physical stimulus.

We must add an important caveat, however, when it comes to applying this distinction to specific cases reported in the first-person mode. Granted that the subject cannot introspectively discriminate whether her reason to act is what *really* moved her to act, it may well be that the action was not voluntary after all, in the sense that the agent was moved by some contextual cue, rather than by her own desire to see her friend. Her belief might rationalize her behaviour while failing to have caused it.

A further important notion is involved in this contrast; in case I go to the window to see whether my friend arrived, I would have acted otherwise and things would have been different. For instance, had there been snipers around, I would not have moved to the window. In this kind of case, I can change my plan flexibly; in the hypnosis or command case I cannot. So the contrast between voluntary and involuntary actions might in a number of cases involve a distinction between actions whose development (i.e. initiation and monitoring) is more or less automatic, and those whose development is more or less sensitive to context. (The 'more-or-less' clause is more plausible than a strict division between two categories. I can pace around in the room absent-mindedly, but still adjust to the context and refrain from doing so when it would involve unwanted consequences. Still, automatic drivers often miss the correct freeway exit).

The B-way of understanding the contrast between voluntary and involuntary actions however does not capture an additional, important aspect of voluntariness, having to do with the fact that an agent may—on-line or retrospectively—*assent* or *dissent* to performing an action while performing it. A subject may have moved voluntarily and have been caused to move by some long-term disposition of hers (thus acting voluntarily in the sense B above), while being unable to resist the force of her drive for performing the action. Her action should then count as C-involuntary. Let us see why.

2.3   Voluntariness as a second-order property of actions

Let us assume that, even when an agent's behaviour is actually controlled by the environment, she represents her action as driven by internal motives. Generally speaking, an agent may or not, while acting, feel a dissonance between the desire or motivation that triggered her action and some higher order desire. This dissonance may be more or less intense, according to the kind of action performed (compare: 'I should not have killed him' with 'I should not have smashed the vase'). Such a dissonance can be understood as a functional property, independent from the notion that the agent would be 'free' to act otherwise. This dissonance implies a third level of analysis of a voluntary action. The possibility of such a dissonance suggests that normally 'be' goals determine the contents of 'do' goals. [On this distinction, see Bayer *et al.* (this volume).]

Let us make sure that the subject matter of free will does not interfere with the present debate. Freedom to act as one wishes is an issue sometimes confused with the disposition to agree or not with one's first-order motivations. What does it mean to say that one acts 'freely'? According to the so-called 'principle of alternate possibilities', a person can act freely only if she could have acted differently from what she did in a particular situation. However, given the fact that all the physical states are what they are, the idea that one could have acted differently from what one did—or thought differently from what one did—is a contentious matter, one which should not be taken for granted in naturalistic approaches to action. Indeed, Wolfgang Prinz has convincingly shown that the notion of free will cannot be incorporated into an empirical psychological theory (Prinz, 1997b). Let us thus assume in this discussion that every single state, mental or physical, is the effect of a set of physical causes such that no other act was possible for a given agent in a given context. This assumption has no bearing on the distinction between the case where an agent simply acts as she does without further ado and the case where she is able to ask herself whether she is right to do what she does. This latter capacity, as Harry Frankfurt (1988) insists, is a purely representational capacity; it is *not* an executive one. It is independent from the ability of the same agent to *resist successfully* her first-order motives. For example, a drug addict craving for heroin may form the second-order desire *not to desire to take* heroin, while being unable—now and later on—to resist the desire to take it.

This kind of case allows distinguishing two C-varieties of a less than voluntary action. We will examine shortly how this distinction applies to our minimal actions.

2.3.1 Non-voluntary action as an impulsive and irreflexive action

A first kind of case consists in acting under the influence of internal or external causes, without being able to represent alternatives, as is the case for an impulsive and irreflexive action (Frankfurt, 1988). An action is *impulsive* when it is performed on the basis of some first-order desire or some current external cue, without any inhibitory mechanism being applicable. An action is *irreflexive* when the agent is not able to entertain second-order desires: she cannot consider alternative courses of actions and order them in the light of her preferences, or she 'does not care' for the kind of desires that guide her actions. Non-human animals and young children seem to belong to this category of impulsive and irreflexive agents: they act on the basis of the stronger will activated, without being able to form a concurrent representation of other courses of action nor to select among their desires the kinds they would rather promote. An impulsive action may thus be perceived as one's own (A-voluntary), and be seen as consonant to some desire one has, or as contextually adequate (B-voluntary), without being voluntary in the sense of being considered in the light of some higher order desire (C_a-voluntary).

It is interesting to observe that an action involuntary in this sense never appears involuntary to an irreflexive agent who performs it. By definition, an irreflexive agent *does not appreciate the fact* that she does not raise the question of her preferences concerning her first-order motivations. Only an agent able to represent her first-order desires can raise this question, a fact with a high moral and legal relevance.

Many minimal actions are impulsive, and their motives fail by definition to be considered. It makes them also involuntary 'by definition' in the C_a sense. However, this sense of the term involuntary does not account for an important difference between minimal actions. Some are in consonance with the general behaviour of the agent, some are not. Driving absent-mindedly and smashing vases are two very different kinds of minimal actions. The following variety of C-non-voluntary actions should account for this crucial difference.

2.3.2 Non-voluntary action as a motivationally dissonant action

In the preceding case of an impulsive-irreflexive agent, non-voluntary actions are necessarily part of a repertoire of exclusively C_a-non-voluntary actions: a non-human animal can never reach the level of a reflexive agent, because it lacks the relevant set of representational-executive abilities. Human minimal actions, on the other hand, seem to be part of a larger repertoire of actions having different kinds of causal background, and more or less susceptible of being integrated with the agent's second-order preferences. Some of the actions of an individual may be performed impulsively, some others inhibited or carefully planned. Among those actions that are planned, some are planned using only first-order desires (as when one plans to prepare a gourmet meal), some involve a selection between the sets of desires to be made efficient (e.g. should I rather eat as I wish and get fat, or follow a diet and get slim?)

In the case of minimal actions, although they are not the product of a conscious intention to act, they can differ with respect to the evaluation that will take place, by necessity, *after* the deed. An agent may perform a large variety of minimal actions under the control of some external cue or present emotion, while being able to reconsider her actions reflexively after she performed them (or at most at the time she performs them). In this late reflexive stage, the subject may or may not, in Frankfurt's words, 'identify to' her first-order motivation. For example, she may recognize that crashing the China vase out of anger involved a substantial loss, that losing her self-control had many unwanted consequences etc., and regret her [minimal] actions. Or she may on the contrary find herself doing something she later finds useful and in agreement with what she should have done (like ducking when a projectile was moving towards her, avoiding a car crash in a split second, etc.).

The important point is that, in all these cases of minimal actions, the agent may have acted involuntarily, in the sense (B) that she did not have the intention to act in such a way, and find herself either pleased or discontent with what she did. In the latter case, her action can be said to be involuntary in the sense (C_b) of being not only under no direct control of her desires, but also *in complete discrepancy with her second-order desires*. Intuitively, this contrast is exemplified in analogy with the situations of two drug addicts described by Frankfurt. It is one thing to take heroin because one desires to take heroin and because one thinks that taking heroin is a behaviour that one wishes to promote; it is another to take heroin because one cannot refrain from doing so, although one desires to stop taking it. In the same way, one can perform a minimal action that one can later identify to. Had she had time to think about it, the agent would have done just what she did, as she herself explains. Ducking was the thing to do. Although she did not duck voluntarily, there is one sense in which she is pleased with was she did and would do it deliberately had she a chance to find herself in the same context.

Now take the vase smasher. Had the agent been given a chance not to smash the vase, she would not have smashed it. The agent here dissents from what she did, because she dislikes this episode of violence; she does not want to be moved by anger to do something. A minimal action of this kind is involuntary in the sense C_b that the agent is made to act against her own preferences.

This third level of analysis of how a minimal action can be seen as voluntary may raise the following objection. Why take an action that the agent *could not have prevented to happen* as voluntary on the basis of counterfactual properties, of the type 'Had I been able to think things over, I would have/would not have done it'. Is not this kind of consideration *too late* to call the corresponding action a voluntary one? Here is the line that an answer to the objection might take.

If one considers the case of a single minimal action, having this third level of analysis of voluntariness may, indeed, appear as a useless sophistication: too late is too late. Granted that actions are reproduced over time, however, the evaluations which an agent produces of her past minimal actions in the light of her second-order desires may in the future help her control impulsions of the same type. The second-order desires and similar *evaluative states* are therefore not idle, even when they arise after the action considered; they have an important role in shaping the future behaviour of the same agent, helping her to act voluntarily, in sense C, when circumstances allow it. The importance of the evaluation is that, in the future, a minimal action of the same type may, through an efficient inhibition, be prevented from happening or, at least, become subject to an inhibitory learning process. Even if one rejects the folk psychological standard account of the will, there is thus room for an interesting role of voluntary action in the evaluative sense of the term to characterize a behaviour that is shaped over time by second-order desires.

References

Bach, K. (1978) A representational theory of action. *Philosoph Stud* **34**, 361–79.

Bratman, M.E. (1987) *Intentions, Plans, and Practical Reason.* Cambridge: Harvard University Press.

Daprati, E., Franck, N., Georgieff, N., Proust, J., Pacherie, E., Daléry, J. & Jeannerod, M. (1997) Looking for the agent: an investigation into self-consciousness and consciousness of the action in schizophrenic patients. *Cognition* **65**, 71–86.

Davidson, D. (1980) *Essays on Actions and Events.* Oxford: Clarendon Press.

Fourneret, P. & Jeannerod, M. (1998) Limited conscious monitoring of motor performance in normal subjects. *Neuropsychol* **36**, 1133–40.

Frankfurt, H. (1988) *The Importance of What We Care About.* Cambridge: Cambridge University Press.

Goldman, A. (1970) *A Theory of Human Action.* New York: Prentice Hall.

Goodale, M.A., Pélisson, D. & Prablanc, C. (1986) Large adjustments in visually guided reaching do not depend on vision of the hand or perception of target displacement. *Nature* **320**, 748–50.

Hursthouse, R. (1991) Arational actions. *J Philos* **88**, 57–68.

Jeannerod, M. (1994) The representing brain, neural correlates of motor intention and imagery. *Behav Brain Sci* **17**, 187–245.

Jeannerod, M. (1997) *The Cognitive Neuroscience of Action.* Oxford: Basil Blackwell.

Lhermitte, F., Pillon, B. & Serdaru, M. (1986) Human autonomy and the frontal lobes. Part I: imitation and utilization behaviour. *Annl Neurol* **19**, 326–34.

Libet, B. (1985) Unconscious cerebral initiative and the role of conscious will in voluntary action. *Behav Brain Sci* **6**, 529–66.

Mele, A.R. (1992) *Springs of Action.* Oxford: Oxford University Press.

Nisbett, R.E. & Wilson, T.D. (1977) Telling more than we can know: verbal reports on mental processes. *Psycholog Rev* **84**, 231–59.

Prinz, W. (1997a) Perception and action planning, *Eur J Cognit Psychol* **9**, 129–54.

Prinz, W. (1997b) Explaining voluntary action: the role of mental content. In Carrier, M. & Machamer, P.K. (eds), *Mindscapes: philosophy, science and the mind.* Konstanz: Universitäts-Verlag/Pittsburgh: Pittsburgh University Press, pp. 153–75.

Proust, J. (1996) Identité personnelle et pathologie de l'action. *Raisons pratiques* 7, 155–76.

Proust, J. (1997) *Comment l'esprit vient aux bêtes*. Paris: Gallimard.

Proust, J. (1999a) Indexes for action. *Rev Int Philos Neurosci* 3, 321–45.

Proust, J. (1999b) Experience, action and theory of mind. *Develop Sci* 2, 286–7.

Proust, J. (2000) Awareness of agency: three levels of analysis. In Metzinger, T. (ed.), *The Neural Correlates of Consciousness*. Cambridge: MIT Press.

Proust, J. (In press) Perceiving intentions. In Roessler, J. & Eilan, N. (eds), *Agency and Self-awareness: issues in philosophy and psychology*. Oxford: Oxford University Press.

Roth, G., Prinz, W. & Maasen, S. (2000) *Voluntary Action: a reader*, Vols I and II. Texts collected to prepare the Conference on Voluntary Action, Delmenhorst, Germany.

Searle, J.R. (1983) *Intentionality: an essay in the philosophy of mind*. Cambridge: Cambridge University Press.

Searle, J.R. (1991) Reference and intentionality. In LePore, E. & Van Gulick, R. (Eds), *John Searle and his Critics*. Oxford: Blackwell, pp. 227–41.

Sperry, R.W. (1950) Neural basis of the spontaneous optokinetic response produced by visual inversion. *J Comp Physiolog Psychol* 43, 482–9.

Von Holst, E. & Mittelstaedt, H. (1950) Das Reafferenzprinzip: Wechselwirkungen zwischen Zentralnervensystem und Peripherie. *Naturwiss* 37, 464–76.

CHAPTER 11

RATIONAL AND IRRATIONAL INTENTIONS: AN ARGUMENT FOR EXTERNALISM

WILHELM VOSSENKUHL

There is plenty of evidence, for instance, in mathematics, the sciences, and economics, that rationality is paramount to all other cognitive powers. There is further evidence that intentions are borne and originate in the mind. We therefore might be inclined to conclude that rational intentions are brought about in the mind internally by the best of all cognitive powers. In this case it would be enough to analyse mental representations that are antecedent to decision making in order to find the basic ingredients causing rational or irrational intentions. However, there is neither evidence for representations of this sort nor for mental causes of rational intentions. It is true that intending is a mental state or act, but it would, indeed, be false to believe that intentions are produced or brought about internally, that is, without reference to the external world. Intentions may well refer indirectly to internal entities. I may, for example, intend to go for a walk in order to relieve my headache, or I may intend to solve a mathematical problem by using a certain method of proof, but I cannot intend any pain, or pleasure, or mathematical operation directly.

Some intentions seem to be irrational, although their mental origin is not different from the origin of rational ones. I shall argue that this indifference of origin of rational and irrational intentions is due to the fact that intentions—like all volitional attitudes—have external meanings. This implies that the criteria of rationality themselves are external to the mental activities of reasoning and intention. 'External' here means that the contents of volitional attitudes are individuated by the objects they are directed to, and not by the mental acts or performances of intentions themselves. This is in accordance with what the late Miss Anscombe wrote in her seminal book *Intention*: '… intention is never a performance in the mind …' (Anscombe, 1957, p. 49). I shall further argue that the indifference in origin of rational and irrational intentions sheds light on the hybrid nature of rationality. For the sake of argument, I shall use examples from the theory of choice. The gist of my argument is that intentional states enable us to choose mental, speech, or non-verbal actions without reflecting on the alternatives beforehand (for arguments to the same effect, see Bach, 1978; Proust, this volume). This links up with the debate about voluntary action in this volume. Proust tries to jump the belief–desire model and follows Bach, holding that some actions—'minimal actions' as they are called—neither presuppose conscious decisions nor intentions. My claims are a lot weaker. From what I argue, actions may be intentional even if they do not result from deliberate choice. I therefore need not tackle the belief–desire model myself.

1   Volitional attitudes and external meanings

It is not obvious why volitional attitudes, like intending or wanting, should have external meanings. It is textbook knowledge that these attitudes are akin to other forms of intentionality or intentional states, such as believing or perceiving. As a common feature, intentional states are directed to some objects. ('Objects' here stands for all sorts of things, like thoughts, spatiotemporal objects, feelings, and ideas.)

If I intend or want to go for a walk, it's the walking that renders content to my intending or wanting. If I believe that two plus two makes four it's a piece of arithmetic that is the content of what I believe. No independent meanings, no 'intending as such' nor 'believing as such' seem to be left if I omit the walking or the arithmetical operation, respectively. Therefore, over and above their word meanings, 'intending', 'believing', and other intentional states have no cognitive or semantic content of their own.

There are some attitudinal differences worth being noted. While the intentional states of believing and knowing represent cognitive attitudes, intending and wanting belong to the group of volitional attitudes. Being members of different families of attitudes, the contents of believing and intending differ significantly in terms of their temporal conditions of satisfaction. While I may believe, or think what is already known, I cannot intend or want what I believe is already the case. Of course, I may intend, for example, to close the front door, not knowing that somebody else already did. From a subjective point of view the external meanings of volitional attitudes are not constitutive to these attitudes as they stand. In other words, the objects or contents that give meaning to these attitudes do not yet exist—at least from the viewpoint of the person who entertains these attitudes. If I intend or want to feel pleasure, or am in fear of pain, it is not the actual pleasure I am intending or wanting, and not the existing pain I fear, but future pleasure and future pain, respectively (cf. Wayne Sumner, 1996, for a similar characterization of wants). Volitional attitudes are, in general, directed to the future, while cognitive attitudes are to all tenses. In terms of tenses there is even a slight difference within the family of volitional attitudes. I may, for instance, have always wished or wanted that some event had never occurred, but it would not make sense to intend that something in the past was or was not the case. It is possible to have intentions concerning the past. I may, for example, intend that some past event is or will not be known by others. The conative attitude here concerns the knowledge of some facts by other people, but not the facts themselves. Wittgenstein's famous note in his *Tractatus* (6.373), that the world is independent from ones own will, is true at least for the past.

2   Intending and choosing spontaneously

The cognitive function of all intentional states may be described as the mental capacity to choose or select objects of knowledge, volition, and action without reflection. 'Choice without reflection' sounds awkward and paradoxical, but we do, indeed, direct our attention to contents or things without consciously considering alternatives. Without being able to offer a reason why we, for example, turn our attention to this person, rather than that one, we choose objects of seeing, thinking, wanting, and intending without knowing why in the moment we do. In a similar vein, T. M. Scanlon proposes: 'Not only perceptual beliefs, but many other attitudes as well arise in us unbidden, without conscious choice or decision' (Scanlon, 1998, p. 22). Let us call the choice brought about by intentional states 'mental choice'. (I shall consider some aspects of mental and rational choice later. Both kinds of choices can be represented in standard and non-standard versions of choice.)

There is some unwelcome vagueness to this kind of choice. While we know mostly what makes us choose what we believe, do, or say, we need not know exactly what makes us choose our intentions and wants. There are two obvious exceptions, first, long-term wants and intentions that already exist, and secondly, rationalizations. Long-term intentions keep arousing deliberation and reasoning. If I always wanted to hike in the Hindu Kush, I shall keep thinking about how to realize this intention until I find the opportunity to really do so. As to rationalizations, we are, of course, in retrospect, always able to answer the question why we intended or wanted to do something, but rationalizations must not be sincere and are not terribly reliable if we are really interested in finding out what made us choose our intentions. Leaving long-term intentions and rationalizations of intentions aside, in order to entertain volitional attitudes we need no reasons to do so. In other words, we need no states of affairs that may count as reasons for intending or wanting. Volitional attitudes may well be taken spontaneously.

Now, 'spontaneity' is a rather vague notion with an air of delusion. It should, therefore, need further qualification if it is to be of any use at all. The spontaneity of choice in the domain of intentional states or acts has two connotations, first, being undetermined and, secondly, being caused or enacted without deliberation. Considering the first, volitional attitudes may count as being spontaneous insofar as they are brought about by mental choices that are—at least from the first person point of view—causally undetermined by any earlier choices. It is important to differentiate between conscious and subconscious causes. If I hold that a consciously taken choice of mine is causally undetermined, this will not preclude that there may be subconscious causes at work. This leaves room for conditions, constraints or causes of choice, which are either presently or generally unknown to the chooser, but possibly subconsciously valid or empirically evident in psychological research. Considering the second of the two connotations of spontaneity, volitional states may be called spontaneous if their choice is not inaugurated by a process of deliberation or reasoning. This leaves further room for all sorts of 'gut reactions' (a phrase borrowed from Calne, 1999, p. 23) determined by instincts, fears, or paranoia. In brief, spontaneous choice of intentions is choice without conscious motive and without deliberate reason.

Both these connotations merge in one and the same kind of example: for instance, my spontaneous intention to go to the cinema after my friend told me she couldn't make our date for dinner this evening. Maybe I am disappointed and angry, maybe not; maybe I just heard good news about the movie before, maybe not. My intention is still spontaneous, independent from whether I could have chosen something else. Probably, after deep and thorough psychological scrutiny, it will become obvious that there are bundles of causal chains that explain why I chose the intention to go to the cinema, as against the theatre or staying home. Subjectively, my choice will still remain as having been taken spontaneously. It is not causally determined by earlier choices of the same or of a similar kind, and it is not taken after reasoning or deliberation. This leaves enough room for long-term intentions, emotions, aesthetic attitudes, and tastes to influence spontaneous mental choices of intentions and wants. These are some of the stronger candidates for the bundles of causal chains that might in the end explain my spontaneous choice of intentions.

3   Mental choice

I have introduced the notion of 'mental choice' claiming that it is the capacity of intentional states to choose their own objects and thus their contents. The exercise of this cognitive function is far from clear. We are, at least conceptually, at a loss to explain in detail the faculty of directing and guiding one's perceptual and cognitive attention to the available contents of intending. We therefore, gladly, take it that these contents individuate what we intend, but, of course, in order to avoid circular explanations, we shall not hold that these contents will direct our attention externally. Otherwise, the intentional contents would cause their respective intentions backwards, as it were.

To direct one's attention to an object seems to be a process of mutual fit in which an individual's attention, and the special features or even attractions of an object merge nicely. It looks as if the direction of one's attention is a co-operative mixture of active and passive between a subject and an object. On the background of a subject's pro-attitudes, including emotional dispositions, liking and disliking, of one particular object seems appealing at a time, but not at another. In the latter case the person will not even take notice of it. If I like walking and I want to take a break, going for a walk may seem appealing, but I may not even think of taking a walk, although I am taking a break. This active–passive interplay is a simple picture of what is going on when we intend to do, say, or know something.

We choose—as I argue above—many of our intentions to do something spontaneously without them being knowingly or consciously determined or caused by earlier mental choices of the same or of a similar kind. It would, for example, not make sense to say that I now intend to go for a walk because I had the same intention before. However, the relationship between intentions, actions, and habits is tricky. Although habits and actions following a rule are repetitive, they are still intentional activities. They express what some-one is up to, that is, his or her intention-in-action. [The causally undetermined role of a person's intention in action is analysed by Miss Anscombe (1957, pp. 34-37).]

The tricky bit is that the expression of intention of each action-token is, in a way, guaranteed by the action-type. A certain action-type or habit is known to express a respec-tive intention-in-action. If I use the common words and gestures to greet people, my behaviour will be identified as greeting independent from further intentions of mine.

Nevertheless, habits do not cause, but represent and express intentions. My habit of greeting people is not the cause of my greeting Paul or Luisa. I don't greet everybody. Habits need some training and if they are well trained they become long-term attitudes we are prone to follow. Thus, habits make it easy to choose affiliated and conventionally used actions, but action types or habits will not cause action tokens. The latter are necessary in order to identify, but are not sufficient to execute the respective action-tokens. The choice of an action-token is open and leaves room for spontaneity. This may be underlined by an example from the realm of the reproductive arts. A pianist performing will know his programme by heart. His maturity to interpret the pieces of music in his own individual way is beyond his technical ease. His individuality and authenticity thrive on top of his technical brilliance. Spontaneity in this case, as in all other cases of intentional actions with strong habitual and repetitive aspects, presupposes a high amount of practical knowledge, which operates successfully without deliberate choice. Spontaneity is neither obviated by subconsciously valid causes, nor by practical knowledge or repetitiveness.

Looking closer to my own intentional actions I might find that some of my intentions—like in the case of greeting—are not really chosen by myself, but rather prompted by the social grid of rules and habits, and their sanctions and gratification. My intentions, in other cases, might even result from evolutionary training to avoid pain and to pursue happiness. Here, again, in the social and in the evolutionary case, emotional dispositions and evaluative attitudes come into play. I might find that consciously acquired and trained emotional dispositions and attitudes often do the whole job of choosing, even without the gravitational forces of evolution and the social grid. Finally, all these dispositions and attitudes are mine, and there is nothing wrong or awkward if I claim authorship for choosing my intentions on the basis of my emotions and psychological dispositions.

Then why 'mental choice' and not just 'choice'? Because choice, even if it is taken after deliberation, calculation, or reasoning, may still be spontaneous. It seems to be an unwarranted prejudice that deliberation, reasoning, and similar mental operations count as being void of or even obviate spontaneity. Choosing mentally is still choosing, that is, deciding about alternatives. All choices can be spontaneously independent from their antecedent conditions. For instance, in order to find an elegant and economic mathematical proof one needs good ideas, and they have to be spontaneous, even if the mathematical techniques and operations are common practice among mathematicians. What is left of the two above-mentioned connotations of spontaneity? Mental choices are spontaneous insofar as they are neither consciously caused after deliberation nor by earlier choices of the same kind. Nevertheless, mental choices may have bundles of subconsciously valid causes and they may be accompanied by conscious operations of reasoning and deliberation, but all these conditions are not sufficient to explain the choice consciously taken.

4   Rationality and rational choice

Like intentionality, rationality, too, has a functional meaning. It is, again, a cognitive function that resembles the type of mental choice just described for intentional states, but while the mental choice of intentions is generally spontaneous, the degree of spontaneity in rational choice is to be clarified. Some differences between mental and rational choice seem obvious. As against mental choice, the choice we perform rationally—so it seems—is caused by conscious motives and explained by deliberate reasons. If it is following deliberation and reasoning the rationality of choice is taken in a wide sense implying non-instrumental aims and purposes like, for example, self-respect or social justice. [Rationality in the wide sense implies a number of models like, e.g. expressive rationality, and bounded rationality. Useful surveys are offered by Wilson (1977), Hahn & Hollis (1979) and Hollis & Lukes (1982). Rationality in the wide sense is often used as a synonym for 'reason'. As mentioned above, deliberation and reasoning does not obviate spontaneity.

In a narrow sense, rationality in terms of rational choice has an instrumental meaning. This type of choice is based on motives of gain relative to some purposes or aims. It seems that these motives make choices successful by making decisions clear and predictable. In its latter sense, the rationality of individual behaviour is unanimously defined by the axioms that determine the maximization of expected utility. (For the sets of axioms for rational choice under certainty and one for rational choice under uncertainty, see Hargreaves *et al.* 1992, pp. 5–11). Nobody will deny the importance of rationality in the wide sense, nor will anybody ignore that the model of rational choice offers a clear and useful normative model of individual decision making under certainty, risk, and uncertainty. Under certainty, every agent knows exactly the utilities of his action. Under risk or uncertainty utilities are gauged by probabilities. The Bayesian rule tells the agent to maximize his subjectively expected utilities. The Bayesian rule contains a subjective probability function and a subjective utility function. Both these functions come down to the value of expected utility. Every rational agent behaves as if he is motivated by the maximization of expected utility. The theory of choice tells us how the agent realizes his motive rationally, that is, with the utmost success relative to some intended aim.

There is no need to go into the details of expected utility theory. Thinking about rational intentions, it will be enough to recall two of the major features of rational choice: its psychological groundwork and its axiomatic structure. The psychological groundwork is more or less expressed by the motivational force of expected utility maximization. Francis Edgeworth's famous conjecture—in his *Mathematical Psychics* (1881)—that all individuals are driven by their pursuit of gain is a possible, but not wholly adequate description of the psychological nature of this motive. It must not necessarily be the case that, in rational decision-making, I am intending benefit myself. It is not greed that motivates my decision, but the optimum of outcomes relative to certain aims, independent from their egotistic or altruistic nature. *Why* humans want to take successful decisions is imbedded in their psychological groundwork and may remain opaque. *What* they want to be successful in is made transparent by the rational decisions themselves. This is how human psychology and mathematical axioms are co-ordinated. On top of the psychological groundwork a small number of axioms tell us how rationality works in order to maximize expected utility. With the axiomatic layer, rational action and social exchange in general is modelled on economic action. Edgeworth described the economy as a bazaar, 'an arena in which everyone is free to haggle with everyone else' (Sugden, 1992a, p. 191). I will not pursue Edgeworth's economic ideas here, but the way he gives pure exchange economy a mathematical face makes it obvious how rationality ascends from the psychological and motivational groundwork via the mathematical structure of exchange to the maximization of expected utility. There is no doubt that rationality in the narrow sense has psychological roots. At least in theory, it originates from non-rational dispositions. However, these dispositions do not explain the decisions people take. The theory explains their rationality externally on the basis of the pay-offs they gain.

5   Rational paradox and the contexts of choice

Historically, we may now remember Hume's notorious plea for the passions as being the masters of reason, but I do not think that this piece of history is any help if we want to understand rational intentions. What we learn from expected utility theory—if we want to—is that the psychology at the bottom of the theory will never carry us anywhere near rational choice on its own. The problem is that non-rational dispositions and motives are blind and clueless without the theoretical scaffolding that is offered by expected utility theory. Therefore, no Humean internalist will be able to explain the rationality or irrationality of choices. On the other hand, expected utility theory is empty and inefficient without the motivational force from some psychological groundwork. It is difficult to explain how motives become forceful without cognitive guidance. One may, of course, try Hume again that the passions press reason into slavery and make them willy-nilly develop the theory needed. Instrumentalism is definitely not void of plausibility. As long as my motives are strong enough I will do anything I can to realize my intentions; this is the message of instrumentalism. However, as we know from the suboptimal results of non-cooperation in the Prisoner's Dilemma, the dictates of the passions will not guarantee maximal success not even with theoretical help. Too easily rationality turns into irrationality. This is, in brief, the message of Amartya Sen (Sen, 1979).

Obviously, the fit between the psychological groundwork and the instruments offered by decision theory to reach success is not quite happy, and I am not trying to improve it. Rather, I am interested in the incongruency itself and what we learn from it. It tells us, first, that we cannot generally proceed from the mental or psychological origin of intentions to rational outcomes even if we know what we should do to behave rationally in terms of the theory. It tells us, further, that our preferences do not agree with those norms of rationality that the standard theory prescribes. The axiomatic structure of the theory seems to be unable to account for what many of us take to be the most rational thing to do. The story I have in mind is the Allais Paradox (Sugden, 1992b, p. 45).

The French economist M. Allais published a paper in which he criticized some of the axioms of expected utility theory (Allais, 1953). His idea was to argue that people choose contrary to some of the assumptions made by the standard theory. [There are other paradoxes of a similar kind trying to question the empirical adequacy of the postulates of utility theory, e.g. the Ellsberg Paradox (Ellsberg, 1961).]

In order to show this, Allais offered two problems that are described by the following lists. The pay-offs on these lists are in money in a theoretical currency.

Problem 1

Choose between

A   2500 with probability 0.33

      2400 with probability 0.66

      0 with probability 0.01

and

B   2400 with certainty

Instead of problem 1 you now face a slightly different problem.

> **Problem 2**
>
> Choose between
> C   2500 with probability 0.33
>   0 with probability 0.67
> and
> D   2400 with probability 0.34
>   0 with probability 0.66

As it turned out in experiments of Kahnemann & Tversky (1979), from where the above-listed pay-offs are taken, many people choose B in Problem 1 and C in problem 2, and only a few people choose A and D, respectively. This is, indeed, what Allais supposed. Let us consider the risks implied in the two problems. A is obviously riskier than B. It seems unreasonable to take the risk of getting nothing for a relatively small increase. Most people will therefore reason that it seems preferable to be on the safe side and choose B instead of A. In problem 2, C looks a bit riskier than D, but here it seems reasonable to take the higher risk for the larger pay-off.

Why should these choices be paradoxical? The paradox is due to expected utility theory. According to the axiomatically grounded recommendations of the theory, if I choose B in problem 1 I shall have to choose D in problem 2; and if I choose A in problem 1 I shall have to choose C in problem 2. The axiom that obliges me to follow this course of decision-making is the independence axiom. It tells us that any preference between A and B should not be influenced by components that are irrelevant. If it is irrelevant for my choosing B (2400 with certainty) that a higher amount (2500) is offered with probability 0.33, this very option must be ignored in problem 2 as well. I must prefer D to C. However, if I prefer A to B in problem 1, I obviously go in for better outcomes even if they are offered with lower probability. I am even prepared to ignore an outcome offered with certainty. In order to choose consistently I have to prefer C to D in this case. Those who choose B in problem 1 and C in problem 2 are sinning against the independence axiom.

It should be easy to correct expected utility theory if it doesn't suit human behaviour. We could, for instance, delete or modify the axiom of independence, as it seems to be too demanding. Allais' paradox arises because people choose options that are irrational in terms of the theory. It seems over-ambitious and counter-intuitive to blame people for behaving irrationally just because they choose—unimpressed by the theory—according to their own expectations of winning. [Scanlon (1998, p. 31) rightly argues that violating axioms of choice is not enough to criticise people as being irrational.] Their intentions to win certain pay-offs seem to be both rational and irrational. Either the theory is wrong or people's choices are, depending on which perspective we choose. This is what I mention at the beginning where I claim that some intentions seem to be irrational, although their mental origin does not differ from the origin of rational intentions. The external meanings that determine the contents of intentions in these cases are either the pay-offs chosen by a great majority of people or the pay-offs offered by the standard theory. However, the rationality or irrationality of both of these options are determined externally by the respective pay-offs.

Both of those pay-offs are external to the psychological groundwork or motivational dispositions of ordinary choosers. People's preferences for pay-offs depend on the contexts in which the pay-offs are offered to them. The preferences for pay-offs neither derive from individual psychological dispositions nor from the individuals' internal representations of long-term preferences, such as life-plans. On the other hand, people's general attitudes towards risks and pay-offs are primed by their characters. My personal character will not explain each of my choices. My timidity, for example, will prompt me to choose a pay-off offered with certainty, but I will not take any of the pay-offs that are certain if the risks of considerably larger pay-offs are reasonable. Secondly, any success of mine will give buoyancy to my taking greater risks in the next round of choices. My former timidity will only return after one or two unfortunate decisions before my confidence to win is strengthened again. Choices will always express timidity or boldness or other characters, but the latter do not explain the choices themselves. This is a further reason why people's intentions to choose are determined externally.

The external nature of the contexts of choice is finally evident in Robert Sugden's Regret Theory (Sugden, 1993). I need not go into the mathematical details of the theory in order to give a brief sketch of Sugden's basic idea. While Allais tries to liberate choosers from the axiom of independence Sugden is prepared to give up the axiom of transitivity for individual preferences. This is illustrated by his example: imagine three situations E, F, and G, and their respective probabilities $p(E) = 0.1$, $p(F) = 0.4$, and $p(G) = 0.5$, where $p(E) = 0.1$ 'the probability that E occurs is 0.1.'

These situations figure in two options of choice A and B:

Option A

0	if	E or F
$1000 + e$	if	G

Option B

1000	if	E or F
0	if	G

The pay-offs are in money and 'e' is an amount slightly larger than 0. As long as the set of options is limited to A and B, almost every theory will recommend A. The picture changes if there is one further option C available.

Option C

5000	if	E
0	if	F or G

Considering the order of preferences (A, B, C), Sugden argues if e is sufficiently small, B is preferable to A. Option C changes the original order of preference of A over B. The switch of preferences from A to B and the implied violation of the axiom of transitivity is easily explained. If we choose A and E occurs our regret will be considerably deeper with option C than without. Of course, it all depends on the negligibility of e. Nevertheless, the change of preferences is brought about externally by a contextual change.

I shall neither discuss the general consequences of weakening the axiom of transitivity nor shall I defend Sugden's Regret Theory. His theory plausibly and convincingly shows that the alternatives of choice are not to be characterized by some intrinsic features of the alternatives themselves, but by their mutual relationships. These change relative to the contexts in which the alternatives of choice are offered. Finally, whenever these contexts change, our preferences change as well.

The incongruency I mentioned earlier between the psychological groundwork of decision-making and the standard theory of rational choice is partly overcome by the different strategies of either weakening the axiom of transitivity or giving up the axiom of independence. In both cases, the norms of rationality are adjusted to the possible changes of individual preferences. It is now possible to proceed without paradox from the psychological groundwork of decision making to the revised standards of rationality. Whatever revision of the set of axioms of the standard theory of rationality we accept, the very possibility of revising the set corroborates the externalist account of rational decision making.

After all, both the analyses of mental and rational choice showed that intentions are individualized by external meanings. While this issues from the spontaneity of mental choice in volitional attitudes, it is due to the contextual character of preferences in rational choice. It first seemed that rational choice was not spontaneous, but was governed by the single motive to maximize expected utility. The advantage of the single motive seemed to be that it makes decisions clear and predictable and that it guarantees maximal success. If this was the case, rational choice would be determined internally by an intrinsic motive of gain. We now see that this is not the case. Obviously, rational decision making is influenced by external factors to be found in its context and these factors are beyond the control of the standard theory of choice. Each individual's psychological groundwork, including character, emotions, and evaluative attitudes, plays a role. [As Donald Calne states: 'We favor certainty if we are dealing with a potential gain and uncertainty if we are facing a potential loss. These attitudes are emotional—we minimize our anxiety by making decisions in this way' (Calne, 1999, p. 288).] This is not surprising, but it shows how inept the internalist Humean picture of the passions pressing reason into slavery is, at least from the viewpoint of rational decision making. The passions are too clueless and changeable to control reason. On the other hand, reason is unable to control the passions to the same effect.

Finally, rational choice can be as spontaneous as the mental choice of intentions. Even if we assume that we all share similar motives the choices we make are not caused by these motives directly. We choose our intentions to maximize our expected utilities in the same way as we choose intentions mentally, that is, independent from the clues and fixations that might have accrued from earlier choices.

At the beginning I mentioned the hybrid nature of rationality. Rationality is, at least in its narrow, instrumental sense, a hybrid. It is partly based on some psychological groundwork or motivational set, and partly on theoretical and axiomatic structure. None of these parts is sufficient for rational decision making, and their relationship is—as we learnt from Allais and Sugden—precarious. Why is rationality a hybrid? Because it combines two incongruent ingredients—psychological groundwork and theoretical structure. The mutual influence of these counterparts to form a coherent whole is *ad hoc* and a matter of compromise.

In order to determine the rationality of intentions we need to know their objects in a context of alternatives. Neither the psychological groundwork nor the theoretical structure of the standard theory offers a universal and conclusive basis to judge whether intentions are rational or not. Rational intentions are determined externally. No intention is intrinsically rational. The consequences of this observation in ethics need to be considered carefully, at least for theories that are based on the intrinsic nature of moral rationality, most prominently that of Immanuel Kant, who, in his *Groundwork of the Metaphysics of Morals*, argues from the intrinsic goodness and moral rationality of 'good will'.

Acknowledgements

I would like to express my gratitude to Martin Rechenauer, Bettina Walde, Sabine Maasen, and Tillmann Vierkant for helpful discussions, and valuable criticisms and recommendations.

References

Allais, M. (1953) Le comportement de l'homme rationnel devant le risque: critique des postulats et axiomes de l'école américaine. *Econometrica* **21**, 503–56.

Anscombe, G.E.M. (1957) *Intention.* Oxford: Blackwell.

Bach, K. (1978) A representational theory of action. *Philosoph Stud* **34**, 361–79.

Calne, D. (1999) *Within Reason. Rationality and Human Behavior.* New York: Vintage Books.

Ellsberg, D. (1961) Risk, ambiguity, and the savage axioms. *Quart J Econ* **75**, 643–69.

Hahn, F. & Hollis, M. (eds) (1979) *Philosophy and Economic Theory.* Oxford: Oxford University Press.

Hargreaves Heap, S., Hollis, M., Lyons, B., Sugden, R. & Weale, A. (eds) (1992) *The Theory of Choice.* Oxford: Blackwell.

Hollis, M. & Lukes, S. (eds) (1982) *Rationality and Relativism.* Oxford: Blackwell.

Kahneman, D. & Tversky, A. (1979) Prospect theory: an analysis of decision under risk. *Econometrica* **43**, 263–91.

Scanlon, T.M. (1998) *What We Owe to Each Other.* Cambridge: Harvard University Press.

Sen, A. (1979) Rational fools: a critique of the behavioural foundations of economic theories. In Hahn, F. & Hollis, M. (eds), *Philosophy and Economic Theory.* Oxford: Oxford University Press, pp. 87–109.

Sugden, R. (1992a) Anarchic order. In Hargreaves Heap, S., Hollis, M., Lyons, B., Sugden, R. & Weale, A. (eds), *The Theory of Choice.* Oxford: Blackwell, pp. 179–95.

Sugden, R. (1992b) How people choose. In Hargreaves Heap, S., Hollis, M., Lyons, B., Sugden, R. & Weale, A. (eds), *The Theory of Choice.* Oxford: Blackwell, pp. 36–50.

Sugden, R. (1993) An axiomatic foundation for regret theory. *J Econ Theory* **60**, 159–80.

Wayne Sumner, L. (1996) *Welfare, Happiness, and Ethics.* Oxford: Oxford University Press.

Wilson, B.R. (ed.) (1977) *Rationality*, 3rd edn. Oxford: Blackwell.

SECTION IV

SECTION IX

BETWEEN THE NORMATIVE AND THE SYMBOLIC: JURIDICAL AND ANTHROPOLOGICAL ACCOUNTS OF VOLUNTARY ACTION

SABINE MAASEN

Thus far, voluntary action has been investigated from three different perspectives: psychologists have inquired into the cognitive processes and social-personality aspects of goal-directed behaviour. Voluntariness, by their account, is either nothing but a convenient manner of speech, that should be abandoned from scientific discourse or, if anything, is a matter of constraining, but not triggering, goal-directed action. As regards the neurosciences, they enquire into the brain functions that process actions that we perceive as conscious or willed. In their view, consciousness, while not the 'lord of the manor' in our brains, can be understood as an automatic mechanism for monitoring actions. Whenever actions fail or remain incomplete, consciousness is understood to be a corrective procedure performed by the acting system. Philosophers differ as to whether these and related findings in the cognitive sciences allow us to dispense with notions such as volition and consciousness altogether, notably, when it comes to explaining actions scientifically.

However, the threat of epiphenomenalism and the role of rationality for voluntary action discussed in the philosophical section are only two examples that show that even philosophical proponents of a strong status for our folk psychological intuitions find it very difficult to say in which way these intuitions could be justified.

In short, in both the cognitive sciences (psychology and neurosciences) and philosophy, voluntary action is a contested phenomenon. Cognitive psychologists and neuroscientists, as well as philosophers, are still attempting to come to terms with dramatic advances in the cognitive sciences, which provide a huge amount of new data on the problem of voluntary action and seem incompatible with our traditional intuitive views. Even those authors who adopt the most radical reductionist stances concede on the sidelines that volition and consciousness do play a significant role in our everyday life. While some find our mentalistic folk psychology pitiful and badly in need of scientific enlightenment (i.e. the Churchlands), others deem it a necessary and indispensable concept for social life. In their view, major social institutions, such as the law, family relationships, and democracy, as well as interpersonal exchanges in general, fundamentally rely on the notion of voluntarily acting subjects. Thus, voluntary action needs to be investigated by the social sciences.

The case of criminology seems most obvious: if actions are considered voluntary, actors are held responsible for them and in cases of unlawful behaviour may justly be punished, according to the circumstances which, in turn, are evaluated by the criterion of responsibility. From a juridical, notably a criminological perspective, voluntary action is a fundamental phenomenon as well—and a contested one. Yet, the aspect of contestation differs sharply from the one mentioned above. Criminologists argue about the question, for instance, on exactly which notion of freedom voluntary action should be based (Burkhardt), and they redirect our attention to the fact that voluntary action is a contested *normative* phenomenon, in need of societal legitimation and subject to historical formation and change (Günther). If it comes to voluntary action as a social and a historical phenomenon, one should also look at its anthropological dimension: here again, one becomes aware of the cultural contingencies that shape specific notions of voluntary action. Particularly, the differing family relationships and their symbolic manifestations in Western and non-Western cultures are telling when it comes to culturally specific concepts of voluntariness (Nuckolls), cultural universal, such as basic attachment patterns, notwithstanding.

Generally speaking, the scientific debate on voluntary action needs to be complemented by social scientific investigations into the how and why of voluntary action in the social sphere. It is time, therefore, to open the floor to social scientists and confront them with two questions: How do criminology and anthropology, respectively, conceive of voluntary action? Moreover, is their discipline-specific view of voluntary action affected by recent findings in the cognitive sciences or pertinent reflections in philosophy—and, if not, should this be the case? One thing to be mentioned at the outset is that all authors, their internal differences in perspective and scope notwithstanding, deem the issue of voluntary action highly appropriate and indispensable for any kind of social discourse. What is more, they all acknowledge recent findings in the cognitive sciences, yet they all are of the opinion that these findings attack the issue at a level that does not truly touch the social sphere or, if they should ever lead to practical consequences such as obligatory brain screening, would imply serious danger for both individual and civil life (see Günther, this volume). Basically, the criminologist insists on an 'as if' perspective toward voluntary action. Society must treat individuals *as if* they were free to choose between right and wrong. The anthropologist gives this stance a reflexive twist: is the project of debunking voluntary action not motivated by 'the fear and fascination, deep down, that we are not in control of our actions even as we act to debunk theories of voluntary control' (Nuckolls)? Whether or not one agrees with this supposition, voluntary action—as a socially induced and historically framed fiction—today serves important needs to organize and harmonize civil order, be it on the level of face-to-face interactions, family structures, organizations, or societies.

In Burkhardt's view, in a scientific world, it is difficult, yet not impossible to reconcile the notion of personal guilt and freedom. More specifically, he suggests that the principle of personal guilt should be based on the subjective experience of freedom to act according to the juridical norms. The acting subject must act *as though* she were free, thereby producing a state in the world that meets the intended effects. From this position, Burkhardt explicitly limits the claims by cognitive scientists: While, from a third-person perspective, freedom of will is a falsifying perception of the causal process producing an action, this scientifically correct order of things is utterly irrelevant for the acting subject. His or her subjective experience of freedom is an intentional state that processes conditions in the world through which this state becomes satisfied. Most importantly, it indicates that the acting subject is, indeed, the author of her action.

In the same vein, Burkhardt counters the social constructivist view according to which voluntary action, ultimately, is a cultural artifact, merely exploiting the resources to be found in the biological hardware of brains (McCrone). Though true, this again is utterly irrelevant for the acting subject. In this respect, Burkhardt (and Günther) refers to the Thomas theorem: if people define a situation as real, they will draw real consequences. Thus, from this viewpoint, a society whose basic institutions are built on a concept of individual responsibility makes its members 'free' in a strong sense of voluntary action. Again, subjects act as though they were free and, if necessary, are punished if they chose to act unlawfully.

In summary, Burkhardt regards both types of deconstruction or enlightenment (neuro-cognitive and social) as true, yet not as truly challenging for criminology—at least not in practice.

Günther puts even more emphasis on voluntary action and responsibility as social an attribution that can be analysed as a social practice throughout history and various cultures. As a case in point, Günther mentions the sea change from welfare state politics, according to which unlawful acts occurred by virtue of unfortunate social circumstances. Nowadays, voices appear that deem this attitude far too permissive. Irritatingly, this paradigm change reinforces an attitude of heightened individual responsibility (which can be noticed in other social arenas as well, such as politics and economics). This paradigm change is neither due to a general refutation of social and psychological explanations that were accepted a few decades before, nor is it affected by modern brain research, which explicitly denies the existence of voluntary action and responsibility in the neurocognitive sphere. Rather, the observation that action is sometimes excused, sometimes not, both diachronically and synchronically (acting out of self-defence is excused, not acting when obliged by profession is not) clearly reveals: Whether and how causal factors of human behaviour influence the attribution of responsibility depends on a normative decision about the rules that govern the attribution process.

Hence, if and to what extent we make allowances for apparent lack of mental capabilities in an acting subject is a matter of norms. 'Accountability' has thus a societal function: it safeguards social order by making people obey the law 'voluntarily', invest money according to their interests, and vote according to their own convictions. Hence, individual responsibility is an organizing principle. It is based upon (self-)discipline and (self-)control, and on a historically evolved distinction between normal/abnormal behaviour (Foucault). Whether or not criminal responsibility requires voluntary action in a strong sense, according to Günther, remains an open question. From a constructivist point of view, voluntary action could be defined in purely sociological and functional terms, changing in time and space. Yet, as this notion seems to be in existence over time and space, if in various appearances, it requires a more reflexive attitude. As Günther pointedly puts it, we should take responsibility for the exact ways in which we specify responsibility. Consequently, he suggests basing the concept of criminal responsibility on the notion of the person as a citizen who has a right to participate in procedures of democratic legitimization.

Both Burkhardt and Günther agree that even if one admits that human behaviour is determined by brain processes—when it comes to the consequences for criminal responsibility and punishment, we are entangled in difficult questions that cannot be answered without any reference to (intersubjectively enacted) concepts like 'responsibility' and 'voluntary action'. This is not to side with the short cuts of common sense, but rather a plea for deconstructing the social processes and functions that shape the concept of voluntary action as they are shaped by it.

From an anthropologist's view, Nuckolls advances the idea that both the concept and perception of voluntary action develops through and is based upon multiple and conflicting childhood-derived concepts of agency and action, all penetrated by the desires and frustrations of development. Throughout early childhood, the infant constructs images of self and world that are at variance with the experience of action and control, and these images gain salience in two directions—toward images of little voluntary control (by way of wilful motor operations) to images of super-abundant autonomy (fantasies of super-human creatures, childhood narcissism). This split conception is a cross-cultural universal: maturing human beings desire both to retain and reject attachments to their primary caregivers, and this generates conflict. Cultural knowledge structures, such as beliefs about voluntary action, come into being and both reproduce conflicts and attempt to resolve these ambivalences in a mutually reinforcing way. First Nuckolls shows that these basic conflicts are transferred into maturity, forming characteristic attachment patterns, as well as vicissitudes in action beliefs. American culture, for instance, has established the contradicting values of autonomy/individuation, as well as of community/common purpose: people must try to balance them. There is thus a dialectic of contradictions, developmental and cultural, that is mutually supportive. As action beliefs are the correlatives of individuation and dependency, one can expect to find different attitudes toward action, voluntary or involuntary. Attribution theory has amply corroborated this expectation that the perceived locus of control shifts considerably with changing contextual information.

Nuckolls is aware of the fact that cognitive psychologists and neuroscientists will only consider anthropological research when it is able to state that the relevant properties of voluntary actions are better explained in universalist terms using a different theoretical framework, 'relevance' meaning transmissibility and memorability over generational time. In a case study on the Jalaris of South India, Nuckolls exemplifies the tendency to view mothers (and by extension, all women) ambivalently, as providers of succor and destroyers of male potency, as a direct result of conflicts of attachment. By way of symbolically transforming them into spirits who possess good (nurturing) and evil (pain inflicting) characteristics, maturing individuals disambiguate their mothers. Ultimately, Nuckolls postulates a psychodynamic ambivalence: just how dependent or independent do we really want to be from the sources of our deepest attachment? While this basic conflict is a universal one, the instantiations differ from culture to culture.

In the following part, the authors introduced here deal with normative, socio-cultural, and historical aspects of voluntary action. The number of contributions is limited, though. One could (and maybe should) have added scholars from further disciplines, such as the political sciences (voluntary action in democratic societies), economics (voluntary action in the market), and pedagogy (voluntary action in education). Moreover, the contributions convened do not touch upon the question as to when and why this capacity has evolved (if in socio-cultural specific ways), and been anchored in brain processes. The limited number of authors and perspective addressed, however, is compensated by the fact that all of them consider more than one disciplinary perspective, but include philosophical

(Burkhardt), political-historical (Günther), and psycho analytic (Nuckolls) dimensions as well. In this, their stances provide promising starting points for reframing the debate among and between the different scientific cultures assembled in this book. Notably, they direct our attention to the fact that voluntary action is not a notion that 'belongs' to any one discipline, but rather is subject of ongoing controversy in various domains. Sure enough, the recent advances in brain research and cognitive psychology have introduced new stimuli that need to be discussed. This, however, is neither to forget nor to diminish other accounts. While philosophy is already struggling with and partly adjusting its notions of intentionality, action, and consciousness to the new findings, the social sciences—mostly arguing from a macro-perspective of societal organization—still doubt whether and where to integrate neurocognitive insights into the processes and functions of voluntary action in order to better explain social practice.

CHAPTER 12

FIRST-PERSON UNDERSTANDING OF ACTION IN CRIMINAL LAW

BJÖRN BURKHARDT

1 Preliminary remarks

Actions—one's own just as much as those of others—can be understood from two different perspectives, but the terminology characterizing these perspectives is not uniform. One widespread approach is to contrast the first- and the third-person point of view (see, e.g. Korsgaard, 1996b; Kim, 1998; Velmans, 2000). Other comparisons can also be found, such as internal and external perspective (Weischedel, 1967; Nagel, 1986), personal and impersonal point of view (Hornsby, 1997), practical and theoretical point of view (Bok, 1998; Korsgaard, 1996a), intentional and deterministic discourse (Kelman, 1987; Boldt, 1992; Herrmann, 1996), or reactive and deliberative interpretation (Pearl, 2000).

The description of the two perspectives is also not completely uniform. To give some examples, Jennifer Hornsby (1997) states:

> From the *personal* point of view, an action is a person's doing something for a reason, and her doing is found intelligible when we know the reason that led her to it. From the *impersonal* point of view, an action would be a link in a causal chain that could be viewed without paying any attention to people, the links being understood by reference to the world's causal working. (p. 129)

Mark Kelman (1987) gives the following description:

> Intentionalist discourse pictures human action in phenomenological, forward-looking, free-will-orientated terms, emphasizing the indeterminacy of action and, correlatively, the ethical responsibilities of actors. Determinist discourse pictures conduct in structuralist, backward-regarding, amoral terms, holding that conduct is simply a last event we focus on in a chain of connected events so predetermined as to merit neither respect nor condemnation. (p. 86)

Finally, Judea Pearl (2000, p. 108) writes:

> The reactive interpretation sees action as a consequence of an agent's beliefs, disposition, and environmental inputs . . . The deliberative interpretation sees action as an option of choice in contemplated decision making, usually involving comparison of consequences.

Pearl also proposes marking the two perspectives terminologically:

> We shall distinguish the two views by calling the first 'act' and the second 'action.' An act is viewed from the outside, an action from the inside. Therefore an act can be predicted and can serve as evidence for the actor's stimuli and motivation (provided the actor is part of our model). Actions, in contrast, can neither be predicted nor provide evidence, since by definition they are pending deliberation and turn into *acts* once executed. (p. 108)

For the time being, let this be an end to these examples, and let us turn to the numerous problems linked to this separation of perspectives. I shall touch briefly on three of these because they play a role in my later considerations:

First, what is the status of introspective (self-)observations and the first-person reports that relate to them? What do we have access to and what not? I shall return to these questions when dealing with the *experience of freedom*. However, even at this stage, it should be noted that there has been remarkably little research on the first-person perspective. Lynne Rudder Baker (1998) suggests that philosophers and cognitive scientists have neglected it at their peril. Varela & Shear (1999, pp. 307–8) have ascertained that psychology and the neurosciences have still done little to clarify the structure of subjective experience. Naturally, I, too, am unable to overcome this deficit.

Secondly, how do the two perspectives relate to each other? Do they compete? Can conflicting descriptions emerge and, if this is the case, which perspective would then have priority? It is well known that answers to these questions are controversial. I assume that the first- and the third-person perspectives are mutually *exclusive* in the sense that one cannot adopt them both at the same time, but that they are *complementary* (and, hence, do not contradict one another) in that both are necessary for a comprehensive description of human behaviour (see Jareborg, 1985, pp. 236–9; Hoche, 1994, pp. 37, 47–8; Korsgaard, 1996a, p. 378; Kim, 1998, pp. 77–81; Varela & Shear, 1999, p. 4; also, Velmans, 2000, pp. 245–262, who talks about an epistemological dualism).

If human behaviour can be understood from two different perspectives and if these perspectives are mutually exclusive in the above-mentioned sense (i.e. cannot be integrated, are incompatible), a third question emerges, namely, which perspective is appropriate within which context (Kelman, 1987, pp. 87–91, talks about the 'issue of discourse choice')? For criminal law, there can be no doubt about the answer: the first-person perspective is not merely the basis of individual responsibility. It is far more the case that criminal law stabilizes this basis by guaranteeing the first-person perspective as the decisive object of evaluation. The guarantee consists in the 'belief principle' that is a component of the principle of blameworthiness. It states 'that a person's criminal liability should be judged on the facts as he [or she] believed them to be' (see Ashworth, 1995, pp. 84, 153; Nagel, 1986, pp. 120–3).

Admittedly, the normative guarantee of the first-person perspective through the principle of blameworthiness does not change the fact that there is a constant tension between the two perspectives (Kelman, 1987; Boldt, 1992). The construction of individual responsibility is unstable precisely because it is based on the acceptability of first-person assumptions. Doubt has repeatedly been cast upon these assumptions, and they have been denounced as vulgar or folk psychology. It has been suggested that the third-person perspective is in a better position to ascertain truth and that the first-person perspective contains assumptions that could prove to be false from the third-person perspective. The discussion over Benjamin Libet's famous experiments provides a good example of this (see, e.g. Prinz, 1996a, p. 99; Roth, 1999, pp. 105–11). In this article, I shall defend the first-person understanding of action (Kim, 1998, p. 75), and the principle of personal responsibility derived from it, against such attempts to bring them into discredit and to destabilize them.

2 Introduction

The construction of individual responsibility in criminal law rests upon folk psychology.[1] Two assumptions are of major importance, namely:[2]

1 The efficacy of conscious experience for bodily behaviour.[3]

2 Freedom, in the sense of self-determination, which involves a decision among genuine alternatives, so that it is true that the agent could have done otherwise.

These assumptions form the basic components of the first-person understanding of action. Although they use the terminology of the third-person perspective, their origin is self-observation, self-description, and self-assessment—in other words, the first-person perspective. From this first-person perspective, it seems absurd to deny the causal role of conscious, intentional states (Honderich, 1988, pp. 91, 293–6, 364–5; Searle, 1992, p. 48; Velmans, 2000, pp. 217–19, 236–8, 253, 276). Experienced (!) freedom of will is built into every normal, conscious action.[4]

Will these assumptions forming the basis for individual responsibility in criminal law outlive the growing insights into the structure and processes of the human brain? Leading German scientists seem to doubt this, and this is also what they have published and proclaimed.

Wolfgang Prinz, director of the Max Planck Institute for Psychological Research at Munich, has gained considerable public attention with his provocative claim that, 'We don't do what we want, but we want what we do' (Prinz, 1996a, p. 87, *translated*). He maintains that folk psychology contains metaphysical and epistemological untenables. He proposes that the 'idea of psychophysical causality should be abandoned' (Prinz, 1996a, pp. 91–2, 1998, pp. 13–15). Phenomena of will should not be assigned 'the role of subjective causes of action, but only the role of subjective *phenomena accompanying* some kind of hidden action-causing process that, in turn, can be explained in neurobiological terms.'[5] A theory claiming that 'persons are autonomous sources of the determinants of their actions and thereby principally free in their action decisions' is also false. It is based on 'far-reaching misconceptions regarding the status of introspective observations' (Prinz, 1996a, p. 93, *translated*).

Gerhard Roth, director of the Institute for Brain Research at Bremen, referring to the experiments of Benjamin Libet, claims that major doubt should be cast on our folk-psychological conception of free will: the experience of engaging in voluntary action is 'not the actual cause of an action, but an *accompanying sensation* that emerges after cortical processes have commenced' (1996, p. 309).[6] Roth does not state whether this finding undermines criminal law theory. However, he assures us that leading legal theorists have long considered that criminal law could do without the principle of personal blameworthiness.[7]

Wolf Singer, director of the Max Planck Institute for Brain Research at Frankfurt, is quoted in a report by the *Deutsche Presse-Agentur* [German Press Agency] dated May 30, 2000, as saying that: 'Neurobiologically speaking, there is no place for freedom. That which we experience as a free decision is nothing other than a subsequent justification for state-transformations that would have occurred anyway.' He links this to the conclusion that 'We must reconsider how we deal with misconduct, blameworthiness, and punishment.'[8] In an interview with the weekly magazine *Der Spiegel* in January 2001, Singer explained that he considered we could do without the principle of guilt and atonement (in a non-religious sense).[9]

I find these statements to be essentially inadequate and, in part, also quite simply unfounded. They, on their part, are based on a number of misconceptions and misinterpretations.[10] My responses are:

1   The folk psychological ideas based on the first-person perspective contain no metaphysical or epistemological untenables.

2   The claim that persons are principally free to choose (and act) otherwise is true from the first-person perspective.

3   If one wants to explain and evaluate actions, then—at least as far as criminal law is concerned—it is the first-person perspective that is fundamentally decisive: 'Our actions are a function of our mental representations of the world, not of the world as it is (unless, of course, it is as we represent it)' (Forguson, 1989, p. 28).

4   Criminal law cannot do without the principle of personal blameworthiness. At the same time, criminal law theory will not be undermined by Benjamin Libet's findings.

I shall try to justify these claims in the following way: my first step will be to recall the content and the normative status of the principle of blameworthiness. Then, I shall address the concept of action in criminal law. I shall demonstrate that experience of freedom of will is an integrative component of this concept of action and that it is inappropriate to dismiss this experience of freedom as an epiphenomenon or illusion. Finally, I shall address the normative relevance of experience of freedom: this experience provides the basis for determining the blameworthiness of a particular actor in a particular case.

3   Some comments on the principle of blameworthiness

One of the basic principles in German criminal law is that 'criminal punishment presupposes a finding of (individual) blameworthiness (personal guilt, culpability)'.[11,12] At this stage, I do not wish to address the question this raises regarding the conditions under which a human being may be found to be personally blameworthy, nor do I wish to address the question of whether these conditions also include freedom of will in a non-deterministic or contracausal sense.[13] Instead, I shall point to an obvious, but infrequently explicated implication of the principle of blameworthiness, namely, the *belief principle* already mentioned above:

> (BP) A person's criminal liability should be judged on the facts as he or she believed them to be. (Ashworth, 1995, pp. 84, 153)[14]

Blameworthiness is accordingly a normative judgment based on an evaluation of the actor's first-person perspective. Hence, it is facts possessing an ontologically subjective mode of existence that are the object of evaluation: the mental representations, the propositional attitudes, or the intentional states of the defendant (including their accompanying background).[15]

The belief principle becomes particularly significant when a defendant's mental representations do not match the rest of the world, in other words, when false beliefs (misrepresentations, misconceptions) are present. Such false beliefs may incriminate or exonerate. A clarification is required: the principle of blameworthiness is essentially negative. It simply prescribes 'no punishment without blameworthiness'. In contrast, it does not state that all behaviour that can be described as blameworthy should also be punished.

The absolute validity of the principle of blameworthiness as provided for in, for example, German, Austrian, Italian, or Spanish criminal law is in no way a matter of course. Various countries such as Israel or Turkey, but also, and above all, Anglo-American criminal law, provide constellations of *criminal liability without blameworthiness*. Particular mention should be given to 'strict liability offences', in which (false) beliefs of the defendant are not relevant, as well as to offences that impose the burden of proof on the defendant.[16] The reasons for such (partial) waivers of the belief principle are self-evident: the concern is to avoid the notorious evidentiary problems that arise when the mental representations of the defendant are considered decisive in the determination of guilt or innocence.[17]

The specific problems involved in proving subjective prerequisites arise because other persons' mental contents are not directly accessible to perception: 'The only person who knows what the defendant's mental processes were is the defendant himself—and probably not even he can recall them accurately' (von Caldwell, 1987, cited in Tur, 1993, p. 228). Hence, there is no alternative to questioning the defendant, to taking his or her self-definition into consideration, to try and place oneself in his or her situation, to adopting his or her perspective vicariously, and to evaluating his or her behaviour in the light of the alternatives available to him or her.[18]

Why should one accept a principle that makes the determination of guilt or innocence dependent on the first-person perspective, thus producing serious evidentiary problems? The answer is simple; it consists of two parts:

1 *If* one wants to retain the principle of *personal blameworthiness*, there is no alternative than to rely upon the actor's perspective on the world. Persons act on the basis of their mental representations, and this is the only basis on which they can grasp and explain their behaviour.[19] Persons who think about what they should do can orientate themselves only by referring to the content of their intentional states (desires, beliefs, expectations, etc.). Only such action options that are represented mentally enter the selection process (and reveal something about the person). In other words, eliminating the subjective perspective of the actor removes the foundation of the principle of blameworthiness.[20]

2 However, this still does not clarify *whether* the principle of blameworthiness should be retained. The reasons in favour of its indispensability culminate, in my opinion, in the following consideration.[21] The principle of blameworthiness has the task of limiting state punishment in such a way that the offender can personally perceive it as being right and just; in other words, so that there is a chance of the punishment being accepted by

the offender. Such an acceptance can be achieved only if criminal law appeals to the offender's insight and rationality. As a result, criminal law may only incriminate actions that are (also) 'blameworthy' from the actor's perspective. This, in turn, will be the case only when the offender believes that he or she has had a fair chance of making his or her behaviour conform to the legal norms.[22]

Here, it is necessary to point to what is perhaps a surprising effect of the belief principle that is usually overlooked: this principle does not just lead to difficulties in proof, but also overcomes some of them, and it does this precisely where they are held to be insurmountable. This requires a short explanation: One very strong opinion in German criminal law theory takes the position that contracausal freedom (the ability to choose otherwise, truly selectable action alternatives) is a prerequisite of personal blameworthiness, and that such free will exists.[23] At the same time, it is admitted that criminal proceedings are unable to prove retrospectively whether the offender could have made another decision at the time of the offence, in other words, whether free will was present. However, this presents a dilemma, namely *either* one must claim that such a proof is not necessary,[24] *or* one must do without personal blameworthiness.[25] The dilemma vanishes when one is guided by the belief principle: Whether a behaviour renders the defendant personally blameworthy does not depend on whether he or she really had an individually attainable behaviour alternative. What is decisive is whether he or she acted in the belief of having one.[26] In other words, it is not objective, but *subjective freedom* (experience of freedom) that is decisive when the concern is whether a behaviour is personally blameworthy.[27] As far as this subjective freedom is concerned, there are normally no serious problems of proof, because the experience of being able to choose and act otherwise is built into every normal, conscious intentional action.[28] This will be discussed below. However, two provisional conclusions can be reached:

1 Criminal law cannot do without the principle of personal blameworthiness.
2 The belief principle contains no assumptions that contradict neuroscientific findings.

4 Comments on the concept of action in criminal law

'All legal systems', according to George Fletcher (1998, p. 44), 'concur that punishment is imposed only for human action or a "human act"'. The Model Penal Code sec. 2.01 (1) of the American Law Institute states accordingly: 'A person is not guilty of an offence unless his liability is based on conduct that includes a voluntary act or the omission to perform an act of which he is physically capable.' Although the German penal code does not contain such a statement, an offence is usually defined as a wrongful and culpable act (i.e. voluntary conduct by act or omission; see, e.g. Roxin, 1997, p. 146). Hence, there is no doubt that 'voluntary action' is a central concept of criminal law, or at least appears to be. However, if one then asks what an act or action is, one stumbles across a variety of different answers in German criminal-law literature.[29] In the following, I shall limit myself to the two definitions of action that are particularly relevant to this interdisciplinary debate and also represent the two extremes of the opinion spectrum. Although both definitions are more than 100 years old, they are still just as relevant today:

4.1   Equating action and imputation

Reinhold Köstlin, one of the most important criminal law theorists of the nineteenth century, defined the concept of action (influenced by Hegel) as follows:

> *Definition 1 (D1):* An action is 'the realized (free) will of the (proper) subject (of imputation)'. (Köstlin, 1855, p. 156, *translated*)[30]

There are five essential points regarding this definition:

1 Köstlin states expressly that 'the concepts of action and imputation coincide' (have the same extension). In other words, only an imputable operation can qualify as an act. A. F. Berner (1868, p. 146, *translated*), a contemporary of Köstlin, formulated this in the following way: 'As far as the concept of action extends, the concept of imputation extends as well; and where the concept of action ends, the concept of imputation ends too.'

2 An action cannot be conceived without freedom (formation of the will through free self-determination) and only proper subjects of imputation, that is, those with criminal capacity, can act. The Supreme Court of the German Reich (*Reichsgericht*) also adopted this point of view in several decisions:

> One can only talk about an 'action' in the sense of criminal law and in any legal sense when that which a person did externally [in the external world] had its origins in this person's free will. This is why the acts of a person whose free determination of will has been negated by mental illness are not acts in the sense of criminal law. If one says that such persons are not responsible for their acts or that their acts cannot be imputed to them . . . this expresses only a legal consequence of the fact that, in actuality, the person has not acted at all.[31]

3 Free will, according to Köstlin (1855, p. 134, *translated*), presupposes 'the act of self-perception of the I as a self-conscious universal subject with respect to its outer and inner nature.' This shifts the focus of attention to the reflective character of the human mind that is constitutive for the experience of freedom. I shall return to this point later.

4 Whether or not the will has been realized can be determined only if the content of the will is known. The intentional (representative) content of the will extends (normally) beyond physical movement and encompasses social facts as well. However, this also means that only the subject can know whether he or she has acted, or as Thomas Nagel (1986, p. 111) puts it: action has its own irreducibly internal aspect.

5 Finally, proper subjects of imputation and reflective (self-)awareness in the above-mentioned sense cannot exist without societal foundations. Accordingly, the concept of action is thoroughly normative.

4.2   Action as an empirically descriptive starting point of imputation

Although the concept of action (D1) has remained topical to this day and currently even seems to be experiencing a renaissance, at the end of the nineteenth century, it was forced into the background by another 'definition of action', namely:

> *Definition 2 (D2):* 'Actions are activities of will [volitions] ... that express and exhaust themselves in movements of the body'. (Mayer, 1901, p. 18, *translated*)[32]

Corresponding definitions can also be found in the criminal law doctrine of common law.[33] One famous formulation is that by Oliver Wendell Holmes from the year 1881: an action is 'a willed muscular contraction, nothing more'. In an important monograph by Michael Moore at the end of the twentieth century, we find that an action is 'a volitionally caused bodily movement'.

This definition calls for four comments:

1 If one tries to characterize this concept of action, the first (negative) thing one notices is that D2 lacks all the features that are essential for D1: according to D2, an action requires neither free will nor criminal capacity, nor conscious attention (awareness). It also excludes the causal consequences of the bodily movement,[34] and thereby everything that could, in any way, have a social relevance. It has been pointed out justifiably that this turns the concept of action into a 'bloodless ghost' (Beling, 1906, p. 17). The defenders of D2 view this as an advantage and it is, indeed, remarkable that the studies by Hans Kornhuber, Benjamin Libet, and others deal specifically with this bloodless ghost.

2 As far as the resolution of the problem of criminal imputation is concerned, the contributions of D2 are meager. The perfect examples for the non-presence of an action are commonly seizures in a person suffering from epilepsy, uncontrollable vomiting, and movements during a high level of delirium. Even the 'abrupt defensive movement' of an automobile driver who suddenly finds herself with an insect in her eye was, in line with D2, classified as an action by a State Superior Court.[35] Hence, D2 does not solve any problems of imputation worth mentioning, but is merely an empirically descriptive starting point for the imputation issue.

3 Even if one takes the point of view that D2 in no way grasps the 'essence of the action', it still has to be admitted that, in any case, this definition has worked out one of the most necessary prerequisites for actions. In my opinion, it can be demonstrated that D2 is at least an implicit basic element of all the concepts of action developed by criminal law doctrine. When, for example, an action is defined as 'individually avoidable causing of an outcome' or as 'avoidability of a transformation of state' (Jakobs, 1991, pp. 136–43, 147, *translated*), this is always a matter of avoidability through performing or refraining from performing a willed bodily movement.

4 Finally, the at least implicit basic element of all action definitions relevant to criminal law consists, of necessity and sufficiently, in a volition (internal side or mental part of the action), and a physical movement that is the object of this volition (and thereby the external side or physical part of the action). Volition as an element of the action can thereby be conceived as an intentional state (not necessarily accompanied by conscious attention) that, in turn, exists only as one element in a sequence of other intentional states.[36] A bodily movement is (then and only then) the object of volition (and thereby an element of the action) if there is a congruence between the content of the volition and the bodily movement including a causal relationship.

4.3   Voluntary action and experience of freedom

Definitions 1 and 2 have one thing in common: subjective freedom (the experience of free-dom)[37] is not mentioned expressly as an element of the action concept. D2 lacks any mention of freedom; D1 seems to presuppose objective freedom ('real freedom', 'genuine choice', 'real, choosable action alternatives').[38] Subjective freedom might be blanked out because it is a *redundant* or a *contingent* element of actions.

There are many indications that subjective freedom should be viewed as a redundant (and thus necessary!) element not only of D1, but also of D2.[39] For D1, this seems compelling: one can only talk about a realized *free* will if there have been mentally represented action alternatives. However, a great deal also speaks for this assumption in D2. The subjective freedom is then found in the element of 'volitional activity.' The question whether subjective freedom is a necessary component of the action concept is discussed only rarely in the literature,[40] although, at times, it is confirmed. For example, Ota Weinberger (1996) states:

> It only makes sense to talk about an action when a *range of different courses of action is available*, when the actor *sees* alternatives for his or her future behaviour, and makes a decision about which action alternative to pursue. Choice based on a real or only *imagined* field of possibilities is an essential characteristic of action (p. 106, *translated, italics added*; see also Strawson, 1986b, pp. 393–400).[41]

Subjective freedom as a necessary element of the action concept is contradicted or seems to be contradicted by the fact that numerous goal-directed activities occur without the accompaniment of conscious attention (so-called automatisms). The question this raises regarding the appropriateness of describing such activities as actions even when they occur without a 'first-person awareness of active control' does not need to be pursued further here. If subjective freedom is not a necessary element of an action, it is, nonetheless, a contingent one, and one that is intrinsic to every normal, conscious, intentional action.[42] However, this means the following: the determination that a person has acted generally includes the determination that the person was aware that he or she had been able to act otherwise. This leaves the question of whether this awareness provides a sound basis for blameworthiness.

5   Remarks on subjective freedom

The entire legal system is built 'on the human consciousness of freedom as an incontrovertible socio-psychological fact' (Roxin, 1993, p. 521, *translated*). Without experiences of freedom, 'there would be no morality, no legal system, no modern national states, and also no revised penal code' (Herrmann, 1996, p. 68, *translated*; see, also, Binding, 1914, p. 56). Yet experienced freedom to choose would be discredited as a basis of criminal responsibility if the mentally represented content of this experience were to contradict scientific knowledge. This assumption is widespread. I wish to show briefly that such a contradiction does not exist. I shall start with the content of the experience of freedom and then address the claim that the experience of freedom is an 'illusion of self-observation.'

5.1   Experienced freedom: the perspective of the acting subject

Generally, science doubts or refutes the idea that 'objective freedom of will' or 'true (real, genuine) self-determination' exists. In contrast, subjective (experienced, perceived) freedom (awareness of self-determination) is accepted as a psychological fact and as a basic experience of most persons. There are thousands of references to this in the literature.[43]

However, the content and the form of subjective freedom are not particularly clear. As far as its *form* is concerned, it is sometimes called a feeling, sometimes an experience, and sometimes a belief.[44] Regarding its *content*, perhaps one can follow Alfred Mele (1995, pp. 133–7), and distinguish between a stronger and a weaker version of the experience of freedom.[45]

The stronger version (deep openness experience) consists in the conviction that our actions cannot be the fixed outcome of prior sufficient conditions, and, thus, in this (non-deterministic, contracausal) sense, they are 'free'. Such a version can be found in the work of Thomas Nagel (1986),[46] who states:

> The sense that we are the authors of our own actions is not just a feeling but a belief ... It
> presents itself initially as the belief that antecedent circumstances, including the condition
> of the agent, leave some of the things we will do undetermined: they are determined only
> by our choices which are motivationally explicable but not themselves causally determined.
> (p. 114)

The weaker version ('up-to-me' experience) consists in the generally latent, but in certain situations, incontestable impression: I can do this or something else; it depends on me.[47] I shall return to the special role of this experience of freedom in decision-making problems below. Here, it should be noted only that this weaker version of the experience of freedom cannot be an 'illusion of indeterminism', simply because it does not possess any indeterministic content.[48]

The experience of freedom has certain necessary *prerequisites* (objective, psychological foundations or constituents). One of these prerequisites is the *reflective structure of the human mind* already mentioned by Köstlin: Without a system that observes itself, without self-perception, without 'I' awareness, without a reflective 'I', there is no experience of freedom.[49] Beyond this, Julius Kuhl (1996a) has named five additional 'system characteristics for the subjective experience of freedom', although he was admittedly concerned with identifying the properties a system must possess in order for it to succumb to a 'subjective illusion of freedom' even when, objectively, its behaviour is determined.[50] Before I address this issue, it is necessary to recall one prerequisite that is not a system characteristic. Numerous authors have pointed out (correctly) that the experience of freedom is a *socially induced artifact*. John McCrone (1999, p. 242) expresses this as follows '... the human mind is bifold with socially-constructed habits of thought being the software that exploits resources to be found in the biological "hardware" of brains'.[51] I have the impression that this sociocultural limitation is, at times, emphasized not just to make the experience of freedom more relative but also to underline its (purportedly) illusionary character. This seems inappropriate. Property, marriage, and honour are also sociocultural artifacts that exist only because we believe them to exist.[52] However, this does not make them any less real. This brings me to my next point.

5.2   The illusion and the problem of decision

The thesis that subjective freedom is the foundation of personal blameworthiness seems to be countered by an objection that appears to be as sound as it is old: Experience of freedom is an 'illusion of self-observation', an 'I illusion', an 'illusion of indeterminism', a 'naïve-realistic self-misunderstanding', and this can hardly form the foundation for the principle of personal blameworthiness (or the concept of action).[53] The counter-question regarding how such an illusion and, in particular, its astonishing stability can be explained has been given numerous answers over the years.[54] Searle stresses that the mentally represented causes of behaviour normally do not suffice to determine behaviour.[55] Luhmann (1987, pp. 29–47) provides the more fundamental comment that no consciousness can reintroduce into the system the totality of its system conditions as objects of its own operations and, as a result, has to remain intrinsically intransparent.[56] Despite, or perhaps precisely because of these (plausible) explanations of experience of freedom, I hold the terms 'illusion' or 'self-deception' to be entirely inadequate, and I do this for two reasons:

1. The first reason is of Kantian origin, but one can also call it simply the 'problem of decision'.[57] A problem of decision arises when one is required to make a decision, but does not know what decision to make. The problem is characterized by a variety of *options for action* presenting themselves to the decision maker (e.g. having an abortion, or giving birth and keeping the child, or giving him or her up for adoption), such that the individual sees him or herself as facing a *choice*. In this situation, it is obviously of no assistance to the individual presented with alternatives to indicate to him or her what he or she *will* do; for the decision maker's concern prior to the decision is only with what he or she *should* do (how he or she should decide). Also, this question can only be asked if it is assumed that the decision maker *is able* to do one thing or the other, and that the decision thus remains open, in other words, it is not yet fixed. However, the crucial point is not that the decision maker in this situation has to *believe* (think, consider) that he or she possesses the freedom to choose, but rather that he or she has to *choose as if* he or she were free.[58] This reveals the Kantian origin of this idea. I am referring to the famous point in the *Foundations of the Metaphysics of Morals* (1990) stating that:

> Now I say that every being which cannot act otherwise than under the idea of freedom is
> thereby really free in a practical respect. That is to say, all laws that are inseparably
> bound with freedom hold for it just as if its wills were proved free in itself by theoretical
> philosophy. (p. 65)[59]

I find that this statement contains no trace of speculative metaphysics, but, instead, is simply an apt characterization of the perspective of the acting subject (internal perspective, first-person point of view), and that this perspective represents the only 'real' one for the acting subject.

Of course, one can also describe the problem of decision from the external perspective (third-person point of view, theoretical standpoint) in such a way that the openness of the decision represents a purely subjective (psychological) phenomenon. One assumes that the 'decision' has already been made, but the decision maker is unaware of this fact and there may even be 'scientific' evidence for this view. The idea of openness of the decision thus proves to be a consequence of a necessary ignorance (because of the intransparency of consciousness) and thus to be an illusory, falsifying perception of a causal process. Such a description is not helpful, because it neither modifies nor advances the problem of decision (Bok, 1998, pp. 108–9). It is of no use to the acting subject from any conceivable point of view, and this is what handicaps the frequently mentioned comparison with the heliocentric view of the world, and the phenomenon of the rising and setting sun. Labelling the perspective of the acting subject as illusionary is, therefore, simply inappropriate (Magill, 1997, pp. 77–8, 105–7).

2. The second reason why I consider it inappropriate to describe belief in freedom of will as an illusion has its starting point in the concept of intentionality developed by John Searle (1983). My thesis, though admittedly based on rather amateur speculations, is:

> The consciousness of freedom is an intentional state whose content can be expressed (principally) in an entire proposition and that has a double direction of fit, namely, 'mind-to-world' and 'world-to-mind'. (see below)

If this thesis is true, consciousness of freedom is a propositional attitude possessing conditions of satisfaction. Conditions of satisfaction are (according to Searle) those conditions in the world (determined by the intentional content) through which the intentional state is actually satisfied. In the case of the consciousness of freedom, the world is not just the external world, but also the imagined ideas (i.e. other intentional states) including their background.[60]

Once one accepts this starting point (as a hypothesis), it becomes necessary to introduce a discrimination between the *consciousness* of freedom and the *experience* of freedom. The relationship of the former, and the latter is comparable to that of *perception* and *visual experience*: 'The notion of perception involves the notion of succeeding in a way that the notion of experience does not. Experience has to determine what counts as succeeding, but one can have an experience without succeeding, i.e. without perceiving' (Searle, 1983, p. 33)—as in the case of hallucination.

I find that the use of such phrases as the 'illusion of self-observation' or the 'illusion of freedom' tends to obscure the above-mentioned difference. It is obvious that one can discriminate between the *consciousness* of freedom and the mere *experience* of freedom, as shown, for example, by post-hypnotic suggestion. My own belief in freedom has the internal condition of satisfaction (whether induced socioculturally or not) that I am not controlled externally. If I then, as in the case of post-hypnotic suggestion, am controlled externally, I may well have an *experience* of freedom (similar to a visual experience in the case of a hallucination), but I do not have the *consciousness* of freedom, because this presumes that I am, in fact, not controlled externally, in other words, that the represented conditions of satisfaction actually are present.[61] Against this background, I find it exceptionally strange when Wolfgang Prinz (1996a, pp. 98–100) bases his contra-intuitive thesis—'We don't do what we want, but want what we do'—on the pathological case of post-hypnotic suggestion. For me, that is not evidence, but its opposite.

Another point that I wish to mention is related to the *double direction of fit*. In my opinion, the experience of freedom does not just have a 'mind-to-world' direction of fit (in line with visual experience), but also a 'world-to-mind' direction of fit (in line with the intention in action). In other words, the consciousness of freedom is not only caused by something (as is the case with visual perception), but it also generates something, namely, leeway for action. It seems to me that although the concept of illusion (as a false interpretation of actual perceptions) fits the perceptual part of the experience of freedom, it does not fit the part that generates reality. It is inappropriate to designate an experience of freedom that generates reality as an illusion, even when this experience is based on a misperception.

There can be no real doubt that the *consciousness* of freedom generates reality.[62] The belief that one can decide in one way or another creates not only room for practical thinking, but is also a basic prerequisite for persons to be able to conceive of themselves as the originators of their actions and to be able to take responsibility.[63] This makes the normative relevance of subjective freedom the focus of attention, which I shall now discuss.

First of all, two points need to be made:

1   The belief of the deliberating subject that he or she can choose, in one way or another, contains no misunderstandings regarding the status of introspective observations. It also contains no epistemological or metaphysical untenables.

2   The conviction of the deliberating subject that he or she can decide in one way or another is (normally) true—relative to that which the subject knows and can know. This means that the mentally represented causes are not sufficient to determine a specific behaviour.

6   Summary comments on the normative relevance of subjective freedom

One famous decision of the German Federal Supreme Court (*Bundesgerichtshof*) contains the following sentences (*translated*):

> Punishment presupposes culpability [*Schuld*]. Culpability is blameworthiness
> [*Vorwerfbarkeit*]. With the verdict of blameworthiness, the offender is blamed for not behav-
> ing legally, for having decided in favour of wrongdoing although he could have acted legally
> and decided in favour of the law. The internal reason for this verdict is that the human being
> is destined to free, responsible, moral self-determination and is therefore enabled to decide
> in favour of the lawful and against the unlawful, to orient his behaviour according to the
> norms of what ought to be, and to avoid that which is forbidden by law ...[64]

Although there has been fundamental agreement with these sentences, they have also been subjected to strong criticism because of a widespread opinion that they are associated with a recognition of indeterminism (see, e.g. Jakobs, 1982). The solution to the problem is to make only a slight change to the formulation of the Federal Supreme Court. Corrected, it should state:

> With the verdict of blameworthiness, the offender is blamed for not behaving legally, for
> having decided in favour of wrongdoing although he or she could have acted legally and
> decided in favour of the law *from his or her own perspective*. The internal reason for this
> verdict is that the human being is destined to act within the *consciousness of freedom*.

This modification places the perspective of the acting subject at the focus of attention and thus recognizes the belief principle. Criminal law treats persons in the way that they normally perceive themselves. There is no alternative to this if one wants to retain the possibility of punishment also being perceived as just by the offenders themselves.[65]

I shall conclude with a comment on the question of how the thesis of the importance of subjective freedom relates to punishment and, in particular, to German statutory rules:

1 With the requirement of intent or 'subjective' (individual) negligence (§§ 15–18 dStGB), the legislature ensures that a punishment without subjective freedom cannot occur.

2 In addition, the legislature specifies constellations in which blame is not imputed, although the offender has acted with the consciousness of having been able to act otherwise. These include §§ 19 (infancy), 20 (insanity and intoxication), 33 (excessive self-defence in a state of shock), and 35 (duress and necessity) dStGB.

Thereby, it is also shown that the reason for the exemption from punishment of children and the insane is, at any rate, not lack of free will, and also has nothing to do with the awareness of being able to choose and act differently. The decisive argument for criminal incapacity is a lack of equality, understood as equality in *reason* (German: Vernunft; see Packer, 1969, p. 135; Jakobs, 1982, pp. 75–6; Moore, 1997, pp. 60–4, 602–9).

7   Final comments

Action theory, writes Stephen J. Morse (1994, p. 1589), 'cannot be avoided by criminal law: the criminal law presupposes precisely the folk psychological [first-person] account of human action based on desires, beliefs, intentions, and other mental states that reductionist theories reject.' Will this 'folk psychological account', will the first-person perspective and the principle of personal blameworthiness derived from it survive the new 'neuroscientific view of humanity?' The criminal sociologist Enrico Ferri (1896, pp. 222–3) claimed at the end of the nineteenth century that 'scientific psychology, that is, physiological psychology' had completely destroyed the belief in free will (or moral freedom), because it was but an illusion of self-observation. In contrast, Karl Binding, one of the greatest scholars of modern German criminal law, spoke of the 'unshakable nature of the consciousness of freedom' and declared the 'ability of self-determination (freedom)' to be the official 'eternal truth in law' (1914, pp. 4–40, 55–6, 78). Up until now, it has been Binding's, rather than Ferri's prediction that has proved correct. Everything indicates that the consciousness of freedom (with all its implications) will also survive the 'new neuroscientific view of humanity.' A system of criminal law that globally (not locally) ignores the representations of the acting subject is literally inconceivable. Hence, the task is 'to deepen the folk psychology on which the law rests, rather than jettisoning it' (Moore, 1997, p. 421). Psychology and neuroscience could also contribute to this if they were to make a greater effort to clarify further the structure of subjective experience and, in particular, the structure and meaning of subjectively experienced freedom.

Notes

1 This is an old insight that most authors mention only in passing (see Huther, 1897, pp. 260–3; Binding, 1914, pp. 3–15; Morse, 1994, p. 1589; Moore, 1997, pp. 420–1, 619).

2 Binding (1914, pp. 3–15, *translated*) talks about the 'basic assumptions of the "psychology of laws"' and the 'esoteric psychology of the law'. Griffin (1998, pp. 33–41) considers these assumptions to belong to the 'hard-core commonsense notions'. The following formulations of the two assumptions are taken from Griffin.

3 A more precise formulation can be found in Ramsey *et al.* (1991, p. 97): '… the crucial folk-psychological tenets … are the claims that propositional attitudes are functionally discrete, semantically interpretable states that play a causal role in the production of other propositional attitudes and ultimately in the production of behaviour'. Greenwood (1991, p. 19) considers that '"propositional attitude" is the conventional term employed by philosophers to reference contentful psychological [intentional] states such as beliefs, desires, and hopes.'

4 This claim has been documented thousands of times in the literature (see, e.g. Searle, 1984, pp. 86–99; Herrmann, 1996, pp. 56–68). Nicolai Hartmann (1926, p. 718, *translated*) talks about the 'awareness of self-determination as a phenomenon that generally accompanies the act.'

5 Prinz (1998, p. 14) himself talks about an 'epiphenomenalistic hypothesis'. I should like to recall only briefly what philosophers have to say about epiphenomenalism: 'Epiphenomenalism—an absurdity' (Holenstein, 1996, p.199, *translated*); 'Epiphenomenalism is a possible thesis, but it is absolutely incredible' (Searle, 2000, p. 16); 'There are not many epiphenomenalists left, at least in philosophy. I know two' (Honderich, 1993, pp. 22, 61).

6 See also Roth *et al.* (2001). The term 'accompanying sensation' also raises the suspicion that Roth takes an epiphenomenalistic stance.

7 See Roth (1999, p. 111), who does not tell us who these legal theorists are. I shall return to this daring (and normatively false) claim below.

8 See <http://vitaweb.salzburg.com/ratgeber/infothek/neurologie/20000605171842.html> (accessed 28 August 2001). Singer is also quoted as saying: 'We shall have to get used to the fact that there are two contradictory but correct descriptive models: on the one side, the subjective sensations; on the other side, the scientific finding.' There are two things one would like to know: (a) How does this assumption relate to the 'law of noncontradiction'? Does one of two contradictory descriptions have to be *false*? (b) If *both* descriptions are correct, why do we need to rethink our approach to misconduct, blameworthiness, and punishment? Why can we not base punishment on the—correct—subjective perspective (see Bok, 1998, pp. 73–5)?

9 *Der Spiegel*, 2001, No. 1, pp. 154, 160.

10 I willingly admit that these misconceptions are at least partially caused by criminal law theory. I shall return to this point later.

11 See *Entscheidungen des Bundesgerichtshofes in Strafsachen*, Vol. 2, pp. 194, 201–2; *Entscheidungen des Bundesverfassungsgerichts*, Vol. 20, pp. 323, 331. The principle of blameworthiness is an (unwritten) element of the German constitution. It is orientated toward the idea of justice and is derived from the 'rule of law' (Rechtsstaatsprinzip; Art. 20 III, 28 I 1 Grundgesetz [GG]), as well as Art. 1 I GG and Art. 2 I GG (see *Entscheidungen des Bundesverfassungsgerichts*, Vol. 50, 125, 133; Vol. 95, 96, 130–1). These articles read as follows:

Article 1 (Protection of human dignity)

(1) The dignity of man shall be inviolable. To respect and protect it shall be the duty of all state authority.

Article 2 (Rights of liberty)

(1) Everyone shall have the right to the free development of his [or her] personality in so far as he [or she] does not violate the rights of others or offend against the constitutional order or the moral code.

Article 20 (Basic principles of the Constitution – Right to resist)

(3) Legislation shall be subject to the constitutional order; the executive and the judiciary shall be bound by law and justice.

Article 28 (Federal guarantee of Laender constitutions)

(1) The constitutional order in the *Laender* (federal states) must conform to the principles of republican, democratic, and social government based on the rule of law, within the meaning of this Basic Law.

12 The Austrian penal code (öStGB) has laid down the principle of blameworthiness expressly. § 4 öStGB states: 'Punishable are only those who act blamefully'. Anglo-American criminal law recognizes many exceptions to the principle of blameworthiness, particularly in the form of so-called 'strict liability offences' that require neither intent nor negligence. See note 16.

13 The discussion of this controversial issue has generated a large body of literature (see, e.g. the references in Lenckner, 2001, pp. 190–1). An end to this entrenched controversy is not in sight. However, its practical significance tends to be low. The German penal code (dStGB) requires intent (in the broadest sense, i.e. including dolus eventualis) or 'subjective' (individual) negligence (§§ 15,18), and otherwise stipulates only the prerequisites that must be fulfilled in order for illegal conduct to be excused. Statutory excuse defences are: mistake of fact (§ 16), mistake of law (§ 17), infancy (§ 19), insanity and intoxication (§ 20), excessive self-defence in a state of shock (§ 33), and duress and necessity (§ 35).

14 See also Packer (1969, p. 121) who states that 'the moral quality of an act inheres not in the act but in the actor's frame of mind with respect to it'. Moore (1997, pp. 404–11, 412) states 'It is the actor's epistemic vantage point–her "information" base, i.e. beliefs—that measures her culpability'.

15 I orientate myself toward the terminology of Searle (1998). He talks about a subjective mode of existence, because the existence of intentional states depends on them being experienced by a subject (pp. 42-45, 69-83). On the concept of propositional attitudes, see also note 3.

16 See Articles 44, 45 of the Turkish and Section 22 of the Israeli penal code and, for Anglo-American law, Ashworth (1995, pp. 158–67), Dressler (1995, pp.125–31), LaFave (2000, pp. 257–65), Smith & Hogan (1996, pp. 101–25). The Anglo-American academic discourse nearly always views these violations of the principle of blameworthiness critically. In the USA, there is doubt whether it is possible to reconcile strict liability offences with the constitution. Robinson (1997, p. 256) considers that strict liability is undercutting criminal law's moral credibility.

17 These problems of proof generate enormous costs. They hinder any rapid and economic reaction. If the first-person perspective is decisive, it opens up the possibility of false defences and unmerited acquittal or mitigation. This, in turn, may reduce the deterrent impact and thereby impair the protection of legal interests.

18 On the difficulties and limits to 'putting oneself in the situation of the offender', see Freund (1987, pp. 5, 26–41). Kim (1998, p. 84) has proposed the plausible thesis that 'we understand the actions of others by projecting to them the way we understand our own actions'. In other words, we regard them as *equals*, as persons who deliberate, make decisions, develop action plans, and put them into practice, and that they do this on the basis of their first-person perspective. On the limits to such a projection, see also Nagel (1986, p. 122).

19 See, in particular, Kim (1998) and Moore (1997, pp. 602–9), as well as the apposite comments by Forguson (1989, pp. 7–8, 28, 31).

20 The validity of this statement is completely independent from the questions whether free will is a precondition of blameworthiness and whether free will exists. This points to a strange cycle: Individual blameworthiness is (like the freedom to make decisions) accessible only from the perspective of the acting subject. By prescribing the perspective of the acting subjects as the

object of evaluation, the principle of blameworthiness guarantees (the foundations of) its own existence.

21 This idea can be found in Pawlowski (1969, pp. 286–91, 1999, p. 280).

22 Usually, this is formulated in *objective* terms, that is, without mentioning the controlling importance of the subjective perspective of the actor. However, this confronts one with the 'principle of alternate possibilities' (PAP). There seems to be a 'fair chance' only when the individual offender could have acted otherwise when committing the offence. It is precisely this intuition that the PAP expresses: 'A person is morally responsible for what he has done only if he could have done otherwise'. See also note 26.

23 See Jähnke (1993, § 20 Rn. 7–12), Jescheck & Weigend (1996, pp. 407–13), Lenckner (2001, pp. 192–5), Tröndle & Fischer (2001, Vorbemerkung § 13 Rn. 28); in addition, *Entscheidungen des Bundesgerichtshofes* (Vol. 2, p. 194, pp. 201–2). Recent Anglo-American criminal law theory tends to be restrained on this point. Nonetheless, see, for example, Hippard (1972).

24 This leads to a degeneration of the thesis that free will is a prerequisite of blameworthiness into pure ideology. In line with this, Smilanski (2000, p. 182) manages to ascertain: 'If we try to characterize the common position regarding free will in Western criminal law in terms of what the laws, lawyers, and judges commonly state or assume, it would seem that "the ideology" is often libertarian while the practice makes sense in control compatibilist terms.'

25 Such a rejection of personal blameworthiness is given when one demands only an 'average' or 'general' ability to act otherwise (see Hassemer, 1990, pp. 229–30). Kienapfel (1985, p. 53, *translated*) states: 'The offender has acted blameworthily if another (i.e. reasonable person) would have, according to general experience, resisted the temptation to offend in the same situation as the offender' (for a similar argument, see Jescheck & Weigend, 1996, pp. 411, 427–8). This no longer has anything to do with personal blameworthiness (see also the criticism in Roxin, 1997, pp. 732–4).

26 The continuing debate over PAP (see note 22) triggered by Harry G. Frankfurt (1969) reveals that something is not quite right with this principle. The main deficit of PAP is that it requires an objective, real ability to act otherwise. However, it is the perspective of the acting subject that is decisive (see also, in this sense, Glannon, 1995, pp. 266–7, 272–4; Kapitan, 1996, pp. 435–41). The principle of alternate possibilities has to be replaced by the principle of *believed alternate possibilities* (PBAP): a person is morally responsible for what she has done only if, from her first-person perspective, she could have done otherwise. See also Anderson (1991, p. 52).

27 The thesis that it is not objective but subjective freedom (epistemic freedom, doxastic freedom, experienced freedom) that forms the basis of personal blameworthiness can be traced back to the nineteenth century (see Burkhardt, 1998). It has found an increasing number of supporters in Anglo-American philosophy; particular mention should be given to Susan Anderson, Hilary Bok, Tomis Kapitan, and Christine Korsgaard.

28 See the reference in note 4. Jareborg (1985, p. 239) states that 'from the point of view of the agent an intentional act is not caused by something else than the agent himself'.

29 Twentieth-century legal scholarship was unable to agree on how to define the concept of action—either in the German-speaking or the Romance countries, or in the domain of common law. I cannot pursue the reasons for these continuing differences of opinion here. In the Anglo-American world, this discussion has been reopened by Michael Moore's (1993) monograph. See the articles in the *University of Pennsylvania Law Review* Vol. 142, 1994.

30 See also Geßler (1860, p. 85), Köhler (1997, p. 9), Schild (1995, pp. 104–5). To be a proper subject of imputation (blame) means to have criminal capacity. This presupposes a theory of personhood (a theory of who or what are proper subjects of responsibility; see Moore, 1997, pp. 60–4).

31 *Entscheidungen des Reichsgerichts in Strafsachen*, Vol. 11, 1885, pp. 56, 58, *translated*. The German Federal Supreme Court (*Bundesgerichtshof*) distinguishes ability to act from criminal capacity (see *Monatsschrift für Deutsches Recht* 1994, p. 127).

32 See also Baumann *et al.* (1995, p. 190); Beling (1906, pp. 10–20).

33 Austin (1885, p. 415), Dressler (1995, pp. 73–4), Holmes (1881, p. 73), Moore (1993, pp. 79–112, 245–301, 350).

34 Moore (1993, pp. 78, 109) talks insofar about the 'identity thesis' and the 'exclusivity thesis'. The exclusion of the consequences is naturally controversial, and this is the case not only in German criminal law, but also in the criminal law doctrine of common law; see Bekker (1859, pp. 243–50, 585–603), Smith & Hogan (1996, pp. 37–8), LaFave (2000, pp. 206–7). If the external side of the act is not restricted to the bodily movement, this leads directly to the problem (and this is a major argument in favour of the above-mentioned limitation) of which consequences of the bodily movement belong to the action. The following solutions are conceivable and also maintained: (a) only the intended consequences; (b) also the non-intended, but foreseen side effects; (c) also the individually (personally) avoidable ones; (d) also the objectively (for the reasonable person) avoidable ones; and, finally, (e) everything that is caused by the voluntary bodily movement.

35 Oberlandesgericht Hamm (*Neue Juristische Wochenschrift* 1975, p. 657).

36 This reconstruction is based on Searle (1983, 1998); see also Moore (1993, pp. 117–33). Beling (1906, p. 9) believes that the question how the will is linked to its realization, whether through psychophysical causality or psychophysical parallelism, may remain open for jurisprudence.

37 Other formulations are, for example, the *sense* that alternate possibilities of action are open to us, the conviction that we could be doing something else right here and now, and the first-person awareness of active control. See also note 44.

38 What this means is freedom to do otherwise in both senses: freedom to choose from among competing courses of conduct and the freedom to do what one chooses.

39 Blanking out the experience of freedom is endemic to criminal law theory. Clearly, this indicates a failure to see that freedom is tied essentially to consciousness (see Finnis, 1983, pp. 137–9; Searle, 2000, pp. 10–13; Strawson, 1986a, pp. 15–21, 173, 293–306).

40 In philosophical action theory, one frequently finds the claim that the possibility of choice is a logically necessary component of the action concept (see Kindhäuser, 1980, pp. 111, 208; Lenk, 1978, p. 316). However, the claim remains in the objective.

41 In my opinion, it can be shown that subjective freedom becomes a necessary element of the action concept when action is defined as 'individually avoidable causing of an outcome' (as in Jakobs, 1991, pp. 136–43). However, I cannot pursue this issue any further here.

42 See note 5.

43 To cite Searle (1984, p. 98) yet again: 'Evolution has given us a form of experience of voluntary action where the experience of freedom, that is to say, the experience of the sense of alternative possibilities, is built into the very structure of conscious, voluntary, intentional human behaviour.' See, further, Galen Strawson (1986a, pp. 61–73, 110–17).

44 The following labels are used in the literature: 'feeling of freedom' (Jareborg, 1985, p. 244; Velleman, 1989, pp. 145–72); 'experience of acting autonomously' (Mele, 1995, pp. 133–7, 246); 'conviction of freedom' (Searle, 1984, pp. 95–9); 'impression of freedom' (Ginet, 1990, pp. 90–3); 'belief in freedom' (Strawson, 1986a; Nagel, 1986, p. 114); 'subjective freedom' (Kuhl, 1996b, p. 743, *translated*); 'awareness of self-determination [*Bewusstsein der Selbstbestimmung*]' (Hartmann, 1926, pp. 717–25); 'experience of freedom' (Double, 1991; Magill, 1997, pp. 77–8); 'consciousness of freedom [*Freiheitsbewusstsein*]' (Bierling, 1905, p. 257; Binding, 1914, pp. 30, 56, 78).

45 Velleman (1989, p. 145) writes: 'The freedom that we feel can be described from two perspectives, one looking outward, or forward, and the other looking inward, or back. When we survey our future conduct, it looks open, unsettled, long on possibilities and short in certainties [the openness of future]. When we reflect to our motives for acting, we feel that they cannot make us decide to act [freedom from our motives]. Both views support us in the conviction that we are free.'

46 See also Patzig (1990, p. 147), Ferré (1973, pp. 170–1); further references in Double (1991, pp. 1–8).

47 See Bierling (1905, pp. 256–74), Ginet (1990, p. 90), Hartmann (1926, p. 718), Kargl (1991, p. 197), Mele (1995, pp. 133–4), Searle (1984, pp. 90–7, 2000, pp. 10–13).

48 A more developed specification of the content of this weaker version of the experience of freedom can be found in the work of Kapitan (1986a, 1989, 2000).

49 See Herrmann (1996, pp. 58–9), Korsgaard (1996b, p. 94), Kuhl (1996a), Luhmann (1987), Metzinger (1999), Strawson (1986a, pp. 161–9).

50 Kuhl (1996a, p. 208) names (alongside self-reflectivity) the following elements (which require further explanation): limitability, access to control, self-congruence, estimation of controllability, dissociation assumption. See also Baker (1998).

51 See also von Cranach (1996, pp. 257, 261–2), Prinz (1996a, pp. 97–8, 1996b, pp. 453, 455, 464–5: it is biological and societal conditions that enter the construction of the 'I'), Artigiani (1996), Claxton (1999, pp. 99–100). See, in addition, Jakobs (1997, p. 34, *translated*): 'To make self-consciousness possible, (at least) two schemes have to be introduced into one and the same consciousness, in other words, the consciousness must contain both schemes simultaneously. In concrete terms, this concerns, on the one hand, pleasure/displeasure; on the other hand, ought and freedom, respectively, duty and arbitrariness. A prerequisite of self-awareness is the awareness of the difference between one's own obligation and one's own pleasure, whereby the "own" has to be understood in each case as "unconstrained", that means, it is not conceivable *per se* as own.'

52 This is addressed by Searle (1997). Nuñez & Freeman (1999, p. XV) comment 'that meaning and concepts are socially and historically mediated, but unlike what many post-modern philosophers suggest, they are not the result of arbitrary social conventions. They are indeed realized through non-arbitrary, species-specific, bodily grounded experiences that are at the basis of consensual spaces and inter-subjectivity.'

53 The criminal sociologist Enrico Ferri (1896, p. 223, *translated*) already wrote more than 100 years ago that '… It can be shown that the consciousness of our purported freedom of will is but an illusion that arises because we are not aware of the psychophysical prerequisites and precursors of volition.' Talk about an illusion is also found in, for example, Kuhl (1996a, p. 208), Metzinger (1999), and Roth (1999, p. 189).

54 See, for example, Binding (1914, p. 55), M. E. Mayer (1901, pp. 98–101), Searle (1984, pp. 94–7).

55 Searle (2000, p. 7): 'In the most general form, we can say that in the case of conscious voluntary actions, the psychological antecedents of the action are not perceived as causally sufficient for the performance of the action. In conscious decision making and acting, my reasons for the action do indeed function causally in the production of the decision, and the decision does function causally in the production of action but in neither case am I aware of either the reasons for the action producing the decision, or the decision producing the action by causally sufficient conditions.' See also McCall (1984, pp. 334–5).

56 See also Weinberger (1996, pp. 189–203, *translated*; principally intransparent determination); Kargl (1991, pp. 187–98, *translated*; epistemic indeterminism). See, further, Kuhl (1996a, p. 210), Prinz (1996b, p. 457). Without the intransparency and uncertainty, according to one thesis, the awareness of freedom would be perfectly abolished; see Kapitan (1991, p. 105), Planck (1978, pp. 282–3). Smilanski (2000, p. 204) therefore views this uncertainty as 'a great blessing'.

57 The following arguments are taken from Pawlowski (2000, pp. 201–6). See also Korsgaard (1996a, p. 370, 1996b, pp. 94–101) who talks about the 'deliberative standpoint', as well as Bok (1998, pp. 92–122), Kapitan (1986a, pp. 230–51; 1986b, pp. 244–54), Magill (1997, pp. 86–107).

58 Korsgaard (1996a, pp. 162–3, 1996b, pp. 94–7) expresses this very clearly. She emphasizes that 'It is important to see that this is quite consistent with believing yourself to be fully determined'. Furthermore, Kapitan (1989, p. 35) states: 'in thinking *himself* free, the agent *qua object of thought* is free and capable of doing otherwise, for it is *his* intentions and actions which are the loci of efficacy and contingency. While it is correct to say that such freedom is a possible object of experience, its doxastic and first-personal character must be insisted on'. Bok (1998, p. 114) emphasizes that 'when we engage in practical reasoning it is not only unavoidable but rational to regard our alternatives as those actions that we would perform if we chose to do so since, for the purposes of deliberation we have no reasons to regard the various actions that we would perform if we chose as differing with respect to their possibility'. McCall (1984, pp. 334–5) writes: 'Intelligent beings act in such a way as to affect what happens in the future, and the first step is to picture the future as an indeterminist would view it'.

59 Interpretations of this section differ, see Adickes (1927, pp. 148–54), Kapitan (1990), Strawson (1986a, pp. 60–73). I agree with the following interpretation: 'One is practically free with respect to A-ing only if one believes one is free to A relative to everything that one already knows'.

60 Searle (1983, pp. 141–59; 1992, pp. 175–96; 1997, pp. 139–47; 1998, pp. 107–9). I agree with Searle in assuming that intentional states (including the consciousness of freedom) function only against a certain 'background'.

61 See also Strawson (1986b, pp. 397–8). He argues that the person *a*, who is compelled by a post-hypnotic command does not act: 'We are deluded into thinking that there is an action precisely because something that must be counted as external to *a* so far as he is considered as an agent is routed through this system, and so causes something that looks just like an action to occur. But it is not really an action …'

62 Particularly not with regard to collective reality, which was pointed out at the beginning of this section (see Binding, 1914; Herrmann, 1996; Roxin, 1993). McCall (1984, p. 334) states: '… conceiving of possible futures is subject to the well-known difficulties of picturing what is not, and their representation is partly a creative act.'

63 In this context, Elsigan (1996, pp. 74–6, *translated*) talks about the 'relevance to practice of the idea of freedom' and the 'way that self-determination is a motive'. He explains this as follows: 'However, if the idea of one's self being the originator of decisions and actions becomes … a *necessary* condition for a certain act, then true freedom is exhibited in the being motivated by the idea of being free. The rare case emerges here, according to the thesis, that the belief in something, properly speaking, the subsequent practice, confirms the content of the belief.' This is exactly what I mean when I talk about the *consciousness* of freedom having a 'world-to-mind' direction of fit. Other authors have also argued 'that a belief in the possibility of choosing one's action so as to shape one's life is itself a source of human freedom'. See the comment in Sappington (1990, p. 25). Montada (1983) focuses attention on 'controllability beliefs' and experienced personal responsibility.

64 *Entscheidungen des Bundesgerichtshofs in Strafsachen* Vol. 2, p. 194, p. 201. Corresponding statements can also be found in Anglo-American criminal law (see Hippard, 1972).

65 In recent years, major arguments have been made in Anglo-American philosophy that the awareness of freedom and thereby the perspective of the acting subject is a legitimate foundation for justifying our ascriptions of moral responsibility. I refer (once again) to the articles by Anderson, Bok, Kapitan and Korsgaard. See also Fischer & Ravizza (1998, pp. 220–39).

References

Adickes, E. (1927) *Kant und die Als-Ob-Philosophie* [*Kant and the philosophy of 'as if'*]. Stuttgart: Frommans.

Anderson, S. L. (1991) A picture of the self which supports moral responsibility. *Monist* **74**, 43–54.

Artigiani, R. (1996) Societal computation and the emergence of mind. *Evolut Cognit* **2**, 2–15.

Ashworth, A. (1995) *Principles of Criminal Law*, 2nd edn. Oxford: Clarendon Press

Austin, J. (1885) *Lectures on Jurisprudence or the Philosophy of Positive Law*, 5th edn. London: Topos Ruggell.

Baker, L.R. (1998) The first-person perspective: a test for naturalism. *Am Philosoph Quart* **35**, 327–48.

Baumann, J., Weber, U. & Mitsch, W. (1995) *Strafrecht Allgemeiner Teil* [*Criminal Law General Part*], 10th edn. Bielefeld: Gieseking.

Bekker, E.I. (1859) *Theorie des heutigen deutschen Strafrecht* [*Theory of Current German Criminal Law*]. Leipzig: Hirzel.

Beling, E. (1906) *Die Lehre vom Verbrechen* [*The Theory of Crime*]. Tübingen, Germany: J.C.B. Mohr.

Berner, A.S. (1868) *Lehrbuch des deutschen Strafrechts* [*Textbook of German Criminal Law*], 4th edn. Leipzig: Tauchnitz.

Bierling, E.R. (1905) *Juristische Prinzipienlehre* [*Theory of Legal Principles*], Vol. 3. Tübingen: J.C.B. Mohr.

Binding, K. (1914) *Die Normen und ihre Übertretung* [*Norms and their Infringement*], Vol. 2, part 1, 2nd edn. Leipzig: Felix Meiner.

Bok, H. (1998) *Freedom and Responsibility*. Princeton: Princeton University Press.

Boldt, R.C. (1992) The construction of responsibility in the criminal law. *Univ Pennsylv Law Rev* **140**, 2245–332.

Burkhardt, B. (1998) Freiheitsbewusstsein und strafrechtliche Schuld. [Consciousness of freedom and criminal culpability]. In Eser, A., Schittenhelm, U. & Schumann, H. (eds), *Festschrift für Theodor Lenckner zum 70. Geburtstag*, Munich: C.H. Beck, pp. 3–24.

Claxton, G. (1999) Whodunnit? Unpicking the 'seems' of free will. In Libet, B., Freeman, A. & Sutherland, K. (eds), *The Volitional Brain: towards a neuroscience of free will*. Thorverton: Imprint Academic, pp. 99–112.

Cranach, M., von (1996) Handlungs-Entscheidungsfreiheit: Ein sozialpsychologisches Modell [Freedom of choice and action: a social psychological model]. In Cranach, M., von & Foppa, K. (eds), *Freiheit des Entscheidens und Handelns*. Heidelberg: Asanger, pp. 253–83.

Double, R. (1991) Determinism and the experience of freedom. *Pacific Philosoph Quart* **72**, 1–8.

Dressler, J. (1995) *Understanding Criminal Law*, 2nd edn. New York: Irwin.

Elsigan, A. (1996) Das Argument von der Praxisrelevanz der Idee der Selbstbestimmung [The argument of the practical relevance of the idea of self-determination]. In Vetter, H. & Liessmann, K.P. (eds), *Philosophia practica universalis; Festgabe für Johann Mader zum 70. Geburtstag*. Vienna: Peter Lang, pp. 57–77.

Ferré, F. (1973) Self-determinism. *Am Philosoph Quart* **10**, 165–76.

Ferri, E. (1896) *Das Verbrechen als sociale Erscheinung* [Crime as a social phenomenon]. Leipzig: Wigand's Verlag.

Finnis, J. (1983) *Fundamentals of Ethics*. Oxford: Oxford University Press.

Fischer, J.M. & Ravizza, M. (1998) *Responsibility and Control: a theory of moral responsibility*. Cambridge: Cambridge University Press.

Fletcher, G.P. (1998) *Basic Concepts of Criminal Law*. New York: Oxford University Press.

Forguson, L. (1989) *Common Sense.* London: Routledge.

Frankfurt, H.G. (1969) Alternate possibilities and moral responsibility. *J Philos* **66**, 829–39.

Freund, G. (1987) *Normative Probleme der 'Tatsachenfeststellung'. Eine Untersuchung zum tolerierten Risiko einer Fehlverurteilung im Bereich subjektiver Deliktsmerkmale.* [*Normative Problems in 'Ascertaining the Facts': a study on the tolerated risk of misjudgment in the field of subjective elements of the offence*]. Heidelberg: C.F. Müller.

Geßler, Th. (1860) *Über den Begriff und die Arten des Dolus* [*On the Concept and Types of Intent*]. Tübingen: Laupp & Siebeck.

Ginet, C. (1990) *On Action.* Cambridge: Cambridge University Press.

Glannon, W. (1995) Responsibility and the principle of possible action. *J Philos* **92**, 261–74.

Greenwood, J.D. (ed.) (1991) *The Future of Folk Psychology.* Cambridge: Cambridge University Press.

Griffin, D.R. (1998) *Unsnarling the World-knot: consciousness, freedom and the mind-body problem.* Berkeley: University of California Press.

Hartmann, N. (1926) *Ethik* [*Ethics*]. Berlin: Walter de Gruyter.

Hassemer, W. (1990) *Einführung in die Grundlagen des Strafrechts* [*Introduction to the Fundamentals of Criminal Law*], 2nd edn. Munich: C.H. Beck.

Herrmann, Th. (1996) Willensfreiheit—eine nützliche Fiktion? [Free will: a useful fiction?]. In Cranach, M., von & Foppa, K. (eds), *Freiheit des Entscheidens und Handelns.* Heidelberg: Asanger, pp. 56–69.

Hippard, J. (1972) The unconstitutionality of criminal liability without fault: An argument for a constitutional doctrine of mens rea. *Houston Law Rev* **10**, 1039–58.

Hoche, H.-U. (1994) Zur Komplementarität von Freiheit und Notwendigkeit des menschlichen Handelns. [On the complementarity of freedom and necessity of human action]. In Byrd, B.S. (ed.), *Jahrbuch für Recht und Ethik 2.* Berlin: Duncker & Humblot, pp. 37–54.

Holenstein, E. (1996) Die kausale Rolle von Bewußtsein und Vernunft. [The causal role of consciousness and reason]. In Krämer, S. (ed.), *Bewußtsein.* Frankfurt am Main: Suhrkamp, pp. 184–212.

Holmes, O.W. (1881) *The Common Law.* Boston: Little & Brown.

Honderich, T. (1988) *Mind and Brain: a theory of determinism,* Vol. 1. Oxford: Clarendon Press.

Honderich, T. (1993) *How Free Are You? The Determinism Problem.* Oxford: Oxford University Press.

Hornsby, J. (1997) *Simple mindedness.* Cambridge, MA: Harvard University Press.

Huther (1897) Die Causalität des Willens im Strafrechte [The causality of volition in criminal law]. *Der Gerichtssaal* **54**, 260–313.

Jähnke, B. (1993) Kommentierung zu § 20 StGB [Commentary of § 20 StGB]. In Jähnke, B., Laufhütte, H.W. & Odersky, W. (eds), *Strafgesetzbuch, Leipziger Kommentar.* Berlin: Walter de Gruyter.

Jakobs, G. (1982) Strafrechtliche Schuld ohne Willensfreiheit? [Criminal culpability without free will?]. *Aspekte der Freiheit. Schriften Univers Regensburg* **6**, 69–83.

Jakobs, G. (1991) *Strafrecht Allgemeiner Teil* [*Criminal Law: general part*], 2nd edn. Berlin: Walter de Gruyter.

Jakobs, G. (1997) Norm, Person, Gesellschaft [Norm, person, society]. *Wissensch Abhand Reden Philos Polit Geistesgesch* **23**.

Jareborg, N. (1985) Determinism, choice and criminal law. In Broekman, J.M., Opalek, K. & Kerimov, D.A.A. (eds), *Social Justice and Individual Responsibility in the Welfare State,* Archiv für Rechts- und Sozialphilosophie, Beiheft 24. Stuttgart: Steiner, pp. 234–60.

Jescheck, H-H. & Weigend, Th. (1996) *Lehrbuch des Strafrechts, Allgemeiner Teil* [*Textbook of Criminal Law: general part*], 5th edn. Berlin: Walter de Gruyter.

Kant, I. (1990) *Foundations of the Metaphysics of Morals and What is Enlightment?* 2nd edn. (L. White Beck, Trans.). New York: Macmillan

Kapitan, T. (1986a) Deliberation and the presumption of open alternatives. *Philosoph Quart* **36**, 230–51.

Kapitan, T. (1986b) Responsibility and free choice. *Noûs* **20**, 241–60.

Kapitan, T. (1989) Doxastic freedom: a compatibilist alternative. *Am Philosoph Quart* **26**, 31–41.

Kapitan, T. (1990) Strawson′s freedom and belief. *Noûs* **24**, 807–10.

Kapitan, T. (1991) Agency and omniscience. *Relig Stud* **27**, 105–20.

Kapitan, T. (1996) Modal principles in the methaphysics of free will. *Philosoph Perspect* **10**, 419–45.

Kapitan, T. (2000) Autonomy and manipulated freedom. *Philosoph Perspect* **14**, 81–103.

Kargl, W. (1991) *Grundlagen einer kognitiven Handlungs- und Straftheorie* [*Fundamentals of a Cognitive Theory of Action and Punishment*]. Berlin: Duncker & Humblot.

Kelman, M. (1987) *A Guide to Critical Legal Studies*. Cambridge: Harvard University Press.

Kienapfel, D. (1985) *Strafrecht Allgemeiner Teil. Eine systematische Darstellung des österreichischen Strafrechts* [General part of criminal law: A systematic treatment of Austrian criminal law]. Vienna: Manzsche Verlagsbuchhandlung.

Kim, J. (1998) Reason and the First Person. In Bransen, J. & Cuypers, S.E. (eds), *Human action, deliberation, and causation*. Dordrecht: Kluwer, pp. 67–87.

Kindhäuser, U.K. (1980) *Intentionale Handlung: Sprachphilosophische Untersuchungen zum Verständnis von Handlung im Strafrecht* [Intentional action: Philosophy of language studies on the comprehension of action in criminal law]. Berlin: Dunker & Humblot.

Köhler, M. (1997) *Strafrecht Allgemeiner Teil* [General part of criminal law]. Berlin: Springer-Verlag.

Köstlin, R. (1855) *System des deutschen Strafrechts* [The system of German criminal law]. Tübingen: Laupp & Siebeck.

Korsgaard, Ch.M. (1996a) *Creating the Kingdom of Ends*. Cambridge: Cambridge University Press.

Korsgaard, Ch.M. (1996b) *The Sources of Normativity*. Cambridge: Cambridge University Press.

Kuhl, J. (1996a) Wille, Freiheit, Verantwortung: Alte Antinomien aus experimentalpsychologischer Sicht [Will, freedom, responsibility: old antinomies from the perspective of experimental psychology]. In von Cranach, M. & Foppa, K. (eds), *Freiheit des Entscheidens und Handelns*. Heidelberg: Asanger, pp. 186–218.

Kuhl, J. (1996b) Wille und Freiheitserleben: Formen der Selbststeuerung. [Will and the experience of freedom: Forms of self-control]. In Kuhl, J. & Heckhausen, H. (eds), *Motivation, Volition und Handlung, Enzyklopädie der Psychologie*, Vol. C/IV/4. Göttingen: Hogrefe, pp. 665–765.

LaFave, W.R. (2000) *Criminal Law*, 3rd edn. St Paul: West Group.

Lenckner, Th. (2001) Vorbemerkungen zu den §§ 13 ff [Initial remarks on §§ 13 ff]. In Schönke, A. & Schröder, H. (eds) *Strafgesetzbuch. Kommentar*, 26th edn. Munich: C.H. Beck, pp. 140–201.

Lenk, H. (1978) Handlung als Interpretationskonstrukt. [Action as an interpretative construct]. In Lenk, H. (ed.), *Handlungstheorien interdisziplinär II*. Munich: Fink, pp. 279–350.

Luhmann, N. (1987) Die Autopoiesis des Bewußtseins [The autopoiesis of consciousness]. In Hahn, A. & Kapp, V. (eds), *Selbstthematisierung und Selbstzeugnis, Bekenntnis und Geständnis*. Frankfurt am Main: Suhrkamp, pp. 24–94.

Magill, K. (1997) *Freedom and Experience*. New York: St Martin's Press.

Mayer, M.E. (1901) *Die schuldhafte Handlung und ihre Arten im Strafrecht* [Culpable action and its typology in criminal law]. Leipzig: Hirschfeld.

McCall, S. (1984) Freedom defined as the power to decide. *Am Philosoph Quart* **21**, 329–38.

McCrone, J. (1999) A bifold model of free will. In Libet, B., Freeman, A. & Sutherland, K. (eds), *The Volitional Brain: towards a neuroscience of free will*. Thorverton: Imprint Academic, pp. 241–59.

Mele, A.R. (1995) *Autonomous Agents: from self-control to autonomy*. Oxford: Oxford University Press.

Metzinger, T. (1999) Willensfreiheit, transparente Selbstmodellierung und Anthropologiefolgenabschätzung [Free will, transparent self-modeling, and assessing the consequences of anthropology]. In Meyer-Krahmer, F. & Lange, S. (eds), *Geisteswissenschaften und Innovation*. Heidelberg: Springer-Verlag, pp. 120–34.

Montanda, L. (1983) Vertantwortlichkeit und das Menschenbied in der Psychologic [Responsibility and the image of man in psychology]. In Jüttemann, G. (ed.), *Psychologic in der Vetänderung*. Weinheim: Beltz, pp. 162–88.

Moore, M.S. (1993) *Act and Crime: the philosophy of action and its implications for criminal law*. Oxford: Clarendon Press.

Moore, M.S. (1997) *Placing Blame*. Oxford: Clarendon Press.

Morse, S.J. (1994) Culpability and control. *Univ Pennsylv Law Rev* **142**, 1587–660.

Nagel, T. (1986) *The View from Nowhere*. New York: Oxford University Press

Nuñez, R. & Freeman, W.F. (eds) (1999) *Reclaiming Cognition: the primacy of action, intention, and emotion*. Thorverton: Imprint Academic.

Packer, H.L. (1969) *The Limits of Criminal Sanction*. Stanford: Stanford University Press

Patzig, G. (1990) Philosophische Bemerkungen zu: Willensfreiheit, Verantwortung, Schuld [Philosophical comments on free will, responsibility, and blame]. In Konrad, T. (ed.), *Schuld: Zusammenhänge und Hintergründe*. Frankfurt am Main: Lang, pp. 147–64.

Pawlowski, H.M. (1969) *Das Studium der Rechtswissenschaft* [*The Study of Jurisprudence*]. Tübingen: J.C.B. Mohr.

Pawlowski, H.M. (1999) *Methodenlehre für Juristen* [*Methodology for Jurists*], 3rd edn. Heidelberg: C.F. Müller.

Pawlowski, H.M. (2000) *Einführung in die Juristische Methodenlehre* [*Introduction to Legal Methodology*], 2nd edn. Heidelberg: C.F. Müller.

Pearl, J. (2000) *Causality: models, reasoning and inference*. Cambridge: Cambridge University Press.

Planck, M. (1978) Vom Wesen der Willensfreiheit [The nature of free will]. In Pothast, U. (ed.), *Seminar: Freies Handeln und Determinismus*. Frankfurt am Main: Suhrkamp, pp. 272–91.

Prinz, W. (1996a) Freiheit oder Wissenschaft? [Freedom or science?] In Cranach, M., von & Foppa, K. (eds), *Freiheit des Entscheidens und Handelns*. Heidelberg: Asanger, pp. 86–103.

Prinz, W. (1996b) Bewußtsein und Ich-Konstitution [Consciousness and the constitution of the self]. In Roth, G. & Prinz, W. (eds), *Kopf-Arbeit: Gehirnfunktionen und kognitive Leistungen*. Heidelberg: Spektrum Akademischer Verlag, pp. 451–67.

Prinz, W. (1998) Die Reaktion als Willenshandlung [The reaction as voluntary action]. *Psycholog Rundsch* **49**, 10–20.

Ramsey, W., Stich, S. & Garon, J. (1991) Connectionism, eliminativism, and the future of folk psychology. In Greenwood, J.D. (ed.), *The Future of Folk Psychology*. Cambridge: Cambridge University Press, pp. 93–119.

Robinson, P.H. (1997) *Criminal Law*. New York: Aspen.

Roth, G. (1996) *Das Gehirn und seine Wirklichkeit:Kognitive Neurobiologie und ihre philosophischen Konsequenzen* [*The Brain and its Reality: cognitive neurobiology and its philosophical consequences*], 5th edn. Frankfurt am Main: Suhrkamp.

Roth, G. (1999) Bewußte und unbewußte Handlungssteuerung aus neurobiologischer Sicht [Conscious and unconscious action control from a neurobiological perspective]. In Meyer-Krahmer, F. & Lange, S. (eds), *Geisteswissenschaften und Innovation*. Heidelberg: Physica-Verlag, pp. 77–119.

Roth, G., Schwegler, H., Stadler, M. & Haynes, J.-D. (2001) *Die funktionale Rolle des bewusst Erlebten*, see <http://www-neuro.physik.uni-bremen.de/~schwegler/Gestalt.html >(28.08.01)

Roxin, C. (1993) Schuldprinzip im Wandel [Changes of the principle of criminal blameworthiness]. InHaft, F., Hassemer, W., Neumann, U., Schild, W. & Schroth, U. (eds), *Strafgerechtigkeit im Wandel. Festschrift für Arthur Kaufmann zum 70. Geburtstag*. Heidelberg: C.F. Müller, pp. 519–35.

Roxin, C. (1997) *Strafrecht Allgemeiner Teil* [*Criminal Law: general part*], Vol. 1, 3rd edn. Munich: C.H. Beck.

Sappington, A.A. (1990) Recent psychological approaches to the free-will versus determinism issue. *Psycholog Bull* **108**, 19–29.

Schild, W. (1995) Strafrechtsdogmatik als Handlungslehre ohne Handlungsbegriff [Criminal law doctrin as an action theory without an action concept]. *Goltdammer's Arch Strafrecht* **142**, 101–20.

Searle, J.R. (1983) *Intentionality*. Cambridge: Cambridge University Press.

Searle, J.R. (1984) *Minds, Brains and Science*. Cambridge: Harvard University Press.

Searle, J.R. (1992) *The Rediscovery of Mind*. Cambridge: MIT Press.

Searle, J.R. (1997) *Die Konstruktion der gesellschaftlichen Wirklichkeit* [*The Construction of Social Reality*]. Hamburg: Rowohlt.

Searle, J.R. (1998) *Mind, Language and Society*. New York: Basic Books.

Searle, J.R. (2000) Consciousness, free action and the brain. *J Conscious Stud* **7**, 3–22.

Smilanski, S. (2000) *Free Will and Illusion*. Oxford: Clarendon Press.

Smith, J. & Hogan, B. (1996) *Criminal Law*, 8th edn. London: Butterworths.

Strawson, G. (1986a) *Freedom and Belief*. Oxford: Clarendon Press.

Strawson, G. (1986b) On the inevitability of freedom (from the compatibilist point of view). *Am Philosoph Quart* **23**, 393–400.

Tröndle, H. & Fischer, Th. (2001) *Strafgesetzbuch und Nebengesetze* [*Penal Code and Accessory Laws*], 50th edn. Munich: C.H. Beck.

Tur, R.H.S. (1993) Subjectivism and objectivism: towards synthesis. In Shute, S., Gardner, J. & Horder, J. (eds), *Action and Value in Criminal Law*. Oxford: Clarendon Press, pp. 213–37.

Varela, F. & Shear, J. (1999) (eds) *The View From Within: first-person approaches to the study of consciousness*. Thorverton: Imprint Academic.

Velleman, D.J. (1989) *Practical Reflection*. Princeton: Princeton University Press.

Velmans, M. (2000) *Understanding Consciousness*. London: Routledge.

Weinberger, O. (1996) *Alternative Handlungstheorie* [*Alternative Action Theory*]. Vienna: Böhlau.

Weischedel, W. (1967) *Philosophische Grenzgänge* [*Philosophical Border Walks*]. Stuttgart: Suhrkamp.

CHAPTER 13

VOLUNTARY ACTION AND CRIMINAL RESPONSIBILITY

KLAUS GÜNTHER

1 Introduction

Discourses on voluntary action often lead to a point where the arguments turn towards possible practical consequences. Among these consequences, one of them seems to make people more upset than others: What follows for crime and punishment from accepting a certain argument within the discourse on voluntary action? If a theory that explains human behaviour denies the possibility of voluntary action because human behaviour is completely determined, then it seems to follow that punishment for having committed a crime does not make any sense because it would mean to punish a person for a behaviour he or she could not have avoided. Such an argument is often based on two unexplained premises: that punishment requires individual responsibility, and that individual responsibility requires voluntary action or, even more, freedom of the will. Because everyone gets upset when imagining how life would be in a society where crimes could not be punished, some people continue to believe in voluntary action even if they have serious doubts. Since punishment seems to be necessary, we should conduct our affairs as if we were persons who were capable of acting voluntarily.

Of course, a theory cannot be refuted simply by its practical consequences – if a theory is wrong, then one has to change institutions and practices to the extent to which they are based on it. When the belief in witchcraft turned out to be false, people had to stop the practice of torturing and punishing women considered to be witches, but the fact that it needed a very long time for this to happen demonstrates that it is very difficult to give up a traditional and collectively accepted social practice, even if some of its basic concepts and theories are clearly refuted. Voluntary action, criminal responsibility and punishment seem to be even more complex and thus complicate the issue. As the debate between St Augustine and Pelagius already demonstrates, there is a long history of arguments against the concept of voluntary action and a long debate about determinism and freedom of the will. Contemporary challenges of 'voluntary action', based on recent discoveries in brain research, are only one part of this long tradition—of course, the most elaborated part and, empirically, much better sustained as compared to, for example, La Mettrie's analysis of the human beings as a machine in his *L'Homme Machine* (1747). Despite this long history of objections to voluntary action, the criminal justice system still persists; it functions quite well and punishment is widely regarded as normal—many people even argue that modern societies in particular are much too permissive with regard to crime and should become more punitive. Especially among scientists it is hard to find anyone who would argue for abolishing the criminal justice system. In the following I would like to start from the irritating fact of the continuity of the criminal justice system.

2 Voluntary action in contemporary criminal law

Among criminal law scholars, the question whether criminal law is inherently dependent upon the reality of some kind of voluntary action is at best an open question. Most of them avoid giving an answer, they hesitate to make statements that presuppose too much 'metaphysics', like a notion of voluntary action that is equated with free will. With regard to deterministic explanations of human behaviour, some scholars argue for a change in the meaning of criminal law's basic concepts and principles such as 'criminal responsibility', as well as for a change in the meaning of punishment (e.g. Roxin, 1997, pp. 721–51). They try to explain and justify criminal law and punishment without any reference to comprehensive notions of voluntary action or to guilt. Punishment is then justified by its consequences for the individual perpetrator or for society as a whole, and criminal responsibility is explained as a means to reach the aims of punishment. These scholars continue to use the term of 'criminal responsibility', but it refers to 'voluntary action' only in a very narrow sense. Most of them omit the word 'guilt' from their vocabulary, speaking only of 'criminal responsibility'.

Nevertheless, presumably all systems of criminal law in modern societies include some rules that are related to some kind of voluntariness. These rules or norms are rooted in everyday objections to the charge of being responsible for doing some harm or other: first of all, the rule that someone who suffers from, say, a mental illness—one that precludes the person from recognizing the wrongfulness of his or her action or from controlling his or her will according to his or her own knowledge—shall not be held responsible for violating the law. Another rule refers to different kinds of mistakes an actor could make with regard to his situation or to the unlawfulness of the act. If someone makes such a mistake he or she shall not be held responsible unless he or she can be reasonably expected to avoid such a mistake. The third rule applies to cases of necessity. A well-known paradigm case since antiquity is 'Karneades' plank': two shipwrecked sailors try to seize a plank, but it can only save one of them. If one sailor kills the other in order to survive, this is considered to be unlawful (it is not allowed by law to kill a person under these circumstances), but is excused (the law does not require a person to give up his or her life in order to save the life of somebody else). Some cases of necessity allow for more than an excuse, they allow for a justification: an act of self-defence is not treated as a violation of the law that can be excused—it is no violation of the law at all and is therefore considered lawful. Whereas justifications are concerned with the question whether an act was right or wrong, unavoidable mistakes, excuses, and insanity defences seem to have something to do with voluntary action. Although the application of these rules leads to a denial of punishment, their relationship to criminal responsibility is different. Whereas severe mental illness counts as a plain denial of responsibility, excuses presuppose responsibility in the sense that the actor has acted intentionally (cf. Gardner, 1998). With respect to these rules, one can, of course, find many statements in criminal law doctrine explaining their meaning and arguing about possible cases of application. However, it is difficult to find a common denominator that gives a clear definition of voluntary action as a basis for attributing criminal responsibility. Criminal law doctrine prefers to take the negative route in avoiding such a definition: If a perpetrator causes harm that is a violation of the law, if this violation is *not* justified, if he made *no* inevitable mistake, if he *cannot* be excused, and if he is *not* mentally insane, then he *is* responsible under criminal law. One could also say that he committed a crime voluntarily, but what is meant by voluntary action here comes down to the *absence* of mistakes, excuses, and insanity defences. To put it bluntly, voluntary action here merely means the everyday understanding that a person acted under 'normal' circumstances, that the person was not forced to do it, and that the person was not out of his or her mind when he or she did it. It would, however, be very difficult to draw conclusions from the existence of criminal law excuses and insanity defences to answer the question whether human beings possess a property that enables them to act voluntarily, whether this property could be identified or not, and whether this property has an appropriate place in a natural world structured by causal chains. These questions are left open. (For a comprehensive discussion of the consequences of the current philosophical debate on freedom of the will for criminal responsibility, see Burkhardt, this volume.)

The criminal justice system with its vocabulary of 'criminal responsibility' functions quite well. Excuses and insanity defences are pleaded for or rejected in the courts; individuals are convicted because there was no excuse or not convicted because an excuse was accepted. The impressive facticity of a functioning criminal justice system leads to the question whether its functioning is more or less independent of the different answers given to the question of voluntary action. Perhaps, the criminal justice system and especially the practice of attributing criminal responsibility to an individual perpetrator have to be understood in a context where controversies about the possibility of voluntary action have no significance.

Following this presumption, I would like to postpone the question whether criminal law requires some kind of voluntary action, whether (or how) voluntary action is possible in a world that can be comprehensively explained by natural laws, and what consequences different answers to these questions would have for criminal law and punishment. Instead of confronting theories of criminal responsibility and voluntary action with results of brain research, I would like to start with the facticity of a social practice in which the notion of responsibility is used by human beings in everyday practice. At the end of the article I shall come back to the tougher questions.

3   Criminal responsibility as a social attribution

'Criminal responsibility' and responsibility in general is not something to which we could refer in the same manner as we refer to objects that are independent of our mind. A person is made responsible, and he or she can make him- or herself responsible. From this point of view, responsibility is *attributed*, and the attribution of responsibility can be understood and analysed as a social practice: person A makes person B responsible for an action or a certain state of affairs or certain consequences of A's behaviour (Shaver, 1985). The term responsibility originates from the Latin word *respondere*, which means to give an answer to someone, usually to give an answer to someone who accuses a person of something he or she imputed to this person. (The same linguistic root can be identified in the German word *Verantwortung.*)

Attribution of responsibility does not come naturally, but is guided by rules and norms for behaviour, ideas, and theories about the world (e.g. causality), and rules of imputation of an event or a state of affairs to a person—like those mentioned above. Attributing responsibility also requires ideas about persons and their capacities, for instance, about voluntariness. All these rules, norms, and concepts form part of a symbolic universe within which most human beings lead their social (and perhaps also their individual) lives. This symbolic universe is neither universal nor homogeneous nor unchangeable. Its basic categories and assumptions are contested, and change in time; it is also linked with culture and power relationships in a society. Whether and how responsibility is attributed or not is more a question of norms than of facts. I would like to argue that responsibility is a contested normative concept.

4   The attribution of criminal responsibility as a changing social practice

History and social anthropology contain many examples of different and changing conceptions of responsibility. Telling examples can be found in criminal law. As Sophocles' play *King Oedipus* demonstrates, it took a long time in human history to accept that the simple fact of a human being causing damage does not suffice to hold him responsible for it, but that one has to take a closer look at the external and internal conditions under which he or she acted (although modern societies reintroduced strict liability in some cases with respect to the use of dangerous machines or products).

One of the most impressive paradigm changes in criminal law with regard to the category of responsibility has taken place during the last two decades. In the sixties and early seventies, when welfare-state policies became central to society, it was perhaps not a common, but certainly a widely accepted opinion that delinquent behaviour is primarily not a matter of individual responsibility, but of social circumstances. David Garland characterized it as the 'welfarist paradigm': 'For modern criminology, crime was a social problem that is presented in the form of individual, criminal acts'(Garland & Sparks, 2000, p. 8). Causal explanations for criminal behaviour were offered by referring to the social and psychological influences of the delinquent person. 'If there was a central explanatory theme, it was the welfarist one of 'social deprivation' and subsequently of 'relative deprivation'. Individuals became delinquent because they were deprived of proper education, or family socialization, or job opportunities, or proper treatment for their social and psychological problems' (Garland & Sparks, 2000, p. 9). A reaction to crime more suitable than imprisonment should therefore be a better social policy. A similar argument was made by psychologists: delinquent behaviour was primarily considered an effect of psychological disorders, caused mainly by damaging experiences made during childhood. Therefore, some kind of rehabilitative treatment and re-socialization was considered a more appropriate reaction than imprisonment. 'The solution for crime was a welfare-state solution—individualized treatment, support and supervision for families, and the enhancement of the plight of the poor though welfare reform'(Garland & Sparks, 2000). In general, these attitudes claimed a better understanding of the perpetrator and his situation instead of holding him individually responsible for violating the law. At the same time, more and more criminal law scholars became sceptical about the possibility of voluntary action in the emphatic sense of a 'free will' as a necessary requirement for criminal responsibility. This scepticism emerged not by pure coincidence. If criminal behaviour could be explained by social circumstances and psychological factors, then it seemed simply *unjust* to single out one individual of society and to attribute responsibility for violation of the law to him or her alone. The practice of criminal law continued, but it was increasingly done with a troubled conscience.

For many different reasons, this attitude has changed. Perpetrators are now again considered to be individually responsible for violating the law. After a cruel and sad killing of a young child by two older children Prime Minister John Major exclaimed that we should be prepared 'to condemn more and to understand less' (Garland, 2001, p. 184). The attitude of understanding is now dismissed as inappropriate and permissive, because it would excuse the perpetrator for the harm and evil he caused to an innocent victim. Examples of an expression of this paradigm change can be found daily in the newspapers. [See, e.g. *The Independent Magazine*, 21 April 2001, reporting on a Rock musician who had an intimate relationship with a 13-year-old girl and was therefore accused of paedophilia. In defence he said: 'These things happen to you in life, and fortunately for me it was the only thing really bizarre that happened in my life. We all have our failings. I'm just glad that my failing was *that*, rather than drug addiction or alcoholism. I mean, I could have been a criminal. I came from that kind of childhood, where you were poor and deprived, so many people went to gaol. I didn't. I was lucky' (p. 13). The commentator remarks: 'W(…) is so blithe on the matter of his lucky escape, it hardly seems fair to bamboozle him with notions of free will and responsibility'.] Being tough on crime became one of the top issues on the political agenda in all Western European and North American societies. These societies become more punitive. The most famous example is the 'Three strikes and you are out' rule in California, which requires life sentence for the third criminal offence.

This change of attitude towards criminal responsibility is irritating, as it has nothing to do with a scientific refutation of the social and psychological explanations of delinquent behaviour accepted during some decades before. Most people continue to believe that crime is related to social and psychological factors, but they nevertheless insist on treating the offender as a person who is individually responsible for his or her crime and therefore should be severely punished. (For a critique of the current practice of granting excuses in the American criminal-justice system, including the famous 'Twinkie' defence of losing control for having consumed too much junk food, see Wilson, 1998.) It is, of course, not clear what is really meant by such a belief in responsibility and punishment—whether it is rooted in a belief in indeterminism and free will so that punishment serves to express blame and retribution, or whether people are convinced that crimes are caused by psychological laws under certain social circumstances so that punishment serves to protect society from those dangerous individuals by locking them up. It was not a debate about the nature of voluntary action with regard to crime that motivated the change of attitude towards criminal responsibility and punishment. What makes this change even more irritating is the observation that it runs parallel to new scientific discoveries in brain research and human biology. The discovery of biochemical laws that govern ontogenetic development of human beings and that, together with environmental influences, determine the functioning of the human brain does simply not question the common punitive attitude towards crime, even though some scientists claim that they cannot find anything like voluntary action and responsibility in their brain research laboratories.

Similar changes in attitude towards responsibility also take place in social areas other than criminal law. 'Individual responsibility' became the key concept for the political critique of the welfare state and it motivates its transformation into a more market-orientated society (Streeck, 1998, Introduction, p. 43). Political decisions concerning the welfare system in many countries of Western Europe and North America today are based on an imperative of individual responsibility: People ought to take more responsibility for their own fate instead of, it is said, depending on the welfare bureaucracies. This claim might also be one of the reasons for the decline of the welfarist paradigm in penal policy. In particular, people should consider themselves as the entrepreneurs of their own capacity for work and compete with one another in a free market. They should also choose their own private insurance against the risks of age, accident, illness, and unemployment in a free market. Instead of being dependent on social solidarity, they should take their future into their own hands.

To make use of one's own creative and innovative capabilities in a free market, and to choose one's own way to take precautions against the risks of life means also that these choices are considered a matter of voluntary action. This becomes obvious in the case of failure. To live under poor conditions is regarded as the consequence of a wrong choice— one could have chosen differently in previous situations and competed in the market in order to earn money instead of being lazy, or spent a considerable part of one's earnings for private insurance instead of buying a new car or going on vacation. Again, this change of attitude has nothing to do with refuting the reasons for a decent welfare state. Individual liberty without social solidarity was regarded as one of the causes for severe social conflicts that could lead to authoritarian political transformations—it was at the time Janis Joplin sang that '… freedom's just another word for nothing left to lose …'. Mutual dependencies of people living in modern societies, which are characterized by a very high degree of division of labour, even increase, and so do the risks and uncertainties of a highly individualistic life style, which in itself depends on a complex social organization. One can observe a controversy in the background about the just distribution of wealth and income: should they be distributed equally or in accordance with individual responsibility (see, e.g. Cohen, 1998)? This can only occur if individual responsibility means that wealth and income are dependent on individual effort, which is primarily based on voluntary action and independent of the social circumstances under which it is earned. Otherwise it would not make sense to say that a person *deserves* the money he or she has. Even if economic success depends less on individual effort than on luck, as well as on market mechanisms that cannot be controlled completely by individual intentional actions (e.g. the gains and losses on the global financial markets), people continue to believe that their gains are somehow deserved, that their wealth is distributed according to individual responsibility, and that their losses must have something to do with a previous mistake, a wrong decision they could have avoided.

5   The normative content of criminal responsibility

These examples of changing concepts of responsibility demonstrate that one has to analyse the changing normative content of responsibility in order to find out what goals are to be reached, what needs are to be served by attributing responsibility. The observation that an action may or may not be excused, that some circumstances are regarded as diminishing responsibility and other circumstances are not, leads to the conclusion that it depends on the rules and principles that define responsibility whether a person is seen as responsible—despite all different kinds of causal chains by which his or her behaviour and deliberation are bound. Whether and how causal factors of human behaviour influence the attribution of responsibility depends on a normative decision about the rules governing the attribution process. It is common knowledge that one's childhood, be it good or bad, causally determines, to a high extent, one's behaviour in adulthood, one's attitudes and mental states. However, it is impossible to draw from this knowledge a simple conclusion on the degree to which a person should be made responsible for a singular action. It depends on the normative context; for example, when in a society a deprived childhood is generally considered to diminish responsibility for an adult's behaviour, as was the case under the 'welfarist paradigm'. However, this is not necessarily so because the normative context may change without any change in the knowledge about causal factors.

Two examples from German criminal law might be helpful (for this and the following example, see detailed explanations in one of the standard commentaries on German criminal law, Schönke, Schroeder *et al.*, 2001, §§ 33, 35, 21). When, in a case of self-defence, the defender starts panicking and acts such that he or she 'transgresses the limits of self-defence' (§ 33 *German Criminal Code*), his or her action (e.g. killing the assailant) might not be justified (as usually in self-defence), but only excused. Such an excuse is granted because the situation of being attacked is regarded as a cause for emotions, which possibly drive the defender out of his or her mind. This excuse, however, is granted only if these emotions are socially acceptable. According to the law, the defender shall be excused only if he or she transgresses the limits of self-defence because of 'bewilderment, fear and fright'. Other emotions that might also be triggered in a defender under the impression of being attacked are not considered excuses, such as feelings of revenge or humiliation. The good emotions as well as the bad ones causally determine the behaviour of a person who transgresses the limits of justifiable self-defence, but only the good ones are considered to be an excuse. A defender who feels severely humiliated by the assailant and acts out of a strong feeling of revenge has to resist his or her feelings—otherwise he or she will be held responsible for his or her action (although punishment might be diminished).

The second example refers to a case of necessity. According to the law (§ 35 *German Criminal Code*), a person who violates criminal law because he or she wants to avert an otherwise inevitable and present danger to his or her life, or to the life of a relative is granted an excuse, even if he or she causes the death of another (innocent) person (see the example of Karneades' Plank above). Again, the argument is that in the presence of severe dangers to one's life (or to one's bodily integrity or liberty) the strong impulse to preserve oneself brings a person beyond his or her capacity for rational self-control. Despite the common knowledge of these causal factors of human behaviour, such an excuse is not acknowledged when the person is required by law to take the risk, like a soldier, a police officer, or a fire fighter. Although soldiers might feel the same need for self-preservation as other persons with regard to a present life-threatening danger, they are obliged to take the risk, and they are held responsible for the violation of the criminal law if they do not. The cultural relativity of this excuse becomes even more obvious from a comparative point of view. English criminal law does not grant an excuse in similar cases, but only mitigating circumstances for punishment (I am indebted to Dr Lucia Zedner for this reference.) As these examples demonstrate, the attribution of responsibility is guided by changing rules and norms that take certain determining causal factors of human behaviour into account, but also draw normative distinctions between these factors. The mere fact that a causal process determines human behaviour, that a certain human action is caused by specific circumstances, does not in itself have any impact on attribution of responsibility. Society has to create a norm, which requires, diminishes, or denies attribution of responsibility with regard to these circumstances. Consequently, the saying that to understand everything means to excuse everything (*Tout comprendre, c'est tout pardonner*) is obviously wrong. (This argument is further elaborated on by Günther, 1998.) Whether a causal explanation of human behaviour suffices to deny the attribution of responsibility for this behaviour is a matter of the normative order of a society. This is even true for a case in which it seems obvious that a causal explanation of human behaviour directly leads to a denial of responsibility—the case of mental illness. Most modern societies have a legal norm or a principle that requires a person who is to be held responsible according to criminal law to be accountable for his or her violation of the law. The rule of accountability (or responsibility, in a narrower sense) excludes persons from being attributed criminal responsibility who suffer from a severe lack of mental capacities at the time they committed the crime and are thus unable to realize that their action was unlawful, or who are unable to control their own will according to their knowledge of right and wrong. Again, exactly what is considered a sufficient lack of mental capability is unclear and depends on a decision about norms.

The case of accountability is a telling example for the normative content of criminal responsibility, because it reveals that the attribution of responsibility is based on a fundamental normative distinction between 'normal' and 'abnormal' circumstances and internal properties of a person. Criminal law is made for 'normal' human beings who act under 'normal' circumstances. A person who commits a crime without acting under abnormal circumstances and who does not suffer from abnormal mental conditions has to be held responsible according to criminal law, and the person has to be punished. Still, what is regarded as 'normal'? It is a social construction, influenced by social and political interests, and power relationships, as well as specific historical circumstances and cultural traditions in a particular society. This becomes obvious in von Liszt's definition of criminal responsibility. He was one of the first German criminal law scholars who explicitly abandoned the doctrine of free will as a necessary requirement of criminal responsibility and defended a pure theory of preventive punishment. According to him, responsibility is nothing but the fact that 'we' hold the mentally sane perpetrator responsible. 'Our' right to do so is based on the perpetrator's accountability, which von Liszt defines as the perpetrator's 'sensitivity to the motivational end of punishment' or as the 'normal determinability by motives'. [The German text runs: 'Verantwortlichkeit ist nicht mehr als die Tatsache, daß wir den geistesgesunden Verbrecher für seine Tat strafrechtlich zur Verantwortung ziehen. Unsere Berechtigung, dies zu tun, liegt einzig und allein in der Zurechnungsfähigkeit des Verbrechers, also in seiner Empfänglichkeit für die durch die Strafe bezweckte Motivsetzung' (von Liszt, 1905, p. 45). 'Zurechnungsfähigkeit ist begründet in der "normalen" Bestimmbarkeit durch Motive' (p. 43).] This means that punishment or, more precisely, the threat of punishment and the fear this threat causes, could become a motive for a person to refrain from violating the law. The concept of a motive is meant as a cause. Motives are causes of action. The mental system or the 'psyche' is thought of as consisting of a bundle of motives. Some systems are able to react to threats like the threat of punishment such that it becomes a motive for refraining from violating the law. If a system has this capability, but follows a different motive, that is, a motive to act in a way that violates the law, then this system is responsible. Such a system is called a 'normal' or a 'sane' system. Von Liszt leaves no doubt as to who the 'we' is that distinguishes here between 'normal' and 'dangerous': 'We, the ruling class, determine today who shall be punished and who shall not' (von Liszt, 1898, p. 256).

6   Functions and contexts of 'criminal responsibility' and 'voluntary action'

Von Liszt's argument could of course be criticized for the many reasons developed in the philosophical debates on free will and responsibility. However, I would prefer to take his argument as a hint for exploring the functions of attributing criminal responsibility. One of its functions seems to be the reproduction of a deeply rooted self-understanding of people living together in a modern society. The organization of society is to be based primarily on individual liberty. 'We' want to live in a society whose basic norms and principles are observed by individuals who make up their own mind, who obey the law voluntarily. Otherwise, people have to be influenced by mechanisms they cannot control, by manipulation, or some kind of training such as that done with dogs. This would mean that the majority of citizens would be controlled and supervised by a minority that has the power and the tools for manipulating the rest. Of course, these two extreme possibilities are not disjunctive. We accept excuses and we do this exactly because we mutually expect that the basic norms of society can be observed by voluntary action under 'normal' circumstances. Those people who are excused for a violation of the law are usually not better off than those who are held responsible. If their crime reveals that they are dangerous individuals, that they are unable to control themselves, they are put under the control of others, primarily psychiatric institutions.

Beyond criminal law, other important institutions of modern societies are based on the presumption of voluntary action as well. The free market rests on the idea that individuals can make up their minds as to when and how to invest money, to produce and sell goods at a certain price, and to buy and consume products. Thus, gains and losses are attributed according to the principle of individual responsibility. The legal framework of markets, that is, property rights and contracts, is built of concepts that always refer to some kind of individual responsibility and voluntary action. Rights, in general, are mostly attributed to individuals, in particular human rights. Democratic government and the idea of political autonomy of a sovereign people who obey nothing but those laws they have given to themselves, are justified by notions of individual autonomy. Despite the huge amount of literature on theories of democracy, it seems obvious that it would make no sense at all to argue for such a complicated and weak political system as democracy, if citizens understood themselves and one another as merely a bundle of motives to be manipulated.

A similar explanation of the needs that are served by the attribution of responsibility was made by Peter Strawson in his famous essay on 'Freedom and Resentment' (Strawson, 1962; for a recent defence, see Fischer & Ravizza, 1998). Strawson's argument is, however, more radical. We treat persons as responsible because they are appropriate candidates for a particular attitude, mostly 'reactive', which differ fundamentally from those we have towards objects other than towards persons. We react differently to a person who harmed us (or another person) 'voluntarily' than to someone who acted under some influence we are convinced was beyond the person's control. When we cannot treat a human being as a responsible person, we change our attitude, and treat him or her like any other that which we have to manipulate in order to get along with it. Feelings like indignation and resentment, reactions like blaming or praise and love, are only appropriate to persons whom we believe *deserve* these attitudes and reactions. The same is true for criminal responsibility, blame, and punishment. According to Strawson, we simply have these attitudes as an important part of our social life, and it would make no sense to claim that we should abandon them because of new discoveries in the causal determination of human behaviour. The world would look completely different to us, and our social life in particular would change dramatically.

In the debate on free will, Strawson's argument belongs to a whole bunch of compatibilist theories that try to reconcile determinism and the possibility of voluntary action. We can talk about an event in 'two different languages' (see McFee, 2000, pp. 79–98). From a participant's point of view, we talk about the event as being an intentional action of a responsible person. From an observer's point of view, we talk about the physical and psychological laws and the initial conditions that caused the event. There is much controversy about the question whether these two languages are somehow related or completely independent of each other, and how it is possible to talk about the same event. Again, what makes Strawson's argument useful for exploring criminal responsibility is the fact that he conceives of this notion and the related concepts of voluntary action or freedom of will as features of the social world human beings live in, despite our knowledge about the causal determination of human behaviour.

To say that we treat people as responsible under certain circumstances, and attribute responsibility to them according to certain rules and principles does not mean that we have an argument for the reality of voluntary action, as is demanded by indeterminist theories and questioned by determinist theories. From the determinist's point of view, it may turn out to be an illusion, but it is an illusion to which the famous sociological *Thomas theorem* can be applied: if people define a situation as real, they will draw real consequences. So one could ask whether a society whose basic institutions are built on the concept of individual responsibility makes its members 'free' in the demanding sense of voluntary action. One can observe that people organize their behaviour and their life, and educate their children according to the standards and norms of individual responsibility. Usually, the language of responsibility is not libertarian, but a language of discipline and control. From this perspective, individual responsibility means that people have to cultivate their passions and to strengthen their character so that they are able to control their will, their passions, and their impulses according to their knowledge about what is right and wrong, good or bad, appropriate or not, and in accordance with the best information available about the circumstances of the intended action, its foreseeable consequences, etc. Voluntary action is action guided by self-control, not by overwhelming impulses that exercise force on one's will, comparable to a blackmailer's threat. Freedom consists in the ability to resist these impulses and to act according to reason—as is regarded in a long tradition ranging from Plato to Kant.

In this tradition, self-control can be equated with reason because control is exercised by an internal 'self' on the person's own will and not externally by somebody else. The defining opposition of an autonomous person is the slave. Slavery means that a person has to substitute his own will for his master's; in legal terminology, a slave is not a person at all, but an object of property. Thus, if unable to resist your passions, you become a slave of these passions.

From an external point of view, the claim that self-control is the most important feature of voluntary action reveals another function of the attribution of responsibility. By treating people according to the ideal of self-control, they gradually become persons who are able to voluntarily obey the basic norms of society, as if these norms were self-imposed. Discipline and control operate most efficiently when people control themselves. Michel Foucault (1991) demonstrated how modern societies built up new forms of discipline, which operate within the soul of each individual instead of torturing the body or threatening the passions by external means. Applied to the concept of criminal responsibility, it turns out that the standard distinction between normal and abnormal, internal and external circumstances of an action also serves to 'normalize' people who become used to seeing themselves and their social world according to these distinctions, and who behave according to them. By attributing criminal responsibility to persons and by punishing them for violations, people continue the social narrative of normal and abnormal behaviour, and they publicly confirm their ideal of self-control. The claim that a person is convicted for a crime because he or she has perpetrated the violation of the law without any mistake, and under normal internal and external circumstances, is then considered to be justified because the same person could have done otherwise under these circumstances, that is, could have controlled him- or herself to the extent of not violating the law.

Again, the normalizing function of the attribution of responsibility and the language of self-control that is used for its justification is not an *a priori* feature of responsibility. It emerged under certain historical circumstances. As Foucault demonstrated, the language of self-control was invented and used in the discourses of criminology, psychiatry, and medicine in early modern societies, and the corresponding institutions of prisons, lunatic asylums, and hospitals were built according to the ideal of the control and discipline of the soul. A closer and more contextual look at the notion of self-control will also reveal that it is deeply rooted in particular cultural assumptions and traditions, as well as in specific historical situations of political and social power struggles. This notion has always been related to an image of the human being divided into a reasonable and an emotional part, into reason and passions. Reason was considered the part that had to dominate, discipline, and cultivate the passions. In the *Stoic* tradition of moral philosophy, self-discipline became the most important virtue. This was also an attempt to cope with a historical and political situation, particularly in late antiquity, when social orders were collapsing, when it became difficult to tell what was right and wrong, and when one could become a slave overnight. It was rediscovered in early modern societies among the Neo-Stoics, in the historical situation of the sixteenth and seventeenth century, with its conflicts about the reformation and its revolutionary political and social consequences. This is, of course, not a sufficient account of the history of the idea of self-control, which is much more complex than my presentation here. The Christian tradition, in particular the notion of conscience, also played an important role in the formation of a mental architecture. I only want to demonstrate that basic notions of the language of voluntary action have a history that should not be ignored in contemporary debates. [For a comprehensive account of the history of the notion of autonomy and related concepts, see Schneewind (1997).] It helped to develop a language for the soul that allowed the organization of philosophical and scientific discourses on its elements, and the forces that drive it. The same Neo-Stoics, such as Justus Lipsius, also wrote about public law and the efficient organization of an army; according to Lipsius, the exercise of the soldier's self-discipline should become the main target of military exercise (see Oestreich, 1997). After all, self-control is only a metaphor whose genesis goes back to the formation of early modern societies with their ideal of a rational political organization of independent individuals. Today we still speak this language, although slightly modified and adapted to changing circumstances, new scientific discoveries, and philosophical elaboration, when we talk about criminal responsibility and voluntary action. Even brain researchers still make use of it when they talk about the architecture of the mental sphere. (See, as an example, the contributions of M. Jeannerod, G. Roth, and R. J. Seitz, this volume. They cannot avoid using an intentionalistic vocabulary when they speak about 'interaction', 'control', and 'steering' with regard to different parts of the human brain.

7 Functional and normative justifications for the attribution of criminal responsibility

As I have tried to demonstrate so far, the notion of criminal responsibility has a normative content, although it also includes some references to the objective world of empirical phenomena. As a notion with a normative content, its social contexts and its functioning can be observed and described empirically. Whether or not criminal responsibility requires voluntary action in the demanding sense of a free will remains an open question. The various notions of voluntary action—which range from a demanding claim to freedom of the will or freedom of 'second-order volitions' that refer to first-order wishes (see Frankfurt, 1971), desires and resulting choices, to less demanding claims like the absence of abnormal internal and external circumstances in the situation where an actor is faced with a choice—can also be explained, understood, and historically reconstructed in a normative context. Even the semantic framework for the discourses on voluntary action— the architecture of the mental sphere that is divided into a reasonable part and an emotional part—is rooted in normative historical contexts, as is the modern notion of control and self-control, which is also an explicit metaphor originating from the political realm.

With regard to criminal responsibility, two different conclusions can be drawn from this argument. Criminal responsibility can be explained in a purely constructivist fashion and thereby be relativized to those historical and socio-political circumstances that govern its construction. The attribution of criminal responsibility has to be justified, and it is justified by its function for the reproduction of a particular society here and now. If criminal responsibility and the notion of responsibility in general have primarily an inter-subjective function for the social world of human beings, then the attribution of criminal responsibility requires no reference to voluntary action at all, because it can be defined in purely sociological and functional terms. A person is responsible under criminal law, if holding him or her responsible—instead of somebody else, society as a whole, nature, or fate—is a necessary means to ensure the general trust in the validity of criminal law. Notions of voluntary action do not refer to empirical phenomena, they have a communicative function only (Duff, 1996). By saying that he or she committed a crime voluntarily (i.e. under normal internal and external circumstances, as explained above), society declares that the perpetrator was not sufficiently motivated to avoid violating the law, and that nobody else can be blamed. The irritating fact that the law is violated can be declared to be the individual mistake of a single person who has to bear the costs—all other citizens can continue believing that criminal law is valid and that their trust in its validity is still justified. From this perspective, voluntary action or freedom of will is not a necessary requirement or, as Günther Jakobs claims, 'Criminal law does not know the category to which the problem of free will belongs' (Jakobs, 1982, p. 80).

However, as Peter Strawson has argued, notions of responsibility (and some kind of voluntary action as a prerequisite) are too deeply rooted in human self-understanding to have their specific translations, realizations, and institutionalizations—such as rules and principles for the attribution of criminal responsibility here and now—left to the power struggles in a particular society. (This assertion is, however, doubted by Martha Klein, 1990, pp. 150–2.) If we cannot avoid reacting such that we hold a person responsible for his or her actions under normal circumstances, then we should take the normative and inter-subjective character of responsibility seriously and take a more *reflexive* attitude towards its specifications. We should take responsibility for the ways in which we specify responsibility, for the rules and principles that are to guide its attribution to a certain person in a certain situation. By doing this, we always interpret and specify our common self-understanding as persons who usually respond to harms and offences, as well as to admirable achievements with our reactive attitudes, based on the attribution of individual responsibility. These interpretations are, of course, *contested*, and we can distinguish legitimate and illegitimate interpretations.

A legitimate concept of criminal responsibility has to take into account the fact that the attribution of criminal responsibility has to be guided by public legal norms in need of public legitimization. My suggestion is to base the concept of criminal responsibility on the notion of the person as a citizen who has a right to participate in procedures of democratic legitimization. Then, the core meaning of criminal responsibility is determined by the self-understanding of a democratic republic of free and equal citizens.

This link between democracy and criminal responsibility is already implicit in the presuppositions of democracy and can be made explicit in three steps (for further elaboration of this argument, see Günther, 1997):

1 Democracy presupposes responsibility in at least two dimensions. On a general level, as a consequence of secularization, citizens in a democracy are responsible for their laws.

Democratic legislation presupposes that the citizens themselves take responsibility for their laws—instead of God, fate, tradition, history, or some kind of exclusive authority being responsible. This responsibility has to be taken by each citizen—it is not a collective responsibility borne by some general subjectivity or collective entity. In this dimension, citizens cannot shirk responsibility for the laws under which they live their lives. Of course, the details of this responsibility vary according to the degree of real participation enjoyed by citizens in democratic legislation. However, in general, it is perhaps the most important part of the public self-understanding of citizens that they themselves and nobody else are, in the last instance, responsible for their legal order.

2   In a second dimension, democracy presupposes responsible citizens; citizens who attribute responsibility to one another as participants in public deliberation. If public deliberation is the most important feature of democratic legislation, then each citizen has to be conceived of as a person who is able to deliberate on the validity of legal norms. This requires the ability to give and accept reasons, as well as the ability to control his or her will according to the reasons he or she accepts. A person able to take a position on a norm, and to act according to his or her own judgements, could be called a *deliberative person*. This is, of course, only a general presupposition—it does not require citizens to behave like deliberative persons. A democracy does not presuppose a duty of each citizen to exercise his or her deliberative capacities, but it considers the participants of public will-formation to be persons who have this capacity—and it requires procedures in which this capacity can be exercised effectively. In the same vein, a democracy does not oblige citizens to act according to their deliberative judgements, but it presupposes that they are able to do so.

3   The deliberative concept of a person that informs the notion of a citizen now finds its mirror image in the *legal person* as the addressee of norms. Citizens who treat one another as responsible authors of their legal norms also have to treat one another as being responsible for obeying their norms. It would not make sense to claim to be a responsible participant in public deliberation, but to plead ignorance when it comes to obeying the law in a concrete situation. Of course, again, this is only a general presupposition. It does not mean that citizens who have exercised their judgement in procedures of public legislative deliberation have a duty to obey the law *because* of their previous participation. Citizens have a duty to follow the law—but this duty is only based on the right and the possibility to participate in legislation, not on the exercise of this right. In the same vein, citizens may obey the law for any reason—it does not matter *why* they obey.

My thesis is that there is an internal link between the citizen as a deliberative person in legislation and as a deliberative addressee of the law in a democracy. However, this link as elaborated above is surely rather general and abstract. The features determining the concept of a legal person who is responsible for obeying the law are, in turn, elaborated in public deliberation. The questions to be answered in this procedure are: How should citizens conceive of one another as responsible legal persons in the role of the addressee? How should they draw the borderline between freedom and coercion with regard to the concrete situation of obeying the law? What excuses should be admitted, what excuses should be excluded from the forensic discourse on a legal person's criminal responsibility? What counts as a situation of necessity in which citizens do not expect of one another obedience of the law? When citizens answer these questions, they express their self-understanding as responsible citizens in the role of the addressee of the law. They do nothing other than spell out the presupposition of responsibility that is an essential requirement of deliberative democracy.

8 Consequences and open questions

Which consequences can be drawn from the argument for the debate about the possibility and reality of voluntary action? The fact that the criminal-justice system and the practice of attributing criminal responsibility to individuals functions well and continues independent of this debate, could lead to the conclusion that the attribution of criminal responsibility is compatible with different accounts of voluntary action. Whether or not determinism is true, human beings have reactive attitudes, they blame and praise one another, and this language of morality has its own grammar and logic that cannot be grasped from an external or observer's point of view, only from an internal, participant's perspective. From an internal viewpoint, we need some kind of distinction between voluntary and involuntary action in order to decide whether a reactive attitude towards a person and his or her action is appropriate or not. It can, of course, be argued whether this defence of compatibility is sound or not. One intriguing problem consists in the relationship between these two languages. If body movements are required for an action and these movements are causally necessitated, how can it still be possible to describe them as the intentional action of a person who did it voluntarily, that is, who could have done otherwise? (For this and other objections, see Blackburn, 1999, p. 109; McFee, 2000, pp. 92–8; Galen Strawson, 1986, pp. 117–20.) The same problem arises on a more general level with regard to the relation between the mental and the physical, between the brain and the mind (Kim, 1998).

Another compatibilist argument is to say that the social practice of attributing criminal responsibility reveals that a certain category of causes of human behaviour is selected, and called 'voluntary' or 'free' as compared to other categories of causes, such as coercion or impulses resulting from malfunctions of the brain. Both categories contain causes that determine human behaviour, but a cause of the first category is called a reason, and an action motivated by certain reasons is called a voluntary action. This argument does, however, face similar difficulties: How could we justify the distinction between different kinds of causes? Could this conceptual framework still justify the imputation of an event to a person and the attribution of criminal responsibility, not to mention punishment, even though his or her bodily movements were caused according to physical and psychological laws? (For this approach and its criticism, see Nagel, 1987, pp. 57–8). As these questions reveal, the problem of the reality of voluntary action is by no means solved with such an account.

Another consequence of the fact that the attribution of responsibility and related categories like voluntary action or person play such an important role in the social interaction of human beings could be a change in the agenda of natural science, particularly in brain research. Instead of insistently searching for an answer to the question whether voluntary action can be located in the brain or not, whether the brain predetermines human action in advance, and what follows from that for our notion of responsibility, one should change the perspective and take responsibility for granted. The question then is: Why did human brains evolve in such a way that they built a symbolic universe in which 'persons' attribute 'responsibility' to one another? Responsibility and voluntary action are less a matter of truth or falsity in the sense of a possible illusion that should be detected and then abolished, more a matter of explanation and understanding. Even if it turns out to be a complete illusion, it remains an important task to discover why human brains obviously are *in need* of such an illusion. It could have something to do with the fact that the ontogenetic development of a human brain is, to a very high degree, influenced by other human brains—the simple fact that the survival of human beings greatly depends on a complex co-operation with others. It was, after all, human brains that invented cultural systems with notions like persons, responsibility, and the fundamental distinction between voluntary and involuntary action. If these notions are an important feature of cultural systems among human brains, then one should try to explain why. One has to be careful, however, not to draw any normative conclusions from such a naturalistic approach to the institution of responsibility. Even if we could find a causal or functional explanation for the formation of this institution in terms of evolution theory and theory of the human brain, these discoveries do not interfere with the internal logic and grammar of the attribution of responsibility, not to say criminal responsibility.

The last conclusion I would like to draw from the argument that criminal responsibility and voluntary action are normative concepts concerns the debate on punishment and responsibility. A highly popular argument about the consequences of brain research for punishment is that brain research demonstrates that human behaviour is not voluntary or free, but causally determined by, among other causes, neuronal transmissions in the human brain. If there is no voluntary action, then it could be doubted whether criminal responsibility makes sense at all and whether punishment for a crime is just. The reaction to this doubt is often punishment has different functions and purposes; for example, it also serves to deter other people from committing a crime or it influences the perpetrator causally by changing his or her habits (cf. Roth & Vollmer, 2000, p. 75). If human behaviour is determined by natural processes within the brain, one should influence these processes such that the person changes his behaviour. Consequently, one can continue punishing criminal behaviour. Nevertheless, one has to be very careful with consequences like this. If punishment is to be legitimate, one has to presuppose that the norms of criminal law whose violation is to be punished are legitimate, too. To claim that society should change the behaviour of an offender by causally influencing his brain might be acceptable with regard to murder, rape and robbery, but should society do the same in cases of tax evasion or illegal gambling? Both are criminal offences in many societies (e.g. § 271 *Abgabenordnung* and §§ 284, 285 *German Criminal Code*). What about the violation of those norms members of a democratic constitutional state consider illegitimate, such as apartheid law? History gives us many examples of authoritarian regimes that treated citizens who refused to obey legal, but illegitimate norms as mentally insane. Another dangerous consequence could be the extension of preventive measures. If criminal behaviour is caused by brain processes that can be influenced, why should society wait until a crime happens? Why not have a general brain screening of all citizens, so that one could single out those who have a predisposition to criminal behaviour in order to give them the treatment that changes their brains? This would lead to vast social control and to further restrictions of individual liberty. A third precarious consequence concerns the status of the person whose brain is to be manipulated. Should the treatment be applied voluntarily to him, i.e. not without his unconstrained agreement, or could it also be applied by coercion? If we want to apply it by agreement only, what then does voluntary treatment mean? Finally, how intrusive should the treatment be; should there be an appropriate relationship or proportionality between the offence and the treatment—and according to which criteria? Even if we admit that human behaviour is determined by brain processes, when it comes to the consequences for criminal responsibility and punishment we are again entangled in difficult questions that, I presume, cannot be answered without some reference to concepts like responsibility and voluntary action.

References

Blackburn, S. (1999) *Think: a compelling introduction to philosophy*. Oxford: Oxford University Press.

Cohen, G.A. (1989) On the currency of egalitarian justice. *Ethics* **99**, 906–44.

Duff, R.A. (1996) Penal communications: recent work in the philosophy of punishment. *Crime Justice: Rev Res* **20**, 1–97.

Fischer, J.M. & Ravizza, M. (1998) *Responsibility and Control: a theory of moral responsibility.* Cambridge: Cambridge University Press.

Foucault, M. (1991) *Discipline and Punish: the birth of the prison.* [Translated by Alan Sheridan.] Harmondsworth: Penguin.

Frankfurt, H. (1971) Freedom of the will and the concept of a person. Reprinted in: Waddel Ekstrom, L. (ed.) (2001) *Agency and Responsibility.* Oxford: Westview Press, pp. 77–91.

Gardner, J. (1998) The gist of excuses. *Buffalo Crim Law Rev* **1**, 575–98.

Garland, D. (2001) *The Culture of Control: crime and social order in contemporary society.* Oxford: Oxford University Press.

Garland, D. & Sparks, R. (2000) Criminology, social theory and the challenge of our times. In Garland, D. & Sparks, R. (eds), *Criminology and Social Theory.* Oxford: Oxford University Press, pp. 1–22.

Günther, K. (1997) Der strafrechtliche Schuldbegriff als Gegenstand einer Politik der Erinnerung in der Demokratie. In Margalit, A. & Smith, G. (eds), *Amnestie oder die Politik der Erinnerung in der Demokratie* [*Amnesty or the Politics of Reminiscence in Democracy*]. Frankfurt/Main: Suhrkamp, pp. 48–98.

Günther, K. (1998) Die Zuschreibung strafrechtlicher Verantwortlichkeit auf der Grundlage des Verstehens. In Lüderssen, K. (ed.), *Aufgeklärte Kriminalpolitik oder Kampf gegen das Böse?* [*Enlightened Criminal Politics or Fight Against Evil?*], Vol. 1. Baden-Baden: Nomos, pp. 319–49.

Jakobs, G. (1982) Strafrechtliche Schuld ohne Willensfreiheit. In Henrich, D. (ed.), *Aspekte der Freiheit* [*Aspects of Freedom*]. Regensburg: Mittelbayerische Druckerei- und Verlagsgesellschaft, pp. 69–83.

Kim, J. (1998) *Mind in a Physical World.* Cambridge: MIT Press.

Klein, M. (1990) *Determinism, Blameworthiness and Deprivation.* Oxford: Oxford University Press.

La Mettrie, J.O. de & Thomson, A. (eds.) (1747/1996) *Machine Man and Other Writings.* Cambridge: Cambridge University Press.

Liszt, F., von (1898) Die strafrechtliche Zurechnungsfähigkeit. *Zeitschr gesam Strafrechtswissensch* **18**, 235–66.

Liszt, F., von (1905) Die deterministischen Gegner der Zweckstrafe. In Liszt, F., von (ed.), *Strafrechtliche Aufsätze und Vorträge*, Vol. 2. Berlin: Guttentag, pp. 25–74.

McFee, G. (2000) *Free Will.* Teddington: Acumen Publishers.

Nagel, T. (1987) *What Does It All Mean?* Oxford: Oxford University Press.

Oestreich, G. (1997) *Antiker Geist und moderner Staat bei Justus Lipsius (1547–1606): Der Neustoizismus als politische Bewegung.* Göttingen: Vandenhoeck & Ruprecht.

Roth, G. & Vollmer, G. (2000) Interview: 'Es geht ans Eingemachte': Neue Erkenntnisse der Hirnforschung verändern unser Bild vom Menschen [Interview: 'We're attacking the core of things now: New findings in brain research change our conception of man.] *Spekt Wissensch* **10**, 72–5.

Roxin, C. (1997) *Strafrecht, Allgemeiner Teil I. [Criminal law, General, part I]*, 3rd edn. München: Beck.

Schneewind, J.B. (1997) *The Invention of Autonomy.* Cambridge: Cambridge University Press.

Schönke, A., Schroeder, H., *et al.* (2001) *Strafgesetzbuch—Kommentar [Criminal Code—Commentary]*, 26th edn. München: Beck.

Shaver, K.G. (1985) *The Attribution of Blame: causality, responsibility and blameworthiness.* New York, Berlin: Springer-Verlag.

Strawson, G. (1986) *Freedom and Belief.* Oxford: Clarendon Press.

Strawson, P. (1962) Freedom and resentment. Reprinted in: Waddel Ekstrom, L. (ed.) (2001) *Agency and Responsibility.* Oxford: Westview Press, pp. 183–204.

Streeck, W. (ed.) (1998) *Internationale Wirtschaft, nationale Demokratie [International Economy, National Democracy]*. Frankfurt/Main: Campus.

Wilson, J.Q. (1998) *Moral Judgement: does the abuse excuse threaten our legal system?* New York: Basic Books (Reprint).

CHAPTER 14

CULTURE AND HUMAN DEVELOPMENT IN A THEORY OF ACTION BELIEFS

CHARLES W. NUCKOLLS

The position advanced in this chapter is that the concept and perception of voluntary action develops through systematic violations of intuitive cognitive assumptions. It bears a resemblance, therefore, to concepts that Pascal Boyer calls 'religious'. Superhuman agencies—the essential characteristic, according to Boyer, of all religious systems—possess features that are salient and memorable chiefly by virtue of their power to violate natural ontologies (Boyer, 1994, 2001; see also Lawson & McCauley, 1990). In other words, we grow up expecting certain things to happen, such as 'things fall when dropped', and these developmentally prescribed intuitions become our 'ontologies'. We fashion our gods by imagining how these expectations can be violated, for example, 'gods float, hover, fly, and otherwise act unconstrained by gravity'. One of these so-called natural ontologies, to extend the Boyer hypothesis, is agency. If it is natural to assume that human actions are voluntary and proceed from the exercise of will, then religiously formulated concepts violate this assumption by postulating the existence of beings who control all of our actions. That is the kind of intuition-violation that makes superhuman agencies, from Christ to Krishna, salient and memorable, and their cults transmissible from generation to generation.

This might be a plausible hypothesis, but it is not the only one. Boyer and his colleagues do not consider emotion, and thus neglect the relationship between action and the desire for attachment—something that psychoanalysts have been discussing for decades. The problem is that cognitivists and psychoanalysts typically do not talk to each other, perhaps out of fear that each side means to swallow the other whole. Still, how would such a combined account work if it could be constructed? Here is one possibility, linking the violation of intuition and emotional development. The human child both wants and needs action directed from the outside, mainly by the parents. At the same time, the self-centeredness of the child—the feeling that actions originate in the self—is strong and persists into maturity, albeit increasingly subject to the constraints of the so-called reality principle. The point is that if the developing mind is predisposed to view human actions as self-directed, that is, voluntary, this assumption is not simple or of a piece. That is because we grow up wanting different and even contradictory things. As children and adults, human beings desire *both* attachment and autonomy, and these competing desires powerfully infuse the perception of actions, voluntary and otherwise.

What is the link to childhood concepts of agency and action? There are two perspectives. One is that the child basks in unchallenged narcissistic grandeur, especially early in life when he views external reality as essentially an extension of the self. The other perspective holds that the omnipotence felt by the child is constantly battered, first by the mother (who does not necessarily respond when bidden) and then by everyone else. Finally, it gives way, replaced by increasingly mature understandings of the relationship between the do-able and doer, and reinforced by the ideals of ego autonomy and independence. However, this view is incomplete and misleading for several reasons. It assumes that the process of development is uni-directional—with the force of change in one direction only—toward the 'ideal of reason' as Kant described it. A more likely hypothesis is that the direction is multiple and the forces at work not in complete synchrony with each other. Factors relevant to the development of the intuitive assumptions of agency remain mixed and confused, not only in childhood, but throughout life. If so, the counter-intuitive assumptions that make up religious ideas of agency are not of a piece, nor are they reducible at any point to only one natural and unitary ontology, as the Boyer hypothesis might suggest. There could be several natural ontologies, based on multiple and conflicting childhood-derived concepts of agency and action, and all penetrated by the desires and frustrations of development.

1   The nature of voluntary action

This volume is taken up with apparently different questions, so it could be asked, why is attention to human development—and the development of ambivalent desires specifically—relevant? The concept of voluntary action, as Proust (this volume) suggests, is typically understood in three senses. All three offer possible foundations for a theory of action, but all three are problematic. In fact, much of the discussion in the volume can be subsumed under the category of debunking, in various ways, the intuitive saliency of voluntariness. Why do you think you act volitionally, when so much of the evidence points in the opposite direction? This line of thinking reaches its culmination, perhaps, in Prinz' assertion that the concept of free will cannot be incorporated in an empirical psychological theory (see also Prinz, 1997). However, to understand why debunking voluntariness still falls short, we must return to the three senses in which the folk psychology of voluntariness is usually understood.

The first is the feeling of will association with the action. The second concerns the causal origin of action, that is, an action is 'voluntary' if its cause is endogenous and accessible. The third involves higher order states of the agent relative to the first-order intentional content of the action. As to the first, 'will', it might be assumed that an agent acquires this awareness through perception of activated motor representations, but as Proust correctly points out, the agent may know which action he is performing, while being wrong about the way he is performing it and vice versa. The agent may identify an action through its goal and through specific movements used to reach it, without being able to identify the author of this action. As to the second, endogenous causal locus, the agent cannot, on the basis of the signals received (e.g. efference copy, perceptual reafferences), tell whether he has done the action deliberately or not. The signals in question do not discriminate, in and of themselves, between actions originating in the agent and in the environment. As to the third, voluntariness as a second-order property of actions, this refers to the distinction between acting and asking oneself whether or not one is right in acting. The conclusion that one could have acted differently reinforces the sensation of voluntariness, but this is purely a representational feature of the action once it has been performed. It does not refer to the executive capacity to act or not act voluntarily, and therefore has no bearing on the question of voluntariness as such.

All of this, and more, can be granted to those who argue that voluntary action is immaterial to the origin of action itself, contrary to the view of Enlightenment philosophers. Indeed, cultural anthropology joins the debunkers of agentive voluntariness in the anti-Enlightenment project of the last century, at least in this sense. As psychology has restricted and narrowed the domain of free will to perceptual systems and brain functions, so likewise anthropology has taken control away from the agent and invested it in 'culture', 'social structure', or 'world system'. Even the currently faddish post-modern anthropological discourse about 'agency' (e.g. Knauft, 1996) only appears to accept that people do what they think they do. Agency anthropologists, ironically, only recognize action as a kind of false consciousness, to be detected in compliance with or resistance to systems of domination. This, to put it simply, is the name of the game and while we employ different vocabularies, it is essentially the same game for psychologists and anthropologists. Instead of debunking agency, however, the question can be asked: Why do we worry about it the first place? For make no mistake, our project is motivated by worry—or, further, by the fear and the fascination, deep down, that we are not in control of our actions even as we act to debunk theories of voluntary control. We are clearly in the realm of the emotions, whether we like it or not. The question addressed below, then, focuses directly on the developmental origins of the question 'why worry about it?' and uses a combined approach—linking the cognitive anthropology of religious concepts with developmental antecedents of emotional attachment.

2   What are natural ontologies?

'Ontology', as cognitivists (like Boyer) use the term, refers to the intuitively grasped relationships between cause and effect. When one speaks of natural ontologies, their postulation and violation, the model of the mind advanced assumes that existential assumptions follows from the observation of perceived regularities. 'Things fall from a height' or 'objects are continuous in time' are examples. The mind records these regularities, and whether or not this capacity is innate or task-derived, the process itself unfolds in orderly succession from earliest childhood. There is nothing terribly novel in this view. What is new is the hypothesized relationship between intuitive natural ontologies and the development of religious concepts. The Boyer hypothesis states that the developing mind violates naturally observed and associated regularities, and this induces conceptualization of superhuman agencies, the basis of all organized religions.

To follow Boyer, how might the cognitivist account of voluntary action work? Here is one possibility. In early development, a child experiences the world as the centre of that world, but with limited ability to exercise control through his own motor operations. Intuitively, then, the child would develop a construct of the world nearly devoid of voluntary action, but that does not mean the experience of voluntary action is absent. On the contrary, as the child matures he violates the assumption of non-voluntariness by constructing and responding to images of wilful agency. Huge creatures with immense supernatural powers—these are stuff of childhood fantasies and the primary raw material from which toys marketed to children are made. Nor does it stop there. At the same time the outside world becomes populated by images of fantastic superhuman agencies, the inner world undergoes a similar transformation, and the child attributes to himself deep or hidden powers. He thinks the world revolves around him. This sometimes goes by the name of 'childhood narcissism'.

Notice what we have here: the developmental origins of both the assumption of outside control (non-voluntary action) by superhuman agencies *and* the assumption of complete volitional control (voluntary action). The opposition between the two is as natural as their origin in human development, and the emotional basis of the anxiety that lies at the root our very interest in the question. Thus, to extend the Boyer hypothesis, the argument is as follows: The child constructs images of self and world that are at variance with the experience of action and control, and these images develop salience accordingly in two directions simultaneously—toward images of little voluntary control to images of super-abundant autonomy.

Before proceeding, we shall review the Boyer hypothesis in more detail. Developmental cognitivism holds that the common properties of culturally postulated superhuman agencies, of the sort found in all religions, derive these properties from systematic violations of intuitive assumptions. Boyer hypothesizes that religious representations (to be defined as such) always postulate the existence of superhuman beings that violate intuitive assumptions about the existential processes associated with persons, artifacts, animals, or plants:

> Spirits and ghosts are commonly represented as intentional agents whose physical properties go against the ordinary physical qualities of embodied gents. They go through physical obstacles, move instantaneously, etc. Gods have non-standard physical and biological qualities. For instance, they are immortal, they feed on the smell of sacrificed foods, etc. Also, religious systems the world over include counter-intuitive assumptions about particular artifacts, statues for instance, which are endowed with intentional psychological processes. They can perceive states of affairs, form beliefs, have intentions, etc. (Boyer, 2001, p. 46).

One might concede this point, but at the same time ask, what makes a violation of intuitive assumptions attention-demanding, rather than simply implausible? Boyer limits representability to counter-intuitive assumptions, yet other assumptions seem to be equally well remembered. How, then, does one account for them? Finally, if all counter-intuitive assumptions are equally memorable, why are only some (out of all that are possible) recurrent?

The Boyer hypothesis does not recognize and cannot theorize about the emotionally complex origin of the assumptions described as 'intuitive'. It misses the most salient of these assumptions by neglecting emotional attachment and the conflicts resident in deep cognition. It is the violation of these assumptions—as natural as any Boyer describes—which explains the development of propositions and anxieties about voluntary action. The most important natural expectation violated by religious propositions is the expectation that early emotional attachments, formed in childhood, will continue forever. The expectation is almost always thwarted in normal development, since childhood attachments cannot continue if adult autonomy is to be achieved. Is it possible to have it both ways—attachment and autonomy?

As Boehm (1989) points out, the paradox of attachment and autonomy is probably inherent in primate evolution, and there is good evidence that the ambivalence it causes is not confined to humans. Tensions among satisfaction quests might even have an adaptive significance, in that they prepare the organism to respond more flexibly in multi-contingency environments. Therefore, if Ingold (2001) is correct, and evolutionary processes must be considered in the development of social constructions, we should focus on the development of attachments, the conflicts that arise, and the ambivalences that result. This leads, inevitably, either to an encounter with Freud or to an avoidance of him, which pointlessly stunts and limits a cognitive theory of voluntary-action beliefs.

3   Toward rapprochement

To construct a theory of voluntary action belief, we need to start from scratch, in what amounts to a basic understanding of how the mind develops concepts of itself and its relationship to the outside world. The purpose, as I suggested earlier, is to come at the issue of voluntary action via human development without neglecting the cross-cultural universal that action beliefs typically split between two conceptions—the first that our actions are *always* controlled from outside, and the second that our actions are *never* controlled from outside. The development of these beliefs is one and the same with the development of a belief in superhuman agencies, and therefore, in addition to being developmentally derived, action beliefs are also inherently religious in Boyer's sense of the term.

How can cognition and depth psychology operate together, and is it possible for us to discuss them using a common vocabulary? Let us posit the existence of a repertoire of relational schemas that contains archaic components, many formed in childhood, which can never be erased. Such early schemas of self and others are constrained by mature concepts of self that contain and integrate immature self-schemas. Nevertheless, in a kind of parallel processing, earlier forms continue an unconscious appraisal of current events, possibly following primitive association and the logic of the 'primary process'.

Unconscious relational schemas, however, tend to conflict. Either they represent mutually unfulfillable desires, or the desires they represent are opposed by mature thought and culturally normative demands. If higher order cultural-knowledge structures are accessible only by activating lower ones in the dynamic unconscious, then higher order structures probably reproduce in their form and function the conflicts of the lower order relational structures. In principle, there is nothing in this proposition at odds with the cognitivist account, for as Boyer remarks, 'adult representation … seem to become more complex by gradual enrichment of principles that can be found in the preschooler' (Boyer, 2001, p. 59). The difference is in the nature of the principles, and the extent to which these bear the imprint of early and ambivalent attachment to one's caregivers.

Where does unresolvable conflict ultimately come from? The most likely hypothesis is that it is a natural outcome of human development in the representation of attachment. Maturing human beings both desire to retain and desire to reject attachments to their primary caregivers, and this generates conflict. At this level, unconscious relational schemas produce ambivalence and the need to deal with it—or in psychoanalytic terms, defend against it. Cultural knowledge structures, including beliefs about voluntary action and superhuman agencies, come into being which both reproduce conflicts and attempt to resolve these ambivalences, in a mutually reinforcing way. In short, our perceptions of action (voluntary and involuntary) could be based on the inevitable developmental conflicts of action orientations and their attachment correlates. To prove this, it must be shown, first, that the cognitive unconscious is conflicted and that conflicts have their origin in the nature of relational attachment; secondly, that attachment conflicts give rise to relational schemas that inform the construction of voluntary action beliefs; and thirdly, that such beliefs exist cross-culturally, and that they might, therefore, be universal. After considering the first two requirements, we will move onto the third, drawing on ethnographic material from India and Japan.

4   First step to a theory of voluntary action: transference and core conflict relational themes

Understanding the properties of mind most relevant to a psychological understanding of religious propositions—including the apparently universal belief that superhuman agencies violate human agency—depends on a central assumption. The assumption holds that thoughts and ideas can have an active influence on people's minds even when they are not conscious and sometimes precisely because they are not conscious. To the first part of this statement most cognitivists and neurophilosophers will agree. No one claims that the assumptions violated by supernatural beliefs are conscious assumptions open to inspection by those who hold them. That is the point of calling them 'intuitive'. As to the second part of the statement, that exclusion from consciousness is actually vital to religious propositions, this is more debatable. Here, I am arguing that unconscious conflict between relational schemas is fundamental to the development of a belief in superhuman agencies—and, by extension, to the experience of voluntary action—because such agencies represent and partially resolve the conflicts that arise in relation to conflicted childhood attachments. In other words, we both desire and reject beliefs in voluntary action, and we do this because of conflicts over attachments that arise predictably and universally in the circumstances of human social development.

Even if developmental conflicts exist in childhood, it must still be shown that these conflicts continue to influence adult relationships well into maturity. Is there evidence that relational patterns shaped can be applied or 'transferred' to present relationships? Freud (1912/1958) described transferences as 'stereotype plates' or representations of early interpersonal relationships that shape and influence current ones. On the surface, this is to suggest no more than what the literature on psychological 'priming' experiments has already demonstrated—that we tend to perceive new people based on mental representations of significant others in the past. Notice that one need not cite case studies in order to provide evidence for this point. In fact, the most important experimental work has been done, not by psychoanalysts, but by cognitive experimentalists like Lester Luborsky. Over the last 30 years, he and his colleagues (Luborsky, 1977; Barber & Crits-Christoph, 1993; Luborsky & Crits-Christoph, 1998) have developed a method for abstracting interpersonal relationship patterns that appear in patient narratives during psychotherapy sessions. Typical narratives are about father, mother, brothers, sisters, friends, bosses, and the therapist. Luborsky developed a method for analysing these narrative in terms of their repeated basic constituents, which he calls a 'core conflict relationship theme (CCRT)'. It describes the relationship patterns and conflict in terms of three components: wishes, needs, or intentions toward the other persons in the narrative, as expressed by the subject; expected or actual responses from others; and responses of self. Within each component the types with the highest frequency across all relationship episodes are identified and this combination constitutes the CCRT. Luborsky and his colleagues found that important themes, because they had been shaped early in life, would tend to recur, making for a powerful transference effect (see also Bond *et al.*, 1987; Crits-Christoph *et al.*, 1988).

First, on the number of transference patterns, there seems to be one main relational theme (just as Freud predicted). Averaging across one sample, for example, the main wish was judged to be present in 80% of each patient's narratives, whereas a secondary wish was present, on the average, in only 16% of each patient's narratives (Luborsky *et al.*, 1986). Moreover, there is strong evidence early in treatment that 60% of patients who relate a narrative about the investigator, describe a pattern that is similar to a theme evident in narratives about a significant other (Connolly *et al.*, 1996, p. 122). One could object that psychodynamically orientated therapy probably tends to elicit this kind of response and thus skew the results, but the same result is evident in patient narratives from non-psychodynamic treatment settings (Connolly *et al.*, 1996, p. 1220).

Secondly, on the consistency of the theme over time, investigators compared CCRTs scored from sessions early in treatment with the same patient's CCRTs scored from sessions later in treatment, about 1 year later. Considerable consistency over time was detected (Luborsky *et al.*, 1986). This suggests that relational schemas are strongly encoded and increases the likelihood that, when established in childhood, they remain active well into adulthood, shaping and constraining new relational information.

Thirdly, on the question of themes' early origins, the hypothesis states that there should be a parallel between the relationship pattern with the therapist and the one with early parent figures. Luborsky and his colleagues compared CCRTs scored from narratives involving a memory of an interaction with early parental figures versus the overall CCRT score from all other narratives. A high degree of similarity was evident for early memory of parents CCRTs paired with the same patient's overall CCRT (see Luborsky *et al.*, 1986; Barber & Crits-Christoph, 1993). It could be argued that, since Luborsky and his colleagues have not done long-term studies, the hypothesis of early childhood origins remains speculative. This has always been a problem with research that purports to demonstrate the validity of psychodynamic processes, but that is changing, and work in the development of attachment styles provides strong evidence that patterns of childhood associations do constitute templates for adult relationships (Brennan & Shaver, 1998; Hazen & Shaver, 1987; see also Feeney & Noller, 1996).

Transference, in short, is an ordinary fact of life, and Freud was right. Even Boyer implicitly concedes this point, when he acknowledges that 'a whole domain of ritual action is based on assumptions that *transfer* properties of live organisms to a non-living natural objects' (Boyer, 2001, p. 52, emphasis mine). However, what remains to be considered is the question of why in the case of relational transferences and its origins are for the most part repressed, and its outcomes in consciousness so varied and different. Here, we must focus not only on transference, but on the nature of the relationships shaped early in childhood.

5   The second step: core conflicts and attachment theory

Simply put, 'attachment' refers to the relationship between infants and their caretakers, and according to John Bowlby, constitutes part of universal human endowment. Attachment theory is essentially a theory of the micro-processes of development that emphasizes the daily interactional exchanges between parent and child and the developing internal working model of the child (Bowlby, 1969, 1973). Attachment theory shares with contemporary psychoanalytic theories a shift in the conceptualization of the unconscious—from a repository of repressed instinctual wishes, to a structure comprising representations of self or object, and of prototypic interactions between the two. The emphasis is on unconscious representations is most clearly expressed in the centrality of the concept of internal working models, similar to the core conflictual relationship themes above. Bowlby notes that people may have more than one internal working model and suggests that different working models may conflict with each other. This fact is crucial to the developing of belief in supernatural agencies.

Observational data reveal that attachment to particular caretakers is recognizable at around 6 months of age and appears to be fully developed at 1 year. A significant attachment figure (usually the biological mother) serves as a secure base for the infant, a place where the child can seek refuge and from which begin to explore the environment. Attachment behaviour is behaviour that has proximity to an attachment figure as a predictable outcome and whose evolutionary function is protection of the infant from danger. Such behaviour is not confined to human beings, of course, and the fact that it is found among most primates is strong evidence for its adaptive significance. For example, Harlow's classic study of cloth-covered and wire-covered 'surrogate mothers' (Harlow & Zimmermann, 1959) demonstrated that rhesus monkeys require secure attachment in childhood in order to develop normally. The importance of clinging contact with the mother, not only as a behavioural prerequisite for the infant that was at least as salient as nursing, but also as the basis for the development of a secure base for subsequent exploration of the environment. Hinde also focused on the normative development of mother–infant relationships in rhesus monkey (e.g. Hinde & Spencer-Booth, 1966). The consistent finding throughout the history of this research has been that mother–infant relationships in Old World monkeys and apes involve common behaviour patterns, follow similar sequences of developmental change, and appear to be subject to the same set of influences, all of which provide empirical support for the basic tenets of Bowlby's attachment theory.

Bowlby assumed that mothers were usually the primary caregivers, but recent research demonstrates that infants and young children can establish relationships with more than a single individual (neither Bowlby nor his colleagues argued otherwise). From the nature of attachment, it follows that dyadic patterns of relating are more resistant to change than individual patterns because of reciprocal expectancies. In general, the more the infant's relationships to such individuals or objects prior to separation resemble that of the typical mother–infant attachment, the more closely their separation reactions follow the prototypical patterns previously described. Thus, the relationship between infant and primary caregiver generates a template, used to understand (via transference) future relationships in adulthood. There is no reason to think that these relationships necessarily involve only people. Via the mechanism of transference, described above, such relationships are mapped onto gods and goddesses, spirits and ghosts, and, probably, all of the other supernatural agencies of interest to Boyer. If one is starting from what every child experiences, then attachment patterns and their symbolic transferences surely rank as high as the perception of solidity or continuity which Boyer considers the bedrock of the intuitive ontologies later flouted by spirit beliefs.

6 The third step: conflict in attachment and its vicissitudes in action beliefs

Now we come to the conflicts inherent in transferred attachment patterns. These, too, are inevitable. Human infants are primed to seek out a primary attachment and, in most cases, this attachment is to the mother—a bond mediated by intimate physical contact (Spiro, 1997). The assumption is that this contact will continue, but the assumption must sooner or later be violated, as the child individuates and the mother withdraws. This is a universal process and no exceptions have ever been noted, although the method and outcome of this transition vary between social groups because of the different values placed on emotional fusion and autonomous individuation. From the beginning, these different valuations play a direct role in the process, making it wrong to assert, as early psychoanalysts did, that human development is the same everywhere or subject only to minor variations. This is probably where psychological anthropology makes its biggest contribution. At the same time, it is misleading to assert, as some cultural relativists have done, that the process is infinitely variable or unconstrained by developmental urgencies.

Action beliefs and assumptions are the correlates of attachment. The assumption of voluntary action, in this view, is simply an extension of the assumption of individuality that arises in relation to the child's development of autonomy. However, the assumption is fraught with emotional ambivalence, since autonomy opposes the desire for attachment. Attachment, in other words, is the source and origin of the assumption of non-voluntary action, and of the belief that outside beings or agencies control us. A quick example from American culture will show it works.

American childrearing (especially in white middle-class families) generally pushes children to early individuation (Hsu, 1981; Bellah *et al.*, 1985; Choi *et al.*, 1999). Parents strive to inculcate greater autonomy in children, and reward them for display of individual achievement and accomplishment. 'My child started ...ing' (fill in the blank with the relevant skill, from walking to talking to playing an instrument), is the usual way parents make judgments about themselves and others, as they compare early acquisition of autonomy skills (Kakar, 1978). Such skills may or may not be important in themselves, but as markers in the development of the supreme value—autonomy—they are crucial, and children who do not measure up are singled out for special remediation or therapy, not uncommonly involving prescription drugs. So, which comes first, the early development of individuation or the cultural value we call individuality?

If the question seems to be of the chicken-and-the-egg variety, it is: there is no point in assigning priority to either one, except in one sense. All children must achieve some degree of individuation from their primary caretakers, but the extent to which this true—and the meaning assigned to it—is dependent on cultural values (Spiro, 1986). Once established, the value of individuation selects for and prefers parenting styles, which encourage the development of personal autonomy. Now, there is another side to this process. No one would argue that 'independence' is the only value American culture seeks to maximize. There is also the value of home and community, of shared dependency and common purpose, and this value also finds expression. American cultural values contradictorily emphasize both individuation and dependency (Bellah *et al.*, 1985; Raeff, 1997), and people must try to balance them or, if they cannot, to adjust to the conflict that accompanies the inability to choose. There is therefore a dialectic of contradictions, developmental and cultural, that is mutually supportive and continuous (Nuckolls, 1998).

Since action beliefs are the correlates of individuation and dependency, we should expect to find that attitudes toward action, voluntary and involuntary, follow accordingly. Studies by attribution psychologists, from Heider (1958) to the present, provide ample evidence that this is so (see Jones & Davis, 1965; Kelley, 1967, 1973; Ross & Fletcher, 1985; Lewis & Daltroy, 1990). Among other things, 'attribution' is a study of causal explanation: when something happens, where is the perceived locus of control—internal to the agent or external to the agent? It is easy to manipulate the perception by subtly changing the context, so that, for example, the subject who attributes control to himself will attribute it to the environment when the context shifts from 'praise' to 'blame'. However, the interesting observation, for our purposes, is the conflict that results when subjects perceive (or are forced to perceive) the contradiction between the two.

Nowhere was this more amply demonstrated than in the famous (or infamous) study of the authoritarian personality by Milgram (1974). He found, surprisingly, that 65% of his subjects, ordinary residents of New Haven, Connecticut, were willing to give apparently harmful electric shocks—up to 450 V—to a pitifully protesting victim, simply because a scientific authority commanded them to and in spite of the fact that the victim did not do anything to deserve such punishment. The victim was, in reality, a good actor who did not actually receive shocks and this fact was revealed to the subjects at the end of the experiment. However, during the experiment itself, the experience was a powerfully real and gripping one for most participants. (Milgram's experiment has been repeated in Australia, South Africa, and in several European countries. In one study conducted in Germany, over 85% of the subjects administered a lethal electric shock to the learner.) The experiment did not end, however, with these results. Ever since, controversy has continued, not over the experiment itself, but over the extent to which we misperceive the voluntariness of our actions. Is this not an index of the ambivalence that results from growing up with two different and sometimes opposed action orientations? Of course, the degree to which people can be 'bothered' by the Milgram experiment varies, but I take the fact that Americans are bothered by it as much today as when it was first reported, as a strong indication that we remain highly conflicted on the sources of our own actions, especially when those actions are ethically questionable.

Cultural patterns like these are interesting, but Boyer is right when he says that the purpose of his theory is not to explain the particularities of religious beliefs. To adumbrate a series of particularistic illustrations, therefore, in the manner of most ethnographers, does not constitute a strong critique of developmental cognitivism. That is why cognitive psychology and neuroscience generally ignore cultural anthropology, and why, one suspects, the discussion of voluntary action is generally not informed by anthropological critique (the two essays by anthropologists in this volume notwithstanding). The critique must be able to state that the relevant properties of superhuman agencies are better explained in universalist terms using a different theoretical framework. By relevance, I mean *transmissibility and memorability over generational time*. These are the criteria Sperber holds up as basic to the endurance of a set of beliefs. We must take as given the cognitivist point of departure in their insistence that these attributes demand explanation.

What does an anthropological study have to do in order to be relevant to the study of action? It must somehow touch on the three conceptual issues already discussed: transference, attachment, and ambivalence. Not only that, but it must also address the finding that cultures do vary in terms of how much or how little emphasis they place on attachment. Finally, there must be some attention to how ideas about action get reinforced in everyday practice.

7   A South-Indian case study

The case to be described resists the criticism that it represents only a particular instance because it exemplifies tendencies that are widely distributed across many social groups. It is equivalent, thus, to Boyer's study of the Fang, except that the processes I call attention to concern the nature of attachment, its relationship to ambivalence, and the salience of religious propositions. My basic point, to set the stage, is that attachment is a fundamental property of intuitive assumptions, and that its vicissitudes in terms of our emotional architecture set the stage for a variety of beliefs, including beliefs about the sources of our own actions. Specifically, the case study exemplifies the tendency to view mothers (and by extension, all women) ambivalently, as providers of succour and destroyers of male potency. This, it will be shown, is a direct result of the conflicts of attachment, something all human share. Certainly, the south Indian case is not unique. The contrast in images of the female is found in many places (see Spiro, 1997), including Greece (Friedl, 1967), Java (Geertz, 1961; Jay, 1969; Brenner, 1995), Spain (Gilmore & Gilmore, 1979), Portugal (Hollos & Lies, 1985), France (Rogers, 1975; Segalen, 1983), Italy (Cornelisen, 1976), and southern Europe generally (Saunders, 1981), among the Kafyar of Nigeria (Netting, 1969), the Swahili of Mombasa (Swartz, 1982), and the Mundurucu (Murphy & Murphy, 1974).

Like most societies, the Jalaris of South India (a Telugu-speaking community of the south-eastern coast) postulate the existence of superhuman agencies that violate a number of intuitive assumptions. Such agencies cannot be seen in ordinary waking experience— they never die, or if they do, usually come back to life; and they have the power to move objects at a distance. There are other assumptions they *could* violate and no doubt, if the Jalaris wished to, they could enumerate them. For example, the spirits defy gravity and move through solid objects, but one would have to elicit this information; the Jalaris would not volunteer it and, indeed, to most Jalaris of my acquaintance, it would seem ridiculously trivial to point it out. So why are some intuitions selected for systematic violation and reference, and not others? This should be at the heart of the question, if, that is, Boyer and the other cognitivists are correct in proposing intuition-violation as the engine of religious concept formation. How do we know that violations are important in constituting supernatural beings, rather than simply incidental trappings—descriptions, that is, attached to superhuman agencies only as a consequence, not a cause, of their postulation?

Starting from the observation that Jalari spirits violate some, but not all, developmentally expected intuitions, we can, in the manner of Boyer, explain some of their attributes. For the purposes of this account, in fact, we can accept the whole of Boyer's explanatory hypothesis. What we *cannot* explain, however, is the fact that the Jalaris always and invariably define these spirits as 'mothers'. This definition is by no means unique to the Jalaris, and a similar belief is one of the most widely encountered facts of anthropological fieldwork. From the fact that they are mothers, all of their other powers and attributes derive, including some of those considered 'violations' of developmentally intuitive assumptions. Mother goddesses nurture, as real mothers do, but they also punish and kill. They are sexually voracious, unlike real mothers are supposed to be, and they can take control of living human bodies through possession. From the perspective of explanatory social science, which is more important: the fact that Jalari spirits violate cognitive assumptions of physical regularity (which they do), or that they are all mothers, in relationship to whom ordinary living people are like children?

The Jalaris posit the existence of a variety of spirits, most of them female, known collectively as *ammavallu* or 'mothers' (Nuckolls, 1996). These spirits possess all the qualities Boyer and Sperber (as well as Lawson & McCauley, 1990) say they should, fulfilling the criteria for supernatural agencies who defy intuitive conceptions. These are supposed to endow them with, to use Boyer's phrase, 'attention-getting' attributes, which also explains their memorability and transmissibility across generations. It is curious, however, that with exposure to so many other similarly posited agencies, including those of mainstream Hinduism (not to mention Christianity and Islam), the Jalaris show remarkably little interest in incorporating most candidates. This is not true across the board, however. Twice in the recent past, new goddesses have arrived in the village, both times accompanied by epidemic diseases. In both cases, it was the disease (smallpox and cholera) that got people's attention, and when they reflected on its origin, they inferred the intervention of mother goddess.

The Jalaris associate terrible calamities, and dramatic events of all kinds (good and bad), with divine females classified as 'mothers'. Goddesses are binary, made up of two aspects, one malign and the other benign. Sometimes goddesses do good things and sometimes they do bad things, but predicting which they will do is impossible. They are fickle. Nevertheless, one must act toward them as if their behaviour could be influenced and that means giving them regular offerings of good things (meat, new clothes, and occasionally alcohol or even marijuana). People regularly forget to do these things and so, when a goddess attacks and punishes them by inflicting disease, they say it was because she felt neglected. However, would it have made any difference if they had made the offerings, in the correct amount and on time? The Jalaris doubt it. Thus, the Jalari cosmos consists of divine beings that are alternately (and unpredictably) good and bad, and of human beings who both love and hate their gods and act toward them accordingly.

Ambivalence of this sort is characteristic of both the goddesses themselves and the people who worship them. The goddess is good and bad; people love them and hate them; no one is sure what to do, only that something must be done. When new calamities befall, as during the epidemic diseases, people interpret events according to the schema just described. It is shot full of conflicted images and emotions, and this, I will argue, is related both to the circumstances of Jalari childhood and to the structure of Jalari cosmology.

Moreover, ambivalence is not merely something 'added on' to a supernatural template already constituted by other means. This is where my account differs substantially from Boyer's. A psychoanalytically informed model of development is better than the cognitivist model at this level and for this purpose—in short, it explains the features of Jalari goddess beliefs that are most salient to their construction and transmission from one generation to the next.

An interesting case in point is the vocabulary concerning 'possession', that is, the belief that the goddesses can temporarily inhabit a human consciousness and invest it with new purposes. In a sense, this is where confusion over the courses of human action (voluntary or involuntary) is most accurately realized in Jalari culture. The observer is often struck by how often the question, 'Is he acting on his own or is it the goddess?' comes up in conversation. The vocabulary of spirit possession is strongly physical, with references to 'holding' and 'handling'. It has often seemed to me, in listening to the Jalaris describe possession experiences, that I was listening to a description of the actions of a parent toward a small child: the picking up, the handling, the directing are all highly reminiscent of the way parents treat their children. A Jalari parent, in fact, expects children to exercise little control or direction on their own part until an age that Americans would consider very late (Kakar, 1989; Kurtz, 1992; Nuckolls, 1996). Even then, the demonstrations of independent initiative and personal responsibility that Americans parents love to praise are almost wholly absent. Is it possible that the vocabulary of possession in Jalari culture represents, through transference, values, and attitudes originally associated with the relationship between mother and child, and thus support the hypothesis that psychodynamic mechanisms mediate language forms and cultural constructions (Nuckolls, 1996)? The answer is that it does. On the one hand, a boy is drawn by memories of his mother's nurturing (far more long-lasting and intense in India than in the West) to idealize the feminine. On the other hand, fear that the mother may reject him or worse, exploit him for the fulfilment of her own sexual needs, compels him to constrain the feminine, to keep its power to envelop him under control. This constitutes what Luborsky and his colleagues term a core conflict relational schema—a pattern formed in childhood that becomes a transference template for understanding future relationships. It is not unique to South Asian societies, but it is present with special prominence.

Let us assume, then, that conflict in the nature of the mother-child relationship—the conflict over attachment—exists and that it is unresolvable in any permanent sense. This is consistent with what we know about child development in Hindu India (Kurtz, 1992), but follows consistently from what Bowlby and other attachment theorists would predict. How, then, do people deal with the ambivalence that must result? It is not the same everywhere, obviously, and India there is a culturally patterned response. Possession-mediumship—also known as 'spirit possession'—offers one culturally sanctioned solution, differently symbolized for the men and women who undergo the experience. Ambivalence in the maternal relationship resolves itself among the men in possession by goddesses, a role that normatively allows certain men to immerse themselves in a nurturing feminine role identity and at the same time to control that identity through the practice of possession-mediumship. The position of the women who become possession-mediums is similar, but reversed. Wanting sons is natural in a culture where fulfilment of a woman's role is contingent on the production of male offspring. However, in having sons, a Jalari mother must eventually acknowledge their loss to a wife, who will supplant her, and (South-Indian culture) to a set of affines who become competitors with her for her son's attention and support. Under some circumstances, ambivalence in the maternal role—between wanting mature sons and knowing that their maturity means some degree of disaffection from her—is intensified and then resolved in the experience of possession by her own dead sons. As a medium, the mother regains total control over her son, whom she incorporates as her permanent tutelary spirit. The son never grows up, he can never leave, and he can never be alienated (Nuckolls, 1996).

Resolution of cultural ambivalence in the relationship of sons and mothers is thus possible in different ways. The first way is through symbolic transformation of the son to make him less problematic for the mother. The second way is through symbolic transformation of the mother to make her less problematic for the son. Male possession-mediums resolve the ambivalence in favour of the son. The 'son', as it were, recovers the mother through his own symbolic transformation and then complete immersion in a female persona, which becomes (for him) a controlled object of devotion. Female possession-mediums resolve the ambivalence in favour of the mother, who then recovers the son through a process of re-absorption into herself. In both cases, the significant other in the mother–son relationship is returned and simultaneously relieved of its ambivalence-generating nature through symbolic transformation into an inalienable possession, as well as into a source of divinatory power. Although these possession experiences are best exemplified in professional mediums, the same dynamic is to be found more generally, since possession is something most people in Jalari culture experience at one time or another.

To be 'caught', 'come to', or 'got down upon' by a possessing spirit called 'mother' is to refer to a relationship that has its origins in childhood. This is no simple thing, because all goddesses—like all mothers—have two aspects: one benign and the other malign. This is one aspect of the ambivalence. If the possessing goddess is in her benign form, and the experience pleasant and useful, then the 'mother' is nurturing. Her purpose in possessing is to do good. If the goddess is in her malign form, and the experience of possession painful, then the 'mother' is angry. Her purpose is to punish and inflict pain. Through regular worship and occasional (male) animal sacrifice, people aim to control the goddesses and insure that the form they most often reveal is the benign one, but they always forget to perform these tasks, with the result that the goddesses become angry and attack.

There are probably many reasons why people forget to make sacrifices to the goddess, but deep down, there is ambivalence. Villagers need the goddess, but they fear she will envelop them, and the fear makes them want to shun her. Doing so directly, however, is too dangerous—and in any case, one should only express devotion to the goddess. 'Forgetting', therefore, while not exactly deliberate, is one of the few means available to express hostility to a supreme being. Seen in a wider context, the relationship between goddesses and devotees is no less problematic and generative of ambivalence than the mother-son relationship, but the trans-active language of worship at least affords some measure of action. One can curse the goddess for her failure to provide sustenance; think of her as either nurturing or punishing, encouraging one and limiting the other; and even imagine sex with her in the appropriate idiom of worship. Of course, the goddess never ages or dies, so the relationship can be prolonged forever. When Jalaris speak of possession by the goddess, using the vocabulary of mother–child interaction, they have transferred the latter and transformed it into the former, where the conflict it generates can be managed in a religious idiom, while at the same time retaining its ambivalence-generating power.

What we see in this example is that religious propositions violate intuitive emotional structures in two ways, first by asserting that the model of early care giving will continue forever, even though it cannot without putting at risk the development of autonomy and, secondly, by claiming that the model will not continue, even though the development of secure attachments in adulthood depends on it. Religious propositions of the kind cognitivists consider fundamental are violations of developmentally derived models of attachment, but since these models are conflictual, religious propositions both represent and attempt to resolve basic contradictions in human experience.

The expectation that childhood dependency will continue, however, is only half of the matter. It is matched by the equal and opposite assumption, common to children, of personal omnipotence—almost as if to say, 'I am completely dependent on you, but it is by my own will that this dependency exists'. The two assumptions arise mutually and bring each other into being, so we should not be surprised that the conflicts of omnipotence—of completely voluntary action—are as fertile a source of religious propositions as the ones already discussed. In fact, they are all intimately related. The child's dependence on or independence from the mother is mirrored by his or her perceptions of natural agency—sometimes high, sometimes low, and always in conflict with each other. The intuitive assumption of continuing childhood dependency, in short, is related to the concept of action that posits limited voluntarism on the part of the self, while the intuitive assumption of childhood omnipotence is related to the concept of action that posits completely self-willed voluntarism. It is the conflict between the two that gives rise, at least in part, to the special salience of action to the understanding of human conduct, and to the realization of this salience in the formation of religious propositions.

All of this may seem far removed from the Boyer thesis and the theory that religious propositions systematically violate intuitive naturalistic assumptions, but it is not, for the simple reason that concepts of independence, dependence, voluntary and involuntary action, all co-vary. Religious propositions clearly involve statements about actions and the characteristics of superhuman agencies, if Boyer is right, violate actions deemed natural for human beings. That is what makes them memorable as well as transmissible through time. My revision of the Boyer hypothesis asserts that these assumptions are not unambiguous, but conflicting. A certain amount of paradox is natural to them. Chief among those assumptions is that actions should be increasingly self-directed with development. This is a human universal. All humans develop from a state of greater dependency to a state of greater individual autonomy. How cultures play on this universal is another matter.

8   Conclusions

The history of thought in the West (especially England and France) usually takes contradictoriness to be a weakness or failure. To be at variance with what one also desires could be taken to be symptomatic of the irrational or the insane. Against monism stands a long tradition of dialectical thinking, especially prominent in Germany, which questions the existence of things in themselves in preference for complex relationships, and the interaction between these relationships and the perceiving consciousness. Paradox is embraced, and understood as the powerful dynamic that drives and develops systems of knowledge, both those that are conscious and those that are unconscious.

The view advanced in this chapter supports the dialectical view and holds that many features of culture—including the concept of voluntary action—result from structural contradictions deep in the development of attachment. These contradictions are insoluble by design. One of the most basic assumptions violated in human development is the assumption that the maternal relationship will continue in its earliest form. At first the child is in close physical proximity to the mother, and the sole object of her affection and attention. Then the child is weaned and privileged position it once enjoyed must now be shared with others. The expectation that the relationship would continue forever is shown to be false and the child must grow up knowing that its most basic expectation about the world is not inviolable. At the same time, the wish itself is contradictory: the desire for continued dependency on the primary attachment figure is opposed by the desire to develop some degree of autonomy. As Spiro notes, 'it is a psychological truism that children's experientially acquired conceptions of their microsocial world of the family form the basis for their initial cognitive orientations to the macrosocial world' (Spiro, 1997, p. 150). Somehow, the contradiction between early experientially derived expectations and their violation in normal development must be resolved, even if it is the form of a paradox that acknowledges no permanent resolution.

Religion as a 'culturally constituted defence mechanism', to use Spiro's (1965) phrase, offers one route to resolution of conflicted attachment wishes. The 'mother' deity, as we have seen, represents at the same time it partly resolves the conflict over childhood-derived wishes for dependence and autonomy on the part of the child, as well as the mother. Conflicted wishes are transferred to the image of the goddess, and in this form they are dealt with through the conventional and trans-active language of worship. The fact that such wishes are never fully and completely realized, of course, partly explains the memorability and transmissibility of such a belief system. Nevertheless, they promise resolution, even if at the same time they make that impossible. This is a paradox, but as I have written elsewhere, culture itself can be understood as built up out of paradox, a complex inter-layering of problems that cannot be solved (Nuckolls, 1998).

Dependency is different from, but related to the contradiction between action as voluntary and action as involuntary. Humans develop with opposing orientations, one that subsumes voluntary action in dependence on a powerful other, and the other that seeks to undo dependency and replace with autonomous self-will. Flouting these expectations is basic to the symbolic construction of superhuman agencies as cultural objects. After all, that is what gods are supposed to do, but there are several ways of doing this. On the one hand, the gods can be imagined as all powerful and thus as determining our actions from one moment to the next without the intervention of human will. On the other hand, human exercise agency when they identify with the gods (as in spirit possession, an almost universal cultural phenomenon) or when they 'forget' to do homage to the gods. I have suggested that the conflict between these orientations—between wanting and rejecting voluntary action—is framed in the language of attachment and that what we are really talking about, deep down, is ambivalence. As subject as this process is to cultural definition, its motivational wellsprings are still to be found in the nature of the maternal bond and in the movement away from it as the human child develops. What 'bothers' us, then, about voluntary/involuntary action is that it resonates with the psychodynamic issue most fraught with ambivalence in our development: just how dependent or independent do we really want to be from the sources of our deepest attachment?

This chapter has not questioned the starting point of the Boyer hypothesis: that the violations of intuitive assumptions inform or direct the construction of superhuman agencies and their attributes. It does question their source. If the development of conflicted attachment is a human universal or nearly so then it would be surprising if ambivalence played no role in the genesis of religious propositions. Indeed, if my argument is correct, then it might even play the primary role, and the ontological expectations adduced by Boyer might function only as enabling conditions. I make no argument as to primacy, however. This is the problem with most arguments framed in exclusively cognitivist terms. They unnecessarily stunt the growth of theory by limiting it to purely operational variables. The point is simply that human attachment and its internal contradictions are too important to overlook in any theory that claims that development, religious beliefs, and action orientations are intimately and inextricably related.

References

Barber, J. & Crits-Christoph, P. (1993) Advances in measures of psychodynamic formulations. *J Consult Clin Psychol* **61**, 574–85.

Bellah, R., Madsen, R., Sullivan, W., Swidler, A. & Tipton, S. (1985) *Habits of the Heart.* New York: Harper & Row.

Boehm, C. (1989) Ambivalence and compromise in human nature. *Am Anthropol* **9**, 921–39.

Bond, J., Hansell, J. & Shevrin, H. (1987) Locating a reference paradigm in psychotherapy transcripts: Reliability of relationship episode location in the Core Conflictual Relationship Theme (CCRT) method. *Psychother* **24**, 736–49.

Bowlby, J. (1969) *Attachment and Loss, Vol. 1: attachment.* New York: Basic Books.

Bowlby, J. (1973) *Attachment and Loss, Vol. 2: separation.* New York: Basic Books.

Boyer, P. (1994) *The Naturalness of Religious Ideas: a cognitive theory of religion.* Berkeley: University of California Press.

Boyer, P. (2001) Cultural inheritance tracks cognitive predispositions. In Whitehouse, H. (ed.), *The Debated Mind.* Oxford: Berg, pp. 57–91.

Brennan, K. & Shaver, P. (1998) Attachment styles and personality disorders: their connections to each other and to parental divorce, parental death, and perceptions of parental caregiving. *J Personal* **66**, 835–78.

Brenner, S. (1995) Why women rule the roost: rethinking Javanese ideologies of gender and self-control. In Ong, A. & Peletz, M. (eds), *Bewitching Women, Pious Men: gender and body politics in Southeast Asia.* Berkeley: University of California Press, pp. 231–55.

Choi, I., Nisbett, R. & Norenzayan, A. (1999) Causal attribution across cultures: variation and universality. *Psycholog Bull* **125**, 47–63.

Connolly, M., Crits-Christoph, P., Demorest, A., Azarian, K., Muenz, L. & Chittams, J. (1996) Varieties of transference patterns in psychotherapy. *J Consult Clin Psychol* **64**, 1213–21.

Cornelisen, A. (1976) *Women of the Shadows.* Boston: Little Brown.

Crits-Christoph, P., Luborsky, L., Dahl, L., Popp, C., Mellon, J. & Mark, D. (1988) Clinicians can agree in assessing relationship patterns in psychotherapy: the Core Conflictual Relationship Theme method. *Arch Gen Psychiat* **45**, 1001–4.

Feeney, J. & Noller, P. (1996) *Adult Attachment.* Thousand Oaks: Sage.

Freud, S. (1912/1958) The dynamics of transference. In Strachey, J. (ed.), *The Standard Edition of the Complete Psychological Works of Sigmund Freud,* Vol. 12. London: Hogarth Press, pp. 99–108.

Friedl, E. (1967) The position of women: appearance and reality. *Anthropol Quart* **40**, 97–108.

Geertz, H. (1961) *The Javanese Family.* Glencoe: Free Press.

Gilmore, M. & Gilmore, D. (1979) Machismo: a psychodynamic approach (Spain) *J Psycholog Anthropol* **2**, 281–300.

Harlow, R. & Zimmermann, R. (1959) Affectional responses in the infant monkey. *Science* **130**, 421.

Hazen, C. & Shaver, P. (1987) Romantic love conceptualized as an attachment process. *J Personal Soc Psychol* **52**, 511–24.

Heider, F. (1958) *The Psychology of Interpersonal Relations.* New York: Wiley.

Hinde, R. & Spencer-Booth, Y. (1966) Effects of six-day maternal deprivation on rhesus monkeys. *Nature* **210**, 1021–3.

Hollos, M. & Lies, P. (1985) The hand that rocks the cradle rules the world: family interaction and decision making in a Portuguese rural community. *Ethos* **13**, 346–57.

Hsu, F. (1981) *American and Chinese: passages to differences.* Honolulu: University of Hawaii Press.

Ingold, T. (2001) From the transmission of representations to the education of attention. In Whitehouse, H. (ed.), *The Debated Mind.* Oxford: Berg, pp. 133–55.

Jay, R. (1969) *Javanese Villagers.* Cambridge: MIT Press.

Jones, E.E. & Davis, K.E. (1965) From acts to dispositions: the attribution process in person perception. In Berkowitz, L. (ed.), *Advances in Experimental Social Psychology*, Vol. 2, 1st edn. New York: Academic Press, pp. 219–26.

Kakar, S. (1978) *The Inner World.* Oxford: Oxford University Press.

Kakar, S. (1989) The maternal-feminine in Indian psychoanalysis. *Int J Psychoanal* **19**, 355–62.

Kelley, H.H. (1967) Attribution in social psychology. *Nebraska Symp Motivat* **15**, 192–238.

Kelley, H.H. (1973) The processes of causal attribution. *Am Psychol* **28**, 107–28.

Knauft, B. (1996) *Genealogies of the Present in Cultural Anthropology.* New York: Routledge.

Kurtz, S. (1992) *All the Mothers Are One.* New York: Columbia University Press.

Lawson, T. & McCauley, R. (1990) *Rethinking Religion: connecting cognition and culture.* Cambridge: Cambridge University Press.

Lewis, F.M. & Daltroy, L.H. (1990) How causal explanations influence health behaviour: Attribution theory. In Glanz, K., Lewis, F.M. & Rimer, B.K. (eds), *Health Education and Health Behaviour: theory, research, and practice.* San Francisco: Jossey-Bass.

Luborsky, L. (1977) Measuring a pervasive psychic structure in psychotherapy: the core conflictual relationship theme. In Freedman, N. & Grand, S. (eds), *Communicative Structures and Psychic Structures.* New York: Plenum Press, pp. 367–95.

Luborsky, L. & Crits-Christoph. P. (1998) *Understanding Transference: the Core Conflictual Relationship Theme Method,* 2nd edn. New York: Basic Books.

Luborsky, L., Crits-Christoph, P. & Millon, T. (1986) Advent of objective measures of the transference concept. *J Consult Clin Psychol* **54**, 39–47.

Milgram, S. (1974) *Obedience to Authority: an experimental view.* New York: Harper & Row.

Murphy, Y. & Murphy, R. (1974) *Women of the Forest.* New York: Columbia University Press.

Netting, R. (1969) Marital relations in the Jos Plateau of Nigeria. *Am Anthropol* **71**, 1037–45.

Nuckolls, C. (1996) *The Cultural Dialectics of Knowledge and Desire.* Madison: University of Wisconsin Press.

Nuckolls, C. (1998) *Culture: a problem that cannot be solved.* Madison: University of Wisconsin Press.

Prinz, W. (1997) Explaining voluntary action: the role of mental content. In Carrier, M. & Machamer, P. (eds), *Mindscapes: philosophy, science, and the mind.* Konstanz: Universitäts-Verlag, pp. 153–75.

Raeff, C. (1997) Individuals in relationships: cultural values, children's social interactions, and the development of an American individualistic self. *Development Rev* 17, 205–38.

Rogers, S. (1975) Female forms of power and the myth of male dominance: a model of female/male interaction in peasant society. *Am Ethnol* 2, 727–56.

Ross, M. & Fletcher, G.J.O. (1985) Attribution and social perception. In Lindzey, G. & Aronson, E. (eds), *The Handbook of Social Psychology*, Vol. II, 3rd edn. New York: Random House, pp. 73–114.

Saunders, G. (1981) Men and women in Southern Europe: a review of some aspects of cultural complexity. *J Psychoanal Anthropol* 4, 435–66.

Segalen, M. (1983) *Love and Power in the Peasant Family: rural France in the nineteenth century.* Chicago: University of Chicago Press.

Spiro, M. (1965) *Context and Meaning in Cultural Anthropology.* New York: Free Press.

Spiro, M. (1986) Some reflections on cultural determinism and relativism with special attention to reason and emotion. In Shweder, R. & LeVine, R. (eds), *Culture Theory: essays on self, mind, and emotion.* Cambridge: Cambridge University Press, pp. 101–22.

Spiro, M. (1997) *Gender Ideology and Psychological Reality.* New Haven: Yale University Press.

Swartz, M. (1982) The isolation of men and power of women: sources of power among the Swahili of Mombasa. *J Anthropolog Res* 38, 26–44.

SECTION V

SECTION V

QUESTIONING THE MULTIDISCIPLINARY FIELD

SABINE MAASEN

This book has attempted to approach the issue of voluntary action anew. The questions we raised seemed simple enough. What counts as an action? What makes an action voluntary? What exactly is it that volition adds to the action? Our folk psychological expertise of what it means to act voluntarily notwithstanding, the concept becomes ever more multi-faceted the closer one looks at it. This is unfortunate because voluntary action is not only a matter of understanding the mental operation of individual minds, but also a matter of social practice. The notion of voluntarily acting persons is an essential ingredient of politics, law, economy, and ethics—therefore, it is high time to assess the available scientific expertise.

Not surprisingly, there is more than just one (sub-)discipline scrutinizing the subject. In particular, psychology, the neurosciences, philosophy, law, and anthropology have made important contributions. Hence, assessing the available scientific expertise requires a multi-disciplinary approach. For a long time, the disciplines mentioned have each pursued their own research agenda; accordingly, cross-disciplinary exchange remained a rare event. In the meantime, this is about to change, mostly due to the fact that the neurocognitive approaches have begun to make stronger claims: in their view, the issue of voluntary action, as well as associated concepts, such as freedom of will or consciousness, could be fully explained within a scientific framework, thereby abandoning the elusive notion cherished by folk psychology. Basically, the neurocognitive approaches, the mental operation called voluntary action, can be understood in terms of neural activity and the cognitive functions operating on them. In principle, this is quite a challenge to certain types of philosophy, but also to various social sciences. In reality, however, they have only just begun to realize that long-standing notions of will-directed action will have to be reconsidered. But, in which way?

The non-scientific articles in this book have given different answers: most of them insist on the notion of voluntary action, however theoretically and/or philosophically conceived. For all practical purposes, thus the general line of reasoning 'wilful action' is an indispensable notion in the realm of social action. Granted that this notion is the result of neural and cognitive processes—among others, the experiential aspect—this very knowledge of being an author of an action, of being responsible for it, cannot be fully explained in neurocognitive terms. Evidently, the exchange between the disciplines is an intricate one. There are, it seems, no obvious ways to bridge the gaps involved. Thus, something else is at stake; namely, the thorny issue of inter-disciplinarity needs to be scrutinized in itself. Hailed by science policy since the late 1960s, inter-disciplinarity is considered a problematic endeavour until today—in both theory and practice (Weingart & Stehr, 2000). The ubiquitous fear of reductionism and the difficulty of finding a common language has accompanied virtually all attempts at inter-disciplinary discourse. At the same time, these experiences should not discourage or even hinder novel attempts, yet they should inform them so as not to repeat old mistakes. Thus, which modes and goals of inter-disciplinary discourse should we adhere to?

If it comes to forefront, the most obvious feature of research on voluntary action is that it addresses a rather limited group of disciplines, including (cognitive) psychology, neurobiology, and (analytical) philosophy. Other types of reasoning (some of which have been quite influential in shaping our knowledge about volition, action, and self) seem to be relegated to the backstage. If anything, they are invited to respond to the neurocognitive challenge—in a way, they seem to be confined to a commenting role. Claiming that a neurocognitive concept of voluntary action is consequential for the social sphere (e.g. politics), the anthropologists, for instance, are invited to engage in some kind of 'anthropology assessment' (Metzinger). As yet, there seems to be no *mutual* exchange between the insights derived from, say, anthropological and neurobiological studies into volition, agency, etc. What may be conceived of as the humble exchange between stakeholders may be caused systematically. What if the implicit reductionist and unifying stance, implied in the neurocognitive approaches, is misleading? What if, by way of discipline-specific processing of concepts, the latter are bound to remain heterogeneous?

In this last section, two papers address these different, albeit complementary, questions. One addresses the 'unity-of-knowledge' approach that is implied in the neurocognitive explanatory claim as regards voluntary action. The other paper traces the highly multi-disciplinary discourse on consciousness, thereby presenting a more minute 'knowledge map' showing the shifting and sifting of inter-disciplinary approaches to consciousness.

First, Richard A. Shweder, anthropologist, pleads polemically against all unwarranted attempts at a unifying knowledge approach towards all phenomena concerning the human sciences, 'and perhaps even in the non-human sciences'. As opposed to this, he pleads energetically for a non-reductionist and decidedly 'polytheistic' approach by way of accepting 'the reality of a loose assemblage of differently focused, rather self-involved, and variably overlapping research communities in both the human and natural sciences' (Geertz). To be sure, there are inspiring forms of cross-talks, the neurocognitive sciences being a case in point, yet, rather than pointing toward a 'unity of knowledge' or a 'new synthesis' (E. O. Wilson), Shweder sees the proliferation of 'disciplinary matrices' (Kuhn): loose assemblage of techniques, vocabularies, assumptions, instruments, and exemplary achievements, some of which are original and creative, some of which are incommensurate with or semi-dependent of each other, some of which are mutually stimulating. This is particularly true of all ambitious endeavours concerning the links between culture, mind, and biology, the so-called mind–body or mind–brain problem being the prototype. Typically, efforts towards inter-disciplinarity are characterized by ignorance, a high level of abstraction, and/or discussing ill-defined concepts. Pointedly, Shweder illustrates this observation with two examples, one being the multi-disciplinary conference on voluntary action upon which this book has been based. Although he considers it a well-designed endeavour, *in actu* it suffered from all weaknesses just mentioned: for example, the neurosciences neither defined their concept of causation nor did they escape a dualism (as soon as they treat something mental as dependent variable or something neurological as dependent variable, or vice versa). This, according to Shweder, is a failure. Philosophers, in turn, adhered to rather different in/compatibilist solutions of the mind–brain problem—no synthesis in sight, neither among philosophers, let alone within the consciousness community. Plurality, however, in Shweder's view, is not a failure, but a characteristic of the game called science. For reality testing is a metaphysical act, based on category systems, background assumptions, metaphors, etc. While there are times when the differences between perspectives appear as illusory, and thus there should be no end to the effort of probing those differences, Shweder does not expect any scientific controversy about fundamental issues to ever come to an end. This is especially so as the humanities and the social science always ask for the 'matterings' of 'matter', that is, meaning, which cannot be completely reduced to neurological processes and cognitive functions.

Sabine Maasen's account of consciousness as a hybrid concept, in a way, substantiates Shweder's view by pointing to the dynamics of knowledge inherent in any lively exchange of concepts. From a sociology-of-knowledge point of view she argues that any concept entering a new field of research will inevitably be changed by it and maybe even change the field in turn. In a way, those terms behave like metaphors in a poem: both term and context have to be processed, that is, interact with each other, in order to make sense. Analogously, the idea of a metaphor view of knowledge dynamics, a term such as consciousness, currently scrutinized by ever more scientific disciplines, will either have to change in the course of the happening or to be sorted out for lack of making sense. As to the importing disciplines, it is also an empirical question whether and which discourses adapt to the (which?) notion of consciousness and, if so, how and to which degree. The article proceeds by first sketching the scientific activity concerning consciousness. This view from the outside reveals a highly fragmented field split into pharmacological, neurocognitive, philosophical, and social scientific accounts. Over almost 30 years of research there has been a noticeable shift toward the neurocognitive approach—philosophical (with the exceptions of analytical philosophy) and social scientific approaches are on the decline. At the same time, psychology splits up into a more cognitive and a more socially-orientated faction, the latter of which seems to play virtually no role in modern consciousness research. This view is then confronted with view from within. First, the paper scrutinizes those (sub-)disciplines that form part of the newly-emerged research front. To put it plainly, while neuroscientists just conquer novel territory without further ado and rearrange the field from the neuroscientific perspective, cognitive psychologists have to re-acknowledge consciousness as an object of scientific inquiry after years of exile, and philosophers, in turn, face the risk of consciousness being used on a case-by-case basis, rather than systematically informing the experimental results. No wonder, perhaps, that this kind of 'scientific inter-disciplinarity' is subject to ongoing criticism, notably due to its lack of accounting for the experiential aspect of consciousness. The criticism comes in various forms, the most obvious one being the foundation of a new *Journal of Consciousness Studies* in 1994. In the editors' view, consciousness research, after having become scientific, should re-open the floor for phenomenal accounts. In a pointed phrase, they hold that the decade of the brain should also be a decade of the mind. This move calls for both *ontological rapprochement* between physicalists and phenomenalists, as well as for *epistemological reconsideration* to overcome the fruitless opposition between reductionist and dualist accounts. A brief analysis of the volumes as yet issued reveals that the journal, indeed, encourages inter-disciplinary efforts without culminating in one over-arching project, which is due to the fact that it did not yet succeed in ontological and epistemological rapprochement—even the new inter-disciplinary neurocognitive group still faces the risk of 'balkanization'—and the social sciences are about to vanish from the discursive arena altogether. In the course of this happening, the concept of consciousness becomes a hybrid (e.g. a loosely coupled ensemble of a neural activity, a cognitive function, a collective representation, a transpersonal event), engaging the disciplines involved in different ways. Due to these inherent tensions, both epistemic and social, consciousness is likely to stay on the academic agenda for quite some time. It will continue to mean many different things to many different discourses.

To repeat, this is not to say that inter-disciplinary efforts in the realm of voluntary action or consciousness, respectively, are just in vain. Rather, the message is to be more modest or more realistic about the goals. Efforts in inter-disciplinary discourse are ultimately about enriching each others' theoretical and methodical tools in order to better grasp the phenomenon at hand. If, in some cases, this leads to overlaps and partial unification, this should be regarded as no more than a by-product of what really is at issue: understanding voluntary action.

References

Weingart, P. & Stehr, N. (eds) (2000) *Practising Interdisciplinarity*. Toronto: Toronto University Press.

CHAPTER 15

A POLYTHEISTIC CONCEPTION OF THE SCIENCES AND THE VIRTUES OF DEEP VARIETY

RICHARD A. SHWEDER

1 Professor Wilson's Sermon

'Can we actually "know" the universe? My God, it is hard enough finding your way around in Chinatown ...' is a line from one of Woody Allen's books. The line seems appropriate as the opening line for an essay in which I plan to examine some of the many problems with the idea of 'unity of knowledge' or 'consilience' as presented by the Harvard University biologist E. O. Wilson (1998). Concerning the gospel of 'consilience' I have doubts about its 'unification metaphysics' (material determination, all the way down) and its 'unified learning' pedagogy (with its emphasis on one particular, even peculiar, 'natural science' conception of knowledge; Wilson, 1998, p. 5, 3). I confess that I am quite dubious of attempts to spread the word of 'science' or promote the quest for knowledge in the human sciences under its name.

Members of the faith of 'consilience' believe that we are now (for the first time, or finally—or is it once again?) on the threshold of (as T. S. Eliot put it, sceptically summarizing the creed) 'rolling the universe up into a ball' (quoted in Converse, 1986). Perhaps that is why I experience Professor Wilson's advocacy of 'consilience' as a kind of 'good news' monotheistic sermon. In effect, Professor Wilson invites us to return to an old time state of pre-Kuhnian, pre-Wittgensteinian, pre-Quinean, pre-Rortyean innocence (see Quine, 1953, 1969; Wittgenstein, 1953, 1969; Kuhn, 1962; Rorty, 1991). Reading his homilies on the nature of human understanding and intellectual curiosity, one might never have imagined that the Enlightenment idealization of the sufficient conditions for producing knowledge ('an innocent eye' plus a logic machine) has pretty much been dismantled or at least seriously critiqued over the past 200 years. One might never have thought to doubt his conviction that unification and convergence of belief are the criteria of maturity in scholarly disciplines. Where T. S. Eliot was sceptical, Professor Wilson remains pious.

There are other sceptics. Clifford Geertz is a cultural anthropologist who specializes in the interpretation of behaviour and who describes his intellectual aim as 'ferreting out the singularities of other people's ways-of-life' (Geertz, 2000, p. xi). As a psychological anthropologist and cultural psychologist, that is my goal as well. Geertz writes about the field of psychology (which was once known as the science of the soul, but is now called the science of the mind, and is scripted to become the science of the body in Wilson's augury for the future) as follows: 'We are not apparently proceeding towards some appointed end where it all comes together, Babel is undone, and Self lies down with Society'.

Apparently, Wilson disagrees and his visions stretch far beyond psychology *per se*. He still dreams Enlightenment dreams of connecting anything and everything (Chinatown and the whole universe) 'in a common skein of cause-and-effect explanation' (Wilson, 2000): validity, simplicity and unity 'all rolled up in a ball'. In his book entitled *Consilience: the unity of knowledge*, Wilson (1998) writes of it as an 'epiphany' or an 'enchantment' that freed him from his Southern Baptist upbringing. I have my doubts. He describes the typical devotee of 'consilience' as being 'under the spell' [his expression] of 'a hoped-for consolidation of theory so tight as to turn the science into a 'perfect' system of thought, which by sheer weight of evidence and logic is made resistant to revision'. In the written version of his keynote address for the New York Academy of Science conference on *Unity of Knowledge: the convergence of natural and human science* he described the natural sciences of the new millennium as having nearly reached a state of perfect 'consilience' (Wilson, 2000). He expressed his conviction that the social sciences and humanities could be similarly unified with each other and with the natural sciences under the banner of biology. He wagered that the royal road to such a comprehensive 'consilience'—a 'resistant to revision', eternal or final solution to all debates and disputations about culture and mind, what might be called the academic 'end time'—would come through work on brain science, human genetics, cognitive psychology, and biological anthropology.

I have my doubts. I would suggest that the idea of consilience—the idea of a seamless coherency and of systematic interconnections across culture, mind and body, across intellectual disciplines, and across units of analysis neatly arranged into decomposable levels of material organization—is far more fictional than factual. At the very least I would suggest that 'consilience' is not a very good description of the current intellectual scene across the human and the non-human sciences.

I recognize, of course, that rather than dismissing the idea of consilience as a fanciful description of the current intellectual scene, it is possible to construe the notion merely as a utopian ideal for guiding research. Even so, I would hope that the aspirations of the members of the church of 'consilience' remain denominational in character and that those ideals are understood to be useful for some intellectual projects but not for others. Why? Because Wilson's ecumenical and monotheistic quest for a 'consilient' unification of knowledge over idealizes one very special and rather limited (even limiting) type of knowledge, the type of knowledge where observations and logic alone make it resistant to revision. There is no universally binding reason to privilege that particular ideal of knowledge and that ideal, while perhaps serviceable in some contexts, may actually get in the way of many valuable forms of systematic inquiry in the human sciences and perhaps even in the non-human sciences as well. At least that is the pluralistic or polytheistic conception of human understanding that I would like to put on the table for discussion.

2 Polycentrism or consilience?

I think it is instructive (by way of contrast to the dogma of consilience) to take a closer look at Clifford Geertz's description of the state of play these days—the actual realities of scholarship and the way interpretative communities are functioning—in the sciences and the humanities. One can find this account in his recent collection of essays entitled

Available Light (already compare the tone and implication of that title with those of the title of Wilson's book). Geertz writes, 'The homogenization of natural science, both over time and across fields, as a constant other, an 'opposing ideal' permanently set off from other forms of thought, as Richard Rorty has put it, 'by a special method [and] a special relation to reality', is extremely difficult to defend when one looks at either its history or its internal variety with any degree of circumstantiality' (Geertz, 2000, pp. 145–6). He continues: 'There is indeed some evidence from within the natural sciences themselves that the continental image of them as an undivided bloc, united in their commitment to Galilean procedures, disengaged consciousness and the view from nowhere, is coming under a certain amount of pressure' (Geertz, 2000, p. 150).

Geertz is impressed by the 'localness' of the knowledge systems constructed by different cultural communities (including scientific communities). He is clearly suspicious of both fanatics and infidels in the academy. In the place of both the hyper-modernist total-systems builders and the radically sceptical anti-science post-modernists, he asks us to take seriously the image and the reality 'of a loose assemblage of differently focused, rather self-involved, and variably overlapping research communities in *both* the human and natural sciences'. Geertz invites us to abandon a conception of 'two continental enterprises, one driven by the ideal of disengaged consciousness looking out with cognitive assurance upon an absolute world of ascertainable fact, the other driven by the ideal of an engaged self struggling uncertainly with signs and expressions to make readable sense of intentional action'. In other words, the story of the academy is not about 'two cultures' (the sciences versus the humanities, the objectivists versus the subjectivists, the 'hard' versus the 'soft'). Nor is it about just one imperial culture (to pick some random examples, human genetics, sociobiology, or cognitive neuroscience) taking over all the others either. Reflecting on claims about the 'unity of knowledge' Geertz doubtfully asks (quoting the philosopher Richard Rorty): '… what method is common to palaeontology and particle physics? What relation to reality is shared by topology and entomology?' Such questions, he argues are hardly more useful than asking 'Is sociology closer to physics than to literary criticism?' or 'Is political science more hermeneutic than microbiology, chemistry more explanatory than psychology?' (Geertz, 2000, p. 150).

I happen to share Geertz's view of the current intellectual scene. The above-mentioned NYAS conference, at which Wilson was the keynote speaker, was held at Rockefeller University in Manhattan in June 2000. When I was first invited by the New York Academy to attend this conference I wrote:

> I am pleased to accept your invitation, although I feel that I should give you some warning that I am quite sceptical of much that is presupposed and implied by the title and subtitle of the meeting. I do not think there is unity either between or within the social and natural sciences. I am not even confident there is unity within biology, although there certainly are similarities between the way certain sorts of biologists and certain sorts of social scientists think about the world.

The similarities and sorts I had in mind were the reductive systems building modernists in the natural and human sciences. They share a mode of explanation and style of research. Non-reductive 'top down' holists, interactionists, and contextualists in the natural sciences and human sciences share a mode of explanation and style of research as well. So there are parallel or comparable splits within the natural and the human sciences. The field of plate tectonics, for example, according to the geologist Frank Richter (1986), makes 'no reference to laws of motion even though it describes motion', is bound to historical circumstances, and has more in common with some varieties of social science scholarship than with some versions of physics.

Biology is not homogeneous either and there are conflicts over some rather fundamental issues in that territory of knowledge. Some of this rather spirited debate was in evidence at the New York Academy conference, especially in the session on *Beyond Nature-Nurture*, which was hardly a consilient event. There appear to be a few items on the 'nature-nurture' agenda that remain unsettled: minor things, such as how to think about the distinction between genes and environments, what precisely it means to say 'it [intelligence, a fear of snakes, Catholicism] is all in your genes', and how to properly measure gene-environment interactions, assuming the distinction between genes and environments can be made precise and coherent in the first place (which, according to some biologists, is very much in doubt).

One thing that is not in doubt is that it is an over-simplification to say that there are only two types of biologists, although at least there is more than just one. The first type is biologists who conceptualize 'phenotypes' in terms of 'epigenetic complexity'. They focus their research on interactions 'between genes, between genes and gene products (proteins), and between all these and environmental signals, including, of course, the individual organismal experience' (see Strohman, 1993, p. 114).[2] The second type is biologists who talk the talk of 'genetic reductionism' and speak the language of direct gene-trait pathways (whether monogenetic or polygenetic, whether simple or complex—in principle, if not in practice, they think they can handle, which means simplify, any complexity that comes along). To identify only two types of biologists is obviously overly simple, but the distinction is revealing. Many of the (type 1) 'epigenetic' biologists are suspicious of genetic interventionism and have rather ambivalent feelings, at best, about the human genome project. Many of the (type 2) genetic reductionists deeply believe that they can make the world a better place through selective alterations in the genetic endowment of particular members of our species. So they promote the human genome project as the paradigm for medical and behavioural research. My main point, however, is this: Whether you are for them or against them, or whether you believe or disbelieve (like or loathe) the message that successful people and their offspring do better in life because they have better genes, there is more than one contentious voice out there, even in biology.

I concluded my response to the NYAS invitation to attend the *Unity of Knowledge* conference as follows:

> And I have some doubts about whether the ideal of substantive 'unity' across the natural and human sciences is any more attainable today than 200 years ago. I even think it is an open question whether (for the sake of human progress and the progress of knowledge) the ideal of substantive unity of belief is even truly desirable. Given those caveats I look forward to a lively meeting in June.

A similar vein of thought is found in *Available Light* (Geertz, 2000). Focusing on the field of psychology, broadly conceived, Geertz sees little 'consilience'. He writes: 'Paradigms, wholly new ways of going about things, come along not by the century, but by the decade, sometimes, it almost seems, by the month'.

> It takes either a preternaturally focused, dogmatical individual, who can shut out any ideas but his or her own, or a mercurial, hopelessly inquisitive one, who can keep dozens of them in play at once, to remain upright amidst this tumble of programs, promises and proclamations. (Geertz, 2000, p. 188)

Programmes, promises, proclamations. 'The Unity of Knowledge'. 'The Convergence of the Natural and Human Sciences'. 'The New Synthesis'. What Geertz thinks we are witnessing, at least in psychology and the cognitive sciences, is not some deep unification of knowledge, but rather a rapid proliferation of what Thomas Kuhn (1962) called disciplinary matrices: '. . . loose assemblages of techniques, vocabularies, assumptions, instruments and exemplary achievements', some of which are original and creative, some of which are incommensurate with each other or semi-independent of each other, some of which are mutually stimulating. No common project—rather 'half-ordered, polycentric collections of mutually conditioned projects' with no ultimate 'consilience' in sight.

The contrast between Wilson's and Geertz's conception of human knowledge and knowledge of humans is dramatic. Unreconstructed and unfazed in substance, monotheistic and modernist in spirit, Wilson (2000) offers us the 'Enlightenment' picture of science as a distinctive and superior mode of thought that is leading us to a new synthesis linking culture, mind and body. This time around (and we have been around this issue many times before both before and after the 'Enlightenment') it would appear that the bygone and misconceived idea of a reductive 'social physics' is now going to be replaced with the fashionable new idea of a reductive 'social biology', based on a set of universal truths generated out of cognitive neuroscience, human genetics, biological anthropology and a species typifying cognitive psychology.[3]

In any case, whatever one thinks of Wilson's Enlightenment picture of how science works (or ought to work, or of its potential public-relations appeal, e.g. to funding agencies or to readers of the New York Times) I submit it is not a good depiction of the current intellectual scene. Clifford Geertz's 'polycentrism' (rather than E. O. Wilson's 'consilience') is the descriptive and normative term that rings more true. I shall try to briefly illustrate what I take to be the polycentric realities of the current scene with some casual glances in a couple of directions.

3   A non-consilient truth

Before glimpsing at some local scenes, however, let me confess that the most rock-bottom truth in my own conception of the human relationship to knowledge (including knowledge of human beings) is fundamentally non-consilient. I associate this truth with an approach to understanding I call 'Confusionism' (not to be confused with 'Confucionism'). According to this non-consilient 'Confusionist' truth, the knowable world is incomplete if seen from any one point of view, incoherent if seen from all points of view at once, and empty if seen from 'nowhere in particular'.

Given the choice between incompleteness, incoherence, and emptiness the best option is to opt for incompleteness, staying on the move between different points of view. The best option is to go ahead and see what each point of view (each genuine cultural tradition, school of thought, theoretical position) illuminates and what each hides, while keeping track of the plural (some might say, polytheistic) character of the humanly knowable world. Coherence can sometimes be achieved, but only within the limits of particular points of view. Findings of great generality across all human beings can also sometimes be uncovered. However, in the human sciences at least, these universal generalizations are often bought at the price of describing the world of culture and mind at a level of abstraction so distanced from lived realities that they are devoid of sufficient content and meaning and have little predictive utility. For example, the psychologist Charles Osgood long ago proposed a simple universal code for characterizing the way all human beings evaluate all objects and events in the universe. They do it, we do it, he proposed by asking of every object and event three questions: 'Is it good or bad?' (Osgood called this the 'evaluation' dimension), 'Is it strong or weak?' (Osgood called this the 'potency' dimension) and 'is it fast or slow?' (Osgood called this the 'activity' dimension; see Osgood *et al.*, 1975). The problem is that this universal code is theorized at such a 'high level' of abstraction that it classifies 'God' and 'ice cream' as equivalent, because they are both judged to be 'good', 'strong', and 'active'. As you can see, a bit too much gets lost in this type of search for universally valid generalizations. That is a common shortcoming (the shortcoming of 'emptiness') of propositions in the human sciences that are designed to be statements about culture and mind true of all human beings.

The 'consilient' aim of synthesizing different points of view is, of course, not inherently evil, but it is equally important to recognize that if different points of view could be fully integrated or synthesized they would not count as different points of view. There *are* times when the supposed difference between two or more points of view is more illusory than real, and at such times a limited unification of knowledge may be possible—but not always or even often when it comes to the types of issues that arise when one examines the links between culture, mind, and biology. In this very broad domain the so-called mind/body (or the mind/brain) problem continues (along with other major issues) to be a major problem and, despite many claims to the contrary, no real resolution is in sight. That is one reason why all interdisciplinary meetings that bring together brain scientists interested in 'organic matter' (and how it functions) with humanists and social scientists interested in 'matterings', meanings, and mental states (and how they function) do, indeed, seem very much like the tower of Babel. Or else at such conferences a fake sense of 'consilience' is achieved by actively repressing any real tower-of-Babel effect. Typically, this fake sense of 'consilience' is a by-product of either:

- not knowing or caring very much about what other researchers are really doing or what they really think (just paying attention to the things you are looking for can also produce a sense of unity);
- formulating propositions at such a 'view from afar' level of abstraction that most of the things that are of interest to social scientists and humanists disappear from sight;
- by sharing words or phrases in common—like Mind or Mental or Consciousness or Cause, or Cognitive Science—without ever asking what those big words or phrases actually and precisely mean.

4   Minds and brains in Bremen

So here is my first glimpse at the current scene. While residing in Germany during the 1999–2000 academic year (where I was a Fellow at the Wissenschaftskolleg zu Berlin), I attended a major interdisciplinary conference held in Bremen on *Voluntary Action*. The experience typified for me the way 'consilience' works (or, more accurately, does not work) as a description of the current intellectual scene in the cognitive sciences. The conference featured philosophers, cognitive neuroscientists, psychologists and anthropologists, and legal scholars. Many of them were there in Bremen ostensibly to explain the fact (or is it just the phenomenal experience? That is the question!) of 'voluntary action'.

Voluntary action is a nice topic for an interdisciplinary meeting. As the conference organizers (Wolfgang Prinz, Gerhard Roth, and Sabine Maasen) pointed out in their invitation, voluntary action:

> ... poses a severe challenge to scientific attempts to form a unitary picture of the working of the human mind and its relation to the working of the body. This is because the notion of mental causation, inherent in the received standard view of voluntary action, is difficult to reconcile with both dualist and monist approaches to the mental and the physical. For dualist accounts it has to be explained what a causal interaction between mind and matter means and how it is possible at all. Conversely, for monist approaches the question of mental causation does not arise and therefore appears to denote a cognitive illusion at best. Dualist and monist accounts can be found in all the disciplines mentioned above [cognitive psychology, neuropsychology, philosophy, ethnology], albeit in different phrasings and/or theoretical frameworks. Moreover, in virtually all disciplines this seemingly insurmountable opposition is [a] subject of ongoing debate.

So 'voluntary action' is a challenge for both mind/body monists and mind/body pluralists (of which mind/body 'dualism' is just one variety). If you are a mind/body monist (and at such conferences the 'monists' are all 'materialists'; apparently the 'idealists' are either hard to find or are not invited), then the 'voluntariness' of 'voluntary action' must be an illusion. That, of course, is the spectacular and breathtaking (or should we say dis-spiriting) implication of mind/body monism. It is spectacular and breathtaking because it amounts to the complete renunciation of all of folk psychology. It amounts to the claim (*involuntarily* arrived at and offered, I suppose, at least according to mind/body monists) that mental states (by which I mean the stuff of 'consciousness'—knowing something, thinking something, wanting something, feeling something, evaluating something as good or bad, or as right or wrong, the 'choice' of something, including one's own truth claims about mental states) are epiphenomenal and have nothing to do with the chain of real events that causes behaviour.

You raise your hand in a situation where you thought that your desire to signal the teacher that you wanted to try to answer the question he or she just posed to the class was the reason that you deliberately, willfully, or 'voluntarily' raised your hand. In a folk psychological sort of way you thought that deliberately communicating that intention was what your hand raising action was all about. 'Not so!' says the mind/body monist. Your hand raising was the end product of material determinants at the neural level, where a human will (and, indeed, even a human self) cannot be observed, and where ideas qua ideas do not exist and, hence, can play no causal role in the movement of your hand.

Given our contemporary-received understanding of the nature (physics, chemistry, and biology) of the material world that is how mind/body monists think they must talk about so-called voluntary action. They talk of it as an epiphenomenon.

However, this leaves the mind/body monists (it is all body, no mind) with a whole lot of explaining to do. Why should such a complex epiphenomenal system (amounting to all of human consciousness and its products) exist at all? How could it evolve, if it plays no causal role in behaviour? Are the ideas of agency, virtue, and human responsibility then incompatible with the 'consilient' teachings of the physical and biological sciences? Should folk psychology (including all the literary, moral, legal and social science disciplines premised on such notions) be banished from the unified curriculum, except perhaps as examples of error, ignorance, and superstition?

Mind/body dualists fare no better when it comes to making sense of 'voluntary' action. As an aside, I would point out that almost all cognitive neuroscience research programmes become tacitly dualist as soon as they treat something mental as an 'independent' variable and something neurological as a 'dependent' variable, or vice versa. In other words, just to carry forward their research agenda they implicitly, usually unselfconsciously, distinguish 'thoughts' (or 'ideas') from 'things' (or neurons) and identify them using ontologically distinct types of criteria.

In any case if you are a reflective mind/body dualist you must explain how something that is immaterial (e.g. the mental state associated with choice, planning, free will, and intentionality) can influence or have an effect on something that is physical (the movement of one's hand). So there is a real and deep problem here with our current understanding of 'voluntary action', and at Bremen an interdisciplinary conference was organized to make some progress on resolving it, in the light of recent research in cognitive neuroscience, psychology, and anthropology, with some assistance from the philosophers. Here is the way 'consilience' operated in that context.

The philosophers were really good at defining the mind/body problem. Each philosopher was terrific at arguing in favour of just one of the several incompatible solutions that have been contenders, while at the same time advancing compelling criticisms against all other 'solutions'. Although not all positions were actually represented at the conference, very little convergence took place among the philosophers who were there, but at least they all knew what the problem was and they tried to address it.

The neuroscientists, on the other hand, came armed with lots of colourful slides, showing this or that brain part lighting up when this or that kind of action took place or sentence got spoken. They named lots of brain parts and they spoke with great confidence, and with a sense of pride and excitement about the technological revolution that had taken place on their watch, which had finally made it possible, or so they thought, to empirically solve the mind/body problem. After about 10 slides one began to realize that they probably had never read Descartes and seemed to think that he would be surprised to find out that when thinking occurs something happens somewhere in the nervous system. After about 20 slides one began to realize that they did not really know what the mind/body problem was in the first place, but they had an imagined solution to the problem, which seemed to excite them a great deal. Upon examination, this 'solution' was simply a form of question-begging in which the very real puzzle of how a non-material thing and a material thing can causally interact is 'solved' by simply substituting a Humean notion of 'causation' for the sense of 'causation' that makes the problem a problem in the first place.

Here, I merely restate a philosophical common place. David Hume was a radical empiricist for whom knowledge had to be based on sensory experience to count as knowledge at all (and, hence, only 'seeing is believing'). According to Hume's epistemology the belief in *any* underlying or inherent causal process is mythic or illusory and 'causal' claims are just reified projections of mental associations. In other words, the empirical world (the perceivable world) is devoid of underlying 'causes' and causal claims should be thought of merely as psychological habits or manners of speaking about subjective impressions that are formed by the perception of things and events that are co-occurring in time and space. For David Hume that is all that counts as knowledge, things and events that are observed and located in time and space. The 'cause' itself, however, cannot be seen and, hence, for Hume, the radical empiricist, it is excluded from his 'positive' science. The neuroscientists 'solved' the mind/body problem by being Humean in their conception of causation, because for them (it became apparent after 20 slides) mind/body 'causation' amounted to little more than the observation that the brain lights up here and there when a person does this or that. This, of course, is hardly a *theoretical* advance over Descartes, but they kept going, slide after slide demonstrating that the mind/body problem had been empirically solved! After 100 slides the only ones awake in the audience (or at least the only ones who really benefited from the presentation) were the other neuroscientists (who were quite genuinely and legitimately interested in questions about the details of brain localization) and a few others who liked the pretty pictures.

Then there were the psychologists, the anthropologists, and the legal scholars. They generally *presupposed* the reality and causal powers of mental states and their ideational content (in other words, they had not expunged folk psychology from their scientific work), and they described the operation of that folk psychology in some detail. One psychologist did present reaction-time evidence, all of it equivocal, trying to prove that mental states are unreal and have no causal powers. In the end, the mind/body problem remained unsolved, when acknowledged, or it remained untouched, but was innocently thought to have been solved by the new technologies for mapping the brain. The everyday experience and/or reality of 'voluntary action' remained as mysterious and fascinating as ever.

5   'Matter' and 'matterings' in the Human Sciences

My second glimpse is a quick look at the crisis literature in the human sciences. This worry about the state of the human sciences compared to the 'natural sciences' goes up and down, and when it is up there emerges a 'crisis literature'. Before examining this literature, however, let me state up-front that I think that social science research institutions are pluralistic hot beds of creative and useful activity. I myself share with Philip Converse (1986) and others the view that disciplined inquiry (use the honorific term 'science' if you like) consists of 'the systematic decoding of observed regularities and the reduction of the regularities to more parsimonious and general principles that account for wide ranges of phenotypic detail'. There is plenty of this type of work going on in the social sciences, and whether or not it moves in the direction of 'consilience' much of this work is exciting and useful.

I myself have tried to contribute to the enterprise in various ways. I work on the cultural psychology of morality, the cultural psychology of the emotions, the cultural psychology of gender, the cultural psychology of illness and suffering, the meaning of family life practices (such as sleeping patterns, dietary practices, and coming of age ceremonies for boys and girls) and on various other issues concerned with the character and social origins of *differences* in psychological functioning across cultural communities. Reports on the substance of this work are available for those who are interested (see, e.g. Shweder & LeVine, 1984; Shweder & Fiske, 1986; Shweder *et al.*, 1996; Shweder, 1991, 1996, 1999; Shweder & Haidt, 2000), but my concerns here go well beyond the discussion of this or that discovery. Any consideration of the substantive issues or questions that concern me—the big 'three' domains (autonomy, community, divinity) of moral reasoning around the world, or the way moral ideas are made manifest and expressed in mundane social practices, such as who eats with whom and who sleeps with whom (that story, by the way, goes well beyond the 'incest taboo'), or why the emotions that are most valued are not the same from culture to culture, or how the experience of 'loss' does not result in the same psychological, or somatic response from society to society or even person to person—must wait for another, less weighty occasion.

However, one of the things I have discovered from my substantive work in cultural psychology is this. The ideal of systematically observing and decoding regularities does not imply that the most useful, significant or even discoverable generalizations in the social sciences are going to be those that characterize all human beings. As Edelson (1984) has remarked 'not all hypotheses of interest to a scientist are universal generalizations'. Indeed, I believe that some of the most reliable, useful, and significant generalizations in the social and psychological sciences are those that are rather restricted in scope, and are 'firmly wedded', as Philip Converse (1986) might have expressed it, to historical, cultural, and institutional circumstances. Rural Oriya Brahmans in India will react this way for these reasons under these circumstances, which is not the way middle-class Anglo-Americans will react, and for these reasons.

Nor must one assume when undertaking the project of disciplined inquiry in the human sciences that real things must exist independent of point of view if they are be considered 'really real'. The realm of 'culture' is a realm occupied and preoccupied with real things— touchdowns, in-laws, child abuse, weeds, the Christmas season—that do not exist independently of the point of view of some specific interpretive community. That is one of the reasons that some of the most reliable and predictively useful generalizations about human behaviour are restricted in scope.

Nor must one assume that the reality of such things is adequately captured from a purely 'naturalistic' or 'materialistic' point of view. Wilson states in the written version of his NYAS conference keynote address: '*After all*, mind and culture, which are the subjects of the social sciences and humanities, are material entities and processes. They do not exist in an astral plane above the tangible world, and are therefore intrinsically open to analysis in the natural scientific mode' (Wilson, 2000; my emphasis).

I find this statement both remarkable and revealing. The current discourse across the sciences and humanities about the character and reality status of culture and mind, I would suggest, is far from 'consilient'. Yet, Wilson seems so untouched by this discourse that a proposition that has been problematic for 3000 years and soundly rejected by many, perhaps most, interpretive social scientists and, for good reason, is asserted as though it were common sense ('After all …'). What do cultural meanings as meanings (e.g. the idea of 'sin') or cultural meanings as made manifest in cultural artefacts (e.g. a 'weapon' or a 'weed') actually look like from a purely material point of view? Is it from a purely material point of view that their very identity is established? For example, a 'utensil' and a 'weapon' may be indistinguishable (it is the same 'knife') from a material point of view. Reference to some non-material element, such as a human purpose, or a human aim, or a human practice, may be required to even identify them in the first place.

This is not a topic that I can examine here in any detail, although one can see the shadow of the mind/body problem once again and I hope one can see how readily many empirical scientists manage to avoid the central issues. Here, let me simply invoke the work of Karl Popper, the well-known twentieth century philosopher of science, as a corrective to Wilson's (in my view) rather dubious assertion that the subjects of the social sciences and humanities are tangible, material, and intrinsically open to naturalistic inspection. Karl Popper believed in three worlds (a world of material objects, a world of subjective mental states and a world of collective meanings) not just one. He was deeply critical of monistic World 1 approaches of the type advanced by Wilson (Popper & Eccles, 1977).

'Mind' and 'culture' refer to 'ideas' or 'meanings' accessible to the mental processes of individual human beings and made manifest in the practices—including linguistic practices—of interpretive communities or social groups. If 'mind' and 'culture' exist at all in the sense that those who study mind and culture think they exist, then certainly they exist in a way that is different from the mode of existence of mere material objects. That, of course, is one big part of what the 3000-year-old argument about the reality status of 'ideas' is about. Can a World 1 science go all the way? The argument is about whether 'ideas' and the mental processes that make them available to human beings actually have more than just a World 1 material existence, and need to be understood in a different sort of way, as ideas and mental processes per se. It seems to me that reference to an 'astral plane' over and above the material world, Popper's World 3 (for example), may not be a bad way to index all that. It is certainly no more mysterious and wondrous than the experience of consciousness itself. Perhaps the 'ideas' made manifest in cultural practices exist in an astral plane not very far away from the place where Gottlob Frege, and at least some philosophers of mathematics, think the truths of logic and mathematics exist (or subsist) before they are discovered. The concept of 'zero' is not a material thing, but enough elaborated on that score in this context. This is not 'consilient' intellectual territory in which 'After all …' is the best way to open a conversation. The mind/body problem is not solved, any more (here moving to the other side of the fence) than issues of 'salvation' are addressed, by taking a picture of the brain activity of sinners in a confessional booth.

My main point, however, is that creative and useful science goes on in social science research centres despite the fact that across and within such research institutions there is a conspicuous absence of 'consilience' and considerable disagreement about whether the unification of knowledge is even a worthy ideal. Most researchers, even those who are totally out of sympathy with each other and find it difficult to credit or make sense of what the other is doing, believe that progress is being made on the problem on which they are working. I would suggest, in many cases, they are right.

6   The crisis literature in the Social Sciences

Finally, then, here is that second glimpse of the current intellectual scene, this time in the social sciences. If one takes a look at the crisis literature in the social sciences one will find four types of complaints, of which I shall focus on three (see Shweder & Fiske, 1986).

6.1   Complaint 1

Social-science generalizations are typically restricted in scope. The modal social science generalization is bound to a particular population studied at a particular historical time in a particular culture and often restricted to the particular methodology used in the investigations (so-called 'method effects'). In other words, as Lee Cronbach (1975) has noted, in the social sciences 'generalizations decay' (as you move from one population to another or across historical eras or across methods). As Donald Campbell (1972) has noted, in the social sciences (including psychology, that ambiguously and ambivalently 'non-social social science') 'higher order interactions are the rule, and main effects, ceteris paribus generalizations, the rare exception'. [For a sustained critique of the quest for 'abstractionism' in the social sciences, see Jerome Kagan's (1998) book *Three Seductive Ideas.*]

Here, I might add that given that 'main effects' are the rare exception, it is generally hazardous in the social sciences to rush to generalizations about all human beings. I suspect that Professor Wilson has been tempted in that hazardous direction in his interpretation of animal phobias. I do not think we really know very much about animal phobias around the world. We need much more good ethnographic and experimental evidence on this topic, but I will bet that when the cross-cultural developmental evidence is actually in, it will be far more complicated and qualified than Wilson (2000) suggests in his keynote address. Even with the limited evidence that is available it is not obvious that we should conclude that there are universal biologically driven rules, readily understandable from a Darwinian adaptationist point of view, for the acquisition of specific animal phobias.

What we know about animal phobias comes mainly from research done in Europe and North America. In that limited database, 90% of those adults who have animal phobias are women, so even in those populations the inclination is restricted to a small subset of one half of the members of the species. More importantly, the list of animals that women with phobias fear the most is not obviously predictable from a Darwinian point of view. What does Darwinian theory actually predict about which animals should be on the list of phobic objects (and which should not) for specific populations of people? North American and European women who have animal phobias are afraid of snakes, and they are afraid of spiders and mice, but they are also afraid of frogs and birds. Yet they are not afraid of wolves or lions or elephants. It seems to me that biological adaptationists (it is all about getting your genes into the next generation) need to tell us a lot more about what their theory actually predicts about the evolution of fears for specific populations. They need to do this before making strong claims about how the current evidence on animal phobias confirms the theory. What if specific non-human animal phobias (e.g. a snake phobia, a bird phobia) are sex-specific in middle-class Anglo-American populations, but not sex-specific among baboons? Is that a point against a Darwinian biological adaptationist theory? What, if anything, does count as a point against this 'theory'?

6.2 Complaint 2

Social science theories and schools of thought do not converge over time. Multiple paradigms persist and the set of concepts and theories that guide research and the interpretation of evidence are as various today as they were 50 or even 100 years ago.

6.3 Complaint 3

Meanings, intentions, ideas, values, emotions, and all other aspects of human consciousness, phenomenological experience or subjectivity cannot be studied scientifically, because they are not the types of things (observable material entities that can be located in time and space) that science was designed to study. In other words, some social scientists (those who are the most 'humanistic') believe that the subject matter of the social sciences puts them outside the proper realm of science. Wilson's response to this, of course, is to argue that their subject matter is not what these humanists thought it was, and that meanings, intentions, and all the other stuff of consciousness is inherently material and, hence, the 'matter' of the natural sciences, after all. Lurking behind these types of complaints are one or more presuppositions about the criteria that distinguish mature science from protoscience from non-science from nonsense; and those presuppositions it turns out make a big difference for whether one perceives a crisis at all. For example, Converse (1986) has argued that 'a model of science that suggests that either we can, in T. S. Eliot's words, 'roll the universe into a ball' with one grand summary expression like $E = MC^2$, or we are not engaging in science is a false model'. He argues that there is a different 'texture' to different fields of rigorous disciplined inquiry depending on their subject matter.

A related point has been made by Roy D'Andrade (1986), who presents us with an ethnographic account of the diversity of models and ideals of science that he finds among practicing researchers. He argues:

> that the sciences contain at least three very different world views, that of the physical sciences, that of the natural sciences, and that of the semiotic sciences; ... that the pursuit of 'general laws' is characteristic primarily of the physical sciences; ... that some of the natural sciences, such as biology, have done well despite the fact that they have not found general laws; ... that in the social sciences there is a considerable division between the natural science approach and the semiotic approach [which involves the interpretation of what something 'means'] without a reasonable synthesis in view ... (D'Andrade, 1986)

Of course, where D'Andrade reports plural scientific world views and a division in relationship to which no synthesis is in sight between natural science and interpretive social science, Wilson senses that a new age of 'consilience' is close at hand.

My answer to all this, as one may have already realized, is to suggest that plurality is inherent in science (just as it is in religion, culture, and society). This is precisely because evidence and logic alone are not sufficient conditions for the development of knowledge systems. Reality testing is a metaphysical act, which relies on various aspects of the imagination, including category systems, background assumptions, metaphors, etc. Hence, I do not expect scientific debate and controversy about fundamental issues to ever come to an end. Because I do not believe that convergence in belief is a mark of the maturity of a scholarly discipline I do not worry, as some do worry, about the future of the social sciences.

I believe that either (a) our current account of the nature of the material world is incomplete (because it cannot handle the role of 'meaning' without terrorizing or eliminating the concept of meaning itself) or (b) human beings have a nature that takes them beyond the material world, in which case reference to other worlds (Popper's World 2—the mental world—and Popper's World 3, the world of 'ideas') must play a central part in any science of human action. Given the central role of meaning as a causal factor for human beings the restriction of scope of generalizations in the social sciences and humanities is thus entirely expectable. The discovery of such meaning-dependent or context-dependent regularities is highly respectable, because it honours the truth.

7   The 'queep' and the 'deep' of life: meaning and divergence in science

Here is a small example (with big implications) of what happens when meaning enters our nervous system. The example comes from Benjamin Lee Whorf and can be found in his writings on *Language, Thought and Reality* (Whorf, 1956, p. 257). He is famous for his work on linguistic relativity, but he was fully aware of the existence of some species typifying affective or synaesthetic responses to stimuli of various kinds. He notes that the semantically meaningless sound pattern 'queep' elicits a universal set of affective or 'feeling-tone' associations when it interacts with the human nervous system. Whether you are in the highlands of New Guinea or in Manhattan, whether you speak English, Guugu Yimidhirr, or Russian, 'queep', the nonsense syllable, is judged to be 'fast' (rather than 'slow'), 'sharp' (rather than 'dull'), 'light' (rather than 'dark'), 'narrow' (rather than 'wide'). Our affective response to 'queep' is automatic and may well be preprogrammed, a feature of our common biology.

However, notice what happens when semantic meaning enters the picture. Whorf asks us to consider the sound pattern 'deep'. As a material thing (and as a pure sound pattern) 'deep' is very similar to 'queep'. For speakers of languages in which 'deep' is a nonsense syllable (i.e. most languages of the world) the sound pattern 'deep' elicits exactly the same set of affective or 'feeling-tone' associations ('fast', 'sharp', 'light', 'narrow') as does 'queep', but 'deep' is not just a physical entity (or pure sound) for English speakers. It is a word in our language. It has semantic meaning, and that meaning totally overrides its impact as pure physical sound (the sound merely becomes the vehicle of the meaning) and completely reverses our nervous system response. For speakers of English, and only for English speakers, 'deep' is judged to be 'slow', 'dull', 'dark', and 'wide'. That is one of the reasons that so many interpretive social scientists are prepared to argue for the duality of human nature, meaning and mind over and above mechanism and body, the 'angel' over and above the 'beast'. There is something more to our nature than just the material realities that meet the ear (or the eye), plus the nervous system that is common to us all. The challenge for the humanities and the social sciences has always been to get 'ideas' and our capacity to be sensitive to what things 'mean' into the picture without completely reducing the 'mental' to the 'material' or 'matterings' to 'matter'. Contemplating a human being as 'a hairless gorilla with a big brain' does not quite do the trick.

Notes

1 This essay was originally presented as an address at the New York Academy of Sciences (NYAS) Conference on *Unity of Knowledge: the convergence of natural and human science* in June 2000, and as a critique of the idea of consilience as represented by E. O. Wilson, Keynote Speaker at the NYAS conference (published 2001 in: *Ann NY Acad Sci* **935**: 217–232). The essay is republished here, slightly revised and abbreviated, in a form that has been edited to read more like a book essay. Parts of the essay are informed by the author's participation in the Bremen 'Voluntary Action' conference (organized by the editors of this volume) that is the catalyst for this book.

2 Richard Strohman (1993) has written a critique of the genetic paradigm in biology and medicine in which he makes the points that 98% of diseases are not monogenetic, and that, although there is a genetic basis for 'speaking French', there probably are no 'speaking-French genes'. Or if there are 'speaking-French genes' it is only in the sense that there is a genetic basis for being a human being who is capable of learning French. This is a very old point, but apparently it still needs to be made.

3 Note that for some reason the expression 'It is not rocket science' has not yet been replaced in popular discourse by such phrases as 'It is not brain science' or 'It is not genetic engineering'. Perhaps this is just a case of cultural lag and the popular recognition of a shift in scientific prestige from nuclear physics to microbiology is only a matter of time. Perhaps the public is waiting to see whether the human genome project is actually going to realize its quite benevolent medical dreams or will turn out instead to be a eugenics nightmare or else just a very expensive dead-end.

References

Campbell, D.T. (1972) Herskovits, cultural relativism, and metascience. In Herskovits, F. (ed.), *Cultural Relativism*. New York: Random House, pp. v-xxiii.

Converse, P.E. (1986) Generalization and the social psychology of 'other worlds'. In Fiske, D.W. & Shweder, R.A. (eds), *Metatheory in Social Science: pluralisms and subjectivities*. Chicago: University of Chicago Press, pp. 42–60.

Cronbach, L.J. (1975) Beyond the two disciplines of scientific psychology. *Am Psychol* **30**, 116–37.

D'Andrade, R.G. (1986) Three scientific world views and the covering law model. In Fiske, D.W. & Shweder, R.A. (eds), *Metatheory in Social Science: pluralisms and subjectivities*. Chicago: University of Chicago Press, pp. 19–41.

Edelson, M. (1984) *Hypothesis and Evidence in Psychoanalysis*. Chicago: University of Chicago Press.

Geertz, C. (2000) *Available Light: anthropological reflections on philosophical topics*. Princeton: Princeton University Press.

Kagan, J. (1998) *Three Seductive Ideas*. Cambridge: Harvard University Press.

Kuhn, T. (1962) *The Structure of Scientific Revolutions*. Chicago: University of Chicago Press.

Osgood, C., May, W. & Miron, M. (1975) *Cross-cultural Universals of affective meaning*. University of Illinois Press. Urbana, Illinois.

Popper, K.R. & Eccles, J.C. (1977) *The Self and its Brain*. New York: Springer-Verlag.

Quine, W.V.O. (1953) Two dogmas of empiricism. In Quine, W.V.O. (ed.), *From a Logical Point of View*. New York: Harper & Row, pp. 20–46.

Quine, W.V.O. (1969) *Ontological Relativity and Other Essays*. New York: Columbia University Press.

Richter, F.M. (1986) Non-linear behaviour. In Fiske, D.W. & Shweder, R.A. (eds), *Metatheory in Social Science: pluralisms and subjectivities* Chicago: University of Chicago Press, pp. 284–92.

Rorty, R. (1991) *Philosophical Papers.* Cambridge: Cambridge University Press.

Shweder, R.A. (1991) *Thinking Through Cultures: expeditions in cultural psychology.* Cambridge: Harvard University Press.

Shweder, R.A. (1996) True ethnography. In Jessor, R., Colby, A. & Shweder, R.A. (eds), *Ethnography and Human Development: context and meaning in social inquiry.* Chicago: University of Chicago Press, pp. 15–52.

Shweder, R.A. (1999) Why cultural psychology? *Ethos: J Soc Psycholog Anthropol* **27**, 62–73.

Shweder, R.A. & **LeVine, R.A.** (1984) *Culture Theory: essays on mind, self and emotion.* Cambridge: Cambridge University Press.

Shweder, R.A. & **Fiske, D.W.** (1986) Uneasy social science. In Fiske, D.W. & Shweder, R.A. (eds), *Metatheory in Social Science: pluralisms and subjectivities.* Chicago: University of Chicago Press, pp. 1–18.

Shweder, R.A., Much, N., Mahapatra, M. & **Park, L.** (1996) The 'Big Three of Morality' (autonomy, community, divinity) and the 'Big Three' explanations of suffering. In Brandt, A. & Rozin, P. (eds), *Morality and Health.* New York: Routledge, pp. 119–72.

Shweder, R.A & **Haidt, J.** (2000) The cultural psychology of the emotions: ancient and new. In Lewis, M. & Haviland, J. (eds), *Handbook of Emotions.* New York: Guilford, pp. 397–414.

Strohman, R.C. (1993) Ancient genomes, wise bodies, unhealthy people: Limits of a genetic paradigm in biology and medicine. *Perspect Biol Med* **37**, 112–45.

Whorf, B.L. (1956) *Language, Thought and Reality.* Cambridge: MIT Press.

Wilson, E.O. (1998) *Consilience: the unity of knowledge.* New York: Alfred Knopf.

Wilson, E.O. (2000) How to unify knowledge. Keynote address at the New York Academy of Science Conference on *The Unity of Knowledge: the convergence of natural and human science*, June 23, 2000. *Ann NY acad Sci*, **935**: 12–17.

Wittgenstein, L. (1953) *Philosophical Investigations.* Oxford: Oxford University Press.

Wittgenstein, L. (1969) *On Certainty.* Oxford: Blackwell.

CHAPTER 16

A VIEW FROM ELSEWHERE: THE EMERGENCE OF CONSCIOUSNESS IN MULTIDISCIPLINARY DISCOURSE

SABINE MAASEN

1 Becoming conscious of consciousness

'The past decade has seen a rising tide of interest in consciousness accompanied by a surge of publications, new journals and scientific meetings' (Zeman, 2001, p. 1264). Today, this is perhaps the best way to open the floor to any review of the field of consciousness. The sheer amount of activities in consciousness research is stunning, indeed, particularly in view of the fact that all studies and approaches are united by one conviction only: 'At our present state of the investigation of consciousness we don't know how it works and we need to try all kinds of different ideas' (John Searle).

Quite fittingly, this statement is quoted on the cover page of the newly established *Journal of Consciousness Studies* [*JCS*, 1994, here: 2 (1), 1995]. Other than journals like *Cognition and Consciousness* or *Psyche*, *JCS* makes a point of inviting international scholarship from a broad array of disciplines, especially focusing—thus the subtitle of *JCS*—on 'controversies in science and the humanities'. It is designed to make progress in consciousness studies by way of providing a platform for multidisciplinary contributions on all issues and approaches that currently may be considered relevant and/or promising. Those considerations, however, vary significantly. While some maintain that phenomenal experience is beyond the reach of science, scientists make strong claims about consciousness that, they hold, will soon render non-scientific accounts obsolete.

Following the editors of *JCS*, however, both the sciences and the humanities have much, if different, things to say about consciousness. Sadly enough, thus far, cross-disciplinary discourse has been insufficient. What is more, debate across disciplinary borders, including, for example, theological or political accounts of consciousness, has been virtually non-existent, and in some cases even actively avoided. The editors themselves consider their project both ambitious and risky, yet worthwhile. Given the history and present state in consciousness studies, which can safely (and undisputedly) be characterized by vividness, yet heterogeneity and a high degree of mutual ignorance as well, multidisciplinary exchange, according to the editors, is called for: mutual enrichment (once again!) nourishes the hope for synergies in research, and some authors even envisage a new and powerful interdiscipline named consciousness (or inter-field, Darden & Maull, 1977).

Clearly, consciousness has become 'an issue' in academic discourse, though this is not to say that consciousness is altogether new on the agenda. On the contrary, it has been an object of contemplation for centuries (e.g. in philosophy and theology); it has been dealt with by political economists (e.g. Karl Marx) and by early psychologists (e.g. William James); it can be found in esoteric speculation and in social scientific studies on feminist, racial, or environmental consciousness. Yet another concern is directed toward the (deep-rooted) notion of self-consciousness. In other words, consciousness has for centuries been a matter of diverse, yet systematic contemplation and concern.

What is new, however, is that it has become the focus of a concerted *scientific* effort. Most notably, the neuro- and the cognitive sciences inquire into the 'brainy bases' of consciousness. At the most provocative end, authors straightforwardly deny any mysterious experiential aspect, that is, they deny the existence of 'qualia', of 'what it is like' to be or to feel (Nagel, 1986). Rather, they insist on consciousness being nothing but the name for the interplay of various regions in the brain upon which cognitive functions operate. Other than that, talking about experiential or phenomenal aspects of consciousness is rejected as folk-psychological wisdom: put to the extreme, its function is claimed to be neither a physiological nor a cognitive, but a purely social one; consciousness is an institution invented to attribute causation and responsibility to a self—it is 'I-talk' (cf. Kusch, 2000).

Such claims have far-reaching implications for notions of voluntary action: in keeping with the stances aforementioned, cognitive psychologists such as Prinz (this volume), for instance, hold that volition does not cause, but follows action.[1] Volition, too, is merely an afterthought produced in the social sphere, regulating individual behaviour in social interaction by way of attributing, for instance, guilt or blameworthiness. Recast in more general psychological terms, the implications of such a stance become all the more evident, if not threatening. The long-cherished notion of the 'I' being the 'lord in the manor' (cf. Roth, this volume) cannot, say the cognitive scientists, be upheld any longer. Accordingly, this claim provokes a heated debate both on the issue of the 'voluntarily acting self' and on the underlying, more general issue of consciousness.[2] Are we indeed and do we just act upon an assembly of neurons and cognitive functions?

In other words, the debate is characterized by bold inputs from the neurosciences and cognitive psychology, and by philosophers, of who only a minor faction responds to the monist challenge at all. In fact, as most philosophers keep reminding us, we discuss the 'mind–body problem', an age-old, self-insistent paradox: While we believe ourselves to be physical beings, we also believe that we are conscious beings whose awareness of physical beings cannot be physical. It thus seems that we are both physical and non-physical. The problem is: how do the physical and non-physical relate? More specifically, how does the physical lead to the non-physical or how does the non-physical lead to the physical? By definition, the physical and the non-physical have no means of 'communication'—hence the problem.[3]

While neurobiology, cognitive psychology, and parts of philosophy engage in research and controversial discussion, sociological, anthropological, juridical, let alone theological and non-science discourses, as yet, seem to be a minority issue—the assemblage and order of disciplines contributing to this book being indicative for their respective input into general discussion and their impact. In this situation, *JCS*, by way of fostering an even broader debate, is interesting in that it highlights the directions and difficulties a general plea for multidisciplinarity consciousness research faces up to. A closer discourse analysis of this journal throughout its existence (1994 until today) will reveal not only the recent shifts in consciousness studies, but also the legitimating narrative and ongoing reflections guiding further efforts in various multidisciplinarities.[4]

In fact, the recent debates on consciousness are all characterized by 'building bridges', in the course of which various multi-, inter-, and trans-disciplinarities emerge.[5] These moves emerge out of the underlying tension between physical and phenomenal aspects of consciousness. This tension does not manifest itself in a linear shift toward a scientific approach to consciousness. Rather, those who regard this shift as impoverished simultaneously explore alternative ways to capture consciousness as both a physical and non-physical phenomenon, thereby focusing on, for example, spiritual, social scientific, aesthetic experiences. Virtually all these attempts are multidisciplinary, convening different assortments of expertise across the scientific cultures. Ultimately, this turns both the concept of consciousness and the field of consciousness studies into hybrids—a state that, in turn, provokes further debates and alliances.

However, before going into the details of the discourse on consciousness, which—not unjustly—has been termed the 'consciousness hype' (Shapiro), I would like to present a view from the outside: What are the dimensions of consciousness research and do they change over time? How many contributions do we have, by which disciplines, and what are their prime concerns? Drawing such a discursive map first will help to go beyond initial impressions (cf. above) and to formulate more precise hypotheses, which will then guide the more thorough discourse analysis of *JCS*. As yet, we can merely suspect that consciousness is a hot topic that, to a large degree, derives its impact from various denials as regards its existence or from its relegation to folk psychology, respectively. As scientific paradigms multiply and philosophical wisdom is challenged, social scientific approaches are struggling against oblivion and folk knowledge may soon be shaken as well. Presently, we observe nothing less than the emergence of a *new concept*, if not a *new interdisciplinary field* called consciousness. We observe the making and remaking of a specific 'piece of knowledge', produced and reproduced (mainly, as yet) in the academic arena. This calls for a different perspective, a sociology-of-knowledge point of view.

After a brief introduction to the issue of metaphor and the method called metaphor analysis, I will present the outline of the broader study. This outline starts by presenting a discursive map and calendar concerning the discourse on consciousness. Based on Science Citation Index and Social Sciences Citation Index (ISI) databanks, I will first inquire into the quantitative dimensions of consciousness research: How many contributions do we have; from which disciplines; what are their prime concerns; do they change over time? This will help to go beyond initial impressions (cf. above), and strictly includes only those discursive contributions that are explicitly concerned with consciousness (as indicated by mentioning the term in either the title or the abstract). These data will lead to more detailed observations, which will then be confronted with views from within cognitive neuroscience. Thereafter, the analysis will be complemented by a brief discourse analysis of the above-mentioned recently established journal, the *Journal of Consciousness Studies*. Its policy is to re-open the scientific debate to phenomenal approaches of various kinds. An overview of the themes published throughout its 8 years of existence will also be confronted with views from within the emerging scientific-cum-humanist community.

The rationale for this sequence of studies, switching between quantitative description and analyses of views from within, is to further disclose the intricacies of the where and how of current, possibly paradigmatic, changes in consciousness studies.

2   Looking from a different angle

From a sociology-of-knowledge point of view, 'consciousness' is but a piece of knowledge circulating in society. Consciousness does not 'belong' to any special discourse—philosophy, or to inner experience, or forefront brain research. Rather, it occurs in various contexts, thereby assuming various meanings or shades of meanings. These different meanings are partly dwelling side by side, happily ignoring each other, but also partly interacting or competing. This holds true for philosophical, psychological, neurobiological, or everyday notions of consciousness; without going into detail, all these notions can be safely said to differ in both scope and impact, maybe even differing in kind.

What difference does a sociology-of-knowledge viewpoint make? A scientist, a philosopher, a theologian, or a guru's task is to discern the 'true meaning' of consciousness in terms of his or her respective interest, and with the help of methods, research, or contemplative strategies, vocabularies, and theories developed in their area (or at the margins of related fields). A sociologist of knowledge, however, has a different viewpoint: She wants to know what a given society or culture over a given period of time conceives of as 'consciousness'. The introduction was meant to emphasize that there are, at present, various conceptions of consciousness and, what is more, they vary *among* and *within* the discourses referring to it. In other words, a sociology-of-knowledge approach, interested in the making of 'knowledges' in society, seeks to reveal the multidiscursive constructions of terms or concepts. In particular, if a certain term or concept is a volatile one, that is, 'voguish' or attractive for various uses in ever-new contexts, it will become more or less heterogeneous—due to its interaction with those contexts.

Therefore, sociology of knowledge is not and cannot be about definitions. To put it bluntly: I will not define what consciousness is. Rather—on a certain level of analysis—I will do something else: I will trace *the emergence of consciousness as a heterogeneous concept*, asking questions such as 'In which discourses does consciousness occur and when? What does the respective discursive context do to the term and, conversely, what does the term do to its respective contexts of application? Do the various shades of meaning ignore, interact, or compete with one another?' Asking those questions implies the conception of consciousness as a site and medium of meaning production.

The idea is that by way of interacting with novel contexts consciousness assumes novel (shades of) meaning. In a way, that is, consciousness acts like a metaphor. According to prominent accounts in metaphor theory, a metaphor is a term or phrase that is somewhat unfamiliar with respect to its poetic context. Both unfamiliar phrase and poetic context need to interact, thereby producing an innovative reading that 'makes sense'. Likewise, consciousness, formerly to be found in non-scientific contexts only, finds itself used in various scientific fields: Interacting with them, it undergoes shifts in meaning and usage, which themselves become the object of affirmation and critique in yet other discourses.

To this end, the next section will introduce the notion of metaphor in more detail by way of sketching some metaphors of consciousness first. Only thereafter will I suggest to treat consciousness itself as a metaphor and explain a special method called metaphor analysis.

The rationale for this sequence of studies, switching between (quantitative) description and analyses of views from within, is to disclose more precisely the intricacies of the wheres and hows of major, possibly paradigmatic, changes in consciousness (studies).

3   Metaphors

3.1   Metaphors of consciousness/consciousness as metaphor

As we turn to metaphor analysis, the reader may well wonder whether this study is about investigating 'metaphors of consciousness'? Although it is not, it might be instructive to take a quick look at some of these metaphors in order to learn more about how they work:

It has frequently been noted that theories of consciousness abound with metaphors. In the domain of psychology, pertinent writings of its founding father, William James, are evidence of this. His *Principles of Psychology* (James, 1890), alongside 'Does "Consciousness" Exist?' (James, 1904), demonstrate how figurative language directs James' study of consciousness. For James, writes Kiss (2000), metaphor does not just describe, but also construct consciousness. It governs his conflicting theories of mind through a series of rhetorical configurations and provokes the continual reconstruction of his ideas of human subjectivity. However, his attitudes toward metaphor are mixed. On the one hand, James presupposes a clearly delineated concept around which one might wrap a verbal expression, while on the other, he also seems painfully aware of the fact that every new metaphor launches an entirely new theory. James therefore creates a series of metaphors out of which consciousness materializes: liquid metaphors, nuclear metaphors, ethereal metaphors, corporeal metaphors. The ultimate principle of Jamesian consciousness seems to be its creative capacity, which he translates into his notion of 'pure experience', while simultaneously remaining committed to figures of speech (especially 'stream of consciousness').

Both before and after James, authors have invented a host of further metaphors of consciousness in order to gain access to an ever-elusive concept. Among many other things, consciousness has been likened to a spotlight, a recursive loop, a stage; likewise, its specific quality has been described as a state, an act, input or output, as a unity, a diversity, or *a unitas multiplex* (cf. Bruner & Fleisher Feldman, 1990, p. 230). An important basic metaphor of consciousness is nakedness ('bare consciousness', 'mere sensing'), put forward by Aristotle (*sensus communis*) and John Locke ('primary qualities'). These metaphors all advance a reproductive or passive view of consciousness: certain ideas are somehow pushed or pulled into the mind. A more productive or active view of consciousness has been advocated by scholars like Kant or Leibniz: From their angle, 'the contents of consciousness are what mind creates rather than what mind encounters' (Bruner & Fleisher Feldman, 1990, p. 232). Both views, however, distinguish between an inside and an outside of consciousness, detailing the various functions of consciousness, such as the function of 'shielding' itself from the demands of the external world and the unconscious (e.g. Freud).

Information-processing models of contemporary cognitive science are recent sources for metaphors of consciousness. It is conceived of as the 'readout' at the end of 'filtering' processes. These filters change over time, depending on what one knows about perceptual processes and depending on the machine analogues (cf. Bruner & Fleisher Feldman, 1990, p. 234).

The difference in reproductive versus productive views of consciousness has been more clearly delineated by metaphors of cognition. On the one hand, there are those that picture the mind as a 'mirror of nature'; on the other, there are metaphors of illumination (e.g. searchlights, spotlights), creative synthesis (e.g. mental chemistry, construction), assignment of meaning (e.g. semantic networks, encoding/decoding), or topography (e.g. cognitive maps, schema). Another set of metaphors centres upon symbolism: Symbolism advances language (icons, indexes, symbols) rather than physics as the most appropriate source for metaphors of cognition. These metaphors, according to Bruner and Fleisher Feldman, highlight what consciousness *does* instead of what it *is*, and ask about the uses to which it may be put in constructing meaning and in assigning interpretations. Whether or not one agrees with this assessment, one may nevertheless feel that the basic message is well argued: The study of consciousness (and cognition) abounds with metaphors and thus is indicative of the psychology involved, the questions it asks, the conceptions it arrives at.[6]

As regards the neurosciences, the theatre metaphor has been suggested by classical and current authors, Pavlov and Crick being pertinent examples. Today, the theatre metaphor branches off into a network of submetaphors: it has been suggested that consciousness might be associated with cortical convergence zones, and that theatres exist to allow numerous convergent influences to shape a coherent performance on stage (cf. Damasio, 1989). However, the theatre metaphor—as any—has met with criticism as well: Dennett and Kinsbourne, for instance, deem it Cartesian and thus misleading (cf. Dennett & Kinsbourne, 1992). Others hold that computers could simulate virtually all hypotheses deriving from the theatre metaphor. Still others claim that some aspects of consciousness are not amenable to explanation, either with or without metaphors, that is. Only few scholars seem to value metaphors as productive, more precisely, that certain metaphors are indeed productive for certain scientific problems. Bernard J. Baars pleads energetically for the value of the theatre metaphor when it comes to scientific reasoning about consciousness. For him, 'the fundamental function of the theatre architecture is to make possible novel, adaptive interactions between the sensory inflow, motor outflow and a range of knowledge sources in the brain' (Baars, 1988, p. 59, 1). Generally speaking, 'the criteria for productive metaphors are the same as for other scientific ideas: they should help organize existing evidence, yield testable hypotheses and suggest conceptual clarifications' (Baars, 1988, p. 59, 2).[7]

Rather than going into these suggestions in any depth, however, I would like to focus on the issue of metaphors in a more general sense. Reviewing the points made by the psychologists and neurobiologists just mentioned, we can broadly summarize them as follows: metaphors

- seem *inevitable*—certainly, they are ubiquitous in scientific as well as in other discourses;
- are *intricate*, that is, irritating and always contested elements of (scientific) discourse;[8]
- have all kinds of impact on (scientific) reasoning, *innovative* ones included.

Indeed, by confronting consciousness with various metaphors, some of its aspects, functions, and modes of operation have been highlighted, whereas others have been shaded or have turned out to be neutral (cf. Hesse, 1974). Every new metaphor provokes new ideas, as well as criticism; sometimes both innovators and critics co-establish a new, elaborated language game, which then guides further research for a while. This is the general message as regards metaphors of consciousness: whatever consciousness is supposed to mean at a given point in time is the result of an encounter with the discourses (and their preferred metaphors) interacting with it. True to its Greek origin (*meta-phorein* = transfer), a metaphor is about transferring and shifting meanings.

The aforementioned mechanism is the point of departure for a more radical idea: one could apply the notion of metaphor to any term or concept that apparently undergoes significant changes. This idea contends that these changes come about due to new discourses interacting with a particular term, thereby instigating shifts and changes in the term's uses and meanings. Why not suppose, along with Mary Hesse and others ('all language is metaphorical', cf. Hesse, 1974), that this is how discourses evolve—by way of terms, concepts, vocabularies, and world views interacting with one another? Adopting this stance, I therefore suggest the re-conceptualization of the notion of metaphors as methodical devices. Hence, instead of analysing metaphors of consciousness I suggest we treat consciousness itself as a metaphor. The study will follow the term consciousness to those discourses in which it happens to occur and will look for the respective interactions. This type of method has been termed metaphor analysis.[9] It aims to provide an account of major instances of knowledge dynamics by looking at metaphors as units of knowledge and discourses and their environments of knowledge, both selecting against each other.

3.2   On metaphor analysis

In order to grasp fully the way in which metaphors can function as sites and media of knowledge transfer (cf. Bono, 1990), one needs to take stock of basic metaphor theoretical insights and to transfer them into a sociology-of-knowledge framework. Semantic, pragmatic, and constructivist theories emphasize different aspects of metaphors.

The *semantic* view of metaphors has been advanced by Max Black (Black, 1962) and Mary Hesse (Hesse, 1972). According to them, metaphors serve to re-describe a phenomenon of a primary system in terms of a secondary system and, in so doing, interact with one another. According to Black, however, this interaction will ultimately lead to a mutual transfer of meanings or aspects of them. Thus, semantic theories are about shifting meanings in both metaphor and context.

Pragmatic theories stress the importance of processing a metaphor within the importing discourse. Donald Davidson advances the idea that a 'metaphor belongs to the domain of use. It is something brought off by the imaginative employment of words and sentences and depends entirely on the ordinary meanings of those words and hence on the ordinary meanings of the sentences they comprise' (cf. Davidson, 1981, p. 202). Thus, pragmatic theories are about new meaning(s) as a product of the interaction between the literal meanings of both metaphor and context.

Thus, when reformulated in *constructivist* terms, an unfamiliar element (i.e. a metaphor), according to Rorty, not only forces us to process both metaphor and its immediate context, but also provokes an entire 'new vocabulary' (Rorty, 1989) in which both the metaphor and its context make sense. On a less radical note, one might learn from 'ethnotheories' in the area of scientific innovation: these regard metaphorical transfer of knowledge as a regular occurrence, since the concepts or models that become analogized have already figured as 'solutions' in other fields. From this perspective, and opposed to Rorty's view, a metaphor is something already known or familiar with respect to a context that is novel or unfamiliar. In both versions, however, constructivist theories are about inventing a new language game capable of integrating metaphor and context in a meaningful way.

Enlightened by the accounts just given, I suggest 'metaphorizing' the concept of metaphors: a discourse-analytical approach conceives of metaphors as single discursive elements within a broader discursive context. Whereas discourses are language games that have become thoroughly familiar, metaphors are (freshly imported) terms or concepts that are (still) unfamiliar to their context (cf. Davidson, Rorty). Thus, speaking of metaphors always means to be speaking of a *relationship* between a concept and a discourse. Secondly, it always implies an aspect of *transience*.[10]

Both the relational and the transient aspects of metaphors turn them into ideal candidates for observing the invention, circulation, and modification of knowledge. From a discourse-analytical level, the discursive processing of a metaphor can be described as one of those mechanisms by which the production of knowledge is controlled, selected, organized, and channelled (cf. Foucault, 1974). That is, if an already established discourse (i.e. cognitive psychology) selects *for* a certain metaphor (i.e. 'consciousness'), it necessarily varies the meaning of consciousness by interpreting it discourse-specifically, and perhaps it retains this new meaning (cf. Luhmann, 1980). Note that this capacity of generating new meaning is not a *feature* of a metaphor, but the *result* of an interaction of a metaphor and its discursive environment.

As to the analytical procedure, these are steps to be taken:

- The first step reads: 'Pick one!'—I pick 'conscious/ness'.

- The second step reads: 'Draw a discursive map!' and: 'Reconstruct a discursive calendar!' With the aid of bibliometric methods I follow the term or concept chosen through all scientific and philosophical discourses in which it appears. The results of this step provide a fair approximation as to the whens and wheres of the metaphor in question. In other words, the dynamics of knowledge are thus represented in quantitative terms: One reveals both the increasing or decreasing occurrences of a certain concept over time and discourses.

- The third step reads: 'Discourse analysis!' Only after the occurrences of a certain metaphor are available, I select a set of publications that seems most productive and enlightening as regards the dynamics of consciousness. Discourse by discourse, I look for specific interaction with the term and confront it with literature commenting on the history, and/or systematicity of any discursive developments (e.g. reviews).

- The fourth step reads: 'Local specificity—global significance?' Do the specific shades of meaning converge on a heterogeneous topic (be it an issue, a paradigm, a cultural matrix ...)? For this is what metaphor analysis is about: It looks for *both* locally specific processing of metaphors *and* for ways in which they—gradually—produce (heterogeneous sets of) meanings across various (types of) discourses for a given period of time.

So what are the dynamics of consciousness now that consciousness itself has become such a highly volatile concept, interacting with cognitive and neurosciences, with philosophy, the social sciences?

4 A metaphor analysis of consciousness

'Consciousness is a word worn smooth by a million tongues. Depending upon the figure of speech chosen it is a state of being, a substance, a process, a place, an epiphenomenon, an emergent aspect of matter, or the only true reality' (Miller, 1963, p. 25). On a very general level, one can isolate a social aspect of the term, that is, joint knowledge shared by a community of people (e.g. Marxist, feminist consciousness) and a mental sense. The latter can be subdivided into the notion of a state concomitant of all thought, feeling, and volition (transitive: conscious of), or as the normal condition of a healthy waking life (intransitive).[11] Thus, stating that consciousness is not one phenomenon today borders on a truism (Chalmers, 1996b, p. 7). Still, it might be worthwhile to look at the most comprehensive databank (the ISI: Science Citation Index/SCI and the Social Science Citation Index/SSCI), which lists journal articles over a broad range of disciplines and covers about 30 years, in order to get a more precise picture:

- How often do the terms 'conscious' and 'consciousness' appear in titles of articles?
- What is the range of disciplines covered by these articles? Does the attention shift from one set of disciplines to another?
- What are the themes associated with consciousness?

At this stage of analysis, the occurrences indicate when, how often, and in which disciplines authors deal with the subject. These observations will be confronted with a view from within the scientific branch of consciousness studies later on.[12]

4.1 Conscious/ness in SCI / SSCI

4.1.1 Absolute and relative occurrence

Throughout a period of 26 years (1975–2000), the terms conscious/ness occur with considerable frequency. Looking at the publications in absolute numbers, the Science Citation Index reveals an increase by a factor of two (from 210 occurrences in 1974 to 435 in 2000) and the Social Science Citation Index an increase by almost a factor of three, although at a lower level (113 in 1974 to 293 in 2000).

The relative frequency of publications paints a different picture: in the natural sciences it remains at about 0.5‰, after a peak of about 0.9‰ in the mid-1980s. In the social sciences, the data show an increase (from 1.25‰ in 1974 to 1.96‰ in 2000; see Figs 16.1 and 16.2).

Taken together, we find noticeable growth in academic publications explicitly dealing with conscious/ness. On the basis of these data one can only speculate about why the natural sciences apparently began to refrain from using the term during the 1990s,

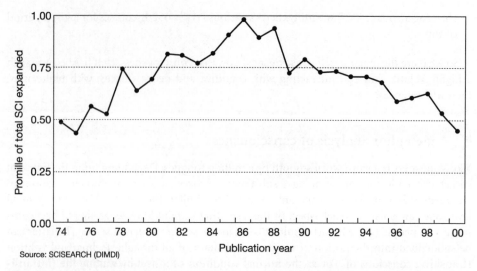

Source: SCISEARCH (DIMDI)

Figure 16.1 Relative frequency of 'consciousness' in titles of articles. Data are based on the Science Citation Index (SCI) 1974–2000.

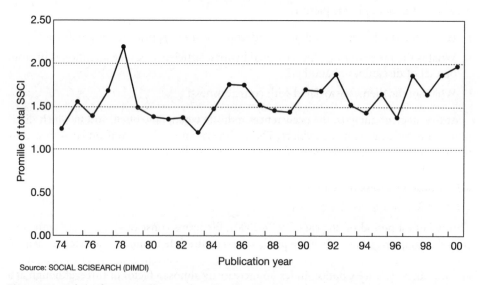

Source: SOCIAL SCISEARCH (DIMDI)

Figure 16.2 Relative frequency of 'consciousness' in titles of articles. Data are based on the Social Science Citation Index (SSCI) 1974–2000.

despite the fact that increased activity on this topic would seem more plausible during that 'decade of the brain'. One reason might be the internal differentiation within the field. When psychologists, philosophers, social scientists, theologians, ethnologists, and scholars in law and politics all write about conscious/ness, scientists may deem it advisable to differentiate, not only in approach and outlook, theory, and method, but also in terms of labels.[13] We can count on the fact that scholars working in the field do use more specific terms in the titles of their publications in order not to become confused with other (i.e. non-scientific) approaches.[14]

4.1.2   Fields

Focusing on selected years (1975, 1980, 1985, 1990, 1995, 2000), I will now investigate the fields in which consciousness studies and research activities are conducted, and those journals that publish the articles we are concerned with here. This line of investigation pursues the breadth and internal structure of scientific interest, i.e. which *disciplines* or *fields* participate in research activities on conscious/ness?

In the SCI, the neurosciences become the most important field dealing with conscious/ness, followed by physiology, pharmacology, and pharmacy. Biology, including cell biology, covers the middle ground. Medicine, general and internal, seems to have become less important over the years, as opposed to those branches of medicine that are orientated toward experimental research.

The SSCI also reveals a broad array of *fields* dealing with conscious/ness, ranging from psychology, psychiatry, and philosophy, through the social, political, and historical sciences to law, anthropology, education, area studies, language, and linguistics. Yet, here as well, we find hierarchies of interest in the issue among the disciplines. The leading field throughout the years is psychology, ranging from 15.66% in 1975 to 56.7% in 2000. While this includes subfields, such as clinical, developmental, and social psychology, there is a noticeable increase in experimental psychology dealing with conscious/ness (1985: 2.29%; 1995: 8.23%; 2000: 33.84%). At the same time (1985, 1990, 1995), the field of neuroscience contributes 8–15% of the publications on conscious/ness. Throughout these years, the academic involvement with conscious/ness becomes more experimental, more cognitive, more 'neuro', and most of all, more pharmacological.

What about philosophy and the social sciences, the two prominent contributors to consciousness throughout the 1970s and 1980s? Philosophy, although under-represented in the ISI data,[15] shows a considerable decrease in publications on conscious/ness. Initially providing about 9% of the articles (1975), they range from 1.21 to 2.13% in 1995/2000. A similar trend can be found in political science and history: starting on the same level, they decrease rapidly in the 1990s (to about 1%). Other fields dealing with sociocultural aspects of consciousness, such as law, anthropology, and religion, mostly contribute about 1 or 2% of all articles per year. Sociology, however, maintains a steady level of about 10%, with the exception of 1995 (5.57%) and a noticeable increase in 2000 (17.37%). Despite the latter finding, it is most obvious that philosophical and social scientific treatment of conscious/ness are a minority issue, especially in view of the fact that the percentages have to be seen in relation to the absolute numbers of publications covered by the SCI and the SSCI, respectively. (The SSCI contains only half as many articles published on consciousness as the SCI!). Although research on consciousness in the social sciences exists, this is evidently not 'where the iron is at its hottest'.

4.1.3 Journals

When it comes to the leading journals that publish scientific articles on conscious/ness, their primary concern with physiology and pharmacology is evident. Journals such as *British Journal of Pharmacology*, *American Journal of Pharmacology*, as well as *Circulation*, for instance, publish the major share of articles on conscious/ness. Yet another community, the neurosciences, figures less prominently: *Behavioral and Brain Sciences*, *Brain Research*, *Neuropsychologia*, and *Neurophysiology* publish 1.27% (1980), 2.2% (1985), 4.99% (1990), and 4.31% (2000) of all articles mentioning conscious/ness in their title. One exception is the year 1995, when more than 10% of all publications appeared in neuroscientific journals. Based on these data, one can conclude that within the natural sciences, research on conscious/ness is primarily a physiological phenomenon, addressed in a variety of different communities, yet most prominently in the context of pharmacological application.

As regards social scientific articles on conscious/ness, they are scattered over a broad spectrum of journals that publish one or two articles at most (in 1975 and 1980). Since 1985, *Behavioral and Brain Sciences* has been listed in the data and has dominated the field (1985: 6.42%; 1990: 9.27%; 1995: 18.8%) from the start, only to be overtaken by *Consciousness and Cognition* in 2000 (28.67%).[16] Next come journals that belong more specifically to the area of psychology. Since 1990, a few journals have been founded that bridge philosophical and psychological concerns with conscious/ness: the *Journal of Mind and Behavior* and *Philosophical Psychology*. Yet not only are they insignificant with respect to those journals that attempt to establish closer links between the neurosciences and cognitive psychology (cf. above), but furthermore, journals trying to establish even broader interdisciplinary perspectives have come into being, most explicitly, the *Journal of Consciousness Studies*. Today, in fact, these journals seem to be the proper place for non-scientific contributions on the study of conscious/ness to appear. A considerable decrease is to be found in, for instance, *Die Deutsche Zeitschrift für Philosophie*, the *Journal of Asian Studies*, or the *Journal of Economic History*. In 1975/1980, one could find 3–7 articles per year in philosophical, social scientific, and other journals, whereas journals publishing such pertinent articles can hardly be found anymore (most notably since 1990). Leaving pharmacologically orientated research on consciousness aside, the data on the growth, breadth and disciplinary distribution of research activities show that conscious/ness has increasingly become a matter of experimental neurocognitive science. In the next step, I will inspect the titles of articles published in order to obtain an overall impression of which particular issues they address, and to see whether they vary among and between disciplines, as well as over time.

4.1.4 Titles/themes

Regarding the specific issues addressed, I will select a few disciplines and examine the lists of full-length titles for the years 1978, 1988, and 1998:

- In *anthropology*, *sociology*, and *law* the term consciousness is regularly connected to certain groups or strata, such as class, ethnic group, or gender. It is a political, historical, or moral/religious concept—national consciousness, epochal consciousness, or Jewish consciousness being pertinent examples. Finally, the term refers to specific practices and technologies: for example, the titles address sorcery as a practice of consciousness or the technocratic consciousness.

* In *philosophy* we find the accounts of metaphors on consciousness used by various philosophers throughout the centuries (Brentano, Descartes, Hobbes, Kant, Husserl, Heidegger, Hegel). Moreover, a number of articles, predominantly published in 1978, deal with political topics, such as social structure and consciousness, or the formation of a Socialist consciousness; that is, specifically Marxist accounts of consciousness. Alongside some esoteric listings, one also finds a slightly increasing number of neuro/evolutionary topics, such as 'consciousness and the brain', 'scientific approaches to consciousness'.

* In *psychology* the titles can be attributed to various fields of studies, too. One group is concerned with the field of social science/psychology and deals with questions of identity formation, self-constitution, self-perception, and self-regulation. Another group addresses various states of consciousness, such as multiple/divided/altered states (sometimes discussing therapeutic interventions), as well as consciousness, while sleeping, in coma, or under hypnosis. Still others address basic phenomena and provide conceptual elaboration; for instance, they discuss the theory-of-mind approach to consciousness. A minority group focuses on general questions, such as 'consciousness in psychology' or 'the history of consciousness'.

* In the *neurosciences*, the situation seems less diverse. A notable group of titles refers to studies on patients in coma, that is, in non-conscious states. Another discusses altered states of consciousness (pathologies, drugs, etc.). Various titles focus on the issue of attention, awareness, and alertness. Finally, and on a more general level, some titles address 'the function of consciousness', or methods '... to study consciousness scientifically'. If titles referring to 'conscious' only are included, one finds a huge amount of publications dealing with methodical issues, such as a particular subject (rat, dog, sheep, patient, child, male/female) and a particular method (EEG, fMRI, etc.).

4.1.5   Frequency of words

Because full-length titles can be very suggestive when one attributes both meanings and frequencies to them, it is highly advisable to take a step back and look at single words and phrases only, as they occur in titles. The frequencies of single words and phrases (pairs of words) may tell a different story.

As far as the frequency of single words is concerned, there are, of course, no surprises at the top. While 'conscious' can be found in 3933 cases, 'consciousness' occurs 1781 times in both SCI and SSCI. Also, immediately below in the ranking, one finds a clear predominance of terms that relate to neuroscientific research, mostly pharmacology. The terms refer to the subjects of study, most often animals, clearly headed by rats (1425), followed by dogs (835), rabbits (260), sheep (91), etc. Secondly, they refer to the state of the subject, e.g. whether under sedation (279), anaesthesia/anaesthetized (108), or unconscious (68). Thirdly, they refer to the locus of research, such as the brain (156) or the heart (128), and fourthly, to all kinds of processes, functions, reactions (inhibition: 127; antagonist: 93), or failures (64). Finally, they postulate effects (693), models (100), and theories (83).

- national consciousness (27), modern national c. (14), class c. (22), mass c. (10), political c. (10)
- environmentally conscious (34)
- historical consciousness (25)
- private self-consciousness (22), self-consciousness (17)
- social (16), public (8), popular (6) consciousness
- Palestinian identity (14), ethnic (9), African American (9), black (9), ethnic self (6) consciousness
- body consciousness (12)
- feminist consciousness (12)
- phenomenal consciousness (11), consciousness explained (10), moral consciousness (10)
- cost consciousness (6)

Figure 16.3   Co-Word Analysis (selective, considering social scientific co-words only).

Only considerably lower in the hierarchy of terms do we find 'self-consciousness' (122), the most frequent term not pertaining to a scientific discourse. Next comes the term 'social' with 59 listings only, and the 'self' with 55. Even more infrequent are terms such as identity (41), national (31), class (35), public (34), political/politics (52), black (24), gender (22), culture (21), or Australia (2). It is worthy of note that the terms just mentioned virtually exhaust the list of words pertaining to non-scientific (i.e. social scientific and/or philosophical) contexts, which is not the case with terms pertaining to a clearly scientific (i.e. predominantly neuroscientific/physiological) context. The latter outnumber non-scientific words by far.

This line of investigation emphasizes that the types of consciousness connected to social scientific and philosophical concerns have become so infrequent that it seems as if they are on the verge of becoming lost, whereas physiological shades of meaning (such as awareness) are coming to dominate the academic discourse on consciousness (Fig. 16.3).

4.1.6   Reviews

Yet another indicator concerns a certain type of publication: the review. The review is designed to inform colleagues of the author's own and/or neighbouring discipline about the state of the art as regards a certain problem or area of study. By implication, there has to be a considerable body of work to write about, which is, in all probability, controversial and/or in need of further investigation, and which is looked at from the reviewer's point of view. Idiosyncratic assessments aside, reviews are indicative of a topic that has a certain stage of vividness and is regarded as 'an issue'. Moreover, reviews contribute to the delineation of fields, they make claims as to which kinds of research activities should prevail and finally, they address—and thereby constitute—scientific communities.

Between 1993 and 2001, the SCI and SSCI list 55 entries for reviews on consciousness. Only 11 of them do not belong to the neurocognitive domain. As to cognitive aspects, the reviews deal with attention and episodic memory, as well as temporal binding/binocular rivalry, etc. In the neuroscientific realm, scholars review the thalamic contributions to attention and consciousness, they inquire into the links between consciousness, pain, and cortical activity, or whether acethylcholine is a neurotransmitter correlate of consciousness, etc.

Of the reviews on non-scientific contributions to consciousness, there are three contributions on legal issues, three in the realm of race/politics, and two in parapsychology, as well as one contribution each to health costs, environmental ethics, and psychology.

The last mentioned review on 'consciousness and the psychological science' (Pickering, 1999) is the only one that explicitly deals with the growing body of experimental neurocognitive research on consciousness and its impact on the science of psychology. All other reviews refer to consciousness as a *façon de parler* (cost consciousness) or to its political connotations. A look at the reviews published since 1993 not only suggests the predominance of neurocognitive approaches once more, but also considerable internal differentiation regarding issues addressed and/or methods used. Last but not least, the SCI/SSCI show no entries for philosophical studies on consciousness.

4.1.7   Most often cited authors

While the data examined thus far did not reveal any special role for philosophers in the field of consciousness studies, the apparent invisibility of philosophy changes dramatically when authors are ranked according to how frequently they are cited in publications addressing consciousness (Fig. 16.4). Again, the dates refer to the SCI and SCCI (1973 until today).

The remainder of the extended list (covering the 'Top 100') includes representatives of philosophy, as well as neuroscientists and cognitive psychologists, yet no social scientist.

Author	Year	Title	Citations
Dennett	1991	*Consciousness Explained*	153
Dennett & Kinsbourne	1992	Time and the observer: the where and when of consciousness in the brain.	39
Paxinos	1986	The rat brain in stereotaxic coordinates.	140
Crick & Koch	1990	Towards a neurobiological theory of consciousness	64
Crick & Koch	1995	Are we aware of neural activity in primary visual cortex?	42
Searle	1992	*The Rediscovery of the Mind*	76
Searle	1983	*Intentionality. An Essay in the Philosophy of Mind*	26
Fenigstein	1975	Public and private self-consciousness: assessment and theory	76
James	1890	*The Principles of Psychology*	76
Baars	1988	*A Cognitive Theory of Consciousness*	64
Nagel	1974	What is it like to be a bat?	51
Block, N.	1995	On a confusion about a function of consciousness. Behavioral and Brain Sciences, 18 (2), 227–247	40
Chalmers, D.J.	1996a	*The Conscious Mind. In Search of a Fundamental Theory*	29

Figure 16.4   List of highly cited authors (selective).

While other indicators did show some activity in the social scientific domain, it borders on insignificance once one looks at data indicating the impact of contributions by single authors from the respective fields. Quite the opposite is true for philosophy: although the group of scholars contributing to the field is much smaller, nevertheless, they have a considerable impact as can be shown by the frequency of quotations pertaining to their field. Yet another pattern is revealed for the neurosciences. Here, there seems to be a pair of star authors (Crick & Koch, cf. Fig. 16.4) and a host of scholars who are cited moderately often. Cognitive psychology seems to have no such stars, yet is represented by a considerable number of scholars who are cited quite often. Although one should be careful when working at the level of counting and categorizing titles, frequencies of words, reviews, and highly cited authors, one can still obtain a reasonable impression of the diversity of issues discussed within and among the various fields. Based on these quantitative data, one might extract some major trends that need further investigation: all indicators considered signal the prevalence of pharmacological studies. Only way below these studies in terms of ranking do we see the beginning of a trend toward a more scientific, especially more cognitive and more neuroscientific approach to consciousness. Other notions are present as well: political, moral, philosophical, educational, they are concerned with different issues, mostly pertaining to collective representations of various kinds. Consciousness research as a whole is characterized by a notable division between scientific accounts and 'others'.

This division, however, not only separates the sciences from the humanities and the social sciences, it also cuts through individual discourses, as is apparent in philosophy and psychology. There is a slightly growing body of studies within philosophy that actively contribute to the neurocognitive debate, thereby significantly rephrasing what was previously referred to as the 'mind-body problem', without special reference to neural processes: 'The key philosophical question posed by consciousness concerns its relationship to the neural processes which correlate with it. How do the events which register in our experience relate to those occurring in our brains?' (Churchland, cited by Zeman, 2001, p. 1282). Likewise, and much more strongly, psychology has become divided. A steadily growing faction within psychology is involved in producing functional theories of consciousness and trying to explain their relevance for producing fitting behaviour: according to them, consciousness is mobilized whenever challenges or unpredictable events require special attention. Hence, consciousness studies seem to create a novel community, to which a certain faction of neurobiologists, psychologists, and philosophers belong. Scholars studying collective approaches to consciousness neither seem to form their own community nor to belong to the emerging one.

The view from outside, it seems, yields a fairly unequivocal result: the paradigm shift in consciousness studies has almost, if not already, happened. Consciousness has become an object of scientific study. This is also reflected in reports from within, that is, from those who now form the inner circle of consciousness studies, constituted by the neurosciences, cognitive psychology, and philosophy. It is to these views from within that I now turn in order to substantiate or differentiate the picture obtained from the view from outside. How do representatives of the evolving neurocognitive field of consciousness conceive consciousness? The answers will differ. To put it boldly: while neuroscientists have simply conquered novel territory without further ado, cognitive psychologists have had to re-acknowledge consciousness as an object of scientific inquiry and philosophers have had to face the risk of being used on a case-by-case basis, rather than systematically informing the experimental results.

4.2   On scientific approaches to consciousness: views from within

4.2.1   Making claims on 'consciousness': neuroscience

A recent review in the realm of the neurosciences is plainly entitled 'consciousness' (Zeman, 2001). This title is a statement: the review should tell us what does and does not reside within the confines of consciousness research today, according to a neuroscientist.

Alongside introducing various concepts of consciousness (as the waking state, as experience, as mind) and self-consciousness (e.g. as self-recognition, as awareness of awareness, as self-knowledge), Zeman highlights two lines of investigation emerging within the field that he regards as 'sciences': the *science of wakefulness* and the *science of awareness*. The former predominantly rests on the study of electrical correlates of states of consciousness, and the discovery that critical structures in the brainstem, thalamus, and basal forebrain regulate conscious states. Consciousness understood as wakefulness inquires into the associated neural, behavioural, and psychological functions, and their—jointly or independently functioning—control systems. The science of awareness predominantly rests on the study of the visual system in animals and man and searches for increasingly fine-grained correlations between cerebral activity and experience, namely in the areas of (visual) perception, memory, and action. As to visual perception, two types of studies are conducted: one looks into visual experiences without any change in external stimuli (e.g. hallucination, ambiguous figures); complementarily, another looks at the difference between explicit neural processes, which give rise to conscious awareness (e.g. conscious vision), and implicit neural processes (e.g. blindsight), which allow visuomotor performance in the absence of awareness. Further studies focus on action: changes in cerebral activity, as consciously directed action becomes automatized or otherwise divorced from conscious control, which may illuminate the neurology of consciousness. Again, pathologies and disorders that disrupt our sense of ownership of our actions are promising sources of insight into the neurological bases of volitional or conscious action (e.g. alien limb syndrome).

While all the studies above operate on locally specific theories, nevertheless, there are some that attempt to provide a more general account. In the next section of his review, Zeman differentiates neurobiological theories, information-processing theories, and social theories. *Neurobiological theories* roughly revolve around the conviction that structures in the upper brainstem core play a critical role in arousal, and that thalamic and cortical activity supplies much of the content of consciousness. Moreover, they agree that the neuronal correlates of consciousness (for short: NCC) are, in all probability, a cell assembly.[17] Disagreement arises on questions such as how large an assembly must be or which regions it has to comprise in order to give rise to consciousness. Basically, neurobiological theories reverberate between the twin poles of neural activity and experience. *Information-processing theories* are concerned with the self in terms of the functions consciousness might have for an organism. In general, while many things we do need little or no attention, consciousness is required whenever the situation involves challenges, is unpredictable or critical. These theories identify consciousness with a stage or aspect of information processing, which directs our waking behaviour. Critics (e.g. Velmans, 2000, Libet, 1996) counter that consciousness rather serves its biological purpose on a longer, more reflective time scale. It provides us with insight into the minds of others, thereby illuminating the workings of our own (Humphreys, 1978; Frith & Frith, 1999). *Social theories*, therefore, suggest going beyond the brains and behaviour of isolated subjects. Other than social scientific theories proper, however, 'social' does not refer to the level of collective representations (e.g. in the Durkheimian sense). Articulated within an individualist methodology, 'social' theories of consciousness are all about an organism's chance to survive with the help of higher-level information processing.

Significantly, Zeman only refers to philosophy after these grander-scale theories. This section is broadly ordered according to the relationship between conscious and neural events that each single theory postulates, yet is in no way connected to the aforementioned theories or findings.

- *Identity theories* hold that neural events are identical to the corresponding conscious events. They offer a reductionist and materialist, or physicalist solution to the mind-body problem—a solution that dates back as far as Lucretius and that was emphasized later on by Thomas Hobbes (today cf., e.g. Churchland, 1983). Critics argue that reductionism leaves out the mind (e.g. Searle, 1992) because, for instance, the blind student of the visual system could never gain a full understanding, as she would never know 'what it is like to see' (Jackson, 1982; Nagel, 1979).

- *Functionalist theories* claim that the essence of consciousness lies in the functions that it serves, that is, in a certain subset of information regarding the inputs or outputs our nervous systems achieve (most prominently, cf. Dennett, 1991). Functionalism reinterprets our experience in terms of a series of judgements made in response to sensory information. Although this approach takes cognitive processes into account, it does not take qualitative properties of consciousness into consideration.

- *Dualist theories* concede a close relationship between neural and conscious events, yet consider them fundamentally distinct classes of phenomena. Dating back to Descartes' separation of material and spiritual substances (Descartes, 1961/1968), today's dualisms refine this argument. Chalmers has proposed a 'naturalistic property dualism' that regards mental features of reality as properties of natural physical entities that bear a lawful relation to their physical ones. Explaining consciousness, on this view, requires a set of psychophysical laws that describe *the relationship between* conscious and neural events.[18]

Concluding, Zeman states: 'Future work in philosophy and science may change the ways in which we think about consciousness so radically that its reduction to physical process begins to look plausible. For the time being we have no alternative but to use all three vocabularies of biology, behaviour, and experience to understand the mind' (Zeman, 2001, p. 1284). Zeman's turn of phrase is revealing: the conundrum of philosophy cannot be resolved without confronting it with different kinds of 'vocabularies'. These assume the role of a heuristics eventually leading to a scientific, brain-based, explanation of the mind. Particularly, wakefulness and awareness are the aspects of consciousness to study. In fact, they *are* what consciousness is about. This is a decisive shift in reasoning about consciousness, that merely grants philosophy a commenting role and largely excludes the social sciences (cf. above).[19]

4.2.2 Rediscovering/reclaiming consciousness: psychology and philosophy

The disciplines considered thus far all have different histories, connected in some way to consciousness: while neurobiologists are just conquering novel territory, the social sciences, philosophy, and psychology already have a history of their dealings with consciousness. Most interestingly, psychology as a scientific discipline has an entire history as to whether or not to study consciousness at all.[20] In a nutshell, this history can be told by sketching William James' attitudes and approaches throughout his scholarly life. He switched from an introspective stance when he discovered consciousness as an entity, yet ultimately denounced consciousness altogether. This same pattern has re-occurred within the discipline of psychology throughout the last 100 years.

In the beginning of psychology as a discipline, introspectionism attempted to give a full description of the mental landscape as it appeared to the subject. Scholars like Külpe or Titchener, having a scientific project in mind, adhered to nothing less than the atomic table of the human mind (Külpe, 1901; Titchener, 1915). However, as they accredited the word of the introspecting subject with ultimate authority—those words that produced different results in different laboratories—introspectionism itself became discredited (Güzeldere, 1995a, p. 38). The emerging positivist attitude thus did away with consciousness as a scientific issue: 'Behaviorism claims that consciousness is neither a definite nor a usable concept' (Watson, 1970, p. 2). Having been an influential paradigm for psychology for over half a century, behaviourism removed the mentalistic vocabulary from the psychological agenda—consciousness can only recently be found once again in textbooks and dictionaries (e.g. Kiefer, 2002). Yet consciousness was always present as a hidden variable: 'Behaviorism owes its *ism* to consciousness. And what would it be without its *ism*? Well it would be physiology' (Boring, 1963, p. 275). Julian Jaynes adds: 'Behaviorism was only a refusal to talk about consciousness' (Jaynes, 1976, p. 15).

With the advent of cognitive psychology in the seventies, consciousness became a kind of component or aspect of information processing models, thereby regaining scientific status. Mandler and Shallice, for instance, insisted on the significance of consciousness research: 'Theoretical developments in cognitive psychology and the increasing use of introspective methods require a rationale, and that this should involve consideration of consciousness ... the common preposition driving the cognitivist research on consciousness was that the basic phenomenological concept—consciousness—can be mapped onto the information-processing concept' (Shallice, 1972, p. 383). This, however, did not occur without objections, such as Neisser's: 'The treatment of consciousness as a processing stage ... does not do justice neither to the usage of the word "consciousness" in ordinary discourse nor to the subtleties of experience. A better conception of consciousness, which has been suggested many times in the history of psychology, would recognize it as an aspect of activity rather than as an independently definable mechanism' (Neisser, 1976, pp. 104–5).

Yet another aspect of rediscovering the issue of consciousness was connected to psychology's rediscovery of the *un*conscious. Other than the Freudian unconscious, which is not inaccessible given appropriate therapeutic treatment, cognitive psychology posits a *cognitive* unconscious. It exists due to the way our perceptual/cognitive system is constituted and is, in principle, inaccessible. This notion has instigated a whole research industry. 'Theorists of diverse persuasions have been led to propose cognitive dichotomies, which have given a rather bewildering array of labels: unconscious vs. conscious, procedural vs. declarative, automatic vs. controlled, reflexive vs. reflective, and many others. These distinctions do not always divide cognition along the same lines … (but) there are tantalizing similarities among the proposed dichotomies. In particular, the first member of each pair is generally viewed as involving unconscious mental processes, a topic that has seen a recent resurgence of interest among experimental psychologists' (Holyoak & Spellman, 1993, p. 265).

Thus, as far as cognitive psychology is concerned, consciousness has regained the status of a scientific object and is currently being investigated by various strands of study. It finds itself re-framed by an impressive number of dual conceptions (cf. above).[21]

As cognitive psychology is mainly driven by a causal intuition, however, little emphasis is generally placed on the phenomenal account (Güzeldere, 1995a, p. 49). This tendency became even more acute once psychology came to form part of the cognitive sciences, which have proved inspiring, not only for the empirical disciplines involved (e.g. neurology, cognitive psychology, and the information sciences), but also for analytical philosophers. Their reasoning on classical problems, such as intentionality, subjectivity, and consciousness, has been enriched with a huge heuristic potential stemming from empirically based theories of information processing in (complex) systems, human and non-human—at least in the view of those (few) philosophers who feel 'cognitively inclined'.

Cognitive science has thus been a major driving force, rendering consciousness studies not only scientific, but interdisciplinary as well. Some, however, find this type of interdisciplinarity far too narrow (cf. below). A good example is Yanina Shapiro's review of 13 (of about 45) books on consciousness by well-known scholars in the field of the biological and neurosciences, as well as in philosophy throughout the first half of the 1990s. It is entitled: 'The Consciousness Hype: What Do We Want Explained?' (Shapiro, 1997). Shapiro's review sketches a story according to which consciousness, as soon as it became 'discovered' by science and analytical philosophy, received special treatment by each author who cared to deal with the issue. Above all, its history is one of theories mutually ignoring each other. If anything, scholars like Edelman (1989) and Calvin (1996) established that consciousness was no longer an outcast of science, but one of its greatest mysteries: consciousness, via neuronal group selection, emerges from a Darwinian machine called the brain; it can best be studied via computational models of visual perception, the best-known of the neuronal pathways; and it can be described as a set of necessary and sufficient conditions (cf. Shapiro, 1997, p. 840). Yet here is where things start to drift apart. Questions such as 'Should a theory of consciousness be consistent with physics? What is the philosophy (e.g. reductionism, functionalism, dualism), the theory should espouse? Should it accept the unconscious as indisputable fact that explains consciousness? What are the necessary and sufficient conditions of consciousness? What can be done about that problem of problems, self-consciousness …?' (Shapiro, 1997, p. 841) seem to allow no consensual answers. Why?

Shapiro's basic critique is that scientists, as yet, have only bits and pieces of scientific facts pertaining to the brain. They glue them together with just the kind of philosophy that seems right to them, whereas the philosophers select neurobiological and cognitive facts as they need them. However, in her view, there is more to be criticized than just this 'quilt-a-theory' approach. In the end, the discussion as a whole suffers from a major flaw in that it disembodies consciousness: '... so far, the discussion has not been about conscious bodies and their thoughts, but about how the unconscious thoughts and feelings become conscious in the brain that is not attached to any body' (Shapiro, 1997, p. 855).

From a discourse analytical point of view, one cannot help but observe that Shapiro, too, is involved in suggesting the right questions in consciousness research. She, too, makes judgements about what is/is not scientific and, finally, she is not at all critical as regards the current breadth of interdisciplinarity. Social, political, and moral aspects, that seems to be clear by now, do not play a role. From a Kuhnian perspective, this situation is intelligible in terms of field formation. While struggling about the right questions to ask, and to determine whether or not being a science is common procedure in pre-paradigmatic states, consciousness studies seems to be on the brink of 'normal science' as concerns the accredited participants.

This is one of the major challenges the *Journal of Consciousness Studies* (*JCS*) faces. On the basis of the renewed interest in consciousness, it wishes to re-open and broaden the forum by welcoming humanists, trans-personalists, and social scientists back into the fold.

5   *JCS*: an exercise in extending and integrating the debate on consciousness

5.1   The legitimating narrative for a multidisciplinary effort

'The 1990s have been christened the "Decade of the Brain" due largely to the remarkable developments in brain research and brain-scanning technology that are set to revolutionize[22] our understanding of cognitive processes. Our purpose in launching the *Journal for Consciousness Studies* is to argue that it should also be the 'decade of the mind', and to point out that the two things are not necessarily synonymous' (The Editors, 1994, p. 4). While the editors acknowledge that neuroscientists have returned consciousness to the academic agenda after nearly a century in exile, they deem it high time to approach consciousness in all its aspects.[23] The application of a scientific approach to consciousness, in their view, has its downside: the threat is that we are but 'a pack of neurons' (Crick). However, will the mystery surrounding consciousness come to an end once we know all about its neuronal correlates and have solved the 'binding problem', that is, the synchronization of different neuronal inputs to form the single unified perception we commonly experience or, alternatively, once we know the natural history of the mind, that is, the evolution of consciousness as something conferring a clear evolutionary advantage? The *JCS* wants its heterogeneous community to acknowledge neuroscientific details, as well as the experiential concerns regarding consciousness. It calls for *ontological rapprochement* between physicalists and phenomenalists, as well as for *epistemological reconsiderations*: An observer-related epistemology might overcome the fruitless opposition between reductionist and dualist accounts. Only then, according to the *JCS*, may we hope to solve what has been termed the 'hard problem' (bridging the gap between neuronal activity and phenomenal experience).[24]

Last, but not least, the editors pursue a social, political, and ethical agenda. What follows for politics, for ethics, for social change, if we are but a 'pack of neurons'? Ethical relativism, uncertainty, and alienation are the concerns they mention explicitly. Most acutely, they hint at the consequences of treating consciousness as nothing but some neuronal activity in the anterior cingulate sulcus: 'Our brave new world might wish to develop a form of "consciousness engineering" to parallel the new technologies in genetics' (The Editors, 1994, p. 9).[25]

In conclusion, the editors insist on their decision *not* to define what consciousness is. In a way, their legitimating narrative goes like this: While peers watch over quality and the editors[26] over diversity, the discourse on consciousness watches over itself, eventually allowing interdisciplinarity/ies to emerge. So what is consciousness about, according to 8 years of multidisciplinary discourse in the *JCS*?

By way of an overview, the following section will focus on the issues addressed and approaches suggested, particularly by way of emphasizing the different types of multidisciplinarity. Secondly, I will analyse two instances of meta-discourse held by the editors of this journal: how do they assess values and shortcomings of their efforts and the reception of their readers, respectively? In addition, the analysis will include reports on the biannual conferences organized by the Association for the Scientific Studies of Consciousness (ASSC), published in the *JCS*. Taken together, these articles will present us with another 'view from within'. This time, we look at those in consciousness research who actively promote a multidisciplinary approach *beyond* the cognitive neuroscientific alliance.

5.2   Themes and approaches in 8 years of the *JCS*

Until today, 40 volumes of the *JCS* have been published, the big issues being the 'hard problem', 'Zombies', neuroscience of consciousness, quantum theories of consciousness, the self. Another bias is toward the basic cognitive functions upon which consciousness operates, such as perception, memory, and awareness, including a discussion of general cognitive theories of consciousness (e.g. 'Global Workspace Theory', Baars, 1988). Moreover, throughout the years, various articles and issues draw connections between cognitive processes and mysticism, particularly Buddhism. Special issues address empathy, morality, and art. Numerous single articles are concerned with the epistemological foundations of consciousness research, with social, emotional, and corporeal aspects of consciousness, and a variety of specific problems (e.g. consciousness in plants, poetry, politics, and psychoanalysis). With one exception (Güzeldere, 1995a,b), there is no paper that gives a general overview of consciousness studies and even the latter is supposed to be an introduction to one of the 'hot' topics (the 'hard problem'), rather than a state-of-the-art account. Highlighting a few issues may show how the issues addressed diverge with respect to the scope of interdisciplinary perspectives they imply or invite:

A considerable portion of articles has been devoted to the *hard problem* (cf. note 21). Although this problem can be mainly driven by the philosophical discourse, the editors still reinforced a broader debate by initiating 'symposia', to which philosophers of various creeds, as well as a few neurobiologists, cognitive psychologists, and computer scientists contributed their views. This procedure of focusing the debate, however, yielded even more contributions: from 1994 to 1997, the *JCS* published six symposia on the hard problem; in 2000, there is one other symposium on the mind-body problem (resulting in a total of 35 contributions). Alongside these symposia, there are a host of individual articles dealing with single problems, such as epistemological stances toward the hard problem (idealist, functionalist, post-functionalist, etc.).

Somewhat related to the hard problem are one symposium and three individual articles on *Zombies,* again predominantly treated by philosophers. Of course, this problem is not about Haitian folklore, the living dead, but about the philosopher's zombies. It is a thought experiment concerning a being for whose cognition a functional description could be exhaustive. According to the experiment, 'given any functional description it will still make sense to suppose that there could be insentient beings that exemplify the description': Zombies (Moody, 1994). Although cognitive psychologists, neurobiologists, and a number of philosophers should, theoretically at least, be keen on this thought experiment, there is not a great deal of interdisciplinary exchange. Prominent philosophers such as Thomas Nagel consider it unsolvable, in principle. Meanwhile, the debates on Zombies are fervently continuing, largely engaging philosophers. This has led to a significant characterization: These are 'qualia wars'.

Not surprisingly, the *neuroscience of consciousness* (18 contributions, including one on neurosurgery) is another 'big issue' of the *JCS*. Unlike the aforementioned debates, however, the pertinent approaches, methods, and insights are covered by individual articles only—thus far, it seems, no real multidisciplinary debate focusing on specific topics has emerged. One of the few exceptions concerns the cortical dysfunction called 'blindsight',[27] which engages philosophers as well. Recently, however, neuroscientific contributions have appeared that try to dampen the general optimism with regard to neuroscientific accounts of consciousness, despite their intricate research instruments. According to Revonsuo (2001), for instance, consciousness, or the phenomenal level of organization, probably resides at higher levels of complex electrophysiological and bioelectrical phenomena in the brain. However, not only do single-cell recordings, PET, fMRI, EEG, and MEG pick up different kinds of signals from different levels of organization in the brain,[28] but also, we as yet lack established theories in neuroscience of how these signals relate to each other. Revonsuo's critique is bold: the correlations that have been detected so far do not allow a reconstruction of the nature or organization of conscious processes on the phenomenal level—while supporting the neuroscientific project, he complains about a lack of deeper theorizing in such an experimentally based discipline.

One particular approach, however, aroused some interest among both cognitive scientists and philosophers alike for quite some time, presumably just because it makes broader theoretical claims. The *quantum-theoretical approach* toward consciousness (nine contributions), championed by Roger Penrose and Stuart Hameroff. According to this approach, consciousness should be viewed as an emergent property of physical systems. While most approaches remain speculative, Hameroff, for example, postulates that cytoskeletal microtubules within neurons could be a possible site for quantum effects. Consciousness is redefined as an 'emergent macroscopic quantum state driven or selected by neurobiological mechanisms (neural networks, attentional scanning circuits, coherent firing of distributed neurons) with origins in quantum coherence in cytoskeletal microtubules with the brain's neurons' (Hameroff, 1994, p. 106). Many contributions are highly critical of this approach: in the *JCS*, Scott, for instance, holds that distinctive features of pertinent brain activity (global coherence, binding of cell assemblies, etc.) are more typical of classical dynamics than of quantum dynamics, which is a linear theory. Therefore, natural scientists should turn to hierarchies of non-linear classical systems (cf., e.g. Scott, 1996). Despite these controversies, quantum theoretical approaches have been (and, to some extent, still are) a striking example of a highly controversial, multidisciplinary debate.

There is another frontier that seems to attract even more interest, however: *transpersonalist* accounts of consciousness. For a long time, they considered consciousness to be a 'pure experiential event', something beyond communication. Yet nine articles and one symposium on 'Cognitive Models and Spiritual Maps' try to bridge this type of gap as well. It is the gap between constructivists (religious experience is wholly constructed from the fabric of pre-existing materials) and so-called perennial psychologists (mystical experiences are defined by some common underlying experiential cores, notably the so-called Pure Consciousness Event). Consciousness, in this volume, is thus meant to be the mediating term between *qualia* or felt experience, and the 'hard' reality we refer to as the external world. Since perceptual systems continually translate between the two systems, it is time to ask how this is accomplished (cf. Andresen & Forman, 2000, p. 7f.).

Only recently, the *JCS* fostered a controversy over the issue of *art* (one symposium, one target paper plus commentaries, two single contributions). Not unlike spiritual, meditative, or psychedelic experiences, for example, aesthetics seem to transcend consciousness as well and, hence, may be another litmus test for empirical investigations pursued from a third-person perspective. The editor of the symposium on art lays down the challenge: 'Nearly all of whatever brain activity it is that corresponds to aesthetic experience is unconscious ... some scholars hold that art is to merge subject and object in an ecstatic epiphany that transcends individual consciousness' (Gogue, 2000, p. 13). Still, given this preconception cherished in the art community, Gogue and some of his colleagues are of the opinion that methods, such as fMRI and theories of embodied consciousness are most promising for yielding further insights into the process of aesthetic experience.[29]

With about the same degree of coverage, one can find contributions on *evolutionary* and *ecological* aspects of consciousness (five articles and a two-part symposium on evolutionary origins of consciousness[30]); only one article concerns itself with consciousness in non-human animals. The symposium on morality, however, does not seem to make any particular effort to attach itself to the consciousness debate: rather, it remains a self-contained issue discussed primarily among evolutionary ethnologists and psychologists who deem morality an evolved capacity. The term consciousness does not even appear once in the introduction to this symposium, thus forcing readers to draw the connections for themselves.

The crossroads at which virtually all the above-mentioned aspects and perspectives meet is the issue called *self*. Inquiries into the nature of the self have a long tradition. We have learned to frame it both within the ancient tradition of Socratic self-knowledge in the context of ethical life and within contemporary discussions of brain function in cognitive science. The variety of responses to the problem of self includes the assertion that there is no self; that the idea is a logical, psychological, or grammatical fiction; that the sense of self is properly understood and defined in terms of brain processes; that it is the centre of personal and public narrative; or that it belongs in an ineffable category all of its own. Accordingly, approaches involve philosophy, psychology, neuroscience, theories of embodiment, and artificial intelligence, all of which try to explore, and, at times, relate various ideas. They address questions of whether or not the self is enduring; is applicable to computer models; can be reduced to neural mechanisms; is a linguistic entity, and/or a social phenomenon (cf. Gallagher & Shear, 1997, pp. 399ff.). *JCS* devotes four volumes (two of which are double issues) to symposia on 'Models of the Self' (edited by Gallagher and Shear), plus eight individual articles. While encompassing most perspectives mentioned above, there is one in particular which is lacking: the social perspective.

The *social* foundation of consciousness is only explicitly addressed on one occasion. Three further articles (since 1998) deal with loosely related issues. The one article targeting the social construction of consciousness deserves closer scrutiny as its authors, Burns & Engdahl (1998a,b), are themselves stunned by the fact that the new research industry on consciousness is proceeding without sociology (and vice versa, one might add).[31] This is all the more surprising as scholars like Durkheim, Schütz, Mead, Bateson, as well as Berger and Luckmann, Goffman, and many others have made significant contributions. Granted that consciousness is a matter of physical or material processes, as well as of sentience and phenomenal processes, socially-based cognitions, representations, reflective processes, and discursive reflections nevertheless need to be accounted for, too. The main thesis is that individual reflectivity, as a defining form of consciousness, *derives from* collective processes. Individuals learn a language, language-mediated collective representations, and a cultural cognitive frame. On this notion, sentience, cognitive processes, and language-based representation and reflectivity entail interactive and feedback effects. Being active cognisers, structuring data and organizing perceptions within established cultural frames, human beings utilize their ability to discriminate, categorize, and react to environmental stimuli and signals. Moreover, they reflect upon, judge, and alter their modes of discrimination, categorization, and reactions to external stimuli. Awareness of self-processes requires a representation of self–states and processes, and thus depends on memory, including collective memory. This is how an enduring self (collective or individual) comes about: because there is a variety of social and cognitive mechanisms that stabilize representations, cognition, and memories.

Consciousness in this sense of reflectivity is a matter not only of awareness that we experience feelings and perceptions, etc., but of the fact that the latter have meaning and can be understood in a larger context. Language and verbal thought enable elaborate articulation, focusing, and awareness of awareness itself; they enable continual and elaborate self-referencing and reflectivity, which is, as is argued here, the characteristic feature of consciousness proper.[32]

In closing, Burns and Engdahl concede that this additional level of analysis may complicate consciousness studies—as yet, however, the multidisciplinary community does not seem to be much disturbed. Consciousness, despite proclamations to the contrary, is not the subject of *one all-encompassing interdisciplinarity*. Rather, consciousness, according to the results of this analysis, is the subject matter of a *specific* interdisciplinarity, which itself consists of various, even *more specific* interdisciplinarities. The most active interdisciplinary level is delineated by all those discourses that engage themselves with the neuro-, cognitive, and experimental challenge (be it affirmatively or critically); there is a less active inter- or perhaps only multidisciplinary level, upon which one finds other frontiers and other common grounds. In one camp, the experiential account talks back (uniting phenomenologists, mysticists, art theorists, and deconstructivists). In another camp, one finds self-accounts uniting all perspectives that reside within the confines of an individualistic methodology (including social psychology, theories of mind). Far less multidisciplinarily organized are debates on the hard problem or zombies—philosophical debates that dominated the discussion until 1997. A host of specific issues combine various perspectives in themselves, like the science-historical study of researches into plant consciousness, for instance, yet they remain unconnected to one of the more general discussions—a fate that may be predetermined for sociological accounts as well. The latter's differentiation of awareness and reflectivity (hence, 'higher-order consciousness') does not concern natural scientists interested in the 'basic (hence brainy) issues' of consciousness.

Finally, a look at both the editorial evaluations of the *JCS* (1996, 1998), as well as at three reports on conferences organized by the scientific association on consciousness studies (conference II–IV, held at Tucson), confronts the observations just made with reference to reflections from within. These are indicative of a renewed effort to both broaden and integrate the knowledge space (*epistemological function*) and at the same time, continually remind the emerging hybrid community to co-operate, epistemological and metaphysical gaps notwithstanding (*social function*).

5.3 On scientific-cum-humanist approaches to consciousness: views from within

5.3.1 Editorials

The first evaluative editorial, issued in 1996 after 3 years of publishing the *JCS*, is mixed. It is quite positive with regard to the stimulating controversy of quantum theoretical approaches toward consciousness. Also, in some cases, cross-talks way beyond the published manifestations have been instigated (e.g. between philosophy and computer theory). More critically, the editors first remark on the abundance of philosophy articles and, secondly, on a shortage of solid experimental work in psychology and neurobiology. This, according to their assessment, is partly due to the fact that the hard problem has been widely misconceived as being a predominantly philosophical problem. To set this balance right, the editors announce the publication of more on NCC (a special issue on blindsight). Thirdly, they note a striking lack of contributions by the arts and the humanities, especially on ethics and social issues (cf. 1996). Fostering a broader dialogue, it seems, did have a promising, if slightly humble start, in need of active guidance on the part of the editors.

A second evaluative editorial appeared 1 year later (1997). In the meantime, as is evident from the outset, there has been much discussion on the part of the editors and other guiding groups as to what a scientific study of consciousness should look like. Although everybody emphasizes that there is no general theory as yet, an increasing number of authors warn against a chaotic, all-encompassing type of interdisciplinarity. Thomas Metzinger, for instance, argued for the debate to be limited to a narrow band of specialists. Particularly, he challenged the interdisciplinary enterprise by stating that he was looking forward to the establishment of a dominant (information processing) paradigm, and the abandonment of all first-person approaches to the 'New Age' Journal (sic!). This leaves, once again, only cognitive psychology, neuroscience, and (analytical) philosophy as legitimate candidates for scientific dialogues on consciousness. The editorial response neither sides with anti-scientism nor with scientism. The message is that non-scientific accounts have to be included, yet they have to follow a standard approach as well, i.e. a hermeneutic one.

Moreover, the editors want to prevent a balkanization of consciousness studies, because even the scientific branch of consciousness studies is less unified than it may seem.

> In practice this means that the 1997 Montreal meeting ... was attended mainly by neuro-scientists, ASSC Claremont ... by psychologists, New School (NY) by philosophers etc. ... given the above-mentioned trends towards premature closure ... our only defense must be a pluralistic one. (The Editors, 1997, p. 388)

The whole discussion, in summary, is about struggling with the *right type* of interdisci-plinarity. In particular, the debate is about *accepting phenomenal accounts*. Do they enrich (as say the editors) or rather disrupt (as say the critics) further insights into the truth of consciousness?[33] Needless to say, the social sciences are not part of this discussion.

5.3.2   Conference reports (ASSC)

Not surprisingly, the reports on the Tucson conferences show a similar pattern. Starting out with an enthusiastic embrace of a broad type of interdisciplinarity (1996 on Tucson II),[34] the next report (1998 on Tucson III) hailed most sessions as very multidisciplinary, yet at the same time, criticized a lack of dialogue among the speakers. In some cases, particular representatives were considered to be missing, such as philosophy in a session on NCC. While certain themes are now ranked as 'standard issues' (e.g. explanatory gap, implicit processes) and other themes have been strongly emphasized (especially cross-cultural and aesthetic approaches), other issues were deemed under-represented, such as the emotional aspects of consciousness. However, there is a reason (and, hence, an apology) for this lack. Due to the cognitive and computational bias in cognitive psychology, pertinent studies are rare (except, e.g. Damasio, 2001).

One observation the report particularly dwells upon is resistance to multidisciplinary communication: Sutherland attacks the division of the conference into two opposing camps (materialists-reductionists vs. transpersonal-experientialists). Interestingly enough, in his view, most materialists take experiential aspects of consciousness seriously, whereas experientialists despise materialist accounts in all forms and fashions. For the first time, the experiential faction is criticized as being unwilling to co-operate. Nevertheless, according to Sutherland, the meeting and the journal, as well as the association aim toward an era in which the transpersonal and humanistic dimension will naturally be included as part of the mainstream science of consciousness (rejections by natural scientists notwithstanding), without the need for some special label (cf. Sutherland, 1998a).[35] From the outside, it seems as if both ends of the continuum are still hesitant to rethink their ontological, epistemo-logical, and pre-theoretical creeds.

In another article, Sutherland emphasizes the point that consciousness studies have found their paradigm in the 'naturalistic triangle':

> The separation between our subjective experience and our scientific descriptions of the world goes back to the writings of Bacon and Descartes. Without the 'Cartesian Cut' the enormous progress of science and technology would not have been possible. But this has also led to a science which, in the end, has to dismiss our most intimate and cherished feel-ing—consciousness, selfhood, and free will—as insupportable illusions. This is increasingly felt unacceptable, as it paints an impoverished picture of the human condition. Therefore,

scientists and theorists are competing to develop a model which does full justice to all the elements in the 'naturalistic triangle' of psychology, neurology, and phenomenology. (Sutherland, 1998b, p. 44)

In his report on Tucson IV, 2 years later, Reimer testifies to the breadth of issues addressed, which cover all aspects of the naturalistic triangle. In particular, he emphasizes David Chalmer's remark that consciousness studies has gone through a transition from primarily comprehensive, incompatible, grand theories, to a spirit of incremental contributions which, according to him, has led to genuine progress in many areas (e.g. studies on NCC, achromats on colour experience, blindsight, facial perception, self-hood).

Most interestingly, he observes that transpersonalists have now struck back. During a session on meditation and consciousness, one scholar suggested that scientists studying neural correlates of meditative states should consider trained meditators as collaborators, not unacquainted subjects. He suggested that the concept of attention, which is most fundamental to both scientific attempts to understand consciousness and to various contemplative traditions, might serve as the best bridge between first- and third-person methodologies. He argued that both scientists and meditators might benefit from such collaboration, the former from sophisticated first-hand reports of mental states, and the latter from information about more natural categories and mechanisms that could result in better meditative techniques (cf. Reimer, 2000). This plea for *mutual* enrichment was followed by a neuroscientific study. The scientist presented results from EEG studies of long-term meditators, a group of professional musicians, and a control group: they clearly indicated that the meditators showed significant differences in the dynamics of their attentional processing. Hence, the over-arching naturalistic paradigm, proclaimed only 2 years earlier, seems to have yielded one instance of *inter*disciplinarity across the physicalist-phenomenalist frontier.

Meanwhile consciousness studies are continuing. Neither is there *one* concept of consciousness, nor *one* community, nor *one* field. At the same time, however, all studies converge on 'consciousness'. Perhaps concept, community, and field are best conceived of as hybrids.

6   Consciousness studies: a hybrid field

This study attempted to reveal the dynamics of consciousness studies by way of, first, tracing the scientification of consciousness, and by completing and commenting on this picture with disciplinary views from within, that is, from within the neurosciences, cognitive psychology, and analytical philosophy. Secondly, the study examined the ongoing efforts of the *JCS* to foster bridges within a broader consciousness community (including phenomenal accounts) and scrutinized their assessments from within. All data were selected and united by the criterion that the articles deal with consciousness (as made explicit in the title or by way of being published in the *JCS*). The sociology of knowledge underlying this approach is based on communications theory and discourse analysis. It is in communications that knowledge emerges, evolves, disappears, depending on whether or not, and if so, how, communications connect to preceding communications. Connecting to communication on consciousness today has become increasingly heterogeneous—the variations, however, are not arbitrary. Rather, if one applies the epistemology of the metaphor analysis, the variations occur via the interaction of the target term (conscious/ness) and the importing discourses. Both the unit of knowledge (conscious/ness) and the importing discourses or fields (e.g. neuroscience, philosophy, cognitive psychology) interact, that is: *they select against each other.*

In the present case, consciousness has been chosen as a unit of knowledge that has a long-standing tradition in itself. On the one hand, it essentially implies an experiential aspect, partly grounded in spiritual metaphysics. On the other hand, it implies social/sociological aspects. Both types of implication are thoroughly challenged by the cognitive and neurosciences. The responses to this challenge throughout the last decade have varied considerably:

- The cognitive and neurosciences have mainly approached consciousness in two ways; first, by denying its experiential aspects, and restricting themselves to phenomena, such as wakefulness or awareness, without making any further-reaching claims. Secondly, others have postulated and explored higher levels of complex electrophysiological and bio-electrical phenomena in the brain that would both ultimately and exhaustively explain the brainy bases of consciousness (including its experiential aspects, that is).

- Philosophy has responded in a split fashion as well. While a considerable number of philosophers have continued to work on standard issues (e.g. reconstructions of classical accounts), others have responded to the cognitive and neuroscientific challenge, either affirmatively or critically with regard to the different claims offered. Philosophers have thereby connected to a variety of accounts to which scientists, in turn, often refer only loosely—if they do so at all.

- Transpersonalists of various branches (religious, meditative, psychedelic) have insisted on the experiential aspect of consciousness. In some instances, they have even denied that experiences of 'pure consciousness' can be studied scientifically. Others, however, have pleaded in favour of the integration of the 'experiential experts' (e.g. long-term meditators) within the scientific study of consciousness, so as to grasp the neural correlates of such states.

- Social scientists have not denied the experiential aspect of consciousness, yet have emphasized that both contents and feelings associated with consciousness are socially co-constituted. While consciousness operates on brains, cognition, and individuals, it is a fundamental social phenomenon. This view, it seems, is a stand-alone, to which neither scientists nor transpersonalists, and only few philosophers, connect.

Other than the neuroscientific challengers proclaim, consciousness is not so easily transformed into a novel unitary concept, guided by neurocognitive insights. Taking all contributions to consciousness into account, its phenomenal aspect (still) concerns quite a few, if not the majority of scholars today. It is the underlying tension between physicalist and phenomenalist approaches that will surely drive the hybrid engine called consciousness for quite some time.

However, a (sociology-of-knowledge) view from elsewhere cannot only register the variety of approaches at hand and reconstruct their non-arbitrary emergence, but does something more. It helps to move beyond the dualism(s) that organize and, hence, stabilize the discourse on consciousness and apply another perspective. In particular, applying a constructivist epistemology would help to re-open some of the dead-ends of this debate. It could do so on two levels:

- *Level 1:* Recast in a constructivist framework, one could conceive of *consciousness as a 'neural, cognitive, ethical, social … construction'.* Depending on the aspect of consciousness to be explained, accounts of various disciplines would thus lend themselves to specific combinations of multiperspectivist conceptions that, in a non-reductive manner, would explain more comprehensively the forms, functions, and feels of consciousness.

- *Level 2:* Applying the level of second-order observation, *the dualism of physicalist and phenomenal accounts of consciousness reveals as a dualism of attributions.* They are cognitive and preconceived frameworks with which we observe either more determinism or more agency with respect to conscious selves. The task for a sociology of knowledge is therefore to find out under which conditions we observe more determinism, as opposed to more agency. Following Fuchs (2001), agency and structure are not opposite natural kinds but variations along a continuum. All other things being equal, 'agency' increases when observers take an intentional stance; determinism increases when observers employ a more structural, mechanical explanatory frame. Seeing behaviour (e.g. consciousness) as simple and repetitive, hence determined, or as unpredictable, foundational, hence agentive, are the *outcomes,* not the *causes* of observations, attributions, and cultural (i.e. scientific) work.

From whichever constructivist level one looks at consciousness, however, the diversity of accounts will not vanish. Yet we render it intelligible by not only reconstructing its emergence, but doing more: on level one, there is hope for converging different explanatory efforts for specific explanatory contexts without resorting to reductionism; on level two, we acknowledge different explanatory frameworks to be observer-related effects rather than being contradictory causes for consciousness. Hence, the view from elsewhere is by no means restricted to a view from afar—the projects lying ahead, however, are not about uniting, but about a social and epistemic endeavour called constructing consciousness. All of the aforementioned is neither to deny recent progress in consciousness studies nor to postulate an unwarranted goal called 'unity of science' or 'new synthesis' (cf. Schweder, this volume). Rather, it pleads for sketching the current landscape of knowledge on consciousness first in order to assess the limits and possibilities for inter-disciplinary action—voluntary and/or discursive.

Notes

1 According to Wegner and Wheatley, the apparent causal relationship between conscious thought and action reflects the fact that thought and action are generally congruent, not that they are causally linked. (In fact, both are caused by related unconscious processes.) While the experience of voluntary action is real, the causal inference that we infer from this experience is not valid (cf. Wegner & Wheatley, 1999).

2 Although this threat to the ego has its own history by now, it does not lose its force throughout the disciplines involved—hard-nosed eliminativists like Dennett being the exception to the rule (yet, do they really mean it while falling in love?).

3 In philosophy, there are two types of a 'solution' (cf. Kuberski, 2000, p. 7):

(1) One branch of philosophy disagrees with the monist stance: consciousness denotes a non-physical dimension of living things that is irreducible to physical processes; if we do reduce consciousness to physical processes, we exclude the very experience of awareness that we are attempting to understand. At the same time, the nature of their interrelationship remains a mystery. This view can sometimes shade into a stronger idealistic version: *Consciousness exists*, yet it needs the brain as an interface between itself and the extended world.

(2) Another branch of philosophy agrees with the monist stance: on this view, consciousness is simply a name for very complex, yet purely physical. Strictly speaking, there is *no consciousness*, no non-physical phenomenon in need of explanation.

4 On the one hand, the analysis will refer to the 'what abouts' and 'hows' of the consciousness studies presented in the journal. On the other hand, it will refer to what one may call a discourse on the consciousness discourse in *JCS*. Namely, as the editors of *JCS* are extremely conscious of their project, they have established a kind of monitoring of their successes and shortcomings in fostering a truly multidisciplinary discourse, documented in print and on the internet. (For pragmatic reasons, the analysis will be restricted to the printed documents as well as to the reports of the conference held by the related 'Association for the Scientific Study of Consciousness'.)

5 The definitions on multi-, inter-, and transdisciplinarity vary. The paper proceeds on the following: both multi- and interdisciplinarity arise from an intellectual problem, multidisciplinarity being a premature stage at which a common ground has not yet been established. Both types are not driven by solutions, whereas transdisciplinarity is driven by socio-economical problems. Instigated more by general problems than by disciplinary questions, the context of application is the decisive frame of reference. The type of communication between the parties is characterized by consulting and negotiation. The organizational setting is flexible and transient. Accordingly, the level of institutionalization is low (cf. mode 2, Gibbons, 1994).

6 Bruner & Fleisher Feldman (1990, p. 237) express themselves boldly: ... at least where psychologists are concerned, it is indeed by their metaphors that we shall know them'.

7 A similar story could be told for the computer metaphor according to which mental life can be mathematically formalized (Haugeland, 1985). While computational accounts have been very inspiring, ranging from the innovative (e.g. Ansell-Pearson, 1997), to the explicit (e.g. Johnson-Laird, 1988), the computer metaphor has been criticized as well, e.g. by Pickering: 'Thus, although it may have refined certain research topics, when generalized into a general theory of human cognition including consciousness, SM, the computational metaphor appears inadequate and restrictive" (Pickering, 1999, p. 614).

8 It is certainly fair to say that metaphors have always been regarded with suspicion and can be found in the midst of various dualistically structured debates: to mention but a few, they have been seen as ornamental, yet inessential; educational, yet lacking genuine insight; as economical carriers of complex meaning, yet easily misleading. Hence, metaphors have been troubling from the very beginning of the reflection on language. Max Black's seminal paper on 'Metaphors' (Black, 1962) eventually endowed the topic with new attraction. Until today, however, many scholars hold that metaphors, invisibly, but nevertheless effectively carry meanings that can be disruptive to the truth of the topic in question. Thus, the analytical task is obvious: metaphors need to be revealed and erased. I will suggest otherwise. We should accept the inevitable and use these metaphors for our own ends, that is, for insights into the dynamics of knowledge (cf. below!).

9 This approach has been developed together with Peter Weingart. For a broader introduction to theoretical underpinnings and methodical refinement, cf. Maasen & Weingart (2000).

10 For instance, it could well be that, in the course of interacting with the neurosciences, consciousness will acquire a different, physicalist meaning, or to put it differently, that neuroscientific efforts are considered to tell us something about, e.g. awareness, yet nothing about consciousness in its experiential aspect. The difference between the physical and the experiential could remain so important that consciousness sharpens its meaning *in contrast to* awareness, thus leading to a separation of terms, consciousness covering the experiential, awareness the scientific aspect.

11 For a brief etymology, cf. for example, Lewis (1960).

12 I wish to thank Matthias Winterhager and Holger Schwechheimer who performed the following bibliometric researches and, above all, provided me with their expert advice.

13 This happened to chaos theory as well. Theoretically inclined authors increasingly reject the label for fear of being misrepresented as belonging to popular uses of the term. It should be noted, though, that earlier on they had been happy to become fashionable by way of piggy-backing on a popular term such as chaos, cf. Weingart & Maasen (1995).

14 There is also a general proviso to be made as regards the indicator (consciousness occurring in titles): on the one hand, it does indicate those authors who explicitly deal with consciousness (even when they tackle very technical issues, which would not 'deserve' such a grand topic in the title). On the other hand, it does not cover those authors who study (some aspect of) consciousness, yet do not mention it in the title. The choice of an approach accounting for only those articles that *explicitly* refer to conscious/ness is justified by discourse theory: neither the participants of a discourse, nor the second-order observer, judge which contributions 'belong' to a discourse, but, in a non-essentialist way, the discourse itself (here, by way of using or not using conscious/ness). This perspective will be complemented later by views from within.

15 Amount of journals covering each field in the ISI 2000 (selective): anthropology: 51; neurosciences: 203; psychology general: 110; experimental: 67; social: 42; philosophy: 23; law: 105; sociology: 94.

16 These journals publish consciousness studies pursued in cognitive psychology. The latter is listed in both SCI and SSCI. Cognitive psychology is, in fact, the only significant overlap between both databanks.

17 Hebb (1949) defined the cell assembly as 'a diffuse structure comprising cells in the cortex and diencephalon ... capable of acting briefly as a closed system, delivering facilitation to other such systems'. On such a view, mental phenomena are subjective by virtue of involving relations to the self: We feel that it is ourselves that are doing the seeing. Other authors hasten to add: 'This view is not homuncular, because we do not envisage that object representations are presented to organism representations, but rather that these two kinds of representations are linked in a neural network whose collective activity generates subjective experience' (Adolphs & Damasio, 1995, p. 83).

18 Dual aspect theories (e.g. Nagel, 1986) go even further: some kinds of events might be inherently neural and mental, by necessity—a necessity the human mind may not be equipped to understand. At present, however, we do not know what kind of properties could render physical events intrinsically mental and, as yet, speculations lead to unwarranted forms of panpsychism.

19 This shift, however, is not a 'conscious' one. Although Zeman claims in a footnote that consciousness and awareness are, for him, synonyms, in his text he seems to differentiate between the two. Generally, there is no clear differentiation of terms; indeed, this is true for the social sciences as well: Burns & Engdahl, for example, consciousness is 'awareness of awareness' (cf. below).

20 In the following, the presentation largely relies on Güven Güzeldere's account (Güzeldere, 1995a,b).

21 This decidedly scientific-experimental stance, as opposed to phenomenal forms of investigation, is of special importance for psychology. Having virtually no 'natural history' of mental phenomena, in psychology the practices came first, whereas equipment and methods modelled on those in experimental physics only came later (e.g. Wundt; cf. Kusch, 1995, p. 128). Not unlike other disciplines struggling for scientific status (e.g. economics), the natural sciences figured as models and sources of true and respectable knowledge—often by way of strictly excluding other ways of investigation, regarded as pre- or non-scientific. In a nutshell, this opposition is re-enacted in psychology's recent rediscovery of consciousness: Scientific approaches (in cognitive, partly social psychology) and non-scientific approaches, such as in psychoanalysis (let alone parapsychology), form two completely different clusters of research activities.

22 By the way, in the discourse on consciousness the revolutionary terminology is not all 'out' (cf. Hagner & Rheinberger, this volume).

23 Important ingredients of its novel success have been: prominent scholars (Dennett, Crick & Koch, Penrose, etc.) addressing consciousness without terminological disguise (they call their respective topics 'consciousness' instead of 'anaesthesiology of cognition'), a host of conferences, scientific associations of or dealing with consciousness, the increase in publications, and the establishment of a specific journal on consciousness (*Journal of Consciousness Studies*).

24 This refers to a distinction of 'hard' and 'easy' problems in the study of consciousness introduced by David Chalmers (1996b). The easy problems refer to the empirical concerns of the cognitive neurosciences, and their investigation of the cognitive and behavioural functions of consciousness. The hard problem is about the question how any physical system could give rise to experience, to first-person perspective. Although we don't have all the answers, we know that easy problems (such as discriminatory abilities, reportability of mental states, the focus of attention, the control of behaviour) can be approached scientifically. The hard problem, namely the problem of subjective experience, resists scientific explanation. Even more, Chalmers asks why all this information processing in the brain does not simply go on 'in the dark', free of any inner feel (cf. Chalmers, 1995, pp. 4–5). Evidently, the hard problem has its roots in the mind-body problem, dating back to Plato's distinction and reformulated by Descartes. As to the so-called explanatory gap, Güzeldere found an interesting quotation by the nineteenth century philosopher and psychologist Charles Mercier: 'The change of consciousness never takes place without the change in the brain; the change in the brain never ... without the change in consciousness. But *why* the two are together, or what the link is that connects them, we do not know, and most authorities believe that we never shall and can never know' (Mercier, 1888). Today, despite computer-based experimental design and instruments such as EEG, MEG, PET, fMRI, some authors still draw the same conclusion.

25 Thomas Metzinger, a cognitive philosopher, holds that the new relationship between brain and consciousness will soon change the ways in which we experience our everyday life. Cognitive science will lead to cognitive technologies (cyberspace) and consciousness technologies (psychoactive substances). Consequently, he suggests that continuous reflections on these issues should be institutionalized: an 'anthropology assessment' is called for (Metzinger, 1994, p. 16). Note that political and ethical issues are discussed as *consequences of*, not as *constitutive for* consciousness.

26 As well as a multidisciplinary advisory board, these include representatives of cognitive science, religion, cognitive studies, psychology, neuropsychiatry, biology, anaesthesiology, physiology, mathematics, sociology, and engineering.

27 This phenomenon can be found in patients with damage to their primary visual cortex. Despite this damage, patients retain the ability to detect, discriminate and localize visual stimuli presented in areas of their visual field in which they report that they are subjectively blind.

28 We look at neuroconsciousness (Revonsuo, 2001, p. 7), for example, at neuroanatomical and neurophysiological levels.

29 Ramachandran & Hirstein (1999, p. 17), for example, suggest artists deploy certain rules or principles (8) to titillate the visual areas of the brain amenable to SCR testing (galvanic skin response) and single-cell recordings.

30 For many scholars, the evolutionary way is the one to go: Despite many scientific findings of neural and cognitive processes we, as yet, do not have more than a correlative, and no transparent theory of consciousness (Nagel). Such a theory, these scholars claim, would 'need to explain how conscious experiences change behaviour so as to provide the increased survival value that would have allowed evolution to select those brain mechanisms that underlie the conscious experiences' (Gray, 1995, p. 9).

31 Hence, the anthropologist Catherine Lutz writes: 'Western social science has generally neglected to consider the cultural aspects of consciousness' (Lutz, 1992, p. 64) and, consequently, pleads for an anthropology of knowledge. In a nutshell, her comparison between American and Ifaluk definitions of consciousness reveals that American definitions of persons have consciousness at their centre (intrapsychic model), whereas Ifaluk focus on the obligations personhood imposes on others in the community (interpersonal model). That is to say, within an anthropological framework, any debate about consciousness is meaningful only insofar it 'examines its cultural foundations and includes the breadth of human experience in its purview' (Lutz, 1992, p. 86).

32 Burns & Engdahl do not fail to mention that this type of consciousness has its roots in the Western world (1998b, pp. 182f). Notably Christianity and modern therapeutic practices brought the self-reflective individual about (cf. also Maasen, 1998).

33 The readers of the *JCS* have been mixed on this issue as well. The results of a poll revealed that about a third wished to have more scientific papers; 10% evaluated the papers published thus far as being too technical already, and 25% wished to read more on literature, art, and transpersonal accounts (Freeman, 1997, p. 389).

34 'Perhaps the most remarkable and creative thing about the conference was the presence of people with starkly different intuitions and backgrounds debating the subject together: fMRI research talks to Eastern writings by Sufi divine Ibn Arabi. Monkey researchers talk to transpersonalists. The atmosphere as a whole was characterized as open yet rigid enquiry' (Sutherland, 1996, p. 285).

35 There is progress to be mentioned with regard to the institutionalization of this kind of multidisciplinary research: In 1997, the Fetzer Institute granted a $1.4 million 3-year grant to establish a centre for consciousness studies at the University of Arizona.

References

Adolphs, R. & Damasio, A.R. (1995) Pain and the brain: advances in pain research and therapy. *Consciousness Neurosci* 22, 83–97.

Andresen, J. & Forman, R.K.C. (2000) Methodological pluralism in the study of religion. *J Consciousness Stud* 7, 7–14.

Ansell-Pearson, K. (1997) *Viroid Life: perspective on Nietzsche and the transhuman condition.* London: Routledge.

Baars, B.J. (1988) *A Cognitive Theory of Consciousness.* New York: Josiah Macy Jr Foundation.

Black, M. (1962) *Models and Metaphors: studies in language and philosophy.* Ithaca: Cornell University Press.

Block, N. (1995) On a confusion about a function of consciousness. *Behav Brain Sci* **18**, 227–47.

Bono, J.J. (1990) Science, discourse, and literature: the role/rule of metaphor in science. In Peterfreund, S. (ed.), *Literature and Science: theory and practice*. Boston: Northeastern University Press, pp. 59–89.

Boring, E. (1963/1932) The physiology of consciousness. In *History, Philosophy & Science: selected papers*. New York: Wiley & Sons, pp. 274–86.

Bruner, J.S. & Fleisher Feldman, C. (1990) Metaphor of consciousness and cognition in the history of psychology. In Leary, D.E. (ed.), *Metaphors in the History of Psychology*. Cambridge: Cambridge University Press, pp. 230–8.

Burns, T. & Engdahl, E. (1998a) The social construction of consciousness. Part 1: collective consciousness and its socio-cultural foundations. *J Consciousness Stud* **5**, 67–85.

Burns, T. & Engdahl, E. (1998b) The social construction of consciousness. Part 2: individual selves, self-awareness and reflectivity. *J Consciousness Stud* **5**, 166–84.

Calvin, W. H. (1996) *How Brains Think: evolving intelligences. Then and Now*. New York: Basic Books.

Chalmers, D. (1995) Facing up to the Problem of Consciousness, *J Consciousness Stud*, **2**, 3, 200–19.

Chalmers, D.J. (1996a) *The Conscious Mind. In Search of a Fundamental Theory*. New York: Oxford University Press.

Chalmers, D. J. (1996) *Toward a Theory of Consciousness*. Oxford: Oxford University Press.

Churchland, P. S. (1983) Consciousness: the transmutation of a concept. *Pacific Philosoph Quart* **64**, 80–95.

Crick, F. & Koch, C. (1990) Towards a neurobiological theory of consciousness. *Sem Neurosci* **2**, 263–75.

Crick, F. & Koch, C. (1995) Are we aware of neural activity in primary visual cortex? *Nature* **375**, 121–3.

Damasio, A. R. (1989) Time-locked multiregional retroactivation: a systems-level proposal for the neural substrates of recall and recognition. *Cognition* **33**, 25–62.

Damasio, A. R. (2001) Fundamental feelings. *Nature* **413**, 781.

Darden, L. & Maull, N. (1977) Interfield theories. *Philos Sci* **44**, 43–64.

Davidson, D. (1981) What metaphors mean. In Johnson, M. (ed.), *Philosophical Perspectives on Metaphor*. Minneapolis: University of Minnesota Press, pp. 190–220.

Dennett, D. (1991) *Consciousness Explained*. London: Allan Lane.

Dennett, D. & Kinsbourne, M. (1992) Time and the observer. *Behav Brain Sci* **15**, 183–247.

Descartes, R. (1961/1968) *Discourse on Method and the Meditations*. Harmondsworth: Penguin.

Edelman, G. M. (1989) *The Remembered Present: a biological theory of consciousness*. New York: Basic Books.

Fenigstein, A., Scheier, M.F., & Buss, A.H. (1975) Public and private self-consciousness: Assessment and theory. *J Consult Clin Psyc*, **43**, 522–27.

Foucault, M. (1974) *Die Ordnung des Diskurses*. Frankfurt/Main: Ullstein.

Freeman, W. (1997) What the readers said. *J Consciousness Stud* **4**, 7–9.

Frith, C.D & Frith, U. (1999) Interacting minds—a biological basis. *Rev Sci* **286**, 1692–5.

Fuchs, S. (2001) Beyond agency. *Sociol Theory* **19**, 24–40.

Gallagher, S. & Shear, J. (1997) Editors' introduction (to 'Models of the Self'). *J Consciousness Stud* **4**, 399–404.

Gibbons, M., *et al.* (eds) (1994) *The New Production of Knowledge*. London: Sage.

Gogue, J. A. (2000) What is art: editorial introduction. *J Consciousness Stud* **7**, 7–15.

Gray, J. (1995) Guest editorial: consciousness—What is the problem and how should it be addressed? *J Consciousness Stud* **2**, 5–9.

Güzeldere, G. (1995a) Consciousness: what it is, how to study it, what to learn from its history. *J Consciousness Stud* **2**, 30–51.

Güzeldere, G. (1995b) Problems of consciousness: a perspective on contemporary issues. *Curr Debates* **2**, 112–43.

Hagner, M. & Rheinberger, H.J. (forthcoming) Prolepsis. *Considerations for Histories of Science* after 2000. In Nowotny, H. & Joerges, B. (eds.), *Social Studies of Science and Technology: Looking Back, Ahead.* Sociology of Science Yearbook, Dordrecht: Kluwer.

Hameroff, S. (1994) Quantum Conference in Microtubules. A neural basis for the emergent consciousness? *J Consciousness Stud*, **1**, 1, 91–118.

Haugeland, J. (1985) *Artificial Intelligence: the very idea.* London: Sage.

Hebb, D. O. (1949) *The Organization of Behaviour.* New York: Wiley.

Hesse, M. (1972) The explanatory function of metaphor. In Bar-Hillel, Y. (ed.), *Logic, Methodology, and Philosophy of Science*, 7th edn. Amsterdam: Elsevier, pp. 249–59.

Hesse, M. (1974) *The Structure of Scientific Interference.* London: Macmillan.

Holyoak, K. & Spellman, B. (1993) Thinking. *Ann Rev Psychol* **44**, 265–315.

Humphreys, N. (1978) Nature's psychologist. *New Scientist* **78**, 900–3.

Jackson, F. (1982) Epiphenomenal Qualia. *Philosophical Quarterly*, XXXII, pp. 127–36.

James, W. (1890) *The Principles of Psychology.* New York: Henry Holt.

James, W. (1904) Does consciousness exist? Reprinted in Perry, R.B. (ed.), *Essays in Radical Empiricism.* New York: Dutton, p. 322.

Jaynes, J. (1976) *The Origin of Consciousness and the Breakdown of the Bicameral Mind.* London: Penguin.

Journal of Consciousness Studies, 2, 1, coverpage.

Johnson-Laird, P.N. (1988) A computational analysis of consciousness. In Mandel, A. & Bisiach, E. (eds), *Consciousness in Contemporary Science.* Oxford: Oxford University Press, pp. 357–68.

Kiefer, M. (2002) Bewusstsein [Consciousness]. In Müsseler, J. & Prinz, W. (eds), *Allgemeine Psychologie.* Heidelberg: Spektrum pp. 178–222.

Kiss, J.M. (2000) Contesting metaphors and the discourse of consciousness in William James. *J Hist Ideas* **61**, 263–82.

Kuberski, P. (2000) A worldly mind: natural history and the experience of consciousness. *Substance* **29**, 7–22.

Külpe, O. (1901) *Outlines of Psychology.* New York: MacMillan.

Kusch, M. (1995) *Psychologism: a case study in the sociology of philosophical knowledge.* London: Routledge.

Kusch, M. (2000) *Folk Psychology and Social Institutions,* Lecture at the Max Planck Institute for Psychological Research, Munich, Germany, February 22.

Lewis, C.S. (1960) Studies in Words. Cambridge: Cambridge University Press.

Libet, B. (1996) Neural processes in the production of conscious experience. In Velmans, M. (ed.), *The Science of Consciousness.* London: Routledge, pp. 96–117.

Luhmann, N. (1980) Gesellschaftliche Struktur und semantische Tradition. In Luhmann, N. (ed.), *Gesellschaftsstruktur und Semantik. Studien zur Wissenssoziologie der modernen Gesellschaft.* Frankfurt/Main: Suhrkamp, pp. 9–71.

Lutz, C. (1992) Culture and consciousness: a problem in the anthropology of knowledge. In Kessel, F.S., Cole, P.M. & Johnson, D.L. (eds), *Self and Consciousness: multiple perspectives*. Hillsdale: Erlbaum, pp. 64–87.

Maasen, S. & Weingart, P. (2000) *Metaphors and the Dynamics of Knowledge*. London: Routledge.

Maasen, S. (1998) *Genealogie der Unmoral. Therapeutisierung sexueller Selbste*. Frankfurt/Main: Suhrkamp.

Mercier, C. (1888) *The Nervous System and the Mind: a treatise on the dynamics of the human organism*. London: Macmillan.

Metzinger, T. (1994) Bewusstseinsforschung und Bewusstseinskultur. In Leuner, H. & Schlichtung, M. (eds), *Jahrbuch des Europäischen Kollegiums für Bewusstseinsstudien*. Berlin: VWB, pp. 7– 29.

Miller, G.A. (1963) *Language and Communication*. New York: McGraw-Hill.

Moody, T. C. (1994) Conversations with zombies. *J Consciousness Stud* 1, 196–200.

Nagel, T. (1974) What is it like to be a bat? *Philosoph Rev* 83, 435–57.

Nagel, T. (1986) *The View from Nowhere*. Oxford: Oxford University Press.

Nagel, T. (1979/1988) *Subjective and Objective, Mortal Questions*. Cambridge: Cambridge University Press.

Neisser, U. (1976) *Cognition and Reality*. San Francisco: Freeman.

Paxinos, G. (1986) *The Rat Brain In Stereotaxic Coordinates*. Sydney: Academic Press.

Pickering, J. (1999) Consciousness and psychological science. *Br J Psychol* 90, 611–24.

Ramachandran, V.S. & Hirstein, W. (1999) The science of art: a neurological theory of aesthetic experience. *J Consciousness Stud* 6, 15–51.

Reimer, J. (2000) Tucson 2000: a whirlwind tour. *J Consciousness Stud* 7, 70–80.

Revonsuo, A. (2001) Can functional brain imaging discover consciousness in the brain? *J Consciousness Stud* 8, 3–23.

Rorty, R. (1989) *Philosophy and the Mirror of Nature*. Princeton: Princeton University Press.

Scott, A. (1996) On quantum theories of mind. *J Consciousness Stud* 3, 484–91.

Searle, J. (1983) *Intentionality. An Essay in the Philosophy of Mind*. Cambridge: Cambridge University Press.

Searle, J. (1992) *The Rediscovery of the Mind*. Cambridge: MIT Press.

Shallice, T. (1972) Dual functions of consciousness. *Psycholog Rev* 79, 383–93.

Shapiro, Y. (1997) The consciousness hype: what do we want explained? *Theory Psychol* 7, 837–56.

Sutherland, K. (1996) Toward a science of consciousness: 1996 conference report. *J Consciousness Stud* 3, 278–85.

Sutherland, K. (1998a) Tucson III—a personal view. *J Consciousness Stud* 5, 497–503.

Sutherland, K. (1998b) Review article: the mirror of consciousness. *J Consciousness Stud* 5, 235–44.

The Editors (1994) Editorial Introduction. *J Consciousness Stud*, 1, 1, 1–9.

Titchener, E.B. (1915) *A Beginner's Psychology*. New York: Macmillan.

Velmans, M. (2000) *Understanding Consciousness*. London: Routledge.

Watson, J. (1970/1924) *Behaviorism*. New York: Norton & Co.

Wegner, D.M. & Wheatley, T.P. (1999) Apparent mental causation: Sources of the experience of will. *American Psychologist*, 54, 480–92.

Weingart, P. & Maasen, S. (1995) The career of chaos as a metaphor. *Configurations* 5, 563–620.

Zeman, A. (2001) Consciousness. *Brain* 124, 1263–89.

AUTHOR INDEX

SUBJECT INDEX